Louise Scholes
June 2007

ENTREPRENEURSHIP, INNOVATION AND ECONOMIC GROWTH

Entrepreneurship, Innovation and Economic Growth

David B. Audretsch

Director at the Max Planck Institute of Economics, Jena, Germany and is the Ameritech Chair of Economic Development, Indiana University, USA

Edward Elgar
Cheltenham, UK • Northampton, MA, USA

Published by
Edward Elgar Publishing Limited
Glensanda House
Montpellier Parade
Cheltenham
Glos GL50 1UA
UK

Edward Elgar Publishing, Inc.
136 West Street
Suite 202
Northampton
Massachusetts 01060
USA

A catalogue record for this book
is available from the British Library

Library of Congress Cataloguing in Publication Data

Audretsch, David B.
  Entrepreneurship, innovation, and economic growth / David B. Audretsch.
     p. cm.
  Includes bibliographical references and index.
  ISBN 1-84542-748-3 (hardcover)
  1. Entrepreneurship. 2. Technological innovations—Economic aspects. 3. Diffusion of innovations—Economic aspects. 4. Research—Economic aspects. 5. Economic development—Effect of technological innovations on. I. Title.

  HB615.A936 2006
  338—dc22
                                                    2005032166

ISBN-13: 978 1 84542 748 1
ISBN-10: 1 84542 748 3

Printed and bound in Great Britain by MPG Books Ltd, Bodmin, Cornwall

Contents

PART VI   POLICY

Acknowledgements

The publishers wish to thank the following who have kindly given permission for the use of copyright material.

The American Economic Association for articles: 'Innovation in Large and Small Firms: An Empirical Analysis', with Zoltan J. Acs, *American Economic Review*, **78**(4), September 1988, 678–90; 'Company-Scientist Locational Links: The Case of Biotechnology', with Paula E. Stephan, *American Economic Review*, **86**(3), June 1996, 641–52; 'R&D Spillovers and the Geography of Innovation and Production', with Maryann P. Feldman, *American Economic Review*, **86**(3), June 1996, 630–40; 'Real Effects of Academic Research: Comment', with Zoltan J. Acs and Maryann P. Feldman, *American Economic Review*, **82**(1), March 1992, 363–7.

Blackwell Publishing Ltd for articles: 'Does Entry Size Matter? The Impact of the Life Cycle and Technology on Firm Survival', with Rajshree Agarwal, *Journal of Industrial Economics*, March 2001, **49**(1), 21–43; 'Impeded Industrial Restructuring: The Growth Penalty', with Martin A. Carree, Adriaan J. van Stel and A. Roy Thurik, *Kyklos*, **55**(1), 2002, 81–97; 'Does Entrepreneurship Capital Matter?', with Max Keilbach, *Entrepreneurship Theory and Practice*, **28**(5), September 2004, 419–29.

Cambridge University Press for chapter: 'Entrepreneurship Policy and the Strategic Management of Places', in *The Emergence of Entrepreneurship Policy*, David Hart (ed.), 2003, 20–38, references.

Elsevier Ltd for articles and chapters: 'University Spillovers and New Firm Location', with Erik E. Lehmann and Susanne Warning, *Research Policy*, **34**, 2005, 1113–22; 'The Knowledge Spillover Theory of Entrepreneurship and Economic Growth', in G.T. Vinig and R.C. van der Voort (eds), *The Emergence of Entrepreneurial Economics*, 2005, 37–54; 'Knowledge Spillovers and the Geography of Innovation', with Maryann P. Feldman, in J. Vernon Henderson and Jacques-François Thisse (eds), *Handbook of Regional and Urban Economics*, Volume 4, 2004, 2713–39; 'Innovation in Cities: Science-Based Diversity, Specialization and Localized Competition', with Maryann P. Feldman, *European Economic Review*, **43**, 1999, 409–29; 'Innovation, Growth and Survival', *International Journal of Industrial Organization*, **13**(4), 1995, 441–57; 'Market Dynamics in the Netherlands: Competition Policy and the Role of Small Firms', with George van Leeuwen, Bert Menkveld and Roy Thurik, *International Journal of Industrial Organization*, **19**(5), 2001, 795–821; 'Does Firm Size Matter? Evidence on the Impact of Liquidity Constraints on Firm Investment Behavior in Germany', with Julie Ann Elston, *International Journal of Industrial Organization*, **20**(1), January 2002, 1–17; 'Competition Policy in Dynamic Markets', with William

Baumol and Andrew Burke, *International Journal of Industrial Organization*, **19**(5), April 2001, 613–34.

MIT Press Journals for articles: 'R&D Rivalry, Industrial Policy, and U.S.–Japanese Trade', with Hideki Yamawaki, *Review of Economics and Statistics*, **70**(3), August 1988, 438–47; 'Innovation, Market Structure, and Firm Size', with Zoltan J. Acs, *Review of Economics and Statistics*, **69**(4), November 1987, 567–74; 'R&D Spillovers and Recipient Firm Size', with Zoltan J. Acs and Maryann P. Feldman, *Review of Economics and Statistics*, **76**(2), May 1994, 336–40; 'New-Firm Survival and the Technological Regime', *Review of Economics and Statistics*, **73**(3), August 1991, 441–50; 'New Firm Survival: New Results Using a Hazard Function', with Talat Mahmood, *Review of Economics and Statistics*, **77**(1), March 1995, 97–103.

Oxford University Press for articles: 'Technological Regimes, Industrial Demography and the Evolution of Industrial Structures', *Industrial and Corporate Change*, 1997, **6**(1), 49–82; 'What's New about the New Economy? Sources of Growth in the Managed and Entrepreneurial Economies', with A. Roy Thurik, *Industrial and Corporate Change*, **10**(1), 2001, 267–315; 'Agglomeration and the Location of Innovative Activity', *Oxford Review of Economic Policy*, 1998, **14**(2), 18–29.

Springer Science and Business Media for articles: 'The Dynamic Role of Small Firms: Evidence from the U.S.', *Small Business Economics*, **18**(1–3), February–May 2002, 13–40; 'Mansfield's Missing Link: The Impact of Knowledge Spillovers on Firm Growth', with Erik E. Lehmann, *Journal of Technology Transfer*, **30**(1–2), 2005, 207–10; 'The Emergence of Entrepreneurship Policy', with Brett Anitra Gilbert and Patricia P. McDougall, *Small Business Economics*, **22**(3–4), 2004, 313–23.

Springer-Verlag for article: 'Knowledge Spillovers in Biotechnology: Sources and Incentives', with Paula E. Stephan, *Journal of Evolutionary Economics*, 1999, **9**, 97–107.

Taylor and Francis Ltd for articles: 'Entrepreneurship Capital and Economic Performance', with Max Keilbach, *Regional Studies*, **38**(8), November 2004, 949–59; 'Growth Regimes over Time and Space', with Michael Fritsch, *Regional Studies*, **36**(2), 2002, 113–24.

Virginia Commonwealth University for article: 'Innovation and Size at the Firm Level', with Zoltan J. Acs, *Southern Economic Journal*, **57**(1), January 1991, 739–44.

Every effort has been made to trace all the copyright holders but if any have been inavertently overlooked the publishers will be pleased to make the necessary arrangements at the first opportunity.

Introduction

Economics attracted me as a student because it dealt with some of the most pressing issues of the day. The 1970s saw the emergence of a new economic problem, the simultaneous existence of high and persistent unemployment combined with worrisome levels of inflation. The twin threats of unemployment and inflation were so menacing as to warrant a new word – *stagflation*, as well as to provide the two factors underpinning the *misery index*, which was designed to record the sum.

While macroeconomics pondered the ineffectiveness of traditional tried-and-true policy prescriptions to alleviate stagflation, the field of industrial organization suggested a different cause – the large corporation along with its accompanying market power. The short-lived theory of administered pricing argued that large corporations, such as General Motors and U.S. Steel, enjoyed sufficient size and market dominance that it could elevate prices even as demand was falling.

In fact, the entire field of industrial organization emerged as a response to a public concern over large corporations possessing too much market power as to corrupt the functioning of markets and ultimately the economy. Industrial organization had its roots as a response to the so-called Trust Problem emerging in the mid to late 1800s. Later, during the Great Depression, scholars such as Berle and Means (1932) attributed large corporations of possessing sufficient market power as to engage in administered pricing, in that they were able to maintain or even raise prices while demand was falling.

However, it wasn't until after the Second World War that the field really took off. In 1956 when Soviet Premier Nikita Khrushchev warned the West that 'We will bury you' the threat was not just militaristic, it was economic. After all the Soviet Union and its Eastern European satellites were free to have complete centralization and concentration of economic activity, forming a single firm within each industry, or what was call the *Kombinate* in East Germany. This single firm approach appeared to be incompatible with the democratic systems to which the West was committed.

Thus, it became the task of the scholars in the field of industrial organization to identify explicitly what exactly was gained and lost as a result of large-scale production and a concentration of economic ownership and decision making. During the post-war period a generation of scholars galvanized the field of industrial organization by developing a research agenda dedicated to identifying the issues involving this perceived trade-off between economic efficiency on the one hand and political and economic decentralization on the other (Scherer, 1970). Scholarship in industrial organization generated a massive literature focusing on three issues: (i) what are the gains to size and large-scale production? (ii) what are the economic welfare implications of having an oligopolistic or concentrated market structure, that is, is economic performance promoted or reduced in an industry with just a handful of large-scale firms? and (iii) given the overwhelming evidence that large-scale production resulting in economic concentration is associated with increased efficiency, what are the public policy implications? Oliver Williamson's classic 1968 article 'Economies as an

Antitrust Defense: The Welfare Tradeoffs,' published in the *American Economic Review*, became something of a final statement demonstrating what appeared to be an inevitable trade-off between the gains in productive efficiency that could be obtained through increased concentration and gains in terms of competition, and implicitly democracy, that could be achieved through decentralizing policies. But it did not seem possible to have both, certainly not in Williamson's completely static model.

Thus, one of the most fundamental policy issue confronting Western Europe and North America during the post-war era was how to live with this apparent trade-off between economic concentration and productive efficiency on the one hand, and decentralization and democracy on the other. The principle public policy question centered on determining *how societies could reap the benefits of the large corporation in an oligopolistic setting while avoiding or at least minimizing the costs imposed by a concentration of economic power.* The policy response was to constrain the freedom of firms to contract. Such policy restraints typically took the form of public ownership, regulation and competition policy or antitrust laws. At the time, considerable attention was devoted to what seemed like significant differences in policy approaches to this apparent trade-off by different countries. France and Sweden resorted to government ownership of private business. Other countries, such as the Netherlands and Germany, tended to emphasize regulation. Still other countries, such as the United States, had a greater emphasis on antitrust. In fact, most countries relied upon elements of all three policy instruments. While the particular instrument may have varied across countries, they were, in fact, manifestations of a singular policy approach – how to restrict and restrain the power of the large corporation. What may have been perceived as a disparate set of policies at the time appears in retrospect to comprise a remarkably singular policy approach.

Western economists and policy makers of the day were nearly unanimous in their acclaim for large-scale enterprises. It is no doubt an irony of history that this consensus mirrored a remarkably similar giantism embedded in Soviet doctrine, fueled by the writings of Marx and ultimately implemented with Stalin's iron fist. This was the era of mass production when economies of scale seemed to be the decisive factor in determining efficiency. This was the world so colorfully described by John Kenneth Galbraith (1956) in his theory of countervailing power, in which big business was held in check by big labor and by big government. This was the era of the man in the gray flannel suit (Riesman, 1950) and the organization man (Whyte, 1960), when virtually every major social and economic institution acted to reinforce the stability and predictability needed for mass production (Piore and Sabel, 1984; Chandler, 1977).

With a decided focus on the role of large corporations, oligopoly and economic concentration, the literature on industrial organization yielded a number of key insights concerning the efficiency and impact on economic performance associated with new and small firms:

1. Small firms were generally less efficient than their larger counterparts. Studies from the USA in the 1960s and 1970 revealed that small firms produced at lower levels of efficiency.

2. Small firms provided lower levels of employee compensation. Empirical evidence from both North America and Europe found a systematic and positive relationship between employee compensation and firm size.
3. Small firms were only marginally involved in innovative activity. Based on research and development (R&D) measures, SMEs accounted for only a small amount of innovative activity.
4. The relative importance of small firms was declining over time in both North America and Europe.

Thus, while a heated debate emerged about which approach best promoted large-scale production while simultaneously constraining the ability of large corporations to exert market power, there was much less debate about public policy concerning small businesses and entrepreneurship. The only issue was whether public policy makers should simply allow small firms to disappear as a result of their inefficiency or intervene to preserve them on social and political grounds. Those who perceived small firms to contribute significantly to growth, employment generation, and competitiveness were few and far between.

In the post-war era, small firms and entrepreneurship were viewed as a luxury, perhaps needed by the West to ensure a decentralization of decision making, but in any case obtained only at a cost to efficiency. Certainly the systematic empirical evidence, gathered from both Europe and North America documented a sharp trend towards a decreased role of small firms during the post-war period.

Public policy towards small firms generally reflected the view of economists and other scholars that they were a drag on economic efficiency and growth, generated lower quality jobs in terms of direct and indirect compensation, and were generally on the way to becoming less important to the economy, if not threatened by long-term extinction. Some countries, such as the Soviet Union, Sweden, and France, adapted the policy stance of allowing small firms to disappear gradually and account for a smaller share of economic activity.

The public policy stance of the United States reflected long-term political and social valuation of small firms that seemed to reach back to the Jeffersonian traditions of the country. After all, in an 1890 Congressional debate, Senator Sherman vowed, 'If we will not endure a King as a political power we should not endure a King over the production, transportation, and sale of the necessaries of life. If we would not submit to an emperor we should not submit to an autocrat of trade with power to prevent competition and to fix the price of any commodity.' Thus, public policy towards small business in the United States was oriented towards preserving what were considered to be inefficient enterprises, which, if left unprotected, might otherwise become extinct.

Even advocates of small business agreed that small firms were less efficient than big companies. These advocates were willing to sacrifice a modicum of efficiency, because of other contributions – moral, political, and otherwise – made by small businesses to society. Thus small business policy was 'preservationist' in nature. For example, the passage of the Robinson-Patman Act in 1936, along with its widespread enforcement in the post-war era, was widely interpreted as an effort to protect small firms, like independent retailers, that would otherwise have been too inefficient to survive in open competition with large corporations.[1] According to Richard Posner

(1976, p. 196), 'The Robinson-Patman Act ... is almost uniformly condemned by professional and academic opinion, legal and economic.' Similarly, Robert Bork (1978, p. 382) observed 'One often hears of the baseball player who, although a weak hitter, was also a poor fielder. Robinson-Patman is a little like that. Although it does not prevent much price discrimination, at least it has stifled a great deal of competition.'

Preservationist policies were clearly at work with the creation of the US Small Business Administration. In the Small Business Act of 10 July 1953, Congress authorized the creation of the Small Business Administration, with an explicit mandate to 'aid, counsel, assist and protect ... the interests of small business concerns.'[2] The Small Business Act was clearly an attempt by the Congress to halt the continued disappearance of small businesses and to preserve their role in the US economy.

If physical capital was at the heart of the Solow economy (Solow, 1956), knowledge capital replaced it in the Romer economy (Romer, 1986). While the policy goals remained relatively unchanged, economic growth, the Romer model reflected the emergence of a new emphasis on a strikingly different policy mechanism, knowledge capital, involving very different policy instruments. Part I of this book deals with a research trajectory focusing on innovative activity. The major questions addressed are which organizational forms, both at the firm and industry levels, are conducive to innovative activity, and what is the performance impact, particularly in terms of global markets, of innovative activity. One of my earliest articles, 'R&D Rivalry, Industrial Policy, and U.S.-Japanese Trade,' co-authored with Hideki Yamawaki and published in the *Review of Economics and Statistics* in 1988 (Chapter 2 this volume), made it clear that economic performance, measured in terms of trade performance at the industry level, is promoted through investments in new knowledge. This article provided a basis suggesting that knowledge investments are conducive to competitive advantage in internationally linked markets.

In terms of the organizational and industry structures most conducive to innovative activity, entrepreneurship and small firms seemed at least as incompatible with the knowledge-based Romer economy as they were in the capital-based Solow economy. The most prevalent theory of innovation in economics, the model of the knowledge production function, suggested that knowledge-generating inputs, such as R&D were a prerequisite to generative innovative output. With their limited and meager investments in R&D, at least in absolute terms, new and small firms did not seem to possess sufficient knowledge capabilities to be competitive in a knowledge-based economy.

It must not be forgotten that as recently as 1992, during Bill Clinton's first election campaign, many scholars and policy makers looked to Japan and Germany to redirect the flagging US economy. This sentiment generally mirrored the influential study, *Made in America* (1989), directed by the leaders of the MIT Commission on Industrial Productivity, Michael L. Dertouzos, Richard K. Lester, and Robert M. Solow. A team of 23 scholars, spanning a broad range of disciplines and backgrounds, reached the conclusion that for the United States to restore its international competitiveness, it had to adapt the types of policies targeting the leading corporations prevalent in Japan and Germany. Lester Thurow bemoaned that the United States was 'losing the economic race,' because, 'Today it's very hard to find an industrial corporation in America that isn't in really serious trouble basically because of trade problems. ... The systematic erosion of our competitiveness comes from having lower rates of growth of manufacturing productivity year after year, as compared with the rest of the world' (Thurow, 1985, p. 23). W.W. Rostow predicted a revolution in economic policy, concluding that, 'The United States is entering a new political era, one in which it will be preoccupied by increased economic competition from abroad and will need better cooperation at home to deal with this challenge.'³ However, neither Rostow nor Thurow predicted that this new focus of public policy to restore US growth and competitiveness in globally linked markets would be on entrepreneurship.

However, in searching for the innovative advantage of different types of firms, Zoltan Acs and I in 'Innovation in Large and Small Firms: An Empirical Analysis,' published in the *American Economic Review* in 1988 (Chapter 1), surprisingly found that small firms provided the engines of innovative activity, at least in certain industries. Similarly, in two of the other chapters contained in Part I, 'Innovation, Market Structure, and Firm Size,' published in the *Review of Economics and Statistics* (Chapter 4), and 'Innovation and Size at the Firm Level' (Chapter 3), we found consistent and compelling evidence challenging the conventional wisdom that large corporations in oligopolisitic industries provided the engine of innovative activity. Rather, small firms and new ventures were also identified as an important source of innovations.

The breakdown of the model of the knowledge production function at the level of the firm raises the question, *Where do innovative firms with little or no R&D get the knowledge inputs?* This question becomes particularly relevant for small and new firms that undertake little R&D themselves, yet contribute considerable innovative activity in newly emerging industries such as biotechnology and computer software. One clue supplied by the literature on the new economic geography identifying the local nature of knowledge spillovers is from other, third-party firms or research institutions, such as universities, that may be located within spatial proximity. Thus, Part III of this volume includes four chapters exploring and identifying the spatial dimensions of innovative active in general, and knowledge spillovers in particular. In 'Real Effects of Academic Research,' published in the *American Economic Review* (Chapter 11), Zoltan Acs, Maryann Feldman and I find empirical evidence that the knowledge production function holds, not just at the firm level as was found in Part I of the volume, but also at spatial units of observation. Another article in this Part, 'R&D Spillovers and the Geography of Innovation and Production' (Chapter 10), also co-authored with Maryann Feldman, and published in the *American Economic Review*, offers not just a theory of knowledge spillovers, but also one of localization, suggesting that spillovers in both knowledge and production tend to be geographically localized. Thus, knowledge spillovers were identified as a source of spatial agglomeration and regional clusters.

An important limitation of the model of the knowledge production function is that, while the magnitude of knowledge resources is linked to innovative output, how those knowledge resources are organized and deployed does not matter. The black box of geographic space is penetrated in 'Innovation in Cities: Science-Based Diversity, Specialization and Localized Competition' (Chapter 12), also published with Maryann Feldman, where the organization of knowledge resources within a spatial unit of observation is linked to the innovative performance of that region. In particular, those regions where knowledge resources tend to be diverse rather than specialized, and where there tends to be a higher degree of local competition, rather than monopoly, exhibit a superior innovative performance. The final chapter in Part III provides a summary and synthesis of theory and empirical evidence of what has been learned about 'Knowledge Spillovers and the Geography of Innovation' (Chapter 13, with Maryann Feldman).

While the articles contained in Parts I and III make it clear that not only is new economic knowledge important for innovative activity, and that innovation promotes economic performance, particularly in globally linked markets, they also leave a number of important questions unanswered. In particular, how can new and small firms access such knowledge spillovers? And why should new and small firms have a competitive advantage accessing knowledge produce elsewhere vis-à-vis their larger counterparts? That is, what are the mechanisms transmitting the spillover of knowledge from the source producing that knowledge, such as the R&D laboratory of a large corporation, or a university, to the small firm actually engaged in commercializing that knowledge? That is, is the spillover of knowledge automatic, and why does entrepreneurship play such an important role in serving as a conduit of knowledge spillovers? In particular their findings suggested that knowledge spillovers are geographically bounded and localized within spatial proximity to the knowledge source. None of these studies, however, identified the actual mechanisms which actually transmit the knowledge spillover; rather, the spillovers were implicitly assumed to automatically exist (or fall like manna from heaven), but only within a geographically bounded spatial area.

The answers to these questions are provided in Part II, which focuses explicitly on entrepreneurship.

The discrepancy in organizational context between the organization creating opportunities and those exploiting the opportunities that seemingly contradicted Griliches' model of the firm knowledge production function was resolved in my 1995 book, *Innovation and Industry Evolution*, by introducing *The Knowledge Spillover Theory of Entrepreneurship*, 'The findings challenge an assumption implicit to the knowledge production function – that firms exist exogenously and then endogenously seek out and apply knowledge inputs to generate innovative output. ... It is the knowledge in the possession of economic agents that is exogenous, and in an effort to appropriate the returns from that knowledge, the spillover of knowledge from its producing entity involves endogenously creating a new firm' (pp. 179–80).

What is the source of this entrepreneurial opportunity that endogenously generated the startup of new firms? The answer seemed to be through the spillover of knowledge that created the opportunities for the startup of a new firm, 'How are these small and frequently new firms able to generate innovative output when undertaking a generally negligible amount of investment into knowledge-generating inputs, such as R&D? One answer is apparently through exploiting knowledge created by expenditures on research in universities and on R&D in large corporations' (p. 179).

The empirical evidence supporting the Knowledge Spillover Theory of Entrepreneurship was provided from analysing variations in startup rates across different industries reflecting different underlying knowledge contexts. In particular, those industries with a greater investment in new knowledge also exhibited higher startup rates while those industries with less investment in new knowledge exhibited lower startup rates, which was interpreted as a conduit transmitting knowledge spillovers.

Thus, compelling evidence was provided suggesting that entrepreneurship is an endogenous response to opportunities created but not exploited by the incumbent firms. This involved an organizational dimension involving the mechanism transmitting knowledge spillovers – the startup of new firms. In the first article contained in Part II, 'Company-Scientist Locational Links: The Case of Biotechnology,' published in the *American Economic Review* (Chapter 5), Paula Stephan and I found evidence that new-firm startups in a knowledge-based industry such as biotechnology tend to be located within close spatial proximity to key knowledge sources, such as key scientists. This suggested that the scientists either starting the new firm, or else working with the new firm, served as conduits for the spillover of knowledge.

The Knowledge Spillover Theory of Entrepreneurship contests the view that entrepreneurial opportunities are exogenous and that only those individual specific characteristics and attributes influence the cognitive process underlying the entrepreneurial decision to start a firm. Rather, the knowledge spillover theory of entrepreneurship explicitly identifies an important source of opportunities – investments in knowledge and ideas made by firms and universities that are not completely commercialized. By linking the degree of entrepreneurial activity to the degree of knowledge investments in a *Standort*, systematic empirical evidence was provided suggesting that entrepreneurial opportunities are not at all exogenous, but rather endogenous to the extent of investments in new knowledge. In a comprehensive study with colleagues at the Max Planck Institute, we found that regions rich in knowledge generated a greater amount of entrepreneurial opportunities than did regions with impoverished knowledge (Audretsch et al., 2005). This empirical evidence confirmed the theory suggesting that entrepreneurial opportunities are not exogenous to the context but, rather, systematically related to the knowledge context.

The Knowledge Spillover Theory of Entrepreneurship identified one such mechanism by which knowledge created with one context and purpose spills over from the organization creating it to the organization actually attempting to commercialize that knowledge. Entrepreneurship has emerged as a vital organizational form for economic growth because it provides the missing link (Acs et al., 2004) in the process of economic growth. By serving as a conduit for the spillover of knowledge, entrepreneurship is a mechanism by which investments, both private and public, generate a greater social return, in terms of economic growth and job creation.

Audretsch et al. (2005) suggest that, in addition to labor, physical capital, and knowledge capital, the endowment of entrepreneurship capital also matters for generating economic growth. Entrepreneurship capital refers to the capacity for the *Standort*, that is the geographically relevant spatial units of observation, to generate the startup of new enterprises.

The concept of *social capital* (Putnam, 1993; Coleman, 1988) added a social component to the traditional factors shaping economic growth and prosperity. Together with Max Keilbach and Erik Lehmann at the Max Planck Institute (Audretsch et al., 2005), we suggest that what has been called social capital in the entrepreneurship literature may actually be a more specific sub-component, which they introduce as *entrepreneurship capital*. The entrepreneurship capital of an economy or a society refers to the institutions, culture, and historical context that is conducive to the creation of new firms. This involves a number of aspects such as social acceptance of entrepreneurial behavior but of course also individuals who are willing to deal with the risk of creating new firms and the activity of bankers and venture capital agents that are willing to share risks and benefits involved. Hence entrepreneurship capital reflects a number of different legal, institutional, and social factors and forces. Taken together, these factors and forces constitute the entrepreneurship capital of an economy, which creates a capacity for entrepreneurial activity.

By including measures of entrepreneurship capital along with the traditional factors of physical capital, knowledge capital and labor in a production function model estimating economic growth, we found pervasive and compelling econometric evidence suggesting that entrepreneurship capital also contributes to economic growth (Audretsch et al., 2005).

Public policy did not wait for the painstaking econometric evidence linking entrepreneurship to economic growth. The mandate for entrepreneurship policy has generally emerged from what would superficially appear to be two opposite directions. One direction emanates from the failure of the traditional policy instruments, corresponding to the Solow model, or those based on instruments promoting investment into physical capital, to maintain economic growth and employment adequately in globally linked markets. The emergence of entrepreneurship policy as a bona fide approach to generating economic growth and job creation has been rampant throughout the old rust belt of the industrial Midwest in the United States, ranging from cities such as Cleveland and Pittsburg to states such as Wisconsin and Indiana which are pinning their economic development strategies on entrepreneurship policies.

The second push for the entrepreneurship policy mandate is from the opposite direction – the failure of the so-called new economy policy instruments, corresponding to the Romer model, or those promoting investment into knowledge capital, to generate economic growth and employment adequately. Recognition of the *European Paradox*, where employment creation and economic growth remain meager, despite world-class levels of human capital and research capabilities prompted the *Lisbon Proclamation* stating that Europe would become the global entrepreneurship leader by 2020.

Although coming from opposite directions, both have in common an unacceptable economic performance. Which is to say that the mandate for entrepreneurship policy is rooted in dissatisfaction – dissatisfaction with the status quo, and in particular, with the status quo economic performance.[4]

For example, confronted not just by economic stagnation but also the worst job creation performance of any modern American President, George W. Bush responded with a policy to promote economic growth that focused on entrepreneurship and small business, '70 percent of the new jobs in America are created by small businesses. I understand that. And I have promoted during the course of the last four years one of the most aggressive, pro-entrepreneur, small business policies ... And so in a new term, we will make sure the tax relief continues to be robust for our small businesses. We'll push legal reform and regulatory reform because I understand the engine of growth is through the small business sector.'[5]

In fact, neither the current US President nor his political party has a monopoly in advocating entrepreneurship policy as an engine of growth and job creation. The decade of the 1990s saw the re-emergence of competitiveness, innovative activity and job generation in the United States. Not only was this economic turnaround largely unanticipated by many scholars and members of the policy community, but what was even more surprising than the resurgence itself was the primary source – small and new firms. As scholars began the arduous task of documenting the crucial role played by small firms and entrepreneurship in the United States as a driving engine of growth, job creation, and competitiveness in global markets, policy makers responded with a bipartisan emphasis on policies promoting entrepreneurship.[6]

For example, in his 1993 State of the Union Address to the country, President Bill Clinton proposed, 'Because small business has created such a high percentage of all the new jobs in our nation over the last 10 or 15 years, our plan includes the boldest targeted incentives for small business in history. We propose a permanent investment tax credit for the small firms in this country.'[7] The Republican response to Clinton was, 'We agree with the President that we have to put more people to work, but remember this: 80 to 85 percent of the new jobs in this country are created by small business. So the climate for starting and expanding businesses must be enhanced with tax incentives and deregulation, rather than imposing higher taxes and more governmental mandates.'[8]

As Bresnahan and Gambardella (2004, p. 1) observe, 'Clusters of high-tech industry, such as Silicon Valley, have received a great deal of attention from scholars and in the public policy arena. National economic growth can be fueled by development of such clusters. In the United States the long boom of the 1980s and 1990s was largely driven by growth in the information technology industries in a few regional clusters. Innovation and entrepreneurship can be supported by a number of mechanisms operating within a cluster, such as easy access to capital, knowledge about technology and markets, and collaborators.' Similarly, Wallsten (2004, p. 229) stated that, 'Policy makers around the world are anxious to find tools that will help their regions emulate the success of Silicon Valley and create new centers of innovation and high technology.'

It is no doubt surprising that such a consensus in the public policy community could emerge concerning the appropriate focus to trigger economic growth and employment that could not just cross party lines within a country, but that is also common across a broad spectrum of disparate nations and regions. But what is even more surprising is the focus of this emerging public policy approach – entrepreneurship. Just a few years earlier entrepreneurship and, in particular new and small firms, were viewed as imposing a burden on the economy.

As first the capital-driven Solow model and more recently the knowledge-driven Romer model alone have not delivered the expected levels of economic performance, a mandate for entrepreneurship policy has emerged and begun to diffuse throughout the entire globe (Lundstrom and Stevenson, 2005). Whether or not specific policy instruments will work in their particular contexts is not the point of this volume. What is striking, however, is the emergence and diffusion of an entirely new public policy approach to generate economic growth – the creation of the entrepreneurial society. It is upon this new mantle the entrepreneurial society that *Standort*, ranging from communities to cities, states and even entire nations hang their hopes, dreams and aspirations for prosperity and security.

Notes

1. According to the Robinson-Patman Act, 'It shall be unlawful for any person engaged in commerce, in the course of such commerce, either directly or indirectly, to discriminate in price between different purchasers of commodities of like grade and quality ...' For example, A&P was found in violation of the Robinson-Patman Act for direct purchases from suppliers and for performing its own wholesale functions. While these activities resulted in lower distribution costs, the gains in efficiency were seen as being irrelevant because small business was threatened.
2. http://www.sba.gov/aboutsba/sbahistory.html
3. W.W. Rostow, 'Here Comes a New Political Chapter in America,' *International Herald Tribune*, 2 January 1987.
4. A third direction contributing to the mandate for entrepreneurship policy may be in the context of less developed regions and developing countries. Such regions have had endowments of neither physical capital nor knowledge capital but still look to entrepreneurship capital to serve as an engine of economic growth.
5. President George W. Bush, Press Conference, November 4, 2004. Transcript: http://www.whitehouse.gov/news/releases/2004/11/20041104-5.html.
6. For example, US News and World Report (16 August, 1993) reported, 'What do Bill Clinton, George Bush and Bob Dole have in common? All have uttered one of the most enduring homilies in American political discourse: That small businesses create most of the nation's jobs.'
7. Cited from Davis, Haltiwanger and Schuh (1996, p. 298).
8. Representative Robert Michel, House Minority Leader, in the Republican Response to the 1993 State of the Union Address, cited from Davis, Haltiwanger and Schuh (1996, p. 298).

References

Acs, Zoltan J., David B. Audretsch, Pontus Braunerhjelm and Bo Carlsson (2004), 'The Missing Link: The Knowledge Filter and Entrepreneurship in Endogenous Growth', Centre for Economic Policy Research (CEPR) Discussion Paper.

Audretsch, David B. (1995), *Innovation and Industry Evolution*, Cambridge, MA: MIT Press.

Audretsch, David B., Max Keilbach and Erik Lehmann (2005), *Entrepreneurship and Economic Growth*, New York: Oxford University Press.

Berle, Adolf A. and Gardiner Means (1932), *The Modern Corporation and Private Property*, New York: Macmillan.

Bork, R. (1978), *The Antitrust Paradox*, New York: Basic Books.

Bresnahan, T. and A. Gambardella (2004), *Building High-Tech Clusters: Silicon Valley and Beyond*, Cambridge: Cambridge University Press.

Chandler, A. (1977), *The Visible Hand: The Managerial Revolution in American Business*, Cambridge: Belknap Press.

Coleman, J.C. (1988), 'Social Capital in the Creation of Human Capital', *American Journal of Sociology*, **94**, S95–S120.

Davis, S., J. Haltiwanger and S. Schuh (1996), 'Small Business and Job Creation: Dissecting the Myth and Reassessing the Facts', *Small Business Economics*, **8**, 297–315.

Dertouzos, M., R. Lester and R. Solow (1989), *Made in America*, Cambridge, MA: MIT Press.

Galbraith, John Kenneth (1956), *American Capitalism*, Boston: Houghton Mifflin.

Lundstrom, A. and L. Stevenson (2005), *Entrepreneurship Policy. Theory and Practice*, International Studies in Entrepreneurship Series, Vol. 9, New York: Springer.

Piore, M. and C. Sabel (1984), *The Second Industrial Divide: Possibilities for Prosperity*, New York: Basic Books.

Posner, R. (1976), *Antitrust Law: An Economic Perspective*, Chicago: University of Chicago Press.

Putnam, Robert D. (1993), *Making Democracy Work*, Princeton: Princeton University Press.

Riesman, David (1950), *The Lonely Crowd: A Study of the Changing American Character*, New Haven: Yale University Press.

Romer, Paul M. (1986), 'Increasing Returns and Long-Run Growth', *Journal of Political Economy*, **94** (5), October, 1002–37.

Scherer, F. (1970), *Industrial Market Structure and Economic Performance*, Chicago: Rand McNally.

Solow, Robert (1956), 'A Contribution to The Theory of Economic Growth', *Quarterly Journal of Economics*, **70**, 65–94.

Thurow, Lester C. (1985), 'Healing with a Thousand Bandages,' *Challenge*, **28**, 1–14.

Wallsten, S.J. (2004), 'The Role of Government in Regional Technology Development: the Effects of Public Venture Capital and Science Parks', in *Building High-Tech Clusters: Silicon Valley and Beyond*, Cambridge: Cambridge University Press, 229–79.

Whyte, William H. (1960), *The Organization Man*, Harmondsworth, Middlesex: Penguin.

Williamson, Oliver E. (1968), 'Economies as an Antitrust Defense: The Welfare Tradeoffs', *American Economic Review*, **58** (1), 18–36.

PART I

INNOVATION

Innovation in Large and Small Firms:
An Empirical Analysis

By Zoltan J. Acs and David B. Audretsch*

We present a model suggesting that innovative output is influenced by R&D and market structure characteristics. Based on a new and direct measure of innovation, we find that (1) the total number of innovations is negatively related to concentration and unionization, and positively related to R&D, skilled labor, and the degree to which large firms comprise the industry; and (2) these determinants have disparate effects on large and small firms.

As Simon Kuznets (1962) observed, perhaps the greatest obstacle to understanding the role of innovation in economic processes has been the lack of meaningful measures of innovative inputs and outputs. More recently, there has been the development of new data sources measuring different aspects of technical change. These new sources of data have included measures of patented inventions from the computerization by the U.S. Patent Office (Bronwyn Hall et al., 1986; Adam B. Jaffe, 1986; Ariel Pakes and Zvi Griliches, 1980), better measures of research and development (John Bound et al., 1984, and F. M. Scherer, 1982), and stock market values of inventive output (Pakes, 1985). While several of these new and improved data sources have been used to examine the relationship between innovative activity and firm size, there have been virtually no studies able to apply a more direct measure of the innovative output. For example, the limita-

tions of using patent data were significant enough to supplement them with renewal data (Pakes and Mark Schankerman, 1984). Further, while most of the empirical research has examined only the innovative activity contributed by relatively large firms, the innovative output of the smallest firms has received only scant attention and quantification.[1] Thus, most of the inferences which have been made about the causes of innovative activity have been based on observing only the behavior of larger firms.[2] Such inferences may be misleading since, as we show, almost half of the number of innovations are contributed by firms which employ fewer than 500 workers.

The purpose of this paper is to add to the literature on new measures examining technical change by introducing a more direct measure of innovative activity, to determine some of its basic properties, and to illustrate its use with a reduced form empirical model. We present a model which investigates the degree to which innovative output is affected by different industry characteristics, and the extent to which small and large firms respond differently to various stimuli. The econometric analysis enables the testing of

*Research Fellows, Wissenschaftszentrum Berlin, Reichpietschufer 50, D-1000 Berlin 30, Federal Republic of Germany. We wish to thank George Bittlingmayer, Bo Carlsson, Paul Geroski, Albert N. Link, Richard R. Nelson, William K. Scheirer, Joachim Schwalbach, J.-Matthias Graf von der Schulenburg, Hideki Yamawaki, Klaus Zimmermann, two anonymous referees, and seminar participants at the U.S. Small Business Administration, Case Western Reserve University, and the University of Bradford for helpful comments. We are especially grateful for the suggestions by F. M. Scherer and the computational assistance of Michael Karge and Jianping Yang. All errors and omissions remain our responsibility.

[1]For a thorough review of the literature relating technical change to innovation activity, see Morton I. Kamien and Nancy L. Schwartz (1975), F. M. Scherer (1980), and Richard C. Levin et al. (1985).

[2]For example, Scherer (1965) related market structure to the number of patents for fewer than 500 of the largest U.S. corporations.

two hypotheses: (1) the degree to which $R \& D$ expenditures produce innovative output is conditioned by the market structure characteristics; and (2) as Sidney G. Winter (1984) suggests, small- and large-firm innovative activity respond to distinct technological and economic regimes.

In Section I of this paper, we introduce the new innovation data and compare them with the more traditional measures of technical change, including patented inventions and $R \& D$ expenditures. After presenting the model in Section II, cross-section regressions estimating the logs of the 1982 total number of innovations, large-firm innovations, small-firm innovations, and the small-firm innovation share for 247 four-digit SIC (Standard Industrial Classification) industries are presented in Section III. Finally, in Section IV, a summary and conclusion of the model and empirical results are provided. We find that innovative output increases with industry $R \& D$ expenditures at a less than proportional rate. While some of the appropriability measures, such as market concentration and unionization, are negatively related to innovation activity, the extent to which an industry is comprised of large firms is positively related to the total number of innovations. Similarly, we find considerable evidence supporting the hypothesis by Winter (1984) that innovation activity for small firms responds to a different technological and economic environment than does innovation activity for large firms.

I. The Innovation Data

The measure of innovative activity used in this paper is the number of innovations in each four-digit SIC industry recorded in 1982. The data, which were only recently released by the U.S. Small Business Administration,[3] consist of 8,074 innovations introduced into the United States in 1982. Of these innovations, 4,476 were identified as occurring in manufacturing industries. The Small Business Administration constructed

this data base by examining over 100 technology, engineering, and trade journals, covering each manufacturing industry. From the sections in each trade journal listing innovations and new products, a data base consisting of the innovations by four-digit SIC industry was formed. The entire list of trade journals used to compile these data is available from the authors. The Small Business Administration defines an innovation as "a process that begins with an invention, proceeds with the development of the invention, and results in the introduction of a new product, process or service to the marketplace." (Keith L. Edwards and Theodore J. Gordon, 1984, p. 1) Because the innovations recorded in 1982 were the result of inventions made, on average, 4.2 years earlier, in some sense the innovation data base represents the inventions made around 1978 that were subsequently introduced to the market in 1982. The data were also checked for duplication. In fact, 8,800 innovations were actually recorded, but it was subsequently found that 726 of them appeared either in separate issues of the same journal or else in different journals. Thus, double counting was avoided. While the Small Business Administration does not claim that every single innovative activity is included in the data base, it does consider the data to be "comprehensive and reliable."

The innovation data were classified according to the industry of origin based on the SIC code of the innovating enterprise. The data were then classified into innovations by large firms, defined as firms with at least 500 employees, and innovations by small firms, defined as firms with fewer than 500 employees. For example, an innovation made by a subsidiary of a diversified firm would be classified by industry according to the SIC industry of the innovating subsidiary (enterprise) and not by the SIC industry of the parent firm. However, the innovation would be classified by size according to the size of the entire firm and not just by the size of the subsidiary.[4]

---

[3]For a more complete explanation of the data, see the Appendix.

[4]Because 67 innovations could not be classified according to firm size, the number of total innovations does not always equal the sum of large- and small-firm innovations.

TABLE 1—NUMBER OF INNOVATIONS AND THE RELATIVE INNOVATIVE ACTIVITY OF
LARGE AND SMALL FIRMS IN THE MOST INNOVATIVE INDUSTRIES, 1982

Industry	Total Innovations	Large-Firm Innovations/ Small-Firm Innovations	Large Firm Employment/ Small-Firm Employment
Electronic Computing Equipment	395	0.696	16.544
Process Control Instruments	165	0.731	1.632
Radio and TV Communication Equipment	157	1.153	4.814
Pharmaceutical Preparations	133	9.231	19.408
Electronic Components	128	0.740	0.894
Engineering and Scientific Instruments	126	0.518	1.096
Semiconductors	122	3.138	5.757
Plastics Products	107	0.268	0.332
Photographic Equipment	88	8.778	18.231
Office Machinery	77	6.700	11.658
Instruments to Measure Electricity	77	0.596	2.077
Surgical Appliances and Supplies	67	4.154	3.566
General Industrial Machinery	67	4.154	0.976
Surgical and Medical Instruments	66	0.833	3.566
Special Industry Machinery	64	2.048	2.717
Industrial Controls	61	0.326	1.732
Toilet Preparations	59	2.278	5.289
Valves and Pipe Fittings	54	0.606	2.436
Electric Housewares and Fans	53	7.833	17.182
Measuring and Controlling Devices	52	0.067	0.866
Food Products Machinery	50	3.083	1.976
Motors and Generators	49	3.900	14.625
Plastic Materials and Resins	45	2.000	6.937
Industrial Inorganic Chemicals	40	4.000	4.917
Radio and TV Receiving Sets	40	8.750	13.925
Hand and Edge Tools	39	2.455	2.125
Fabricated Platework	38	3.222	1.597
Fabricated Metal Products	35	0.706	0.495
Pumps and Pumping Equipment	34	1.125	3.484
Optical Instruments and Lenses	34	0.571	1.179
Polishes and Sanitation Goods	33	0.684	2.937
Industrial Trucks and Tractors	33	0.650	6.404
Medicinals and Botanicals	32	5.400	4.376
Aircraft	32	31.000	111.111
Environmental Controls	32	2.200	3.566
Total	2,617	1.272	8.440

Source: U.S. Small Business Administration.

There are several other important qualifications which should be made concerning the innovation data. The trade journals report relatively few process, service, and management innovations and tend to capture mainly product innovations. The most likely effect of this bias is to underestimate the number of innovations emanating from large firms, since larger enterprises tend to produce more process innovations than do their smaller counterparts. However, because it was found that the large-firm innovations are more likely to be reported in trade journals than are small-firm innovations, the Small Business Administration considers the biases to be at least somewhat offsetting.

Table 1 lists the total number of innovations in those industries which had the greatest number of innovations in 1982, along with the corresponding ratios of large-firm innovation to small-firm innovation and large-firm employment to small-firm employment (also for 1982). Large firms are defined as firms with at least 500 employees and small firms are defined as firms with fewer than 500. In some industries, the large firms exhibit considerably more innovative activity than do their smaller counterparts, while in other industries the small firms are apparently more innovative. One potential concern might be that the significance and "quality" of the innovations vary considerably between large and small firms. Based on 4,938 of the innovations, the Small Business Administration classified each innovation according to one of the following levels of significance: (1) the innovation established an entirely new category of product; (2) the innovation is the first of its type on the market in a product category already in existence; (3) the innovation represents a significant improvement in existing technology; and (4) the innovation is a modest improvement designed to update an existing product. While none of the innovations in the sample were in the highest level of significance, 80 were in the second level, 576 in the third level, and 4,282 were classified in the fourth level. Within each level of significance, the distribution between large- and small-firm innovations proved to be remarkably constant. In both the second and third significance categories, the large firms accounted for 62.5 percent of the innovations and the small firms for the remaining 37.5 percent. In the fourth significance category, the large firms accounted for just a slightly smaller share of the innovations, 56.6 percent, while the small firms contributed the remaining 43.4 percent. A chi-square test for the hypothesis that there is no difference in the frequency of innovation with respect to innovation significance and firm size cannot be rejected at the 99 percent level of confidence (Edwards and Gordon, 1984).[5] Thus, based on the U.S. Small Business Administration's classification of the significance level of innovations, there does not appear to be a great difference in the "quality" and signifi-

cance of the innovations between large and small firms. However, the extent of innovative activity does not necessarily correspond to the market values of the innovations. It is conceivable that larger firms may tend to focus on innovations with a higher market value.

The second column of Table 1 shows that while the number of large-firm innovations exceeded that of small firms in twenty-one of the thirty-five most innovative industries, the small firms were more innovative in the remaining fourteen. By contrast, the third column indicates that large firms accounted for a greater share of 1982 industry employment in all but five of these highly innovative industries. For the entire sample of manufacturing industries the simple correlation between these two measures is only 0.316. While the ratio of the innovations-per-employee is 6.64 times greater for small firms than for large firms for the most innovative industries, small firms were only 43 percent more innovative than their larger counterparts for the entire sample of manufacturing industries.[6]

Table 2 shows the distribution of manufacturing industries according to innovation frequency. About one-quarter of the innovating industries contributed at least sixteen innovations, while slightly more than one-half of these industries had fewer than six innovations.

In order to compare the new innovation measures with the more traditional measures of technical change, Table 3 provides a correlation matrix of input and output measures of innovative activity. There is a striking difference in the simple correlation of 0.481

---

[5] Unfortunately, no further information regarding the distribution of innovations by significance category has been released by the U.S. Small Business Administration. Therefore, no comparisons across industries can be made.

[6] It should be noted that while there were a total of 8,074 innovations identified in the data base, some innovations occurred outside of manufacturing and others were contributed from firms which could not be found in publishing company directories. While some of these were subsidiaries of large firms, many more were small companies. A random sample of 600 firms (with 375 responses) was used to allocate the entire set of innovations into 55 percent from small firms and 45 percent from large firms, resulting in an innovation-per-employee ratio 2.38 times greater in small firms than in large firms.

TABLE 2—THE DISTRIBUTION OF MANUFACTURING INDUSTRIES ACCORDING TO INNOVATION FREQUENCY

| | \multicolumn{8}{c}{Number of Innovations[a]} |
	1–5	6–10	11–15	16–20	21–25	26–30	31 >	Total
Total Innovations	149	36	21	13	15	6	36	276
(percent)	(53.99)	(13.04)	(7.61)	(4.71)	(5.43)	(2.17)	(13.04)	(99.99)
Large-Firm Innovations	127	28	24	6	7	8	18	218
(percent)	(58.26)	(12.84)	(11.01)	(2.75)	(3.21)	(3.67)	(8.26)	(100.00)
Small-Firm Innovations	129	33	16	9	4	1	13	205
(percent)	(62.93)	(16.10)	(7.80)	(4.39)	(1.95)	(0.49)	(6.34)	(100.00)

Source: U.S. Small Business Administration.
[a] Only industries in which there is at least some innovation activity are included in this table.

TABLE 3—CORRELATION MATRIX OF INPUT AND OUTPUT MEASURES
OF INNOVATIVE ACTIVITY

	Total Innovations	Large-Firm Innovations	Small-Firm Innovations	Total R&D Expenditures	Company R&D Expenditures
Large-Firm Innovations	0.920	–			
Small-Firm Innovations	0.922	0.698	–		
Total R&D Expenditures	0.481	0.532	0.379	–	
Company R&D Expenditures	0.746	0.737	0.672	0.764	–
Patents	0.467	0.482	0.382	0.327	0.440

between total $R\&D$ expenditures (also from the 1977 FTC Line of Business) and total innovations, and of 0.746 between company $R\&D$ expenditures and total innovations. That the correlation between company $R\&D$ and innovative activity is stronger than the correlation between total $R\&D$ and innovative activity is consistent with the findings by Griliches (1986) that privately financed $R\&D$ has a larger effect on private productivity and profitability than does government-financed $R\&D$. The somewhat lower correlation between the $R\&D$ measures and the total number of patented inventions[7] between 1970 and 1972 is not surprising, as Pakes and Griliches (1980, p. 378) observe

[7] The correlations involving the patents are at the three-digit SIC level. (The corresponding variables were also aggregated to the three-digit SIC level.) All other correlations are for the four-digit SIC level.

that "patents are a flawed measure (of innovative output); particularly since not all new innovations are patented and since patents differ greatly in their economic impact." Still, the correlation between the output measures, total innovations, and patents is greater than that between the $R\&D$ measures and patents. Also of interest is that, just as the correlation between innovations and $R\&D$ is greater for large firms than for small ones, the correlation between patents and innovations is greater for large firms than for small ones.

The relationships between the input and output measures of innovative activity are somewhat sensitive to the total amount of innovative activity. That is, in industries in which there is little innovative activity, defined as those with fewer than seven innovations, the correlation between all of the measures of technical change become considerably weaker. In particular, the correla-

TABLE 4—COMPARISON OF INNOVATION DATA WITH $R\&D$ AND PATENT MEASURES[a]

Industry Group	Total Innovations	Patents	Patents/ Innovation	Company $R\&D$ (millions)	$R\&D$ (millions)/ Innovation
Food and Tobacco	206	311	1.51	272	1.32
Textiles and Apparel	29	147	5.07	65	2.24
Lumber and Furniture	83	50	0.60	37	0.45
Paper	61	292	4.79	150	2.46
Chemicals (excluding drugs)	332	3,492	10.52	1,260	3.80
Drugs	170	868	5.11	449	2.64
Petroleum	24	1,046	43.58	360	15.00
Rubber and Plastics	129	637	4.94	287	2.22
Stone, Clay, and Glass	59	477	8.09	149	2.53
Primary Metals	74	424	5.73	239	3.23
Fabricated Metal Products	340	450	1.32	246	0.72
Machinery (excluding office)	612	1,657	2.71	852	1.39
Computers and Office Equipment	566	1,045	1.85	1,054	1.86
Industrial Electrical Equipment[b]	444	836	1.88	210	0.47
Household Appliances	64	232	3.63	78	1.22
Communications Equipment	262	2,384	9.10	1,136	4.34
Motor Vehicles and Other Transportation Equipment[c]	152	809	5.32	1,791	11.78
Aircraft and Engines	48	501	10.44	653	13.60
Guided Missiles and Ordnance	16	173	10.81	103	6.44
Instruments	736	1,351	1.84	652	0.89
Total[d]	4,407	17,182	3.90	10,043	2.28

[a] Company $R\&D$ (1974) and patent (June 1976–March 1977) data are from Scherer (1983).
[b] Includes SIC 361, 362, 364, and 367.
[c] Includes SIC 371, 373, 374, 375, and 379.
[d] Includes only industries in this table.

tion between large-firm innovations and patents falls to 0.107, while that between small-firm innovations and patents is nearly twice as great. Similarly, the correlation between each of the $R\&D$ measures and small-firm innovations falls to less than 0.070 while that between each of the $R\&D$ measures and the large-firm innovations is not so greatly affected. In addition, the correlation between patents and each of the $R\&D$ measures falls to below 0.100 for the low-innovative industries. In the high-innovative industries, defined as those with at least fifteen innovations, the correlation between small-firm innovations and patents is also considerably weaker, as is that between the $R\&D$ measures and small-firm innovations.

Table 4 provides a more detailed comparison of an input measure—company $R\&D$ expenditures (from the FTC Line of Business Survey)—and two output measures, the total number of innovations and the total number of patented inventions between June 1976 and March 1977 (from Scherer, 1983). As the simple correlation of 0.74 indicates, there is a fairly strong relationship between the ratio of patents-per-innovation and $R\&D$ expenditures (millions of dollars)-per-innovation.[8] Of particular interest is that the patent-per-innovation ratio in drugs is about one-half of that in the rest of the broader chemical sector. This is remarkably similar to the pattern of patents-per-scientists and engineers identified by Robert E. Evenson (1984). The relatively high ratios of patents-per-innovation in the chemical and petroleum sectors, and the relatively low ratios in the computers, electrical machinery, lumber, and instruments sectors is explained by Edwin Mansfield (1984, p. 462): "The value

---

[8] Patents represent 59 percent of all invention patents issued to U.S. corporations during the sample period and 61 percent of patents issued to industrial corporations (Scherer, 1983).

TABLE 5—WEIGHTED MEAN NUMBER OF TOTAL INNOVATIONS, SMALL-FIRM INNOVATION, AND EMPLOYMENT SHARES BY TWO-DIGIT SECTOR[a]

Sector	Total Innovations	Small-Firm Innovation Share	Small-Firm Employment Share
Food	3.739	0.228	0.220
	(1.977)	(0.052)	(0.175)
Textiles	0.333	0.133	0.325
	(0.062)	(0.161)	(0.156)
Apparel	0.576	0.099	0.565
	(0.605)	(0.159)	(0.220)
Lumber	0.647	0.088	0.564
	(0.338)	(0.228)	(0.264)
Furniture	5.539	0.365	0.596
	(0.422)	(0.074)	(0.264)
Paper	3.588	0.161	0.234
	(0.103)	(0.022)	(0.199)
Printing	1.471	0.191	0.524
	(0.368)	(0.048)	(0.245)
Chemicals	17.929	0.313	0.135
	(0.014)	(0.041)	(0.163)
Petroleum	4.800	0.400	0.113
	(2.400)	(0.200)	(0.163)
Leather	0.546	0.273	0.422
	(0.776)	(0.230)	(0.182)
Stone,	2.185	0.219	0.347
Clay, and Glass	(0.036)	(0.013)	(0.264)
Primary Metals	2.846	0.276	0.227
	(1.631)	(0.043)	(0.167)
Fabricated Metal	9.556	0.388	0.524
Products	(4.301)	(0.038)	(0.192)
Machinery	25.886	0.485	0.289
(nonelectrical)	(1.355)	(0.014)	(0.199)
Electrical	20.946	0.411	0.164
Equipment	(1.824)	(0.008)	(0.155)
Transportation	9.000	0.149	0.075
Equipment	(1.000)	(0.029)	(0.325)
Instruments	56.615	0.506	0.221
	(16.344)	(0.017)	(0.121)

[a]The sector means are weighted averages (by 1977 value-of-shipments) of the four-digit SIC industry values. The small-firm innovation share is defined as the percentage of total innovations contributed by small firms. The small-firm employment share is defined as the percentage of industry employment accounted for by firms with fewer than 500 employees. The data come from the U.S. Small Business Administration, Small Business Data Base, 1982. Standard deviations are listed in parentheses.

and cost of individual patents vary enormously within and across industries... Many inventions are not patented. And in some industries, like electronics, there is considerable speculation that the patent system is being bypassed to a greater extent than in the past. Some types of technologies are more likely to be patented than others."

A broader comparison of the distribution of the innovations classified according to firm size, both between and within two-digit SIC sectors is presented in Table 5. For example, the first column shows that the mean number of total innovations in the 47 industries (weighted by the 1977 value-of-shipments) comprising the food sector was 3.74. The second column shows the small-firm innovation share, measured as the percentage of total innovations contributed by small firms, and indicates that in certain sectors the mean number of innovations contributed by the large firms far exceeded the mean number contributed by small firms, while in other sectors the pattern is reversed. As the third column indicates, in about half of the sectors the small-firm employment share exceeds the small-firm innovation share, and in the other half the innovation share of small firms exceeds the employment share.

II. The Empirical Model

We follow others (Jaffe, 1986; Scherer, 1982; and Mansfield, 1981) and assume innovative output is related to innovation-inducing inputs in the previous period according to a log relationship. The independent variables we expect to be important are: $R \& D$ expenditures (either total or company), 1977; capital intensity, measured as gross assets divided by value-of-shipments, 1977; the four-firm concentration ratio, 1977; the mean percentage of employees belonging to a union between 1973 and 1975; advertising expenditures divided by value-of-shipments; the share of 1977 industry employment accounted for by large firms (enterprises with more than 500 employees); a measure of skilled labor, defined as the percentage of employment consisting of professional and kindred workers, plus managers and administrators, plus craftsmen and kindred workers, 1970. Finally, to control for industry size, the 1977 value-of-shipments is included in the empirical model. All variable sources are listed in the Appendix.

Concentration, advertising, and capital intensity have all been hypothesized to facilitate appropriability and therefore encourage innovation (William S. Comanor, 1967; and Kamien and Schwartz, 1975). More recently, several models have been developed arguing that unions capture rents from intangible capital investments, and, in particular, those accruing from innovation-producing $R \& D$ (Robert A. Connolly, Barry Hirsch, and Mark Hirschey, 1986; and Hirsch and Albert N. Link, 1986). To the extent to which unions are successful in such rent-seeking activities, the ease of appropriability by the innovative firm is clearly reduced. Therefore, a negative

relationship between unionization and total innovative activity is expected.

By substituting the number of large-firm innovations and small-firm innovations as dependent variables into the regression model, the hypothesis by Winter (1984) that two technological regimes exist can be examined. According to Winter (1984, p. 297), "An entrepreneurial regime is one that is favorable to innovative entry and unfavorable to innovative activity by established firms; a routinized regime is one in which the conditions are the other way round." To the extent to which innovations from small and large firms emanate from different technological regimes, a difference in the parameters in the small- and large-firm innovation equations would offer support for Winter's hypothesis that large- and small-firm innovations are promoted under differing economic and technological conditions.[9] The relative small-firm innovative advantage "is likely to be roughly proportional to the number of people exposed to the knowledge base from which innovative ideas might derive." (Winter, 1984, p. 297)

While the exact dynamic relationship between the endogenous and exogenous variables is not known, this should not pose a significant problem in the context of cross-sectional analysis where each of the industry-specific attributes remains relatively invariant over time. While this model assumes the traditional view that technical change is endogenous to market structure, Partha Dasgupta and Joseph Stiglitz (1980) argue that, in fact, certain aspects of market structure are endogenous to technical change.

III. Regression Results

Using the logged value of the number of total innovations in 1982 as the dependent

---

[9] While we have seen a major shift in the twentieth century, with the large firm and the industrial research laboratory playing a much more important role in innovation, individual entrepreneurs, who are not associated with established firms (Joseph Schumpeter, 1934, p. 62), continue to survive and thrive in a number of industries (Kenney Martin, 1986).

TABLE 6 — REGRESSIONS OF LOG OF TOTAL NUMBER
OF INNOVATIONS
(*t*-statistics in parentheses)

	1	2
Log Total $R \& D$	0.364	—
	$(6.434)^a$	
Log Company $R \& D$	—	0.409
		$(7.424)^a$
Log Capital/Output	0.007	−0.040
	(0.045)	(−0.278)
Log Concentration	−0.613	−0.631
	$(−3.853)^a$	$(−4.061)^a$
Log Unionization	−0.460	−0.425
	$(−3.078)^a$	$(−2.907)^a$
Log Advertising	−0.061	−0.056
	(−1.169)	(−1.096)
Log Large-Firm Employment Share	0.438	0.400
	$(2.170)^a$	$(2.023)^a$
Log Skilled Labor	0.505	0.559
	$(2.257)^a$	$(2.620)^a$
Log Industry Size	0.032	0.621
	(0.372)	$(4.301)^a$
Constant	1.883	1.821
	(1.251)	(1.492)
Sample Size	247	247
R^2	0.457	0.482
F	25.040^a	27.730^a

^{a} Statistically significant at the 95 percent level of confidence, two-tailed test.

variable, the cross-section regressions for 247 four-digit SIC manufacturing industries are shown in Table 6. While equation (1) uses the measure of total expenditures on $R \& D$, equation (2) uses company expenditures on $R \& D$. There are two major results from this table. First, the negative coefficient of concentration suggests that lower, and not higher, levels of concentration tend to be associated with increased innovation activity. While the emergence of a negative and significant relationship is consistent with the findings of Connolly and Hirschey (1984), it is a much stronger result than found by Scherer (1965). Second, the elasticity of both company and total $R \& D$ with respect to the total number of innovations is considerably less than one. Even when the measure of company $R \& D$, which apparently explains innovative activity better than total $R \& D$, is used in equation (2), the elasticity of $R \& D$ remains below 0.5. This is somewhat less

than the elasticity of about one found between firm $R \& D$ and patents by Bound et al. (1984).

The positive coefficient of the large-firm employment share indicates that the greater the proportion of an industry consisting of firms with more than 500 employees, the greater is the innovation activity. Of the other variables representing appropriability, only unionization apparently is negatively associated with the total number of innovations, providing support for the Hirsch and Link (1986) hypothesis.[10]

Table 7 shows the results for analogous regressions where the log of the number of large-firm innovations, log of the number of small-firm innovations, and the small-firm innovation share are the dependent variables. Since the error terms in the large- and small-firm innovation regressions are presumably interrelated, the generalized least squares method for seemingly unrelated regressions was estimated using the Aitken procedure (Jan Kmenta, 1971). Skilled labor and advertising apparently have disparate relationships with small- and large-firm innovations. While skilled labor is positively and advertising negatively associated with small-firm innovations, neither is statistically associated with large-firm innovations. Although concentration is negatively associated with both large- and small-firm innovation, the elasticity of concentration with respect to small-firm innovations is more than double that for large firms. A perhaps somewhat surprising result is that not only is

---

[10] Regressions analogous to those in Table 6 were estimated substituting the patent measure used in Table 3 as the dependent variable. The results are quite similar to those using the innovation measure in Table 6. Total $R \& D$, capital/output, the large-firm employment share, and skilled labor are found to be positively related to the number of patents, while concentration is negatively related to patents. Neither advertising, which has a negative coefficient, nor unionization, which has a positive coefficient, can be considered statistically significant. Thus, substituting the patent measure for the innovation measure yields very similar results. Only unionization and capital/output have different qualitative relationships between the patent and innovation measures.

TABLE 7—REGRESSIONS OF THE LOG OF THE NUMBER OF LARGE- AND SMALL-FIRM INNOVATIONS, AND THE SMALL-FIRM INNOVATION SHARE (t-statistics listed in parentheses)[a]

Equation	Total R&D	Company R&D	Concentration	Capital/Output	Unionization	Advertising	Large-Firm Employment Share	Skilled Labor	Industry Size	Constant	Sample Size	R^2	F
1 Large-Firm Innovations	0.251 (4.711)[c]	—	-0.276 (-1.836)[b]	0.107 (0.763)	-0.415 (-2.937)[c]	-0.042 (-0.854)	0.371 (1.943)[b]	0.294 (1.388)	0.150 (1.825)[b]	0.020 (0.017)	247	0.372	—
2 Small-Firm Innovations	0.278 (5.850)[c]	—	-0.705 (2.036)[c]	-0.060 (-0.481)	-0.442 (-3.517)[c]	-0.082 (-1.866)[b]	0.437 (2.572)[c]	0.383 (2.036)[c]	-0.158 (-2.155)[c]	3.802 (1.056)	247	0.366	—
3 Large-Firm Innovations	—	0.294 (5.612)[c]	-0.294 (-1.987)[c]	0.078 (0.568)	-0.388 (-2.785)[c]	-0.038 (-0.787)	0.339 (1.802)[b]	0.318 (1.567)	0.110 (1.361)	-0.022 (-0.019)	247	0.393	—
4 Small-Firm Innovations	—	0.324 (7.015)[c]	-0.723 (-5.556)[c]	-0.093 (-0.769)	-0.412 (-3.356)[c]	-0.078 (-1.813)[b]	0.401 (2.423)[c]	0.411 (2.300)[c]	-0.202 (-2.842)[c]	3.756 (3.669)[c]	247	0.398	—
5 Small-Firm Innovation Share	-0.389 (-1.765)[b]	—	-0.505 (-2.811)[c]	-0.001 (-3.077)[c]	(0.569)	-7.306 (-0.456)	0.355 (2.535)[c]	0.785 (2.881)[c]	-0.154 (-0.367)	0.168 (1.459)	247	0.117	3.94[b]
6 Small-Firm Innovation Share	—	-0.138 (-0.463)	-0.004 (-2.837)[c]	-0.484 (-2.934)[b]	-0.001 (0.637)	-7.194 (-0.446)	0.330 (2.327)[c]	0.666 (2.482)[c]	-0.400 (-0.903)	0.209 (1.834)[b]	247	0.116	3.92[b]

[a] The method of generalized least squares (Aitken procedure) was used to estimate large-firm innovations and small-firm innovations. The logs for all explanatory variables are used to estimate log large-firm innovations and log small-firm innovations but not for the small-firm innovation share.
[b] Statistically significant at the 90 percent level of confidence, two-tailed test.
[c] Statistically significant at the 95 percent level of confidence, two-tailed test.

the coefficient of the large-firm employment share positive and significant for small-firm innovations, but it is actually greater in magnitude than for large firms. This suggests that, *ceteris paribus*, the greater extent to which an industry is composed of large firms, the greater will be the innovative activity, but that increased innovative activity will tend to emanate more from the small firms than from the large firms. Perhaps this indicates that, in industries composed predominantly of large firms, the existing small firms must resort to a strategy of innovation in order to remain viable. This is consistent with the findings of Richard E. Caves and Thomas A. Pugel (1980) that smaller firms in an industry tend to perform better if they use different strategies from those followed by the larger firms.[11]

Equations (5) and (6) address a slightly different question. Rather than considering what determines the extent of innovative activity in small firms, small-firm innovative activity is examined relative to that in the entire industry.[12] The small-firm innovation share, or the number of small-firm innovations divided by the number of total innovations, is used as the dependent variable. The negative coefficients of total R&D, concentration, and capital/output, suggest that the number of small-firm innovations tends to be small relative to that in the entire industry in industries which are high in R&D, capital-intensive, and which are concentrated. The positive coefficients of the large-firm employment share and skilled labor imply that the innovation activity of small firms is high relative to the industry level in in-

[11] The disparate effect of the large-firm employment share on small- and large-firm innovation rates is perhaps implied by Scherer (1980, p. 422), "...the most favorable industrial environment for rapid technological progress would appear to be a firm size distribution that includes a predominance of companies with sales below $500 million, pressed on one side by a horde of small, technologically oriented enterprises bubbling over with bright new ideas and on the other by a few larger corporations with the capacity to undertake exceptionally ambitious developments."

[12] For further analysis of the difference between large- and small-firm innovation rates, see our 1987 paper.

TABLE 8—HYPOTHESES TESTS FOR THE
DIFFERENCES IN THE DETERMINANTS OF
INNOVATION BETWEEN LARGE AND
SMALL FIRMS (BASED ON REGRESSIONS
3 AND 4 IN TABLE 7)

Variable Hypothesized[a]	SSR[b]	F
Company $R \& D$	118.21	3.665[d]
Capital/Output	120.80	0.279
Concentration	118.25	3.625[d]
Unionization	120.71	0.398
Advertising	120.73	0.359
Large-Firm Employment Share	120.73	0.359
Skilled Labor	118.23	3.630[d]
All Variables[c]	104.276	2.731[d]

[a] The variable hypothesized and therefore constrained to have an identical effect on large-firm innovations and small-firm innovations. Each hypothesis is tested by comparing the sum of the squares explained by the regression from the regression with the restricted coefficient to that from the unrestricted regression. For further explanation of the hypothesis test, see Kmenta (1971).
[b] SSR refers to the sum of squares explained by the estimated regressions for small-firm innovations with the restricted coefficient.
[c] The coefficients of all the explanatory variables are constrained to be identical for the large-firm innovation and small-firm innovation equations.
[d] Statistically significant at the 95 percent level of confidence.

dustries in which there is only a small share of small firms, and in which skilled labor plays an important role.

The results from Table 7 do not support an unequivocal conclusion regarding the exact differences in innovation behavior between large and small firms. While the first four equations imply that skilled labor, advertising, and perhaps concentration and the large-firm employment share, account for the different patterns in innovative activity between large and small firms, the last two equations suggest that total $R \& D$, concentration, capital/output, large-firm employment share, and skilled labor account for the differences in relative innovative activity. Thus, in Table 8 the hypotheses that each variable has an identical effect on small- and large-firm innovation activity are tested. The resulting F-test is statistically significant for skilled labor, company $R \& D$, and con-

centration, as well as for the hypothesis that all of the variables jointly have an identical effect on small- and large-firm innovation activity. Thus, while there still remains ambiguity regarding the exact patterns between $R \& D$, appropriability, and innovation activity for large and small firms, there is considerable support for Winter's (1984) hypothesis that different economic and technological regimes may account for at least some of the differences between the innovation activity of large and small firms.

IV. Conclusion

We have introduced a new and more direct measure of innovative activity in this paper and found that, while the total number of innovations is closely related to $R \& D$ expenditures (particularly after excluding federal $R \& D$), and patented inventions, especially at the more aggregated level, the exact relationship between $R \& D$ and innovation is somewhat different from that between $R \& D$ and patents. While Bound et al. (1984) found that, based on firm data, the elasticity of $R \& D$ expenditures with respect to patented inventions is about one, we find that the number of innovations increases with increased industry $R \& D$ expenditures but at a decreasing rate. Similarly, while the literature has found a somewhat ambiguous relationship between concentration and various measures of technical change, our results are unequivocal—industry innovation tends to decrease as the level of concentration rises. In addition, there is evidence supporting the hypothesis that unionization is negatively related to innovation activity. Of course, these results are at best an introduction of the innovation data and need to be qualified, particularly in light of the likely simultaneity between industry technology and market structure. Future research may be able to incorporate the endogeneity of market structure in a manner suggested by Levin and Peter Reiss (1984).

This paper has also provided evidence supporting Winter's (1984) prediction that the innovation activity of small and large firms responds to considerably different technological and economic environments.

These findings are not without ambiguity. Further research should apply the patent measure in a similar framework to determine whether its performance differs from that of the innovation measure used here.

APPENDIX: DATA SOURCES AND FURTHER EXPLANATIONS

The data on innovations and employment for small and large firms come from the U.S. Small Business Administration (Edwards and Gordon, 1984). These data can be obtained upon request from the authors. The U.S. Department of Commerce, Bureau of the Census, *Annual Survey of Manufactures*, 1977, *Industry Profiles*, Washington: USGPO, issued 1981, is the source for capital/output (gross assets divided by value-of-shipments), concentration, and value-of-shipments. The advertising measure was derived by using the value-of-shipments data described above and advertising expenditures, from the 1972 U.S. Input-Output Table.

The unionization data are from Richard B. Freeman and James L. Medoff (1979). The percentage of total employment that is unionized for three-digit SIC industries between 1973 and 1975 is reported. We repeat these three-digit SIC values at the four-digit level. The measure of skilled labor is from the U.S. Department of Commerce, Bureau of the Census, Census Population 1970, Subject Report PC (2)-7C, *Occupation by Industry*, Washington: USGPO, issued 1972.

The total *R&D* and company *R&D* data are from the 1977 Federal Trade Commission Line of Business Report. The patent measure used for the disaggregated three-digit SIC correlations in Table 3 is from the Office of Technology Assessment and Forecast of the U.S. Patent Office. Both the patent and skill measures are taken from the *U.S. International Trade Commission's Industrial Characteristics and Trade Performance Data Bank*, June 1975, Office of Economic Research, Washington, D.C. The USITC data bank is described by Edward J. Ray (1981) and these measures are available from the authors on request.

REFERENCES

Acs, Zoltan J. and Audretsch, David B., "Innovation, Market Structure, and Firm Size," *Review of Economics and Statistics*, November 1987, *69*, 567–75.

Bound, John, Cummins, Clint, Griliches, Zvi, Hall, Bronwyn H. and Jaffe, Adam, "Who Does *R&D* and Who Patents?," in Zvi Griliches, ed., *R&D, Patents, and Productivity*, Chicago: University of Chicago, 1984, 21–54.

Caves, Richard E. and Pugel, Thomas A., *Intraindustry Differences in Conduct and*

Peformance: Viable Strategies in U.S. Manufacturing Industries, New York University Press, 1980.

Comanor, William S., "Market Structure, Product Differentiation, and Industrial Research," *Quarterly Journal of Economics*, November 1967, *81*, 639–57.

Connolly, Robert A., Hirsch, Barry T. and Hirschey, Mark, "Union Rent Seeking, Intangible Capital, and the Market Value of the Firm," *Review of Economics and Statistics*, November 1986, *68*, 567–77.

_____ and Hirschey, Mark, "*R&D*, Market Structure and Profits: A Value-Based Approach," *Review of Economics and Statistics*, November 1984, *66*, 682–86.

Dasgupta, Partha and Stiglitz, Joseph, "Industrial Structure and the Nature of Innovative Activity," *Economic Journal*, June 1980, *90*, 266–93.

Edwards, Keith L. and Gordon, Theodore, J., "Characterization of Innovations Introduced on the U.S. Market in 1982," The Futures Group, U.S. Small Business Administration, Contract No. SBA-6050-0A-82, March 1984.

Evenson, Robert E., "International Invention: Implications for Technology Market Analysis," in Zvi Griliches, ed., *R&D, Patents, and Productivity*, Chicago: University of Chicago, 1984, 55–70.

Freeman, Richard B. and Medoff, James L., "New Estimates of Private Sector Unionism in the United States," *Industrial and Labor Relations Review*, January 1979, *32*, 143–74.

Griliches, Zvi, "Productivity, *R&D*, and Basic Research at the Firm Level in the 1970's," *American Economic Review*, March 1986, *76*, 141–54.

Hall, Bronwyn H., Griliches, Zvi and Hausman, Jerry A., "Patents and R&D: Is There a Lag?," *International Economic Review*, June 1986, *27*, 265–302.

Hirsch, Barry T. and Link, Albert N., "Labor Union Effects on Innovative Activity," unpublished manuscript, University of North Carolina-Greensboro, 1986.

Jaffe, Adam B., "Technological Opportunity and Spillovers of *R&D*: Evidence from Firms' Patents, Profits, and Market Value," *American Economic Review*, December 1986, *76*, 984–1001.

Kamien, Morton I. and Schwartz, Nancy L., "Market Structure and Innovation: A Survey," *Journal of Economic Literature*, March 1975, *13*, 1–37.

Kmenta, Jan, *Elements of Econometrics*, New York: Macmillan, 1971.

Kuznets, Simon, "Inventive Activity: Problems of Definition and Measurement," in R. R. Nelson, ed., *The Rate of Direction of Inventive Activity*, Princeton: Princeton University Press, 1962, 19–43.

Levin, Richard C., Cohen, Welsley M. and Mowery, David C., "*R&D* Appropriability, Opportunity, and Market Structure: New Evidence on Some Schumpeterian Hypotheses," *American Economic Review*, May 1985, *75*, 20–24.

_____, and Reiss, Peter C., "Tests of a Schumpeterian Model of *R&D* and Market Structure," in Zvi Griliches, ed., *R&D, Patents, and Productivity*, Chicago: University of Chicago Press, 1984, 462–64.

Mansfield, Edwin, "Comment on Using Linked Patent and *R&D* Data to Measure Interindustry Technology Flows," in Zvi Griliches, ed., *R&D, Patents, and Productivity*, Chicago: University of Chicago, 1984, 175–204.

_____, "Composition of R and D Expenditures: Relationship to Size of Firm, Concentration, and Innovative Output," *Review of Economics and Statistics*, November 1981, *63*, 610–15.

Martin, Kenney, "Schumpeterian Innovation and Entrepreneurs in Capitalism," *Research Policy*, February 1986, *1*, 21–33.

Pakes, Ariel, "On Patents, *R&D*, and the Stock Market Rate of Return," *Journal of Political Economy*, April 1985, *93*, 390–409.

_____, and Griliches, Zvi, "Patents and *R&D* at the Firm Level: A First Report," *Eco-*

nomics Letters, 1980, *4*, 377–81.

_____, and Griliches, Zvi, "Patents and *R&D* at the Firm Level: A First Look," in Zvi Griliches, ed., *R&D, Patents, and Productivity*, Chicago: University of Chicago, 1984, 55–70.

_____, and Schankerman, Mark, "The Rate of Obsolescence of Patents, Research Gestation Lags, and the Private Rate of Return to Research Resources," in Zvi Griliches, ed., *R&D, Patents, and Productivity*, Chicago: University of Chicago, 1984, 73–88.

Ray, Edward J., "The Determinants of Tariffs and Nontariff Trade Restrictions in the United States," *Journal of Political Economy*, February 1981, *89*, 105–21.

Scherer, F. M., "The Propensity to Patent," *International Journal of Industrial Organization*, 1983, *1*, 107–28.

_____, "Inter-Industry Technology Flows and Productivity Growth," *Review of Economics and Statistics*, December 1982, *64*, 627–34.

_____, *Industrial Market Structure and Economic Performance*, Chicago: Rand McNally College Publishing, 1980.

_____, "Market Structure and the Employment of Scientists and Engineers," *American Economic Review*, June 1967, *57*, 524–30.

_____, "Firm Size, Market Structure, Opportunity, and the Output of Patented Inventions," *American Economic Review*, December 1965, *55*, 1097–125.

Schumpeter, Joseph, *The Theory of Economic Development*, Cambridge: Harvard University Press, 1934.

Winter, Sidney G., "Schumpeterian Competition in Alternative Technological Regimes," *Journal of Economic Behavior and Organization*, September–December 1984, *5*, 287–320.

R&D RIVALRY, INDUSTRIAL POLICY, AND U.S.–JAPANESE TRADE

David B. Audretsch and Hideki Yamawaki*

Abstract—We examine how the strategic aspect of Japanese research and development expenditures and industrial policies affected U.S.–Japanese bilateral trade during the late 1970s, and investigate which component of R&D—expenditures on process innovation, product quality improvements, new products or new technology, and technology transfer—proved to be most effective. We find that while Japanese R&D expenditures have generally promoted Japan's trade advantage, certain components of R&D have proved more effective than others. The depreciation subsidy and special status with the MITI is positively related to the Japanese trade performance, while legal cartelization status has not had any apparent effect.

I. Introduction

THE significance of U.S.–Japanese trade has not gone unnoticed in the popular press. This is reflected in the Economic Report of the President, which reports that, particularly with respect to Japan, "Concern over the international competiveness of the United States is as high as it has ever been" (1983, p. 52). While U.S.–Japanese trade has often been thought to be an important factor contributing to Japan's high growth rate between 1955 and 1970 (Ueno, 1980), the recent U.S. trade deficits with Japan have been considered to be a catalyst for the new wave of protectionist pressures in the United States during the 1980s as well as for the September 1985 agreement for multilateral intervention to precipitate a decline in the value of the dollar. Despite this preeminence, there is a scarcity of empirical research attempting to identify the determinants of U.S.–Japanese trade (see Petri, 1984, and Baldwin, 1971). The purpose of this paper is to examine how the strategic aspect of Japanese research and development (R&D) expenditures and industrial policies affected the balance of U.S.–Japanese trade during the late 1970s.

Received for publication October 14, 1986. Revision accepted for publication December 31, 1987.

* Wissenschaftszentrum Berlin für Sozialforschung.

We are grateful to George Bittlingmayer, Richard Caves, Paul Geroski, Thomas Pugel, and the anonymous referees, as well as to seminar participants at the Catholic University Leuven and the International Institute of Management, Berlin for their helpful comments. We thank Michael Karge and Talat Mahmood for their research and computational assistance. We are also thankful to Edward J. Ray for making some of the data available to us.

This paper is unique in two ways. First, we focus on Japanese expenditures on R&D as a strategic instrument for rivalry, as well as the level of R&D in the United States, as a significant determinant of bilateral trade. In particular, we examine which component of R&D—expenditures on process innovation, product quality improvements, new products or new technology, and technology transfer—proved to be most effective. Previous work has tended to estimate trade only on the basis of R&D intensity in one country, typically the United States, presumably due to data limitations, and has not considered how the different components of R&D have had differential impacts on trade. Second, we have included direct measures of industrial policies, such as the tax depreciation subsidy and special treatment from the Ministry of International Trade and Industry (MITI), and legal cartelization status. No previous study, to our knowledge, has considered industrial policy as a determinant of trade.[1]

After the hypothesis is introduced in the second section of the paper, the Japanese R&D and technology data are described in the third section. In the fourth section a cross-section regression model estimating the 1977 U.S.–Japanese balance of trade at the four-digit standard industrial classification (SIC) level is presented. Finally, in the last section, a summary and conclusion from the empirical results is provided. We find that while Japanese R&D generally has promoted the comparative advantage, certain components, such as expenditures on improving the quality of existing products, and process innovation reducing costs for existing products have proved more effective than have expenditures on developing new products and technologies and on applications emanating from technology transfer. Similarly, we find that although the depreciation subsidy and special status with the MITI is negatively related to the U.S. bilateral trade balance, legal cartelization status has not had any apparent effect.

[1] Several studies have included measures of trade policy, including tariff and non-tariff barriers. For examples, see Ray (1981a and 1981b).

II. The Model

We test the hypotheses that (1) R&D served as a strategic instrument for Japanese firms which promoted the comparative advantage, (2) the four major components of R&D—Japanese expenditures on process innovation, product quality improvements, new products or new technology, and technology transfer—had disparate effects on the trade balance, and (3) Japanese industrial policy was related to the trade performance in the targeted industries, by estimating a model which decomposes the determinants of trade into four general components:

$$TB = \alpha + \beta_1 (R\&D_J - R\&D_{US}) + \beta_2 R\&D_{US}$$
$$+ \sum_{i=1}^{l} \gamma_{1i} IP_i + \sum_{j=1}^{m} \gamma_{2j} MS_j$$
$$+ \sum_{k=1}^{n} \gamma_{3k} FE_k + \epsilon \qquad (1)$$

The U.S.–Japanese trade balance, TB, is defined as $(X - M)/(X + M)$, where X is U.S. exports to Japan in 1977, and M is U.S. imports from Japan in 1977. This trade measure weights net exports, $X - M$, by the total amount traded between the two countries, $X + M$, and has the advantage of implicitly controlling for transportability, while providing a direct measure of comparative advantage. As Pugel (1978) notes, although this measure has the disadvantage of perhaps overstating the importance of the low balance of trade in industries in which there is only little international trade, it is the best comprehensive measure of comparative advantage.

$R\&D_J$ and $R\&D_{US}$ indicate the relative R&D intensities between Japanese and U.S. firms in a given industry. While Spencer and Brander (1983) suggest that process R&D serves as a strategic instrument for enhancing market share, we extend this concept to product R&D. Thus, to the extent that R&D expenditures are not evenly distributed between the two countries for any given industry, the bilateral trade balance, ceteris paribus, should reflect the asymmetry.

From this model two important hypotheses regarding R&D rivalry between the United States and Japan can be tested. The first hypothesis is that, as has been the implicit assumption in most empirical trade models, the R&D behavior of the trading partner of the United States has no effect

on trade patterns, or H_0: $\beta_1 = \beta_J = 0$. The alternative hypothesis is that Japanese R&D expenditures had a beneficial impact on the Japanese trade performance, or H_1: $\beta_J < 0$. The second hypothesis is that the expenditures on R&D by both countries had an identical impact on the bilateral trade balance, or $\beta_1 = -\beta_{US} = \beta_J$. Since

$$\beta_1(R\&D_J - R\&D_{US}) + \beta_2 R\&D_{US}$$
$$= \beta_1 R\&D_J - \beta_1 R\&D_{US} + \beta_2 R\&D_{US} \qquad (2)$$

the effect of additional R&D expenditures by Japan is $\beta_J = \beta_1$, while for the United States it is $\beta_{US} = -\beta_1 + \beta_2$.[2]

Because there have been virtually as few empirical tests of the relationship between trade and government intervention as there have been conjectures, we consider that Japanese industrial policy, represented by IP_i, may be statistically related to trade performance. The influences of market structure characteristics, represented by MS_j, on trade relationships have been shown by White (1974), Pugel (1978), and Caves et al. (1980). While the factor endowments, represented by FE_k, such as capital–labor and human capital, play perhaps the most crucial role in determining trade balances, there exists a full literature explaining and estimating their influences (see Urata (1983) for Japan; Stern and Maskus (1981) for the United States). These variables derived from the theory of international trade are included to provide the full and appropriate specification of the model. However, because our focus is on the R&D and industrial policy aspects of trade, and the literature concerning the factor endowments has been so fully developed, we restrict our discussion and are concerned primarily with the first two components.

The impact of Japanese R&D as an instrument for strategic rivalry is analyzed by including two types of Japanese R&D and technology variables in the regression model—the Japanese R&D/Sales ratio, along with the allocation of the R&D budget among four different major categories of expendi-

---

[2] It should be noted that the same hypotheses could be tested by including RD_J and RD_{US} as separate variables in the regression model. However, the ensuing hypotheses tests, while yielding the identical results, are considerably more complicated and require a t-test using the variance-covariance matrix. The same hypothesis tests based on estimating equation (1) require only the standard t-ratios based on the estimated coefficients for β_1 and β_2.

tures, and the total Japanese payments for purchased technology (as a percentage of sales), as well as the allocation of technology purchases from the United States, Europe and Japan. To measure the direct impact, the difference in the 1977 R&D/Sales ratio between Japan and the United States is represented along with the U.S. R&D/Sales ratio. If R&D expenditures do not serve as an instrument for strategic rivalry, the coefficient of the difference between the two countries' R&D/Sales should be insignificant. If, however, as we suspect, R&D/Sales ratios serve as a strategic instrument for rivalry, its coefficient, β_1, should be negative, while the net effect $(\beta_1 + \beta_2)$ of the U.S. R&D/Sales ratios should be positive.

To address the question of which type of R&D expenditure proved to be the most successful, 1969 Japanese R&D expenditures on process innovation, product quality improvements, new products or new technology, and technology transfer are included as four separate variables. We follow the example of Griliches (1986) by measuring these as a percentage of total R&D expenditure, to examine how the allocation of R&D was related to the trade balance. According to Peck and Tamura (1976), and Ueno (1980), productivity in Japanese industry has benefited more from importation of foreign technology and exploitation of existing technology than from the development of new domestic technology. To the extent that this is true, R&D expenditures on improving the quality of existing products and on reducing costs through process innovation should have a stronger negative effect on the balance of trade than do expenditures on developing new products and new technology. However, since Caves and Uekusa (1976) found that aggregate purchases of foreign technology had no net effect on productivity, the pattern of significance among these four variables cannot confidently be predicted a priori.

Similarly, to address the question of which type of purchased technology proved to be the most successful, Japanese purchases from the United States, Europe and from domestic sources are included as three distinct variables. Again, following the example of Griliches (1986), these are measured as a percentage of the total amount of technology purchased in 1969. As with the components of R&D expenditure, no a priori pattern of significance can be predicted for the sources of purchased technology.

Japanese industrial policy, or at least one aspect of it, is reflected by including a dummy variable taking on a value of one when the industry had been a target for Japanese industrial policy in the form of preferential depreciation allowance status between 1962 and 1973, and zero otherwise. Specifically, those industries with 10% or more of total depreciation covered by a special depreciation allowance (the average was 8%) are classified as recipients of preferential status. Thirty-three industries were categorized as having been the recipients of preferential depreciation allowance status and therefore were assigned a value of one, while the remaining 180 industries were assigned a value of zero for this variable. These 33 industries are in the broadly classified shipbuilding, automobiles, steel, machinery, and textile sectors, which Ogura and Yoshina (1984) identified as having the most generous depreciation allowances.[3] When an industry was granted such status, it signalled that the MITI considered the industry to be strategic (Ito et al., 1984). According to Ueno, "A subsidy is important in itself, but it is more important as a signal indicating that the industry or the product receiving the subsidy is publicly recognized as one under government protection" (1980, p. 388). If Japanese industrial policy has been effective, the regression coefficient is expected to be negative. Similarly, the percentage of an industry granted legalized cartel status in 1970 through exemption from the Japanese Antimonopoly Law is included.[4]

Of these variables measuring industrial policy and R&D expenditures in Japan, only the industrial policy and cartelization measures represent direct government intervention into the economy. The remaining variables represent essentially the decisions of private firms. Prior to 1967 the MITI exerted considerable influence over purchases of foreign technology through controlling the allocation of foreign currency.[5] However, following the Kennedy Round the MITI lost this

---

[3] Specifically, the special depreciation allowance as a percentage of total depreciation between 1962–1973 was 15% in shipbuilding, 13% in autos, 12% in steel, 13% in machinery, and 10% in textiles. The average in manufacturing industries was 8% (Ogura and Yoshino, 1984).

[4] Of the 886 exempted cartels in 1970, 52.9% were classified under "Medium and Small Enterprises Organization Law," 24.6% under "Export-Import Transactions Law," 2.5% under "Provisional Measures Laws," and 1.10% under "Rationalization Cartels" (Imai, 1980, p. 111).

[5] The relative importance of imported technology upon

influence. Subsequently, annual average purchases of foreign technology increased from 103 between 1950–59 and 469 between 1960–67, to 1,154 in 1969. Thus, the measures of technology purchases could no longer be considered to be under the province of the MITI by 1969 (Goto and Wakasugi, 1984).

Similarly, Japanese expenditures of R&D were largely autonomous from MITI influence by the late 1960s. Although the MITI had earlier exerted considerable influence over R&D expenditures in the form of subsidies and special tax credits, this policy was largely abandoned by 1965. Thus, the percentage of R&D expenditures (including technology transfers) that was subsidized by the government, either directly or else through special tax credits, fell from 10.34% during 1955–59 to 5.88% in 1960–64, and to 3.43% in 1965–69. By 1975–79 this percentage had fallen to 2.52%, indicating the autonomy of private R&D expenditures from government intervention (Goto and Wakasugi, 1984).

The industrial organization variables included are the 1977 four-firm concentration ratio and advertising–sales ratio. Whereas White (1974) demonstrated that market concentration is conducive to imports through the incentive of elevated price–cost margins, Koo and Martin (1984) found a negative and statistically significant relationship between concentration and net exports. The advertising intensity, measured as advertising expenditures divided by 1977 value of shipments, is included to represent industries in which product differentiation plays an important role and thus may present a barrier to Japanese firms in penetrating the U.S. market.

The traditional trade variables, which have been included to complete the specificity of the model, are the 1977 capital–labor ratio, human capital, relative U.S. tariff rates, and the relative non-tariff barriers between the United States and Japan. The capital–labor ratio has been found to be negatively related to U.S. net exports in most empirical studies (Baldwin, 1971; Stern and Maskus, 1981).

The human capital variable is a measure of the difference between the annual average industry wage per employee and the annual wage for persons with less than eight years' education, capitalized at 10% for 1970. The identical measure has been frequently used in the trade literature (Baldwin, 1971). Empirical studies generally find that human capital is positively related to the U.S. trade balance.

The relative tariff measure is the ratio of average U.S. tariff rates in 1970 to the average tariff rates of other major industrialized countries in 1970. Similar tariff measures were used by Ray (1981a and 1981b), who argues that tariff barriers should not have a strong effect on exports and imports. Although, as Ray finds, tariff rates are certainly endogenous to trade performance, the seven-year lag between the relative tariff values and the dependent variable suggests that we can consider the relative tariff measure as a predetermined variable. Similarly, relative non-tariff barriers are represented by the ratio of non-tariff barriers in the United States to non-tariff barriers in Japan. Ray argues, and found, that non-tariff barriers should have a larger effect on trade than do tariff barriers. Like tariff barriers, the non-tariff barrier measure can also be classified as predetermined because of the seven-year lag.

The model presented here represents an evolution from previous research by including the R&D behavior, technology policies, and industrial policies of a trading partner of the United States, rather than merely including U.S. industry-specific characteristics (see Badwin, 1971, Ray, 1981b, and Stern and Maskus, 1981). While including the relevant characteristics of all variables for both trading partners is a desirable goal of this research, data limitations severely limit such a possibility at this point (see Yamawaki and Audretsch, forthcoming, for preliminary work on including paired variables for both countries for all characteristics).

III. Data

To estimate the model discussed in the previous section, several variables measuring R&D intensity, the allocation of R&D, technology purchases, and the allocation of technology purchases, all for Japan have to be introduced. A summary of these variables is included in table 1, along with all

---

Japan's economy had diminished even by 1960. The proportion of the total value of output that was produced with imported technology was only 10% in 1960. Similarly, the proportion of total investment in plant and equipment that was based on imported technology was only 15% in 1960 (Goto and Wakasugi, 1984, p. 160).

TABLE 1. — VARIABLE DEFINITIONS, MEANS AND STANDARD DEVIATIONS

Variable Name	Definition	Mean/Std. Deviation
TB	U.S.–Japanese bilateral trade balance, 1977	−0.1734 (0.7013)
USR&D	U.S. R&D expenditures/sales (%), 1977	2.5423 (2.6179)
JR&D	Japanese R&D expenditures/sales (%), 1977	1.4256 (0.9571)
JR&D-USR&D	Difference between Japanese and U.S. R&D intensities, 1977	−1.1166 (2.0370)
JProcess Innovation R&D	Japanese R&D expenditures on process innovation for existing products/Total R&D expenditures (%), 1969	16.0030 (6.1920)
JProduct Quality R&D	Japanese R&D expenditures on product quality improvements for existing products/Total R&D expenditures (%), 1969	33.3730 (8.5020)
JNew Products Technology R&D	Japanese R&D expenditures for developing new products and technology/Total R&D expenditures (%), 1969	37.9370 (10.9230)
JTechnology Transfer R&D	Japanese R&D expenditures on applications from technology transfer/Total R&D expenditures (%), 1969	5.1192 (3.8766)
JTechnology Purchases	Total Japanese purchases on technology/sales, 1969	0.0263 (0.0266)
JTechnology from US	Japanese technology purchases from US/Total technology purchases, 1969.	0.6133 (0.2342)
JTechnology from Europe	Japanese technology purchases from Europe/Total technology purchases, 1969	0.2437 (0.2316)
JTechnology from Japan	Japanese domestic technology purchases/ Total technology purchases, 1969	0.0949 (0.1589)
JIndustrial Policy	Dummy variable equal to one if 10% or more of total depreciation was covered by the special depreciation allowance in Japan, 1962–1973	0.1549 (0.3627)
JCartelization	Percentage of industry granted legalized cartel status in Japan, 1970	30.1300 (19.5980)
USAD/Sales	U.S. advertising expenditures/value-of-shipments (%), 1977	0.9200 (1.5800)
USCR4	U.S. four-firm concentration ratio (%), 1977	41.3240 (21.5040)
USK/L	U.S. assets/employment, 1977	17,725 (22,929)
USHumanK	U.S. difference between the annual average wage per employee and the annual wage for persons with less than eight years' education (capitalized at 10%), 1970	3.0074 (0.7819)
USNTB	U.S. non-tariff barrier index, 1970	0.6743 (1.9229)
JNTB	Japanese non-tariff barrier index, 1970	0.7078 (2.1514)
USTB	U.S. average tariff rates (%), 1970	10.7850 (7.8905)
WTB	Average tariff rates of non-U.S. major industrial countries (%), 1970	9.4160 (3.7750)

variable definitions, means and standard deviations for the 213 industries used in the regression analysis. All data sources and additional explanations are given in appendix A, which is available upon request. Table 1 shows that while an average of 2.54% of sales in the United States was allocated towards R&D expenditures (*USR&D*) in 1977, only 1.43% of sales in Japan went towards R&D (*JR&D*). Although the mean difference between the Japanese and U.S. R&D intensities was 1.12%, these two measures tend to move together

across manufacturing industries as the simple correlation of 0.720 reflects. An alternative measure of R&D intensity, the percentage of industry employment consisting of scientists and engineers, which is not included in table 1, yields a similar pattern. While there was an average of 2.84% of the labor force consisting of scientists and engineers in the United States in 1970, in Japan the equivalent ratio was 1.80% in 1969. However, while the R&D/Sales measure between the United States and Japan is virtually identical, and thus conducive to comparison, the measure for scientists and engineers is somewhat different between the two countries, particularly in the way in which engineers are defined. Thus, we use only the superior measure, the R&D-sales ratio, in comparing R&D intensities between the United States and Japan.

While the trade data are at the four-digit SIC level, the R&D data for Japan, like all of the Japanese technology variables, are available only at a more aggregated level, for broadly defined industries which roughly correspond between two-digit and three-digit SIC industries. In making the data sets congruous, we followed the same procedure as Caves and Uekusa (1976), who used the same Japanese data set, in assuming that the value of the Japanese technology variable was common among all appropriate four-digit industries.[6] As Caves and Uekusa noted, this most likely introduces errors of measurement into the regression analysis. However, as they also suggest, because the industries which are grouped together are similar in their technological opportunity classes, their patterns in R&D should be quite similar. Further, because all of the other data are at the four-digit SIC level, including the dependent variable, the measurement error is most likely minimized through this procedure, rather than by aggregating all of the other variables, including net trade.

All of the other Japanese R&D and technology purchase variables are from the Japanese Industrial and Science Agency. The data are based on a 1970 survey covering 582 large companies with more than 500 million Yen of capital. There are two potential sources of bias involved in using these data. The first is the greater degree of aggregation of the Japanese R&D, technology, industrial policy, and cartel variables than that of the dependent and other explanatory variables. Among other things, this exacerbates the multicollinearity problem by repeating values across four-digit industries common to more broadly defined sectors. For example, there is a simple correlation of 0.716 between *JR&D* and *JTechnology Purchases*, and 0.311 between *JIndustrial Policy* and *JTechnology Purchases*. The second potential

source of bias involves the eight-year lag between the Japanese technology variables and the bilateral trade measure. However, while 1970 is the only year available for these data, a rather lengthy time lag may be appropriate for explaining subsequent trade patterns. Goto and Wakasugi (1987) argue that Japanese industrial and technology policies were implemented with long time horizons approaching a decade for expected results. Similarly, Griliches (1986) and Sveikauskas (1983), among others, have pointed out that the impact of technology-oriented investments does not typically materialize for a number of years. This would suggest that the lag between the Japanese technology variables and the bilateral trade measure may be quite appropriate and not a debilitating source of bias.

IV. Regression Results

Using the balance of trade between the United States and Japan as the dependent variable, the cross-section regression results for 213 four-digit SIC manufacturing industries are shown in table 2. Because the dependent variable by definition varies between minus one and plus one, the logit method of estimation was used to compare with the ordinary least squares (OLS) results.[7] Two important hypotheses can be tested from the estimated coefficients of *JR&D-USR&D* and *USR&D*. The first addresses the question, "Did Japanese expenditures on R&D have any impact on the bilateral trade balance?" or $H_0: \beta_J = 0$. As the negative and statistically significant coefficient of *JR&D-USR&D* implies, this hypothesis is rejected, suggesting that with an additional dollar of R&D in Japan, its trade balance improved by 0.1492.

The second important hypothesis addresses the question, "Was the impact of additional R&D expenditures on the trade performance equivalent for the United States and Japan?" or $H_0: \beta_1 = \beta_J = -\beta_{US}$. As the statistically significant coefficient of *USR&D* implies, this hypothesis can also be rejected, suggesting that R&D expenditures in the two countries do not have identical impacts on the trade balance. Finally, the impact of additional expenditures on R&D is considerably less in the

---

[6] Note that while Caves and Uekusa (1976) used 99 industries, we use 213. This reflects a greater level of disaggregation in our dependent variable than in theirs.

[7] In order to use the logit estimation method, the variable had to be transformed to varying between zero and plus one.

TABLE 2.— REGRESSIONS OF THE BALANCE OF TRADE BETWEEN THE UNITED STATES AND JAPAN

	OLS		Logit	
	1	2	3	4
JR&D-USR&D	−0.1492	−0.1486	−0.6622	−0.6590
	(0.0816)[a]	(0.0814)[a]	(0.3501)[a]	(0.3493)[a]
USR&D	−0.1242	−0.1238	−0.5350	−0.5329
	(0.0747)[a]	(0.0745)[a]	(0.3205)[a]	(0.3198)[a]
JTechnology Purchases	4.8121	4.7392	21.6960	21.2690
	(2.9474)	(2.9266)	(12.6450)[a]	(12.5580)[a]
JIndustrial Policy	−0.3673	−0.3602	−1.3147	−1.2730
	(0.1442)[b]	(0.1411)[b]	(0.6185)[b]	(0.6054)[b]
JCartelization	0.0006	—	0.0035	—
	(0.0024)		(0.0101)	
USAD/Sales	0.3013	0.2889	0.5098	0.4368
	(0.3284)	(0.3240)	(1.4089)	(1.3901)
USCR4	−0.0047	−0.0047	−0.0201	−0.0200
	(0.0023)[b]	(0.0023)[b]	(0.0099)[b]	(0.0099)[b]
USK/L	0.6821	0.6812	2.6941	2.6885
	(0.2050)[b]	(0.2044)[b]	(0.8793)[b]	(0.8773)[b]
USHumanK	−0.2082	−0.2094	−1.0169	−1.0244
	(0.0731)[b]	(0.0728)[b]	(0.3138)[b]	(0.3124)[b]
USNTB/JNTB	0.1904	0.1880	0.7577	0.7434
	(0.1051)[a]	(0.1044)[a]	(0.4508)[a]	(0.4480)[a]
Intercept	0.5462	0.5695	2.9144	3.0513
	(0.2769)[b]	(0.2606)[b]	(1.1880)[b]	(1.1182)[b]
$\bar{R}^2$	0.146	0.150	0.129	0.133
F	4.624[b]	5.154[b]	4.147[b]	4.614[b]

Note: The dependent variable is the balance of trade between the United States and Japan. The numbers in parentheses are the standard errors. The regression coefficient and standard error for the capital–labor ratio have been multiplied by 100,000.
[a] Statistically significant at the 90% level of confidence, two-tailed test.
[b] Statistically significant at the 95% level of confidence, two-tailed test.

United States than in Japan, since $\beta_{US} = \beta_1 + \beta_2 = 0.1492 - 0.1242 = 0.0250$.

The insignificant coefficient of Japanese technology purchases as a percentage of sales implies that aggregate Japanese purchases of technology have not promoted the comparative advantage of Japanese industries. More insight is gained into this when the distribution of technology purchases by region is included in table 3. The negative and significant coefficient of Japanese industrial policy suggests that subsidized depreciation and special status from the MITI has been related to those industries which have attained international competitiveness, even after controlling for the traditional factors which determine trade flows. However, the positive and statistically insignificant coefficient of the cartelization measure implies that, whatever else it may have accomplished, legalized cartel status has not been effective in promoting the comparative advantage among Japanese industries.

The OLS results indicate that the USCR4 and USHumanK exert a negative influence on the U.S. bilateral trade performance, and that USK/L and

USNTB/JNTB are positively related to TB. While the pattern for capital intensity and human capital in the U.S.–Japanese bilateral trade relationship apparently differs from that typically found for the general U.S. trade structure (Stern and Maskus, 1981, and Baldwin, 1971 and 1979), these results are consistent with the more recent findings of Sveikauskas (1983).[8]

Virtually identical results emerged when the relative tariff barriers (USTB/WTB) were included in the regression model, but the coefficient of the tariff measure was very insignificant ($t = 0.44$). As Ray (1981b) found, non-tariff barriers are apparently a more effective instrument for altering the trade balance than are tariff barriers. Using the logit method of estimation in equations (3) and (4) yields results which are qualitatively unchanged for JR&D–USR&D, USR&D, and JIndustrial Policy, as well as for all the other

[8] Excluding the 53 "Ricardo" industries, defined as high natural resource industries (taken from Stern and Maskus, 1981), leaves the results of the capital–labor variable unaffected. The coefficient of the human capital variable remains negative but is no longer statistically significant.

TABLE 3. — REGRESSIONS OF THE U.S.-JAPAN BALANCE OF TRADE USING JAPANESE COMPONENTS OF R&D AND TECHNOLOGY EXPENDITURES

	OLS		Logit	
	1	2	3	4
J Process Innovation R&D	−3.6170	—	−19.5340	—
	(1.6295)[b]		(6.9176)[b]	
J Product Quality R&D	−3.8892	—	−18.9710	—
	(1.9593)[b]		(8.3177)[b]	
J New Products &	−2.5811	—	−13.3440	—
Technology R&D	(1.8657)		(8.0000)	
J Technology Transfer R&D	−2.9156	—	−11.8250	—
	(2.1141)		(8.9747)	
J Industrial Policy	−0.4436	−0.2875	−1.7811	−0.9060
	(0.1462)[b]	(0.1343)[b]	(0.6206)[b]	(0.5666)
US R&D	−0.0065	−0.0304	−0.0408	0.1718
	(0.0226)	(0.0196)	(0.0959)	(0.0831)[b]
US AD/Sales	0.1038	0.1239	−0.4567	−0.4186
	(0.3153)	(0.3178)	(1.3386)	(1.3457)
US CR4	−0.0038	−0.0043	−0.0154	−0.0177
	(0.0022)[b]	(0.0023)[a]	(0.0097)	(0.0096)[a]
US K/L	0.6221	0.7265	2.5585	2.9062
	(0.2124)[b]	(0.2016)[b]	(0.9015)[b]	(0.8534)[b]
US Human K	−0.1675	−0.1911	−0.8126	−1.0014
	(0.0774)[b]	(0.0801)[b]	(0.3287)[b]	(0.3390)[b]
US NTB/JNTB	0.1359	0.1383	0.4908	0.4726
	(0.1051)	(0.1084)	(0.4460)	(0.4591)
J Technology from US	—	−0.5442	—	−0.3340
		(0.3021)[a]		(0.1279)[b]
J Technology from Europe	—	0.0148	—	−0.0526
		(0.3220)		(0.1364)
J Technology from Japan	—	0.3881	—	0.1429
		(0.4211)		(0.1783)
Intercept	3.4457	0.6900	17.6010	4.4398
	(1.6168)[b]	(0.4428)	(6.8636)[b]	(1.8752)[b]
$\bar{R}^2$	0.181	0.173	0.183	0.178
F	5.269[b]	5.422[b]	5.311[b]	5.596[b]

Note: The dependent variable is the balance of trade between the United States and Japan. The numbers in parentheses are the standard errors.
[a] Statistically significant at the 90% level of confidence, two-tailed test.
[b] Statistically significant at the 95% level of confidence, two-tailed test.

explanatory variables. Thus, the results appear to be quite robust with respect to the OLS and logit methods of estimation.[9]

In table 3 specific components of Japanese R&D and technology expenditures are included in regressions estimating the U.S.–Japanese balance of trade to answer the questions, "Which components of R&D expenditures are most effective at promoting the Japanese comparative advantage?" and "Are any types of technological purchases effective at promoting the Japanese comparative advantage?"

[9] U.S. and Japanese R&D intensity apparently do not have a disparate effect in low R&D industries. When duplicating the model for a sample limited to the third of the industries (71) with the lowest U.S. R&D/sales ratios, the coefficient of *J R&D-US R&D* was negative and statistically significant but the coefficient of *US R&D* was insignificant.

In equation (1) (and equation (3) for the logit estimation) two of the R&D components are shown to be more effective at promoting the Japanese comparative advantage than are the other two. The coefficient of the process innovation variable implies that, holding the total budget of R&D constant, an increase of one percentage point (0.01) in expenditures on product innovation leads to a decrease in the U.S. trade balance of 0.036. While the signs of R&D expenditures on product quality improvements and on process innovation are negative and statistically significant, the coefficients of R&D expenditures on technology transfer and on new products and technology are also negative but statistically insignificant. Further, the elasticity of R&D expenditures on product quality improvements is 7.48 at the mean and 3.34 for process innovation R&D. This supports the thesis of Peck and Tamura (1976), that Japanese R&D expenditures which have been oriented towards improving upon the quality or reducing the costs of existing products have been more effective than R&D allocated towards developing new products and technology. As the F-ratio of 3.500 (D.F. = 4,201) suggests, the hypothesis that the Japanese R&D components have no joint effect on the bilateral trade balance is rejected at the 95% level of confidence. The hypothesis that the first two components, process innovation and product quality R&D, have no combined effect on TB is similarly reflected at the 90% level of confidence. However, as the F-ratio of 0.916 (D.F. = 2,201) implies, the hypothesis that Japanese R&D expenditures on new products and technology and on technology transfer jointly have no effect on TB cannot be rejected. Finally, the hypothesis that the first two categories of R&D expenditure have an identical impact on the bilateral trade balance cannot be rejected at the 90% level of confidence.

Equation (2) (and equation (4) for the logit estimation) includes variables representing different categories of technology purchased by Japanese firms. The negative and statistically significant coefficient of technology purchased from the United States, combined with the positive and statistically insignificant coefficients of purchases from Europe and purchases from domestic sources, implies that technology purchased from the United States has been effective in promoting the subsequent Japanese comparative advantage, while technology purchased from either European or domestic firms has not been effective. Both the hypothesis that the three technology purchase variables jointly have no effect on the bilateral trade balance ($F = 3.589$) and that they have an identical effect are rejected at the 95% level of confidence. This result is not surprising, since most studies have found the United States to be the world technological leader in the 1960s (Baldwin, 1971, Gruber et al., 1967).

V.   Conclusions

The major finding of this paper is that expenditures by Japanese firms on R&D served as an effective mechanism for promoting the trade balance. This tends to support the view that R&D expenditures in an industry are more than just a market structure characteristic representing the extent of technological opportunity; rather, R&D is a strategic instrument which apparently has been successfully implemented by firms to enhance market share, even in a cross-country context. However, certain types of R&D may have been more effective than others in promoting the Japanese trade advantage. While the United States generally has had the comparative advantage for industries that are R&D intensive, Japanese firms were able at least somewhat to offset this through their own expenditures on improving the quality of existing products and on cost-reducing process innovation for existing products, which have proven to be more effective than analogous expenditures on developing new products and technology, and on applications from technology transfer. Similarly, the effectiveness of purchased technology apparently has been dependent upon the source. While technology purchased from Europe and from other domestic firms has been ineffective, similar purchases from the United States have promoted the comparative advantage. However, this does not at all preclude the possibility that such purchases from non-U.S. sources promoted the trade advantage elsewhere.

We also find that certain types of Japanese industrial policy are positively related to Japan's trade advantage. That is, those industries which enjoyed a relatively high subsidized depreciation and presumably special status with the MITI in the 1960s also tended to demonstrate a relatively strong trade preformance in the late 1970s, even after accounting for the traditional factors that determine trade performance. Whether this observed statistical relationship implies that MITI's policies were actually responsible for the strong trade performance cannot be unequivocally be ascertained here.[10] For example, it is conceivable that the MITI, in fact, had a policy of targeting industries that were relatively strong and likely to succeed in the world market. However, in such a case, the factors providing such success lay outside the traditional international trade and industrial organization variables which were included in the regression equations. It does seem clear that whatever the goals and accomplishments of legalized cartel status were in Japan, it did not prove to

---

[10] For the opposite conclusion see Saxonhouse (1983).

be an effective instrument for promoting Japan's trade balance.

Based on the balance of U.S.–Japanese trade in 1977, it appears that certain types of R&D expenditures served as a successful strategy for promoting the trade advantage. At least some of Japan's trade success during this period can be attributed to the procurement of existing U.S. technology and the subsequent application of domestic R&D resources towards improving upon the quality of existing products. Whether that R&D strategy will continue to be as effective in the future should prove to be a significant question for future research. Similarly, future research should evolve towards considering U.S. trade patterns as the result of all relevant industry-specific characteristics for the major developed trading partners of the United States as well as those for the United States.

REFERENCES

Baldwin, Robert E., "The Determinants of the Commodity Structure of U.S. Trade," *American Economic Review* 61 (Mar. 1971), 126–146.

_____, "Determinants of Trade and Foreign Investment: Further Evidence," this REVIEW 61 (Feb. 1979), 40–48.

Caves, Richard E., Michael E. Porter and A. Michael Spence with John T. Scott, *Competition in the Open Economy* (Cambridge: Harvard University Press, 1980).

Caves, Richard E., and Masu Uekusa, *Industrial Organization in Japan* (Washington, D.C.: The Brookings Institution, 1976).

Goto, Akira, and Ryuhei Wakasugi, "Gijutsu seisaku" ("Technology Policy"), in Ryutaro Komiya, M. Okuno, and K. Suzumura (eds.), *Nihon no sangyo seisaku* (*Industrial Policy in Japan*) (Tokyo: University of Tokyo Press, 1984).

_____, "Technology Policy in Japan: A Short Review," *Technovation* 5 (1987), 269–279.

Griliches, Zvi, "Productivity, R&D and Basic Research at the Firm Level in the 1970's," *American Economic Review* 76 (Mar. 1986), 141–154.

Gruber, W. H., D. Mehta, and R. Vernon, "The R&D Factor in International Trade and International Investment of the United States," *Journal of Political Economy* 75 (Feb. 1967), 20–37.

Imai, Ken'ichi, "Japan's Industrial Organisation," in Kazuo Sato (ed.), *Industry and Business in Japan* (White Plains, NY: M.E. Sharpe, 1980), 74–135.

Ito, Motoshige, Masahiro Okuno, Kazuharu Kiyono and Kotaro Suzumura, "Sijo no shippai to hoseiteki-sangyoseisaku" ("Market Failure and Industrial Policy"), in Ryutaro Komiya, M. Okuno, and K. Suzumura (eds.), *Nihon no sangyo seisaku* (*Industrial Policy in Japan*) (Tokyo: University of Tokyo Press, 1984).

Koo, Anthony Y. C., and Stephen Martin, "Market Structure and U.S. Trade Flows," *International Journal of Industrial Organization* 2 (Sept. 1984), 173–198.

Ogura, Seiritsu, and Naoyuki Yoshino, "Zeisei to Zaisei toyushi," (The Tax System and Public Finance"), in Ryutaro Komiya, M. Okuno, and K. Suzumura (eds.), *Nihon no sangyo seisaku* (*Industrial Policy in Japan*) (Tokyo: University of Tokyo Press, 1984).

Peck, Merton J., and Shuji Tamura, "Technology," in Hugh Patrick and Henry Rosovsky (eds.), *Asia's New Giant* (Washington, D.C.: The Brookings Institution, 1976), 525–586.

Petri, Peter A., *Modelling Japanese-American Trade: A Study of Asymmetric Interdependence* (Cambridge: Harvard University Press, 1984).

Pugel, Thomas A., *International Market Linkages and U.S. Manufacturing: Prices, Profits, and Patterns* (Cambridge, MA: Ballinger, 1978).

Ray, Edward J., "The Determinants of Tariffs and Nontariff Trade Restrictions in the U.S.," *Journal of Political Economy* 89 (Feb. 1981a), 105–121.

_____, "Tariff and Nontariff Barriers to Trade in the United States and Abroad," this REVIEW 63 (May 1981b), 161–168.

Saxonhouse, Gary R., "The Micro- and Macroeconomics of Foreign Sales to Japan," in William R. Cline (ed.), *Trade Policy in the 1980's* (Cambridge, MA: MIT Press, 1983).

Spencer, Barbara J., and James A. Brander, "International R&D Rivalry and Industrial Strategy," *Review of Economic Studies* 30 (Oct. 1983), 707–722.

Stern, Robert M., and Keith E. Maskus, "Determinants of the Structure of U.S. Foreign Trade, 1958–76," *Journal of International Economics* 11 (May 1981), 207–224.

Sveikauskas, Leo, "Science and Technology in United States Trade," *The Economic Journal* 64 (Sept. 1983), 542–554.

Ueno, Hiroya, "The Conception and Evaluation of Japanese Industrial Policy," in Kazuo Sato (ed.), *Industry and Business in Japan* (White Plains, NY: M.E. Sharpe, 1980), 375–436.

Urata, Shujiro, "Factor Inputs and Japanese Manufacturing Trade Structure," this REVIEW 69 (Nov. 1983), 678–684.

White, Lawrence J., "Industrial Organization and International Trade: Some Theoretical Considerations," *American Economic Review* 64 (Dec. 1974), 1013–1020.

Yamawaki, Hideki, and David B. Audretsch, "Import Share Under International Oligopoly with Differentiated Products: Japanese Imports in U.S. Manufacturing," this REVIEW, forthcoming 1988.

[3]

Innovation and Size at the Firm Level*

DAVID B. AUDRETSCH
Wissenschaftszentrum Berlin für Sozialforschung
Berlin, Germany

ZOLTAN J. ACS
University of Baltimore
Baltimore, Maryland

I. Introduction

Empirical studies examining the relationship between firm size and innovative activity have produced what superficially might appear to be contradictory results.[1] While some studies have found a positive relationship between firm size and technological change, still others have identified no relationship or even a negative one. There are two main reasons for these seemingly inconsistent findings. The first is that different measures have been used to quantify technical change. These measures have typically involved either some measure of inputs into the innovative process, such as R&D expenditures, or else the number of patented inventions. While neither of these are direct measures of innovative output, they clearly represent different aspects of the innovative process. Thus, it is perhaps not too surprising that different results have tended to emerge when the R&D input measures are used than for the patent measures.

The second reason is that virtually every study examining the relationship between firm size and technical change has had to use a truncated distribution of firm sizes where either no or only a few small firms were included. For example, Scherer's [14, 234–35] conclusion that the empirical results, ". . . tilt on the side of supporting the Schumpeterian Hypothesis that size is conducive to vigorous conduct of R&D" was based on the responses of 443 large corporations participating in the Federal Trade Commission's Line of Business Survey. Similarly, Scherer [15] used the *Fortune* annual survey of the 500 largest U.S. industrial corporations and found that the number of patented inventions increases less than proportionately along with firm size. Soete [16] found that R&D expenditures tend to increase more than proportionately along with firm size using a sample from *Business Week*, consisting of the most R&D intensive firms. Bound et al. [6] were able to include a considerably wider spectrum of firm sizes in their sample of 1,492 firms from the 1976 COMPUSTAT data. They found that R&D increases more than proportionately along with firm size for the smaller firms in their sample, but that a fairly linear relationship exists for the largest firms.

Inferences about the relationship between firm size and technical change based on a severely

*We thank F. M. Scherer and an anonymous referee for helpful suggestions, as well as Sigrid Raasch and Jianping Yang for their computational assistance. All errors and omissions remain our responsibility.
1. For a thorough review of the literature see Baldwin and Scott [5] and Cohen and Klepper [7].

739

truncated distribution of firm sizes could be misleading. If small firms contribute to innovative activity as much as Scherer [11] and Acs and Audretsch [3] suggest, their omission from virtually all of the previous statistical tests limits the reliability and generality of the findings. Similarly, inferences about innovation based on studies of R&D and patent behavior must be severely qualified. As Scherer [13] warns, the finding that patents tend to increase only at a decreasing rate along with firm size could indicate that larger firms actually have a lower propensity to patent inventions and not that they are less innovative.

The purpose of this paper is to apply a new data source that remedies both of the deficiencies inherent in the measures and truncated samples used in previous studies. We use the individual firm records of the innovation data base introduced at the aggregated industry level in our 1987 and 1988 papers. This enables us to measure innovative activity directly for a broad spectrum of firm sizes.

II. The Data

The measure of a firm's innovative activity is the number of innovations recorded by the U.S. Small Business Administration in 1982 which were attributed to that firm. The data base was created by recording innovations appearing in new-product sections of technology, engineering and trade journals. While an innovation is defined as the commercial introduction of a new product, process, or service, in fact, by nature of the construction of the data base, most of the innovations are product innovations. Although these data are described in detail in our 1990 study, several points should be emphasized.

First, 862 of the 1,695 firms included in our analysis or slightly more than half, have fewer than 500 employees and can therefore be considered to be small according to the standard used by the U.S. Small Business Administration. There are also 85 firms with at least 50,000 employees included in the sample, so there is little doubt that the sample includes a full spectrum of firm sizes. Table I shows that, as for the overall firm-size distribution, the size distribution of innovating firms is skewed towards small firms. However, large and very large enterprises account for a substantially greater share of innovating firms than they do of firms in general. This is presumably due to the greater propensity to innovate for large than for small firms.

Table I also reveals the mean number of innovations per firm according to employment size class. For example, firms with fewer than 100 employees contributed an average of 2.617 innovations per firm. Below 1,000 employees, the mean number of innovations decreases as the firm employment size class increases. The smallest firms are over 50 percent more innovative than firms with between 500 and 999 employees. The mean number of innovations increases throughout the larger firm size classes, so that the largest 85 firms contributed an average of 7.093 innovations each.

Thus, a U-shaped relationship emerges between firm size and innovative activity. It should be noted that in our 1987 paper we used the number of innovations-per-employee as a measure of innovative intensity. Based on that standard the smallest firms are clearly the most innovative-intensive, and the largest firms produce the fewest innovations-per-employee.

The second point regarding these data is that the sample includes only innovative firms. Including non-innovative firms in the sample would presumably tend to reduce the innovative intensity of small firms more than that of the larger firms.

Table I. Mean Number of Innovations per Firm According to Employment Size Class

Firm Employment Size Class	Number of Firms [a]	Mean Number of Innovations [b]
1–99	428	2.617
	(25.25)	(2.948)
100–199	197	2.117
	(11.62)	(1.970)
200–499	237	1.894
	(13.98)	(1.662)
500–999	147	1.699
	(8.67)	(1.303)
1,000–1,999	119	1.871
	(7.02)	(1.623)
2,000–4,999	165	2.136
	(9.74)	(1.752)
5,000–9,999	91	2.146
	(5.37)	(1.616)
10,000–19,999	105	3.704
	(6.20)	(4.068)
20,000–49,999	121	4.558
	(7.14)	(4.847)
50,000+	85	7.093
	(5.02)	(8.646)

a. The percentage of the total number of firms in this size class is listed in parentheses.
b. The standard deviation is listed in the parentheses.

III. Empirical Results

While there has been considerable ambiguity in the results in studies relating various measures of technological change to firm size, one conclusion has been consistently confirmed in several studies, among others Scherer [15; 13]: the market structure and technological environment in which the firm operates, or the technological opportunity class, play decisive roles in shaping the relationship between firm size and technical change. Thus, in order to control for market structure and to ensure that the technological environment is held relatively constant, we include measures of the 1978 four-firm concentration, the capital-sales ratio, the advertising-sales ratio, and a measure of the extent of skilled labor used in the industry, defined as the percentage of employment consisting of professional and kindred workers, plus managers and administrators, plus craftsmen and kindred workers, 1970.[2] Since all of these are market structure characteristics measured at the four-digit standard industrial classification (SIC) level, and the innovation records are for

2. The capital-sales ratio (gross assets divided by value-of-shipments), four-firm concentration, and value-of-shipments measures are from the U.S. Department of Commerce, Bureau of the Census, *Annual Survey of Manufacturers, 1977, Industry Profiles*, Washington: USGPO, issued 1981. The advertising measure was derived by using the value-of-shipments data and advertising expenditures from the 1972 U.S. Input-Output Table. The measure of skilled labor is from the U.S. Department of Commerce, Bureau of the Census, Census Population, 1970, Subject Report PC(2)-7C, *Occupation by Industry*, Washington: USGOP, issued 1972.

Table II. Regressions for Firm Innovations (*t*-statistics in parentheses)

	All Industries		High Technology[c]	Low Technology[d]
	(1)	(2)	(3)	(4)
Sales	0.0013	0.0012	0.0036	0.0014
	(10.704)[b]	(15.580)[b]	(10.639)[b]	(1.811)[a]
Sales^2	-0.3173×10^{-7}	-0.1927×10^{-6}	-0.1203×10^{-6}	-0.4772×10^{-6}
	(−3.633)[b]	(−12.070)	(−7.740)[b]	(−1.986)[b]
Sales^3	0.1782×10^{-12}	—	—	0.4789×10^{-10}
	(1.452)			(2.576)[b]
Concentration	−0.0002	−0.0009	−0.0112	0.0023
	(−0.026)	(0.140)	(−0.495)	(0.181)
Capital/Sales	−0.9236	−0.8276	10.9690	−0.1646
	(−0.826)	(−0.741)	(1.708)[a]	(0.091)
Advertising/Sales	−4.9377	−2.1731	770.6500	−173.0500
	(−0.086)	(−0.038)	(0.775)	(−1.190)
Skilled Labor	4.5235	4.5210	10.4980	2.7079
	(2.910)[b]	(2.9063)[b]	(1.075)	(0.780)
Constant	0.411	0.3880	−4.5369	0.8285
	(0.563)	(0.532)	(−0.846)	(0.832)
R^2	0.242	0.240	0.370	0.421
F	41.529[b]	48.041[b]	25.446[b]	6.853[b]

a. Statistically significant at the 90 percent level of confidence, two-tailed test.
b. Statistically significant at the 95 percent level of confidence, two-tailed test.
c. Includes four-digit SIC industries within sectors 38, 357, 366, 367, and 283.
d. Includes four-digit SIC industries within sectors 20, 22–25, 331–332, and 3398–3399.

individual firms, these industry variables were matched with the appropriate industry assigned to each innovating firm.

To examine the relationship between firm size and innovative output, we follow the examples of Scherer [15] and Soete [16], among others, in estimating cubic and quadratic regressions.[3] The regression results are reported in Table II. Equation (1) includes all innovating firms for all manufacturing industries. There are two particularly striking results from Equation (1). First, there is no evidence supporting the existence of increasing returns to firm size in generating innovative output. Not only does the coefficient of the cubic term for sales fail to be statistically significant, but only two firms Dow Chemical ($11.870 billion) and DuPont ($13.650 billion) had 1982 sales exceeding the second turning point of $9.024 billion.

The second major result is that the only industry structure variable which proves to be statistically significant is the measure of skilled labor, which exerts a positive influence on innovative output. This result is hardly surprising, and merely confirms that the technological opportunity class essentially shifts the relationship between firm size and innovative output.

These two results are confirmed in Equation (2), where the cubic term for sales has been deleted from the regression. Taken together, Equations (1) and (2) imply that the quadratic func-

3. Logarithmic regressions were also estimated but are not reported. These produced results consistent with the regressions reported in Table II.

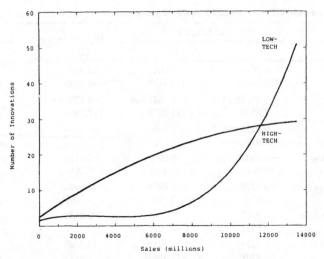

Figure 1. Firm Size and Innovative Activity in Low- and High-Technology Industries

tion provides a better description of the relationship between firm size and innovative output than does the cubic function.

In Equations (3) and (4), the innovating firms are grouped according to "high-technology" and "low-technology"[4] industries based on 1982 R&D/sales ratios.[5] Because the coefficient of the cubic term for sales for the high-technology group is not statistically significant, only the quadratic regression is reported in Equation (3). As for the entire sample of manufacturing firms, firms in these high-technology industries show no evidence of exhibiting increasing returns to firm size in generating innovative output. However, as the positive and statistically significant coefficient of the capital-sales ratio suggests, innovative activity is apparently greater in capital-intensive industries. As Comanor [8] and others have argued, this may reflect the ability of firms to appropriate economic rents accruing from innovative activity in industries where the cost of entry is relatively high. The lack of statistical significance of the measure of skilled labor may reflect the relatively homogeneous technological opportunity class of these high-technology industries.

As the positive and statistically significant coefficient of the cubic term for sales in Equation (4) suggests, those industry groups classified as low-technology apparently exhibit increasing returns to firm size in generating innovative activity. There were numerous firms in 1982 with sales exceeding the second turning point of $4.520 billion, so, as Figure 1 indicates, the relationship between firm size and innovative activity is better characterized by the cubic equation for the low-technology industries, rather than by a quadratic equation, as is the case for the high-technology industries.

The contrast between the high-technology and low-technology groups may reflect that in high-technological opportunity industries only relatively small increments to existing knowledge are required to innovate, while in low-technological industries an innovation requires a firm to

---

4. The high-technology industry group includes four-digit SIC industries within sectors 38, 357, 366, 367, and 282. The low-technology industry group includes four-digit SIC industries within sectors 20, 22–25, 331–332 and 3398–3399.
5. The industry group R&D/sales ratios are taken from National Science Foundation [9].

invest in a substantial addition to the stock of existing knowledge. In any case, the contrasting relationship between firm size and innovative activity in low- and high-technological opportunity industries supports Scherer's [12] contention that the underlying technological environment plays a decisive role in influencing the innovative performance of firms.

IV. Conclusions

Application of a new direct measure of innovative activity over a broad spectrum of firm sizes suggests that the relationship between firm size and innovation tends to be more similar to that found when the number of patented inventions is used to measure technical change than for R&D inputs. As Scherer [15; 13] and Bound et al. [6] found for patents, most industries exhibit decreasing returns to scale with respect to the output of innovations. However, this relationship is apparently sensitive to the technological environment. In low-technology industries there is at least some evidence of increasing returns.

An important qualification of these results is that the sample includes only innovative firms. Inclusion of non-innovative firms in the sample could alter the results somewhat, since small firms may have a lower propensity to innovate than do the very largest enterprises. This points to the need for additional data sources measuring the amount of R&D, number of patents and extent of innovative activity covering firms of all sizes.

References

1. Acs, Zoltan J. and David B. Audretsch. *Innovation and Small Firms*. Cambridge, Mass.: MIT Press, 1990.
2. —— and ——, "Innovation in Large and Small Firms: An Empirical Analysis." *American Economic Review*, September 1988a, 678–90.
3. —— and ——, Testimony before the Subcommittee on Monopolies and Commercial Law, Committee on the Judiciary, U.S. House of Representatives, 24 February 1988b.
4. —— and ——, "Innovation, Market Structure and Firm Size." *Review of Economics and Statistics*, November 1987, 567–75.
5. Baldwin, William L. and John T. Scott. *Market Structure and Technological Change*. London and New York: Harwood Academic Publishers, 1987.
6. Bound, John, Clint Cummins, Zvi Griliches, Bronwyn H. Hall and Adam Jaffee. "Who Does R&D and Who Patents?", in *R&D, Patents, and Productivity*, edited by Zvi Griliches. Chicago: University of Chicago, 1984, pp. 21–54.
7. Cohen, Wesley M. and Steven Klepper. "Firm Size versus Diversity in the Achievement of Technological Advance," in *Innovation and Technological Change: An International Comparison*, edited by Zoltan J. Acs and David B. Audretsch. Ann Arbor: University of Michigan Press, 1991.
8. Comanor, William S., "Market Structure, Product Differentiation, and Industrial Research." *Quarterly Journal of Economics*, November 1967, 639–57.
9. National Science Foundation. *National Patterns of Science and Technology Resources 1986*. Washington, D.C., 1986.
10. Scherer, F. M., "Changing Perspectives on the Firm Size Problem," in *Innovation and Technological Change: An International Comparison*, edited by Zoltan J. Acs and David B. Audretsch. Ann Arbor: University of Michigan Press, 1991.
11. ——. Testimony before the Subcommittee on Monopolies and Commercial Law, Committee on the Judiciary, U.S. House of Representatives, 24 February 1988.
12. ——. *Innovation and Growth: Schumpeterian Perspectives*. Cambridge, Mass.: MIT Press, 1984.
13. ——, "The Propensity to Patent." *International Journal of Industrial Organization*, March 1983, 107–28.
14. ——, "Inter-Industry Technology Flows in the United States." *Research Policy*, 1982, 227–45.
15. ——, "Firm Size, Market Structure, Opportunity, and the Output of Patented Inventions." *American Economic Review*, December 1965, 1097–125.
16. Soete, Luc L. G., "Firm Size and Inventive Activity: The Evidence Reconsidered." *European Economic Review*, 1979, 319–40.

4

The Review *of* Economics *and* Statistics

VOL. LXIX   NOVEMBER 1987   NUMBER 4

INNOVATION, MARKET STRUCTURE, AND FIRM SIZE

Zoltan J. Acs and David B. Audretsch*

Abstract—The hypothesis that the relative innovative advantage between large and small firms is determined by market concentration, the extent of entry barriers, the composition of firm size within the industry, and the overall importance of innovation activity is tested. We find that large firms tend to have the relative innovative advantage in industries which are capital-intensive, concentrated, highly unionized, and produce a differentiated good. The small firms tend to have the relative advantage in industries which are highly innovative, utilize a large component of skilled labor, and tend to be composed of a relatively high proportion of large firms.

I. Introduction

WHILE the two fundamental tenets of the Schumpeterian hypothesis—that innovative activity is promoted by large firms[1] and by imperfect competition—have been subjected to several empirical tests,[2] most studies have examined only one aspect in isolation from the other (Link, 1980). That is, the exact interaction between these two tenets has been largely overlooked, mainly because of the availability of data. However, as we show in the second section of this paper, large firms, in fact, are not more innovative than their smaller counterparts in every industry. While large firms have proven to be more innovative in a number of industries, the opposite is true in still others. In considering what accounts for these differences in innovative activity between large and small firms, we provide an empirical test of a somewhat modified Schumpeterian hypothesis which combines both of the central tenets. That is, we test the hypothesis that large firms have the innovative advantage in markets characterized by imperfect competition, but that small firms have

the innovative advantage in markets more closely approximating the competitive model.

A particularly unique feature of this paper is that, by using data newly released from the U.S. Small Business Administration, we are able to apply a direct measure of innovation, for both large and small firms, over a broad sample of four-digit standard industrial classification (SIC) industries. After describing these new data in the second section of the paper, we present in the third section the hypothesis that market imperfections account for the relative innovative superiority of large firms over their smaller counterparts. In the fourth section, two different samples consisting of 172 innovative and 42 highly innovative industries are used in a model estimating the difference between large- and small-firm innovative rates. We find that large firms tend to have the relative innovative advantage in industries which are capital-intensive, concentrated, and advertising-intensive. By contrast, small firms tend to have the relative innovative advantage in highly innovative industries and in industries which tend to be composed of a relatively high proportion of large firms. Thus, in the last section, we conclude that the results support the hypothesis that large firms have the relative innovative advantage in markets characterized by imperfect competition, while small firms have the relative advantage in markets more closely approximating the competitive model.

II. Innovative Activity and Firm Size

Virtually all of the empirical studies testing the Schumpeterian hypotheses, or the relationships between firm size and innovative activity, and between market structure and innovative activity, have had to rely on relatively deficient measures of innovative activity. Typically, these measures have involved either some measure of an input into the innovative process, such as R & D (Scherer, 1965), or else a proxy measure of innovative output, such as patented inventions (Mansfield, 1968). While R & D measures suffer from indicating only the budgeted resources allocated towards trying to produce innovative activity, but not the actual

Received for publication September 4, 1986. Revision accepted for publication May 8, 1987.

*Wissenschaftszentrum Berlin für Sozialforschung.

We thank George Bittlingmayer, Al Link, J.-Matthias Graf von der Schulenburg, Joachim Schwalbach, Hideki Yamawaki, Klaus Zimmermann and two anonymous referees for their helpful comments, and Michael Karge for his computational assistance. Any errors or omissions remain our responsibility.

[1] Kamien and Schwartz (1975, p. 15) characterize the Schumpeterian debate as, "A statistical relationship between firm size and innovative activity is most frequently sought with exploration of the impact of firm size on both the amount of innovational effort and innovational success."

[2] For an excellent survey of this literature, see Kamien and Schwartz (1975).

[567]

amount of resulting innovations, the measures of patents suffer because not all patented inventions prove to be innovations, and many innovations are never patented.[3]

We are able to avoid these inherent problems in the traditional measures of innovation activity by using a new direct measure of innovation (Acs and Audretsch, 1987). The innovative measure we adopt in this paper is the number of innovations in each four-digit SIC industry recorded in 1982. The U.S. Small Business Administration identified innovations which were introduced in 1982 and appeared in the sections listing new innovations from over 100 technology, engineering, and trade journals, spanning every manufacturing industry. The entire list of trade journals used to compile these data is available from the authors. Although the innovations were recorded in 1982, the Small Business Administration found that they were the result of inventions made, on average, 4.2 years earlier. Thus, the innovation data in some sense represent inventions occurring around 1978. The Small Business Administration defines an innovation as "...a process that begins with an invention, proceeds with the development of the invention, and results in the introduction of a new product, process or service to the marketplace" (Edwards and Gordon, 1984, p. 1). The innovation data were classified into two firm-size categories, according to the employment level of the innovating firm. Innovations from firms with fewer than 500 employees were considered to constitute "small-firm innovations," while innovations from firms with at least 500 employees constitute "large-firm innovations." Unfortunately, these definitions of large and small firms by employment level are fixed and do not enable alternative measures of firm size to be constructed for comparison. Because not all of the innovations could be classified according to firm size, the number of total innovations does not always equal the sum of large- and small-firm innovations.

Table 1 shows the twenty four-digit SIC industries where the large-firm innovation rate

most greatly exceeds the small-firm innovation rate, and the twenty four-digit industries where the small-firm innovation rate most greatly exceeds the large firm innovation rate. The large-firm innovation rate (LIE) is defined as the number of innovations made by firms with at least 500 employees, divided by the number of employees (thousands) in large firms.[4] The small-firm innovation rate (SIE) is defined as the number of innovations made by firms with fewer than 500 employees, divided by the number of employees (thousands) in small firms.

The innovation rate, or the number of innovations per employee, is used because it measures innovative activity relative to the industry size. The absolute number of innovations contributed by an industry may be a misleading measure of innovative activity, since it is not standardized by some equivalent measure of industry size. The innovation rate is presumably a more reliable measure of innovation activity because it is weighted by industry and firm size. Thus, while large firms in manufacturing introduced 2,608 innovations in 1982, and small firms contributed slightly fewer, 1,923, small-firm employment was only about half as great as large-firm employment, yielding an average small-firm innovation rate in manufacturing of 0.322, compared to a large-firm innovation rate of 0.225.

Of course, standardizing the innovation measures on the basis of employment may introduce bias to the extent that large firms might differ from their smaller counterparts in the capital-intensity of their production process. That is, if large firms tend to be more capital-intensive, their innovation rates will tend to be overstated, and the small-firm innovation rates will tend to be understated. Similarly, the extent to which small firms in the Bureau of Census SIC industry classification actually manufacture different product class lines than the larger firms also introduces bias into the measures. A third source of bias may be that innovation rates affect firm size (see Acs and Audretsch, 1986). While no adjustments can be made to address the second two sources of bias, an alternative measure of the innovation rates, defined as the number of innovations divided by sales (divided by 10,000), provides a

---

[3]According to Shepherd (1979, p. 400), "patents are a notoriously weak measure. Most of the eighty thousand patents issued each year are worthless and are never used. Many are of moderate value, and a few are bonanzas. Still others have negative social value. They are used as "blocking" patents to stop innovation, or they simply are developed to keep competition out."

[4]The employment data are from 1977 (see appendix A).

TABLE 1.— THE INDUSTRIES WITH THE LARGEST DIFFERENCES BETWEEN THE
LARGE- AND SMALL-FIRM INNOVATION RATES[a]

	LIE	SIE	DIE	DIS
Tires and inner tubes	8.4615	0.0000	8.4615	2.5000
Agricultural chemicals	2.2642	0.0000	2.2642	1.7940
General industrial machinery	2.2041	0.3939	1.8101	3.9210
Food products machinery	2.0109	0.6704	1.3405	3.6520
Ammunition, except for small arms	1.2281	0.0000	1.2281	5.2764
Cottonseed oil mills	1.1111	0.0000	1.1111	1.9342
Cheese, natural and processed	1.1258	0.0862	1.0396	1.9667
Wet corn milling	1.0000	0.0000	1.0000	0.1301
Storage batteries	0.9649	0.0000	0.9649	4.6968
Converted paper products	0.9848	0.0617	0.9231	5.2486
Truck and bus bodies	0.7643	0.0000	0.7643	0.9384
Paper industries machinery	0.8696	0.1053	0.7643	2.5401
Metal office furniture	1.1628	0.4000	0.7628	0.9827
Woodworking machinery	0.7500	0.0000	0.7500	2.5641
Building paper and board mills	0.6452	0.0000	0.6452	1.1468
Pens and mechanical pencils	0.6154	0.0000	0.6154	0.3194
Flat glass	0.5882	0.0000	0.5882	0.4395
Raw cane sugar	0.5455	0.0000	0.5455	0.6967
Industrial furnaces and ovens	1.6667	1.1250	0.5417	0.1242
Primary metal products	1.3793	0.9375	0.4418	0.8299
Scales and balances, except laboratory	0.8511	8.7500	−7.8989	−6.8472
Electronic computing equipment	0.9570	8.2246	−7.2676	−8.3290
Process control instruments	1.8785	9.0291	−7.1507	−3.8790
Synthetic rubber	0.0000	6.6667	−6.6667	−1.3788
Fluid meters and counting devices	0.4380	4.5455	−4.1075	−5.1517
Engineering and scientific instruments	1.5751	5.5333	−3.9582	−2.9035
Measuring and controlling devices	0.1442	3.9130	−3.7688	−4.2051
Gum and wood chemicals	0.2500	3.7500	−3.5000	−1.6155
Primary copper	0.0000	3.3333	−3.3333	−8.9286
Industrial controls	0.3538	3.5385	−3.1847	−3.6549
Surface active agents	0.5405	3.4483	−2.9077	−2.0639
Power driven handtools	0.5512	3.0435	−2.4923	−1.4856
Instruments to measure electricity	0.5534	2.9560	−2.4026	−2.4434
Surgical and medical instruments	0.9524	3.0769	−2.1245	−1.7433
Plastics materials and resins	0.5894	2.3810	−1.7916	−0.5038
Transformers	0.1344	1.8033	−1.6689	−0.9757
Electric lamps	0.0000	1.5789	−1.5789	−0.2908
Industrial trucks and tractors	0.6701	2.1277	−1.4576	−1.0488
Measuring and dispensing pumps	0.0000	1.4286	−1.4286	−1.1884
Environmental controls	0.6452	2.0408	−1.3957	−0.5742

[a] The twenty industries where the large-firm innovation rate (*LIE*) most greatly exceeds the small-firm innovation rate (*SIE*), and the twenty industries where the small-firm innovation rate most greatly exceeds the large-firm innovation rate The innovation rate is measured as the number of innovations divided by total employment for *LIE, SIE,* and *DIE*, and by sales for *DIS.*

comparative measure of innovative activity. The last column in table 1 lists the corresponding differences in innovation rates, *DIS*, when the innovations are standardized by the sales accounted for by large and small firms. As table 1 shows, the correspondence between the innovation measures standardized by employment (*DIE*) and by sales (*DIS*) is fairly strong. In fact, for the entire sample of 247 four-digit SIC manufacturing industries, the simple correlation between the two measures is 0.707. While this is somewhat reassuring, standardizing the innovation rates by sales is susceptible to bias from differences in the vertical

level at which the sales are made between large and small firms. For example, if the large firms tend to sell products which are further downstream, then the innovation rates would tend to be overstated for small firms and understated for the large firms.

That the average innovation rate for small firms was about 43% higher than that of large firms in 1982 does not imply that the answer to the question, "Which firm size is more innovative?" is unequivocally "the small firm." Rather, table 1 suggests that the correct answer is: "it depends—on the particular industry." For example, in the tires industry, the large-firm innovation rate exceeded the small-firm innovation rate by 8.46, or by about eight innovations per thousand employees. Just as the innovation rate is relatively higher for the large firms in the tires, chemicals, industrial machinery, and food machinery industries, it is relatively higher for the small firms in the scales and balances, computing equipment, control instruments, and synthetic rubber industries.

III. The Hypothesis

While the Schumpeterian position has generally been interpreted as asserting that large firms are more innovative than their smaller counterparts,[5] this is clearly not validated in every manufacturing industry, as table 1 suggests. However, considering the other major tenet of the Schumpeterian hypothesis, that markets characterized by imperfect competition are particularly conducive to innovation activity, a modified Schumpeterian hypothesis is that the large firms should have the relative innovative advantage in concentrated markets imposing significant entry barriers, while the small firms should have the innovative advantage in markets more closely resembling the competitive model. In particular, the literature has identified three aspects of market structure which have been suggested to affect significantly the relative innovative advantage of large and small firms—the size distribution of firms, the existence of certain barriers to entry, and the stage of the industry in the product life-cycle.

Galbraith (1956) and Scherer (1980), among others, have noted that scale economies in production may provide scope economies for research and development (R & D).[6] To the extent that this view that innovative activity is positively related to the extent of scale economies is correct, the existence of capital-intensity in an industry should tend to provide a barrier to small-firm innovation, while relatively promoting large-firm innovation. Simply put, large firms, rather than small firms, are in a better position to exploit the gains yielded from innovation in an industry requiring capital-intensity.

Similarly, the extent of product differentiation through advertising intensity has been considered to yield a greater innovative advantage to large firms, while inhibiting the innovative activity of smaller firms (Comanor, 1967). Scherer (1980) notes that economies of scale in promotion facilitate the market penetration of new products, thus enabling larger firms with a greater profit potential from innovation in advertising-intensive industries.

The most obvious index measure for the extent of imperfect competition in a market is the degree of concentration.[7] As Kamien and Schwartz (1975) summarize the Schumpeterian hypothesis, market power and the potential for accruing economic rents is a necessary condition for innovation. Only firms that are large enough to attain at least temporary market power will therefore choose innovation as a means for profit-maximization. Concentration, in particular, should provide the large firms with an innovative advantage over their smaller counterparts because, according to Galbraith (1956, p. 87), innovation can occur only in the presence of such market power and " . . . only by a firm that has the resources which are associated with considerable size." [8]

On the other hand, the extent of unionization in an industry might be considered to be more of a barrier to large-firm innovation than to small-firm innovation. Hirsch and Link (1986) provide a model and empirical evidence suggesting that, through the rent-seeking activities of unions, rents accruing from innovation are captured to some extent by strong unions (see also Connolly et al., 1986). Since employees in small firms tend to have lower union participation rates than do employees in large firms (Hirsch and Addison, 1986), a high

---

[5] According to Schumpeter, "What we have got to accept is that (the large-scale establishment) has come to be the most powerful engine of progress . . . " (1950, p. 106).

[6] According to Scherer "(R)esearch and development projects may benefit from scale economies realized in other parts of the large firm's operations" (1980, p. 414).

[7] As Scherer (1980) notes, caution must be applied when interpreting the actual meaning of market concentration. Concentration ratios are a weak measure of market power at best, and in practice contain substantial error.

[8] It should be noted that Phillips (1965) argued that concentration should promote the innovative activity of small firms more than that of large firms. He reasoned that if concentration inhibits price competition, it is also likely to deter non-price competition, such as product innovation. However, the smaller firms are less likely to be bound by such tacit agreements restraining innovation. This argument runs contradictory to the literature in the Schumpeterian and Galbraithian tradition.

degree of unionization in an industry might adversely impact large-firm innovation relative to small-firm innovation.

Finally, several studies, including Pavitt and Wald (1971), suggest that the opportunity for small-firm innovation tends to be the highest when the industry is in the early stages of the product life-cycle. The introduction and growth stages of the life-cycle are defined by Vernon (1966) as the absence of a standardized product concept in the market. Because the product design is subject to rapid change and evolution, a relatively high level of skilled labor is required, while the production process remains fairly labor-intensive. Thus, the innovative opportunities for the small firms are presumably the greatest during the early life-cycle stages, and the least in the mature and declining stages, when product innovation plays a relatively minor role but capital-intensity becomes a more prominent feature.

To test the hypothesis that the difference between the large- and small-firm innovation rates is attributable to the extent of imperfect competition in the market, we estimate the following model:

$$DIE = \beta_0 + \beta_1 CAPVS + \beta_2 PROD$$
$$+ \beta_3 CON + \beta_4 CB + \beta_5 GROWTH$$
$$+ \beta_6 LFI + \beta_7 HK + \beta_8 TIE + \mu \qquad (1)$$

where the dependent variable, DIE, is defined as the difference between the large-firm innovation rate (LIE) and the small-firm innovation rate (SIE), $DIE = LIE - SIE$, and the innovation rate is defined as the number of innovations per employee (thousands) in a four-digit SIC industry. An alternative measure of the difference between large- and small-firm innovation rates, DIS, is also estimated, where the innovation rates are defined as the number of innovations per sales (ten thousand dollars) in a four-digit SIC industry. To measure the discussed barriers, we include as explanatory variables the 1977 capital-output ratio ($CAPVS$), the percentage of employees in the industry covered by collective bargaining between 1973 and 1975 (CB), the 1977 four-firm concentration ratio (CON), and the 1977 advertising-to-sales ratio ($PROD$). A substitute measure of product differentiation is also used ($PRODC$), where $PRODC = PROD \times D$, and D is a dummy variable taking on the value of one in consumer industries which are also convenience goods and zero otherwise. This follows the procedure used by Porter (1976) and Pugel (1978), who argue that product differentiation plays a more significant role only in these industries.

To measure the stage of the industry life-cycle we also include the percentage growth rate between 1972 and 1977, divided by five ($GROWTH$), a measure of human capital (HK), defined as the professional and kindred workers, as a percentage of total employment, 1970, and the total innovation rate (TIE), defined as the total number of innovations, divided by total industry employment. Since an industry tends to rely on the highest component of skilled labor during the early stages of the life-cycle, and the least amount of skilled labor after the product has become standardized in the mature and declining phases, HK is expected to be negatively related to DIE. Similarly, since industries in the early life-cycle stages tend to be the most innovative, and small firms are presumably relatively more innovative during the early life-cycle stages, high levels of TIE are expected to be conducive to small-firm relative to large-firm innovation, implying a negative relationship between TIE and DIE. Finally, the percentage of an industry which is accounted for by firms with at least 500 employees in 1977 (LFI) is included as an explanatory variable. Caves and Pugel (1980) have argued that small firms can perhaps offset their inherent size disadvantage through pursuing a strategy of product innovation. That is, after controlling for the negative influences of entry barriers on small-firm innovation, small firms may tend to rely on a strategy of innovation in the presence of an industry dominated largely by large firms, suggesting a negative relationship between LFI and DIE. All variable sources and further data explanations are provided in appendix A.[9]

IV. Regression Results

Although 247 four-digit SIC industries were compatible for estimating the above model, a large number (170 or 38%) of four-digit industries experienced no innovation. In these industries the

---

[9] Quadratic terms for *CON, GROWTH, HK,* and *TIE* were also included in the model but did not lead to a qualitative change in the results.

TABLE 2.—ESTIMATES OF MODEL FOR THE DIFFERENCE IN LARGE- AND SMALL-FIRM INNOVATION RATES

Independent Variable	High Innovative Industries				Innovative Industries	
	(1) (DIE)	(2) (DIE)	(3) (DIS)	(4) (DIS)	(5) (DIE)	(6) (DIE)
Intercept	1.737 (1.602)	2.093 (1.575)[a]	11.245 (17.921)	13.758 (17.504)	0.780 (0.361)[b]	0.748 (0.355)[b]
CAPVS	5.972 (3.382)[b]	5.371 (3.332)[a]	68.252 (37.843)[b]	64.329 (37.034)[b]	0.684 (0.671)	0.651 (0.666)
PROD	169.970 (117.890)[a]	—	12.480 (13.191)	—	61.614 (50.816)	—
PRODC	—	148.620 (125.580)	—	11.509 (13.959)	—	74.630 (58.360)[a]
CON	0.029 (0.021)[a]	0.031 (0.021)[a]	0.301 (0.234)[a]	0.317 (0.237)[a]	-0.004 (0.006)	-0.003 (0.005)
CB	0.023 (0.017)[a]	0.023 (0.018)[a]	0.189 (0.195)[a]	0.187 (0.197)[a]	-0.001 (0.006)	-0.001 (0.006)
GROWTH	4.196 (4.632)	3.329 (4.581)	62.952 (51.825)	56.882 (50.927)	1.565 (1.458)	1.556 (1.457)
LFI	-6.601 (2.451)[b]	-6.776 (2.518)[b]	-57.038 (27.424)[b]	-58.599 (27.994)[b]	-0.797 (0.571)[a]	-0.893 (0.577)[a]
HK	2.123 (5.244)	1.658 (5.266)	9.867 (58.671)	7.010 (58.537)	-2.934 (2.016)[a]	-2.883 (2.019)[a]
TIE	-1.789 (0.409)[b]	-1.753 (0.411)[b]	-14.067 (4.576)[b]	-13.827 (4.565)[b]	-1.021 (0.183)[b]	-1.007 (0.181)[b]
Sample Size	42	42	42	42	172	172
R^2	0.524	0.515	0.376	0.372	0.295	0.296
F	4.538[b]	4.371[b]	2.448[b]	2.446[b]	8.527[b]	8.556[b]

Note: The dependent variables are the industry difference between large- and small-firm innovation rates (DIE and DIS). Standard errors are listed in parentheses. The coefficients of PROD and PRODC have been divided by 100 in equations (3) and (4).
[a]Statistically significant at the 90% level of confidence for a one-tailed test.
[b]Statistically significant at the 95% level of confidence for a one-tailed test.

difference between the large- and small-firm innovation rates is, of course, zero. Hence, the sole determinant of *DIE* in these industries is the lack of innovation. That is, when considering what determines the differences in innovation rates between large and small firms, it seems appropriate only to examine industries where a difference can possibly exist—industries with at least some innovation activity. Thus, the above model is estimated for two different samples: (1) high innovative industries, which include the highest-fourth of industries that had at least some innovative activity; and (2) innovative industries, which include those industries that had some innovative activity.

Using the 1982 differences between the large- and small-firm innovation rates as the dependent variables, the cross-section regressions were estimated for the different samples of innovative intensity, and are shown in table 2. Equation (1) includes *DIE* as the dependent variable for the high innovative industries. The positive and statistically significant coefficient of *CAPVS* indicates that, ceteris paribus, large firms tend to

have the relative innovative advantage over their smaller counterparts in the more capital-intensive industries. Conversely, the smaller firms tend to be relatively more innovative in the less capital-intensive industries. This lends support to a slightly reinterpreted Schumpeterian view: Where capital-intensity plays an important role in the industry, innovation tends to be promoted in large firms and impeded in small firms.

The coefficient of *PROD* is also positive and statistically significant. This suggests that, like capital-intensity, advertising-intensity deters innovation by smaller firms. The coefficient of *CON* is also positive and significant, suggesting that the larger firms tend to have the relative innovative advantage in the highly concentrated industries, and that the smaller firms tend to have the relative innovative advantage in the less concentrated industries. The positive and statistically significant coefficient of *CB* suggests that large firms tend to have the innovative advantage in industries that are highly unionized, while small firms tend to have the innovative advantage in industries that are relatively non-unionized. The coefficient of

GROWTH is not statistically significant, implying that, among the high innovative industries, the growth rate has a similar effect on large- and small-firm innovation rates. Because the coefficient of *LFI* is negative and statistically significant, it appears that the less an industry is composed of small firms, the greater is the relative innovative advantage of those existing small firms over their larger counterparts. Perhaps this reflects the use of a strategy of innovation by small firms to remain viable in industries dominated by large firms.

The statistical insignificance of *HK* is somewhat surprising; the explanation may lie in the fact that virtually all of the industries in the high innovative industry sample are skilled-labor intensive. Thus, the lack of variation in *HK* may explain its statistical insignificance in equation (1). Finally, the negative and statistically significant coefficient of *TIE* implies that, even among the high innovative industries, the relative innovative advantage of the small firms increases as the total innovation rate of the industry also increases.

In equation (2), the high innovative industry sample is again used, but *PRODC* is substituted for *PROD*. The results remain virtually unchanged, except that the coefficient of *PRODC* is statistically insignificant, whereas the coefficient of *PROD* is statistically significant in equation (1). It appears, therefore, that advertising-intensity is a significant barrier to small-firm innovation across manufacturing in the high innovative industries and not just in the consumer goods industries.

In equations (3) and (4), the innovative measure standardizing large- and small-firm innovation by sales, *DIS*, is substituted for *DIE*. While the regression results remain mostly unchanged, the major difference is that the coefficient of *PROD* and *CB* are no longer significant. Accordingly, the coefficient of determination falls to 0.376 in equation (3) from 0.524 in equation (1), and to 0.372 in equation (4) from 0.515 in equation (2). However, while the results are somewhat weaker for *DIS* than for *DIE*, the signs and significance of the coefficient of *CAPVS, CON, LFI,* and *TIE* remain similar between the different sets of regressions.

The same model is estimated using the sample of innovative industries—where there was at least some innovative activity—in equations (5) and (6), which use *DIE* as the dependent variable. The coefficients of *CAPVS, CON,* and *CB* are not statistically significant, although all are significant in equations (1) and (2). However, the coefficients of *LFI* and *TIE* remain statistically significant, and *HK* emerges as a statistically significant variable in both equations (5) and (6). Thus, when a broader spectrum of skilled-labor industries is considered, *HK* is found to have a significant effect on the differential between large-firm and small-firm innovation rates. The smaller firms tend to have the relative innovative advantage in the industries utilizing a fairly high component of skilled labor, whereas the large firms tend to have the relative innovative advantage in the industries utilizing less skilled labor. Since the regression results using *DIS* as the dependent variable were virtually identical to those in equations (5) and (6), they were not included in table 2 to save space.

V. Conclusion

In general, the empirical results support the modified Schumpeterian hypothesis that the relative innovative advantage of large and small firms is determined by the extent to which a market is characterized by imperfect competition. Industries which are capital-intensive, concentrated, and advertising-intensive tend to promote the innovative advantage in large firms. The small-firm innovative advantage, however, tends to occur in industries in the early stages of the life-cycle, where total innovation and the use of skilled labor play a large role, and where large firms comprise a high share of the market. At least for these industries, the conclusion of Scherer (1980) that markets composed of a diversity of firm sizes are perhaps the most conducive to innovative activity is reinforced.

Our findings suggest that the focus of the Schumpeterian debate should perhaps be redirected. Rather than posing the issue as, "Which firm size is most conducive to innovation?" the more relevant question may be, "Under which circumstances do large firms have the relative innovative advantage, and under which circumstances do small firms have the relative innovative advantage?" The evidence presented here implies that both sides of the debate—those arguments supporting the innovative superiority of large firms and those supporting the superiority of small firms—are, in fact, correct. However, neither side is correct universally across manufacturing industries. Although the mean manufacturing innovation rate of small firms exceeds that of large firms, in many industries the large firms are more innovative, just as in many others, the small firms are more innovative. We have found that the extent to which the market is characterized by imperfect competition accounts for at least some of this disparate innovation activity between large and small firms. Because innovation rates may also have a significant effect on firm size and market structure, these results must be somewhat qualified. An important topic for future research is the extent to which the firm size distribution is influenced by the relative innovative activity of large and small firms.

REFERENCES

Acs, Zoltan J., and David B. Audretsch, "Entrepreneurial Strategy, Entry Deterrence, and the Presence of Small Firms in Manufacturing," discussion paper IIM/IP 86-28, Wissenschaftszentrum Berlin für Sozialforschung (Oct. 1986).
———, "Innovation in Large and Small Firms," *Economic Letters* 23 (1987), 109–112.
Caves, Richard E., and Thomas A. Pugel, *Intraindustry Differences in Conduct and Performance: Viable Strategies in U.S. Manufacturing Industries* (New York: New York University Press, 1980).
Comanor, William S., "Market Structure, Product Differentiation and Industrial Research," *Quarterly Journal of Economics* (Nov. 1967), 639–657.
Connolly, Robert A., Barry T. Hirsch, and Mark Hirschey, "Union Rent Seeking, Intangible Capital, and Market Value of the Firm," this REVIEW 68 (Nov. 1986), 567–577.
Edwards, Keith L., and Theodore J. Gordon, "Characterization of Innovations Introduced in the U.S. Market in 1982," prepared for the U.S. Small Business Administration under contract no. SBA-6050-A-82, Mar. 1984.
Galbraith, John K., *American Capitalism*, revised edition (Boston: Houghton Mifflin, 1956).
Hirsch, Barry T., and John T. Addison, *The Economic Analysis of Unions: New Approaches and Evidence* (Boston: George Allen and Unwin, 1986).
Hirsch, Barry T., and Albert N. Link, "Labor Union Effects on Innovative Activity," mimeo (June 1986).
Kamien, Morton I., and Nancy L. Schwartz, "Market Structure and Innovation: A Survey," *The Journal of Economic Literature* 13 (Mar. 1975), 1–37.
Link, Albert N., "Firm Size and Efficient Entrepreneurial Activity: A Reformulation of the Schumpeterian Hypothesis," *Journal of Political Economy* 88 (Aug. 1980), 771–782.

Mansfield, Edwin, *Industrial Research and Technological Change* (New York: W.W. Norton, 1968).
Pavitt, K., and S. Wald, "The Conditions for Success in Technological Innovation," OECD, Paris, 1971.
Phillips, A., "Market Structure, Innovation and Investment," in W. Alderson, B. Terpstra and J. Shapiro (eds.), *Patents and Progress: The Sources and Impact of Advancing Technology* (Homewood, Ill.: Irwin, 1965), 37–58.
Porter, Michael E., *Interbrand Choice, Strategy and Bilateral Market Power* (Cambridge: Harvard University Press, 1976).
Pugel, Thomas A., *International Market Linkages and U.S. Manufacturing: Prices, Profits, and Patterns* (Cambridge, MA: Ballinger, 1978).
Scherer, F. M., "Size of Firm, Oligopoly and Research: A Comment," *Canadian Journal of Economics and Political Science* 31 (May 1965), 256–266.
———, *Industrial Market Structure and Economic Performance*, 2nd edition (Chicago: Rand McNally, 1980).
Schumpeter, Joseph A., *Capitalism, Socialism and Democracy*, third edition (New York: Harper and Row, 1950).
Shepherd, William J., *The Economics of Industrial Organization* (Englewood Cliff, N.J.: Prentice Hall, 1979).
Vernon, Raymond, "International Investment and International Trade in the Product Life Cycle," *Quarterly Journal of Economics* 80 (May 1966), 190–207.

APPENDIX A

Data Sources

DIE, LIE, SIE, TIE, DIS, LIS, SIS, and *LFI* are calculated from the innovation and employment data from the U.S. Small Business Administration (Edwards and Gordon, 1984). *HK* was constructed by the U.S. International Trade Commission and is reported in U.S. International Trade Commission, *Industrial Characteristics and Trade Performance Data Base,* Washington, D.C., 1975. A description of the data base can be found in Edward J. Ray, "The Determinants of Tariffs and Nontariff Trade Restrictions in the U.S.," *Journal of Political Economy* 89 (Feb. 1981), 105–121. *CAPVS, CON,* and *GROWTH* are from U.S. Department of Commerce, Bureau of the Census, Annual Survey of Manufacturers, 1977, *Industry Profiles* (Washington, D.C.: U.S. Government Printing Office, issued 1981). (The same source for 1972 is also used to calculate *GROWTH*.) *PROD* uses the value-of-shipments data from the above source along with advertising expenditures from the 1972 United States Input-Output Table. *PRODC* is based on the classification of consumer goods industries which are also convenience goods, identified by Pugel (1978) and Porter (1976). *CB* is from Richard B. Freeman and James L. Medoff, "New Estimates of Private Sector Unionism in the United States," *Industrial and Labor Relations Review* 32 (Jan. 1979), 113–174. The percentage of total employment that is unionized for three-digit SIC industries is reported. We repeat these three-digit SIC values at the four-digit level.

PART II

ENTREPRENEURSHIP

5

Company-Scientist Locational Links:
The Case of Biotechnology

By DAVID B. AUDRETSCH AND PAULA E. STEPHAN*

The emergence of a recent literature (re)-discovering the importance of economic geography[1] might seem paradoxical in a world increasingly dominated by E-mail, faxes, and electronic communications superhighways. Why should geographic proximity matter when technology has advanced in a manner that has drastically reduced the cost of transmitting information across geographic space? This paper explores why geography matters more in certain economic relationships than in others by focusing on the locational incidence of contacts between firms in the biotechnology industry and university-based scientists affiliated with these firms. In particular, we suggest that the specific role played by the scientist shapes the importance of geographic proximity in the firm-scientist link.

* Audretsch: Wissenschaftszentrum Berlin für Sozialforschung and the Centre for Economic Policy Research (CEPR), Reichpietschufer 50, D-10785 Berlin, Germany; Stephan: Department of Economics and Policy Research Center, Georgia State University, Atlanta, GA 30303. This paper was started while Paula Stephan was a visiting professor at the Wissenschaftszentrum Berlin für Sozialforschung. We would like to acknowledge financial support from the North Atlantic Treaty Organization (NATO) under grant number CRG.940792, the College of Business Administration, Georgia State University, and the Policy Research Center of Georgia State University. Richard Hawkins, Meghan Crimmins, Anne Gilbert and Janet Keene coded the data. Steve Everhart provided computer assistance. Earlier versions of this paper were presented at the 1995 meetings of the American Economics Association in Washington, DC; the May 1995 Conference on R&D, Innovation, and Productivity at the Institute for Fiscal Studies in London; the September 1995 annual conference of the European Association for Research in Industrial Economics (EARIE) at Juan-Les-Pins, France; and an October 1995 seminar at INSEAD, Fontainebleau, France. We are also grateful to the suggestions and comments of James Adams, Maryann P. Feldman, Mary Beth Walker and an anonymous referee of this journal. Any remaining errors or omissions are our responsibility.

[1] See for examples Paul Krugman (1991a, b), Robert E. Lucas (1993), Paul Romer (1990), and Audretsch and Maryann P. Feldman (1996).

We shed light on two questions concerning biotechnology companies and the university-based scientists associated with the companies:

1) To what extent are the links between university scientists and biotechnology companies geographically bounded?
2) Is the spatial dimension of geographic links between biotechnology firms and scientists shaped by the role and characteristics of the scientist?

We are able to answer these questions by linking the location of the biotechnology firm with the location of the university-based scientists affiliated with the firm. Thus, while Krugman (1991a) may be correct in pointing out that no "paper trail" exists to facilitate measuring and tracking networks, in this paper we develop a trail of geographic linkages between scientists and firms in biotechnology.

The method used to identify and measure linkages between scientists and biotechnology firms is described in Section I. In particular, we employ a new data base, which includes virtually the entire population of biotechnology firms that prepared an initial public offering (IPO) in the early 1990's, to examine the extent to which the firms and the university-based scientists involved with the firms are located within the same region. In Section II we provide a theory suggesting that the relationship between the locations of a biotechnology firm and a university scientist will be shaped by the potential economic knowledge residing in that scientist and the role that she or he plays in working with the firm. In Section III a probit analysis is undertaken to link the likelihood that a scientist is located in the same region as the biotechnology firm with which she or he is involved and to characteristics specific to the scientist and to the role played with the biotechnology firm. Finally, a summary and conclusions are presented.

I. Measuring Links Between Scientists and Firms

Biotechnology is a new industry that is knowledge based and predominantly composed of new small firms having close ties with university-based scientists. The relative small scale of most biotechnology firms is arguably attributable to the diseconomies of scale inherent in the "bureaucratic process which inhibits both innovative activity and the speed with which new inventions move through the corporate system towards the market" (Albert N. Link and John Rees, 1990 p. 25). Lynne G. Zucker et al. (1994 p. 1) provide considerable evidence suggesting that the timing and location of new biotechnology firms is "primarily explained by the presence at a particular time and place of scientists who are actively contributing to the basic science." More specifically, they find that biotechnology firms are likely to be found in close geographic proximity to where scientists who have published articles on gene sequencing are located. Their work, however, does not explore the geographic linkages among scientists at these institutions and biotech firms. That is, while Zucker et al. show that a region such as the San Francisco Bay Area, which produces a disproportionate amount of research in biotechnology, is home to a disproportionate number of biotech firms, their work sheds virtually no light upon the extent to which biotech firms, once located in the region, establish networks with university-based scientists located in the area. The implicit assumption, of course, is that the networks are overwhelmingly local. Their research design, however, lacks a paper trail linking firms and scientists, and thus can neither affirm nor deny the assumption. Furthermore, they do not explore the variety of roles that university scientists play with biotech firms, but instead focus exclusively on the role of knowledge transfer.[2]

The uniqueness of our approach is that it allows us to determine the actual geographic location of the firm as well as the geographic location of the university-based scientists affiliated with the firm. We are also able to make

inferences about the role the scientist plays with the firm since we are able to identify the title they hold with the firm as well as whether the scientist was a founder of the firm. We do this by collecting data from the prospectuses of biotechnology companies that prepared an initial public offering in the United States during the period March 1990 to November 1992. All told, 54 firms affiliated with 445 university-based scientists meet this criterion.[3] By carefully reading these prospectuses, we determine the names of university-based scientists affiliated with each firm, the role they play in the firm, and the name and location of their home institution. Universities and firms are then grouped into regions which are generally larger than a single city but considerably smaller than a state. Certain areas, for example, metropolitan New York, cross several state lines. A straightforward way to examine our data is to determine the percentage of university-based scientists affiliated with the firm that are from universities in the same region as the firm. This is done in the Data Appendix.

Four major conclusions can be drawn from Table A1. First, firms are geographically concentrated in three primary regions (the San Francisco Bay Area, San Diego and Boston), two secondary regions (Philadelphia and New York), and a number of smaller clusters.[4] Second, the degree to which regions rely upon local scientific talent varies substantially. For example, the Boston area firms draw nearly one-half of their scientists from universities located within the region. By contrast, firms located in the San Diego area draw only about one-quarter of their scientists from universities in the region. Third, the degree to which firms rely upon local scientists varies significantly across individual firms. Eighty percent of the scientists employed by Anergen are located in

---

[2] See also Zucker et al. (1995).

---

[3] The study includes several firms for which the initial public offering was prepared but postponed at the last minute.

[4] Although these data are drawn from a two and one-half year time period, the geographic distribution of the 54 firms in our sample is virtually identical to the entire population of biotechnology firms in the United States. Ernst and Young identify three primary regions, two secondary regions, several other regions with at least 20 companies, and a host of smaller clusters (G. Steven Burrill and Kenneth B. Lee, 1992).

TABLE 1—LOCATION OF SCIENTISTS BY REGION OF UNIVERSITY

	Contacts	Unique firms	Contacts in region	Percentage in region
San Francisco Bay Area	66	28	44	66.7
Stanford University	37	17	24	64.9
University of California, San Francisco	26	14	17	65.4
San Diego, CA	27	13	21	77.8
Scripps College	7	5	5	71.4
University of California, San Diego	16	10	14	87.5
Boston, MA	69	26	41	59.4
Harvard University	43	21	24	55.8
Massachusetts Institute of Technology	15	9	7	46.7
Philadelphia, PA	17	14	8	47.1
University of Pennsylvania	9	8	3	33.3
New York, NY	36	22	9	25.0
Albert Einstein College of Medicine	7	6	1	14.3
Columbia University	11	8	3	27.3
Rockefeller	11	7	4	36.4
Maryland	11	9	1	9.1
Johns Hopkins University	5	4	0	0.0
Seattle, WA	6	5	2	33.3
University of Washington	6	5	2	33.3
Boulder, CO	3	3	1	33.3
Kansas	0	0	0	0.0
Research Triangle, NC	8	8	2	25.0
Los Angeles, CA	13	9	0	0.0
California Institute of Tech	7	5	0	0.0
Dallas, TX	9	5	1	11.1
University of Texas, South Western Medical Center	5	3	0	0.0
Houston, TX	22	9	8	36.4
University of Texas, Anderson Center	11	3	7	63.6
Baylor College of Medicine	7	6	0	0.0
East	37	25	0	0.0
Penn State University	6	5	0	0.0
Pittsburgh University	5	5	0	0.0
Yale University	8	7	0	0.0
Foreign Countries	33	21	0	0.0
Midwest	39	21	0	0.0
Michigan	13	10	0	0.0
South	24	15	0	0.0
Alabama, Birmingham	6	4	0	0.0
West	25	19	0	0.0
University of California, Davis	5	4	0	0.0
Total	445	138		

the San Francisco Bay Area. By contrast, only one of Genta's 19 university-based scientists is located in the same geographic area as the company. The final conclusion to be drawn from Table A1 is that the propensity to draw upon local networks appears unrelated to firm density. For example, the region with the most firms, the San Francisco Bay Area, does not have the greatest propensity to rely upon local-based scientific networks.

Table 1 explores geographic linkages between universities and firms. Eighteen educational regions are defined and within each region institutions with at least five scientific contacts to biotechnology firms are listed. The Table also gives the number of scientist-firm contacts that exist by region and institution as well as the number of firms involved in these contacts. Six important points should be emphasized from Table 1. First, although universities in the San Francisco Bay Area and the Boston-Cambridge Area together supply approximately 30 percent of the scientists, the supply of talent is much less regionally concentrated than are the firms. Second, three institutions are major producers of contacts: Harvard, with 43; Stanford, with 37; and the University of California at San Francisco (UCSF), with 26. Third, universities that are major producers send talent to a large number of firms. Harvard scientists had contact with 40 percent of the firms in our sample; Stanford and UCSF scientists each had contact with over 25 percent of the firms.

Fourth, *commuting patterns* vary by region. For example, two thirds of the university-based scientists in the San Francisco Bay Area work with biotechnology firms located in the Bay Area. By contrast, one fourth of the scientists located in the New York area work with firms in their area. Fifth, commuting patterns also vary considerably according to institutional affiliation. For example, only one in eight of the scientists at the University of California at San Diego (UCSD) commute while six out of seven scientists at the Albert Einstein College of Medicine are affiliated with firms outside the region. Finally, Table 1 indicates the existence of regions in the United States rich in scientific talent but not in biotechnology firms. For example, although 13 of the university-based scientists are located at the University of Michigan, there were no new public offerings filed by biotechnology firms located in the Ann Arbor/Detroit area during our two and one-half year window of observation.

In Table 2 firms are classified into 13 regions and universities into 18 geographic areas. The final row at the bottom indicates the number of scientists drawn from the 18 distinct university regions and is identical to the summary statistics found in Table 1. The column at the extreme right of the last group indicates the number of university-based scientists affiliated with biotechnology companies from the 13 distinct regions and is identical to the summary entries of Table A1.

The virtue of Table 2 is that it reflects the regional location of biotech talent as well as commuting patterns of university-based scientists. For the 13 regions in which there are both firms and universities, the entries on the diagonal represent the number of university-based scientists involved with firms located within that region. Off-diagonal row entries in Table 2 report the regional source of imported talent.

Table 2 invites two conclusions. First, geographic proximity does not play an important role for most company-scientist location links. Only 138 of the 445 observations lie on the diagonal. Yet, a Chi-square test implies that the null hypothesis of factor independence can be rejected at better than the 0.001 level. Linkages may not be overwhelmingly local but neither are they random. Second, distance does not appear to affect commuting patterns. For example, the hypothesis that scientists are just as likely to make a 2500 mile trip as a 250 mile trip cannot be rejected at the 10-percent level of significance.

II. The Role of University-Based Scientists

The results from the previous section clearly show that in some cases the geographic link between a biotechnology company and a university scientist occurs within the same region, while in other cases geographic proximity does not matter. Here we hypothesize that the locational incidence of contacts between firms and university-scientists is shaped by the particular role played by the scientist with the firm. When university-based scientists are actively involved in knowledge transfer, their knowledge is more easily tapped if the firm is located in the same region as the scientist. But when the scientist plays other roles geographic proximity is considerably less important. Balanced against the benefits of local proximity to the scientist is proximity to other firms and research organizations and also to better inputs. The fewer firms there are in a region, holding all else constant, the less likely the firm would be to locate near scientists in that region with which it has contacts. Also relevant would be unobserved features of the firm,

TABLE 2—GEOGRAPHIC DISTRIBUTION OF FIRM-UNIVERSITY LINKS

	Region of University					
	SF Bay	Los Angeles	San Diego	Boulder	Kansas	Boston
Region of Firm:						
SF Bay	44	9	2	1	0	13
Los Angeles	1	0	0	0	0	0
San Diego	5	1	21	0	0	3
Boulder	1	0	0	1	0	1
Kansas	1	0	0	0	0	0
Boston	4	3	3	1	0	41
Maryland	1	0	0	0	0	1
RTI	0	0	0	0	0	0
New York	5	0	0	0	0	6
Philadelphia	0	0	1	0	0	4
Dallas	0	0	0	0	0	0
Houston	1	0	0	0	0	0
Seattle	3	0	0	0	0	0
Total	66	13	27	3	0	69

	Region of University					
	Maryland	RTI	New York	Philadelphia	Dallas	Houston
Region of Firm:						
SF Bay	2	3	11	2	3	1
Los Angeles	0	0	0	0	0	0
San Diego	2	0	5	4	1	5
Boulder	0	1	0	0	0	0
Kansas	0	0	0	0	0	0
Boston	4	1	6	2	0	0
Maryland	1	0	2	0	0	3
RTI	0	2	0	0	0	0
New York	1	1	9	1	4	1
Philadelphia	1	0	3	8	0	1
Dallas	0	0	0	0	1	3
Houston	0	0	0	0	0	8
Seattle	0	0	0	0	0	0
Total	11	8	36	17	9	22

	Region of University						
	Seattle	East	Foreign	Midwest	South	West	Total
Region of Firm:							
SF Bay	2	9	11	12	10	10	145
Los Angeles	0	2	1	3	1	1	9
San Diego	1	5	9	7	3	5	77
Boulder	0	0	0	0	0	0	4
Kansas	0	0	1	2	1	1	6
Boston	0	4	7	3	3	3	85
Maryland	1	3	0	0	1	0	13
RTI	0	1	0	1	1	1	6
New York	0	3	5	1	1	1	39
Philadelphia	0	8	0	2	1	2	31
Dallas	0	1	1	2	2	0	10
Houston	0	2	1	0	0	1	13
Seattle	2	0	0	2	0	0	7
Total	6	37	33	39	24	25	445

such as where the main participants in the firm that are not university scientists reside.

University-based scientists provide three key functions to biotech firms: they facilitate knowledge transfer from university laboratories to the firm; they signal the quality of the firm's research to both capital and resource markets; and they help chart the scientific direction of the company. The knowledge transfer function of university-based scientists has received the most attention (Gary P. Pisano et al., 1988; Zucker et al., 1994; Zucker et al., 1995; and Henry Etzkowitz, 1983). It occurs, for example, whenever a university-based scientist founds a firm for the explicit purpose of developing knowledge created in the scientist's lab or when a university-based scientist is extensively involved in the research agenda of the firm. It is not the only way that knowledge moves from university labs and companies. Companies can also learn about the research occurring in university labs through social contacts between employees and university scientists and by sending employees to participate in workshops and seminars at the university (Zucker et al., 1995).

In addition to providing knowledge to newly formed biotechnology companies, university-based scientists also signal the quality of the firm to the scientific and financial communities. An effective way to recruit young scientists is to have a scientific advisory board (SAB) composed of the leaders in the field. According to George B. Rathmann, former president and CEO of Amgen, some of the young scientists that Amgen recruited would not have come "without the knowledge that an outstanding scientific advisory board took Amgen seriously" (Burill, 1987 p. 77). University-based scientists can also serve as *bait* to the investment community. In the early stages of development, biotechnology firms miss no opportunity to signal the abilities of their scientists as well as the science they are undertaking. It is not uncommon for prospectuses to read like proposals to the National Institutes of Health, both in terms of the projects they describe and the accomplishments of the scientists. Stephan (1994) has shown that the proceeds raised from an initial public offering as well as the "day one" value of the firm is positively and significantly related to the reputation of the university-based scientist affiliated with the firm.

University-based scientists also help chart the scientific direction of the company. Most biotech companies go public long before they have a flagship product ready for clinical tests. Some go public in the earliest stages of development.[5] Having few employees, and working in what has proved to be an exceptionally risky environment with regard to product effectiveness, firms seek guidance from the scientific community.[6]

The tacit nature of knowledge in biotechnology (Pisano et al., 1988) suggests that knowledge transfer between university-based scientists and biotechnology firms is facilitated by face to face contact and thus geographic proximity. On the other hand, the geographic proximity of all major researchers in a particular subfield is unlikely given the opportunity cost universities face in buying into a single research agenda. The broad-based nature of the knowledge used in biotechnology (Luigi Orsenigo, 1989) also suggests that knowledge links may not be exclusively local.

Scientists whose primary function is to signal the quality of the company are less likely to be local than are scientists who provide essential knowledge to the company. Their quality signal is produced by lending prestige to a venture they have presumably reviewed, a task that can be accomplished with credibility from a distance. The only reason that university-based scientists fulfilling the role of signal bearer might be geographically linked with the company is that the company may find it useful to locate near talent on the assumption that it makes scientific stars that much more willing to be involved. A similar line of reasoning can be made concerning the geographic proximity of scientists whose primary function is to chart the scientific course of the company.

It is, of course, difficult to know the exact functions the university-based scientist fulfills and many scientists undoubtedly fulfill multi-

---

[5] This was particularly true in the early 1990's when companies, sensing an open financial "window," rushed to go public in fear that the window would close and they would find themselves without the resources needed for product development.

[6] Such guidance is also often required by the financial backers and underwriters. Recent examples of product failure in biotechnology underscores the risky nature of the industry (Jim Shrine, 1994).

TABLE 3—ROLE OF SCIENTIST

	Founder	SAB	SAB chair	Majorstock
Nonlocal	16	249	7	20
$n = 307$	(42.1)	(68.2)	(33.3)	(50.0)
Local	22	116	14	20
$n = 138$	(57.9)	(31.8)	(66.7)	(50.0)
Total	38	365	21	40
χ^2	14.04[a]	0.56	13.10[a]	7.41[b]

Note: Percentages of the total are given in parentheses.
 [a] Significant at 0.000 or better.
 [b] Significant at 0.02 or better.

ple functions. The title the scientists holds at the firm, however, gives some insight into the function performed, and the genesis of the firm also allows for inference. In particular, we expect university-based founders to be a source of knowledge transfer. Presumably scientists start new biotechnology companies because their knowledge is not transferable to other firms for the expected economic value of the knowledge.[7] If this were not the case, there would be no incentive to start a new and independent company. Chairs of scientific advisory boards arguably also play a key role in knowledge transfer. Members of SABs, on the other hand, provide ballast to the masthead and help chart the course of the company. They can also facilitate knowledge transfer by providing the firm, at minimal cost, a full roster of key players doing research in the area.[8]

Table 3 explores the hypothesis that the role played by the scientist in the firm relates to the probability that the linkage is local. Consistent with the above discussion concerning knowledge transfer, we find, using a Chi-square test, that scientific founders are significantly more likely to have a local linkage than are non-

---

[7] Kenneth Arrow (1962), Oliver E. Williamson (1975), and Audretsch (1995) have argued that when new economic knowledge cannot be easily transferred to established firms, perhaps due to organization factors, the holder of such knowledge must start a new firm in order to appropriate the potential economic value of the knowledge.

[8] Members of scientific advisory boards usually receive compensation in the neighborhood of $10,000 per year. In addition, they are often granted options which prove in some cases to be quite valuable (Stephan and Stephen Everhart, 1996).

founders. We also find that the university scientists who are chairs of scientific advisory boards are significantly more likely to have a local linkage than are nonchairs.[9] One cannot, however, conclude that chairs and founders who (presumably) provide a source of knowledge do so exclusively for firms in close geographic proximity to where they work. Over 40 percent of the university-based founders establish firms outside of the region of their university; a third of the chairs of SABs are not in the same geographic region as the firm. This is consistent with the idea that while tacit knowledge requires face to face interaction, such interaction does not require that the scientist and the firm be permanently located in the same area.

The table also indicates that the 40 scientists who have sufficient equity holdings in the company (Majorstock) to require disclosure at the time of the initial public offering are more likely to have local ties than those scientists who are not major stockholders. This relates not only to the fact that major stockholders are often founders.[10] It is also consistent with the hypothesis that monitoring is facilitated through geographic proximity. Once again, however, the ties are far from exclusively local. The table also shows that we cannot reject the hypothesis that networks of the 365 SAB members are any more local than networks of other scientists in the data base, as indicated by the Chi-square value of 0.56.

III. Probit Analysis

While suggestive, the results from Table 3 examine geographic linkages only in terms of the role played by the university-based scientist in the firm. No attempt is made to control for personal characteristics of the scientists. Yet, the willingness of a scientist to be involved, as well as the attractiveness of a scientist to a company, undoubtedly influences the extent to which linkages between firms and scientists are geographically bounded. In order

---

[9] Twenty-two of the 54 firms designate the chair of the SAB in the prospectus. In all but two instances the chair is employed by a university. In another instance the SAB has co-chairs, both of whom work at a university.
[10] Fifty percent of the major stockholders are founders.

to examine these relations, we estimate a probit model of the probability that a scientist is located in the same region as the biotechnology firm with which she or he is involved. The probit model permits us to determine how various factors affect the likelihood of being part of a local network as opposed to a nonlocal network. Individual characteristics introduced into the analysis include age, citation history, and Nobel status.[11] Before presenting the results, we discuss the variables and link them to the main hypotheses introduced above. In interpreting the results, it is important to remember that the data do not permit us to examine *who* on university faculties is involved with a biotechnology firm. By definition, *everyone* in our sample is involved. Rather, the analysis focuses upon the geographic dimension of the link between university-based scientists and biotechnology companies—that is, under what circumstances this link occurs within the same geographic space and under which circumstances the scientist and the firm are located in different regions.

A necessary condition for participation is that the firm is aware of the capabilities of the scientist. The dispersion of such information is clearly shaped by the geographic breadth of the scientist's network (contacts). Scientists with limited networks are more likely to be constrained to participate within a local rather than a nonlocal sphere. This suggests that, other things equal, a younger person is more likely to be involved with a local firm than with a nonlocal firm. The expected sign is not only based on factors affecting the size of networks. Life-cycle models of the allocation of time by scientists (David Levy, 1988; and Sharon G. Levin and Stephan, 1991) suggest that in the early stages of their lives scientists invest in human capital in order to build a reputation, while in the later stages of their career scientists trade or *cash in* their reputation for economic return. That is, early in their careers, scientists invest in the creation of knowledge in order to establish a reputation reflecting the scientific value of that new knowledge; with maturity, scientists cash in by seeking ways to

appropriate the economic value of that new knowledge. Thus, we expect older scientists to accept multiple offers of firm involvement. By contrast, younger scientists who have a higher opportunity cost of travel are expected to focus contacts within their own geographic region.

Age is not the only factor shaping the geographic extent of a scientist's network. Scientists who publish are much more likely to be known outside their local network than are nonpublishers. This is especially true if the publications are heavily cited, indicating that the scientific community has a high regard for the work (Robert Merton, 1957; Jonathan R. Cole and Stephen Cole, 1973; and Eugene Garfield, 1979). Thus, just as the involvement of older scientists is likely to be nonlocal in nature, the involvement of scientists with many citations is also likely to be nonlocal. An analogous argument suggests that Nobel laureates are more likely to have nonlocal than local ties.

A major qualification, however, relating to what we call *drawing power*, must be made to the above line of reasoning. Scientists become involved with start-up firms when venture capitalists find the scientist and science she or he is doing sufficiently attractive to warrant financing. Thus, mature scientists with strong reputations have the drawing power to attract firms to locate near them. For example, venture capital and other components of a start-up team for a new biotechnology company will be attracted to locations near scientists with extraordinary reputations to increase the probability that a contact can be established. Whether this drawing power effect outweighs the more general reputation effect is an empirical question.

A different type of qualification is that the higher the density of firms in the region in which any given scientist is located, the greater is the extent of opportunities for her or him within that region. To control for this effect, we include the density of biotechnology firms in the region, measured by the share of the 54 firms located in the scientist's geographic region. The probit model also controls for the role played by the scientist in the biotechnology firm by including a dummy variable defined to be 0 if the scientist founded the firm or chairs the SAB and 0 if she or he did not.

---

[11] Nine of the 445 scientists are Nobel prize recipients and have 10 contacts with biotechnology firms.

The probit regression is estimated for the 312 scientists for whom there is information identifying both their age and citation history. The results are reported in Table 4.[12] The dependent variable is equal to 1 if the link between the scientist and firm is local, and 0 if it is nonlocal. In addition to presenting the probit coefficients and asymptotic standard errors, Table 4 also presents the marginal effect that a one unit change in an independent variable has on the probability of commuting.[13]

The results are striking. The negative and statistically significant coefficient of the age variable suggests that, ceteris paribus, older scientists, are more likely than younger scientists to have contacts with biotechnology firms located outside of the regions of their universities. The marginal effect of an additional year is to increase the probability of a scientist commuting by 0.6 percent; of a decade is 6.0 percent. As expected, the specific role played by the scientist in the biotechnology firm also shapes the geographic dimension of the contact. Those scientists serving as founders of biotechnology firms have a significantly higher propensity to be located in the same region as the firm than those who are not founders. According to the marginal effect, a shift in status from nonfounder to founder increases the likelihood of a contact being local by more than 20 percent. The combined impact (equation (2)) of serving as a founder *or* chair of a SAB is slightly larger.

Having been awarded a Nobel prize significantly increases the propensity for the scientist to engage in local contacts with biotechnology firms.[14] This may reflect the willingness of venture capitalists and other key members of new biotechnology start-ups to locate close to a Nobel prize recipient, and suggests that for scientific stars drawing power overwhelms general reputational effects. On the other hand, there is no evidence that the citation history of a scientist influences the propensity of a scientist to engage in local versus nonlocal contacts.[15] This presumably reflects the offsetting effects of reputation and drawing power discussed in Section II.

One of the concerns in the probit model is that the majority of scientist-firm contacts are concentrated in just two sections of the country: California, which spans the three areas of the San Francisco Bay Area, Los Angeles and San Diego, and the North East, which includes the three areas of Boston, Philadelphia and New York. Because of the proximity of opportunities in neighboring areas, after controlling for density we would expect scientists in the North East and California to have a higher propensity to commute than scientists located in alternative regions of the country. In order to test this hypothesis, we include two dummy variables, the first taking on a value of 1 for scientists located in California, and the other taking on a value of 1 for scientists located in the North East. The results suggest a type of asymmetry between west coast and east coast scientific networks. The positive and statistically significant coefficient on the North East dummy variable implies that despite the large number of opportunities in neighboring areas, scientists located in the North East tend to be insular in their propensity to engage in contacts with firms located in their specific area. By contrast, the coefficient on the California dummy variable, which cannot be considered statistically significant, suggests that proximity of opportunity does not affect commuting patterns for California scientists.

IV. Conclusions

A key finding of this paper is that while a substantial number of university-based scientists participate in networks that are

---

[12] Thirty-one scientists working for three firms are excluded because citation histories were not collected for scientists working for these firms. Of the remaining 414 scientists we found birth dates (and citation histories) for 312, yielding a sample retention rate of 75 percent.

[13] For the continuous variables the marginal effect is evaluated at the mean of the explanatory variable. For the dummy variables the marginal effect reflects the difference between having the characteristic versus not having the characteristic.

[14] The dummy variable for the Nobel prize indicates receipt of the prize since 1970. One scientist received the prize in 1958. The inclusion of this scientist reduces the statistical significance of the coefficient of the Nobel prize dummy variable to being statistically significant at the 10-percent level of significance, for a two-tailed test.

[15] The citation history measure is not statistically significant regardless of the specification by which it is included in the probit equation.

TABLE 4—PROBIT RESULTS FOR PROBABILITY OF SCIENTIST-FIRM CONTACT BEING LOCAL[a]

	(1)	Marginal effect[b]	(2)	Marginal effect[b]	(3)	Marginal effect[b]	(4)	Marginal effect[b]
Constant	−0.45 (0.47)	—	−0.42 (0.47)	—	−0.59 (0.48)	—	−0.56 (0.48)	—
Age	−0.018* (0.008)	−0.006	−0.019* (0.008)	−0.006	−0.022* (0.009)	−0.007	−0.023** (0.009)	−0.008
Citations	0.74×10^{-4} (0.56×10^{-3})	0.25×10^{-4}	0.32×10^{-4} (0.56×10^{-3})	0.10×10^{-4}	0.79×10^{-4} (0.59×10^{-3})	0.25×10^{-4}	0.12×10^{-3} (0.58×10^{-3})	0.40×10^{-4}
Nobel prize	1.13* (0.49)	0.427	1.14* (0.50)	0.430	1.12* (0.50)	0.420	1.12* (0.49)	0.420
Founder	0.62* (0.27)	0.233	—	—	0.67* (0.27)	0.240	—	—
Founder/chair	—	—	0.65** (0.25)	0.242	—	—	0.68** (0.25)	0.250
Firm density[c]	7.39** (0.31)	0.250	7.36** (0.82)	0.248	6.25** (1.37)	0.198	6.15** (1.37)	0.209
California	—	—	—	—	0.38 (0.38)	0.13	0.41 (0.38)	0.14
North East	—	—	—	—	0.87** (0.28)	0.30	0.87** (0.28)	0.30
Log-Likelihood	−142.02		−141.27		−134.72		−134.07	
Sample size	312		312		312		312	

[a] Asymptotic standard errors are listed in parentheses.
[b] See the text for how the marginal effect is computed.
[c] The marginal effect is calculated for a 0.10 change in firm density.
* Statistically significant at the 95-percent level of confidence, two-tailed test.
** Statistically significant at the 99-percent level of confidence, two-tailed test.

geographically bounded, approximately 70 percent of the links between biotechnology companies and the university-based scientists are nonlocal. We conclude that while proximity matters in establishing formal ties between university-based scientists and companies, its influence is anything but overwhelming.

The results clearly suggest that the importance of proximity is shaped by the role played by the scientist. Proximity matters more in the case of founders than for members of scientific advisory boards. It also matters more for chairs of SABs. This presumably reflects the qualitative difference in the services provided by the scientist. In addition, characteristics specific to the scientist shape the geographic dimension of the scientist-firm contact. The status of being a *star*, as reflected by receipt of a Nobel prize, for example, reduces the need to commute outside of the region in which the scientist is located. Apparently, other key components comprising a biotechnology start-up, such as venture capital and managerial competence, may be willing to locate within close proximity to such stars. In addition, we

find that older scientists, other things being equal, are more likely to have links with biotechnology firms that are not geographically bounded. This apparently reflects both the desire of mature scientists to cash in and the geographic breadth of their networks.

Our findings also suggest that the links between scientists and companies involve a multiplicity of dimensions, only one of which is knowledge transfer, and that the importance of local proximity varies considerably across these dimensions. The results also suggest that even in the case of knowledge transfer, scientists and firms are often geographically separated. For example, 40 percent of the university-based founders of biotech firms in the data base are affiliated with firms outside their region. Does this mean that the proponents of the new growth economics may have overemphasized the importance that geography plays? Not necessarily, if one recalls that much of this work stresses the informality of knowledge spillovers while our work focuses on relationships that have been intentionally formed to capitalize on the scientist's knowledge. In both the informal and formal case, the marginal cost of transmitting new economic knowledge, particularly tacit knowledge, across geographic space is nontrivial. This means, as the studies by Audretsch and Feldman (1996) and Adam B. Jaffe et al. (1993) imply, that geographic proximity matters when knowledge spillovers are *informal*. But an important conclusion of this paper is that when knowledge is transmitted through *formal* ties between researchers and firms, geographic proximity is not necessary, since face to face contact does not occur by chance but instead is carefully planned.

Finally, it is important to realize that while geographic proximity between university scientists and firms is valuable, other factors that are related to agglomeration, such as the location of other firms and research organizations, play an important role in mediating the geographic proximity of firms and their affiliated university scientists. These broader types of spillovers have not been examined in this paper. Perhaps future research should shift away from asking *if* geography plays a role to exploring in more depth *how* the role of geography varies by function as well as by characteristics of the region.

APPENDIX TABLE A1—LOCATION OF BIOTECH FIRMS BY REGION

| | University-based scientists | Scientists from within region | | | University-based scientists | Scientists from within region | |
		Number	Percent			Number	Percent
San Francisco Bay Area, CA				*Philadelphia, PA*			
Anergen	5	4	80.0	Affinity Biotech	5	1	20.0
Applied Immune Sciences	8	1	12.5	Cephalon	5	1	20.0
Biocircutis	4	2	50.0	DNX	5	2	40.0
Biotime	6	2	33.3	Magainin Pharmaceuticals	6	2	33.3
Cell Genesis	16	2	12.5	Medarex	6	0	0.0
COR Therapeutics	15	5	33.3	Zynaxis	4	2	50.0
Cygnus	5	1	20.0	Total	31	8	25.8
Genelabs Technologies	13	6	46.2				
Genpharm	15	0	0.0	*New York, NY*			
Gilead Sciences	7	1	14.3	Alteon	6	4	66.6
Neurex	22	6	27.3	Biomatrix	6	1	16.7
Oclassen Pharmaceuticals	7	1	14.3	Biospecifics Technologies	5	2	40.0
Protein Design Labs	7	4	57.1	Medicis	9	0	0.0
Sciclone	8	7	87.5	Regeneron Pharmaceuticals	13	2	15.4
Systemix	7	2	28.9	Total	39	9	23.0
Total	145	44	30.3				
				Maryland			
San Diego, CA				Genetic Therapy	7	0	0.0
Amylin	10	3	30.0	Univax Biologics	6	1	16.7
Corvas	9	3	33.3	Total	13	1	7.7
Cytel	9	1	33.3				
Genta	19	1	5.2	*Seattle, WA*			
Idec Pharmaceuticals	2	1	50.0	Cell Pro	7	2	28.6
Immune Response	7	2	28.6				
Ligand Pharmaceuticals	7	4	57.1	*Boulder, CO*			
Protein Polymer Technologie	7	1	14.3	Somatogen	4	1	25.0
Vical	7	3	42.3				
Total	77	21	27.2	*Kansas*			
				Deprenyl	6	0	0.0
Boston, MA							
Alpha-Beta Technology	7	7	100.0	*Research Triangle, NC*			
Cambridge Neuroscience	10	4	40.0	Sphinx Pharmaceuticals	6	2	33.3
Creative Biomolecules	11	4	36.4				
Cytotherapeutics	14	4	28.6	*Los Angeles, CA*			
Epigen	8	2	25.0	Watson Pharmaceuticals	9	0	0.0
Immulogie	11	5	45.5				
Matritech	8	3	37.5	*Dallas, TX*			
Sepracor	7	3	42.8	Carntech	10	1	10.0
Seragen	3	3	100.0				
Vertex Pharmaceuticals	6	6	100.0	*Houston, TX*			
Total	85	41	48.2	Argus Pharmaceuticals	13	8	61.5
				Total	**445**	**138**	**31.0**

REFERENCES

Arrow, Kenneth. "Economic Welfare and the Allocation of Resources for Invention," in Richard R. Nelson, ed., *The rate and direction of inventive activity.* Princeton, NJ: Princeton University Press, 1962, pp. 609–26.

Audretsch, David B. *Innovation and industry evolution.* Cambridge, MA: MIT Press, 1995.

Audretsch, David B. and Feldman, Maryann P. "R&D Spillovers and the Geography of Innovation and Production." *American Economic Review*, June 1996, *86*(3), pp. 630–40.

Burrill, G. Steven. *Biotech 88: Into the marketplace.* San Francisco: Arthur Young High Technology Group, 1987.

Burrill, G. Steven and Lee, Kenneth B., Jr. *Biotech 93: Accelerating commercialization.* San Francisco: Ernst & Young, 1992.

Cole, Jonathan R. and Cole, Stephen. *Social stratification in science.* Chicago: University of Chicago Press, 1973.

Etzkowitz, Henry. "Entrepreneurial Scientists and Entrepreneurial Universities in American Academic Science." *Minerva*, 1983, *21*(2), pp. 198–233.

Garfield, Eugene. *Citation indexing: Its theory and application in science, technology and humanities.* New York: Wiley, 1979.

Jaffe, Adam B.; Trajtenberg, Manuel and Henderson, Rebecca. "Geographic Localization of Knowledge Spillovers as Evidenced by Patent Citations." *Quarterly Journal of Economics*, August 1993, *63*(3), pp. 577–98.

Krugman, Paul. "Increasing Returns and Economic Geography." *Journal of Political Economy*, June 1991a, *99*(3), pp. 483–99.

──────. *Geography and trade.* Cambridge, MA: MIT Press, 1991b.

Levin, Sharon G. and Stephan, Paula E. "Research Productivity over the Life Cycle: Evidence for Academic Scientists." *American Economic Review*, March 1991, *81*(4), pp. 114–32.

Levy, David. "The Market for Fame and Fortune." *History of Political Economy*, Winter 1988, *20*(4), pp. 615–25.

Link, Albert N. and Rees, John. "Firm Size, University Based Research, and the Returns to R&D." *Small Business Economics*, 1990, *2*(1), pp. 25–32.

Lucas, Robert E., Jr. "Making a Miracle." *Econometrica*, March 1993, *61*(2), pp. 251–72.

Merton, Robert. "Priorities in Scientific Discovery: A Chapter in the Sociology of Science." *American Sociological Review*, December 1957, *22*(6), pp. 635–59.

Orsenigo, Luigi. *The emergence of biotechnology: Institutions and markets in industrial innovation.* New York: St Martins Press, 1989.

Pisano, Gary P.; Shan, Wiejnian and Teece, David. "Joint Ventures and Collaboration in the Biotechnology Industry," in David Mowery, ed., *International collaborative ventures in U.S. manufacturing.* Cambridge, MA: Ballinger Publishers, 1988, pp. 183–222.

Romer, Paul. "Endogenous Technological Change." *Journal of Political Economy*, October 1990, *98*(5) Part 2, pp. S71–102.

Shrine, Jim. "Telios Offers to Buy Back Shares from Offering." *Bioworld Today*, October 1994, *10*, p. 1.

Stephan, Paula E. "Differences in the Post-Entry Value of Biotech Firms: The Role of Human Capital." Presented at the Conference on the Post-Entry Performance of Firms," hosted by the Bank of Portugal, Lisbon, May 22–28, 1994.

Stephan, Paula E. and Everhart, Stephen. "The Changing Rewards to Science: The Case of Biotechnology." *Small Business Economics*, forthcoming 1996, *8*.

Stephan, Paula E. and Levin, Sharon G. *Striking the mother lode in science.* New York: Oxford University Press, 1992.

Williamson, Oliver E. *Markets and hierarchies: Antitrust analysis and implications.* New York: Free Press, 1975.

Zucker, Lynne G.; Darby, Michael R. and Armstrong, Jeff. "Intellectual Capital and the Firm: The Technology of Geographically Localized Knowledge Spillovers." National Bureau of Economic Research (Cambridge, MA) Working Paper No. 4946, 1995.

Zucker, Lynne G.; Darby, Michael R. and Brewer, Marilynn B. "Intellectual Capital and the Birth of U.S. Biotechnology Enterprises." National Bureau of Economic Research (Cambridge, MA) Working Paper No. 4653, 1994.

R&D SPILLOVERS AND RECIPIENT FIRM SIZE

Zoltan J. Acs, David B. Audretsch, and Maryann P. Feldman*

Abstract—The findings in this paper provide some insight into how small firms are able to innovate. Using a production function approach to relate knowledge generating inputs to innovative output, the empirical results suggest that small firms are the recipients of R&D spillovers from knowledge generated in the R&D centers of their larger counterparts and in universities. Such R&D spillovers are apparently more decisive in promoting the innovative activity of small firms than of large corporations.

I. Introduction

A recent series of studies for both the United States (Acs and Audretsch, 1987, 1988, and 1990) and Great Britain (Pavitt, Robson, and Townsend, 1987) found that while large corporations have the innovative advantage in certain industries, in other markets small firms are more innovative. This finding posed something of a paradox, because it is well known that the

bulk of R&D is concentrated among the largest industrial corporations (Scherer, 1991). And, according to one of the most prevalent models of technological change (Griliches, 1979), innovative output is the product of knowledge generating inputs, most notably R&D. That small enterprises are the engine of innovative activity in certain industries despite an obvious lack of formal R&D activities,[1] raises the question, "Where do small firms get the innovation producing inputs?"

One possible answer is from other firms and institutions investing in R&D (Link and Rees, 1990; and Dorfman, 1983). An important finding of Jaffe (1986 and 1989) was that investment in R&D made by private corporations and universities "spills over" for economic exploitation by third party firms. However, while Jaffe (1986 and 1989) identified the extent to which corporate and university research spills over onto the generation of inventions by other firms, he

Received for publication August 5, 1991. Revision accepted for publication October 16, 1992.

* University of Baltimore, Wissenschaftszentrum Berlin für Sozialforschung, and Carnegie-Mellon University, respectively.

[1] Kleinknecht (1987 and 1989) has found that informal R&D activity plays a larger role in small firms than in large enterprises.

shed little light on which type of firm is the recipient of such spillovers. The purpose of this paper is to explicitly identify the degree to which university and corporate R & D spills over to small firms, and the extent to which university R & D spills over to large firms. By focusing on the recipients of the spillovers, rather than just upon the source, the manner by which large and small firms produce innovations can be more accurately identified.

We find substantial evidence that corporate R & D is a relatively more important source for generating innovations in large firms, while spillovers from university research laboratories are more important in producing innovative activity in small firms. In the following section, the "knowledge production function" model of innovation activity is applied for large and small firms. The data are introduced in the third section. In the fourth section, the empirical results from Tobit estimation are presented.

II.   R & D Inputs and Innovative Output

According to the model of technological change introduced by Griliches (1979), innovative output is the product of knowledge generating inputs. Jaffe modified this production function approach for adoption to a model specified for spatial and product dimensions:

$$I_{si} = CRD_{si}^{\beta 1} * UR_{si}^{\beta 2} * (UR_{si} * GC_{si})^{\beta 3} * e_{si} \qquad (1)$$

where I is innovative output, CRD is private corporate expenditures on R & D, UR the research expenditures undertaken at universities, and e represents a stochastic error term. The unit of observation is at the spatial level, s, and product level, i.[2] To overcome the conceptual problem of using state level data to measure geographic spillovers, Jaffe constructs an index of the geographic coincidence of university and industrial research labs, GC.[3] Jaffe argued that the proximity of

[2] Jaffe (1989) used "technological areas" for the product dimension.

[3] The geographic coincidence index is calculated as

$$GC_S = \frac{\sum_c UNIV_{ci} TP_{ci}}{\left[\sum_c UNIV_{ci}^2\right]^{1/2} \left[\sum_c TP_{ci}^2\right]^{1/2}};$$

where TP_{ci} is the total number of industrial R & D lab workers in a city or SMSA. The geographic coincidence index is calculated as the uncentered correlation of the vectors U_i and TP_i across SMSAs within a state. Jaffe's (1989) hypothesis is that research will yield more innovative activity if university and industrial labs are geographically concentrated. For example, more patents would be expected in Illinois, where industrial and research labs are concentrated around Chicago, than in Indiana where university labs are located in different SMSAs from industrial labs.

university research to corporate laboratories should raise the potency of spillovers from the universities.

Using the number of patented inventions to proxy innovative activity, Jaffe (1989) estimated equation (1) and found that university research does, in fact, spill over to promote corporate patent activity. That is, not only does patent activity increase in the presence of high private corporate expenditures on R & D, but also from research expenditures undertaken by universities within the state.

Jaffe's results made it clear that spillovers play an important role as an input in generating innovations in third party firms,[4] but they shed little light on the recipients of the spillovers. By estimating equation (1) for the innovative activity contributed by large firms separately from the innovative activity contributed by small firms, and directly comparing the magnitude of the coefficients of CRD, UR, and $UR * GC$, the relative importance of R & D spillovers from universities and corporate laboratories for large and small firms can be explicitly ascertained.

III.   Measurement

Although Jaffe (1989) used patent counts to proxy innovative activity, we use a direct measure—the number of innovations in 1982. This measure comes from the U.S. Small Business Administration's Innovation Data Base and is explained and analyzed in considerable detail in Acs and Audretsch (1987, 1988, and 1990). Griliches (1990), Scherer (1983), and Mansfield (1984) have all observed that patent counts measure an intermediate output in the entire process of producing an innovation. According to Griliches (1990, p. 1669), "Ideally, we might hope that patent statistics would provide a measure of the (innovative) output.... The reality, however, is very far from it. The dream of getting hold of an output indicator of inventive activity is one of the strong motivating forces for economic research in this area."

In contrast to patent data, which mark the certification of an invention, innovation citations announce the market introduction of a commercially viable product.[5] Thus, the resulting data base provides a more direct measure of innovative activity than does the number of patented inventions. Not only are inventions which were not patented but ultimately introduced into the market included in the data base, but those inventions which were patented but never developed into innovations are excluded.

[4] Acs, Audretsch, and Feldman (1992) confirm that Jaffe's results for R & D spillovers onto patenting activity hold using the direct measure of innovative activity used in this paper.

[5] Another distinction is that an innovating firm did not necessarily make the invention.

TABLE 1.—INNOVATIVE OUTPUT IN LARGE AND SMALL FIRMS AND R & D INPUTS BY STATE[a]

State	Total Innovations	Large Firm Innovations	Small Firm Innovations	Industry R & D Expenditures	University Research
CALF	974	315	659	3883	710.4
NY	456	180	276	1859	371.0
NJ	426	162	264	1361	70.8
MASS	360	148	212	954	245.3
PA	245	104	141	1293	139.2
ILL	231	100	131	894	254.9
OHIO	188	76	112	926	76.2
CONN	132	77	55	650	54.7
MICH	112	61	51	1815	103.2
MINN	110	64	46	399	55.7
WISC	86	33	53	224	65.0
FLA	66	21	45	375	70.1
GA	53	20	33	78	57.8
IND	49	20	29	398	51.3
COLO	42	13	29	167	77.2
ARIZ	41	23	18	201	37.4
VA	38	19	19	207	45.9
NC	38	16	22	193	64.6
RI	24	4	20	32	14.9
OKLA	20	12	8	93	19.9
IOWA	20	12	8	135	46.4
KANS	15	3	12	66	26.6
UTAH	11	2	9	72	32.5
NEB	9	1	8	9	20.4
KY	9	6	3	72	17.5
LA	5	0	5	65	33.4
ARK	5	5	0	9	12.0
ALA	5	0	5	54	28.3
MISS	4	1	3	420	61.4

[a] Industry R & D and University Research expenditures are in millions of 1972 dollars and are taken from Jaffe (1989). Data are available for 29 states.

The innovation data are classified according to the size of the innovating firm. Large firms are defined as having at least 500 employees, and small firms are defined as having fewer than 500 employees. Innovations are attributed to the state in which the establishment responsible for the commercial development of the innovation is located. The data base distinguishes between the location of the innovating establishment and the location of the parent firm. In the case of a multi-establishment firm, the innovation would be classified by size on the basis of the employment of the entire parent firm, but would be located at the innovating establishment and not at the headquarters of the parent firm.

Table 1 ranks the states according to innovative activity and shows the distribution of innovations across large and small firms, along with the corresponding industry R & D expenditures and expenditures on research by universities. The two innovative inputs included in table 1 are taken from Jaffe (1989). The industry and university expenditures are based upon the average value measured (in constant 1972 million dollars) over the eight year period, 1972–1977, 1979, and 1981. We follow Jaffe (1989) by including the population of each state to control for size differentials

across the geographic unit of observation. We also include the geographic coincidence index to control for within state variation. The geographic coincidence index is explained and documented by Jaffe (1989, p. 959) and our footnote 3. While Jaffe rescaled the index "for estimation purposes" so that its log had a mean of zero, we see no advantage in doing so and leave the geographic coincidence index unscaled.

IV. Empirical Results

The dependent variable is the number of innovations (alternatively by all firms, by large firms, and by small firms) in a specific technological area and within a particular state. Since data are available for five technological areas over 29 states, the entire sample size is 145 observations.[6] There are no innovations registered for certain technological areas within particular states. Thus, equation (1) is estimated using the Tobit model. The results for the innovative output for all firms and

[6] For a detailed description of these technological areas as well as the manner by which they were selected, see Jaffe (1989, appendix A).

TABLE 2.—TOBIT REGRESSIONS OF INNOVATIVE ACTIVITY BY STATE
AND TECHNOLOGICAL AREA
(*t*-statistics listed in parentheses)

	(1) All firms	(2) Large firms	(3) Small Firms
Log Industry R & D	0.615	0.950	0.550
	(5.457)[b]	(7.133)[b]	(4.184)[b]
Log University Research	0.550	0.446	0.661
	(5.635)[b]	(4.569)[b]	(5.848)[b]
Log Geographic Coincidence	0.089	0.033	0.111
× University Research	(1.802)[a]	(0.687)	(1.965)[b]
Log Population	−0.246	−0.554	−0.314
	(−3.653)[b]	(−6.558)[b]	(−3.914)[b]
Log-Likelihood	−233.21	−202.19	−225.86
Sample Size	145	145	145

[a] Statistically significant at the 90% level of confidence for a two-tailed test.
[b] Statistically significant at the 95% level of confidence for a two-tailed test.

separately for large and small firms are shown in table 2.[7]

The first equation estimates the innovative activity of all firms, the second equation estimates the innovative activity of large firms, and the third equation estimates the innovative activity of small firms. Regardless of firm size, the knowledge production function for innovative output holds. Additional inputs in knowledge generating R & D, both by private corporations and by universities, lead to increases in innovative output.

However, the relative importance of industry R & D and university research as inputs in generating innovative output clearly varies between large and small firms. That is, for large firms, not only is the elasticity of innovative activity with respect to industry R & D expenditures more than two times greater than the elasticity with respect to expenditures on research by universities, but it is nearly twice as large as the elasticity of small-firm innovative activity with respect to industry R & D. By contrast, for small firms the elasticity of innovative output with respect to expenditures on research by universities is about one-fifth greater than the elasticity with respect to industry R & D. And the elasticity of innovative activity with respect to university research is about fifty percent greater for small enterprises than for large corporations.[8]

These results support the hypothesis that private corporation R & D plays a relatively more important role in generating innovative activity in large corpora-

tions than in small firms.[9] By contrast, spillovers from the research activities of universities play a more decisive role in the innovative activity of small firms.[10]

Geographic proximity between university and corporate laboratories within a state clearly serves as a catalyst to innovative activity for firms of all sizes. However, the impact is apparently greater on small firms than on large firms. The elasticity of innovative activity with respect to the geographic coincidence index multiplied by university research is nearly four times greater for small firms than for their larger counterparts.

A particular concern with the estimates in table 2 is multicollinearity between the log of industrial R & D expenditures and the log of university research expenditures. The simple correlation coefficient between the two variables is 0.61. When the log of industry R & D is omitted from the regressions, the coefficient of the log of university research rises somewhat to 0.592 (*t*-ratio of 8.733) in estimating large-firm innovative activity and to 0.828 (*t*-ratio of 8.036) in estimating small-firm innovative activity. Similarly, when the log of university research is omitted from the regressions, the coefficient of the log of industry R & D rises to 1.289 (*t*-ratio of 9.541) in estimating large-firm innovative activity and to 0.790 (*t*-ratio of 10.465) in estimating small-firm innovative activity. Thus, even when only one source of knowledge generating R & D is included in the regression equation, the results hold. The innovative activity of small enterprises responds more to university research, while the innovative activity of large corporations responds more to industry R & D.

---

[7] The logarithmic transformation of the left-hand side of equation (1) uses a linear transformation of $((I_{si} + 1) * 10)$. The Tobit censoring boundary is set to correspond to a zero observation.

[8] There may be greater measurement error for the small firm equation because large firms generate most of the state R & D expenditures. The size of any resulting bias is difficult to predict.

[9] There is a statistically discernible difference in the coefficients of industry R & D for small and large firms at the 95% level of confidence using a two-tailed test.

[10] There is a statistically discernible difference in the coefficients of university research expenditures for small and large firms at the 95% level of confidence using a two-tailed test.

V. Conclusions

The findings in this paper provide some insight into the puzzle posed by the recent wave of studies identifying vigorous innovative activity emanating from small firms in certain industries. How are these small, and frequently new, firms able to generate innovative output while undertaking generally negligible amounts of investment into knowledge generating inputs, such as R & D? At least one answer, implied by the findings in this paper, is that small firms innovate through exploiting knowledge created by expenditures on research in universities and on R & D in large corporations.

The empirical results suggest that the innovative output of all firms rises along with an increase in the amount of R & D inputs, both in private corporations as well as in university laboratories. However, R & D expenditures made by private companies play a particularly important role in providing inputs to the innovative activity of large firms, while expenditures on research made by universities serve as an especially key input for generating innovative activity in small enterprises. Apparently large firms are more adept at exploiting knowledge created in their own laboratories, while their smaller counterparts have a comparative advantage at exploiting spillovers from university laboratories.

REFERENCES

Acs, Zoltan J., and David B. Audretsch, *Innovation and Small Firms* (Cambridge, MA: MIT Press, 1990).
_____, "Innovation in Large and Small Firms: An Empirical Analysis," *American Economic Review* 78 (Sept. 1988), 678–690.
_____, "Innovation Market Structure and Firm Size," this REVIEW 69 (Nov. 1987), 567–575.

Acs, Zoltan J., David B. Audretsch, and Maryann P. Feldman, "Real Effects of Academic Research: Comment," *American Economic Review* 82 (Mar. 1992).
Dorfman, Nancy S., "Route 128: The Development of a Regional High Technology Economy," *Research Policy* 12 (Dec. 1983), 299–316.
Griliches, Zvi, "Patent Statistics as Economic Indicators: A Survey," *Journal of Economic Literature* 28 (Dec. 1990), 1661–1707.
_____, "Issues in Assessing the Contribution of R & D to Productivity Growth," *Bell Journal of Economics* 10 (Spring 1979), 92–116.
Jaffe, Adam B., "Real Effects of Academic Research," *American Economic Review* 79 (Dec. 1989), 957–970.
_____, "Technological Opportunity and Spillovers of R & D: Evidence from Firms' Patents, Profits and Market Value," *American Economic Review* 76 (Dec. 1986), 984–1001.
Kleinknecht, Alfred, "Firm Size and Innovation: Observations in Dutch Manufacturing Industry," *Small Business Economics* 1 (4) (1989), 215–222.
_____, "Measuring R & D in Small Firms: How Much Are We Missing?" *Journal of Industrial Economics* 36 (Dec. 1987), 253–256.
Link, Albert N., and John Rees, "Firm Size, University Based Research, and the Returns to R & D," *Small Business Economics* 2 (1), (1990), 25–32.
Mansfield, Edwin, "Comment on Using Linked Patent and R & D Data to Measure Interindustry Technology Flows," in Zvi Griliches (ed.), *R & D, Patents, and Productivity* (Chicago, IL: University of Chicago Press, 1984), 462–464.
Pavitt, Keith, M. Robson, and J. Townsend, "The Size Distribution of Innovating Firms in the U.K.: 1945–1983," *The Journal of Industrial Economics* 55 (Mar. 1987), 291–316.
Scherer, F. M., "Changing Perspectives on the Firm Size Problem," in Z. J. Acs and D. B. Audretsch (eds.), *Innovation and Technological Change: An International Comparison* (Ann Arbor: University of Michigan Press, 1991), 24–38.
_____, "The Propensity to Patent," *International Journal of Industrial Organization* 1 (Mar. 1983), 107–128.

7

Available online at www.sciencedirect.com

SCIENCE @ DIRECT·

Research Policy 34 (2005) 1113–1122

research
policy

www.elsevier.com/locate/econbase

University spillovers and new firm location[☆]

David B. Audretsch [a,*], Erik E. Lehmann [b], Susanne Warning [c]

[a] *Indiana University and CEPR, Entrepreneurship, Growth and Public Policy, Max Planck Institute Jena,*
Kahlaische Strasse 10, D-07745 Jena, Germany
[b] *University of Augsburg, Universitaetstrasse 16, 86159 Augsburg, Germany*
[c] *IAAEG, University of Trier, Behringstrasse, 54296 Trier, Germany*

Available online 29 June 2005

Abstract

This paper examines the impact of locational choice as a firm strategy to access knowledge spillovers from universities. Based on a large dataset of publicly listed, high-technology startup firms in Germany, we test the proposition that proximity to the university is shaped by different spillover mechanisms—research and human capital—and by different types of knowledge spillovers—natural sciences and social sciences. The results suggest that spillover mechanisms as well as spillover types are heterogeneous. In particular, the evidence suggests that new knowledge and technological-based firms have a high propensity to locate close to universities, presumably in order to access knowledge spillovers. However, the exact role that geographic proximity plays is shaped by the two factors examined in this paper—the particular knowledge context, and the specific type of spillover mechanism.
© 2005 Elsevier B.V. All rights reserved.

JEL classification: M13; L20; R30

Keywords: University spillovers; New firm location; Spillover mechanisms

1. Introduction

The assets that really count are those accountants cannot count.

(T.A. Stewart 1995, in Fortune 137 (7), p. 157)

In proposing a new theory of economic geography, Krugman (1991) asks, "What is the most striking feature of the geography of economic activity? The short answer is surely concentration [...] production [...] which is remarkably concentrated in space." As for other fields of economics, the impact of geography has not escaped the attention of scholars of entrepreneurship. Recent studies have focused on the locational decision of new-firm startups (Sorenson and Audia, 2000; Baum and Sorenson, 2003). Indeed, an important finding of this literature is that the impact of geographic characteristics on locational choice is

---

[☆] Large parts of the paper were written while the second two authors were at the University of Konstanz.
[*] Corresponding author.
E-mail addresses: audretsch@mpiew-jena.mpg.de
(D.B. Audretsch), Erik.Lehmann@wiwi.uni-augsburg.de
(E.E. Lehmann), warning@iaaeg.de (S. Warning).

anything but neutral. For example, the collection of European-country studies included in the special issue of *Regional Studies*, on "Regional Variations in New Firm Formation" (Reynolds et al., 1994), identified a number of geographic-specific characteristics that impact the location of new firms. These characteristics were generally based on factors identified in earlier studies by Carlton (1983) and Bartik (1985).

However, none of these studies focused on the role of accessing knowledge spillovers in the locational choice decision of new firms. This oversight is surprising, given that the growing literature on technology management and the economics of innovation has found that knowledge spillovers play an important role in fostering entrepreneurship and innovative activity (Sorenson and Audia, 2000; Baum and Sorenson, 2003). In addition, spillovers from universities, as well as from private firms, have been identified as key sources promoting firm innovation and performance (Stuart and Sorenson, 2003; Hall et al., 2003).

The purpose of this paper is to address these significant gaps in the literature that relates locational choice as a strategic decision by firms to knowledge externalities in general and spillovers from universities in special. We do this by linking the locational choice of firms, in terms of proximity to a university, to both the type of knowledge produced at universities, as well as the actual spillover mechanism transmitting that knowledge. In particular, the importance of locational proximity to a university is analyzed in terms of two distinct types of knowledge and two distinct spillover mechanisms in order to identify whether the role of geographic proximity to a knowledge source is heterogeneous with respect to the type of knowledge as well as the actual spillover mechanism. Thus, we assume that location is a strategic choice of an entrepreneur and that the locational decision is influenced by both research activities and the provision of human capital of universities.

In Section 2, we explain why proximity to a university should yield benefits to knowledge-based startups. In Section 3, the different types of knowledge outputs and different mechanisms used by firms to access knowledge spillovers from universities are discussed. Not only are the types of knowledge and spillover mechanisms heterogeneous, but also the capacity to generate knowledge spillovers varies considerably across universities. Thus, in Section 4, a new database

consisting of 281 publicly listed firms in German high-technology and knowledge industries is used to identify empirically in Section 5 how locational choice varies for different types of knowledge and spillover mechanisms. In Section 6, a summary and conclusion are provided. In particular, the evidence suggests that, in general, new knowledge and technological-based firms have a high propensity to locate close to universities, presumably in order to access knowledge spillovers. However, the exact role that geographic proximity plays is shaped by the two factors examined in this paper—the particular knowledge context, and the specific type of spillover mechanism.

2. Proximity to universities as a locational strategy

There are two streams of literature linking locational choice as a strategic decision to access and absorb knowledge spillovers. The first strand of the literature focuses on the existence and geographic distribution of university spillovers. The second set of studies deals with the impact of location on the entrepreneurial choice to start and sustain a new firm. While the first strand of literature establishes that knowledge not only has spillovers from universities but is also spatially bounded, an implication for the model of entrepreneurial choice is that the prospects for a new firm are greater in locations conducive to accessing and absorbing those knowledge spillovers. Thus, the major premise of the location argument is that new firms would like to reduce their knowledge acquisition costs by locating close to the knowledge source, the university. However, those benefits must bear the higher costs of locational proximity to a university (see also Link and Scott, in press).

The prevalent theoretical framework analyzing the decision to start a firm has been the general model of entrepreneurial choice. The model of entrepreneurial choice dates back at least to Knight (1921), but was more recently extended and updated by Khilstrom and Laffont (1979), Holmes and Schmitz (1990), Jovanovic (1994), Lazear (2002), Alvarez and Barney (2004) among others. None of the above models or studies consider the role of location in the context of the entrepreneurial choice framework. However, geographic location should influence the entrepreneurial decision by altering the expected return from entrepreneurial activity.

The theory of localized knowledge spillovers suggests that profits will be greater in agglomerations and spatial clusters, since access to tacit knowledge is easier. Because firms access external knowledge at a cost that is lower than the cost of producing this value internally or of acquiring it externally from a geographic distance (Harhoff, 2000), they will exhibit higher expected profits. The cost of transferring such knowledge is a function of geographic distance and gives rise to localized externalities (Siegel et al., 2003). Thus, the empirical analysis of university spillovers assumes that the geographical dimension is a significant factor explaining the innovative activities of firms.

University spillovers could be defined by externalities towards firms, for which the university is the source of the spillover but is not fully compensated (Harris, 2001). Some models assume that geography plays no role in the cost of accessing that knowledge (Spence, 1984; Cohen and Levinthal, 1990). However, theories of localization suggest that just because universities are the sources of knowledge, spillovers do not mean that knowledge transmits costlessly across geographic space. In particular, these theories argue that geographic proximity reduces the cost of accessing and absorbing knowledge spillovers. Thus, a basic tenet in the literature is that university spillovers lower the costs of firms accessing and absorbing knowledge spillovers. If an entrepreneur decides to locate nearby a university, the benefits must outweigh the costs. Locating close to universities, mostly in city center, is associated with high costs of living, housing, and others. Thus, firms also have to pay higher wages to their employees. If the basic resources gathered from a university are not essential to bear those costs, it is more advantageous to locate outside such a metropolitan area.

There are both theoretical reasons and empirical evidence to believe that such knowledge spillovers generated by universities are not accessed and absorbed at costs that are invariant to geographic location (Bottazzi and Peri, 2003). Rather, because university spillovers tend to be spatially bounded, the costs of absorbing spillovers increases with distance from a university. An implication of the geographic distribution of knowledge spillovers is not only that

they are spatially clustered around universities, but also that the entrepreneurial opportunities to start a new firm are also geographically linked to the spatial distribution of knowledge spillovers. The limited geographic reach of such channels for the exchange of information and know-how is one of the leading causes of the impact of geographical proximity. Or, with the words of Marshall (1890) more than a century ago, "the mysteries of the industry are in the air". Thus, a key hypothesis of this paper is that the value of locating within close geographic proximity to a university will depend upon the university output. In particular, the locational strategy of firm geographic proximity to a university should be greater when the knowledge output of the university is high.

3. Spillover mechanisms—research and human capital

There are at least two principle mechanisms facilitating the knowledge spillovers from universities to firms. The first one involves scientific research published in scholarly journals. Such published research is codified knowledge. This is because knowledge provided by articles can be transferred and transmitted with low cost, or with costs which are independent from the location. Academic papers can be downloaded from the Internet, obtained from publishers or found in libraries. This suggests that an important testable hypothesis is that the amount of scientific articles published by a university has no effect on firm location, since accessing (codified) knowledge is more or less invariant to locational distance from the university producing that knowledge.

However, an important qualification is that not all university knowledge is the same. In fact, the knowledge output of a university is heterogeneous. One useful distinction differentiates natural and social science knowledge. Social science knowledge is not based on a unified and established scientific methodology, but it rather is idiosyncratic to very specific disciplines, sub-disciplines and even research approaches. Compared to the natural sciences, research in the social sciences is considerably less codified. Thus, geographic proximity to high output universities may be more important for accessing social science research than for accessing natural science research.

The second type of spillover mechanism involves human capital embodied in students graduating from the university. As Saxenian (1994) points out, one of the important mechanisms facilitating knowledge spillovers involves the mobility of human capital, embodied in graduating students, as they move from the university to a firm. Spatial proximity to universities can therefore generate positive externalities that can be accessed by the firm through the spillover mechanism of human capital. As Varga (2000) shows, university graduates may be one of the most important channels for disseminating knowledge from academia to the local high-technology industry. In addition, other related externalities may result from close geographic proximity. For example, local proximity lowers the search costs for both firms and students. This may lead to some competitive advantage over similar firms, which are not located close to universities, especially when high skilled labor is a scarce resource and there is intense competition about high potentials.[1]

Central to the theories of localized knowledge spillovers is the distinction between codified and tacit knowledge (Kogut and Zander, 1992). Tacit knowledge needs oral communication and reciprocity, which may be ineffective or infeasible over longer distances. Such elements of know-how and operations cannot be codified easily in a blueprint or a contractual document (Mowery and Ziedonis, 2001). Thus, technology transfer or exchange is associated with personal contacts. Such spillovers could be transmitted through certain conduits across geographic space such as the channels of communication, the social system, or a kind of technology diffusion process. Most of those benefits could not be obtained by markets or ensured by contractual arrangements. If personnel contacts are the main source for absorbing, the number of students of a university should have a positive impact on firm location. Thus, the relative importance of tacit knowledge is reflected by the number of students of a university, which serves as a measure for the intense demand for labor and interpersonal communication. Otherwise, the access to students also captures factors like network effects, social contacts and other sources of tacit knowledge. Furthermore, students in Germany are quite immobile (Fabel et al., 2002). This

suggests that the higher the human capital output of a university, the lower the distance between a university and the firm. Apart from the spillover mechanism, there might be at least two other groups of variables influencing the distance between a university and a new knowledge-based firm: location variables and firm characteristics.

Previous studies have shown that firm location decisions are influenced by such factors as the size of a city or region. It is possible that firms locate close to the areas where universities are located for network reasons. A drawback of most studies on the impact of university spillover on firm location is to explain their finding of a negative sign of spillover sources. One possible interpretation is that such knowledge sources—patents, citations, and articles—are not essential to locate close towards a university. However, there is no rational argument for this "push away" effect as expressed by the negative sign. Since our basic assumption is that locating close towards a university is associated with high costs, we also include a measure for these costs. Now, the negative sign could be interpreted in the way that the trade-off between the costs and benefits of locating close to the universities is more influenced by the costs, i.e. the costs of the close location exceed the benefits of spillover effects.

As pointed out by Audretsch and Thurik (2001) among others, the impact of such spillovers may be more important for young firms than for established firms. This is because new firms may rely on external knowledge produced by either other firms or universities (see also Link and Scott, in press; Hall et al., 2003). It has been observed (Scherer, 1991) that small and new firms do not devote a large share of resources to formal R&D. In contrast, larger and more established enterprises are able to generate their own formal R&D, and therefore are less dependent upon external knowledge. This implies that geographic proximity to universities is a source of competitive advantage for young firms, when the competitive advantage is based on intangible assets, such as ideas and the human capital of the employees. This suggests that locational strategy of firm geographic proximity is more important for young firms. Finally, previous research has shown that spillover effects differ between industries in their necessity and capability to absorb spillover effects (Jaffe, 1989; Cohen and Levinthal, 1990; Henderson and Cockburn, 1994).

---

[1] See also Stephan et al. (in press), analyzing the firm's placement of Ph.D. students.

D.B. Audretsch et al. / Research Policy 34 (2005) 1113–1122   1117

4. Data and methodology

4.1. The data

The link between proximity and university spillovers is tested by using a unique dataset of all of knowledge and high-technology German firms that were publicly listed on the *Neuer Markt*, Germany's equivalent of the *NASDAQ*. Between 1997 and 2002, the total number of firms listed in this index was 341. We excluded all firms located outside Germany as well as holding companies. Though, the underlying dataset consists of 281 publicly listed German firms, collected from IPO prospectuses, and publicly available information from on-line data sources including the *Deutsche Boerse AG*. First, this database includes firms from highly innovative industries, like biotechnology, medical devices, life sciences, e-commerce and other high-technology industries, which represent the knowledge-based economy. Secondly, there is strong evidence from the U.S. for a growth effect of clusters influenced by active research universities (Feldman, 2000) and thus we follow this line of research. Finally, this dataset represents the technological change in the German business sector from the predominance of medium sized firms in the production and manufacturing towards the high-technology and service sector.

The university-related data are collected from different sources. Information about the number of students is provided by the Federal Statistical Office. Publication data are hand-collected from the research database ISI (Information Sciences Institutes, see also Warning, 2004).

As we examine the impact of university output on locational proximity to the university, the distance of a new knowledge-based firm to the closest university is applied as endogenous variable (*distance*). This measure is sensible enough to ensure capturing also small differences in firm–university distances that is especially necessary in Germany as universities are much more geographically concentrated compared to the United States. The online database of the *German Automobile Club* (www.adac.de) is used to determine the distance between the firm and the closest university. Firms located within a radius of 1.5 km are classified as belonging in the distance category of 1 km.

Table 1 shows the descriptive statistics for the endogenous variable *distance* as well as for the exogenous variables. The median distance of a firm and a university is 7 km while the mean is more than double as high with 16.75 km. Thus, the variable distance is highly skewed, as shown in graph 1. The 92% percentile shows of the endogenous variable is 50 km and means that the 92% of the shortest distances from a firm to a university are 50 km or even shorter. This quantile is chosen for several reasons. First, we assume that within this circle, the firm is located in the metropolitan area of the university town. Second, we assume that this distance is the maximum distance for employees to travel each day to the respective firm. However, all the universities, which are taken as the nearest university of those firms, are universities located in big cities.

The independent variables are categorized into three main groups. The first group contains spillover mechanism variables for research and human capital. The second group consists of location variables, which contain university location variables as well as

Table 1
Descriptive statistics

	Mean	S.D.	Min	Max	Median
Distance	16.75	23.93	1	177	7
No. of publications in natural sciences	5139.43	4603.16	0	14,176	4069
No. of publications in social sciences	253.86	220.01	0	659	204
No. of students in natural sciences	7304.89	3988.45	0	20,570	7725
No. of students in social sciences	20,321	15,409.63	0	47,112	15,741
Inhabitants of the city of the university	916,796	830,554	76,000	3,410,000	615,000
Hotel price in the university town in Euro	180.81	68.44	55	319	179
No. of universities in the city	1.84	0.960	1	3	1
Inhabitants of firm location	640,442	897,371	1850	3,387,000	190,000
Firm age	10.400	10.025	<1	90	8

firm location variables. And finally, the third group considers firm-specific variables.

To capture the first spillover mechanism research, we include the number of articles published in high quality journals (see Zucker et al., 1998; Audretsch and Stephan, 1996). Since university spillovers are neither restricted to patent inventions[2] nor solely in the natural sciences, we include separate measures for social science research output and natural science output. This enables us also to discriminate between the types of spillover effects. Since knowledge-based industries include services such as media and entertainment, service, or e-commerce, spillovers can also be generated by fields without high patent activities. Research in the social sciences is captured by the number of articles published in journals listed in the Social Science Citation Index (SSCI). The number of publications in the Science Citation Index (SCI) indicates the research activity of universities in the natural sciences. We include the number of listed papers of both indices for each university published from 1997 until 2000.[3]

Table 1 clearly shows that the universities differ in their research activities, both in natural sciences and social sciences. Of course, the number of articles in natural sciences cannot be compared to those in social sciences, as articles in natural science are typically shorter and written by a larger number of co-authors. However, the median university published in this time period 204 articles in the social sciences and 4069 in the natural sciences. In both fields, the mean value exceeds the median value, which suggests that some universities are more research intensive than others.

The second spillover mechanism, "human capital", is captured by the number of students enrolled at each university. Consistent with our approach to the research mechanism, we consider students from the natural sciences and from the social sciences separately to control for the different types of spillover. We calculated the number of students in natural sciences and social sciences by adding the number of students from different disciplines. The natural sciences students' variable contains the study fields biology,

chemistry, physics, mathematics, computing, agriculture, forestry, dietetics, engineering, and medicine. The social science variable consists of students from the fields of languages, cultural studies, law, economics, social science, and arts. For two reasons, all student data are taken from the year 1997. First, those data are not always available for every year and university. Second, the *Neuer Markt* started in 1997 and thus, we take this year as the base year. As shown in Table 1, the number of new graduates in the social sciences is twice as much as those in natural sciences.

The second group of exogenous variables consists of location variables for the university as well as for the firm. The number of inhabitants form the location of the university is taken from the official statistics based on 1997 as proxy for the size of the city where the university is located. In the lack of adequate data for the costs of living at the university location, we include the average price of a basic single room from the most expensive hotel in the city where the university is located. These prices differ significantly across cities with the most expensive in Frankfurt, which is also the most expensive city in Germany as measured by the OECD. The number of universities in the town captures a cluster effect but also a competition effect between the universities. The variables of firm location include the number of inhabitants where the firms is located and a dummy variable that indicates location of the firm in the former western part of Germany.

In the third group of exogenous variables, we control for specific industry effects by including dummy variables for the following industries: software, e-services, e-commerce, computer and hardware, telecommunication, biotechnology, medicine and life science, media and entertainment, and high-technology. Finally, the age of the firm is considered.

4.2. Analysis and methodology

We use OLS regressions to estimate the impact of the spillover mechanisms on the endogenous variable distance, as measured in kilometers first. A closer examination of Fig. 1 shows that the endogenous variable "kilometer" is highly skewed. Thus, we not only use the natural log of the distance variable but also quantile regressions. This semi-parametric technique provides a general class of models in which the conditional quantiles have a linear form. In its

---

[2] For an analysis of university patenting, see Henderson et al. (1998) and Jaffe et al. (1993). For university patenting, see Jensen and Thursby (2001) and Jensen et al. (2003).

[3] The publications in social science and natural science did not vary across the universities during time (see Warning, 2004).

D.B. Audretsch et al. / Research Policy 34 (2005) 1113–1122   1119

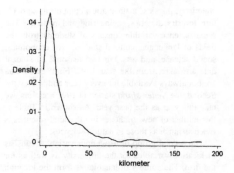

Fig. 1. Kernel density estimation of kilometer (Epanechnikow).

simplest form, the least absolute deviation estimator fits medians to a linear function of covariates. The method of quantile regression is potentially attractive for the same reason that the median or other quantiles are a better measure of location than the mean. Other useful features are the robustness against outliers and that the likelihood estimators are in general more efficient than least square estimators. Besides the technical features, quantile regressions allow that potentially different solutions at distinct quantiles may be interpreted as differences in the response of the dependent variable, namely the distance, to changes in the regressors at various points in the conditional distinction of the dependent variable. Thus, quantile regressions reveal asymmetries in the data, which could not be detected by simple OLS estimations (see Buchinsky, 1998). While the median regression focuses on the median firm, the regression on the 92% percentile focuses on the firms 50 km away from the university.

5. Empirical results: startup proximity to a university

In order to identify the impact of university output on the importance of locational proximity to the university, Table 2 shows the mean, median and the 92%-quantile regression results. Using these different estimations enables us to examine the impact of startups with greater distance from the university (compared to the median and mean).

The first column shows the results from the OLS regression with the natural logarithm of kilometers as the endogenous variable. In this approach, none of the spillover mechanisms enters the regression significantly. Next, we include the absolute number of kilometers. Now, the number of students in the natural science enters the regression significantly. The larger the number of students in the natural sciences, the closer a firm is to a university.

However, the mean distance between a firm and the closest university is about 16 km, while the median distance is only 7 km. To consider this skewed distribution, we apply quantile regressions. The results are shown in column three and four. The third column shows the results from the median regression. As the positive and statistically significant coefficient of the number of publications in the natural sciences suggests, new firms do not have a high propensity to locate within close proximity to universities with a high research output in the natural sciences. In fact, as the research output increases, the distance of the new startup from the university also tends to increase. Thus, there is no statistical evidence suggesting that new firms locate close to research universities in order to access the spillover of knowledge using the research mechanism for the knowledge type represented by the natural sciences.

However, as the negative and statistically significant coefficient of the number of publications in the social sciences indicates, the importance of locating within close geographic proximity to a university may not be invariant to the type of knowledge. This result suggests that knowledge transmitted through published research in the social sciences may, in fact, be less codified and more tacit, leading new firms to locate closer to the university in order to access the knowledge spillover.

The results in the third column of Table 2 also suggest that the magnitude of university output in the form of human capital also affects locational decisions. As the negative and statistically significant coefficient of the number of students in the natural sciences indicates, new firms tend to locate more closely to universities with a large output of students. However, this result does not hold in the social sciences. This may indicate that human capital in the natural sciences is more specific and less general than in the social sciences. The results also indicate that the other location-specific characteristics also impact the locational choice of new firms. The size of the city in which the university is

Table 2
Regressions on the mean, median and the 92%-quantile

Variables	OLS (semi-log)	OLS	Median	0.92-quantile
Spillover mechanism research				
Natural science research	−0.00009 (1.05)	−0.001 (0.10)	0.0012 (3.22)***	−0.0016 (0.26)
Social science research	0.00093 (0.42)	0.0144 (0.39)	−0.0303 (3.80)***	0.1116 (0.69)
Spillover mechanism human capital				
Natural science human capital	−0.00003 (1.46)	−0.0006 (1.95)**	−0.0005 (4.93)***	−0.0002 (0.10)
Social science human capital	0.00001 (0.91)	−0.0007 (0.36)	0.0001 (2.31)**	−0.0011 (0.88)
Location variables				
City size (for university)	0.0080 (0.85)	0.0246 (0.94)	0.0153 (11.01)***	0.0323 (1.45)
Cost of living (for university)	0.0121 (0.64)	−0.0129 (0.47)	−0.00258 (3.58)***	−0.0895 (0.56)
Number of universities in town	0.5340 (3.74)***	1.5741 (0.65)	−2.0271 (2.16)**	−13.822 (0.82)
West location	0.5826 (1.40)	−11.882 (1.87)*	3.8011 (2.31)***	−12.180 (0.91)
City size (for firm)	−0.0080 (5.98)***	−0.0122 (4.34)***	−0.0013 (15.71)***	−0.0365 (2.58)***
Firm characteristics				
Firm age	0.0151 (2.06)**	0.0744 (0.49)	0.0507 (1.37)	−0.3421 (0.64)
Software	−0.0029 (0.03)	0.4810 (0.73)	0.4966 (1.26)	−0.3421 (0.11)
Service	−0.2311 (0.82)	1.2914 (0.28)	−1.1929 (1.16)	9.7641 (0.45)
E-commerce	0.0425 (0.11)	4.5571 (0.51)	1.8528 (1.16)	35.874 (1.12)
Hardware	−0.0984 (0.29)	8.4662 (0.86)	−1.1422 (0.80)	22.321 (0.85)
Telecom	−0.0066 (0.21)	−4.7332 (1.22)	0.7564 (0.50)	−4.315 (0.25)
Biotechnology	0.5687 (1.28)	−7.8921 (1.25)	−5.0633 (3.13)***	−4.4202 (0.12)
Medical devices	−0.9444 (1.56)	−13.445 (1.87)*	−1.0453 (0.55)	2.8956 (0.15)
Media	−0.8593 (3.33)***	−8.293 (2.67)**	−4.0047 (3.24)***	−5.9651 (0.25)
Constant	2.0104 (3.99)***	32.3856 (3.93)***	11.9244 (6.05)***	96.441 (3.33)
R-squared	0.1235	0.1479	0.1603	0.2848

The endogenous variable is the distance from the new firm to the closest university. *t*-values are in parenthesis. The baseline is firms in the technology sector. The asterisks, *, **, and *** indicate significance at the 10%, 5%, and 1% level, respectively. The number of observations is 281. The variables for city size (for university) and city size (for firm) are multiplied with 1000.

located, the cost of living in which the university is located, and the city size where the firm is located are all found to influence the locational decision of new firms. Since we focus only on academic research, as expressed by the number of articles published in academic journals and the number of students, we restrict our analysis extremely on those two aspects. However, there are several aspects which also influence the strategic choice of founders which are captured by variables like the size of a city or the cost of living.

As column three in Table 2 shows, the results are considerably different when the 92.5%-quantile estimation is used. Neither the spillover mechanisms nor the knowledge types have a statistically significant impact on the location of new firms. This would suggest that the knowledge spillovers are geographically bounded within a small distance from the university. The same holds for the mean regression in column two, where the mean distance is about 16 km. Thus,

we prefer the median regression to capture the effect that half of the firms are located within a small circle about 7 km around a university.

6. Conclusions

Recent studies suggest that regional characteristics have a critical impact on the locational decisions made by new firms. Our findings are consistent with this view, but we also identify an additional locational factor: the presence of a university. New firms in high-technology industries are influenced not only by the traditional regional characteristics, but also by the opportunity to access knowledge generated by universities.

An important finding of this paper, however, is the impact of university output on new firm location is sensitive to both the type of knowledge and mechanism used to access that knowledge. Thus, the role of geographic proximity to access university knowledge is not simple and straightforward, but rather depends on the knowledge type and spillover mechanism.

The emergence of knowledge as a basic resource of competitiveness, along with the propensity for knowledge to remain localized, means that locations have new policy opportunities. Entrepreneurs flourish under supportive public policy regimes. By providing high skilled and well-educated students, cities help entrepreneurs find the necessary human capital, which will, subsequently, help develop new ideas and faster growth. Increasing university spending leads to better educated and trained students, as well as improving research activities and enhancing spillovers. Finally, regional and local initiatives can lower the costs of locating close to universities for entrepreneurs. However, the impact of entrepreneurship policy on entrepreneurship is affected by factors which are not considered in this paper.

Future research may be expected to focus less on uncovering the existence of knowledge spillovers and more on identifying the heterogeneity inherent in both types of knowledge generated by universities, as well as the various mechanisms that firms use to access knowledge spillovers.

Acknowledgments

Financial support by the German Research Foundation (DFG) through the research group #FOR454 "Heterogeneous Labor" at the University of Konstanz and the ZEW, Mannheim, is gratefully acknowledged. We would also like to thank Paula Stephan, Al Link, Don Siegel, Frank T. Rothaermel, Adam Lederer, Dieter Sadowski, the participants of the Technology Transfer Society (T2S) Meeting 2004, and two anonymous referees for their helpful comments. The usual disclaimer applies.

References

Alvarez, S.A., Barney, J.B., 2004. Organizing rent generation and appropriation: toward a theory of the entrepreneurial firm. Journal of Business Venturing 19, 621–635.

Audretsch, D.B., Stephan, P.E., 1996. Company-scientist locational links: the case of biotechnology. American Economic Review 86, 641–652.

Audretsch, D.B., Thurik, R., 2001. What's new about the new economy? Sources of growth in the managed and entrepreneurial economies. Industrial and Corporate Change 10, 267–315.

Bartik, T.J., 1985. Business location decisions in the United States: estimates of the effects of unionization, taxes, and other characteristics of states. Journal of Business and Economic Statistics 3, 14–22.

Baum, J.A.C., Sorenson, O., 2003. Advances in Strategic Management: Geography and Strategy, vol. 20. JAI Press, Greenwich, CT.

Bottazzi, L., Peri, G., 2003. Innovation and spillovers in regions: evidence from European patent data. European Economic Review 47, 687–710.

Buchinsky, M., 1998. Recent advantages in quantile regression models. Journal of Human Resources 33, 88–126.

Carlton, D.W., 1983. The location and employment choices of new firms: an econometric model with discrete and continuous endogenous variables. Review of Economics and Statistics 54, 440–449.

Cohen, W.M., Levinthal, D.A., 1990. Absorptive capacity: a new perspective on learning and innovation. Administrative Science Quarterly 35, 128–152.

Fabel, O., Lehmann, E.E., Warning, S., 2002. Der relative Vorteil deutscher wirtschaftswissenschaftlicher Fachbereiche im Wettbewerb um studentischen Zuspruch. Zeitschrift für betriebswirtschaftliche Forschung 54, 509–526 (with an English summary).

Feldman, M.P., 2000. Location and innovation: the new economic geography of innovation. In: Clark, G., Feldman, M.P., Gertler, M. (Eds.), Oxford Handbook of Economic Geography. Oxford University Press, Oxford.

Hall, B.A., Link, N., Scott, J.T., 2003. Universities as research partners. Review of Economics and Statistics 85, 485–491.

Harhoff, D., 2000. R&D spillovers, technological proximity, and productivity growth—evidence from German panel data. Schmalenbach Business Review 52, 238–260.

Harris, R.G., 2001. The knowledge-based economy: intellectual origins and new economic perspectives. International Journal of Management Review 3, 21–41.

Henderson, R., Jaffe, A., Trajtenberg, M., 1998. Universities as a source of commercial technology: a detailed analysis of university patenting 1965–1988. Review of Economics and Statistics 65, 119–127.

Henderson, R., Cockburn, I., 1994. Measuring competence? Exploring firm effects in pharmaceutical research. Strategic Management Journal 15 (Special Issue), 63–84.

Holmes, T.J., Schmitz, J.A., 1990. A theory of entrepreneurship and its application to the study of business transfer. Journal of Political Economy 98, 265–294.

Jaffe, A.B., 1989. Real effects of academic research. American Economic Review 79, 957–970.

Jaffe, A.B., Trajtenberg, M., Henderson, R., 1993. Geographic localization of knowledge spillovers as evidenced by patent citations. Quarterly Journal of Economics 63, 577–598.

Jensen, R.A., Thursby, M., 2001. Proofs and prototypes for sale: the licensing of university inventions. American Economic Review 91, 240–259.

Jensen, R.A., Thursby, J.G., Thursby, M.C., 2003. Disclosure and licensing of university inventions: 'The Best We Can Do with the S**t We Get to Work With'. International Journal of Industrial Organization 21, 1271–1300.

Jovanovic, B., 1994. Entrepreneurial choice when people differ in their management and labor skills. Small Business Economics 6 (3), 185–192.

Khilstrom, R., Laffont, J.-J., 1979. A general equilibrium entrepreneurial theory of firm formation based on risk aversion. Journal of Political Economy 87, 719–748.

Krugman, P., 1991. Geography and Trade. Leuven University, MIT Press.

Knight, F., 1921. Risk, Uncertainty and Profit. Augustus Kelly, New York.

Kogut, B., Zander, U., 1992. Knowledge of the firm, combinative capabilities, and the replication of technology. Organizational Science 3, 383–397.

Lazear, E.P., 2002. Entrepreneurship. NBER Working Paper No. 9109.

Link, A.N., Scott, J.T., in press. U.S. science parks: the diffusion of an innovation and its effects on the academic mission of universities. Journal of Productivity Analysis.

Marshall, A., 1890. Principles of Economics. MacMillan, London.

Mowery, D.C., Ziedonis, A.A., 2001. The geographic reach of market and non-market channels of technology transfer: comparing citations and licenses of university patents. NBER Working Paper No. 8568.

Reynolds, P.D., Storey, D.J., Westhead, P., 1994. Regional variations in new firm formation—special issue. Regional Studies 28, 343–456.

Saxenian, A., 1994. Regional Advantage: Culture and Competition in Silicon Valley and Rte., vol. 128. Harvard University Press, Cambridge, MA.

Scherer, F.M., 1991. Changing perspectives on the firm size problem. In: Acs, Z.J., Audretsch, D.B. (Eds.), Innovation and Technological Change: An International Comparison. University of Michigan Press, Ann Arbor, pp. 24–38.

Siegel, D.S., Westhead, P., Wright, M., 2003. Assessing the impact of science parks on the research productivity of firms: exploratory evidence from the United Kingdom. International Journal of Industrial Organization 21, 1217–1225.

Sorenson, O., Audia, G., 2000. The social structure of entrepreneurial activity: geographic concentration of footwear production in the U.S. 1940–1989. American Journal of Sociology 106, 324–362.

Spence, M.A., 1984. Cost reduction, competition, and industry performance. Econometrica 52, 101–121.

Stephan, P.E., Sumell, A.J., Black, G.C., Adams, J.D., in press. Public knowledge, private placements: new Ph.D.s as a source of knowledge spillovers. Economic Development Quarterly.

Stuart, T.E., Sorenson, O., 2003. The geography of opportunity: spatial heterogeneity in founding rates and the performance of biotechnology firms. Research Policy 25, 1139–1157.

Varga, A., 2000. Local academic knowledge transfers and the concentration of economic activity. Journal of Regional Science 40, 289–309.

Warning, S., 2004. Performance differences in German higher education. Empirical analysis of strategic groups. Review of Industrial Organization 24, 393–408.

Zucker, L.G., Darby, M.R., Armstrong, J., 1998. Intellectual human capital and the birth of U.S. biotechnology enterprises. American Economic Review 88, 290–306.

8

J Evol Econ (1999) 9: 97–107

—Journal of—
**Evolutionary
Economics**
© Springer-Verlag 1999

Knowledge spillovers in biotechnology: sources and incentives

David B. Audretsch[1], Paula E. Stephan[2]

[1] Indiana University, Institute for Development Strategies, SPEA, Bloomington, IN 47405-2100, USA (e-mail: daudrets@indiana.edu)
[2] School of Policy Studies, Georgia State University, Atlanta, 6A 30303, USA

The late twentieth century has witnessed a scientific gold rush of astonishing proportions; the headlong and furious haste to commercialize genetic engineering. This enterprise has proceeded so rapidly – with so little outside commentary – that its dimensions and implications are hardly understood at all.
Michael Crichtron. Introduction to **Jurassic Park**

Abstract. This paper sheds light on the questions, *Why does knowledge spill over?* and *How does knowledge spill over?* The answer to these questions we suggest lies in the incentives confronting scientists to appropriate the expected value of their knowledge considered in the context of their path-dependent career trajectories. In particular, we focus on the ability of scientists to appropriate the value of knowledge embedded in their human capital along with the incentive structure influencing if and how scientists choose to commercialize their knowledge. We conclude that the spillover of knowledge from the source creating it, such as a university, research institute, or industrial corporation, to a new-firm startup facilitates the appropriation of knowledge for the individual scientist(s) but not necessarily for the organization creating that new knowledge in the first place.

Key words: Biotechnology – Knowledge spillovers – Science – Entrepreneurship – Startups

JEL-classification: LO; O1; O3

1 Introduction

A recent wave of empirical studies has confirmed the validity of the knowledge production function, which links knowledge inputs to innovative output. However, the exact unit of observation at which the knowledge production function exists is less certain, due to the presence of knowledge spillovers, which obscure the links between knowledge sources and innovative output. The answers to where knowledge comes from, and how and

---

Correspondence to: D.B. Audretsch

why it spills over are thus often elusive. This has moved Paul Krugman (1991a, p. 53) to argue that economists should abandon any attempts at measuring knowledge spillovers because "...knowledge flows are invisible, they leave no paper trail by which they may be marked and tracked."

While Krugman's (1991a) observation is undeniably true, the creation of a new firm, especially in a high-technology, science-based industry, such as biotechnology, produces an event that leaves traces for studying the knowledge production function. One of the most striking features of firms making Initial Public Offerings (IPOs) in biotechnology is that they are typically able to raise millions of dollars in the absence of having a viable product at the time when they go public. Indeed, new firms are founded and receive financing on the prospects of transforming technological knowledge created at another source into economic knowledge at a new firm through the development and introduction of an innovative product.

The purpose of this paper is to shed some light on the questions, *Why does knowledge spill over?* and *How does knowledge spill over?* We suggest that the answer to these questions lies in the incentives confronting scientists to appropriate the expected value of their knowledge considered in the context of their path-dependent career trajectories. In the metaphor provided by Albert O. Hirschman (1970), if voice proves to be ineffective within incumbent organizations, and loyalty is sufficiently weak, scientists will resort to exit from a corporation or university to form a new biotechnology company.

The plan of this paper is as follows. Section 2 focuses on the production of new economic knowledge and problems encountered in estimating the knowledge production function due to the presence of spillovers. The ability of scientists to appropriate the value of knowledge embedded in their human capital is also examined as well as the incentive structure influencing if and how scientists choose to commercialize their knowledge. Section 3 describes the data base. The links between knowledge sources and flows are examined in Section 4, and the incentives confronting scientists are examined in Section 5. A conclusion and summary are presented in Section 6.

2 New economic knowledge

2.1 Production

The starting point for most theories of innovation is the firm.[1] In such theories the firm is assumed to be exogenous and its performance in generating technological change is endogenous.[2] For example, in the most prevalent model found in the literature of technological change, the *knowledge production function*, formalized by Zvi Griliches (1979), the firm exists exogenously and then engages in the pursuit of new knowledge as an input into the process of generating innovative activity. As Cohen and Klepper (1992a,b) conclude, the most important source of new knowledge

---

[1] For reviews of this literature see Baldwin and Scott (1987).

[2] For examples see Scherer (1992), Cohen and Klepper (1992a,b) and Arrow (1962).

is generally considered to be R&D. Certainly a large body of empirical work has found a strong and positive relationship between knowledge inputs, such as R&D, and innovative outputs.

The knowledge production function has been found to hold most strongly at broader levels of aggregation. For example, the most innovative countries are those with the greatest investments in R&D. Little innovative output is associated with less developed countries, which are characterized by a paucity of production of new knowledge. Similarly, the most innovative industries also tend to be characterized by considerable investments in R&D and new knowledge. Not only are industries such as computers, pharmaceuticals and instruments high in R&D inputs that generate new economic knowledge, but also in terms of measured innovative outputs (Audretsch, 1995). By contrast, industries with little R&D, such as wood products, textiles and paper, also tend to produce only a negligible amount of innovative output. Thus, the model of the knowledge production function linking knowledge generating inputs to outputs certainly holds at aggregated levels of economic activity.

The relationship becomes less compelling, however, at the disaggregated microeconomic level of enterprise, establishment, or even line of business. For example, with Acs and Audretsch (1990) found that the simple correlation between R&D inputs and innovative output was 0.84 for four-digit standard industrial classification (SIC) manufacturing industries in the United States, it was only about half, 0.40, among the largest U.S. corporations.

The model of the knowledge production function becomes even less compelling in view of the recent wave of studies revealing that small enterprises serve as the engine of innovative activity in certain industries. These results are startling, because as Scherer (1992) observes, the bulk of industrial R&D is undertaken in the largest corporations; small enterprises account for only a minor share of R&D inputs. Thus, the model of the knowledge production function seemingly implies that, as the *Schumpeterian Hypothesis* predicts, innovative activity favors those organizations with access to knowledge-producing inputs – the large incumbent organization. The more recent evidence identifying the sources of innovative activity raises the question, *Where do new and small firms get the innovation producing inputs, that is the knowledge?*

One answer, proposed by Audretsch (1995), is that although the model of the knowledge production function may certainly be valid, the implicitly assumed unit of observation – at the level of the establishment or firm – may be less valid. The reason why the model of the knowledge production function holds more closely for more aggregated degrees of observation may be that investment in R&D and other sources of new knowledge spills over for economic exploitation by third-party firms.

This view is supported by theoretical models which have focused on the role that spillovers of economic knowledge across firms play in generating increasing returns and ultimately economic growth (Romer, 1986; Krugman; 1991a,b; Grossman and Helpman, 1991). These theories have been supported by the emergence of a wave of recent studies that have identified the existence of knowledge spillovers (Jaffe, 1989; Jaffe et al.,

1993; Audretsch and Feldman, 1996; Feldman, 1994a,b). Stephan (1996) identifies three distinct lines of inquiry which establish that such a relationship is present.

What happens within the black box of the knowledge production function, however, is vague and ambiguous at best. The exact links between knowledge sources and the resulting innovative output remain invisible and unknown. In many instances external knowledge is absorbed and used by existing firms. In other cases, however, the development of new knowledge provides an incentive for the establishment of new firms. Sometimes these firms are established by individuals who have played a central role in the creation of the new knowledge; in other instances the firms are established by individuals who grasp the opportunity that the new knowledge may provide. Thus, the establishment of a new firm in a knowledge-based industry provides an opportunity for examining properties of the knowledge production function. At the same time it should be recognized that this reveals only a particular aspect of knowledge flows occurring within the framework of the knowledge production function.

2.2. Appropriability and incentives

A large literature has emerged focusing on what has become known as the appropriability problem.[3] The underlying issue revolves around how firms which invest in the creation of new knowledge can best appropriate the economic returns from that knowledge (Arrow, 1962). Audretsch (1995) proposes shifting the unit of observation away from exogenously assumed firms to individuals – agents with endowments of new economic knowledge. As J. de V. Graaf observed nearly four decades ago, "When we try to construct a transformation function for society as a whole from those facing the individual firms comprising it, a fundamental difficulty confronts us. There is, from a welfare point of view, nothing special about the firms actually existing in an economy at a given moment of time. The firm is in no sense a 'natural unit'. Only the individual members of the economy can lay claim to that distinction. All are potential entrepreneurs. It seems, therefore, that the natural thing to do is to build up from the transformation function of men, rather than the firms, constituting an economy. If we are interested in eventual empirical determination, this is extremely inconvenient. But it has conceptual advantages. The ultimate repositories of technological knowledge in any society are the men comprising it, and it is just this knowledge which is effectively summarized in the form of a transformation function. In itself a firm possesses no knowledge. That which is available to it belongs to the men associated with it. Its production function is really built up in exactly the same way, and from the same basic ingredients, as society's."

When the lens is shifted away from the firm to the individual as the relevant unit of observation, the appropriability issue remains, but the question becomes, *How can economic agents with a given endowment of new*

---

[3] See Baldwin and Scott (1987).

knowledge best appropriate the returns from that knowledge? Different work contexts have different incentive structures. The academic sector encourages and rewards the production of new scientific knowledge. Thus the goal of the scientist in the university context is to establish priority. This is done most efficiently through publication in scientific journals (Stephan, 1996). By contrast, in the industrial sector, scientists are rewarded for the production of new economic knowledge but not necessarily new scientific knowledge *per se*. In fact, scientists working in industry are often discouraged from sharing knowledge externally with the scientific community through publication. As a result of these differential incentive structures, industrial and academic scientists develop distinct career trajectories.[4]

The appropriability question confronting academic scientists can be considered in the context of the human capital model. Life-cycle models of scientists suggest that early in their careers scientists invest heavily in human capital in order to build a reputation (Levin and Stephan, 1991). In later stages of their career, scientists trade or *cash in* this reputation for economic return. Thus, early in their careers, scientists invest in the creation of knowledge in order to establish a reputation that signals the value of that knowledge to the scientific community. With maturity, scientists seek ways to appropriate the economic value of the new knowledge. But how should a scientist best appropriate the value of her/his human capital? Alternatives abound, such as working full-time or part time with an incumbent firm, licensing the knowledge to an incumbent firm, or starting or joining a new firm.

Scientists working in the private sector are arguably more fully compensated for the economic value of their knowledge. This will not be the case for academic scientists unless they *cash out*, in terms of Dasgupta and David (1994) by selling their knowledge to a private firm. This suggests that academic scientists seek affiliation with a commercial venture in a life-cycle context. By contrast, industrial scientists consider leaving the incumbent firm when a disparity arises between the firm and the individual concerning the expected value of their knowledge. In the former situation, age is a good predictor of when the scientist establishes ties with industry. In the latter case, factors other than age are expected to play a more important role in determining when the scientist leaves the incumbent firm.

Once a scientist has decided to commercialize his knowledge, why should (s)he choose to do this by starting a new firm? In fact, in a model of perfect information with no agency costs, any positive economies of scale or scope will ensure that the appropriability problems of the firm and individual converge. If a scientist has an idea for doing something differently than is currently being practiced by the incumbent enterprises, that idea can be sold to an incumbent enterprise. Because of the assumption of perfect knowledge, both the firm and the scientist would agree upon the expected

---

[4] One must not overstate the effect that institutional affiliation has on the willingness and ability of scientists to share information. Some firms make the results of their research public. Some academics engage in practices that lead to the privatization of knowledge (Stephan, 1996).

value of the innovation.[5] The incumbent firm and the inventor of the idea would be expected to reach a bargain splitting the value added to the firm contributed by the (potential) innovation. The payment to the scientist, either in terms of a higher wage or some other means of remuneration, would be bounded between the expected value of the innovation if it is implemented by the incumbent enterprise on the upper end, and by the return that the agent could expect to earn if (s)he used it to launch a new enterprise on the lower end.[6]

3 Measurement

This paper uses a new database drawn from the prospectuses of 60 firms that made an initial public offering (IPO) in biotechnology during the period March 1990 to November 1992 to study the sources and incentives for commercializing new knowledge (Audretsch and Stephan, 1996). Prospectuses for the offerings were carefully read in order to identify the scientific founders of the new firms. In cases where it proved difficult to identify founders from the prospectuses, telephone calls were made to the firm. In addition, firm histories were checked and confirmed in *BioScan*. Founders having a Ph.D. or an M.D. were coded as scientific founders for the purposes of this research. In addition, several individuals who did not have a doctorate but were engaged in research were included as scientific founders. All told, we were able to identify 101 scientific founders for 52 firms making an initial public offering during this period.

Biographical information was also collected from the prospectuses and was supplemented by entries from standard references works such as *American Men and Women of Science*. Four types of job experience were identified – academic experience (which includes positions at hospitals, research foundations and the government); experience with pharmaceutical companies; training experiences (as a student, post-doc, or resident), and "other" experience. This information was used to distinguish among five distinct career trajectories followed prior to the founding of the company:

1. The *academic trajectory* describes scientists who had spent all of their time since completing their training employed in the academic research sector;

---

[5] In his 1911 treatise, Schumpeter argued that the gap between those firms creating knowledge and those appropriating it triggered a process of creative destruction. However, by 1942, Schumpeter had modified his theory, arguing instead that, "Innovation itself is being reduced to a routine. Technological progress is increasingly becoming the business of teams of trained specialists who turn out what is required to make it work in predictable ways" (p. 132).

[6] As Frank Knight (1921, p. 273) observed more than seventy years ago. "The laborer asks what he thinks the entrepreneur will be able to pay, and in any case will not accept less than he can get from some other entrepreneur, or by turning entrepreneur himself. In the same way the entrepreneur offers to any laborer what he thinks he must in order to secure his services, and in any case not more than he thinks the laborer will actually be worth to him, keeping in mind what he can get by turning laborer himself."

2. The *pharmaceutical trajectory* describes those scientists whose careers subsequent to receiving training had been entirely spent working in the drug industry;
3. The *mixed trajectory* describes scientists who had worked in both the pharmaceutical industry and the academic research sector;
4. The *student trajectory* describes individuals who went directly from a training position to founding a biotechnology firm; and
5. The "other trajectory", which includes scientists who have been employed by non-pharmaceutical firms.

Additional biographical information coded was ascertained concerning date of birth and educational background. Citation counts to first-authored published scientific articles were measured using the 1991 *Science Citation Index* produced by ISI and are used here as an indicator of scientific reputation.

4 Knowledge sources and flows

Summary data, presented in Table 1, show that fifty percent of the scientific founders' careers followed an academic trajectory; slightly more than 25 percent a pharmaceutical trajectory. Half of this latter group had established their careers exclusively with large pharmaceutical companies such as SmithKline and Beckman; half had come from smaller pharmaceutical firms, some of which, like Amgen, were first generation biotech firm. Table 1 also indicates that approximately an eighth of the founders had a mixed career in the sense that prior to founding the firm they had held positions in both a pharmaceutical company as well as a university or non-profit research organization. A handful of founders moved directly from a training position such as a residency or post-doctorate appointment to the startup firm, thereby short-circuiting the traditional trajectories from pharmaceutical firms and/or academe. The career trajectory of the

Table 1. The age and citation record of founders

	Birth date				Citations		
	N	M	SD	N_{known}	M	SD	N_{known}
All scientific founders	101	1943.18	10.20	96	92.13	171.05	99
All academic founders	50	1940.55	10.06	49	149.32	226.51	49
Part time	35	1938.79	10.29	34	172.71	259.03	35
Full time	15	1945.06	8.54	15	72.21	78.70	15
All drug founders	28	1945.61	9.20	28	29.71	46.28	28
Small	14	1945.93	9.84	14	30.30	57.40	14
Big	12	1947.00	7.67	12	34.00	34.41	14
Mixed career	13	1943.80	8.76	13	62.69	57.56	13
Student career	6	1957.00	3.54	5	58.17	83.72	6
All full time	57	1945.64	9.61	57	46.59	60.69	57
All part time	40	1939.42	10.03	37	159.30	245.52	37

remaining scientists was either indeterminate or followed another type of path.

The employment status of the founders with the biotechnology company was also determined. We find that 59 of the 101 scientific founders were working full time with the new firm at the time of the public offering; 41 were working part time, and almost all (35) of these had followed an academic trajectory. This means that 70 percent of the academic founders maintain full-time employment with their academic institutions, serving as consultants or members of the Scientific Advisory Boards to the startup firms. Only 15 of the academic founders had moved to full-time employment with the firm by the time the IPO was made. By contrast, all 28 scientists whose careers had been exclusively in the pharmaceutical sector held full-time positions with the firm at the time of the IPO; 9 of the 13 whose careers followed a mixed trajectory were full time.

5 Incentives

The evidence from Table 1 supports the hypothesis that the incentive structure varies considerably between the pharmaceutical founders and the academic founders. Those founders coming from universities and non-profit research organizations have the option of eating their cake and having it too, by maintaining formal contacts with their previous employer, often in a full-time position. Even those from the academic sector who are full time with the new firm are often able to maintain some connection with the non-profit sector as adjunct or clinical faculty. By contrast, those who have a career path in pharmaceuticals take full-time positions with the company, at least by the time that the company goes public.

There are other differences between those coming from an academic trajectory and those coming from a pharmaceutical trajectory. The most notable is the difference in age at the time the public offering was made. On average, those coming from academe were born approximately five years earlier than those coming from the pharmaceutical sector, a difference which is statistically significant at the 95 percent level of confidence. As would be expected, we also find that those following the academic trajectory have significantly more citations than those coming from a pharmaceutical trajectory. Of perhaps even greater interest are the differences between the part-time academics and the full-time academics. Academic founders who remain full-time with their institution, working but part-time for the new firm, were, for example, born more than six years earlier than academic founders who leave their institution to go full time with the firm. The part-timers are not only older; they are also more eminent, have significantly more cations than academics who go full time with the firm. This suggests that eminence gives these scientists the luxury of hedging their bets; both the firm and their research institution welcome a chance to claim them as affiliates. And, although we did not measure the incidence, such individuals often serve as directors and members of Scientific Advisory Boards of *additional* start-up firms. The full-timers, by contrast, have developed sufficient human capital to be recognized as experts but lack the luster to hold "dual" citizenship. In terms of both citation counts and date of birth they are remarkably similar to their fellow founders who followed a pharmaceutical trajectory.

The above discussion suggests that the incentive structure depends crucially upon the career trajectory that the scientists has followed as well as upon whether the scientist has established sufficient eminence to be able to sustain multiple roles. Scientists working in incumbent pharmaceutical firms face the well known problem, described in the appropriability literature, of deciding whether to remain with the firm or start a new firm. Furthermore, the goal of industry to capture their economic knowledge seldom permits them to establish reputations based solely on publication. Instead, their scientific reputations are often established in terms of the products they helped to develop and are known primarily to "insiders" in the industry. Scientists in academe, however, face a different incentive structure. They live in a world where publications are essential for the establishment of reputation. Early in their careers they invest heavily in human capital in order to build a reputation. In the later stages of their career, scientists may trade or cash in on this reputation for economic returns. A variety of avenues are available to do this, including the establishment of a new firm.

The data suggest that this *cashing out* pattern is determined in part by eminence. As noted, a number of academic founders have established sufficiently strong reputations to eat their cake and have it too. They maintain their full-time jobs in academe, while seeking part-time opportunities to gain economically from their knowledge and scientific reputation. The economic returns are tied to the shares they own in the startup companies. A subset of academic scientists, however, go full time with the firm. They, too, hold stock in the firm. But, their rewards are more immediate in terms of the salaries paid to executives in the companies.[7] And, while they have established solid reputations, they are considerably less cited than those academic founders who maintain full-time positions in academe. Although this may be a result of age (they are, after all, about five years younger), it is more likely a characteristic that age cannot alter. Science, as numerous researchers have established, is noteworthy for persistent inequality which age merely amplifies.[8]

Conclusions

This paper has attempted to penetrate the black box of the knowledge production function. In addressing the questions how and why knowledge spills over, an assumption implicit to the model of the knowledge production function is challenged – that firms exist *exogenously* and then

---

[7] Note that our data do not permit us to compare the *full-timers* and *part-timers* to university-based scientists who *do not* found firms. One would expect that this group is younger, and less eminent than either of the other groups.

[8] Scientific productivity is not only characterized by extreme inequality at a point in time (Lotka, 1926); it is also characterized by increasing inequality over the career of a cohort of scientists (Weiss and Lillard, 1982; Stephan, 1996).

endogenously seek out and apply knowledge inputs to generate innovative output. Although this may be valid some, if not most of the time, the evidence from the biotechnology suggests that, at least in some cases, it is the knowledge in the possession of economic agents that is *exogenous*. In an effort to appropriate the returns from that knowledge, the scientist *endogenously* creates a new firm. Thus, the spillover of knowledge from the source creating it, such as a university, research institute, or industrial corporation, to a new-firm startup facilitates the appropriation of knowledge for the individual scientist(s) but not necessarily for the organization creating that new knowledge in the first place.

This paper also has shed some light on questions which has plagued economists for decades, *Where do new industries, like biotechnology, come from*? The answer appears to have something to do with new knowledge created with perhaps one purpose in mind, but is, in fact, valuable in a very different context. We observe that the participants in the biotechnology industry come from a broad range of diverse backgrounds. Because no biotechnology industry has traditionally existed, no set career paths have been established. Rather, the participants in an emerging industry choose to leave what otherwise would be established career trajectories in more traditional industries. Through the flow of scientists into this new industry, knowledge which was generated with a more traditional context in mind becomes applied in the process of creating a new industry.

References

Acs ZJ, Audretsch DB (1990) Innovation and small firms. MIT Press, Cambridge

Arrow K (1962) Economic welfare and the allocation of resources for invention. In: Nelson R (ed) The rate and direction of inventive activity. Princeton University Press, Princeton, NJ, pp 609–626

Audretsch DB (1995) Innovation and industry evolution. MIT Press, Cambridge

Audretsch DB, Feldman MP (1996) R&D spillovers and the geography of innovation and production. American Economic Review 86(3): 630–640

Audretsch DB, Stephan PE (1996) Company-scientist locational links: the case of biotechnology. American Economic Review 86(3): 641–652

Baldwin WL, Scott JT (1987) Market structure and technological change. Harwood Academic Publishers, New York

Cohen WM, Klepper S (1992a) The tradeoff between firm size and diversity in the pursuit of technological progress. Small Business Economics 4(1): 1–14

Cohen WM, Klepper S (1992b) The anatomy of industry R&D intensity distributions. American Economic Review 82(4): 773–799

Dasgupta P, David PA (1994) Toward a new economics of science. Research Policy 23(5): 487–521

Feldman MP (1994a) The geography of innovation. Kluwer, Boston

Feldman MP (1994b) Knowledge complementarity and innovation. Small Business Economics 6(5): 363–372

Graf J, de V (1957) Theoretical welfare economics. Cambridge University Press, Cambridge

Griliches Z (1979) Issues in assessing the contribution of R&D to productivity growth. Bell Journal of Economics 10(10): 92–116

Grossman G, Helpman E (1991) Innovation and growth in the global economy. MIT Press, Cambridge

Hirschman AO (1970) Exit, voice, and loyalty. Harvard University Press, Cambridge
Jaffe AB (1989) Real effects of academic research. American Economic Review 79(5): 957–970
Jaffe AB, Trajtenberg M, Henderson R (1993) Geographic localization of knowledge spillovers as evidenced by patent citations. Quarterly Journal of Economics 63(3): 577–598
Knight FH (1921) Risk, uncertainty and profit. Houghton Mifflin, New York
Krugman PA (1991a) Geography and trade. MIT Press, Cambridge
Krugman PA (1991b) Increasing returns and economic geography. Journal of Political Economy 99(3): 483–499
Levin SG, Stephan PE (1991) Research productivity over the life cycle: evidence for academic scientists. American Economic Review 81(4): 114–132
Lotka AJ (1926) The frequency distribution of scientific productivity. Journal Washington Academy Science 16(12): 317–323
Romer P (1986) Increasing returns and long-run economic growth. Journal of Political Economy 94(5): 1002–1037
Scherer FM (1992) Schumpeter and plausible capitalism. Journal of Economic Literature 30(3): 1416–1433
Schumpeter JA (1911) Theorie der wirtschaftlichen Entwicklung: Eine Untersuchung über Unternehmergewinn, Kapital, Kredit, Zins und den Konjunkturzyklus. Duncker und Humblot, Berlin
Schumpeter JA (1942) Capitalism, socialism and democracy. Harper and Row, New York
Stephan PE (1996) The economics of science. Journal of Economic Literature 34(3): 1199–1235
Stephan PE, Levin SG (1992) Striking the mother lode in science. Oxford University Press, New York
Weiss Y, Lillard LA (1982) Output variability, academic labour contracts, and waiting times for promotion. In: Ehrenberg RG (ed) Research in labor economics, vol 5, pp 157–188

[9]

THE KNOWLEDGE SPILLOVER THEORY OF ENTREPRENEURSHIP AND ECONOMIC GROWTH

David B. Audretsch

INTRODUCTION

Why should entrepreneurship matter for economic growth, employment creation and international competitiveness? The entrepreneurship literature has traditionally suggested that entrepreneurship matters to individuals and firms, but rarely for economic growth.

This chapter presents the knowledge spillover theory of entrepreneurship, which suggests that entrepreneurship is the missing link in the process of economic growth because it facilitates the spillover of knowledge from universities and private firms, resulting in commercialization of ideas that otherwise might remain uncommercialized.

The knowledge spillover theory of entrepreneurship inverts the traditional approach to entrepreneurship. Traditional theories of entrepreneurship have held the context within which the individual finds oneself and probed why certain individuals will make the decision to start a new firm. This typically leads to a focus on variations in characteristics, attributes and inclinations across individuals.

By contrast, the knowledge spillover theory of entrepreneurship instead assumes the individual characteristics to be constant and then analyzes how

The Emergence of Entrepreneurial Economics
Research on Technological Innovation, Management and Policy, Volume 9, 37–54
ISSN: 0737-1071/doi:10.1016/S0737-1071(05)09003-7

37

the cognitive process inducing the entrepreneurial decision is influenced by placing that same individual in different contexts. In particular, high knowledge contexts are compared with impoverished knowledge contexts. A strikingly different view of entrepreneurship emerges. Instead of being a phenomenon that is exogenously determined by preconditioned personal attributes and family history, entrepreneurship instead becomes seen as an endogenous response to opportunities generated by investments in new knowledge made by incumbent firms and organizations, combined with their inability to completely exhaust the ensuing opportunities to commercialize that knowledge. Thus, the knowledge spillover theory of entrepreneurship shows how entrepreneurship can be an endogenous response to investments in new knowledge where commercialization of that knowledge is constrained by the existence of a formidable knowledge filter.

The next section explains how entrepreneurship combines the cognitive process of recognizing opportunities with pursuing those opportunities by starting a new firm. The third section introduces the knowledge spillover theory of entrepreneurship, which suggests that entrepreneurship is an endogenous response to investments in knowledge that are not fully appropriated by incumbent firms. The fourth section links endogenous entrepreneurship based on knowledge spillovers to economic growth. Finally, the summary and conclusions are provided in the last section. In particular, we suggest that entrepreneurship education and the transfer of technology from universities for commercialization make a key contribution to the societal values of economic growth, employment creation and competitiveness in globally linked markets by reducing the knowledge filter and facilitating the missing link to economic growth – entrepreneurship.

ENTREPRENEURIAL OPPORTUNITY: EXOGENOUS VERSUS ENDOGENOUS

Entrepreneurship involves the recognition of opportunities and the commercialization of those opportunities (Venkataraman, 1997). This has resulted in a focus on the cognitive process by which individuals reach the decision to start a new firm. As Krueger (2003, p. 105) explains, "The heart of entrepreneurship is an orientation toward seeing opportunities". Thus, the literature on entrepreneurship has been concerned with, "What is the nature of entrepreneurial thinking and What cognitive phenomena are associated with seeing and acting on opportunities?" (Krueger, 2003, p. 105).

According to Sarasvathy, Dew, Velamuri, and Venkataraman (2003, p. 142), "An entrepreneurial opportunity consists of a set of ideas, beliefs and actions that enable the creation of future goods and services in the absence of current markets for them".

The methodological approach in the literature on entrepreneurship has been to hold the context constant and then to analyze how the cognitive process inherent in the entrepreneurial decision varies across different individual characteristics and attributes (Shaver, 2003; McClelland, 1961). As Shane and Eckhardt (2003, p. 187) summarize the entrepreneurship literature, the focus is on "the process of opportunity discovery and why some actors are more likely to discover a given opportunity than others".

Some of these differences involve the willingness to incur risk, others involve the preference for autonomy and self-direction, while still others involve differential access to scarce and expensive resources, such as financial capital, human capital, social capital and experiential capital. This approach, focusing on individual cognition in the entrepreneurial process, has generated a number of important and valuable insights, such as the contribution made by social networks, education and training, and familial influence. The literature certainly leaves the impression that entrepreneurship is a personal matter largely determined by DNA, familial status and access to crucial resources.

While entrepreneurship theory revolves around opportunities, in fact such entrepreneurial opportunities are taken as being exogenous to the individual. By contrast, a very different literature suggests that opportunities are endogenous. In the model of the knowledge production function, introduced by Griliches (1984), innovation is the result of purposeful firm-specific investments in knowledge inputs. The unit of analysis in this literature is the firm. Innovative opportunities are generated through investing resources in R&D and other types of knowledge, such as human capital.

Thus, the firm is exogenous while the opportunity is created endogenously. An important implication is that the opportunity recognition and exploitation take place within the same organizational unit creating those opportunities – the firm. Just as the firm serves as the organizational unit generating the opportunities, that same firm appropriates the returns to those purposeful knowledge investments through innovative activity.

The empirical evidence from systematic empirical testing of the model of the knowledge production function contradicted the assumption of singularity between the organization creating the opportunities and the organization exploiting the opportunities. In particular, the empirical evidence pointed to a much more vigorous contribution to small and new-firm innovative activity than would have been warranted from their rather limited investments in new knowledge, as measured by R&D and human capital (Audretsch, 1995).

THE KNOWLEDGE SPILLOVER THEORY OF ENTREPRENEURSHIP

The discrepancy in organizational context between the organization creating opportunities and those exploiting the opportunities that seemingly contradicted Griliches' model of the firm knowledge production function was resolved by Audretsch (1995), who introduced the Knowledge Spillover Theory of Entrepreneurship, "The findings challenge an assumption implicit to the knowledge production function – that firms exist exogenously and then endogenously seek out and apply knowledge inputs to generate innovative output. It is the knowledge in the possession of economic agents that is exogenous, and in an effort to appropriate the returns from that knowledge, the spillover of knowledge from its producing entity involves endogenously creating a new firm" (pp. 179–180).

The knowledge spillover theory of entrepreneurship suggests that knowledge spillovers serve as the source of knowledge creating the entrepreneurial opportunities for small and new firms. "How are these small and frequently new firms able to generate innovative output when undertaken a generally negligible amount of investment into knowledge-generating inputs, such as R&D? One answer is apparently through exploiting knowledge created by expenditures on research in universities and on R&D in large corporations" (p. 179).

The empirical evidence supporting the knowledge spillover theory of entrepreneurship was provided from analyzing variations in startup rates across different industries reflecting different underlying knowledge contexts. In particular, those industries with a greater investment in new knowledge also exhibited higher startup rates while those industries with less investment in new knowledge exhibited lower startup rates, which was interpreted as a conduit, transmitting knowledge spillovers (Audretsch, 1995; Caves, 1998).

Thus, compelling evidence was provided suggesting that entrepreneurship is an endogenous response to opportunities created but not exploited by the incumbent firms. This involved an organizational dimension involving the mechanism transmitting knowledge spillovers – the startup of a new firm.

In addition, Jaffe (1989), Audretsch and Feldman (1996) and Audretsch and Stephan (1996) provided evidence concerning the spatial dimension of knowledge spillovers. In particular, their findings suggested that knowledge spillovers are geographically bounded and localized within spatial proximity to the knowledge source. None of these studies, however, identified the actual mechanisms which actually transmit the knowledge spillover; rather, the spillovers were implicitly assumed to automatically exist (or fall like manna from heaven), but only within a geographically bounded spatial area.

As the second section emphasized, while much has been made about the key role played by the recognition of opportunities in the cognitive process underlying the decision to become an entrepreneur, relatively little has been written about the actual source of such entrepreneurial opportunities. The knowledge spillover theory of entrepreneurship identifies one source of entrepreneurial opportunities – new knowledge and ideas. In particular, the knowledge spillover theory of entrepreneurship posits that it is new knowledge and ideas created in one context, but left uncommercialized or not vigorously pursued by the source actually creating those ideas, such as a research laboratory in a large corporation or research undertaken by a university, that serves as the source of knowledge generating entrepreneurial opportunities. Thus, in this view, one mechanism for recognizing new opportunities and actually implementing them by starting a new firm involves the spillover of knowledge. The organization creating the opportunities is not the same organization that exploits the opportunities. If the exploitation of those opportunities by the entrepreneur does not involve full payment to the firm for producing those opportunities, such as a license or royalty, then the entrepreneurial act of starting a new firm serves as a mechanism for knowledge spillovers.

LINKING ENTREPRENEURSHIP TO GROWTH

In the Romer (1986) model of endogenous growth, new technological knowledge is assumed to automatically spillover. Investment in new technological knowledge is automatically accessed by third-party firms and economic agents, resulting in the automatic spillover of knowledge. The assumption that knowledge automatically spills over is, of course, consistent with the important insight by Arrow (1962) that knowledge differs from the traditional factors of production – physical capital and (unskilled) labor – in that it is non-excludable and non-exhaustive. When the firm or economic agent uses the knowledge, it is neither exhausted nor can it be, in the absence of legal protection, precluded from use by third-party firms or other economic agents. Thus, in the spirit of the Romer model, drawing on the earlier insights about knowledge from Arrow, a large and vigorous literature has emerged obsessed with the links between intellectual property protection and the incentives for firms to invest in the creation of new knowledge through R&D and investments in human capital.

However, the preoccupation with the non-excludability and non-exhaustibility of knowledge first identified by Arrow and later carried forward and assumed in the Romer model, neglects another key insight in the original Arrow (1962) article. Arrow also identified another dimension by which knowledge differs from the traditional factors of production. This other dimension involves the greater degree of uncertainty, higher extent of asymmetries and greater cost of transacting new ideas. The expected value of any new idea is highly uncertain, and as Arrow pointed out, has a much greater variance than would be associated with the deployment of traditional factors of production. After all, there is relative certainty about what a standard piece of capital equipment can do, or what an (unskilled) worker can contribute to a mass-production assembly line. By contrast, Arrow emphasized that when it comes to innovation, there is uncertainty about whether the new product can be produced, how it can be produced, and whether sufficient demand for that visualized new product might actually materialize.

In addition, new ideas are typically associated with considerable asymmetries. In order to evaluate a proposed new idea concerning a new biotechnology product, the decision-maker might not only need to have a Ph.D. in biotechnology, but also a specialization in the exact scientific area. Such divergences in education, background and experience can result in a divergence in the expected value of a new project or the variance in outcomes anticipated from pursuing that new idea, both of which can lead to divergences in the recognition and evaluation of opportunities across economic agents and decision-making hierarchies. Such divergences in the valuation of new ideas will become greater if the new idea is not consistent with the core competence and technological trajectory of the incumbent firm.

Thus, because of the conditions inherent in knowledge – high uncertainty, asymmetries and transactions cost – decision-making hierarchies can reach the decision not to pursue and try to commercialize new ideas that individual economic agents, or groups or teams of economic agents think are potentially valuable and should be pursued. The basic conditions characterizing new knowledge, combined with a broad spectrum of institutions, rules and regulations impose what could be termed as the knowledge filter. The knowledge filter is the gap between new knowledge and what Arrow (1962) referred to as economic knowledge or commercialized knowledge. The greater is the knowledge filter, the more pronounced is this gap between new knowledge and new economic, or commercialized, knowledge.

The knowledge filter is a consequence of the basic conditions inherent in new knowledge. Similarly, it is the knowledge filter that creates the opportunity for entrepreneurship in the knowledge spillover theory of entrepreneurship. According to this theory, opportunities for entrepreneurship are the duality of the knowledge filter. The higher is the knowledge filter, the greater are the divergences in the valuation of new ideas across economic agents and the decision-making hierarchies of incumbent firms. Entrepreneurial opportunities are generated not just by investments in new knowledge and ideas, but in the propensity for only a distinct subset of those opportunities to be fully pursued by incumbent firms.

Thus, the knowledge spillover theory of entrepreneurship shifts the fundamental decision-making unit of observation in the model of the knowledge production function away from exogenously assumed firms to individuals, such as scientists, engineers or other knowledge workers – agents with endowments of new economic knowledge. As Audretsch (1995) pointed out, when the lens is shifted away from the firm to the individual as the relevant unit of observation, the appropriability issue remains, but the question becomes: how can economic agents with a given endowment of new knowledge best appropriate the returns from that knowledge? If the scientist or engineer can pursue the new idea within the organizational structure of the firm developing the knowledge and appropriate roughly the expected value of that knowledge, one has no reason to leave the firm. On the other hand, if one places a greater value on his ideas than do the decision-making bureaucracy of the incumbent firm, one may choose to start a new firm to appropriate the value of his knowledge.

In the knowledge spillover theory of entrepreneurship the knowledge production function is actually reversed. The knowledge is exogenous and embodied in a worker. The firm is created endogenously in the worker's effort to appropriate the value of his knowledge through innovative activity. Typically, an employee from an established large corporation, often a scientist or engineer working in a research laboratory, will have an idea for an invention and ultimately for an innovation. Accompanying this potential innovation is an expected net return from the new product. The inventor would expect to be compensated for his/her potential innovation accordingly. If the company has a different, presumably lower, valuation of the potential innovation, it may decide either not to pursue its development, or that it merits a lower level of compensation than that expected by the employee.

As investments in new knowledge increase, entrepreneurial opportunities will also increase. Contexts where new knowledge plays an important role are associated with a greater degree of uncertainty and asymmetries across economic agents evaluating the potential value of new ideas. Thus, a context involving more new knowledge will also impose a greater divergence in the evaluation of that knowledge across economic agents, resulting in a greater variance in the outcome expected from commercializing those ideas. It is this gap in the valuation of new ideas across economic agents, or between economic agents and decision-making hierarchies of incumbent enterprises, that creates the entrepreneurial opportunity.

The knowledge spillover theory of entrepreneurship posits that, ceteris paribus, entrepreneurial activity will tend to be greater in contexts where investments in new knowledge are relatively high. In a high-knowledge context, new ideas will generate entrepreneurial opportunities by exploiting (potential) spillovers of that knowledge. By contrast, a paucity of new ideas in an impoverished knowledge context will generate only limited entrepreneurial opportunities. Thus, the knowledge spillover theory of entrepreneurship provides a clear link, or prediction that entrepreneurial activity will result from investments in new knowledge and that entrepreneurial activity will be spatially localized within close geographic proximity to the knowledge source.

In their 2005 book, Audretsch, Keilbach, and Lehmann derive a series of hypotheses emanating from the Knowledge Spillover Theory of Entrepreneurship. The first hypothesis is the Endogenous Entrepreneurship Hypothesis, which suggests that entrepreneurship will be greater in the presence of higher investments in new knowledge, ceteris paribus. Entrepreneurial activity is an endogenous response to higher investments in new knowledge, reflecting greater entrepreneurial opportunities generated by knowledge investments.

Systematic empirical evidence supporting the endogenous entrepreneurship hypothesis has been provided by Audretsch, Keilbach, and Lehmann (2005) and Acs et al. (2004). Both studies find that where investments in new knowledge are higher, the propensity for economic agents to start a new firms also tends to be higher. In particular, Audretsch et al. (2005) find that even after controlling for other sources of entrepreneurial opportunities access to entrepreneurial resources, those regions with a greater investment in new knowledge induce a greater degree of entrepreneurial start-ups, particularly in high-technology and other knowledge-based industries.

Jaffe (1989) and Audretsch and Feldman (1996) provided systematic empirical evidence that spatial proximity is a prerequisite to accessing such knowledge spillovers. However, they provided no insight about the actual mechanism transmitting such knowledge spillovers. As for the Romer, Lucas and Jones models, investment in new knowledge automatically generates knowledge spillovers. The only additional insight involves the spatial dimension – knowledge spills over but the spillovers are spatially bounded. Thus, the second hypothesis emerging from the knowledge spillover theory of entrepreneurship is the locational hypothesis, which posits that Empirical evidence of the locational hypothesis has been provided by Audretsch et al. (2005) and Audretsch and Lehmann (2005), who analyze a database consisting of technology and knowledge-based start-ups making an initial public offering (IPO). Their results suggest that those with a higher knowledge capacity and greater knowledge output also generate a higher number of knowledge and technology start-ups, suggesting that university spillovers are geographically bounded.

The knowledge spillover theory of entrepreneurship, which focuses on how new knowledge can influence the cognitive decision-making process inherent in the entrepreneurial decision links entrepreneurship and economic growth, is consistent with theories of industry evolution (Jovanovic, 1982; Ericson & Pakes, 1995; Audretsch, 1995; Hopenhayn, 1992; Klepper, 1996). A distinguishing feature of these evolutionary theories is the focus on change as a central phenomenon. Innovative activity, one of the central manifestations of change, is at the heart of much of this work. Entry, growth, survival and the way firms and entire industries change over time are linked to innovation. The dynamic performance of regions and even entire economies, that is the Standort, or location, is linked to the efficacy of transforming investments in new knowledge into innovative activity.

For example, Audretsch (1995) analyzes the factors that influence the rate of new firm start-ups. He finds that such start-ups are more likely in industries in which small firms account for a greater percentage of the industry's innovations. This suggests that firms are started to capitalize on distinctive knowledge about innovation that originates from sources outside of an industry's leaders. This initial condition of not just uncertainty, but greater degree of uncertainty vis-à-vis incumbent enterprises in the industry is captured in the theory of firm selection and industry evolution proposed by Jovanovic (1982). Jovanovic presents a model in which the new firms, which he terms entrepreneurs, face costs that are not only random but also differ across firms. A central feature of the model is that a new firm does not know what its cost function is, that is its relative efficiency, but rather discovers this through the process of learning from its actual post-entry performance. In particular, Jovanovic (1982) assumes that entrepreneurs are unsure about their ability to manage a new-firm startup and therefore their prospects for success. Although entrepreneurs may launch a new firm based on a vague sense of expected post-entry performance, they only discover their true ability – in terms of managerial competence and of having based the firm on an idea that is viable on the market – once their business is established. Those entrepreneurs who discover that their ability exceeds their expectations expand the scale of their business, whereas those discovering that their post-entry performance is less than commensurate with their expectations will contact the scale of output and possibly exit from the industry. Thus, Jovanovic's model is a theory of noisy selection, where efficient firms grow and survive and inefficient firms decline and fail. The links between entrepreneurship on the one hand and growth and survival on the other have been found across a number of social science disciplines, including economics, sociology and regional studies.

One of the important findings of Glaeser et al. (1992) and Feldman and Audretsch (1999) is that economic performance is promoted by knowledge spillovers. However, their findings, as well as the corroborative results from a plethora of studies, focused on a spatial unit of observation, such as cities, regions and states. For example, Glaeser et al. (1992) found compelling empirical evidence suggesting that a greater degree of knowledge spillover leads to higher growth rates of cities. If the existence of higher knowledge spillovers bestow higher growth rates for cities, this relationship should also hold for the unit of observation of the (knowledge) firm. The performance of entrepreneurial firms accessing knowledge spillovers should exhibit a superior performance. Thus, the Competitive Advantage Hypothesis states that the performance of knowledge-based start-ups should be superior when they are able to access knowledge spillovers through geographic proximity to knowledge sources, such as universities, when compared to their counterparts without a close geographic proximity to a knowledge source.

Evidence supporting the Competitive Advantage Hypothesis at the firm level has been provided by Audretsch et al. (2005), Audretsch and Lehmann (2005) and Gilbert et al. (2004), all of whom find that the competitive advantage of new-firm start-ups within close geographic proximity to knowledge sources, such as universities. In particular, Audretsch, Keilbach and Lehmann (2005) and Audretsch and Lehmann (2005) show the exact relationship between location and the competitive advantage of entrepreneurial start-ups is complex. Whether or not geographic proximity to a knowledge source, such as a university, bestows competitive benefits to an entrepreneurial firm depends on a number of factors. In particular, the impact of geographic proximity on competitive advantage is shaped by the amount and type of knowledge produced at a particular university. If the research output of a university is meager, close geographic proximity to a university will not bestow a superior competitive advantage. However, close geographic proximity to a university with a strong research output and spillover mechanisms enhances the competitive advantage of entrepreneurial start-ups. Similarly, Audretsch and Lehman (2005) and Audretsch et al. (2006) show that the benefits of geographic proximity in enhancing competitive advantage are not homogeneous but apparently vary across academic fields and disciplines.

However, the Competitive Advantage Hypothesis and supporting empirical evidence not be interpreted as attributing the entire impact of entrepreneurship on growth to be restricted to the growth of entrepreneurial firms themselves. Such an extreme assumption of no external impacts is implicit in the analyses of new and small enterprises found in the path-breaking Birch (1979) study, as well as the more recent Davis et al. (1996a, b) update. While there is severe methodological disagreement between the Davis and Birch approaches to measuring the impact of small firms on economic performance, both implicitly agree in an absence of external impact. Thus, in a type of statistical apartheid or segregation, in the Birch and Davis studies, the impact of small and new firms is measured only within that set of firms.

By contrast, the impact of entrepreneurship on economic growth is not constrained to be limited to manifest itself solely in those entrepreneurial firms, but rather has an external impact of far greater significance. The link between entrepreneurship and economic growth should also exist at the more aggregated level of economic activity. A location, or Standort endowed with a higher degree of what is Audretsch et al. (2005) and Audretsch and Keilbach (2004) term as Entrepreneurship Capital, will facilitate knowledge spillovers and the commercialization of knowledge, thereby generating greater economic growth. The Growth Hypothesis states, "Given a level of knowledge investment and severity of the knowledge filter, higher levels of economic growth should result from greater entrepreneurial activity, since entrepreneurship serves as a mechanism facilitating the spillover and commercialization of knowledge".

In introducing the model of the production function, Solow (1956) argued that economic growth is determined explicitly by the stocks of capital and labor. Technical change entered the production function exogenously as a shift factor. More recently, Romer (1986), Lucas (1993) and others extended the neoclassical model of growth by suggesting that not only is knowledge an important factor generating growth, but because it spills over for use by third-party firms, it is actually the most potent factor.

The knowledge spillover theory of entrepreneurship explained in the previous section suggests that this assessment of the role of knowledge overlooks some of the most fundamental mechanisms driving the process of economic growth. The spillover process that Romer and the endogenous growth theory assumes to be automatic is not at all automatic. Rather, it is a process that is actively driven by economic agents. According to Audretsch et al. (2005), Entrepreneurship Capital serves as a mechanism facilitating the spillover of knowledge.

While Romer and Lucas added the factor of knowledge capital to the traditional factors of physical capital and labor, Audretsch et al. (2005) do not dispute the importance of the traditional factors, but suggest an additional factor as well – the degree of entrepreneurship capital specific to a Standort, or location. By entrepreneurship capital Audretsch et al. (2005) mean the capacity for the Standort, that is the geographically relevant spatial units of observation, to generate the start-up of new enterprises.

While the neoclassical tradition identified investment in physical capital as the driving factor of economic performance (Solow, 1956), the endogenous growth theory (Romer, 1986, 1990; Lucas, 1988) put the emphasis on the process of the accumulation of knowledge, and hence the creation of knowledge capital. The concept of social capital (Putnam, 1993; Coleman, 1988) could be considered as a further extension because it added a social component to those factors shaping economic growth and prosperity. According to Putnam (2000, p. 19), "Whereas physical capital refers to physical objects and human capital refers to the properties of individuals, social capital refers to connections among individuals – social networks and the norms of reciprocity and trustworthiness that arise from them. In that sense social capital is closely related to what some have called 'civic virtue'. The difference is that 'social capital' calls attention to the fact that civic virtue is most powerful when embedded in a sense network of reciprocal social relations. A society of many virtues but isolated individuals is not necessarily rich in social capital".

Putnam also challenged the standard neoclassical growth model by arguing that social capital was also important in generating economic growth, "By analogy with notions of physical capital and human capital – tools and training that enhance individual productivity – social capital refers to features of social organization, such as networks, norms and trust, that facilitate coordination and cooperation for mutual benefits".

A large and robust literature has emerged trying to link social capital to entrepreneurship (Aldrich & Martinez, 2003; Thorton & Flynne, 2003). However, while it was clear that Putnam was providing a link between social capital and economic welfare, this link did not directly involve entrepreneurship. The components of social capital Putnam emphasized the most included associational membership and public trust. While these may be essential for social and economic well being, it was not obvious that they involved entrepreneurship, per se.

Social capital and entrepreneurship capital are distinctive concepts that should not be confused. According to Putnam (2000, p. 19), "Social capital refers to connections among individuals – social networks and the norms of reciprocity and trustworthiness that arise from them. In that sense social capital is closely related to what some have called 'civic virtue'. (...) Social capital calls attention to the fact that civic virtue is most powerful when embedded in a sense network of reciprocal social relations. (...) Social capital refers to features of social organization, such as networks, norms and trust, that facilitate coordination and cooperation for mutual benefits".

Audretsch et al. (2005) and Audretsch and Keilbach (2004) argue that what has been called social capital in the entrepreneurship literature may actually be a more specific sub-component, which we introduce as entrepreneurship capital. Entrepreneurship has typically been defined as an action, process or activity. Entrepreneurship involves the start-up and growth of new enterprises. Entrepreneurship capital involves a milieu of agents and institutions that is conducive to the creation of new firms. This involves a number of aspects such as social acceptance of entrepreneurial behavior but of course also individuals who are willing to deal with the risk of creating new firms[1] and the activity of bankers and venture capital agents that are willing to share risks and benefits involved. Hence, entrepreneurship capital reflects a number of different legal, institutional and social factors and forces. Taken together, these factors and forces constitute the entrepreneurship capital of an economy, which creates a capacity for entrepreneurial activity (Hofstede, Noorderhaven, Thurik, Wennekers, & Uhlaner, Wildeman, 2002).

It should be emphasized that entrepreneurship capital should not be confused with social capital. The major distinction is that, in our view, not all social capital may be conducive to economic performance, let alone entrepreneurial activity. Some types of social capital may be more focused on preserving the status quo and not necessarily directed at creating challenges to the status quo. By contrast, entrepreneurship capital could be considered to constitute one particular sub-set of social capital. While social capital may have various impacts on entrepreneurship, depending on the specific orientation, entrepreneurship capital, by its very definition, will have a positive impact on entrepreneurial activity.

Audretsch et al. (2005) and Audretsch and Keilbach (2004) include a measure of entrepreneurship capital, along with the traditional factors of production of labor, physical capital and knowledge capital, in a production function model to estimate economic growth. Their evidence suggests that entrepreneurship capital exerts indeed a positive impact on economic growth. This finding holds for difference measured of entrepreneurship capital, ranging from the more general to the more risk oriented.

While the findings by Audretsch et al. (2005) and Audretsch and Keilbach (2004) certainly do not contradict the conclusions of earlier studies linking growth to factors such as labor, capital and knowledge, their evidence points to an additional factor, entrepreneurship capital, that also plays an important role in generating economic growth.

The results from including measures of entrepreneurship capital in the context of estimating economic growth in a production function model are consistent with other studies also finding a positive relationship between various measures of entrepreneurship and economic growth. For example, Acs, Audretsch, Braunerhjelm, and Carlsson (2004) find a positive relationship between entrepreneurship and growth at the country level. Carree et al. (2000) provided empirical evidence from a 1984–1994 cross-sectional study of the 23 countries that are part of the Organization for Economic Co-operation and Development (OECD), that increased entrepreneurship, as measured by business ownership rates, was associated with higher rates of employment growth at the country level. Similarly, Audretsch et al. (2002) and Carree et al. (2000) find that OECD countries exhibiting higher increases in entrepreneurship also have experienced greater rates of growth and lower levels of unemployment.

In a study for the OECD, Audretsch and Thurik (2002) undertook two separate empirical analyses to identify the impact of changes of entrepreneurship on growth. Each one uses a different measure of entrepreneurship, sample of countries and specification. This provides some sense of robustness across different measures of entrepreneurship, data sets, time periods and specifications. The first analysis uses a database that measures entrepreneurship in terms of the relative share of economic activity accounted for by small firms. It links changes in entrepreneurship to growth rates for a panel of 18 OECD countries spanning five years to test the hypothesis that higher rates of entrepreneurship lead to greater subsequent growth rates. The second analysis uses a measure of self-employment as an index of entrepreneurship and links changes in entrepreneurship to unemployment at the country level between 1974 and 1998. The different samples including OECD countries over different time periods reach consistent results – increases in entrepreneurial activity tends to result in higher subsequent growth rates and a reduction of unemployment.

CONCLUSIONS

The prevalent and traditional theories of entrepreneurship have typically held the context constant and then examined how characteristics specific to the individual impact the cognitive process inherent in the model of entrepreneurial choice. This often leads to the view that, given a distribution of personality characteristics, proclivities, preferences and tastes, entrepreneurship is exogenous. One of the great conventional wisdoms in entrepreneurship is "Entrepreneurs are born not made". Either you have it or you don't. This leaves virtually no room for policy or for altering what nature has created.

The knowledge spillover theory of entrepreneurship suggests an alternative view. In the knowledge spillover theory, the individual attributes constant and instead focus on variations in the context. In particular, we consider how the knowledge context will impact the cognitive process underlying the entrepreneurial choice model. The result is a theory of endogenous entrepreneurship, where (knowledge) workers respond to opportunities generated by new knowledge by starting a new firm. In this view, entrepreneurship is a rationale choice made by economic agents to appropriate the expected value of their endowment of knowledge. Thus, the creation of a new firm is the endogenous response to investments in knowledge that have not been entirely or exhaustively appropriated by the incumbent firm.

In the endogenous theory of entrepreneurship, the spillover of knowledge and the creation of a new, knowledge-based firm are virtually synonymous. Of course, there are many other important mechanisms facilitating the spillover of knowledge that have nothing to do with entrepreneurship, such as the mobility of scientists and workers, and informal networks, linkages and interactions. Similarly, there are certainly new firms started that have nothing to do with the spillover of knowledge. Still, the spillover theory of entrepreneurship suggests that there will be additional entrepreneurial activity as a rationale and cognitive response to the creation of new knowledge. Those contexts with greater investment in knowledge should also experience a higher degree of entrepreneurship, ceteris paribus. Perhaps, it is true that entrepreneurs are made. But more of them will discover what they are made of in a high knowledge context than in an impoverished knowledge context. Thus, we are inclined to restate the conventional wisdom and instead propose that entrepreneurs are not necessarily made, bur are rather a response – and in particular a response to high knowledge contexts that are especially fertile in spawning entrepreneurial opportunities.

By endogenously facilitating the spillover of knowledge created in a different organization and perhaps for a different application, entrepreneurship may serve as the missing link to economic growth. Confronted with a formidable knowledge filter, public policy instruments emerging from the new growth theory, such as investments in human capital, R&D and university research may not adequately result in satisfactory economic growth.

By serving as a conduit for knowledge spillovers, entrepreneurship is the missing link between investments in new knowledge and economic growth. Thus, the knowledge spillover theory of entrepreneurship provides not just an explanation of why entrepreneurship has become more prevalent as the factor of knowledge has emerged as a crucial source for comparative advantage, but also why entrepreneurship plays a vital role in generating economic growth. Entrepreneurship is an important mechanism permeating the knowledge filter to facilitate the spillover of knowledge and ultimately generate economic growth. Entrepreneurship education and the transfer of technology from universities to commercialization in the private sector makes a significant contribution to economic growth by reducing the knowledge filter and facilitating the crucial missing link – entrepreneurship.

NOTES

1. As Gartner and Carter (2003) state, "Entrepreneurial behavior involves the activities of individuals who are associated with creating new organizations rather than the activities of individuals who are involved with maintaining or changing the operations of on-going established organizations".

REFERENCES

Acs, Z. J., Audretsch, D. B., Braunerhjelm, P., & Carlsson, B. (2004). *The missing link: The knowledge filter and endogenous growth* (Discussion paper). Stockholm: Center for Business and Policy Studies.

Aldrich, H. E., & Martinez, M. (2003). Entrepreneurship, networks and geographies. In: Z. J. Acs & D. B. Audretsch (Eds), *Handbook of entrepreneurship research* (pp. 359–400). Boston: Kluwer Academic Publishers.

Arrow, K. J. (1962). Economic welfare and the allocation of resources for invention. In: R. R. Nelson (Ed.), *The rate and direction of inventive activity* (pp. 609–626). Princeton: Princeton University Press.

Audretsch, D., & Keilbach, M. (2004). Entrepreneurship and regional growth: An evolutionary interpretation. *Journal of Evolutionary Economics, 14,* 605–616.

Audretsch, D., & Lehmann, E. (2005). Mansfield's missing link: The impact of knowledge spillovers on firm growth. *Journal of Technology Transfer, 30,* 207–210.

Audretsch, D. B. (1995). *Innovation and industry evolution.* Cambridge: MIT Press.

Audretsch, D. B. (2006). *The entrepreneurial socity.* New York: Oxford University Press, forthcoming.

Audretsch, D. B., Carree, M. A., van Stel, A. J., & Thurik, A. R. (2002). Impeded industrial restructuring: The growth penalty. *Kyklos, 55,* 81–98.

Audretsch, D. B., & Feldman, M. P. (1996). R&D spillovers and the geography of innovation and production. *American Economic Review, 86,* 630–640.

Audretsch, D. B., Keilbach, M., & Lehmann, E. (2006). *Entrepreneurship and economic growth.* Oxford: Oxford University Press, forthcoming.

Audretsch, D. B., & Stephan, P. E. (1996). Company-scientist locational links: The case of biotechnology. *American Economic Review, 86,* 641–652.

Audretsch, D. B., & Thurik, R. (2002). *Linking entrepreneurship to growth.* OECD STI Working Paper 2081/2.

Birch, D. (1979). *The job generation process. MIT Program on Neighborhood and Regional Change.* Cambridge: MIT.

Carree, van Stel, A., Thurik, R., & Wennekers, S. (2000). Business ownership and economic growth in 23 OECD countries. Tinbergen Institute Discussion Paper. Available online: http://www.tinbergen.nl/discussionpapers/00001.pdf

Caves, R. E. (1998). Industrial organization and new findings on the turnover and mobility of firms. *Journal of Economic Literature, 36,* 1947–1982.

Coleman, J. (1998). Social capital in the creation of human capital. *American Journal of sociology, 94,* 95–121.

Davis, S., Haltiwanger, J., & Schuh, S. (1996a). *Job creation and destruction.* Cambridge: MIT Press.

Davis, S., Haltiwanger, J., & Schuh, S. (1996b). Small business and job creation: Dissecting the myth and reassessing the facts. *Small Business Economics, 8,* 297–315.

Ericson, R., & Pakes, A. (1995). Markov-perfect industry dynamics: A framework for empirical work. *Review of Economic Studies, 62,* 53–82.

Feldman, M., & Audretsch, D. (1999). Innovations in cities: Science-based diversity, specialization and localized monopoly. *European Economic Review, 43,* 409–429.

Gartner, W. B., & Carter, N. M. (2003). Entrepreneurial behaviour and firm organizing processes. In: Z. J. Acs & D. B. Audretsch (Eds), *Handbook of entrepreneurship research* (pp. 195–222). Boston: Kluwer Academic Publishers.

Gilbert, B., Audretsch, D., & McDoughall, P. (2004). The emergence of entrepreneurship policy. *Small Business Economics, 22,* 313–323.

Glaeser, E., Kallal, H., Scheinkman, J., & Shleifer, A. (1992). Growth in cities. *Journal of Political Economy, 100,* 1126–1152.

Griliches, Z. (1984). *R&D, patents and productivity*. Chicago: University of Chicago Press.

Hofstede, G., Noorderhaven, N., Thurik, A., Wennekers, A., Uhlaner, L., & Wildeman, R. (2002). Culture's role in entrepreneurship: Self-employment out of dissatisfaction. In: *Innovation, entrepreneurship and culture: The interaction between technology, progress and economic growth*. Brookfield, UK: Edward Elgar.

Hopenhayn, H. A. (1992). Entry, exit and firm dynamics in long run equilibrium. *Econometrica, 60*, 1127–1150.

Jaffe, A. B. (1989). Real effects of academic research. *American Economic Review, 79*, 957–970.

Jovanovic, B. (1982). Selection and evolution of industry. *Econometrica, 50*, 649–670.

Klepper, S. (1996). Entry, exit, growth, and innovation over the product life cycle. *American Economic Review, 86*, 562–583.

Krueger, N. F. (2003). The cognitive psychology of entrepreneurship. In: Z. J. Acs & D. B. Audretsch (Eds), *Handbook of entrepreneurship research* (pp. 105–140). Boston: Kluwer Academic Publishers.

Lucas, R. (1988). On the mechanics of economic development. *Journal of Monetary Economics, 22*, 3–42.

Lucas, R. (1993). Making a miracle. *Econometrica, 61*, 251–272.

McClelland, D. (1961). *The achieving society*. Boston: Kluwer Academic Publishers.

Putnam, R. D. (1993). *Making democracy work. Civic traditions in modern Italy*. Princeton: Princeton University Press.

Putnam, R. D. (2000). *Bowling alone: The collapse and revival of American community*. New York: Simon & Schuster.

Romer, P. M. (1986). Increasing returns and long-run growth. *Journal of Political Economy, 94*, 1002–1037.

Sarasvathy, S. D., Dew, N., Velamuri, S. R., & Venkataraman, S. (2003). Three views of entrepreneurial opportunity. In: Z. J. Acs & D. B. Audretsch (Eds), *Handbook of entrepreneurship research* (pp. 141–160). Boston: Kluwer Academic Publishers.

Shane, S., & Eckhardt, J. (2003). The individual-opportunity nexus. In: Z. J. Acs & D. B. Audretsch (Eds), *Handbook of entrepreneurship research* (pp. 161–194). Boston: Kluwer Academic Publishers.

Shaver, K. G. (2003). The social psychology of entrepreneurial behaviour. In: Z. J. Acs & D. B. Audretsch (Eds), *Handbook of entrepreneurship research* (pp. 331–358). Boston: Kluwer Academic Publishers.

Solow, R. (1956). A contribution to the theory of economic growth. *Quarterly Journal of Economics, 70*, 65–94.

Thorton, P. H., & Flynne, K. H. (2003). Entrepreneurship, networks and geographies. In: Z. J. Acs & D. B. Audretsch (Eds), *Handbook of entrepreneurship research*. Boston: Kluwer Academic Publishers.

Venkataraman, S. (1997). The distinctive domain of entrepreneurship research. In: *Advances in entrepreneurship, firm emergence and growth*. Greenwich: JAI Press.

PART III

GEOGRAPHY

[10]

R&D Spillovers and the Geography of Innovation and Production

By David B. Audretsch and Maryann P. Feldman*

More than most other economic activities, innovation and technological change depend upon new economic knowledge. Thus, Paul Romer (1986), Paul Krugman (1991a, b), and Gene Grossman and Elhanan Helpman (1991), among others, have focused on the role that spillovers of economic knowledge across agents and firms play in generating increasing returns and ultimately economic growth. In fact, several recent studies have identified the existence of spatially-mediated knowledge spillovers. An important finding of Adam B. Jaffe (1989), Zoltan Acs et al. (1992, 1994), and Feldman (1994a, b) is that investment in R&D by private corporations and universities "spills over" for third-party firms to exploit. If the ability to receive knowledge spillovers is influenced by distance from the knowledge source, then geographic concentration should be observed, especially in industries where knowledge spillovers are likely to play a more important role. The purpose of this paper is to examine the extent to which industrial activity clusters spatially and to link this geographic concentration to the existence of knowledge externalities. Of course,

as Jaffe et al. (1993) point out, one obvious explanation why innovative activity in some industries tends to cluster geographically more than in other industries is that the location of production is more concentrated spatially. Thus, in explaining why the propensity for innovative activity to cluster geographically varies across industries, we need first to explain, and then to control for, the geographic concentration of the location of production.

As Alfred Marshall (1920) and, later Krugman (1991b) argue, there may be geographic boundaries to information flows or knowledge spillovers, particularly tacit knowledge, among the firms in an industry. Although the cost of transmitting information may be invariant to distance, presumably the cost of transmitting knowledge rises with distance. That is, proximity and location matter. While there is considerable evidence supporting the existence of knowledge spillovers, neither Jaffe (1989), Jaffe et al. (1993), nor Acs et al. (1992, 1994), and Feldman (1994a) actually examine the propensity for innovative activity to cluster spatially. But implicit in the knowledge production function model is the assumption that innovative activity should concentrate geographically in those industries where the direct knowledge-generating inputs are the greatest and where knowledge spillovers are the most prevalent. No one, to date, has examined the underlying propensity for industrial activity to cluster spatially. While one of the central themes in the industrial organization literature is to explain the degree of concentration of economic activity within an industry (F. M. Scherer and David Ross, 1990), the focus has typically been on the extent of dispersion across different enterprises and establishments within a single spatial unit—the country. The emerging importance of location as a unit of observation argues for examining both production and innovation within a geographic context. We empirically

* Audretsch: Wissenschaftszentrum Berlin für Sozialforschung and the Centre for Economic Policy Research, Reichpietschufer 50, D-10785 Berlin, Germany; Feldman: Institute for Policy Studies, Johns Hopkins University, Baltimore, MD 21218. This article was written while Maryann Feldman was visiting at the Heinz School of Public Policy and Management, Carnegie Mellon University. We thank Richard Baldwin, Paul Krugman, James Markusen, and participants at the CEPR Conference on the "Location of Economic Activity: New Theories and New Evidence," 17–20 December, 1993, Vigo, Spain, for their useful comments. We also thank Jim Adams, Zvi Griliches, Bronwyn Hall, Frank Lichtenberg, Richard Nelson and Mike Scherer and the participants in the discussion at the 1995 AEA Meetings. We would also like to thank the anonymous referees for useful comments and suggestions. Gail Cohen Shaivitz provided invaluable research assistance.

630

test for the importance of geographic location to different types of industries by linking the geographic concentration in manufacturing industries to industry specific characteristics, most notably the relative importance of knowledge spillovers.

In the following section of this paper, we examine the spatial distribution of innovative activity as well as the geographic concentration of production. An empirical model is specified in Section II, and the results are presented in Section III. In the final section, we provide a summary and conclusion. The empirical evidence suggests that, even after controlling for the degree of geographic concentration in production, innovative activity tends to cluster more in industries where knowledge spillovers play a decisive role. Although such industries also tend to exhibit a greater geographic concentration of production, the results suggest that the propensity for innovative activity to cluster is more attributable to the role of knowledge spillovers and not merely the geographic concentration of production.

I. The Spatial Distribution of Innovation and Production

To measure the spatial distribution of innovative activity we rely on the most recent and most ambitious major data base that provides a direct measure of innovative activity. The United States Small Business Administration (the Small Business Administration's Innovation Data Base or the SBIDB) compiled a data base of 8,074 commercial innovations introduced in the United States in 1982. A private firm, The Futures Group, compiled the data and performed quality control analyses for the United States Small Business Administration. A data base consisting of innovations by four-digit standard industrial classification (SIC) industries was formed from the new product announcement sections in over 100 technology, engineering and trade journals that span every industry.[1] These data were

used by Acs and Audretsch (1988, 1990) to analyze the relationships between firm size and technological change, and market structure and technological change, and by Acs et al. (1992, 1994), Feldman (1994a, b), and Feldman and Richard Florida (1994) to examine the geography of innovation.

We adopt the state as the spatial unit of observation. While this is at best a crude proxy of the relevant economic market,[2] it does have one obvious appeal other than that it conforms to a number of data sources—the most relevant unit of policy-making is at the level of state. Still, states are certainly not an entirely satisfactory unit of observation for the analysis of spatial phenomena. The analyses of spatial processes are handicapped by a lack of data for what might be considered to be the ideal observation. Certainly considerable progress would be made if data sources identifying innovation activity at the city or county level were made available.

Using the citation data base described above, an innovation is attributed to the state in which the establishment responsible for the development of that innovation is located. Some innovations are, in fact, developed by subsidiaries or divisions of companies with headquarters in other states. Since headquarters may announce new product innovations, the data base discriminates between the location of the innovating establishment and the location of the larger, innovating entity (Edwards and Gordon, 1984). For our purposes, the state identifier of the establishment is used to investigate the spatial distribution of innovation. Of the total number of innovations recorded in the data base, 4,200 were manufacturing innovations with information specifying location.[3]

Figure 1 shows the distribution of innovations by states. California is the state in which

---

[1] A detailed description of the U.S. Small Business Administration's Innovation Citation Data Base can be found in chapter two of Acs and Audretsch (1990), as well as in Acs and Audretsch (1988).

[2] As Krugman (1991b p. 57) emphasizes, "States aren't really the right geographical units," because of the lack of concordance between economic markets and political units.

[3] The SBIDB contains a total of 4,476 innovations in manufacturing industries. Of these, there are 276 innovations which are not used because they were developed by establishments outside the United States or did not have complete location information.

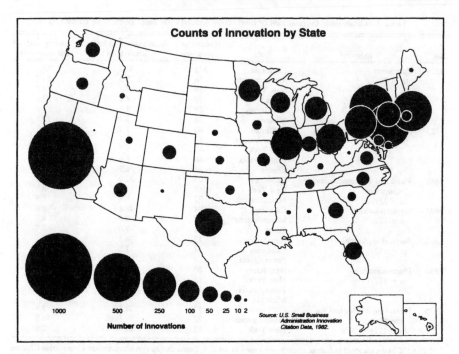

FIGURE 1. NUMBER OF INNOVATIONS BY STATE

the greatest number of innovations were registered, followed by New York, New Jersey, and Massachusetts. A particularly striking feature shown in Figure 1 is that the bulk of innovative activity in the United States occurs on the coasts, and especially in California and in New England. By contrast, no innovative activity is registered in certain Midwestern states such as North Dakota, South Dakota, Montana, and Wyoming.[4] States in the traditional manufacturing belt such as Ohio, Illi-

[4] Of course, simply comparing the absolute amount of innovative activity across states ignores the fact that the manufacturing base of some states is larger than others. Presumably one of the most important determinants of innovative activity is the location of manufacturing activity. Additional information on the geographic distribution of the innovation data can be found in Feldman (1994b) and Feldman and Florida (1994).

nois, Michigan, and Pennsylvania are not at all particularly innovative. Thus, while the location of manufacturing activity may explain the spatial distribution of innovative activity to some degree, it is certainly not the only factor.

This presentation of the aggregate geographic distribution of innovative activity in the United States obscures the propensity for innovative activity to cluster spatially within specific industries. Thus, the distribution of innovative activity for the seven most innovative four-digit standard industrial classification (SIC) industries is shown in Table 1. A striking result is that the spatial concentration of innovative activity in particular industries is considerably greater than for all of manufacturing. For example, in the computer industry, 342 of the 821 innovations recorded, or 41.7 percent, are in California. And an additional 10 percent are recorded in Massachusetts.

TABLE 1—GEOGRAPHIC DISTRIBUTION OF INNOVATIVE ACTIVITY FOR MOST INNOVATIVE INDUSTRIES

SIC[a]	Industry[b]	State	Number of innovations	State share of industry innovations	Industry share of state innovations
3573	Computers	California	342	41.7	35.1
	(n = 821)	Massachusetts	78	9.5	21.7
		New York	58	7.1	12.7
		Texas	39	4.8	23.1
		New Jersey	38	4.6	8.9
		Illinois	28	3.4	12.1
3823	Process control instruments	California	80	17.2	8.2
	(n = 464)	Massachusetts	61	13.1	16.9
		New York	45	9.7	9.9
		Pennsylvania	40	8.6	16.5
		Illinois	32	6.9	13.9
3662	Radio and TV communications	California	105	31.0	10.8
	equipment	New York	40	11.8	8.8
	(n = 339)	Massachusetts	32	9.4	8.9
3674	Semiconductors	California	84	48.8	8.6
	(n = 172)	Massachusetts	17	9.9	4.7
		Texas	13	7.6	7.7
3842	Surgical appliances	New Jersey	43	28.3	10.1
	(n = 152)	California	17	11.2	1.7
		Pennsylvania	10	7.9	4.1
2834	Pharmaceuticals	New Jersey	50	39.4	11.7
	(n = 127)	New York	18	14.2	3.9
		Pennsylvania	10	7.9	4.1
		Michigan	8	6.3	7.1
3825	Measuring instruments for	California	37	32.2	3.8
	electricity	Massachusetts	22	19.1	16.9
	(n = 115)	New York	13	11.3	2.9

[a] The SIC is the standard industrial classification used in the U.S. Small Business Administration's Innovation Citation Data Base.
[b] The total number of innovations recorded in the four-digit industry is listed in parentheses.

Thus, these two states alone account for over one half of all the innovations in the computer industry. At the same time, the last column indicates that innovations in the computer industry accounted for slightly more than one third of all the innovations in California and a little more than one fifth of all innovations in Massachusetts. Similarly, nearly 40 percent of the 127 innovations in the drug industry (pharmaceuticals) were recorded in New Jersey, while an additional 14 percent were made in New York. Thus, over one-half of pharmaceutical innovations were in the New Jersey-New York area. At the same time, pharmaceutical innovations account for over one tenth of all innovations registered in New Jersey.

To measure the extent to which manufacturing in specific industries is concentrated geographically and the extent to which innovative activity tends to cluster spatially, we follow Krugman's (1991b) example and calculate Gini coefficients for the geographic concentration of innovative activity and for the location of manufacturing.[5] Table 2 provides

[5] The locational Gini coefficients for production are based on industry value-added. We calculate the amount of value-added in an industry and state divided by the national value-added for the industry. This ratio is normalized by the state share of total manufacturing value-added in order to account for the overall distribution of manufacturing activity. An industry which is not geographically concentrated more than is reflected by the overall distribution of manufacturing value-added would have a coefficient of 0. The closer the industry coefficient is to 1, the more geographically concentrated the industry would be. Cases in which state or industry data have been suppressed are omitted from the analysis. The Gini coefficients for innovation are based on the count of innovation in a state and industry and are calculated in a similar way. Further details are available from the authors upon request.

TABLE 2—GEOGRAPHIC CONCENTRATION OF PRODUCTION
AND INNOVATIVE ACTIVITY FOR MANUFACTURING
SECTORS (MEAN GINI COEFFICIENTS)[a]

Manufacturing sector	Value added	Employment	Innovations
Food and	0.6973	0.5584	0.2567
beverages	(0.1685)	(0.1828)	(0.2226)
Tobacco	0.6589	0.4137	0.3319
	(0.2559)	(0.1444)	(0.2043)
Textiles	0.7040	0.5670	0.1659
	(0.1149)	(0.1430)	(0.2347)
Apparel	0.6179	0.5160	0.0583
	(0.1589)	(0.1687)	(0.1469)
Lumber	0.6309	0.5605	0.1180
	(0.1007)	(0.1208)	(0.1235)
Furniture	0.5815	0.4632	0.4204
	(0.1373)	(0.1366)	(0.2347)
Paper	0.6036	0.5580	0.2363
	(0.1525)	(0.1568)	(0.3253)
Printing	0.5977	0.5325	0.1762
	(0.1491)	(0.1485)	(0.2220)
Chemicals	0.7003	0.5987	0.3881
	(0.1612)	(0.1790)	(0.1945)
Petroleum	0.6786	0.4766	0.2598
	(0.1512)	(0.1493)	(0.3674)
Rubber and	0.5771	0.4569	0.3932
plastics	(0.3089)	(0.2434)	(0.1952)
Leather	0.7186	0.5552	0.0646
	(0.1150)	(0.1300)	(0.1119)

[a] Standard deviations are given in parentheses.

the weighted mean Gini coefficients for value-added, employment, and innovative activity within each broad two-digit SIC manufacturing sector. Those sectors exhibiting the greatest geographic concentration of manufacturing activity include primary metals, transportation equipment, textiles, food and beverages, leather and chemicals. By contrast, those manufacturing sectors exhibiting the highest propensity for innovative activity to cluster spatially include transportation equipment, instruments, and electronics. That the propensity for innovative activity to spatially cluster cannot be simply explained by the geographic concentration of the location of manufacturing activity is evident from Table 2. This points to the importance of controlling for the geographic concentration of production in explaining the propensity for innovative activity to spatially cluster.

II. The Model

Why should innovations tend to cluster spatially more in some industries than in other

industries? One obvious answer is simply that the location of production is more geographically concentrated in some industries than in others. This raises the issue of endogeny. Jaffe et al. (1993) identify two related critical issues which must be considered in trying to identify why the propensity for innovative activity to cluster spatially varies across industries. First, the extent to which the location of production is geographically concentrated must be controlled for, so that the relevant question becomes: *even after accounting for the geographic concentration of the production location, why does the propensity for innovative activity to cluster vary across industries?* And second, in trying to account for the degree to which the location of production is geographically concentrated, an important factor is the role which knowledge spillovers play in the industry. It is only after the geographic concentration of production has been controlled for, that the degree to which innovative activity clusters spatially can be addressed. Thus, to explain the propensity for innovative activity to cluster spatially we begin with the extent to which production is geographically concentrated.

While it is not possible to directly measure the extent to which knowledge externalities exist, as Kenneth J. Arrow (1962) and Krugman (1991a) point out, it is possible to identify industries in which new economic knowledge plays a relatively more important role. This is done on the basis of the industry R&D intensity, or R&D-sales ratio. The crucial assumption we make here is Arrow's (1962) argument that knowledge spillovers are more important in, and reflected at least to some degree by, highly R&D-intensive industries. By contrast, such knowledge externalities, while perhaps still present, play a less important role where the creation of new economic knowledge, as reflected by R&D intensity, is negligible. Thus, the location of production would be expected to be more concentrated in those industries where knowledge spillovers are prevalent, that is in industries which are R&D intensive.

Similarly, skilled workers endowed with a high level of human capital are a mechanism by which economic knowledge is transmitted. The greater the extent to which the industry

TABLE 3—DESCRIPTION OF VARIABLES

Variable	Description and source	Mean	Standard deviation
Gini of production	Gini coefficient of four-digit SIC industry value-added across states, weighted by national value-added for the industry in 1982 (U.S. Department of Commerce, Bureau of the Census, 1982 Economic Census).	0.56	0.13
Gini of innovation	Gini coefficient of four-digit SIC industry count of innovations across states, weighted by national innovation count for the industry in 1982 (Edwards and Gordon, 1984).	0.30	0.23
Natural resources	Share of total industry inputs purchased from mining and agriculture in 1976 (Input-output data as provided by U.S. International Trade Commission databank).	0.09	0.16
Scale	Mean size of the largest establishments accounting for one half of the industry value-of-shipments divided by industry value of shipments in 1982 (U.S. Department of Commerce, Bureau of the Census, 1982).	2.13	3.97
Transportation costs	Radius of the mean distance shipped in 1967 (Commodity Transport Survey of the United States Census of Transportation for 1967, taken from Weiss [1991]).	7.9549	4.0574
Industry R&D/sales	Industry expenditures on research and development divided by sales in 1977 (Line of Business Survey, U.S. Federal Trade Commission, 1977).	1.66	1.69
Skilled labor	Share of industry employment accounted for by professional and kindred workers, managers and administrators, plus craftspeople and kindred workers in 1970 (U.S. Department of Commerce, Bureau of the Census, 1972).	0.35	0.09
University research	Expenditures on university research for departments relevant to industry (Yale Survey of Industrial Managers in Levin et al. [1987] and National Science Foundation's (NSF) Survey of Science Resources Survey)	17.5946	13.851

work force is composed of skilled workers, the more important knowledge spillovers are likely to be. Thus, industries which rely on a higher component of skilled workers should tend to exhibit a greater tendency towards spatial concentration of industrial location.

Of course, while knowledge externalities may be important in influencing the degree to which the location of production is spatially concentrated, they are certainly not the only factors. Krugman (1991a) points out that the extent to which the location of production is geographically concentrated will be shaped by transportation costs. Transportation costs are inversely related to the mean distance shipped, so that a higher value of transportation costs should be associated with a lower geographic concentration of production. Similarly, industries which are highly dependent upon natural resource inputs are also going to tend to be geographically concentrated—presumably close to the source of those inputs. Augustus

Loesch (1954) and Victor R. Fuchs (1962) argue that firms in industries with a high dependency on natural resource inputs will tend to locate in close proximity to those resources. Therefore, a higher content of natural resource inputs in an industry should result in a greater geographic concentration of the location of production. In addition, Robert C. Shelburne and Robert W. Bednarzik (1993) argue that industries which are more capital-intensive will tend to be geographically concentrated, since production will be concentrated among fewer enterprises. That is, as capital intensity and the importance of scale economies rise, fewer large establishments will be able to exist at a level of output in excess of the minimum efficient scale (MES) level of output.

The main hypothesis of this paper suggests that innovative activity will tend to cluster in industries where new economic knowledge plays an especially important role. In estimating the main influences on the geographic

TABLE 4—CORRELATION MATRIX

	Gini of production	Gini of innovation	Natural resources	Scale	Transportation costs	Industry R&D/sales	Skilled labor	University research
Gini of production	1.0	—	—	—	—	—	—	—
Gini of innovation	0.0090	1.0	—	—	—	—	—	—
Natural resources	0.1292	−0.1130	1.0	—	—	—	—	—
Scale	−0.2370	−0.1158	0.1009	1.0	—	—	—	—
Transportation costs	0.2076	0.1013	−0.1400	0.3010	1.0	—	—	—
Industry R&D/sales	0.3241	0.2254	−0.2148	0.2420	0.3225	1.0	—	—
Skilled labor	0.0563	0.2540	−0.2848	0.0997	0.0702	0.3961	1.0	—
University research	0.8730	0.5100	0.1199	−0.1077	0.0819	0.1946	0.0239	1.0

concentration of innovation we consider three sources of economic knowledge—industry R&D, skilled labor, and the size of the pool of basic science for a specific industry. Conceptually, there are great differences in the scope and commercial applicability of university research undertaken in different fields. Academic research will not necessarily result in useful knowledge for every industry; however, scientific knowledge from certain academic departments is expected to be more important for certain industries than for others. To capture the relevant pool of knowledge, academic departments are assigned to industries using the survey of industrial R&D managers by Richard C. Levin et al. (1987).[6] For example, basic scientific research in medicine, biology, chemistry and chemical engineering is found to be relevant for product innovation in drugs (SIC 2834).

III. The Results

Descriptive statistics for the variables used to estimate the model are provided in Table 3,

and Table 4 provides the correlation matrix. There are 163 four-digit SIC industries for which comparable data for the different measures could be compiled.

Table 5 presents the regression results using ordinary-least-squares (OLS) estimates. Table 6 presents the results estimating the system of equations using three-stage least squares (3SLS).[7] The statistical results are generally quite consistent between the OLS and 3SLS methods of estimation.

In equation (1) of Table 5, the positive and statistically significant coefficient of the measure of natural resource utilization suggests that the degree to which inputs in an industry are composed of natural resources clearly tends to shape the geographic concentration of production. Resource dependent industries tend to be more geographically concentrated. The negative and statistically significant coefficient on the scale measure suggests that industries tend to be less, and not more, geographically concentrated when scale economies play a more important role. This result emerges even after controlling for the size of the industry. One explanation for this result

---

[6] To measure the relevance of a discipline to an industry a survey of industrial R&D managers was used. The question was asked, "How relevant were the basic sciences to technical progress in this line of business over the past 10–15 years?" The survey uses a Likert scale of 1 to 7 to assess relevance. We consider relevant science to be those academic departments that are rated with a relevance greater than a value of 5 on the scale.

[7] The system of equations was also estimated using two-stage least-squares estimation. The differences in the standard errors indicate the presence of cross-equation correlation. Thus, we estimate the model with 3SLS. The instruments used include all of the exogenous variables appearing on the right-hand side of the equations in the model.

TABLE 5—OLS REGRESSION RESULTS ESTIMATING GINI COEFFICIENTS ACROSS STATES[a]

	Gini of production			Gini of innovation		
	(1)	(2)	(3)[b]	(4)	(5)	(6)[b]
Gini of innovation	—	0.768	−0.125	—	—	—
		(0.143)	(−1.741)			
Natural resources	0.326	0.330	0.384	—	—	−0.108
	(4.950)	(5.261)	(5.058)			(−1.228)
Scale	−0.137	−0.160	−0.244	—	—	−0.007
	(−4.162)	(−4.173)	(−0.695)			(1.986)
Transportation costs	1.223	1.419	1.741	—	—	0.006
	(4.439)	(4.838)	(5.631)			(1.674)
Industry R&D/sales	0.455	0.436	0.608	0.469	0.565	0.543
	(7.791)	(7.170)	(2.860)	(2.137)	(2.405)	(2.341)
Skilled labor	1.094	1.058	1.318	0.466	0.657	0.645
	(15.044)	(12.483)	(15.031)	(4.910)	(4.581)	(4.686)
University research	—	—	0.034	0.108	0.116	0.118
			(2.147)	(7.920)	(8.093)	(8.139)
Gini of production	—	—	—	—	−0.119	−0.146
					(−1.587)	(−1.741)
Sample size	163	163	163	163	163	163
R^2	0.951	0.952	0.970	0.827	0.908	0.921
Standard error	0.15034	0.15079	0.18601	0.21443	0.21469	0.18487

[a] t values are given in parentheses.
[b] Columns (3) and (6) provide the unrestricted regression results. When the regression estimated for the Gini of production in column (2) is compared with the estimate of the unrestricted regression in column (3), the F test statistic (2,156) of 0.087 is computed for the overidentifying restrictions. Similarly, when the regression estimated for the Gini of innovation in column (5) is compared to the estimate of the unrestricted regression in column (6), the F test statistic (3,156) equals 2.662 for the overidentifying restrictions.

may be that this measure limits the size of the market to the United States, but when many manufacturing industries are global in scale, this measure will be understated.

There is little ambiguity concerning the two measures that are the primary focus of this paper—the relative importance of industry R&D in an industry and the extent to which the labor force is composed of skilled workers. The coefficient of industry R&D is positive and clearly statistically significant, supporting the hypothesis that industries where new economic knowledge tends to play a more important role will have a higher propensity to cluster together. Similarly, industries where skilled labor is relatively important also tend to exhibit a greater degree of geographic concentration of production.

An alternative specification which includes the Gini coefficient of innovation is presented in equation (2) of Table 5. To the extent that geographic proximity between R&D labs and production facilities is important to gain the benefits of R&D, we might expect that industries with closely clustered innovations may also have closely clustered factories. However, the coefficient of this variable cannot be considered to be statistically different from 0.

Equations (4) and (5) of Table 5 present the OLS regression results estimating the Gini coefficients of innovative activity across states. Equation (4) indicates that, when the extent to which production activity is geographically concentrated is not controlled for, the coefficients of all three types of knowledge-generating measures included—industry R&D, skilled labor, and university research—are positive and statistically significant. However, industries in which new economic knowledge plays a more important role also tend to exhibit a greater degree of spatial concentration. That is, without first controlling for the extent to which the location of production is geographically concentrated, it is not at all clear whether

TABLE 6—3SLS REGRESSION RESULTS ESTIMATING GINI COEFFICIENTS ACROSS STATES[a]

	Gini of production	Gini of innovation	Gini of production	Gini of innovation
Gini of innovation	—	—	0.224	—
			(0.416)	
Natural resources	0.331	—	0.347	—
	(5.145)		(5.261)	
Scale	−0.160	—	−0.166	—
	(−4.333)		(−3.589)	
Transportation costs	1.432	—	1.506	—
	(5.052)		(3.974)	
Industry R&D/sales	0.440	0.572	0.460	0.557
	(7.290)	(2.421)	(6.723)	(2.341)
Skilled labor	1.075	0.687	1.193	0.683
	(14.846)	(3.707)	(5.599)	(3.736)
University research	—	0.119	—	0.140
		(7.887)		(3.480)
Gini of production	—	−0.135	—	−0.158
		(−1.247)		(−1.391)
Sample size	163	163	163	163
Standard error	0.15523	0.21733	0.15571	0.21767

[a] *t* values are given in parentheses.

the greater propensity for innovative activity to cluster in industries where knowledge spillovers are more prevalent is attributable to the fact that knowledge externalities are more conducive to innovative activity or simply that the firms are already located within a relatively tight geographic area.

Thus, in equation (5) of Table 5, the Gini measure of the value-added across states is included. The coefficient of this variable is statistically insignificant, but the coefficients of the other explanatory variables remain virtually unchanged. Which is to say that, even after controlling for the extent to which the location of production is geographically concentrated, the three knowledge-generating variables are still found to have a significant impact on the propensity for innovative activity to cluster spatially.

Table 6 presents the 3SLS method of estimation. In the first set of equations the Gini coefficient of innovative activity across states is endogenous in both equations. In the second set of equations a fully specified simultaneous version of the model is presented in which the Gini coefficients of both innovative activity and production are endogenously included. Most importantly, the propensity for innovative activity to spatially cluster is found to be

the result of new economic knowledge and not merely the existing geographic concentration of production.

The positive coefficients of industry R&D, skilled labor, and university research, even after controlling for the degree of concentration of production, using both the OLS and 3SLS methods of estimation, are certainly consistent with the following hypothesis. The propensity for innovative activity to cluster will tend to be higher in industries where new economic knowledge plays a more important role. Presumably, it is in such industries where new economic knowledge which generates innovative activity is transmitted tacitly through what has been described as knowledge spillovers. Therefore, innovative activity is more likely to occur within close geographic proximity to the source of that knowledge, be it a university research laboratory, the research and development department of a corporation, or exposure to the knowledge embodied in a skilled worker.

Industries where new economic knowledge plays a more important role also tend to exhibit a greater geographic concentration of production. However, based on the statistical results reported above it appears that the propensity for innovative activity to cluster spatially is more attributable to the influence of knowledge spillovers and not merely the geographic concentration of production.

IV. Conclusions

This paper examines the geography of innovation and production. In particular, by examining the concentration of economic phenomena, we re-focus the lens from the usual product dimension to a geographic or spatial dimension. A key assumption we make in examining the link between knowledge spillovers in an industry and innovative activity clustering spatially is that knowledge externalities are more prevalent in industries where new economic knowledge plays a greater role. New economic knowledge is captured by industry R&D, university R&D, and skilled labor.

One obvious complication in testing for this link is that innovative activity will be more geographically concentrated in industries where production is also geographically concentrated, simply because the bulk of firms are located within close proximity. Even more problematic, though, is the hypothesis that new economic knowledge will tend to shape the spatial distribution of production as well as that of innovation. Indeed, we find that a key determinant of the extent to which the location of production is geographically concentrated is the relative importance of new economic knowledge in the industry. Even after controlling for the concentration of production we find evidence that industries in which knowledge spillovers are more prevalent—that is where industry R&D, university research and skilled labor are the most important—have a greater propensity for innovative activity to cluster than industries where knowledge externalities are less important.

REFERENCES

Acs, Zoltan J. and Audretsch, David B. "Innovation in Large and Small Firms: An Empirical Analysis." *American Economic Review*, September 1988, *78*(4), pp. 678–90.

_____. *Innovation and small firms.* Cambridge, MA: MIT Press, 1990.

Acs, Zoltan J.; Audretsch, David B. and Feldman, Maryann P. "Real Effects of Academic Research: Comment." *American Economic Review*, March 1992, *82*(1), pp. 363–67.

_____. "R&D Spillovers and Recipient Firm Size." *Review of Economics and Statistics*, May 1994, *76*(2), pp. 336–40.

Arrow, Kenneth J. "Economic Welfare and the Allocation of Resources for Invention," in Richard R. Nelson, ed., *The rate and direction of inventive activity.* Princeton, NJ: Princeton University Press, 1962, pp. 609–26.

Edwards, Keith L. and Gordon, Theodore J. "Characterization of Innovations Introduced on the U.S. Market in 1982." The Futures Group, prepared for the U.S. Small Business Administration under Contract No. SBA-6050-0A-82, March 1984.

Feldman, Maryann P. "Knowledge Complementarity and Innovation." *Small Business Economics*, October 1994a, *6*(5), pp. 363–72.

_____. *The geography of innovation.* Boston: Kluwer Academic Publishers, 1994b.

Feldman, Maryann P. and Florida, Richard. "The Geographic Sources of Innovation: Technological Infrastructure and Product Innovation in the United States." *Annals of the Association of American Geographers*, May 1994, *84*(2), pp. 210–29.

Fuchs, Victor R. *Change in the location of manufacturing in the United States since 1929.* New Haven: Yale University Press, 1962.

Grossman, Gene and Helpman, Elhanan. *Innovation and growth in the global economy.* Cambridge, MA: MIT Press, 1991.

Jaffe, Adam B. "Real Effects of Academic Research." *American Economic Review*, December 1989, *79*(5), pp. 957–70.

Jaffe, Adam B.; Trajtenberg, Manuel and Henderson, Rebecca. "Geographic Localization of Knowledge Spillovers as Evidenced by Patent Citations." *Quarterly Journal of Economics*, August 1993, *63*(3), pp. 577–98.

Krugman, Paul. "Increasing Returns and Economic Geography." *Journal of Political Economy*, June 1991a, *99*(3), pp. 483–99.

_____. *Geography and trade.* Cambridge, MA: MIT Press, 1991b.

Levin, Richard C.; Klevorick, Alvin K.; Nelson, Richard R. and Winter, Sidney G. "Appropriating the Returns from Industrial Research and Development." *Brookings Papers on Economic Activity,* 1987 (3), pp. 783–820.

Loesch, Augustus. *The economics of location.* New Haven: Yale University Press, 1954.

Marshall, Alfred. *Principles of economics,* 8th ed. London: Macmillan, 1920.

Romer, Paul. "Increasing Returns and Long-Run Growth." *Journal of Political Economy,* November 1986, *94*(5), pp. 1002–37.

Scherer, F. M. and Ross, David. *Industrial market structure and economic performance,* 3rd ed. Boston: Houghton Mifflin, 1990.

Shelburne, Robert C. and Bednarzik, Robert W. "Geographic Concentration of Trade-Sensitive Employment." *Monthly Labor Review,* June 1993, *116*(6), pp. 3–13.

Weiss, Leonard W. "The Geographic Size of Markets in Manufacturing," in David B. Audretsch and Hideki Yamawaki, eds., *Structure, conduct, and performance.* New York: New York University Press, 1991, pp. 64–91.

[11]

Real Effects of Academic Research: Comment

By Zoltan J. Acs, David B. Audretsch, and Maryann P. Feldman*

A fundamental issue which remains unresolved in the economics of technology is the identification and measurement of R&D spillovers, or the extent to which a firm is able to exploit economically the investment in R&D made by another company. In a 1989 paper in this *Review*, Adam Jaffe extended his pathbreaking 1986 study measuring the total R&D "pool" available for spillovers to identify the contribution of spillovers from university research to "commercial innovation" (Jaffe, 1989 p. 957). Jaffe's findings were the first to identify the extent to which university research spills over into the generation of inventions and innovations by private firms.

To measure technological change, Jaffe relies upon the number of patented inventions registered at the U.S. patent office, which he argues is "a proxy for new economically useful knowledge" (Jaffe, 1989 p. 958). In order to relate the response of this measure to R&D spillovers from universities, Jaffe modifies the "knowledge production function" introduced by Zvi Griliches (1979) for two inputs:

$$(1) \quad \log(P_{ik}) = \beta_{1k} \log(I_{ik}) + \beta_{2k} \log(U_{ik})$$
$$+ \beta_{3k}[\log(U_{ik}) \times \log(C_{ik})]$$
$$+ e_{ik}$$

where P is number of patented inventions, I represents the private corporate expenditures on R&D, U represents the research expenditures undertaken at universities, C is a measure of the geographic coincidence

*Acs: Department of Economics and Finance, University of Baltimore, Baltimore, MD; Audretsch: Wissenschaftszentrum Berlin für Sozialforschung, Berlin, Germany; Feldman: Carnegie Mellon University and Goucher College. We thank two referees for their helpful comments and suggestions. All errors and omissions remain our responsibility.

of university and corporate research, and e represents stochastic disturbance. The unit of observation is at the level of the state, i, and what Jaffe terms the "technological area," or the industrial sector, k. In addition, Jaffe includes the state population (Pop_{ik}) in his estimating equation in order to control for the size differential across the geographic units of observation.

Jaffe's (1989) statistical results provide evidence that corporate patent activity responds positively to commercial spillovers from university research. Not only does patent activity increase in the presence of high private corporate expenditures on R&D, but also as a result of research expenditures undertaken by universities within the state. The results concerning the role of geographic proximity in spillovers from university research are clouded, however, by the lack of evidence that geographic proximity *within the state* matters as well. According to Jaffe (1989 p. 968), "There is only weak evidence that spillovers are facilitated by geographic coincidence of universities and research labs within the state."

While Jaffe's (1989) model is constructed to identify the contribution of university research to generating "new economically useful knowledge" (p. 958), F. M. Scherer (1983), Edwin Mansfield (1984), and Griliches (1990) have all warned that measuring the number of patented inventions is not the equivalent of a direct measure of innovative output. For example, Ariel Pakes and Griliches (1980 p. 378) argued that "patents are a flawed measure (of innovative output); particularly since not all new innovations are patented and since patents differ greatly in their economic impact." In addressing the question "Patents as indicators of what?" Griliches (1990 p. 1669) concludes that "Ideally, we might hope that patent statistics would provide a measure of the (innovative) output.... The reality, however, is very far from it. The dream of

TABLE 1—COMPARISON AMONG PATENT, UNIVERSITY RESEARCH, AND INNOVATION MEASURES

Measure	Mean	Standard deviation	Minimum	Maximum	Number of innovations yielded per unit of input
University research expenditures (millions of dollars)	98.8	144.0	12.0	710.4	1.3
Drugs	28.5	35.3	2.2	142.3	3.3
Chemicals	5.7	9.7	0.5	46.7	1.9
Electronics	21.0	49.2	0.3	239.0	2.8
Mechanical	12.7	25.6	0.9	126.1	3.5
Corporate patents	879.4	975.7	39.0	3,230.0	0.148
Drugs	71.7	99.4	1.0	418.0	0.132
Chemicals	201.2	249.0	6.0	908.0	0.054
Electronics	225.0	295.3	7.0	1,142.0	0.263
Mechanical	300.8	319.9	20.0	993.0	0.146
Innovations	130.1	206.4	4.0	974.0	—
Drugs	9.5	16.0	0.0	75.0	—
Chemicals	10.9	17.7	0.0	80.0	—
Electronics	59.2	100.5	1.0	475.0	—
Mechanical	44.5	79.7	0.0	416.0	—

Notes: All dollar figures are millions of 1972 dollars. Data on university research funds by state are available for the four broad technical areas of drugs and medical technology; chemicals; electronics, optics and nuclear technology; and mechanical arts. These groups, along with the data for university research expenditures and corporate patents, are from Jaffe (1989).

getting hold of an output indicator of inventive activity is one of the strong motivating forces for economic research in this area."

The use of patent counts to identify the effect of spillovers from university research might be expected to be particularly sensitive to what Scherer (1983 p. 108) has termed the "propensity to patent." Just as Albert N. Link and John Rees (1990) found that small new entrepreneurial firms tend to benefit more than their established larger counterparts from university research spillovers, Griliches (1990) and Scherer (1983) both concluded that the propensity to patent does not appear to be invariant across a wide range of firm sizes.

A different and more direct measure of innovative output was introduced in Acs and Audretsch (1987), where the measure of innovative activity is the number of innovations recorded in 1982 by the U.S. Small Business Administration from the leading technology, engineering, and trade journals in each manufacturing industry. A detailed description and analysis of the data can be found in Acs and Audretsch (1988, 1990).

Because each innovation was recorded subsequent to its introduction in the market, the resulting data base provides a more direct measure of innovative activity than do patent counts. That is, the innovation data base includes inventions that were not patented but were ultimately introduced into the market and excludes inventions that were patented but never proved to be economically viable enough to appear in the market.

The extent to which university-research spillovers serve as a catalyst for private-corporation innovative activity can be identified by using the direct measure of innovative activity in the model introduced by Jaffe in equation (1). This enables a direct comparison of the influence of university R&D spillovers on innovation with the results that Jaffe reported using the patent measure.

Table 1 compares the mean measures of university research expenditures and corporate patents for all 29 states used by Jaffe with the mean number of innovations per state. It should be noted that, while Jaffe's university-research and patent measures are

TABLE 2—A COMPARISON BETWEEN REGRESSION RESULTS USING JAFFE'S PATENT MEASURE AND
THE INNOVATION MEASURE

Independent variable	All areas		Electronics		Mechanical arts	
	Patents (i)	Innovations (ii)	Patents (iii)	Innovations (iv)	Patents (v)	Innovations (vi)
$Log(I_i)$	0.668 (8.919)	0.428 (4.653)	0.631 (5.517)	0.268 (1.370)	0.643 (6.712)	0.649 (4.720)
$Log(U_{ik})$	0.241 (3.650)	0.431 (6.024)	0.265 (2.598)	0.520 (2.977)	0.059 (0.490)	0.329 (1.999)
$Log(U_{ik}) \times Log(C_i)$	0.020 (0.244)	0.173 (1.914)	.063 (0.531)	0.272 (1.331)	−0.046 (−0.406)	0.224 (1.436)
$Log(Pop_i)$	0.159 (1.297)	−0.072 (−1.287)	0.076 (1.263)	0.076 (0.742)	0.177 (3.767)	−0.143 (−2.051)
$\hat{S}$:	0.444	0.451	0.203	0.348	0.181	0.247
R^2:	0.959	0.902	0.992	0.951	0.994	0.974
N:	145	125	29	29	27	27

Note: Numbers in parentheses are t statistics.

based upon an eight-year sample (1972–1977, 1979, and 1981), the innovation measure is based upon a single year, 1982. Both the number of innovations per university research dollar (millions) and the number of innovations per patent vary considerably across the four industrial sectors included in Jaffe's sample. The number of innovations yielded per dollar of university research is apparently highest in the mechanical industries and lowest in the chemical industries. As in Acs and Audretsch (1988), the amount of innovative activity yielded per patent is highest in the electronics sector and lowest in chemicals.

While Jaffe (1989) was able to pool the different years across each state observation in estimating the production function for patented inventions, this is not possible using the innovation measure, due to data constraints. Thus, it is important first to establish that Jaffe's (1989) results do not differ greatly from estimates for a single year. This is done in equation (i) of Table 2, where Jaffe's (1989) patent measure for 1981 is used in the same estimating equation found in his table 4B, based on all (technological) areas. All of the data sources and a detailed description of the data and measures can be found in Jaffe (1989). Using the patent measure for a single year yields

virtually identical results to those based on the pooled estimation reported in Jaffe's article. That is, both private corporate expenditures on R&D and expenditures by universities on research are found to exert a positive and significant influence on patent activity. Similarly, both the geographic coincidence effect and the population variables have positive coefficients. The estimated coefficient of 0.668 for $log(I_i)$ in equation (i) of Table 2 is remarkably close to the coefficient of 0.713 estimated by Jaffe using the pooled sample. We conclude that using a single estimation year does not greatly alter the results obtained by Jaffe (1989) using several years to measure the extent of patent activity.

The number of 1982 innovations is substituted for the number of registered patents as the dependent variable in equation (ii) of Table 2, which estimates the impact of spillovers on all technological areas combined.[1] There are two important differences that emerge when the innovation measure is used instead of the patent measure. First, the elasticity of $log(U_{ik})$ almost doubles,

[1]The sample sizes differ between the patent and innovation estimations because the observations with the value of zero had to be omitted.

from 0.241 when the patent measure is used in equation (i) to 0.431 when the innovation measure is used in equation (ii). That is, the impact of university spillovers is apparently greater on innovations than on patented inventions. Second, the impact of the geographic coincidence effect also is much greater on innovation activity than on patents, suggesting that spillovers from geographic proximity may be more important than Jaffe (1989) concluded.

Jaffe (1989) also estimated knowledge-production functions for what he calls specific technical areas.[2] Equations (iii) and (iv) in Table 2 compare the estimations based on the patent and innovation measures for the electronics area, and equations (v) and (vi) compare the estimations based on the two measures for the mechanical-arts area. The patent and innovation measures yield somewhat different results. For the electronics area, expenditures on R&D by private corporations are found to have a positive and significant influence on patents but not on innovative activity. By contrast, in the mechanical-arts area, both patent and innovative activity respond positively to private R&D spending. This may reflect the difference in what Sidney G. Winter (1984) termed the "technological regime" between the electronics and mechanical-arts areas. That is, under the "entrepreneurial regime," the underlying technological information required to produce an innovation is more likely to come from basic research and from outside of the industry. By contrast, under the "routinized regime," an innovation is more likely to result from technological information from an R&D laboratory within the industry. Since the electronics area more closely corresponds to Winter's notion of the entrepreneurial regime, while the mechanical-arts area more closely resembles the routinized regime, it is not surprising that company R&D expenditures are relatively less important and university expenditures on research are relatively more impor-

tant in producing innovations in electronics but not in the mechanical arts. Further, as Mansfield (1984 p. 462) noted, innovations may have a particular tendency not to result from patented inventions in industries such as electronics: "The value and cost of individual patents vary enormously within and across industries.... Many inventions are not patented. And in some industries, like electronics, there is considerable speculation that the patent system is being bypassed to a greater extent than in the past."

Substitution of the direct measure of innovative activity for the patent measure in the knowledge-production function generally strengthens Jaffe's (1989) arguments and reinforces his findings. Most importantly, use of the innovation data provides even greater support than was found by Jaffe: as he predicted, spillovers are facilitated by the geographic coincidence of universities and research labs within the state. In addition, there is at least some evidence that, because the patent and innovation measures capture different aspects of the process of technological change, results for specific sectors may be, at least to some extent, influenced by the technological regime. Thus, we find that the importance of university spillovers relative to private-company R&D spending is considerably greater in the electronics sector when the direct measure of innovative activity is substituted for the patent measure.

REFERENCES

Acs, Zoltan J. and Audretsch, David B., "Innovation, Market Structure and Firm Size," *Review of Economics and Statistics*, November 1987, *69*, 567–75.

_____ and _____, "Innovation in Large and Small Firms: An Empirical Analysis," *American Economic Review*, September 1988, *78*, 678–90.

_____ and _____, *Innovation and Small Firms*, Cambridge, MA: MIT Press, 1990.

Griliches, Zvi, "Issues in Assessing the Contribution of R&D to Productivity Growth," *Bell Journal of Economics*, Spring 1979, *10*, 92–116.

_____, "Patent Statistics as Economic In-

---

[2]The technological areas are based on a technological classification and not on an industrial classification. For further explanation see appendix A in Jaffe (1989).

dicators: A Survey," *Journal of Economic Literature*, December 1990, *28*, 1661–1707.

Jaffe, Adam B., "Technological Opportunity and Spillovers of R&D: Evidence from Firms' Patents, Profits, and Market Value," *American Economic Review*, December 1986, *76*, 984–1001.

_____, "Real Effects of Academic Research," *American Economic Review*, December 1989, *79*, 957–70.

Link, Albert N. and Rees, John, "Firm Size, University Based Research, and the Returns to R&D," *Small Business Economics*, March 1990, *2*, 25–32.

Mansfield, Edwin, "Comment on Using Linked Patent and R&D Data to Measure Interindustry Technology Flows," in Zvi Griliches, ed., R&D, *Patents, and Productivity*, Chicago: University of Chicago Press, 1984, pp. 462–4.

Pakes, Ariel and Griliches, Zvi, "Patents and R&D at the Firm Level: A First Report," *Economics Letters*, 1980, *5* (4), 377–81.

Scherer, F. M., "The Propensity to Patent," *International Journal of Industrial Organization*, March 1983, *1*, 107–28.

Winter, Sidney G., "Schumpeterian Competition in Alternative Technological Regimes," *Journal of Economic Behavior and Organization*, September-December 1984, *5*, 287–320.

ELSEVIER   European Economic Review 43 (1999) 409–429

Innovation in cities:
Science-based diversity, specialization and localized competition

Maryann P. Feldman[a], David B. Audretsch[b,c,*]

[a] *Institute for Policy Studies, Johns Hopkins University, 3400 N. Charles St., Wyman Park 5th Floor, Baltimore, MD 21218-2696, USA*
[b] *Institute for Development Strategies, Indiana University, Bloomington, IN 47405-2100, USA*
[c] *Centre for Economic Policy Research, London, UK*

Received 1 September 1997; accepted 19 May 1998

Abstract

Whether diversity or specialization of economic activity better promotes technological change and subsequent economic growth has been the subject of a heated debate in the economics literature. The purpose of this paper is to consider the effect of the composition of economic activity on innovation. We test whether the specialization of economic activity within a narrow concentrated set of economic activities is more conducive to knowledge spillovers or if diversity, by bringing together complementary activities, better promotes innovation. The evidence provides considerable support for the diversity thesis but little support for the specialization thesis. © 1999 Elsevier Science B.V. All rights reserved.

JEL classification: O3, O1

Keywords: Innovation; Geography; Economic development; Agglomeration; Spillovers

*Correspondence address: School of Public and Environmental Affairs (SPEA), Institute for Developmental Strategies, Indiana University, Bloomington, IN 47405-2100, USA. Tel.: 1 812 855 6766; fax: 1 812 855 0184; e-mail: daudretsch@indiana.edu.

1. Introduction

In proposing a new theory of economic geography, Paul Krugman (1991b, p. 5) asks, 'What is the most striking feature of the geography of economic activity? The short answer is surely concentration ... production is remarkably concentrated in space.' Perhaps in response to Krugman's concern, a literature has recently emerged which focuses on the implications of the concentration of economic activity for economic growth. Models posited by Romer (1986, 1990), Lucas (1993), and Krugman (1991a,b) link increasing returns to scale yielded by externalities within a geographically bounded region to higher rates of growth. The results of Jaffe (1989), Jaffe et al. (1993), Feldman (1994) and Audretsch and Feldman (1996) suggest that R&D and other knowledge spillovers not only generate externalities, but the evidence also suggests that such knowledge spillovers tend to be geographically bounded within the region where the new economic knowledge was created. New economic knowledge may spill over, but the geographic extent of such knowledge spillovers is bounded. Lucas (1993) emphasizes the most natural context in which to understand the mechanics of economic growth is in metropolitan areas where the compact nature of the geographic unit facilitates communication. Indeed, Lucas (1993) asserts that the only compelling reason for the existence of cities would be the presence of increasing returns to agglomerations of resources which make these locations more productive.

None of these studies, however, ask the question, 'Does the specific type of economic activity undertaken within any particular geographic region matter?' This question is important because a recent debate has arisen focusing precisely on the composition of economic activity within an agglomeration and how such externalities will be shaped by that composition of economic activity. One view, which Glaeser et al. (1992) attribute to the *Marshall–Arrow–Romer* externality, suggests that an increased concentration of a particular industry within a specific geographic region facilitates knowledge spillovers across firms.[1] By contrast, Jacobs (1969) argues that it is the exchange of complementary knowledge across diverse firms and economic agents which yields a greater return to new economic knowledge.

There are clear policy implications of this debate in terms of policies directed towards innovation and technological change. If the specialization thesis is correct, then policy should focus on developing a narrow set of economic activities within a geographic region in order to yield greater innovative output. On the other hand, if the diversity thesis is correct, then a geographic region comprised of a diverse set of economic activities will tend to yield greater output

---

[1] This mirrors an earlier debate summarized by Loesch (1954).

M.P. Feldman, D.B. Audretsch / European Economic Review 43 (1999) 409–429 411

in terms of innovative activity. The key policy concerns would then become how to identify the commonalties and how to foster such diversity.

The purpose of this paper is to penetrate the black box of geographic space by identifying the extent to which the organization of economic activity is either concentrated, or alternatively consists of diverse but complementary economic activities, and how this composition influences innovative output. To consider this question we link the innovative output of product categories within a specific city to the extent to which the economic activity of that city is concentrated in that industry, or conversely, diversified in terms of complementary industries sharing a common science base. We use results on the relevance of academic departments to R&D from Levin et al. (1987) to identify complementary industries across which knowledge spillovers may be realized. We find a tendency for innovative activity in complementary industries sharing a common science-base to cluster together in geographic space. Industries which use the same base of scientific knowledge exhibit a strong tendency to locate together for both the location of production and the location of innovation.

In Section 2, we introduce the main theories alternatively favoring diversity or specialization in generating innovative activity. Issues concerning the measurement of innovative activity, the geographic unit of observation and the concepts of science-based diversity and specialization are examined in Section 3. After the model is presented in the Section 4, the empirical results are provided in Section 5. To explore the validity of our results, we extend our analysis to consider the impact of specialization versus diversity of economic activity within the firm on innovative activity in Section 6. We find considerable evidence rejecting the specialization thesis and in support of the diversity thesis. Based on the findings for both industries within specific cities as well as for individual firms, an organizational structure of economic activities that are diverse, but still complementary, apparently yields a greater innovative output than a specialization of economic activity.

2. Diversity versus specialization

The importance of location to innovation in a world increasingly relying upon E-mail, fax machines, and electronic communications superhighways may seem surprising, and even paradoxical at first glance. The resolution of this paradox lies in the distinction between knowledge and information. While the costs of transmitting information may be invariant to distance, presumably the cost of transmitting knowledge, especially what Von Hipple (1994) refers to as *sticky knowledge*, rises with distance. Von Hipple persuasively demonstrates that highly contextual and uncertain knowledge is best transmitted via face-to-face interaction and through frequent contact. Proximity matters in transmitting knowledge because, as Arrow (1962) pointed out, such sticky knowledge is inherently non-rival in nature and knowledge developed for any particular application can easily spill over and be applied to different use and applications. Indeed, Griliches (1992) has defined knowledge spillovers as 'working on similar things and hence benefiting much from each other's research'.[2]

Despite the general consensus that knowledge spillovers within a given location stimulate technological advance, there is little consensus as to exactly how this occurs. Glaeser et al. (1992) characterize three different models from the literature that would influence the production of innovation in cities. The *Marshall–Arrow–Romer* model formalizes the insight that the concentration of an industry in a city promotes knowledge spillovers between firms and therefore would facilitate innovation in that city-industry observation. This type of concentration is also known as industry localization (Loesch, 1954). An important assumption is that knowledge externalities with respect to firms exist, *but only for firms within the same industry*. Thus, the relevant unit of observation is extended from the firm to the region in the theoretical tradition of the Marshall–Arrow–Romer model and in subsequent empirical studies, but spillovers are limited to occur within the relevant industry. The transmission of knowledge spillovers across industries is assumed to be non-existent or at least trivial.

Restricting knowledge externalities to occur only within the industry may ignore an important source of new economic knowledge–inter-industry spillovers. Jacobs (1969) argues that the most important source of knowledge spillovers are external to the industry in which the firm operates and that cities are the source of innovation because the diversity of these knowledge sources is greatest in cities. Thus, Jacobs develops a theory that emphasizes that the variety of industries within a geographic region promotes knowledge externalities and ultimately innovative activity and economic growth. Of course, there should be some basis for interaction between diverse activities. A common science base facilitates the exchange of existing ideas and generation of new ones across disparate but complementary industries. Thus, in Jacobs' view, diversity rather than specialization is the operative mechanism of economic growth.

A second controversy involves the degree of competition prevalent in the region, or the extent of local monopoly. The Marshall–Arrow–Romer model predicts that local monopoly is superior to local competition because it

---

[2] Considerable evidence suggests that location and proximity clearly matter in exploiting knowledge spillovers. Not only have Jaffe et al. (1993) found that patent citations tend to occur more frequently within the state in which they were patented but Audretsch and Stephan (1996) and Audretsch and Feldman (1996) found that the propensity for innovative activity to cluster geographically tends to be greater in industries where new economic knowledge plays a more important role.

maximizes the ability of firms to appropriate the economic value accruing from their innovative activity. By contrast, Jacobs (1969) and Porter (1990) argue that competition is more conducive to knowledge externalities than is local monopoly.[3] It should be emphasized that by local competition, Jacobs (1969) does not mean competition within product markets as has traditionally envisioned within the industrial organization literature. Rather, Jacobs is referring to the competition for the new ideas embodied in economic agents. Not only does an increased number of firms provide greater competition for new ideas, but in addition, greater competition across firms facilitates the entry of a new firm specializing in some particular, new, product niche. This is because the necessary complementary inputs and services are likely to be available from small specialist niche firms but not necessarily from large, vertically integrated producers.[4]

3. Measurement issues

Krugman (1991a, p. 53) has argued that economists should abandon any attempts at measuring knowledge spillovers because ' ... knowledge flows are invisible, they leave no paper trail by which they may be measured and tracked'. But as Jaffe et al. (1993, p. 578) point out, 'knowledge flows do sometimes leave a paper trail' – in particular in the form of patented inventions and new product introductions.

In this paper we rely upon a direct measure of innovative output, rather than on a measure of intermediate output, such as patented inventions.[5] This United States Small Business Administration's Innovation Data Base (SBIDB) is the primary source of data for this paper.[6] The database consists of new product

---

[3] Porter (1990) provides examples of Italian ceramics and gold jewelry industries in which numerous firms are located with a bounded geographic region and compete intensively in terms of product innovation rather than focusing on simple price competition.

[4] A recent series of country studies assembled by Reynolds et al. (1994) show that new-firm start-up rates tend to be greatest in those geographic regions where the average number of firms per employee is the greatest.

[5] Scherer (1983), Mansfield (1984) and Griliches (1990) have all warned that the number of patented inventions is not the equivalent of a direct measure of innovative output. For example, Pakes and Griliches (1984, p. 378) argue that 'patents are a flawed measure of innovative output; particularly since not all new innovations are patented and since patents differ greatly in their economic impact'. In addressing the question, 'Patents as indicators of what?' Griliches (1990, p. 1669) concludes that, 'Ideally, we might hope that patent statistics would provide a measure of the innovative output ... The reality, however, is very far from it. The dream of getting hold of an output measure of inventive activity is one of the strong motivating forces for economic research in this area'.

[6] A detailed description of the SBIDB is contained in Audretsch (1995).

introductions compiled form the new product announcement sections of over 100 technology, engineering and trade journals spanning every industry in manufacturing. From the sections in each trade journal listing new products, a database consisting of the innovations by four-digit standard industrial classification (SIC) industries was formed. These innovation data have been implemented by Audretsch (1995) to analyze the relationship between industry dynamics and technological change, and by Audretsch and Feldman (1996), Feldman (1994) and Feldman and Florida (1994) to examine the spatial distribution of innovation.

There are several important qualifications that should be made concerning the SBIDB. The trade journals report mainly product innovations. Thus, as is the case in the studies by Audretsch (1995) and Audretsch and Feldman (1996), the empirical analyses undertaken in this paper capture product innovation but not process innovation.

Another potential concern might be that the significance and 'quality' of the innovations vary considerably. In fact, each innovation was classified according to one of the following levels of significance: (1) the innovation established an entirely new category of product; (2) the innovation is the first of its type on the market in a product category already in existence; (3) the innovation represents a significant improvement in existing technology; and (4) the innovation is a modest improvement designed to update an existing product. About 87% of the innovations were in this fourth category and most of the remaining innovations were classified in the third category. However, the preliminary nature of such classifications leads us to treat the innovations as being homogeneous. While such an assumption will hopefully be improved upon in the future, it is consistent with the voluminous body of literature treating dollars of R&D, numbers of scientists and engineers, and numbers of patents as being homogeneous.[7]

An important strength of the database is that the innovating *establishment* is identified as well as the innovating *enterprise*. While this distinction is trivial for single-plant manufacturing firms, it becomes important in multi-plant firms. This is because some innovations are made by subsidiaries or divisions of companies with headquarters in other states. Even though the headquarters may announce new product innovations made by the company, the database still identifies the individual establishment responsible for the majority of the work leading to the innovation.

---

[7] An anonymous referee points out that the implicit assumption that innovations are homogeneous in their impact is found in most studies attempting to measure innovative activity. As Griliches (1990) emphasizes, this limitation has plagued studies using counts of patents, just as it has in those based on R&D expenditures or R&D scientists and engineers.

The innovations from the SBIDB are then classified according to the four-digit SIC industry of the new product and the city where the innovating establishment was located. We adapt either the Consolidated Metropolitan Statistical Area (CMSA) or the Metropolitan Statistical Area (MSA) as the spatial unit of observation. The analysis here is based on 3969 new manufacturing product innovations for which the address of the innovating establishment could be identified.[8]

In 1982 the most innovative city in the United States was New York. Seven hundred and thirty-five, or 18.5%, of the total number of innovations in the country were attributed to firms in the greater New York City area. Four hundred and seventy-seven (12.0%) were attributed to San Francisco and 345 (8.7%) to the Boston area and 333 (8.4%) to the Los Angeles area. In total, 1890, or 45% of the innovations, took place in these four consolidated metropolitan areas. In fact, all but 150 of the innovations included in the database are attributed to metropolitan areas. That is, less than 4% of the innovations occurred outside of metropolitan areas. This contrasts with the 70% of the population which resided in these areas.

Of course, simply comparing the absolute amount of innovative activity across cities ignores the fact that some cities are simply larger than others. Cities vary considerably in terms of measures of city size, and we expect that city scale will have an impact on innovative output. Table 1 presents the number of innovations normalized by the size of the geographic unit. Population provides a crude but useful measure of the size of the geographic unit. Cities in Table 1 are ranked in descending order by innovation rate or the number of innovations per 100,000 population. While New York has the highest count of innovation, it has the third highest innovation rate. The most innovative city in the United States, on a per capita measure of city size, was San Francisco, with an innovation rate of 8.90, followed by Boston, with an innovation rate of 8.69. By contrast, the mean innovation rate for the entire country is 1.75 innovations per 100,000 population. The distribution of innovation rates is considerably skewed. Only 14 cities are more innovative than the national average. Clearly, innovation appears to be a large city phenomenon.

To systematically identify the degree to which specific industries have a common underlying science and technology base, we rely upon a deductive approach that links products on their closeness in technological space. We use the widely acknowledge and established *Yale Survey of R&D managers*. This survey is documented in great detail in Levin et al. (1987) and has been widely used in studies linking various mechanisms of appropriability to R&D activity (Cohen

---

[8] Feldman (1994) provides a description of the data collection procedure. The results are invariant to using PMSAs.

Table 1
Counts of innovation normalized by population

Consolidated metropolitan statistical area	Innovations (1982)	1980 population (thousands)	Innovations per 100,000 population
San Francisco – Oakland	477	5368	8.886
Boston – Lawrence	345	3972	8.686
New York – Northern New Jersey	735	17539	4.191
Philadelphia – Wilmington	205	5681	3.609
Dallas – Fort Worth	88	2931	3.002
Hartford	30	1014	2.959
Los Angeles – Anaheim	333	11498	2.896
Buffalo – Niagara	35	1243	2.816
Cleveland – Akron	77	2834	2.717
Chicago – Gary	203	7937	2.558
Providence – Pawtucket	25	1083	2.308
Portland – Vancouver	25	1298	1.926
Cincinnati - Hamilton	30	1660	1.807
Seattle – Tacoma	37	2093	1.768
Pittsburgh	42	2423	1.733
Denver – Boulder	28	1618	1.731
Detroit – Ann Arbor	68	4753	1.431
Houston – Galveston	39	3101	1.258
Miami – Fort Lauderdale	13	2644	0.492

Source: 1980 Population is from the Statistical Abstract.

and Levinthal, 1990; Levin et al., 1987). The survey uses a Likert scale of 1 to 7, from least important to most important, to assess the relevance of basic scientific research in biology, chemistry, computer science, physics, mathematics, medicine, geology, mechanical engineering and electrical engineering. We assume any academic discipline with a value greater than 5 to be relevant for a product category. For example, basic scientific research in medicine, chemistry and chemical engineering is found to be relevant for product innovation in drugs (SIC 2834).

We then identify six groups of industries which rely on similar rankings for the importance of the different academic disciplines. These six groups, shown in Table 2, reflect distinct underlying common scientific bases. To facilitate identification of the groupings we assigned a name to each group that reflects not only the underlying science base but also the application to which this knowledge is directed. Thus, what we term as the 'chemical engineering' and 'industrial machinery' groups actually include the same critical academic departments (ranked differently), but applied to different types of industries.

While each industry within the group shares a common scientific base, the geographic space and product space differ across industries. For example, there

Table 2
The common science bases of industry clusters

Cluster	Critical academic departments	Most innovative industries
Agra-business	Chemistry (6.06); Agricultural Science (4.65); Computer Science (4.18); Biology (4.09).	SIC 2013: Sausages SIC 2038: Frozen Specialities SIC 2087: Flavoring Extracts SIC 2092: Packaged Foods
Chemical engineering	Materials Science (5.32); Chemistry (4.80); Computer Science (4.50); Physics (4.12).	SIC 3861: Photographic Equipment SIC 3443: Fabricated Plate Work SIC 2821: Plastic Materials SIC 3559: Special Ind. Machinery
Office machinery	Computer Science (6.75); Medical Science (5.75); Math (5.49); Applied Math (4.64).	SIC 3576: Scales and Balances SIC 3579: Office Machinery SIC 3535: Conveyors SIC 2751: Commerial Printing
Industrial machinery	Materials Science (5.03); Computer Science (4.76); Physics (3.94); Chemistry (3.88).	SIC 3551: Food Processing Equipment SIC 3523: Machinery SIC 3546: Hand Tools SIC 3629: Industrial Apparatus
High-tech computing	Materials Science (5.92); Computer Science (5.63); Physics (5.45); Math (4.76).	SIC 3573: Computing Machinery SIC 3662: Radio/TV Equipment SIC 3823: Process Control Instruments SIC 3674: Semiconductors
Biomedical	Chemistry (5.53); Medical Science (5.47); Computer Science (5.32); Materials Science (5.02).	SIC 3842: Surgical Appliances SIC 3841: Medical Instruments SIC 2834: Pharmaceuticals SIC 3811: Scientific Instruments

are 15 distinct industries included in the biomedical group. On average, each industry contributed 3.22 innovations. Their shared underlying knowledge base consists of chemistry, medical sciences, computer sciences and material sciences. Surgical Appliances (SIC 3842), Surgical and Medical Instruments (SIC 3841), and Pharmaceuticals (SIC 2834) are three of the 15 industries heavily dependent on this common underlying scientific knowledge base. There are 21 industries included in the Agra-Business group, 34 industries included in the Chemical Engineering group, 7 industries in the Office Machinery group and 11 industries included in the Industrial Machinery group. The largest science-based group is what we term High-tech Computing, which includes 80 industries.

The most innovative cities within each science-based industrial cluster are identified in Table 3. This recalls the well-known association between cities and

Table 3
Innovation in science-based industry clusters

Cluster	Prominent cities	Mean industry innovations per 100,000 workers
Agra-business	Atlanta	92.40
	Dallas	41.15
	Chicago	33.03
	St. Louis	91.74
Chemical engineering	Dallas	38.09
	Minneapolis	66.67
	San Francisco	43.89
	Wilmington	85.47
Office machinery	Anaheim-Santa Ana	92.59
	Minneapolis	31.86
	Rochester	72.20
	Stanford	68.40
Industrial machinery	Anaheim-Santa Ana	54.95
	Cincinnati	66.01
	Cleveland	141.51
	Passaic, NJ	90.90
High-tech computing	Boston	73.89
	Houston	62.08
	San Jose	44.88
	Minneapolis	181.74
Biomedical	Boston	38.71
	Cleveland	68.76
	Dallas	35.22
	New York	188.07

industries. For example, Atlanta is a prominent center for innovative activity stemming from the common science base of agra-business. While the national innovation rate was 20.34 innovations per 100,000 manufacturing workers, agra-business in Atlanta was almost five times as innovative.

A Chi-Squared test on the independence of the location of city and science-based industrial activity reveals that neither the distribution of employment nor the distribution of innovative activity is random. Industries which rely on a common science base exhibit a tendency to cluster together geographically with regard to the location of employment and the location of innovation. We conclude that the distribution of innovation within science-based clusters and cities appears to reflect the existence of science-related expertise.

4. Modeling framework

To test the hypothesis that the degree of specialization shapes the innovative output of an industry, we estimate a model where the dependent variable is the number of innovations attributed to a specific four-digit SIC industry in a particular city. To reflect the extent to which economic activity within a city is specialized, we include as an explanatory variable a measure of industry specialization which was used by Glaeser et al. (1992) and is defined as the 1982 share of total employment in the city accounted for by industry employment in the city, divided by the share of United States employment accounted by that particular industry. This variable reflects the degree to which a city is specialized in a particular industry relative to the degree of economic activity in that industry that would occur if employment in the industry were randomly distributed across the United States. A higher value of this measure indicates a greater degree of specialization of the industry in that particular city. Thus, a positive coefficient would indicate that increased specialization within a city is conducive to greater innovative output and would support the *Marshall–Arrow–Romer* thesis. A negative coefficient would indicate that greater specialization within a city impedes innovative output and would support Jacobs' theory that diversity of economic activity is more conducive to innovation than is specialization.

To identify the impact of an increased presence of economic activity in complementary industries, the presence of science-based related industries is included. This measure is constructed analogously to the index of industry specialization, and is defined as the share of total city employment accounted for by employment in the city in industries sharing the science base, divided by the share of total United States employment accounted for by employment in that same science base. This variable measures the presence of complementary industries relative to what the presence would be if those related industries were distributed across the United States. A positive coefficient of the presence of science-based related industries would indicate that a greater presence of complementary industries is conducive to greater innovative output and supports for the diversity thesis. By contrast, a negative coefficient suggests that a greater presence of related industries sharing the same science base impedes innovation and argues against Jacobs' diversity thesis.

The usual concept of product market competition in the industrial organization literature is typically measured in terms of the size-distribution of firms. By contrast, Jacobs' concept of *localized competition* emphasizes the extent of competition for the ideas embodied in individuals. The greater the degree of competition among firms, the greater the extent of specialization among those firms and the easier it will be for individuals to pursue and implement new ideas. Thus, the metric relevant to reflect the degree of localized competition is not the

Table 4
Variable definitions and descriptive statistics

Variable name	Definition	Mean	Standard deviation
Specialization	$\dfrac{\text{Industry employment in city/total employment in city}}{\text{Industry employment in US/total employment in US}}$	0.96	1.47
Science base diversity	$\dfrac{\text{Employment in cluster in city/total employment in city}}{\text{Employment in cluster in US/total employment in US}}$	0.37	0.51
Competition	$\dfrac{\text{Firms in city} - \text{industry/workers in city} - \text{industry}}{\text{Firms in US industry/workers in US industry}}$	0.57	2.08

size of the firms in the region relative to their number (because, after all, many if not most manufacturing product markets are national or at least inter-regional in nature) but rather the number of firms relative to the number of workers. In measuring the extent of localized competition we again adopt a measure used by Glaeser et al. (1992), which is defined as the number of firms per worker in the industry in the city relative to the number of firms per worker in the same industry in the United States. A higher value of this index of localized competition suggests that the industry has a greater number of firms per worker relative to its size in the particular city than it does elsewhere in the United States. Thus, if the index of localized competition exceeds one then the city is locally less competitive than in other American cities.

The data for these measures are from County Business Patterns. Table 4 presents the variable definitions and descriptive statistics for the measures of science-based diversity, specialization and competition.

5. Results

Table 5 presents the regression results based on the 5946 city-industry observations for which data could be collected. The Poisson regression estimation method is used because the dependent variable is a limited dependent variable with a highly skewed distribution.[9]

---

[9] The number of innovations in a city and product category is either zero or some positive integer. The mean of the distribution is 0.26 and the standard deviation is 2.96.

Table 5
Poisson regression estimation results

	Model 1	Model 2	Model 3	Model 4
Industry specialization	−0.209	−0.334	−0.527	−0.142
	(−8.360)	(−14.522)	(−17.684)	(−5.680)
Science-based related	0.168	0.104	0.089	0.069
industries	(3.812)	(2.122)	(2.405)	(2.091)
Localized competition	−0.175	0.576	0.221	0.168
	(−3.365)	(7.481)	(0.269)	(1.976)
City scale		1.044		1.004
		(28.216)		(20.917)
Technological opportunity			0.079	0.034
			(26.333)	(1.700)
n	5946	5946	5946	5946
Log-likelihood	−1296.793	−901.489	−693.046	−652.264

Note: The *t*-values of the coefficient is listed in parentheses.

Model 1 provides the results for the three measures which reflect the degree of specialization, diversity and localized competition. The negative and statistically significant coefficient of industry specialization suggests that innovative activity tends to be lower in industries located in cities specialized in economic activity in that industry. The positive and statistically significant coefficient for science-based related industries indicates that a strong presence of complementary industries sharing a common science base is particularly conducive to innovative activity. Taken together, these results provide support for the diversity thesis but not for the specialization thesis. The negative coefficient on the measure of localized competition suggests that less and not more localized competition promotes the innovative activity of an industry in a particular city.

One concern regarding the estimation of Model 1 is that larger cities might be expected to generate a greater amount of innovation in any particular industry, *ceteris paribus*, simply because of a greater degree of economic activity. In addition, the extent of localized competition might tend to be greater as the size of the city grows. Thus, when the total employment is included in the estimation of Model 2, the sign of the coefficient for localized competition switches from negative to positive, suggesting that a greater degree of localized competition is conducive to innovative activity. At the same time, the signs of the coefficients of the measures of industry specialization and science-based related industries remain unchanged.

Another concern regarding the estimation of Model 1 is that some industries are more innovative, or in a higher technological opportunity class than others. But even after controlling for the number of innovations recorded for the relevant industry in the estimation of Model 3 and Model 4, the basic results remain the same.[10]

The results in Table 5 generally provide support that it is diversity and not specialization that is more conducive to innovation. It should be emphasized here that even after we control for city scale and technological opportunity, specialization appears to have a negative effect on innovation, while science-based diversity has a positive impact on innovative output. In addition, the evidence suggests that a greater extent of localized competition and not monopoly tends to promote innovative output: Of course, the cross-sectional city level data do not provide any insight into whether these patterns are stable over time.

6. Diversity versus specialization at the firm level

The debate between specialization and diversity of economic activity and the impact on technological change is also relevant at the level of the firm and allows a further test of the effects of these influences on innovation. We expect a similar result in the organization of innovation within the firm – undertaking innovative activity across a range of science-based complementary activities will lead to greater innovative output than concentrating innovative activity within one industry. With this test we seek to ascertain if analogous processes operate at both the firm and the geographic level.

Jewkes et al. (1958) examined the histories of 61 innovations and found that a variety of different approaches within the firm are often pursued. It appears that diversity in terms of the number and the type of approaches used serves to reduce the uncertainty inherent in innovation by providing a greater number of unique ideas and outcomes. In an empirical examination of this question, Cohen and Malerba (1995) find a strong relationship between technological diversity and the rate of technical advance at the industry level. Our consideration of specialization examines the degree to which the firm focuses its innovative activity on one product category.

In order to model the effects of science-based diversity and specialization at the level, we follow the pioneering study of Scherer (1983) to estimate a

---

[10] The extent to which these relationships are non-linear was examined in the estimation with the inclusion of quadratic terms for industry specialization and localized competition. The results indicate that, in fact, cities which are highly specialized in economic activity may actually generate more innovative output in that industry. This result does not hold when city scale is included. It appears that scale is more important than the rate of change in the degree of specialization. The quadratic of localized competition suggests that there may be increasing returns to innovative output resulting for increased localized competition. Again, this result does not hold when urban scale is considered.

non-linear model which links R&D[11] to innovative output:

$$I_i = \alpha + \beta_1 RD_i + \beta_2 RD_i^2 + \beta_3 Innovative\ Diversity_i$$

$$+ \beta_4 Innovative\ Specialization_i + \varepsilon,$$

where I represents the total number of innovations attributed to firm I in the 1982 SBIDB.[12] RD represents the R&D expenditures of firm I.[13] To measure the extent to which the innovative activity of firm I is diversified across related product categories we calculate the share of innovations in the same common science base product categories divided by the total number of innovations introduced by the firm. Similarly, specialization, or own industry share, is measured as the proportion's of the firm's innovative activity in the primary industry identified with the firm.

R&D expenditures are taken from the *Business Week* 1975 sample of over 700 corporations for which R&D expenditures play an important role. An important feature of this sample is that it included more than 95% of the total company R&D expenditures undertaken in the United States. There is a seven year lag between the 1982 innovations and the 1975 R&D expenditures. This lag may be somewhat long in view of a number of studies in the literature. However, as long as firm R&D expenditures are relatively stable over a short period of time, differences in the assumed lag structure should not greatly impact the results.[14]

Table 6 indicates the most innovative firms in the database along with the corresponding R&D expenditures, sales, R&D/sales ratio and the number of innovations per R&D dollar. As we might expect a positive relationship can be observed between the size of the R&D budget and innovative output, but there is also great variation in the productivity of R&D. Some firms such as Data General appear to obtain a relatively high degree of innovation per R&D dollar expended. Other firms such as General Electric and RCA exhibit a considerably lower R&D yield.

The regression results from estimating the model of firm innovative activity are shown in Table 7. The positive relationship between R&D inputs and

---

[11] R&D is generally observed to be the most decisive source of economic knowledge generating innovative activity.

[12] A log-log specification was estimated as well as the quadratic specification. The results for both specifications are consistent. We only report the results from the quadratic equations to facilitate comparisons with the earlier studies mentioned in the text.

[13] Note that the firm-level models are for the entire country and not for MSAs or states. It is not possible to identify firm-level R&D by location at this point.

[14] As an anonymous referee emphasizes, future research needs to explore distributed lags between R&D and innovative output.

Table 6
Firm innovation

	Number of innovations	R&D expenditure ($ million)	Sales ($ million)	R&D/ sales ratio	Innovation/ R&D[a]
Hewlett Packard Company	55	981.00	89.6	9.1	5.61
Minnesota Mining & Mfg.	40	3127.00	143.4	4.6	1.28
General Electric	36	13399.00	357.1	2.7	0.27
General Signal	29	548.00	21.2	3.9	5.29
National Semiconductor	27	235.00	20.7	8.8	11.49
Xerox	25	4054.00	198.6	4.9	0.62
Texas Instruments	24	1368.00	51.0	3.7	1.75
Pitney Bowes	22	461.00	10.5	2.3	4.77
RCA	21	4790.00	113.6	2.4	0.44
IBM	21	14437.00	946.0	6.6	0.15
Digital Equipment	21	534.00	48.5	9.1	3.93
Gould	20	773.00	23.1	3.0	2.59
Motorola	19	13112.00	98.5	7.5	1.45
Wheelabrator Frye	18	332.00	2.0	0.6	5.42
United Technologies	18	3878.00	323.7	8.3	0.46
Hoover	18	594.00	4.3	0.7	3.03
Honeywell	18	2760.00	164.2	5.9	0.65
Rockwell International	17	4943.00	31.0	0.6	0.34
Johnson & Johnson	17	2225.00	97.9	4.4	0.76
Eastman Kodak	17	4959.00	312.9	6.3	0.34
Data General	17	108.00	11.6	10.8	15.74
Exxon	16	4486.05	187.0	0.4	0.36
Du Pont	16	7222.00	335.7	4.6	0.22
Stanley Works	15	464.00	3.5	0.7	3.23
Sperry Rand	15	3041.00	163.5	5.4	0.49
Pennwalt	15	714.00	15.7	2.2	2.10
North American Philips	14	1410.00	22.5	1.6	0.99
Harris	14	479.00	21.1	4.4	2.92
General Motors	14	3572.05	1113.9	3.1	0.39

[a] Scaled by 100.

innovative output can be observed in Model 1. The negative coefficient of the quadratic term suggests that although innovative output tends to respond positively to increased investments in R&D inputs, the rate of increase in innovative output diminishes as R&D inputs increase.

When the measure of innovation diversity within industries sharing a common science base is included in Model 2, the positive coefficient provides support for the hypothesis that diversification across complementary economic activities is conducive to greater innovative output. When the measure of innovation specialization is included in Model 3, the positive coefficient suggests

Table 7
Regression results estimating firm innovative activity

	1	2	3	4
R&D	0.02804	0.0119	0.0178	0.0081
	(6.051)	(3.320)	(1.624)	(2.481)
R&D^2	−1.6945	−0.4157	−0.8940	−0.0323
	(−2.603)	(−0.878)	(−1.732)	(−0.075)
Innovative diversity	–	3.3081	–	9.2466
		(9.510)		(9.988)
Innovative specialization	–	–	2.8116	−7.4357
			(6.218)	(−6.819)
Number of observations	209	203	203	203
R^2	0.189	0.466	0.350	0.568
F	23.980	57.905	35.677	64.980

Notes: The t-value of the coefficient is listed in parentheses. The coefficients of R&D^2 have been divided by 100,000 for presentation purposes.

that greater specialization in innovation yields greater innovative output. When both specialization and diversity are included together in Model 4, the coefficient of specialization exhibits a negative coefficient suggesting that greater innovation specialization is less conducive to greater innovative output. On the other hand, holding R&D expenditures constant, greater innovative diversity within the common science base results in more innovative output.

The firms can also be grouped according to major two-digit SIC sectors. Results for six specific industrial sectors are listed in Table 8. There is interesting variation in these results across manufacturing sectors. For example, in instruments and telecommunications diminishing returns to R&D inputs can be observed. By contrast, increasing returns to R&D can be observed in the group of firms classified as conglomerates, and in electrical equipment and transportation no significant relationship can be observed between R&D and innovative output.

While the links between R&D inputs and innovative output vary substantially across sectors in Table 8, the relationships between specialization, innovation diversity and innovation remain remarkably constant across sectors. For all six sectors the coefficient of the measure of science-based innovation diversity remains positive and statistically significant, and the coefficient of the measure of innovation specialization also remains negative and statistically significant in all six sectors. Thus, the main finding that diversity in innovation activities within a common science base tends to promote innovative output more than does the specialization of innovation within just one single industry holds across a broad range of industrial sectors.

Table 8
Regression estimating firm innovative activity for specific sectors

Sector	R&D	R&D^2	Innovative diversity	Innovative specialization	n	R^2	F
Instruments	0.1796	−46.7294	7.7780	−7.3747	23	0.756	13.918
	(2.863)	(−2.344)	(3.167)	(−2.311)			
Telecommunications	0.0426	−81.0826	12.1458	−10.5068	31	0.681	13.857
	(1.757)	(−1.955)	(3.995)	(−2.888)			
Pharmaceuticals	0.0579	−21.2919	5.0999	−4.1984	24	0.732	12.951
	(1.162)	(−0.496)	(1.840)	(−1.501)			
Electrical	0.0328	−2.6788	11.8368	−9.5924	27	0.694	12.455
equipment	(0.908)	(−0.249)	(3.471)	(−2.310)			
Transportation	0.0025	0.5888	10.1231	−8.7190	20	0.859	22.934
	(0.357)	(0.880)	(4.985)	(−3.960)			
Conglomerates	−0.1074	0.0019	7.5160	−5.5113	25	0.926	62.866
	(−2.671)	(6.970)	(3.941)	(−2.671)			

Notes: The t-value of each coefficient is listed in parentheses. The coefficients of R&D^2 are multiplied by 100,000 for presentation purposes.

Table 9
Regression results estimating firm innovative activity for specific science bases

	High-tech computing (1)	High-tech computing (2)	Biomedical (3)	Biomedical (4)
R&D	0.0100	0.0059	0.6000	0.0501
	(2.293)	(1.497)	(2.056)	(1.723)
R&D^2	−0.2928	−0.1683	−25.7484	−18.6446
	(−0.522)	(0.300)	(−1.222)	(−0.889)
Innovation share within science base	3.7691	9.8348	1.4761	5.2878
	(7.831)	(8.524)	(1.925)	(2.120)
Innovation share within industry	–	−8.2150	–	−4.0457
		(−5.670)		(−1.601)
Number of observations	134	134	32	32
R^2	0.454	0.563	0.680	0.708
F	35.983	41.493	35.677	64.980

Notes: The t-value of the coefficient is listed in parentheses. The coefficients of R&D^2 have been divided by 100,000 for presentation purposes.

The results are confirmed in Table 9, which groups the firms according to two of the largest science bases – high-tech computing and biomedical products. Not only is the knowledge production function found to hold for firms in each of these distinct science bases, but again, diversity in innovation across economic activities with a common science base is found to increase innovation.

7. Conclusions

The nature and utility of knowledge is at the heart of the economics of R&D, innovation and technological change. Whether diversity or specialization of economic activities better promotes technological change has been the subject of a heated debate in the economics literature. This paper has attempted to shed light on that debate by linking the extent of diversity versus specialization of economic activities to innovative output. By focusing on innovative activity for particular industries at specific locations, we find compelling evidence that specialization of economic activity does not promote innovative output. Rather, the results indicate that diversity across complementary economic activities sharing a common science base is more conducive to innovation than is specialization. In addition, the results indicate that the degree of local competition for new ideas within a city is more conducive to innovative activity than is local monopoly.

A second perspective explored in this paper is the effect of diversity and specialization at the firm level. The results indicate that innovative activity tends to be lower when that innovation is specialized within a narrow industry than when it is diversified across a complementary set of industries sharing a common science base. Thus, the results at both the level of the firm as well as for the industry across geographic space present a consistent view of the returns to specialization versus diversity of economic activity. Our results suggest that diversity across complementary industries sharing a common base – a crucial qualification – results in greater returns to R&D.[15]

Increasingly scholars of technological change realize that external sources of knowledge are critical to innovation. Our results suggest that the boundaries of the firm are but one means to organize and harness knowledge. An analogous means of organizing economic activity are spatially defined boundaries. Geographic location may provide another useful set of boundaries within which to organize innovation. Geography may provide a platform upon which knowledge may be effectively organized.

---

[15] We underscore the descriptive nature of these results since there may be alternative explanations. Specifically, the relationships may be endogenous in a way that we have not considered. Firms which are more innovative may be more profitable and therefore, more likely to be able to engage in diverse activities. Similarly, regions which are successful at innovation in one industry may attract other activities. The cross-sectional nature of the data we use here does not allow us to examine these issues.

Acknowledgements

We are grateful to the comments and suggestions of two anonymous referees and an editor of this journal, Elhanan Helpman. An earlier version of this paper was presented at the Center for Economic Policy Research (CEPR) conference on R&D Spillovers at Lausanne, Switzerland, 27–28 January 1995 and at the 1997 annual meetings of the American Economic Association at San Francisco. We would like to thank Zvi Griliches, Bronwyn Hall, Frank Lichtenberg and F.M. Scherer for their comments and suggestions.

References

Arrow, K.J., 1962. Economic welfare and the allocation of resources for innovation. In: Nelson, R.R. (Ed.), The Rate and Direction of Inventive Activity. Princeton University Press, Princeton, NJ, pp. 609–626.

Audretsch, D.B., 1995. Innovation and Industry Evolution. MIT Press, Cambridge.

Audretsch, D.B., Feldman, M.P., 1996. R&D spillovers and the geography of innovation and production. American Economic Review 86 (3), 630–640.

Audretsch, D.B., Stephan, P.E., 1996. Company-scientist locational links: The case of biotechnology. American Economic Review 86, 641–652.

Cohen, W., Levinthal, D., 1990. Absorptive capacity: A new perspective on learning and innovation. Administrative Science Quarterly 35, 1288–1352.

Cohen, W.M., Malerba, F., 1995. Is the tendency to variation a chief cause of progress? Unpublished manuscript, Carnegie-Mellon University.

Feldman, M.P., 1994. The Geography of Innovation. Kluwer Academic Publishers, Boston.

Feldman, M.P., Florida, R., 1994. The geographic sources of innovation: Technological infrastructure and product innovation in the United States. Annals of the Association of American Geographers 84, 210–229.

Glaeser, E.L., Kallal, H.D., Scheinkman, J.A., Shleifer, A., 1992. Growth of cities. Journal of Political Economy 100, 1126–1152.

Griliches, Z., 1990. Patent statistics as economic indicator: A survey. Journal of Economic Literature 28, 1661–1707.

Griliches, Z., 1992. The search for R&D spill-overs. Scandinavian Journal of Economics 94, 29–47.

Jacobs, J., 1969. The Economy of Cities. Random House, New York.

Jaffe, A.B., 1989. Real effects of academic research. American Economic Review 79, 957–970.

Jaffe, A.B., Trajtenberg, M., Henderson, R., 1993. Geographic localization of knowledge spillovers as evidenced by patent citations. Quarterly Journal of Economics 63, 577–598.

Jewkes, J., Sawers, D., Stillerman, M., 1958. The Sources of Innovation. MacMillan, London.

Krugman, P., 1991a. Increasing returns and economic geography. Journal of Political Economy 99, 483–499.

Krugman, P., 1991b. Geography and Trade. MIT Press, Cambridge.

Levin, R.C., Klevorick, A.K., Nelson R.R., Winter, S.G., 1987. Appropriating the returns from industrial research and development. Brooking Papers on Economic Activity, 783–820.

Loesch, A., 1954. The Economics of Location. Yale University Press, New Haven.

Lucas, R.E. Jr., 1993. Making a miracle. Econometrica 61, 251–272.

Mansfield, E.J., 1984. Comment on using linked patent and R&D data to measure interindustry technology flows. In: Griliches, Z. (Ed.), R&D, Patents and Productivity. University of Chicago Press, Chicago, pp. 415–418.

Pakes, A., Griliches, Z., 1984. Patents and R&D at the firm level: A first look. In: Griliches, Z. (Ed.), R&D, Patents and Productivity. University of Chicago Press, Chicago, pp. 139–161.

Porter, M.P., 1990. The Comparative Advantage of Nations. The Free Press, New York.

Reynolds, P., Storey, D., Westhead, P., 1994. Cross-national comparisons of the variation in new firm formation rates. Regional Studies 28, 443–456.

Romer, P., 1990. Endogenous technological Change. Journal of Political Economy 94 (1), 71–102.

Romer, P., 1986. Increasing returns and long-run growth. Journal of Political Economy 94 (5), 1002–1037.

Scherer, F.M., 1983. The propensity to patent. International Journal of Industrial Organization 1 (1), 107–128.

Von Hipple, E., 1994. Sticky information and the locus of problem solving: Implications for innovation. Management Science 40, 429–439.

[13]

KNOWLEDGE SPILLOVERS AND THE GEOGRAPHY OF INNOVATION

DAVID B. AUDRETSCH[1]

Max-Planck-Institut für die Erforschung von Wirtschaftssystemen, Germany
e-mail: audretsch@mpiew-jena.mpg.de

MARYANN P. FELDMAN

University of Toronto, Toronto, Canada
e-mail: maryann.feldman@rotman.utoronto.ca

Contents

[1] Also affiliated with CEPR.

Handbook of Regional and Urban Economics, Volume 4. Edited by J.V. Henderson and J.F. Thisse
DOI: 10.1016/S0169-7218(04)07061-3

Abstract

This chapter focuses on the geographic dimensions of knowledge spillovers. The starting point comes from the economics of innovation and technological change. This tradition focused on the innovation production function however it was aspatial or insensitive to issues involving location and geography. However, empirical results hinted that knowledge production had a spatial dimension. Armed with a new theoretical understanding about the role and significance of knowledge spillovers and the manner in which they are localized, scholars began to estimate the knowledge production function with a spatial dimension. Location and geographic space have become key factors in explaining the determinants of innovation and technological change. The chapter also identifies new insights that have sought to penetrate the black box of geographic space by addressing a limitation inherent in the model of the knowledge production. These insights come from a rich tradition of analyzing the role of both localization and urbanization economies, by extending the focus to the organization of economic activity within a spatial dimension and examine how different organizational aspects influence economic performance. While the endogenous growth theory emphasizes the importance of investments in research and development and human capital, a research agenda needs to be mapped out identifying the role that investments in spillover conduits can make in generating economic growth. It may be that a mapping of the process by which new knowledge is created, externalized and commercialized, hold the key to providing the microeconomic linkages to endogenous macroeconomic growth.

Keywords

spillovers, knowledge, clusters, entrepreneurship, innovation, technological change, regions

JEL classification: O3, R1

1. Introduction

In proposing a new theory of economic geography, Paul Krugman (1991, p. 55) asks: "What is the most striking feature of the geography of economic activity? The short answer is surely concentration... production is remarkably concentrated in space". Feldman (1994a) provided evidence that what Krugman observed to be true for production was even more pronounced for innovative activity. This finding helped trigger a new literature with the goal of *understanding the spatial dimension of innovative activity*, specifically the determinants and mechanisms that underlie the propensity of innovative activity to cluster spatially. Knowledge spillovers figure prominently in addressing these issues. This chapter introduces the reader to the path that scholars have taken to understand the geographic dimensions of knowledge spillovers.

The starting point on this intellectual journey is the literature that analyzes the economics of innovation and technological change. This tradition, reviewed in Section 2, focused on the innovation production function; however, it was *aspatial* or insensitive to issues involving location and geography. However, empirical results hinted that knowledge production had a spatial dimension. Armed with a new theoretical understanding about the role and significance of knowledge spillovers and the manner in which they are localized, scholars began to estimate the knowledge production function with a spatial dimension.

As Section 3 makes clear, *location and geographic space have become key factors in explaining the determinants of innovation and technological change*. There is a long and insightful literature that considers the spatial dimension of innovative activity and the factors that influence industrial clustering. A piece that had been missing in this older tradition was the role that knowledge spillovers play in providing access to new economic knowledge and increasing the productivity of economic actors.

Section 4 examines studies that have sought to penetrate the black box of geographic space by addressing a limitation inherent in the model of the knowledge production. These studies follow a rich tradition dating back at least to Hoover Jr. (1936) of analyzing the role of both localization and urbanization economies, by extending the focus to the organization of economic activity within a spatial dimension and examine how different organizational aspects influence economic performance.

While identifying the importance of geographic location in general, and agglomeration in particular, was a significant step in generating innovative activity, it provided little insight as to *how and why knowledge spills over*, nor did it illuminate the mechanisms that serve as conduits for the transmission of knowledge. Section 5 considers various potential spillover mechanisms and studies that examine these different mechanisms.

Section 6 examines one spillover mechanism which has generated a large body of research – entrepreneurship. Just as entrepreneurs have been found to originate in locations with strong knowledge assets, empirical evidence suggests that high rates of entrepreneurial activity contribute to higher growth performance. Finally, the last section provides a summary and conclusion.

2. The knowledge production function

The traditional starting point in the literature on innovation and technological change for most theories of innovation has been the firm [Baldwin and Scott (1987), Cohen and Levin (1989), Scherer (1984, 1991), Griliches (1979)]. In such theories firms are exogenous and their performance in generating technological change is endogenous [Scherer (1984, 1991), Cohen and Klepper (1991, 1992)]. For example, in the most prevalent model of technological change, the model of the knowledge production function [Griliches (1979)], incumbent firms engage in the pursuit of new economic knowledge as an input into the process of generating innovative activity. The most important input in this model is new economic knowledge. As Cohen and Klepper (1991, 1992) point out, the greatest source generating new economic knowledge is generally considered to be R&D. Other inputs in the knowledge production function have included measures of human capital, skilled labor, and educational levels. Thus, the model of the knowledge production function from the literature on innovation and technological change can be represented as

$$I_i = \alpha RD_i^\beta HK_i^\gamma \varepsilon_i,\tag{1}$$

where I stands for the degree of innovative activity, RD represents R&D inputs, and HK represents human capital inputs. The unit of observation for estimating the model of the knowledge production function, reflected by the subscript i, has been at the level of countries, industries and enterprises.

The logic of the production function held: innovative output was a function of innovative inputs. However, empirical estimation of the model of the knowledge production function, represented by Equation (1), was found to be stronger at broader levels of aggregation such as countries or industries. For example, at the unit of observation of countries, the empirical evidence [Griliches (1984)] clearly supported the existence of the knowledge production function. This is intuitively understandable, because the most innovative countries are those with the greatest investments to R&D. Less innovative output is associated with developing countries, which are characterized by a paucity of new economic knowledge. Similarly, the model of the knowledge production function was strong at the level of the industry [Scherer (1984), Griliches (1984)]. Again, this seems obvious as the most innovative industries also tend to be characterized by considerable investments in R&D and new economic knowledge. Not only are industries such as computers, pharmaceuticals and instruments high in R&D inputs that generate new economic knowledge, but also in terms of innovative outputs [Acs and Audretsch (1990)]. By contrast, industries with little R&D, such as wood products, textiles and paper, also tend to produce only a negligible amount of innovative output.

Where the relationship became less robust was at the disaggregated microeconomic level of the enterprise, establishment, or even line of business: there is no direct deterministic relationship between inputs and innovation.[2] Thus, the finding that the knowledge production model linking knowledge generating inputs to outputs holds at the more aggregated levels of economic activity suggests the presence of an externality.

The model of the knowledge production function also became less compelling in view of a wave of studies that found that small enterprises were an engine of innovative activity in certain industries. For example, Acs and Audretsch (1988, 1990) found that while large enterprises (defined as having at least 500 employees) generated a greater number of new product innovations than did small firms (defined as having fewer than 500 employees), once the measures were standardized by levels of employment, the innovative intensity of small enterprises was found to exceed that of large firms.[3] These results are startling, because as Scherer (1991) documented, the bulk of industrial R&D is undertaken in the largest corporations; and small enterprises account only for a minor share of R&D inputs. This raises the question of *how small firms obtained access to R&D inputs.* Either the model of the knowledge production did not hold, at least at the level of the enterprise (for a broad spectrum across the firm-size distribution), or else the appropriate unit of observation had to be reconsidered. In searching for a solution, scholars chose the second interpretation, leading them to move towards spatial units of observation as an important unit of analysis for the model of the knowledge production function.

3. Geography and the role of spillovers

As it became apparent that the firm was not completely adequate as a unit of analysis for estimating the model of the knowledge production function, scholars began to look for externalities. In refocusing the model of the knowledge production to a spatial unit of observation, scholars confronted two challenges. The first one was theoretical. What was the theoretical basis for knowledge to spill over yet, at the same time, be spatially within some geographic unit of observation? The second challenge involved measurement. How could knowledge spillovers be measured and identified? More than

---

[2]   For example, while Acs and Audretsch (1988, 1990) found that the simple correlation between R&D inputs and innovative output was 0.84 for four-digit standard industrial classification (SIC) manufacturing industries in the United States, it was only about half, 0.40 among the largest U.S. corporations.

[3]   The innovation rates, or the number of innovations per thousand employees, have the advantage of measuring large- and small-firm innovative activity relative to the presence of large and small firms in any given industry. That is, in making a direct comparison between large- and small-firm innovative activities, the absolute number of innovations contributed by large firms and small enterprises is somewhat misleading, since these measures are not standardized by the relative presence of large and small firms in each industry. When a direct comparison is made between the innovative activity of large and small firms, the innovation rates are presumably a more reliable measure of innovative intensity because they are weighted by the relative presence of small and large enterprises in any given industry. Thus, while large firms in manufacturing introduced 2445 innovations, and small firms contributed slightly fewer, 1954, small-firm employment was only half as great as large-firm employment, yielding an average small-firm innovation rate in manufacturing of 0.309, compared to a large-firm innovation rate of 0.202.

a few scholars heeded Krugman's warning (1991, p. 53) that empirical measurement of knowledge spillovers would prove to be impossible because "knowledge flows are invisible, they leave no paper trail by which they may be measured and tracked".[4]

In confronting the first challenge, which involved developing a theoretical basis for geographically bounded knowledge spillovers, scholars turned to the emerging literature of the new growth theory. In explaining the increased divergence in the distribution of economic activity between countries and regions, Krugman (1991) and Romer (1986) relied on models based on increasing returns to scale in production. By increasing returns, however, Krugman and Romer did not necessarily mean at the level of observation most familiar in the industrial organization literature – the plant, or at least the firm – but rather at the level of a spatially distinguishable unit. In fact, it was assumed that the externalities across firms and even industries would generate increasing returns in production. In particular, Krugman (1991), invoking Marshall (1920), focused on "external increasing returns" arising from spillovers from: (i) a pooled labor market; (ii) pecuniary externalities enabling the provision of non-traded inputs to an industry in a greater variety and at lower cost; and (iii) information or technological spillovers.

That knowledge spills over was barely disputed. Some thirty years earlier, Arrow (1962) identified externalities associated with knowledge due to its non-exclusive and non-rival use. However, what has been contested is the geographic range of knowledge spillovers: knowledge externalities are so important and forceful that there is no reason that knowledge should stop spilling over just because of borders, such as a city limit, state line, or national boundary. Krugman (1991), and others, did not question the existence or importance of such knowledge spillovers. In fact, they argue that such knowledge externalities are so important and forceful that there is no reason for a political boundary to limit the spatial extent of the spillover.

In applying the model of the knowledge production function to spatial units of observation, theories of why knowledge externalities are spatially bounded were needed. Thus, it took the development of localization theories explaining not only that knowledge spills over but also why those spillovers decay as they move across geographic space. An older but insightful literature addressed these concerns.

Jacobs (1969), writing about cities, suggests that *information*, such as the price of gold on the New York Stock Exchange, or the value of the Yen in London, has a familiar meaning and interpretation. By contrast, *knowledge* or what is sometimes referred to as *tacit knowledge*, is vague, difficult to codify and often only serendipitously recognized. While information is codified and can be formalized, written down, tacit knowledge, by definition, is non-codifiable and cannot be formalized and written down. Geographic proximity matters in transmitting knowledge, because tacit knowledge is inherently non-rival in nature, and knowledge developed for any particular application

---

[4] Lucas (2001) and Lucas and Rossi-Hansberg (2002) impose a spatial structure on production externalities in order to model the spatial structure of cities. The logic is that spatial gradients capture some of the externalities associated with localized human capital accumulation.

can easily spill over and have economic value in very different applications. Manski (2000) considers that many of the interactions in R&D and human capital formation that are important to endogenous growth theory occur in non-market environments and are influenced by the expectations, preferences and constraints of related economic agents. Moreover, social interactions have economic value in transmitting knowledge and ideas. Von Hipple (1994) explains that high context, uncertain knowledge, or what he terms *sticky knowledge*, is best transmitted via face-to-face interaction and through frequent and repeated contact. An implication of the distinction between information and tacit knowledge is that the marginal cost of transmitting information across geographic space has been rendered invariant by the revolution in telecommunications while *the marginal cost of transmitting knowledge, especially tacit knowledge, is lowest with frequent social interaction, observation and communication*. After all, geographic proximity matters in transmitting knowledge, because as Glaeser et al. (1992, p. 1126) observe, "intellectual breakthroughs must cross hallways and streets more easily than oceans and continents".

Feldman (1994a, 1994b) developed the theory that location mitigates the inherent uncertainty of innovative activity: *proximity enhances the ability of firms to exchange ideas and be cognizant of important incipient knowledge*, hence reducing uncertainty for firms that work in new fields. Innovation clusters spatially where knowledge externalities reduce the costs of scientific discovery and commercialization. In addition, Feldman (1994a) suggests that firms producing innovations tend to be located in areas where there are necessary resources: resources that have accumulated due to a region's past success with innovation. In this way, firms and resources are endogenous.

Studies identifying the extent of knowledge spillovers are based on the model of the knowledge production function applied at spatial units of observation. In what is generally to be considered to be the first important study re-focusing the knowledge production function, Jaffe (1989) modified the traditional approach to estimate a model specified for both spatial and product dimensions:

$$I_{si} = \alpha IRD^{\beta_1} * UR_{si}^{\beta_2} * \left(UR_{si} * GC_{si}^{\beta_3} \right) * \varepsilon_{si}, \tag{2}$$

where I is innovative output, IRD is private corporate expenditures on R&D, UR is the research expenditures undertaken at universities, and GC measures the geographic coincidence of university and corporate research. The unit of observation for estimation was at the spatial level, s, a state, and industry level, i. Estimation of Equation (2) essentially shifted the knowledge production function from the unit of observation of a firm to that of a geographic unit. Implicitly contained within the knowledge production function model is the assumption that innovative activity should take place in those regions, s, where the direct knowledge-generating inputs are the greatest, and where knowledge spillovers are the most prevalent. Jaffe (1989) dealt with the measurement problem raised by Krugman (1991) by linking the patent activity within technologies located within states to knowledge inputs located within the same spatial jurisdiction.

Estimation of Equation (1) essentially shifted the model of the knowledge production function from the unit of observation of a firm to that of a geographic unit. Jaffe (1989) found empirical evidence that $\beta_1 \geqslant 0$, $\beta_2 \geqslant 0$, $\beta_3 \geqslant 0$ supporting the notion knowledge spills over for third-party use from university research laboratories as well as industry R&D laboratories. Acs, Audretsch and Feldman (1992) confirmed that the knowledge production function represented by Equation (2) held at a spatial unit of observation using a direct measure of innovative activity, new product introductions in the market. Feldman (1994b) extended the model to consider other knowledge inputs to the commercialization of new products. The results confirmed that the knowledge production function was robust at the geographic level of analysis: the output of innovation is a function of the innovative inputs in that location.

Other studies concur that knowledge spillovers tend to be geographically bounded within the region where new economic knowledge was created [Agrawal (2002a, 2002b), Anselin, Acs and Varga (1997), Black (2003), Orlando (2000), Autant-Bernard (2001a, 2001b)]. Scholars have continued to work in this tradition adding new measures of innovative output and refining the measures of innovative inputs and outputs. For example, Black (2003) developed a measure of innovation based on awards made in the United States Small Business Innovation Research (SBIR) Program. In estimating a knowledge production function along the lines of Equation (2) for a variety of geographic units and using different measure of innovative output, the results concur that the logic of the knowledge production function is robust across geography. Autant-Bernard (2001a, 2001b) and Orlando (2000) model the interplay between geographic and technological proximity for inter-firm spillovers. Their results suggest the importance of geographic proximity for spillovers is dependent on the propensity of similar industrial activity to agglomerate geographically.

Estimation of the knowledge production function has typically varied the spatial unit from relatively broad geographic units of observations, such as states, to much more focused geographic units of observations such as cities, counties or even zip codes. Most scholars concur that states are probably too broad to represent an appropriate geographic unit of observation. Some have tried to estimate the geographic extent of knowledge spillovers in miles using the concept of distance decay [Adams and Jaffe (2002), Adams (2002), Wallsten (2001)]. Others contend that geography is more a platform for organizing economic activity and that "as the crow flies" measures of distance do not capture complex social relationships [Feldman (2002), Branstetter (2002)]. The role of social relationships will be explicitly discussed when we examine the literature on industrial districts.

There are also good reasons to believe that knowledge spillovers are not homogeneous across firms [Feldman (1993)]. In estimating Equation (1) for large and small enterprises separately, Acs, Audretsch and Feldman (1994) provide some insight into the puzzle about how small, and frequently new, firms able to generate innovative output while undertaking generally negligible amounts of investment into knowledge generating inputs, such as R&D. The answer appears to be through exploiting knowledge created by expenditures on research in universities and on R&D in large corporations. Their findings suggest that the innovative output of all firms rises along with an increase in the amount of R&D inputs, both in private corporations as well as in university laboratories.

However, R&D expenditures made by private companies play a particularly important role in providing knowledge inputs to the innovative activity of large firms, while expenditures on research made by universities serve as an especially key input for generating innovative activity in small enterprises. Apparently large firms are more adept at exploiting knowledge created in their own laboratories, while their smaller counterparts have a comparative advantage at exploiting spillovers from university laboratories.

Jaffe, Trajtenberg and Henderson (1993) and Jaffe and Trajtenberg (2002) analyze patent families – patents that reference or cite each other and indicate the flows of knowledge from one invention to another.[5] Specifically, they compare the probabilities of patents citing prior patents with inventors from the same city against a randomly drawn control sample of cited patents. Their results suggest that citations are significantly more localized than the control group. The same methodology has been applied by Almeida and Kogut (1997) to study patenting in the semiconductor industry. The basic results agree: patent citations are highly localized, indicating that location and proximity clearly matter in exploiting knowledge spillovers.

Audretsch and Feldman (1996) found that the propensity of innovative activity to cluster geographically tends to be greater in industries where new economic knowledge plays a more important role. This effect was found to hold even after holding the degree of production at that location constant. Audretsch and Feldman (1996) follow Krugman's (1991) example, and calculate Gini coefficients for the geographic concentration of innovative activity to test this relationship.[6] The results indicate that a key determinant of the extent to which the location of production is geographically concentrated is the relative importance of new economic knowledge in the industry. Even after controlling for the geographic concentration of production, the results suggest a greater propensity for innovative activity to cluster spatially in industries in which industry R&D, university research and skilled labor are important inputs. In this work, skilled labor is included as a mechanism by which knowledge spillovers may be realized as workers move between jobs in an industry taking their accumulated skills and know-how with them.

The spatial distribution of innovative output can be seen in Table 1. The measure of innovative output is new product innovations introduced to the U.S. market. The majority of new product innovations were located in cities indicating that innovation is an

---

5 Griliches (1990) provides a survey of the uses and limitations of patent data.

6 The Gini coefficients are weighted by the relative share of economic activity located in each state. Computation of weighted Gini coefficients enables us to control for size differences across states. The Gini coefficients are based on the share of activity in a state and industry relative to the state share of the national activity for the industry. The locational Gini coefficients for production are based on industry value-added. We calculate the amount of value added in an industry and a state divided by national value-added for the industry. This ratio is normalized by the state share of total manufacturing value-added in order to account for the overall distribution of manufacturing activity. An industry which is not geographically concentrated more than is reflected by the overall distribution of manufacturing value-added would have a coefficient of 0. The closer the industry coefficient is to 1, the more geographically concentrated the industry would be. Cases is which data are suppressed are omitted from the analysis. The Gini coefficients for innovation are based on counts of innovation in a state and industry are calculated in a similar way.

Table 1
Innovative activity in cities

Consolidated metropolitan statistical area	Innovations	Population (thousands)	Innovations per 100,000 population
San Francisco–Oakland	477	5368	8.886
Boston–Lawrence	345	3972	8.686
New York–Northern New Jersey	735	17,539	4.191
Philadelphia–Wilmington	205	5681	3.609
Dallas–Fort Worth	88	2931	3.002
Hartford	30	1014	2.959
Los Angeles–Anaheim	333	11,498	2.896
Buffalo–Niagara	35	1243	2.816
Cleveland–Akron	77	2834	2.717
Chicago–Gary	203	7937	2.558
Providence–Pawtucket	25	1083	2.308
Portland–Vancouver	25	1298	1.926
Cincinnati–Hamilton	30	1660	1.807
Seattle–Tacoma	37	2093	1.768
Pittsburgh	42	2423	1.733
Denver–Boulder	28	1618	1.731
Detroit–Ann Arbor	68	4753	1.431
Houston–Galveston	39	3101	1.258
Miami–Fort Lauderdale	13	2644	0.492

Source. Feldman and Audretsch (1999).

Table 2
The innovative advantage of U.S. cities (MSA and count)

	Industry	N	Most innovative MSA
3573	Electronic computing machinery	787	San Jose (166); Boston (48); Los Angeles (48); Anaheim (35)
3823	Process control instruments	464	Boston (45); Philadelphia (31); Chicago (26)
3662	Radio/TV equipment	311	San Jose (58); Boston (25); New York (17); Los Angeles (14)
3674	Semiconductors	168	San Jose (53; Boston (10); Dallas (10); Los Angeles (10)
3825	Instruments to measure electricity	114	San Jose (22); Boston (20)
2834	Pharmaceuticals	116	Newark (27); Philadelphia (11); New York (10)
3842	Surgical appliances	101	Newark (20); Nassau–Suffolk (10); Bergen–Passaic (8); Philadelphia (6)
3494	Values and pipe fittings	81	Anaheim (6); Los Angeles (6); Cleveland (6); Cincinnati (5)
3679	Electronic components	72	San Jose (19); Anaheim (7); Boston (6)
3561	Pumps and pumping equipment	68	Philadelphia (8); Aurora–Elgin (7)
3861	Photographic equipment	57	Rochester (8); Minneapolis (7)
3579	Office machines	54	New York (11); Philadelphia (7); Stamford (5)
3622	Industrial controls	51	San Jose (7); Cleveland (4)
3841	Surgical and medical instruments	51	Nassau–Suffolk (10); Bergen–Passaic (8)

Source. Feldman and Audretsch (1999).

urban activity. Table 2 shows that the propensity for innovative activity to cluster spatially is even greater for specific industries, such as computers and process control instruments, pharmaceuticals, etc. Even more mundane types of industrial activities such as industrial pumps and pumping equipment demonstrate a tendency to concentrate in certain locations.

In sum, *the empirical evidence suggests that location and proximity clearly matter in exploiting knowledge spillovers.* The geographic estimation of the knowledge production function, however, is limited because there is no understanding of the way in which spillovers occur and are realized at the geographic level. The pre-existing pattern of technology related activities makes it difficult to separate spillovers from the correlation of variables at the geographic level. Economic activity may be co-located, but the pattern of causality is difficult to decipher.

4. Penetrating the black box of geographic space

The contribution of the new wave of studies described in the previous section was simply to shift the unit of observation away from firms to a geographic region. But does it make a difference how economic activity is organized within the black box of geographic space? Geographers, political scientists and sociologists have long argued that the differences in the culture of a region and relationships between actors may contribute to differences in innovative performance across regions, even holding knowledge inputs such as R&D and human capital constant [see Malecki (1997) for a review of the literature]. For example, Saxenian (1994) argues that a culture of greater interdependence and exchange among individuals in the Silicon Valley region has contributed to a superior innovative performance than is found around Boston's Route 128, where firms and individuals tend to be more isolated and less interdependent.

Such observations suggest a limitation inherent to the general knowledge production function approach described in the previous section. While economists tend to avoid attributing differences in economic performance to cultural differences, there has been a series of theoretical arguments suggesting that differences in the underlying structure between regions may account for differences in rates of growth and technological change. In fact, a heated debate has emerged in the literature about the manner in which the underlying economic structure within a geographic unit of observation might shape economic performance [see Rosenthal and Strange (2004) in this volume]. In this section we review the debate that revolves around two key structural elements – the degree of diversity versus specialization and the degree of monopoly versus local competition.

One view, which Glaeser et al. (1992) attribute to the *Marshall–Arrow–Romer externality*, suggests that an increased concentration of a particular industry within a specific geographic region facilitates knowledge spillovers across firms. This model formalizes the insight that the concentration of an industry within a city promotes knowledge spillovers among firms and therefore facilitates innovative activity. To the degree that individuals in the population are identical and engaged in identical types of activities, the costs of communication and transactions are minimized. Lower costs of transaction in communication result in a higher probability of knowledge spilling over across individuals within the population. An important assumption of the model is that knowledge externalities with respect to firms exist, but only for firms within the same industry. Thus, the relevant unit of observation is extended from the firm to the region in the tradition of the Marshall–Arrow–Romer model, but the spillovers are limited to occur solely within the relevant industry.

By contrast, restricting knowledge externalities to occur only within the same industry may ignore an important source of new economic knowledge – inter-industry knowledge spillovers. After all, Griliches (1992, p. 29) defined knowledge spillovers as "working on similar things and hence benefiting much from each others research". Jacobs (1969) argues that the most important source of knowledge spillovers is external to the industry in which the firm operates and that cities are the source of considerable innovation because the diversity of these knowledge sources is greatest in cities. According to Jacobs, it is the exchange of complementary knowledge across diverse firms and economic agents which yield a greater return on new economic knowledge. She develops a theory that emphasizes that the variety of industries within a geographic region promotes knowledge externalities and ultimately innovative activity and economic growth.[7]

The extent of regional specialization versus regional diversity in promoting knowledge spillovers is not the only dimension over which there has been a theoretical debate. A second controversy involves the degree of competition prevalent in the region, or the extent of local monopoly. The Marshall–Arrow–Romer model predicts that local monopoly is superior to local competition because it maximizes the ability of firms to appropriate the economic value accruing from their investments in new knowledge. By contrast, Jacobs (1969) and Porter (1990) argue the opposite – that competition is more conducive to knowledge externalities than is local monopoly.[8] It should be emphasized that by local competition Jacobs does not mean competition within product markets as has traditionally been envisioned within the industrial organization literature. Rather, Jacobs is referring to the competition for the new ideas embodied in economic agents. Not only do an increased number of firms provide greater competition for new ideas, but in addition, greater competition across firms facilitates the entry of a new firm specializing in some particular new product niche. This is because the necessary complementary inputs and services are likely to be available from small specialist niche firms but not necessarily from large, vertically integrated producers.

A test of the specialization versus diversity debate measured economic performance in terms of employment growth. Glaeser et al. (1992) employ a data set on the growth

---

[7] For an extension, see Henderson (1997), Henderson, Shalizi and Venables (2001) and Rosenthal and Strange (2003).

[8] Porter (1990) provides examples of Italian ceramics and gold jewelry as industries in which numerous firms are located within a bounded geographic region and compete intensively for new ideas.

of large industries in 170 cities between 1956 and 1987 in order to identify the relative importance of the degree of regional specialization, diversity and local competition play in influencing industry growth rates. The authors find evidence that contradicts the Marshall–Arrow–Romer model but is consistent with the theories of Jacobs. However, their study provided no direct evidence as to whether diversity is more important than specialization in generating innovative activity.

Feldman and Audretsch (1999) identify the extent to which the organization of economic activity is either concentrated, or alternatively consists of diverse but complementary economic activities, and how the underlying structure of economic activity influences innovative output. They link the innovative output of product categories within a specific city to the extent to which the economic activity of that city is concentrated in that industry, or conversely, diversified in terms of complementary industries sharing a common science base. Feldman and Audretsch (1999) identify the extent to which the organization of economic activity is either concentrated, or alternatively consists of diverse but complementary economic activities, and how the underlying structure of

Table 3
Innovation in science-based industry clusters

Cluster	Prominent cities	Mean industry innovations per 100,000 workers
Agra-business	Atlanta	92.40
	Dallas	41.15
	Chicago	33.03
	St. Louis	91.74
Chemical engineering	Dallas	38.09
	Minneapolis	66.67
	San Francisco	43.89
	Wilmington	85.47
Office machinery	Anaheim–Santa Ana	92.59
	Minneapolis	31.86
	Rochester	72.20
	Stanford	68.40
Industrial machinery	Anaheim–Santa Ana	54.95
	Cincinnati	66.01
	Cleveland	141.51
	Passaic, NJ	90.90
High-tech computing	Boston	73.89
	Houston	62.08
	San Jose	44.88
	Minneapolis	181.74
Biomedical	Boston	38.71
	Cleveland	68.76
	Dallas	35.22
	New York	188.07

Source. Feldman and Audretsch (1999).

economic activity influences innovative output. They link the innovative output of product categories within a specific city to the extent to which the economic activity of that city is concentrated in that industry, or conversely, diversified in terms of complementary industries sharing a common science base.

Table 3 shows the innovative activity of cities sharing a common science base. Their results indicate that diversity across complementary economic activities sharing a common science base is more conducive to innovation than is specialization. In addition, their results indicate that the degree of local competition for new ideas within a city is more conducive to innovative activity than is local monopoly. Perhaps the most important conclusions from these two studies, however, is that more than simply an endowment of knowledge inputs is required to generate innovative activity. The underlying economic and institutional structure matters, as do the microeconomic linkages across agents and firms. These findings do not address the path that spillovers take or the mechanisms by which spillovers are realized. These have been examined by work reviewed in the following sections.

5. Spillover mechanisms

Romer (1986), Lucas (1988, 1993) and Grossman and Helpman (1991) established that knowledge spillovers are an important mechanism underlying endogenous growth. However, they shed little light on the actual mechanisms by which knowledge is transmitted across firms and individuals. By necessity, the knowledge production function focused on the quantifiable aspects of innovation. However, formal R&D data ignore the complex processes of technological accumulation whereby tacit knowledge is built up and accumulates meaning – complex transactions that involves local institutions, social convention and legal rights as well as economic interests [Feldman et al. (2002)]. Thus, *the literature on knowledge spillovers and the geography of innovation has begun to consider the mechanisms by which knowledge spills over and is put into economic use and the degree to which these process are geographically localized.* Understanding these issues are important because a policy implication commonly drawn from the new economic growth theory is that, as a result of convexities in knowledge and the resultant increasing returns, knowledge resources, such as R&D should be publicly supported. While this may be valid, it is also important to recognize that the mechanisms for spillover transmission may also play a key role and may also serve as a focus for public policy enhancing economic growth and development.

The concepts of localized knowledge spillovers and absorptive capacity – the ability of economic agents to recognize, assimilate and apply new scientific knowledge, are closely linked [Agrawal (2002a, 2002b)]. Cohen and Levinthal (1989, 1990) suggest that firms that invest in R&D develop the capacity to adapt knowledge developed in other firms and are therefore able to appropriate some of the returns accruing to external investments in new knowledge. Cockburn and Henderson (1998) build on this concept to suggest that firms that are connected to the community of open science are able to increase their investment in R&D by absorbing knowledge spillovers. Firms are able to acquire and benefit from external knowledge by cultivating relationships with universities, participating in research consortia and partnering with academics that do related scientific work.

Edwin Mansfield was perhaps the earliest to point out that research laboratories of universities provide one source of innovation-generating knowledge that is available to private enterprises for commercial exploitation [Mansfield (1995, 1998)]. The empirical work reviewed previously supported that finding. For example, Jaffe (1989) and Acs, Audretsch and Feldman (1992), Audretsch and Feldman (1996) and Feldman and Audretsch (1999) found that the knowledge created in university laboratories spills over to contribute to the generation of commercial innovations by private enterprises [Feldman and Desrochers (2003)]. Even after controlling for the location of industrial R&D, knowledge created at universities results in greater innovation. The ability of research universities to create benefits for their local economies has created a new mission for research universities and a developing literature examines the mechanism and the process of technology transfer from research universities [Mowery and Shane (2002)].

A different literature has emphasized the impact of networks and social capital found within a geographic region. Relational networks exist at multiple levels of analysis because they can link together individuals, groups, firms, industries, geographic regions, and nation-states. In addition, they can tie members of any one of these categories to members of another category. For example, Powell, Koput and Smith-Doerr (1996), Florida and Cohen (1999) and Feldman et al. (2002) demonstrate the ways in which research universities provide a link that facilitates knowledge spillovers in the form of recruiting talent to the region, transferring technology through local linkages and interactions, placing students in industry, and providing a platform for firms, individuals and government agencies to interact. Similarly, Florida and Kenney (1988) examine the connections and special access to talent and resources that venture capital firms provide to link their new high technology startups clients. Gompers and Lerner (1999) have shown how geography affects the location of venture capital. In particular, they show that the geographic distribution of venture capital is highly spatially skewed with California, New York, and New England as the major location of venture capital funds. Furthermore, Sorenson and Stuart (2001) show that location matters in obtaining venture capital. By analyzing the determinants of venture capital investment in the United States between 1986 and 1998, they find that the likelihood of a venture capitalist investing in a given target declines with geographical distance between the venture capitalist and the company.

Malecki (1997) was perhaps the first to note *the importance of skilled labor as a mechanism for knowledge transfer in technology based industrial clusters*. It is also the case that for certain science based industries that the location and preferences of scientists influence the geographical location of innovation. Zucker, Darby and Brewer (1998) and Prevenzer (1997) show that in biotechnology, an industry based almost exclusively on new knowledge and cutting edge scientific discoveries, firms tend to cluster together in just a handful of locations and find that this is due to the location of star scientists – those individuals with high amounts of human capital who are able to appropriate their knowledge through start-up firms. This finding is supported by Audretsch and Stephan (1996) who examine the geographic relationships of scientists working with biotechnology firms. The importance of geographic proximity is clearly shaped by the role played by the scientist. The scientist is more likely to be located in the same region as the firm when the relationship involves the transfer of new economic knowledge. However, when the scientist is providing a service to the company that does not involve knowledge transfer, local proximity becomes much less important.

6. Entrepreneurship as a spillover mechanism

The literature identifying mechanisms actually transmitting knowledge spillovers is sparse and remains underdeveloped. However, one important area where such transmission mechanisms have been identified is entrepreneurship. Entrepreneurship is concerned with the startup and growth of new enterprises.

Why should entrepreneurship serve as a mechanism for the spill over of knowledge from the source of origin? At least two major channels or mechanisms for knowledge spillovers have been identified in the literature. Both of these spillover mechanisms revolve around the issue of appropriability of new knowledge and absorptive capacity. This view of spillovers is consistent with the traditional model of the knowledge production function, where the firm exists exogenously and then undertakes (knowledge) investments to generate innovative output.

By contrast, Audretsch (1995) proposes shifting the unit of observation away from exogenously assumed firms to individuals, such as scientists, engineers or other knowledge workers – agents with endowments of new economic knowledge. When the lens is shifted away from the firm to the individual as the relevant unit of observation, the appropriability issue remains, but the question becomes: *How can economic agents with a given endowment of new knowledge best appropriate the returns from that knowledge?* If the scientist or engineer can pursue the new idea within the organizational structure of the firm developing the knowledge and appropriate roughly the expected value of that knowledge, he has no reason to leave the firm. On the other hand, if he places a greater value on his ideas than do the decision-making bureaucracy of the incumbent firm, he may choose to start a new firm to appropriate the value of his knowledge. Small enterprises can compensate for their lack of R&D is through spillovers and spin-offs. Typically an employee from an established large corporation, often a scientist or engineer working in a research laboratory, will have an idea for an invention and ultimately for an innovation. Accompanying this potential innovation is an expected net return from the new product. The inventor would expect to be compensated for his/her potential innovation accordingly. If the company has a different, presumably lower, valuation of the potential innovation, it may decide either not to pursue its development, or that it merits a lower level of compensation than that expected by the employee.

In either case, the employee will weigh the alternative of starting his/her own firm. If the gap in the expected return accruing from the potential innovation between the inventor and the corporate decision maker is sufficiently large, and if the cost of starting a new firm is sufficiently low, the employee may decide to leave the large corporation and establish a new enterprise. Since the knowledge was generated in the established corporation, the new start-up is considered to be a spin-off from the existing firm. Such start-ups typically do not have direct access to a large R&D laboratory. Rather, these small firms succeed in exploiting the knowledge and experience accrued from the R&D laboratories with their previous employers.

In the metaphor provided by Albert O. Hirschman (1970), if voice proves to be ineffective within incumbent organizations, and loyalty is sufficiently weak, a knowledge worker may resort to exit the firm or university where the knowledge was created in order to form a new company. In this spillover channel the knowledge production function is actually reversed. The knowledge is exogenous and embodied in a worker. The firm is created endogenously in the worker's effort to appropriate the value of his knowledge through innovative activity.

One group of studies has focused on how location has influenced the entrepreneurial decision, or the decision to start a new firm. Within the economics literature, the prevalent theoretical framework has been the general model of income choice. The model of entrepreneurial choice dates back at least to Knight (1921), but was more recently extended and updated by Lucas (1978), Kihlstrom and Laffont (1979), Holmes and Schmitz Jr. (1990) and Jovanovic (1994). In its most basic rendition, individuals are confronted with a choice of earning their income either from wages earned through employment in an incumbent enterprise or else from profits accrued by starting a new firm. The essence of the entrepreneurial choice model is made by comparing the wage an individual expects to earn through employment, W^*, with the profits that are expected to accrue from a new-firm startup, P^*. Thus, the probability of starting a new firm, $\Pr(s)$, can be represented as

$$\Pr(s) = f(P^* - W^*). \tag{3}$$

The model of entrepreneurial choice has been extended by Kihlstrom and Laffont (1979) to incorporate aversion to risk, and by Lucas (1978) and Jovanovic (1994) to explain why firms of varying size exist, and has served as the basis for empirical studies of the decision to start a new firm by Evans and Leighton (1989a, 1989b, 1990).

Geographic location should influence the entrepreneurial decision by altering the expected return from entrepreneurial activity, P^*. The theory of knowledge spillovers suggests that P^* will tend to be greater in agglomerations and spatial clusters, since access to tacit knowledge is greater. Geography and spatial location also influences entrepreneurship. The important role that geographic clusters and networks play as a determinant of entrepreneurial activity was identified in Europe and only recently has been discovered within the North American context [Porter (1990, 2000), Saxenian (1994)]. By contrast, there is a longer and richer tradition of research linking entrepreneurship to spatial clusters and networks in Europe. However, most of these studies have been in social science fields other than economics. For example, Becattini (1990) and Brusco (1990) identified the key role that spatial clusters and networks play in promoting SMEs in Italy. With the development of recent theoretical models by Soubeyran and Thisse (1999) and Soubeyran and Weber (2002), it became clear and accepted that spatial agglomerations were also important in the North American context.

An important distinction between the European literature and the emerging literature in North America was the emphasis on high technology and knowledge spillovers in the North American context. By contrast, the European tradition focused much more on the role of networks and clusters in fostering the viability of SMEs in traditional industries, such as textiles, apparel and metalworking. For example, seminal studies by Becattini (1990) and Brusco (1990) argue that small and new firms enjoy a high degree of stability when supported by networks in Italy. A rich literature has provided a body of case studies, spanning the textile industries of northern Italy to the metal working firms of Baden Wuerttenberg [Piore and Sabel (1984)], documenting the long-term viability and stability of small and new firms embedded in the so-called industrial districts of Europe. Pyke and Sengenberger (1990) argue that through the support of an industrial district, small firms in European spatial clusters have been able to compensate for what would otherwise be an inherent size disadvantage. According to Pyke and Sengenberger (1990), an industrial district is a geographically defined production system, involving a large number of enterprises engaging in production at a wide range of stages, and typically involved in the production of a well-defined but differentiated product. A particularly significant feature of Italian industrial districts is that almost all of the firms are small or even micro-enterprises. Examples of such industrial districts include Prato, Biella, Carpi and Castelgoffredo, which specialize in textile (coolants in Castelgoffredo); Vigevano, Montebellune and Montegranaro where shoes are manufactured (ski boots in Montebellune); Pesaro and Nogara which manufacture wooden furniture; Sassuolo where ceramic tiles are produced.

Brusco (1990) emphasizes the cooperation among network firms within an industrial district. Such cooperation presumably reduces any size-inherent disadvantages and improves the viability of small firms operating within the network. According to Pyke and Sengenberger (1990, p. 2), "A characteristic of the industrial district is that it should be conceived as a social and economic whole. That is to say, there are close inter-relationships between the different social, political and economic spheres, and the functioning of one, say the economic, is shaped by functioning and organization of the others." Grabher (1993) similarly argues that the social structure underlying industrial networks contributes to the viability of small firms that would otherwise be vulnerable if they were operating in an isolated context.

Feldman (2001) and Feldman and Francis (2002) examine the formation of innovative clusters and argue that entrepreneurs are key agents. Based on an analysis of the development of an Internet and biotechnology cluster around Washington, DC, Feldman (2001) provides evidence that clusters form not because resources are initially located in a particular region, but rather through the work of entrepreneurs. Entrepreneurship is a local phenomenon as most entrepreneurs were previously employed in the region.

Moreover, entrepreneurs are endogenous and organize resources and institutions to support their firms. An industry agglomeration is simply a collection of localized firms with a common focus and there are gains to collective action. As their businesses begin to thrive, resources such as money, networks, experts, and related services develop in, and are attracted to, the region. With this infrastructure in place, more entrepreneurial ventures locate and thrive in the region, which ultimately may create a thriving cluster where none previously existed. Feldman and Francis (2002) develop a conceptual model to formalize the process of cluster formation through entrepreneurism. Using simulations, Zhang (2002) demonstrates how a small number of successful entrepreneurs can generate a cluster.

A series of studies, spanning a broad spectrum of countries, has attempted to link entrepreneurial activity to characteristics specific to a geographic region, including measures of knowledge, such as R&D and human capital. Entrepreneurship activity has been typically measured as new-firm startups (rates), self-employment (rates), business ownership (rates), or a combination of startups and exits referred to as turbulence (rates). For example, the collection of European country studies included in the special issue of *Regional Studies* on "Regional Variations in New Firm Formation" [Reynolds, Storey and Westhead (1994)], along with the survey by Storey (1991) suggest that the empirical evidence has been generally unambiguous with respect to the findings for population density (a positive impact on startup rates), population growth (positive impact on startup rates), skill and human capital levels of the labor force (positive impact), and mean establishment size (negative impact on startup rates). By contrast, the empirical evidence about the impact of unemployment on startup rates is considerably more ambiguous. But an unambiguous positive relationship has emerged between measures of human capital and entrepreneurial activity at the regional level.[9]

Audretsch and Fritsch (1996) examined the impact that location plays on entrepreneurial activity in (West) Germany. Using a data base derived from the social insurance statistics, which covers about 90 percent of employment, they identify the birth rates of new startups for each of 75 distinct economic regions. These regions are distinguished on the basis of planning regions, or *Raumordungsregionen*. They find that, for the late 1980s, the birth rates of new firms are higher in regions experiencing low unemployment, which have a dense population, a high growth rate of population, a high share of skilled workers, and a strong presence of small businesses.

Similarly, Pfirrmann (1994) has found that the innovative activity of small- and medium-sized firms in West Germany is shaped by regional factors. He uses a database consisting of innovative small and medium-sized firms and finds that the innovative activity of small- and medium-sized enterprises tends to be greater in those regions where there is a strong presence of knowledge resources. However, his results also indicate

---

[9]   The positive relationship between entrepreneurship activity and economic growth could also be at least partially explained by the fact that a large number of entrepreneurs implies a greater number of firms and a stronger accumulation of physical capital.

that factors internal to the firm are more important for the innovation efforts of a small firm than is the regional environment.

If entrepreneurship serves as a mechanism for knowledge spillovers, it should not only be reflected by the model of entrepreneurial choice, or the decision to start a new firm. Rather, measures of entrepreneurial activity should also be positively linked to the growth performance of regions. The view of entrepreneurship is based on its role as an agent of change in a knowledge-based economy implies that a positive economic performance should be linked to entrepreneurial activity. This hypothesis has raised two challenges to researchers: (1) what is meant by economic performance and how can it be measured and operationalized? and (2) over which units of analysis should such a positive relationship between entrepreneurship and economic performance be manifested? In fact, these two issues are not independent from each other. The answer to the second question, the appropriate unit of analysis, has influenced the first question, the performance criteria and measure.

The most prevalent measures of performance has been employment growth. The most common and most exclusive measure of performance is growth, typically measured in terms of employment growth. These studies have tried to link various measures of entrepreneurial activity, most typically startup rates, to economic growth. Other measures sometimes used include the relative share of SMEs, and self-employment rates.

For example, Audretsch and Fritsch (1996) analyzed a database identifying new business startups and exits from the social insurance statistics in Germany to examine whether a greater degree of turbulence leads to greater economic growth, as suggested by Schumpeter in his 1911 treatise, *A Theory of Economic Development*. These social insurance statistics are collected for individuals. Each record in the database identifies the establishment at which an individual is employed. The startup of a new firm is recorded when a new establishment identification appears in the database, which generally indicates the birth of a new enterprise. While there is some evidence for the United States linking a greater degree of turbulence at the regional level to higher rates of growth for regions [Reynolds (1999)], Audretsch and Fritsch (1996) find that the opposite was true for Germany during the 1980s. In both the manufacturing and the service sectors, a high rate of turbulence in a region tends to lead to a lower and not a higher rate of growth. They attribute this negative relationship to the fact that the underlying components – the startup and death rates – are both negatively related to subsequent economic growth. Those areas with higher startup rates tend to experience lower growth rates in subsequent years. Most strikingly, the same is also true for the death rates. The German regions experiencing higher death rates also tend to experience lower growth rates in subsequent years. Similar evidence for Germany is found by Fritsch (1997).

Audretsch and Fritsch (1996) conjectured that one possible explanation for the disparity in results between the United States and Germany may lie in the role that innovative activity, and therefore the ability of new firms to ultimately displace the incumbent enterprises, plays in new-firm startups. It may be that innovative activity did not play the same role for the German *Mittelstand* as it does for SMEs in the United States. To the degree that this was true, it may be hold that regional growth emanates from SMEs only when they serve as agents of change through innovative activity.

The empirical evidence suggested that the German model for growth provided a sharp contrast to that for the United States. While Reynolds (1999) had found that the degree of entrepreneurship was positively related to growth in the United States, a series of studies by Audretsch and Fritsch (1996) and Fritsch (1997) could not identify such a relationship for Germany. However, the results by Audretsch and Fritsch were based on data from the 1980s.

Divergent findings from the 1980s about the relationship between the degree of entrepreneurial activity and economic growth in the United States and Germany posed something of a puzzle. On the one hand, these different results suggested that the relationship between entrepreneurship and growth was fraught with ambiguities. No confirmation could be found for a general pattern across developed countries. On the other hand, it provided evidence for the existence of distinct and different national systems. The empirical evidence clearly suggested that there was more than one way to achieve growth, at least across different countries. *Convergence in growth rates seemed to be attainable by maintaining differences in underlying institutions and structures.*

However, in a more recent study, Audretsch and Fritsch (2002) find that different results emerge for the 1990s. Those regions with a higher startup rate exhibit higher growth rates. This would suggest that, in fact, Germany is changing over time, where the engine of growth is shifting towards entrepreneurship as a source of growth. The results of their 2002 paper suggest a somewhat different interpretation. Based on the empirical evidence that the source of growth in Germany has shifted away from established incumbent firms during the 1980s to entrepreneurial firms in the 1990s, it would appear that a process of convergence is taking place between Germany and the United States, where entrepreneurship provides the engine of growth in both countries. Despite remaining institutional differences, the relationship between entrepreneurship and growth is apparently converging in both countries.

The positive relationship between entrepreneurship and growth at the regional level is not limited to Germany in the 1990. For example, Foelster (2000) examines not just the employment impact within new and small firms but on the overall link between increases in self-employment and total employment in Sweden between 1976–1995. By using a Layard–Nickell framework, he provides a link between micro behavior and macroeconomic performance, and shows that increases in self-employment rates have had a positive impact on regional employment rates in Sweden.

Hart and Hanvey (1995) examine measures of new and small firms start-ups to employment generation in the late 1980s for three regions in the United Kingdom. While they find that employment creation came largely from SMEs, they also identify that most of the job losses also came from SMEs.

Callejon and Segarra (2000) use a data set of Spanish manufacturing industries between 1980–1992 to link new-firm birth rates and death rates, which taken together constitute a measure of turbulence, to total factor productivity growth in industries and regions. They adopt a model based on a vintage capital framework in which new entrants embody the edge technologies available and exiting businesses represent marginal obsolete plants. Using a Hall type of production function, which controls for imperfect competition and the extent of scale economies, they find that both new-firm startup rates and exit rates contribute positively to the growth of total factor productivity in regions as well as industries.

The evidence linking entrepreneurship to growth at the regional level may actually be more convincing in the European context than in the North American context. Only a handful of studies have been undertaken for North America, while the evidence from Europe is considerably more robust and consistent.

In the U.S., a series of studies [Wilson (1996), Bates (1998)] have attempted to identify whether the determinants of entrepreneurial activity differ for different immigrant and ethnic minority groups. In one of the most important studies, Saxenian (2001) documents that the decision to become an entrepreneur is shaped by immigrant group status. In particular, she provides evidence that the fastest-growing groups of immigrant engineers in Silicon Valley are from Mainland China and India. Chinese, in particular, are increasingly visible in the computer science and engineering departments on university campuses located in the Silicon Valley region. Saxenian (2001) suggests that these immigrant entrepreneurs provide a mechanism for a two-way flow of ideas and knowledge between Silicon Valley and their home regions in Asia.

7. Conclusions

Perhaps the greatest development in the literature on the economics of innovation and technological change in the last decade has been the insight that geography matters. A long tradition of analyzing the innovative process within the boundaries of the firm and devoid of spatial context has given way to the incorporation of spatial context in models of innovation and technological change.

Incorporating spatial relationships into the model of the knowledge production function has redeemed the view that knowledge inputs are linked to innovative output. While the boundaries of the firm still matter, so do the boundaries of spatial agglomerations. Geography has been found to provide a platform upon which new economic knowledge can be produced, harnessed and commercialized into innovations. Thus, *the model of the knowledge production has been found to hold better for spatial units of observation than for enterprises in isolation of spatial context.*

This is not to say that the research agenda of the geography of innovation and knowledge spillovers is in any way complete. Rather, a broad spectrum of research issues and questions remain open and virtually unexplored. One important but relatively unchartered area for future research involves the life cycle of spatial units, such as agglomerations, clusters and regions. Due to data constraints, most of the research reported in the chapter is based on cross-sectional analyses. *While research has determined that geographic space matters for innovation, it has yet to unravel how agglomerations are formed, where they come from, how they are either sustained and strengthen, or else deteriorate over time*. With the prevalence of new longitudinal panel data, we look forward to answers to these questions being provided by a new generation of scholars researching the spatial dimensions of innovative activity.

As this chapter concludes, scholars have confirmed that knowledge spills over and that such knowledge spillovers matter in the formation of clusters and agglomerations. But to move beyond this insight much work remains to be done. The concept of knowledge spillovers has been generally treated as being homogeneous. Yet, surely not all knowledge is the same. We look for a greater taxonomy identifying the rich heterogeneity involved in knowledge and the process by which it spills over. Just as the Eskimos have names for the many different types of snow, scholars must begin the arduous task of identifying and distinguishing among the many types of knowledge spillovers.

Similarly, the mechanisms transmitting knowledge spillovers remain relatively unexplored and unknown. How and why does knowledge spill over is more than an academic question. Firms would like to know how spillovers can be accessed and places – cities, states, regions and countries – would like to know how strategically invest in the development of absorptive capacity to enhance the spillover of knowledge. Thus, while the endogenous growth theory emphasizes the importance of investments in research and development and human capital, a research agenda needs to be mapped out identifying the role that investments in spillover conduits can make in generating economic growth. It may be that a mapping of the process by which new knowledge is created, externalized and commercialized, hold the key to providing the microeconomic linkages to endogenous macroeconomic growth.

Acknowledgements

We acknowledge the comments of Vernon Henderson, Jacque Thisse, Will Strange and the participants at the CEPR Meetings in December 2002. We are also grateful to the comments and suggestions made by Luigi Guiso. Feldman acknowledges financial support of the Connaught Fund at the University of Toronto. Comments are welcome and appreciated.

References

Acs, Z.J., Audretsch, D.B. (1988). "Innovation in large and small firms: an empirical analysis". American Economic Review 78, 678–690.
Acs, Z.J., Audretsch, D.B. (1990). Innovation and Small Firms. MIT Press, Cambridge, MA.
Acs, Z.J., Audretsch, D.B., Feldman, M.P. (1992). "Real effects of academic research". American Economic Review 82, 363–367.
Acs, Z.J., Audretsch, D., Feldman, M.P. (1994). "R&D spillovers and recipient firm size". Review of Economics and Statistics 100 (1), 336–367.
Adams, J.D. (2002). "Comparative localization of academic and industrial spillovers". Journal of Economic Geography 2, 253–278.

Adams, J.D., Jaffe, A.B. (2002). "Bounding the effects of R&D: an investigation using matched firm and establishment data". RAND Journal of Economics 27, 700–721.

Agrawal, A. (2002a). "Importing scientific inventions: direct interaction, geography and economic performance". Mimeo. MIT.

Agrawal, A. (2002b). "Innovation, growth theory and the role of knowledge spillovers". Innovation Analysis Bulletin 4 (3), 3–6.

Almeida, P., Kogut, B. (1997). "The exploration of technological diversity and the geographic localization of innovation". Small Business Economics 9 (1), 21–31.

Anselin, L., Acs, Z.J., Varga, A. (1997). "Local geographic spillovers between university research and high technology innovations". Journal of Urban Economics 42, 422–448.

Arrow, K. (1962). "Economic welfare and the allocation of resources for invention". In: Nelson, R. (Ed.), The Rate and Direction of Inventive Activity. Princeton Univ. Press, Princeton, NJ.

Audretsch, D.B. (1995). Innovation and Industry Evolution. MIT Press, Cambridge, MA.

Audretsch, D.B., Feldman, M.P. (1996). "R&D spillovers and the geography of innovation and production". American Economic Review 86 (4), 253–273.

Audretsch, D.B., Fritsch, M. (1996). "Creative destruction: turbulence and economic growth". In: Helmstädter, E., Perlman, M. (Eds.), Behavioral Norms, Technological Progress, and Economic Dynamics: Studies in Schumpeterian Economics. Univ. of Michigan Press, Ann Arbor, pp. 137–150.

Audretsch, D.B., Fritsch, M. (2002). "Growth regimes over time and space". Regional Studies 36 (2), 113–124.

Audretsch, D.B., Stephan, P. (1996). "Company–scientist locational links: the case of biotechnology". American Economic Review 86 (4), 641–652.

Autant-Bernard, C. (2001a). "Science and knowledge flows: evidence from the French case". Research Policy 30 (7), 1069–1078.

Autant-Bernard, C. (2001b). "The geography of knowledge spillovers and technological proximity". Economics of Innovation and New Technology 10 (4), 237–254.

Baldwin, W.L., Scott, J.T. (1987). Market Structure and Technological Change. Harwood Academic, London.

Bates, T.M. (1998). Self-Employment and Upward Mobility: An Illusive American Dream. Johns Hopkins Univ. Press, Baltimore.

Becattini, G. (1990). "The Marshallian industrial district as a socio-economic notion". In: Becattini, G., Pyke, F., Sengenberger, W. (Eds.), Industrial Districts and Inter-Firm Co-operation in Italy. International Labor Studies, Geneva, pp. 37–51.

Black, G. (2003). The Geography of Small Firm Innovation. Kluwer Academic, Dordrecht.

Branstetter, L. (2002). "Measuring the link between academic science and innovation: the case of California research universities". Mimeo. University of California, Davis.

Brusco, S. (1990). "The idea of the industrial district, its genesis". In: Becattini, G., Pyke, F., Sengenberger, W. (Eds.), Industrial Districts and Inter-Firm Co-operation in Italy. International Labour Studies, Geneva, pp. 10–19.

Callejon, M., Segarra, A. (2000). "Business dynamics and efficiency in industries and regions: the case of Spain". Small Business Economics 13 (4), 253–271.

Cockburn, I.M., Henderson, R. (1998). "Absorptive capacity, coauthoring behavior and the organization of research in drug discovery". The Journal of Industrial Economics 66 (2), 157–182.

Cohen, W.M., Klepper, S. (1991). "Firm size versus diversity in the achievement of technological advance". In: Acs, Z.J., Audretsch, D.B. (Eds.), Innovation and Technological Change: An International Comparison. Univ. of Michigan Press, Ann Arbor, pp. 183–203.

Cohen, W.M., Klepper, S. (1992). "The tradeoff between firm size and diversity in the pursuit of technological progress". Small Business Economics 4 (1), 1–14.

Cohen, W.M., Levin, R.C. (1989). "Empirical studies of innovation and market structure". In: Schmalensee, R., Willig, R. (Eds.). North-Holland, Amsterdam, pp. 1059–1107.

Cohen, W.M., Levinthal, D.A. (1989). "Innovation and learning: the two faces of R&D". Economic Journal 99 (3), 569–596.

Cohen, W.M., Levinthal, D.A. (1990). "Absorptive capacity: a new perspective on innovation and learning". Administrative Sciences Quarterly 35, 128–152.

Evans, D.S., Leighton, L.S. (1989a). "Some empirical aspects of entrepreneurship". American Economic Review 79 (3), 519–535.

Evans, D.S., Leighton, L.S. (1989b). "The determinants of changes in U.S. self-employment". Small Business Economics 1 (2), 11–120.

Evans, D.S., Leighton, L.S. (1990). "Small business formation by unemployed and employed workers". Small Business Economics 2 (4), 319–330.

Feldman, M.P. (1993). "An examination of the geography of innovation". Industrial and Corporate Change 4, 451–470.

Feldman, M.P. (1994a). The Geography of Innovation. Kluwer Academic, Boston.

Feldman, M. (1994b). "Knowledge complementarity and innovation". Small Business Economics 6 (3), 363–372.

Feldman, M.P. (2001). "The entrepreneurial event revisited: firm formation in a regional context". Industrial and Corporate Change, 861–891.

Feldman, M.P. (2002). "The internet revolution and the geography of innovation". International Social Science Journal 54, 47–56.

Feldman, M.P., Audretsch, D. (1999). "Innovation in cities: science-based diversity, specialization and localized competition". European Economic Review 43, 409–429.

Feldman, M.P., Desrochers, P. (2003). "The evolving role of research universities in technology transfer: lessons from the history of Johns Hopkins University". Industry and Innovation 10, 5–24.

Feldman, M.P., Francis, J.L. (2002). "The entrepreneurial spark, individual agents and the formation of innovative clusters". In: Quadrio Curzio, A., Fortis, M. (Eds.), Complexity and Industrial Clusters. Springer-Verlag, Heidelberg.

Feldman, M.P., Feller, I., Bercovitz, J.E.L., Burton, R.M. (2002). "University-technology transfer and the system of innovation". In: Feldman, M.P., Massard, N. (Eds.), Institutions and Systems in the Geography of Innovation. Kluwer Academic, Boston, pp. 55–78.

Florida, R.L., Cohen, W.M. (1999). "Engine or infrastructure? The university role in economic development". In: Branscomb, L.M., Kodama, F., Florida, R. (Eds.), Industrializing Knowledge: University–Industry Linkages in Japan and the United States. MIT Press, Cambridge, MA, pp. 589–610.

Florida, R.L., Kenney, M. (1988). "Venture capital, high technology and regional development". Regional Studies 22 (1), 33–48.

Foelster, S. (2000). "Do entrepreneurs create jobs?" Small Business Economics 14 (2), 137–148.

Fritsch, M. (1997). "New firms and regional employment change". Small Business Economics 9 (5), 437–448.

Glaeser, E., Kallal, H., Scheinkman, J., Shleifer, A. (1992). "Growth of cities". Journal of Political Economy 100, 1126–1152.

Gompers, P., Lerner, J. (1999). The Venture Capital Cycle. MIT Press, Cambridge, MA.

Grabher, G. (Ed.) (1993). The Embedded Firm. On the Socio-Economics of Industrial Networks. Routlegde, London and New York.

Griliches, Z. (1979). "Issues in assessing the contribution of R&D to productivity growth". Bell Journal of Economics 10, 92–116.

Griliches, Z. (1984). R&D, Patents, and Productivity. Univ. of Chicago Press, Chicago.

Griliches, Z. (1990). "Patent statistics as economic indicators: a survey". Journal of Economic Literature 28 (4), 1661–1707.

Griliches, Z. (1992). "The search for R&D spill-overs". Scandinavian Journal of Economics 94, 29–47.

Grossman, G.M., Helpman, E. (1991). Innovation and Growth in the Global Economy. MIT Press, Cambridge, MA.

Hart, M., Hanvey, E. (1995). "Job generation and new and small firms: some evidence from the late 1980s". Small Business Economics 7, 97–109.

Henderson, J.V. (1997). "Externalities and industrial development". Journal of Urban Economics 42, 449–470.

Henderson, J.V., Shalizi, Z., Venables, A. (2001). "Geography and development". Journal of Economic Geography 1, 81–106.

Hirschman, A.O. (1970). Exit, Voice, and Loyalty. Harvard Univ. Press, Cambridge, MA.

Holmes, T.J., Schmitz Jr., J.A. (1990). "A theory of entrepreneurship and its application to the study of business transfers". Journal of Political Economy 98 (4), 265–294.

Hoover Jr., E.M. (1936). "The measurement of industrial localization". Review of Economics and Statistics 18 (4), 162–171.

Jacobs, J. (1969). The Economy of Cities. Random House, New York.

Jaffe, A.B. (1989). "Real effects of academic research". American Economic Review 79 (5), 957–970.

Jaffe, A.B., Trajtenberg, M. (2002). Patents, citations, and innovations: a window on the knowledge economy. MIT Press, Cambridge, MA.

Jaffe, A.B., Trajtenberg, M., Henderson, R. (1993). "Geographic localization of knowledge spillovers as evidenced by patent citations". Quarterly Journal of Economics 63, 577–598.

Jovanovic, B. (1994). "Entrepreneurial choice when people differ in their management and labor skills". Small Business Economics 6 (3), 185–192.

Kihlstrom, R.E., Laffont, J.J. (1979). "A general equilibrium entrepreneurial theory of firm formation based on risk aversion". Journal of Political Economy 87 (4), 719–748.

Knight, F.H. (1921). Risk, Uncertainty and Profit. Houghton Mifflin, New York.

Krugman, P. (1991). Geography and Trade. MIT Press, Cambridge, MA.

Lucas, R.E. (1978). "On the size distribution of business firms". Bell Journal of Economics 9, 508–523.

Lucas, R.E. (1988). "On the mechanics of economic development". Journal of Monetary Economic 22, 3–39.

Lucas, R.E. (1993). "Making a miracle". Econometrica 61, 251–272.

Lucas, R.E. (2001). "Externalities and cities". Review of Economic Studies 4, 245–274.

Lucas, R.E., Rossi-Hansberg, E. (2002). "On the internal structure of cities". Econometrica 70, 1445–1476.

Malecki, E. (1997). Technology and Economic Development: The Dynamics of Local, Regional and National Competitiveness, second ed. Addison–Wesley, Longman, London.

Mansfield, E. (1995). "Academic research underlying industrial innovations: sources, characteristics, and financing". Review of Economics and Statistics 77 (1), 55–65.

Mansfield, E. (1998). "Academic research and industrial innovation: an update of empirical finding". Research Policy 26, 773–776.

Manski, C.F. (2000). "Economic analysis of social interactions". Journal of Economic Perspectives 14, 115–136.

Marshall, A. (1920). Principles of Economics. Macmillan, London.

Mowery, D.C., Shane, S. (2002). "Introduction to the special issue on university entrepreneurship and technology transfer". Management Science 48 (1), 1–6.

Orlando, M.J. (2000). "On the importance of geographic and technological proximity for R&D spillovers: an empirical investigation". Federal Reserve Bank of Kansas City Research Working Paper.

Pfirrmann, O. (1994). "The geography of innovation in small and medium-sized firms in West Germany". Small Business Economics 6 (1), 27–41.

Piore, M.J., Sabel, C.F. (1984). The Second Industrial Divide: Possibilities for Prosperity. Basic Books, New York.

Porter, M.E. (1990). The Comparative Advantage of Nations. Free Press, New York.

Porter, M.E. (2000). "Locations, clusters, and company strategy". In: Clark, G.L., Feldman, M.P., Gertler, M.S. (Eds.), The Oxford Handbook of Economic Geography. Oxford Univ. Press, Oxford, pp. 253–274.

Powell, W., Koput, K.W., Smith-Doerr, L. (1996). "Interorganizational collaboration and the locus of innovation: networks of learning in biotechnology". Administrative Science Quarterly 42 (1), 116–145.

Prevenzer, M. (1997). "The dynamics of industrial clustering in biotechnology". Small Business Economics 9 (3), 255–271.

Pyke, F., Sengenberger, W. (1990). "Introduction". In: Pyke, F., Becattini, G., Sengenberger, W. (Eds.), Industrial Districts and Inter-Firm Co-Operation in Italy. International Institute for Labour Studies, Geneva, pp. 1–9.

Reynolds, P.D. (1999). "Creative destruction, source or symptom of economic growth?". In: Acs, Z.J., Carlsson, B., Karlsson, C. (Eds.), Entrepreneurship, Small and Medium-Sized Enterprises and the Macroeconomy. Cambridge Univ. Press, Cambridge, MA, pp. 97–136.

Reynolds, P., Storey, D.J., Westhead, P. (1994). "Cross-national comparisons of the variation in new firm formation rates". Regional Studies 28 (4), 443–456.

Romer, P.M. (1986). "Increasing returns and long-run growth". Journal of Political Economy 94 (5), 1002–1037.

Rosenthal, S.S., Strange, W. (2003). "Geography, industrial organization and agglomeration". The Review of Economics and Statistics 85 (2), 377–393.

Rosenthal, S.S., Strange, W. (2004). "Evidence on the nature and sources of agglomeration economies". In: Henderson, J.V., Thisse, J.-F. (Eds.), Handbook of Regional and Urban Economics, vol. 4. Elsevier, Amsterdam, pp. 2119–2171. This volume.

Saxenian, A. (1994). Regional Advantage: Culture and Competition in Silicon Valley and Route 128. Harvard Univ. Press, Cambridge, MA.

Saxenian, A. (2001). "The role of immigrant entrepreneurs in new venture creation". In: Schoonhoven, C.B., Romanelli, E. (Eds.), The Entrepreneurship Dynamic. Stanford Univ. Press, Palo Alto, pp. 40–67.

Scherer, F.M. (1984). Innovation and Growth: Schumpetrian Perspectives. MIT Press, Cambridge, MA.

Scherer, F.M. (1991). "Changing perspectives on the firm size problem". In: Acs, Z.J., Audretsch, D.B. (Eds.), Innovation and Technological Change. An International Comparison. University of Michigan Press, Ann Arbor, pp. 24–38.

Schumpeter, J.A. (1911). Theorie der wirtschaftlichen Entwicklung. Eine Untersuchung, ueber Unternehmergewinn, Kapital, Kredit, Zins und den Konjunkturzyklus. Duncker und Humbolt, Berlin.

Sorenson, O., Stuart, T. (2001). "Syndication networks and the spatial distribution of venture capital investments". American Journal of Sociology 106 (6), 1546–1588.

Soubeyran, A., Thisse, J.-F. (1999). "Learning-by-doing and the development of industrial districts". Journal of Urban Economics 45, 156–176.

Soubeyran, A., Weber, S. (2002). "District formation and local social capital: a (tacit) co-opetition approach". Journal of Urban Economics 52, 65–92.

Storey, D.J. (1991). "The birth of new firms – does unemployment matter? A review of the evidence". Small Business Economics 3 (3), 167–178.

Von Hipple, E. (1994). "Sticky information and the locus of problem solving: implications for innovation". Management Science 40, 429–439.

Wallsten, S.J. (2001). "An empirical test of geographic knowledge spillovers using geographic information systems and firm-level data". Regional Science and Urban Economic 31, 571–599.

Wilson, W.J. (1996). When Work Disappears: The World of the New Urban Poor. Knopf, New York.

Zhang, J. (2002). Growing Silicon Valley on a landscape: an agent-based approach to high technology industrial clusters. Public Policy Institute of California.

Zucker, L.G., Darby, M.R., Brewer, M.B. (1998). "Intellectual human capital and the birth of U.S. biotechnology enterprises". American Economic Review 88, 290–306.

PART IV

EVOLUTION

14

NEW-FIRM SURVIVAL AND THE TECHNOLOGICAL REGIME

David B. Audretsch*

Abstract—The survival rates of over 11,000 firms established in 1976 are compared across manufacturing industries. The variation in ten-year survival rates across industries is hypothesized to be the result of differences in the underlying technological regime and industry-specific characteristics, especially the extent of scale economies and capital intensity. Based on 295 four-digit standard industrial classification industries, new-firm survival is found to be promoted by the extent of small-firm innovative activity. The existence of substantial scale economies and a high capital–labor ratio tends to lower the likelihood of firm survival. However, these results apparently vary considerably with the time interval considered. Market concentration is found to promote short-run survival, while it has no impact on long-run survival.

I. Introduction

A rather startling result has emerged in the empirical literature of industrial organization—entry by new firms into an industry is apparently not substantially deterred in capital-intensive industries where scale economies play an important role. For example, Acs and Audretsch (1989a and 1989b) found that even small firms are not significantly deterred from entering industries which are relatively capital-intensive. This raises a fundamental question at the core of intra-industry dynamics: What happens to new firms subsequent to entry? And how are they able to survive?

In fact, little is known about the ability of firms to survive subsequent to entry. In trying to test the validity of Gibrat's Law, both Hall (1987) and Evans (1987a and 1987b) found that not only do smaller firms have significantly higher growth rates, but they also have a substantially greater propensity to exit the industry than do their larger counterparts. Evans (1987a), for example, was able to use the U.S. Small Business Data Base (compiled by the U.S. Small Business Administration) to identify the existence of a strong positive relationship between the likelihood of survival and firm size in 81 of the 100 four-digit standard industrial classification (SIC) industries he examined.

Phillips and Kirchhoff (1989) also used the U.S. Small Business Data Base to confirm Evans' (1989a) finding that firm survival tends to increase with enterprise age.[1] Based on 200,000 plants that were classified by the U.S. Census of Manufactures as being established between 1966 and 1977, Dunne et al. (1989) found that failure rates tend to decrease as plant size increases and decrease along with an increase in the age of the plant.

However, none of these studies provide any insight as to whether the ability of firms to survive varies across industries, and if so, to which factors such variation in firm survival can be attributed.[2] The absence of any such studies is particularly striking since a growing body of literature on firm entry, exit, mobility, and turbulence has shown that industry-specific characteristics play an important role in explaining intra-industry dynamics.[3]

The purpose of this paper is to fill this gap in the literature by identifying the extent to which new-firm survival varies across a broad spectrum of manufacturing industries, along with the determinants of new-firm survival. In particular, the hypothesis introduced by Winter (1984) and Gort and Klepper (1982) that the technological and knowledge conditions determine the relative ease with which new firms are able to innovate and therefore survive is tested. In addition, the models of learning-by-doing introduced by Jovanovic (1982) and Pakes and Ericson (1987) suggest that firms may enter an industry at sub-optimal scale

---

[1] Preisendörfer et al. (1989) also find that firm survival tends to increase with enterprise age for over 100,000 West German firms established between 1980 and 1984.

[2] Dunne et al. (1989) do analyse the relationships between plant age, size, and probability of failure for twenty broadly defined two-digit SIC industry sectors. However, they make no attempt to relate variations in the failure rate to sector-specific characteristics.

[3] For a comprehensive group of studies relating firm entry and exit to industry-specific characteristics, see Geroski and Schwalbach (1991). Oster (1982) provides a careful study of intra-industry mobility between strategic groups, and Beesley and Hamilton (1984) and Acs and Audretsch (1990, chapter seven) relate intra-industry turbulence to market structure.

Received for publication March 6, 1990. Revision accepted for publication November 30, 1990.
* Wissenschaftszentrum Berlin für Sozialforschung
I wish to thank two anonymous referees, and Bo Carlsson, Tim Dunne, and Paul Geroski for their suggestions, and Jianping Yang for his computational assistance with this paper. All errors and omissions remain my responsibility.

[441]

in order to obtain the opportunity to learn and subsequently expand if successful. An implication tested in this paper is that, especially in the presence of substantial scale economies and capital intensity, those firms unable to successfully learn and adapt will be forced to exit the industry.

In the second section of the paper the manner in which new-firm survival is measured along with the underlying data base is explained. The hypotheses that firm survival rates are related to the technological regime and industry-specific characteristics, especially the extent of scale economies and capital intensity, are developed in the third section. The U.S. Small Business Data Base is used to estimate survival rates of 295 four-digit SIC industries for varying periods between 1976 and 1986 in the fourth section. Finally, a summary and conclusion are provided in the fifth section. New-firm survival rates are found to be positively related to the extent of small-firm innovative activity. In addition, the existence of scale economies and capital intensity is identified as decreasing the likelihood of firm survival. However, these relationships are considerably different when four-year survival rates are examined rather than ten-year survival rates.

II.   Measuring New-Firm Survival

The greatest obstacle to directly measuring firm survival has been the lack of panel data sets tracking the evolution of firms subsequent to their birth.[4] The USELM file of the U.S. Small Business Data Base (SBDB) is a relatively new source of data that enables newly-created firms and plants to be followed over time. The SBDB has been used by Evans (1987a and 1987b) to analyse the relationships between firm growth, age, and size; Phillips and Kirchhoff (1989) to examine the relationship between small-firm growth and size; and Acs and Audretsch (1989a, 1989b, and 1990) to investigate intra-industry dynamics, including entry across firm-size classes and the extent of turbulence within an industry.

The SBDB data have been derived from the Dun and Bradstreet (DUNS) market identifier file (DMI). The essential unit of observation in the data base is an establishment, defined as an economic entity operating at a specific and single location. Establishments are then linked by ownership to their parent firms. Over the period of 1976 to 1986, the SBDB provides biennial observations on about 4.5 million U.S. business establishments. While the raw data provided by Dun and Bradstreet have been criticized for several weaknesses, such as missing branch records (Armington and Odle, 1982; Storey and Johnson, 1987), the U.S. Small Business Administration, in conjunction with the National Science Foundation and the Brookings Institution has restructured, edited and supplemented the SBDB with data from other sources.[5]

To measure new-firm survival, all establishments that were classified by the SBDB as being founded in 1976 were identified. Those new establishments belonging to an established firm or identified as a branch or subsidiary of a new firm were then discarded. The remaining establishments thus represent newly created firms. Most of these are single-plant firms, although some are multi-plant firms.

Table 1 shows that the number of new firms established in 1976 varied considerably across two-digit SIC manufacturing industries. For example, 16.18% of the new firms were in the printing sector, 13.62% were in the non-electrical machinery sector, 8.62% were in fabricated metal products, and 7.75% were in the apparel sector. Thus, nearly 50% of all new firms were established within these four industrial sectors.

The number of these newly formed firms that were still in existence over the ensuing decade is also shown in table 1. The survival rate in each year is defined as the number of firms still in existence, as a percentage of the total number of new firms that were established in that industry in 1976. There are four important points that emerge from the survival patterns over time. First, and least surprising, the probability of a firm surviving over any given time period is negatively related to the length of that time period. That is, for the entire cohort of firms established in 1976, slightly more than three-quarters were still in existence after two years, slightly fewer than

---

[4] The major data base which has been used to track the evolution of plants over time is the U.S. Census of Manufactures (Dunne et al., 1989 and 1988).

[5] The procedures used by the U.S. Small Business Administration to adjust the raw data provided by Dun and Bradstreet are explicitly explained in detail in U.S. Small Business Administration (1987), Boden and Phillips (1985), and Acs and Audretsch (1990, chapter two).

NEW-FIRM SURVIVAL AND THE TECHNOLOGICAL REGIME   443

TABLE 1.—NEW-FIRM (1976) SURVIVAL RATES OVER TIME BY MANUFACTURING SECTOR

Sector	Year					
	1976	1978	1980	1982	1984	1986
Food	474	340	277	203	152	144
		(71.7)	(58.4)	(42.8)	(32.1)	(30.4)
Tobacco	2	2	2	1	1	1
		(100.0)	(100.0)	(50.0)	(50.0)	(50.0)
Textiles	308	225	165	111	88	84
		(73.1)	(53.6)	(36.0)	(28.6)	(27.3)
Apparel	864	622	477	332	256	236
		(72.0)	(55.2)	(38.4)	(29.6)	(27.3)
Lumber	794	601	514	349	267	256
		(75.7)	(64.7)	(44.0)	(33.6)	(32.2)
Furniture	531	393	310	196	161	141
		(74.0)	(58.4)	(36.9)	(30.3)	(28.4)
Paper	126	99	80	67	58	57
		(78.6)	(63.5)	(53.2)	(46.0)	(45.2)
Printing	1,805	1,482	1,255	931	799	768
		(82.1)	(69.5)	(51.6)	(46.0)	(45.2)
Chemicals	322	248	197	146	119	114
		(77.0)	(61.2)	(45.3)	(37.0)	(35.4)
Petroleum	41	27	18	14	11	11
		(69.5)	(43.9)	(34.1)	(26.8)	(26.8)
Rubber	430	341	280	207	181	176
		(79.3)	(65.1)	(48.1)	(42.1)	(40.9)
Leather	124	89	75	41	33	30
		(71.8)	(60.5)	(33.1)	(26.6)	(24.2)
Stone, Clay, Glass	545	429	341	246	197	182
		(78.7)	(62.6)	(45.1)	(36.1)	(33.4)
Primary Metals	168	135	108	82	74	72
		(80.4)	(64.3)	(48.8)	(44.0)	(42.9)
Fabricated Metal Products	962	758	638	493	414	394
		(78.8)	(66.3)	(51.2)	(43.0)	(41.0)
Machinery (non-electrical)	1,519	1,243	1,054	820	708	675
		(81.8)	(69.4)	(54.0)	(46.6)	(44.4)
Electrical Equipment	635	489	378	259	220	196
		(77.0)	(59.5)	(40.8)	(33.1)	(30.9)
Transportation Equipment	420	304	229	144	103	97
		(72.4)	(54.5)	(34.3)	(24.5)	(23.1)
Instruments	312	251	205	147	123	120
		(80.4)	(65.7)	(47.1)	(39.4)	(38.5)
Miscellenous	772	559	432	272	200	185
		(72.4)	(56.0)	(35.2)	(25.9)	(24.0)
Total	11,154	8,637	7,035	5,061	4,155	3,949
		(77.4)	(63.1)	(45.4)	(37.3)	(35.4)

Note: The survival rate is defined as the number of firms surviving in an industry in a given year, as a percentage of the total number of new firms established in 1976.

one-half were still operating after six years, and about one-third had survived ten years.

Second, as Evans (1987a and 1987b) found, the probability of survival generally increases with the age of the firm. Thus, firms which were two years old in 1978 had an 81.45% chance of surviving until 1980; those firms that were four years old in 1980 had a 71.94% chance of surviving until 1982; six-year old firms in 1982 had an 82.10% chance of surviving another two years; and eight year old firms in 1984 had a 95.04% chance of surviving

until 1986. Of course, these aggregate survival rates in no way control for the business cycle—a qualification which will be made more explicitly in the concluding section of this paper. Still, the overall trend generally confirms the stylized fact identified by Evans that the probability of a firm surviving an additional increment of time increases with the amount of time that the firm has already survived.

Third, the survival rate apparently varies considerably across manufacturing sectors. For example, the ten-year survival rate is relatively high in paper, non-electrical machinery, primary metals, and fabricated metal products, all of which had survival rates in 1986 exceeding 40%.[6] By contrast, over the same time interval the survival rate is relatively low in the petroleum, apparel, furniture, transportation equipment, and leather sectors. None of these sectors experienced a ten-year survival rate in excess of 27%.

Finally, there is no apparent relationship between the number of newly created firms and the probability of surviving. Both the paper and non-electrical machinery sectors had ten-year survival rates of about 45%. However, the non-electrical machinery sector experienced the greatest number of newly established firms, while there were only 126 new firms established in the paper sector. Similarly, in both the chemical and textile sectors there were slightly more than three hundred new firms established in 1976. However, the ten-year survival rate in the chemical sector was nearly one-third greater than the survival rate in the textile sector.

III. The Technological Regime and Firm Survival

It has been widely observed (Scherer, 1980, p. 248; Phillips and Kirchhoff, 1989; Acs and Audretsch, 1990) that most new entrants are small and tend to operate at a suboptimal scale of output, at least in capital-intensive industries.[7] Thus, the greatest detriment to the survival of new firms may be the extent to which scale economies play an important role in the industry. That is, the greater the minimum efficient scale (MES) level of output, the less likely a firm is to survive, unless it experiences sufficient growth to attain MES.

However, Weiss (1976 and 1979) has argued that the existence of suboptimal capacity firms, that is those firms operating at a scale of output less than the MES level, is promoted in industries where price has been elevated above the minimum level of average costs (for firms with output exceeding the MES). To the extent that price

exceeds the minimum average cost of the most efficient firms, the probability of a newly established firm surviving will be higher.

Each firm must decide whether to maintain its output at the same level, expand, contract, or exit from any industry, i. The probability of any given firm, j, of age t, remaining in industry i, or Pr $(Y_{it}^j > 0)$, is essentially determined by the extent to which a firm is burdened with an inherent size disadvantage, the degree to which the industry price is elevated beyond average cost at the MES level of output, and the probability of innovative activity:

$$\Pr(Y_{it}^j > 0) = f(I_t, P_i - c(Y_i^*),$$
$$c(Y_i) - c(Y^*)) \qquad (1)$$

where I_t is the probability of a firm with t years of experience making an innovation, $c(Y_i)$ is the average cost of producing at a scale of output Y_i, P_i is the price level in industry i, and $c(Y_i^*)$ is the average cost of producing at the MES level of output, or the minimum level of production required to exhaust scale economies, Y^*.

The probability of making an innovation, I, affects a firm's decision to remain in, or exit from, an industry because innovative activity is a vehicle by which a firm can grow and attain the MES level of output.[8] An implication of the Jovanovic (1982) and Pakes and Ericson (1987) learning-by-doing models is that firms begin at a small scale of output and then, if merited by subsequent performance, expand. While entrepreneurs may be unsure about their ability to innovate upon establishing a new firm, this becomes clearer with the passage of time. Those firms which successfully innovate can expect future sales growth, while those that face only dim prospects of innovating are more likely to exit from the industry.

The ability of a firm to innovate after t years of experience in the industry is influenced by what Nelson and Winter (1974 and 1982) term as the underlying technological regime: "An entrepreneurial regime is one that is favorable to innovative entry and unfavorable to innovative activity by established firms; a routinized regime is one in which the conditions are the other way around" (Winter, 1984, p. 297). At least some

---

[6] Because only two new firms were established in the tobacco sector (SIC 21), it is excluded from these comparisons among two-digit SIC sectors.

[7] Of the 11,662 establishments started in 1976, only 589 (5.05%) had more than 50 employees. Thus, virtually all new establishments can be considered to be small.

[8] Caves and Pugel (1980) found that a strategy of product innovation is an instrument used by small firms to compete in high-MES industries.

empirical evidence was provided by Acs and Audretsch (1987, 1988, and 1990) supporting the existence of these two distinct technological regimes.

Gort and Klepper (1982) posited, and found evidence, that the relative innovative advantage between newly established enterprises and incumbent firms depends upon the source of information leading to innovative activity. If information based on non-transferable experience in the market is an important input in generating innovative activity, then incumbent firms will tend to have the innovative advantage over new firms. This is consistent with Winter's (1984) notion of the routinized regime, where the accumulated stock of non-transferable information is the product of experience within the market, which firms outside of the industry, by definition, cannot possess.

By contrast, when information outside of the industry is a relatively important input in generating innovative activity, newly established firms will tend to have the innovative advantage over the incumbent firms. Arrow (1962), Mueller (1976), and Williamson (1975) have all emphasized that when such information created outside of the industry cannot be easily transferred to those firms existing within the industry, perhaps due to organizational factors, the holder of such knowledge must enter and expand in the industry in order to exploit the market value of his/her knowledge.

Thus, the probability of a given firm making an innovation, I, is dependent upon the extent to which an industry can be characterized by an entrepreneurial regime, u, or a routinized regime, r, as well as the age of the firm, t:

$$I = A/(1 + re^{-ut}) \tag{2}$$

where A is a constant determining the asymptotic conditions.

Under the routinized regime, r is relatively large and u is relatively small, implying that the probability of a firm making an innovation increases as t increases, or as the firm gains experience in the industry. Under the entrepreneurial regime the opposite technological conditions hold —r is relatively small and u is relatively large—so that the probability of a firm making an innovation decreases as t increases.

One implication of the passive and learning models by Jovanovic (1982) and Pakes and Ericson (1987) is not only that firms that are unable to learn and adapt must exit the industry, but that the greater the cost disadvantage incurred by such firms, the more rapid will be their departure. This implies that industries which are capital-intensive and where scale economies play an important role may be particularly subject to low rates of survival. High-MES industries may be particularly subject to a low rate of survival, because those newly established firms unable to innovate, or find some other vehicle for growth, will be forced to exit.

IV. Empirical Results

To test the hypotheses that new-firm survival is attributable to the technological regime, market structure, and the extent of scale economies characterizing an industry, survival rates for firms established in 1976 were calculated for 295 four-digit SIC industries for 1978, 1980, 1982, 1984, and 1986. While the concept of technological regimes does not lend itself to precise measurement, the major conclusion of Acs and Audretsch (1987, 1988, and 1990) was that the existence of these distinct regimes can be inferred by the extent to which small firms are able to innovate relative to the total amount of innovative activity in an industry. That is, when the small-firm innovation rate is high relative to the total innovation rate, the technological and knowledge conditions are more likely to reflect the entrepreneurial regime. The routinized regime is more likely to exhibit a low small-firm innovation rate relative to the total innovation rate.

The total innovation rate is defined as the total number of innovations recorded in 1982 divided by industry employment. The small-firm innovation rate is defined as the number of innovations contributed by firms with fewer than 500 employees divided by small-firm employment.[9] The rates

---

[9] The innovation data are from the U.S. Small Business Administration's Innovation Data Base. The data base consists of 8,074 innovations introduced into the United States in 1982. Of the manufacturing innovations for which firm size could be identified, 55.81% came from large firms (with at least 500 employees), while 44.19% came from small firms (with fewer than 500 employees) (Acs and Audretsch, 1990, p. 19). A detailed analysis of the distribution of innovations according to significance levels and firm size can be found in Acs and Audretsch (1990, chapter 2).

are used to standardize the amount of innovative and small-firm innovative activity in an industry for the size of that industry (as Acs and Audretsch do in their 1987 and 1990 studies). Since high small-firm innovation rates, given a total innovation rate, presumably reflect the entrepreneurial regime, the small-firm innovation rate is expected to have a positive influence on new-firm survival.

The challenge presented in measuring the extent of scale economies has been discussed in some detail in Scherer (1980), and Caves et al. (1975). As a proxy measure for MES, the Comanor-Wilson (1967) approach is adapted, where MES is measured as the mean size of the largest plants accounting for one-half of the industry value-of-shipments. To transform the MES measure into the share of the market required to exhaust scale economies, MES is divided by the 1977 industry value-of-shipments. In addition, the 1977 capital–labor ratio is included as an explanatory variable, since, as White (1982) points out, higher capital–labor ratios tend to be associated with greater scale economies.[10] This is partially because capital equipment tends to be "lumpy" in nature. Also, by enabling firms to take advantage of increased specialization and greater rates of utilization, the use of larger machines tends to reduce costs per unit of output. Since newly established enterprises generally operate at a suboptimal scale in capital-intensive industries where MES is high, both of these measures are expected to have a negative influence on the survival rate.

Advertising intensity, measured as industry expenditures on advertising divided by 1977 value-of-shipments, is also expected to be negatively related to new-firm survival for at least two reasons. First, the effect of advertising on firm revenues is subject to economies of scale that result from the increasing effectiveness of advertising message per unit of output.[11] Second, to the extent that scale economies exist in either production or advertising, the need to obtain funds for advertising will tend to aggravate the inherent size disadvantage of newly established firms.

As explained in the previous section, factors contributing to the elevation of price above the long-run average cost for firms at the MES level of output may facilitate the survival of suboptimal scale firms. According to Weiss (1976 and 1979) the existence of suboptimal scale firms may be promoted in concentrated industries, where the price level is more likely to be elevated.[12] Thus, ceteris paribus, the 1977 four-firm concentration ratio is expected to have a positive influence on new-firm survival rates. Similarly, Bradburd and Caves (1982) found that industry growth has a positive influence on the price-cost margin. The 1976–1986 industry growth rate (measured as the percentage change in value-of-shipments) is therefore expected to exert a positive effect on new-firm survival rates.

One of the more striking results to emerge in the Dunne et al. (1989) study is that plant growth and failure is influenced by the ownership structure of the firm. They found that the expected growth rate tends to decline with size for single-plant firms, whereas expected growth increases with size for plants owned by multiplant firms. Therefore, the share of newly established firms in 1976 accounted for by single-plant firms is also included as an explanatory variable. A negative coefficient would be consistent with the Dunne et al. findings. All data sources and further explanations are provided in the data appendix.

Table 2 shows the regression results estimating the ten-year survival rates for firms established in 1976. Because the dependent variable can vary only between 0 and 1 by definition, ordinary least squares estimation would produce inefficient variances of the estimated coefficients, rendering the appropriate hypothesis tests unreliable. Following the procedure recommended by Judge et al. (1980), this statistical inefficiency is corrected by using the logit estimation.

The regression results provide considerable support for the hypothesis that new-firm survival is influenced by the technological regime. The positive and statistically significant coefficient of the small-firm innovation rate in equations (1)–(3) suggests that, holding the total amount of innovative activity in the industry constant, an increase

---

[10] It should be recognized that the production function is not homothetic.

[11] The hypothesis that there are scale economies in advertising has been challenged by Arndt and Simon (1983), Boyer (1974), and Simon (1970).

[12] For a comprehensive group of studies providing at least some evidence that the price level tends to be elevated in concentrated industries see Weiss (1990).

NEW-FIRM SURVIVAL AND THE TECHNOLOGICAL REGIME 447

TABLE 2.—LOGIT REGRESSIONS OF NEW-FIRM SURVIVAL RATES, 1976–1986
(*t*-statistics listed in parentheses)

	(1)	(2)	(3)	(4)
Intercept	67.8190	63.9800	73.0430	70.5430
	(7.408)[b]	(7.539)[b]	(6.430)[b]	(6.268)[b]
Innovation Rate	−4.959	−4.6525	−5.4503	—
	(−0.592)	(−0.555)	(−0.648)	
Small-Firm Innovation Rate	0.6070	0.6080	0.6372	
	(2.019)[b]	(2.021)[b]	(2.100)[b]	
Small-Firm/Total Innovation Rate	—	—	—	1.2045
				(1.758)[a]
Scale Economies	−2.2565	−2.2632	−1.6447	−1.8035
	(−1.915)[a]	(−1.920)[a]	(−1.160)	(−1.257)
Capital Intensity	−0.4148	−0.4063	−0.3764	−0.3661
	(−2.138)[b]	(−2.095)[b]	(−1.879)[a]	(−1.825)[a]
Concentration	—	—	−0.1905	−0.2477
			(−0.778)	(−0.984)
Advertising/Sales	27.1970	22.998	30.213	30.870
	(0.942)	(0.803)	(1.036)	(1.055)
Growth	1.7336	1.8601	1.7619	1.1644
	(0.479)	(0.514)	(0.487)	(0.320)
Single-Plant Share	−3.9765	—	−4.1132	−3.9493
	(−1.116)		(−1.152)	(−1.105)
Log-Likelihood	−299.973	−300.611	−299.662	−300.030
Sample Size	295	295	295	295

Note: The dependent variable has been multiplied by 100 for presentation purposes.
[a] Statistically significant at the 90% level of confidence, two-tailed test.
[b] Statistically significant at the 95% level of confidence, two-tailed test.

in the ability of small firms to innovate leads to a higher survival rate. By contrast, when the small-firm innovation rate is relatively low, the survival rate tends to be lower. This is also consistent with the positive and statistically significant coefficient of the ratio between the small-firm innovation rate and the total innovation rate in equation (4).

There is also evidence that, as expected, the survival rate is negatively influenced by the extent of scale economies and capital intensity characterizing an industry. In equations (1) and (2) both the measure of MES and the capital–labor ratio are negative and statistically significant. When the four-firm concentration ratio is included in the regression in equations (3) and (4), the coefficient of the MES measure remains negative but can no longer be considered statistically significant.[13] Although the growth rate has a positive coefficient and the share of firms consisting of single-plant enterprises has a negative coefficient, as expected, neither coefficient can be inferred to be statistically different from zero.

[13] It should also be reported that when the scale economies variable and both the scale economies and capital intensity variables are dropped from equations (3) and (4) in table 2, the four-firm concentration ratio is found to exert a negative and statistically significant influence on new-firm survival rates.

Survival rates for shorter time periods are substituted as the dependent variable in table 3. The first two equations estimate the four-year survival rates between 1976 and 1980. Two striking differences emerge between the determinants of the four- and ten-year survival rates. As the low *t*-statistics for the total innovation rate and small-firm innovation rate suggest, the technological regime apparently has no significant influence on survival within the first four years subsequent to establishment of a new firm. Second, as the positive and statistically significant coefficients of the measures of scale economies, capital-intensity, and market concentration all indicate, high-MES markets exert a positive influence on the ability of new firms to survive in the short run. All three of these measures have been usually identified as being positively related to industry price–cost margins (Schmalensee, 1988). It may be that the elevated price–cost margins enable new and presumably suboptimal scale firms to survive in the short run, but not in the longer run.

In fact, none of these variables is significantly different from zero in equation (3), where the time period has been lengthened to six years. Extending the time period further in equation (4) yields a negative and statistically significant rela-

TABLE 3.—LOGIT REGRESSIONS OF NEW-FIRM SURVIVAL RATES FOR VARYING TIME PERIODS
(*t*-statistics listed in parentheses)

	1976–1980		1976–1982	1976–1984	1978–1982	1980–1984
	(1)	(2)	(3)	(4)	(5)	(6)
Intercept	−52.5330	−66.1610	12.0060	53.8720	−7.6916	−37.2850
	(−5.951)[b]	(−6.243)[b]	(−1.424)	(5.727)[b]	(−0.167)	(−1.300)
Innovation Rate	4.9880	6.2177	−2.5144	1.6693	13.8140	−7.5336
	(0.681)	(0.853)	(−0.331)	(0.198)	(1.235)	(−0.906)
Small-Firm	0.1096	0.0324	0.1437	−0.0091	0.2294	0.8709
Innovation Rate	(0.415)	(0.123)	(0.525)	(−0.030)	(0.689)	(3.152)[b]
Scale Economies	2.866	1.2972	−0.5808	−1.6072	3.1614	5.3727
	(2.771)[b]	(1.050)	(−0.542)	(−1.355)	(1.947)[a]	(2.660)[b]
Capital Intensity	0.4950	0.3969	0.1430	−0.3587	−0.0320	0.0827
	(2.912)[b]	(2.280)[b]	(0.810)	(−1.838)[a]	(−0.131)	(0.381)
Concentration	—	0.4879	—	—	—	—
		(2.286)[b]				
Advertising/Sales	39.6470	31.8110	56.1270	37.3370	−9.7024	27.5830
	(1.566)	(1.254)	(2.130)[b]	(1.283)	(−0.272)	(1.023)
Growth[c]	−3.1061	−3.001	3.1576	2.8424	−2.0817	1.1503
	(−0.631)	(−0.615)	(0.807)	(0.733)	(−1.177)	(0.234)
Single-Plant Share	1.2150	1.5661	−1.9080	−3.5004	1.4825	7.1377
	(0.388)	(0.504)	(−0.588)	(−0.975)	(0.339)	(0.235)
Log-Likelihood	−261.587	−258.915	−272.130	−302.083	−259.730	213.087
Sample Size	295	295	295	295	236	232

Note: The dependent variable has been multiplied by 100 for presentation purposes.
[a] Statistically significant at the 90% level of confidence, two-tailed test.
[b] Statistically significant at the 95% level of confidence, two-tailed test.
[c] Industry growth is measured over the relevant time period corresponding to the dependent variable.

tionship between capital-intensity and the eight-year survival rate.[14] Thus, there is considerable evidence that, just as the technological regime affects the ability of new firms to survive over a fairly long period but has no influence in the short run, the existence of high market concentration, scale economies and capital intensity facilitates survival shortly following the establishment of a new firm, but impedes survival in the longer run.

One qualification about the generality of the statistical results is the impact that the stage of the business cycle has on the pattern of survival rates across manufacturing industries. In order to shed at least some light on the extent to which macroeconomic volatility affects cross-section survival rates, the four-year survival rate for firms established in 1978 is estimated in equation (5) and for firms established in 1980 in equation (6). The results are generally consistent with those in equation (1). The presence of scale economies is found to increase the survival rate for all three time periods. However, while the small-firm innovation rate exerts no impact on the ability of firms to survive for the first two time periods, it has a

[14] Including the four-firm concentration ratio in equations (3) and (4) results in a coefficient that is not statistically significant.

positive and statistically significant effect during the 1980–1984 period. This ambiguity would suggest that the relationship between survival rates across industries and the business cycle needs to be more thoroughly examined in subsequent research.

V. Conclusions

The findings of this paper provide at least some resolution to the apparent paradox that the entry of new firms is not substantially deterred in capital-intensive industries which exhibit scale economies. While entry may still occur in such industries, the likelihood of survival is considerably less. This is consistent with the observation that most new firms are sufficiently small as to operate at a suboptimal scale of output in high MES and capital-intensive industries. According to Jovanovic's (1982) theory, only those firms that are somehow able to adapt and grow will survive, while the others will be forced to exit from the industry.

One instrument that may enhance the survival of new firms, at least under the entrepreneurial regime, is innovative activity. As the empirical results imply, those technology and knowledge conditions conducive to small-firm innovation tend to promote the survival of new firms. Under the routinized regime, where small firms are at an innovative disadvantage, the survival rate is distinctly lower.

However, the influence of the technological regime and market structure on firm survival apparently varies considerably with the time interval considered. Just as the technological regime has no impact on four-year survival rates, the extent of scale economies and capital-intensity has a positive effect on the ability of firms to survive in the short run. In addition, the four-year survival rate for 1976–1980 is positively related to concentration. This is consistent with the hypothesis posited by Weiss (1976 and 1979) and others that factors associated with higher price-cost margins will tend to promote the entry of suboptimal scale firms. As the ten-year survival results indicate, however, this is a short-run and not a long-run effect.

These results need to be qualified by several considerations. First, the likelihood of survival is conditional upon an enterprise having already made the decision to enter an industry. However, the decision to establish a new enterprise is surely not independent of the probability of survival. To some extent there is a self-selection bias affecting the cohort of firms established in any given year —presumably those potential entrants which actually do establish a new firm would be expected to be influenced by their prospects of survival. The interaction between the decision to enter and the likelihood of survival needs to be explicitly examined in future research.

Second, there is at least some evidence that the observed survival rates are affected by the business cycle. In order to disentangle observed survival rates from business cycle effects, panel data sets with frequent observations must be constructed over long time intervals. The results from this paper make it clear, however, that the technological regime and market structure play an important role in explaining the variation in firm survival across manufacturing industries.

APPENDIX

Data Sources and Further Explanations

The data on firm survival and the share of new firms accounted for by single-plant firms come from the USELM file of the U.S. Small Business Data Base. More detailed description of the data can be found in Phillips and Kirchhoff (1989), Acs and Audretsch (1990, Chapter two), Boden and Phillips (1985), and U.S. Small Business Administration (1987).

The innovation data for the number of small-firm innovations and total innovations, which are used to construct the innovation rates, come from the U.S. Small Business Data Base. This is explained in detail in Acs and Audretsch (1988 and 1990, chapter two).

The measures of MES (scale economies), capital–labor ratio (defined as gross fixed assets divided by total employment (thousands)), value-of-shipments, and the four-firm concentration ratio come from the U.S. Department of Commerce, Bureau of the Census, Census of Manufactures, 1977, Washington, D.C.: U.S. Government Printing Office. The growth measure is derived from the U.S. Department of Commerce, Bureau of the Census, Annual Survey of Manufactures, Industry Profiles, Washington, D.C.: U.S. Government Printing Office, various years.

REFERENCES

Acs, Zoltan J., and David B. Audretsch, *Innovation and Small Firms* (Cambridge, MA: MIT Press, 1990).

———, "Small-Firm Entry in U.S. Manufacturing," *Economica* 56 (May 1989a), 255–265.

———, "Births and Firm Size," *Southern Economic Journal* 55 (Oct. 1989b), 255–265.

———, "Innovation in Large and Small Firms: An Empirical Analysis," *American Economic Review* 78 (Sept. 1988), 678–690.

———, "Innovation, Market Structure and Firm Size," this REVIEW 69 (Nov. 1987), 567–575.

Armington, Catherine, and Marjorie Odle, "Small Business—How Many Jobs," *The Brookings Review* 1 (Winter 1982), 14–17.

Arndt, Johan, and Julian L. Simon, "Advertising and Economies of Scale: Critical Comments on the Evidence," *Journal of Industrial Economics* 32 (Dec. 1983), 229–243.

Arrow, Kenneth J., "Economic Welfare and the Allocation of Resources for Invention," in R. R. Nelson (ed.), *The Rate and Direction of Inventive Activity* (Princeton: Princeton University Press, 1962), 609–626.

Beesley, M. E., and R. T. Hamilton, "Small Firms' Seedbed Role and the Concept of Turbulence," *Journal of Industrial Economics* 33 (Dec. 1984), 217–232.

Boden, Richard, and Bruce D. Phillips, "Uses and Limitations of USEEM/USELM Data," Office of Advocacy, U.S. Small Business Administration, Washington, D.C., Nov. 1985.

Boyer, Kenneth D., "Information and Goodwill Advertising," this REVIEW 56 (Nov. 1974), 541–548.

Bradburd, Ralph, and Richard E. Caves, "Closer Look at the Effect of Market Growth on Industries' Profits," this REVIEW 64 (Nov. 1982), 635–645.

Caves, Richard E., and T. A. Pugel, *Intraindustry Differences in Conduct and Performance: Viable Strategies in U.S. Manufacturing Industries* (New York, NY: New York University Press, 1980).

Caves, Richard E., J. Khalilzadeh-Shirazi, and M. E. Porter, "Scale Economies in Statistical Analyses of Market Power," this REVIEW 57 (May 1975), 133–140.

Comanor, William S., and Thomas A. Wilson, "Advertising, Market Structure, and Performance," this REVIEW 49 (Nov. 1967), 423–440.

Dunne, Timothy, Mark J. Robert, and Larry Samuelson, "The Growth and Failure of U.S. Manufacturing Plants," *Quarterly Journal of Economics* 104 (Nov. 1989), 671–698.

Dunne, Timothy, Mark J. Robert, and Larry Samuelson, "Patterns of Firm Entry and Exit in U.S. Manufacturing Industries," *Rand Journal of Economics* 19 (Winter 1988), 495–515.

Evans, David S., "The Relationship between Firm Growth, Size, and Age: Estimates for 100 Manufacturing Industries," *Journal of Industrial Economics* 35 (June 1987a), 567–581.

_____, "Tests of Alternative Theories of Firm Growth," *Journal of Political Economy* 95 (Aug. 1987b), 657–674.

Geroski, Paul, and Joachim Schwalbach (eds.), *Entry and Market Contestability: An International Comparison* (London: Basil Blackwell, 1991).

Gort, Michael, and Steven Klepper, "Time Paths in the Diffusion of Product Innovations," *Economic Journal* 92 (Sept. 1982), 630–653.

Hall, Bronwyn H., "The Relationship Between Firm Size and Firm Growth in the U.S. Manufacturing Sector," *Journal of Industrial Economics* 35 (June 1987), 583–605.

Jovanovic, Boyan, "Selection and Evolution of Industry," *Econometrica* 50 (May 1982), 649–670.

Judge, George G., E. Griffiths, R. Carter-Hill and Tsoung-Chao-Lee, *The Theory and Practice of Econometrics* (New York, NY: John Wiley & Sons, 1980).

Mueller, Dennis, "Information, Mobility, and Profit," *Kyklos* 29 (1976), 419–448.

Nelson, Richard R., and Sidney G. Winter, *An Evolutionary Theory of Economic Change* (Cambridge: Harvard University Press, 1982).

_____, "Neoclassical vs. Evolutionary Theories of Economic Growth: Critique and Prospectus," *Economic Journal* 84 (Dec. 1974), 886–905.

Oster, Sharon, "Intraindustry Structure and the Ease of Strategic Change," this REVIEW 64 (Aug. 1982), 376–383.

Pakes, A., and R. Ericson, "Empirical implications of Alternative Models of Firm Dynamics," manuscript, Department of Economics, University of Wisconsin-Madison, 1987.

Phillips, Bruce D., and Bruce A. Kirchhoff, "Formation, Growth and Survival: Small Firm Dynamics in the U.S. Economy," *Small Business Economics* 1 (1989), 65–74.

Preisendörfer, Peter, Rudolf Schüssler, and Rolf Ziegler, "Bestandschancen neugegründeter Kleinbetriebe," *Internationales Gewerbearchiv* 37 (1989), 237–248.

Scherer, F. M., *Industrial Market Structure and Economic Performance*, 2nd edition (Chicago, IL: Rand McNally College Publishing Co., 1980).

Schmalensee, Richard, "Industrial Economics: An Overview," *Economic Journal* 98 (Sept. 1988), 619–642.

Simon, Julian L., *Issues in the Economics of Advertising* (Urbana: University of Illinois Press, 1970).

Storey, David J., and Steven Johnson, *Job Generation and Labour Market Changes* (London: Macmillan, 1987).

U.S. Small Business Administration, Office of Advocacy, *Linked 1976–1984 USEEM User's Guide* (Washington, D.C., July 1987).

Weiss, Leonard W. (ed.), *Concentration and Price* (Cambridge, MA: The MIT Press, 1990).

_____, "The Structure-Conduct-Performance Paradigm and Antitrust," *University of Pennsylvania Law Review* 127 (Apr. 1979), 1104–1140.

_____, "Optimal Plant Scale and the Extent of Suboptimal Capacity," in Robert T. Masson and P. D. Qualls, (eds.), *Essays on Industrial Organization in Honor of Joe S. Bain* (Cambridge, MA: Ballinger, 1976), 126–134.

_____, "The Survival Technique and the Extent of Suboptimal Capacity," *Journal of Political Economy* 72 (June 1964), 246–261.

White, Lawrence J., "The Determinants of the Relative Importance of Small Business," this REVIEW 64 (Feb. 1982), 42–49.

Williamson, Oliver E., *Markets and Hierarchies* (New York, NY: Macmillan Publishing Co., 1975).

Winter, Sidney G., "Schumpeterian Competition in Alternative Technological Regimes," *Journal of Economic Behavior and Organization* 5 (Sept.–Dec. 1984), 287–320.

15

N·H

ELSEVIER

International Journal of Industrial Organization
13 (1995) 441–457

International Journal of
Industrial
Organization

Innovation, growth and survival

David B. Audretsch

Wissenschaftszentrum Berlin für Sozialforschung, Reichpietschufer 50, D-10785, Berlin 30,
Germany
CEPR, 25–28 Old Burlington Street, London, W1X 1LB, UK

Abstract

The purpose of this paper is to explain why the likelihood of survival and post-entry growth rates vary systematically from industry to industry. In particular, the post-entry performance of new firms is linked to the underlying technological conditions in an industry. In industries where innovative activity, and especially the innovative activity of small firms, plays an important role, the likelihood of new entrants' surviving over a decade is lower than in industries where innovative activity is less important. At the same time, those entrants that are able to survive exhibit higher growth rates. In addition, the conditional likelihood of surviving an additional two years for entrants that have already survived the first few years is actually greater, and not lower, in highly innovative industries.

The evidence therefore suggests that a highly innovative environment exerts a disparate effect on the post-entry performance of new entrants. Those new firms that are able to adjust and offer a viable product apparently experience higher rates of growth and a greater likelihood of survival. But overall, entrants and certainly new firms that are not able to adjust and produce a viable product are confronted by a lower likelihood of survival in highly innovative environments.

Keywords: Innovation; Growth; Survival; Industry evolution

JEL classification: L1; O3

1. Introduction

A recent wave of studies has established what Paul Geroski (1995, p. 20) has classified as a stylized fact, that "Both firm size and age are correlated with the survival and growth of entrants." Starting with the studies by Evans (1987a,b), Hall (1987), and Dunne, Roberts and Samuelson (1988, 1989) a consistent finding suggests that the likelihood of survival is positively related to firm size but growth rates, at least for small and young firms, tend to be negatively related to firm size. Subsequent studies for Canada (Baldwin, 1995), Portugal (Mata and Portugal, 1994; Mata et al., 1995) and Germany (Wagner, 1994) have confirmed that these relationships are not specific to the United States.

One of the major findings of Dunne, Roberts and Samuelson (1988, 1989) is that the survival rates and growth rates of new firms vary systematically across industries. However, they provided no insight as to why such variation in survival rates should exist. The purpose of this paper it to examine explicitly why the propensity for firms to survive as well as their growth rates vary systematically across manufacturing industries. In particular, we focus upon the hypothesis posited by Geroski (1995, p. 21), that "the growth and survival prospects of new firms will depend on their ability to learn about their environment, and to link changes in their strategy choices to the changing configuration of that environment . . . (t)he more turbulent is the market environment, the more likely it is that firms will fail to cope. If the process of entry continually throws up new aspirants for market places, then slow learning coupled with a turbulent environment means that high entry rates will be observed jointly with high failure rates." That is, it is variations in the opportunity for new firms to innovate that shape variations in their survival and growth rates across industries.

In the second section of this paper the methodology for measuring new-firm survival and growth is introduced. We find that the variance in survival rates across manufacturing industries is greater than the variance in entry rates. The hypotheses explaining why survival rates and growth rates vary systematically across industries are introduced in the third section. In the fourth section these hypotheses are tested using a large longitudinal data base consisting of 11,000 U.S. manufacturing firms established in 1976. Finally, in the fifth section a summary and a conclusion are provided. In particular, there is considerable evidence supporting the Geroski (1995, p. 21) hypothesis that the likelihood of survival tends to be systematically lower in industries where the innovative opportunities available to small firms tend to be the greatest, i.e. where the "process of entry continually throws up new aspirants for market places". However, for those entrants having survived the first several years, being in an innovative industry actually raises the likelihood of survival

2. Measuring survival and growth rates

The longitudinal data base used to analyze the post-entry performance of new firms is taken from the United States Small Business Administration's

Small Business Data Base (SBDB).[1] The SBDB identifies the startup of new firms and establishments (plants in manufacturing). The USELM file of the SBDB makes it possible to track the subsequent performance of these entrants over time and thus is well-suited for such a longitudinal study.[2]

Businesses are identified at both the establishment and enterprise levels by the SBDB. Observations are reported biannually between 1976 and 1986. The SBDB has been used by Audretsch (1991, 1995) and Evans (1987a, 1987b) to examine the relationships between firm age, size, growth and survival, and by Audretsch and Mahmood (1995) to estimate a hazard function for new firms.

As Table 1 indicates, there are 11 154 new-firm entrants in U.S. manufac-

Table 1
New firm entry and survival rates compared across manufacturing sectors, 1976–1986

Sector	New firm entry, 1976	Entry rate (%), 1976	Surviving firms, 1986	Survival rate (%), 1986
Food	474	2.53	144	30.4
Textiles	308	3.91	84	27.3
Apparel	864	3.76	236	27.3
Lumber	794	3.72	256	32.2
Furniture	531	3.70	141	28.4
Paper	126	2.98	57	45.2
Printing	805	2.90	768	42.5
Chemicals	322	2.95	114	35.4
Petroleum	41	3.21	11	26.8
Rubber	430	4.72	176	40.9
Leather	124	3.00	30	24.2
Stone, clay, glass	545	3.86	182	33.4
Primary metals	168	2.97	72	42.9
Fabricated metal products	962	3.19	394	41.0
Machinery (non-electrical)	1519	3.14	675	44.4
Electrical equipment	635	4.41	196	30.9
Transportation equipment	420	4.01	97	23.1
Instruments	312	3.94	120	38.5
Miscellaneous	772	3.62	185	24.0
Total	11154	3.56	3949	35.4

Note: The startup rate is defined as the share (percentage) of the total number of firms accounted for by new-firm startups. The survival rate is defined as the number of firms surviving in an industry in a given year, as a percentage of the total number of new firms established in 1976.

[1] For a detailed description of the SBDB see Boden and Phillips (1985) and the Small Business Administration (1987).
[2] The individual records in the SBDB are derived from the Dun and Bradstreet (DUNS) market identifier file (DMI). There are around 4.5 million establishments included in the SBDB.

turing identified in 1976.[3] When entry activity is compared across aggregated two-digit standard industrial classification (SIC) sectors in manufacturing, the number of new-firm entrants ranges from 41 in the petroleum sector to 1805 in printing. Of course, some sectors contain a larger population of firms than others. Thus, when the *entry rate* is formed by dividing the number of new firms by the population of firms in 1976, it is found to range from 2.53% in the food and beverage sector, to 4.72% in rubber.

Based on the number of firms identified by the SBDB as still existing in 1986, the survival rate is measured as the share of 1976 entrants surviving one decade. As Table 1 indicates, the mean survival rates for the aggregated manufacturing sectors ranges from a low of 24.2% in rubber to 45.2% in paper.

A particularly striking result emerging when comparing the entry rates with the survival rates is that the variance of the survival rates across manufacturing industries is actually considerably greater than is the variance of the entry rates across manufacturing industries. The coefficient of variation is 0.228 for the survival rate and only 0.160 for the entry rate. The lower variance in entry rates than survival rates across industries is consistent with Geroski's (1995, p. 4) observation that, "In fact, most of the total variation in entry across industries and over time is 'within' industry variation rather than 'between' industry variation." By contrast, while the propensity for new firms to enter is relatively more constant across manufacturing industries, the likelihood of those firms' surviving over one decade varies considerably more. Thus, while Geroski's (1995, p. 23) conclusion that "entry appears to be relatively easy, but survival is not," not only is true, but apparently the degree to which the likelihood of survival varies across industries is substantial and greater than the degree to which entry varies across industries. Barriers to survival appear to be more severe than barriers to entry.

Table 2 shows that not only does the post-entry growth of firms vary systematically between cohorts of surviving firms and exiting firms, but it also varies systematically across manufacturing industries. The growth rate is measured as employment in the last year divided by employment in 1976, multiplied by one hundred, to yield a percentage growth rate. Between 1976 and 1978 the cohort of 1986 survivors registered a mean employment growth

---

[3] It should be pointed out that Table 1 includes only new-firm entry in 1976. Dennis Mueller (1991) points out that at least five different forms of entry can be distinguished, only one of which involves a newly created firm. The other four types are (1) entry by an existing firm that builds a new plant in the industry; (2) entry by an existing firm that purchases a plant or firm already existing in the industry; (3) entry by an existing firm that alters the product mix in an existing plant; and (4) entry by a foreign-owned firm in one of the above ways. Still, a new firm not only represents the entry of a new firm, but as Dunne, Roberts and Samuelson (1988, 1989) show, it is by far the most prevalent and common form of entry.

Table 2
Employment growth rates (%) in exiting firms and 1986 survivors

Sector	Period									1976–1986
	1976–1978		1976–1980		1976–1982		1976–1984			
	Exiting firms	1986 survivors	Exiting firms	1986 survivors	Exiting firms	1986 survivors	Exiting firms	1986 survivors	1986 survivors	1986 survivors
Food	11.4	8.4	44.9	22.5	106.7	27.5	64.4	32.6	44.8	
Textiles	34.0	62.0	50.0	100.4	143.0	92.9	86.6	116.3	115.5	
Apparel	39.2	39.1	57.4	131.7	35.5	132.6	164.2	181.8	176.0	
Lumber	34.2	36.3	66.9	44.7	25.3	48.0	112.5	82.1	98.0	
Furniture	59.4	68.7	68.4	121.7	27.5	150.3	99.0	179.9	213.7	
Paper	28.8	48.1	72.0	73.7	263.7	101.9	83.3	157.3	205.7	
Printing	21.7	32.7	23.9	69.2	39.3	96.1	131.3	127.4	160.4	
Chemicals	6.7	20.5	48.9	33.5	34.5	79.0	131.7	135.9	113.9	
Petroleum	44.0	12.1	46.3	3.0	72.7	-15.2	78.9	-24.2	6.1	
Rubber	44.7	51.6	34.4	89.6	151.0	109.8	104.3	138.0	160.5	
Leather	67.4	9.4	82.4	74.5	18.7	135.2	158.3	130.9	134.2	
Stone, clay, glass	37.6	36.7	91.2	65.7	5.4	53.7	44.6	73.9	95.5	
Primary metals	2.6	21.7	103.6	48.7	69.1	48.2	191.0	52.8	76.2	
Fabricated metal products	20.1	41.7	26.1	78.4	80.5	94.4	146.5	105.1	125.0	
Machinery (non-electrical)	36.6	54.6	52.4	109.4	101.8	136.4	135.5	140.4	177.6	
Electrical equipment	48.1	73.9	39.8	166.2	125.5	174.6	176.3	272.5	279.5	
Transportation equipment	125.1	113.6	62.1	140.1	125.3	186.8	60.1	252.1	273.4	
Instruments	45.0	46.0	84.0	137.7	16.0	269.2	232.0	339.7	420.4	
Total	36.2	44.8	51.2	90.3	66.0	106.1	127.2	135.2	154.8	

rate of 44.8%, while firms exiting prior to 1986 grew at a somewhat slower rate of 36.2%. The four-year growth rates, measured between 1976 and 1980, were 90.3% for the cohort of surviving firms and only about half as great, 51.2%, for the firms that exited. While this large gap in growth rates between the cohort of surviving firms and exiting firms continued through six years subsequent to entry, it closed somewhat after eight years.

There are striking differences in the post-entry growth rates across sectors. These differences involve not just the growth rates, but also the differences in the growth rates between the cohorts of surviving firms and the cohorts of exiting firms. That is, the difference in the growth rates between the cohort of surviving firms and exiting firms tends to be the greatest within the first six years subsequent to entry. However, after six years the gap in growth rates between the survivors and exiting firms tends to close.

Entrants in industries such as transportation equipment, electrical equipment, and instruments registered the highest mean growth rates, while entrants in food, lumber, and petroleum exhibited the lowest growth rates. The gap between the growth rates of the surviving and exiting firms tended to be the greatest in the transportation equipment and electrical equipment sectors. By contrast, in the food, lumber, printing, and leather sectors the mean growth rates of the exiting firms tended to actually exceed that of the cohort of firms that survived throughout the entire ten-year period.

Comparing Tables 1 and 2 a tendency can be observed for the post-entry survival rates to be relatively greater in those industries where the growth rates of the surviving firms tend to be the lowest. These also tend to be the sectors with the smallest differences in growth rates between the cohorts of surviving and exiting firms. By contrast, the likelihood of survival tends to be lower in those industries where the difference in the growth rates of the surviving firms tend to be higher. And it is in these industries where the growth rates between the cohorts of surviving and exiting firms tend to be the greatest.

3. Why do survival and growth rates vary across industries?

Why should the likelihood of survival and growth rates vary systematically across industries, and even to a greater extent than entry rates? As Geroski (1995, p. 23) points out, "Perhaps the most striking thing that we know about entry is that small-scale, de novo entry seems to be relatively common in most industries, but that small-scale, de novov entrants generally have a rather short life expectancy. *That is, entry appears to be relatively easy, but survival is not*" (my italics). Geroski goes on to identify a seeming paradox posed by the relative high degree of entry activity, and its relative stability across industries in light of the literature emphasizing the importance of entry barriers: "it is a little difficult to reconcile high entry barriers with high entry rates, not least because entry barriers are commonly thought of as an obstacle which prevents firms from entering a market." Geroski then offers a possible reconciliation: "If, however, barriers to entry are thought of as an obstacle which prevents new firms from surviving long in a market, then the data present less of a puzzle." *That is, the same industry structure characteristics that have been posited to pose a barrier to entry can be interpreted to pose, if not instead of, then at least in addition, a barrier to survival.*

In particular, dating back to Joe Bain (1956), such structural barriers have generally reflected some aspect of the extent of scale economies in the industry and the importance of product differentiation. While studies linking product differentiation to entry have generally focused on measures of advertising as a barrier to entry, a different dimension of product differentiation may be more important as constituting a barrier to survival – the degree of which new products play an important role in the industry. This is generally referred to as innovative activity. And as Arrow (1962) pointed out, there is a high degree of uncertainty inherent in new economic knowledge. While virtually every economic good is subject to uncertainty, almost none is exposed to the degree of risk involved with introducing new products and technologies. There are two additional elements of uncertainty inherent in innovative activity that are not present in other goods. The first is in the realm of production. How a new good can be produced is typically shrouded in uncertainty. The second involves marketing the product. To whom the product can be sold and involving which types of marketing is a conjecture at best. Even if the knowledge can result in a new product, it is not at all clear that the product can be profitably sold. That is, knowledge leading to new goods can be produced, but there is no guarantee that the new knowledge is economic knowledge.

Geroski (1995) has observed that entry is typically used as a vehicle for appropriating the value of potential innovative activity. But due to the uncertainty inherent in highly innovative environments not all entrants will successfully innovate. This means that the likelihood of survival on the condition that the entrant successfully innovates should be relatively high. But the likelihood of survival on the condition that the entrant does not successfully innovate should be correspondingly low.

Baldwin and Scott (1987) and Cohen and Levin (1989) emphasize that the degree of technological opportunity, or importance of innovative activity is anything but constant across manufacturing industries. Similarly, as Acs and Audretsch (1988) show for the United States and Pavitt, Robson and Townsend (1987) show for the United Kingdom, with the degree of technological opportunity or innovative activity in an industry held constant, the extent to which small firms contribute to that innovative activity varies

448   *D.B. Audretsch / Int. J. Ind. Organ. 13 (1995) 441–457*

considerably from industry to industry. That is, as Acs and Audretsch (1988) conclude, the small-firm innovative advantage tends to be in very different industries from those where the large firms have the innovative advantage.

The findings of distinct differences across industries between the small-firm innovative advantage and the large-firm innovative advantage are consistent with Nelson and Winter's (1982) contention that the underlying knowledge conditions generating innovative activity vary from industry to industry. In some industries new economic knowledge generating innovative activity tends to be relatively routine and can be processed within the context of incumbent organizations. In other industries, however, innovations tend to come from knowledge that is not of a routine nature and therefore tends to be rejected by the incumbent organizations. Sidney Winter (1984, p. 297) described these different underlying knowledge conditions as reflecting two distinct technological regimes – "the entrepreneurial regime is one that is favorable to innovative entry and unfavorable to innovative activity by established firms; a routinized regime is one in which the conditions are the other way around."

Why should distinct technological regimes, alternatively favoring the innovative activity of incumbent firms and new entrants, exist? Gort and Klepper (1982) posited and found evidence that the relative innovative advantage between newly established enterprises and incumbent firms depends on the source of information generating innovative activity. If information based on non-transferable experience in the market is an important input in generating innovative activity, then incumbent firms will tend to have the innovative advantage over new firms. This is consistent with Winter's (1984) notion of the routinized regime, where the accumulated stock of non-transferable information is the product of experience within the market, which firms outside of the industry, by definition, cannot possess.

By contrast, when information outside of the routines practiced by the incumbent firms is a relatively important input in generating innovative activity, newly established firms will tend to have the innovative advantage over the incumbent firms. Kenneth Arrow (1962), Dennis Mueller (1976), and Oliver Williamson (1975) have all emphasized that when such information created outside of the incumbent firms cannot be easily transferred to those incumbent firms, the holder of such knowledge must enter the industry to exploit the market value of his knowledge.

Thus, Geroski's (1995) observation that entry serves as a vehicle for innovative activity may vary from industry to industry not only because the relative importance of innovative activity varies systematically across industries, but also because the opportunities for new firms to generate that innovative activity, i.e. the technological regime, also vary from industry to industry. That is, while Geroski (1989a) finds that entry rates tend to be higher in industries exhibiting a greater degree of innovative activity, Acs and Audretsch (1990) find that new-firm entry tends to be even greater in industries where small firms have the innovative advantage (which corresponds to Winter's entrepreneurial regime) than in industries where the large firms have the innovative advantage (which corresponds to Winter's routinized regime). And as Geroski (1995) predicts, the likelihood of survival should tend to be lower for new firms in industries where the degree of uncertainty with respect to the viability of the product is greater.

There is an important distinction to be emphasized between the likelihood of survival for new entrants that successfully innovate versus any given new entrant in a highly innovative environment. As Geroski (1995) points out, numerous case studies have suggested that entry is often used as a vehicle for introducing new innovations. But these case studies typically focus on entrants that have successfully innovated. What about those entrants which attempt to innovate and fail – that is, base their entry on the introduction of a new product that does not prove to be viable in the market? The inability of entrants to adjust to market conditions leads Geroski (1995) to predict that both high entry and failure rates should be observed in innovative industries. The key distinction to be made here is that any particular entrant that successfully innovates will have a greater likelihood of survival. But, on average, the typical entrant in a highly innovative industry incurs a greater risk of not producing a product which will ultimately be viable in the market. Thus, as Acs and Audretsch (1990) find, the entry of new firms may be greater in industries where small firms are particularly innovative, but the likelihood that any one of these new entrants successfully innovates and ultimately survives may in fact be lower. That is, new firms may be induced to enter highly innovative industries with the hopes of innovating, but not all will succeed.

Systematic differences in the growth rates of surviving firms across manufacturing industries will presumably also reflect the degree to which barriers to survival exist in the industry. For example, holding the startup size of an entrant constant, those firms surviving in industries characterized by a high degree of scale economies should, on average, exhibit higher rates of growth than firms in industries where scale economies are relatively unimportant. That is, in the first case new firms not growing are more likely to be confronted with a cost disadvantage – which essentially is the cost disadvantage traditionally considered to be a barrier to entry. Only through attaining a relatively larger size can this barrier be alleviated. By contrast, in an industry where scale economies are relatively unimportant, no such size barrier exists. The consequences of not growing, in terms of any cost disadvantage, remain relatively unimportant. Such an industry corresponds to what has traditionally been referred to as an industry with no or only low barriers to entry. In such an industry, firms with low or even no growth will not be forced to exit out of the industry as a result of any cost disadvantages, so that, on average, lower mean growth rates should tend to be observed in industries exhibiting only a trivial degree of scale economies.

The growth rates of *surviving firms* are also expected to be systematically greater in highly innovative industries than in less innovative industries. This is attributable to the process of learning or discovery about the viability of the new product subsequent to entering. The only way that the entrant can know for certain about the viability of the new product is through entry. If the new product proves to be viable, the firm will tend to grow, since the typical startup size is so small. (Audretsch, 1995, shows that the mean startup size in United States manufacturing industries in 1976 was fewer than eight employees.) If the new product proves not to be viable, the new form is more likely to exit (hence the lower predicted survival rate), resulting in higher observed growth rates exhibited by surviving firms in highly innovative industries.

The theory of strategic groups operating in an industry where barriers to mobility are prevalent suggests that a strategy of product differentiation will facilitate viability even at a small scale of output (Caves and Porter, 1977). While the potential for new entrants to seek and maintain product niches might seemingly suggest that lower and not higher growth rates should be expected from surviving entrants in highly innovative industries, such a prediction overlooks the small mean startup size of new firms. The introduction of a successful new product in manufacturing is likely to induce growth beyond a handful of employees, even if the new entrant does pursue the type of niche strategy described by Porter (1979).

4. Empirical results

To test the hypothesis that what have traditionally been considered to pose as barriers to entry actually serve as barriers to survival, a logit regression equation is estimated for 11 322 new-firm entrants in U.S. manufacturing in 1976, where the value of one defines a firm that has survived until 1986 and the value of zero defines a firm which has exited prior to 1986. Thus, the unit of observation for the logit regression is a firm (founded in 1976) which either survived or exited. And to test the hypothesis that the observed growth rates of surviving entrants are also shaped, at least to some extent, by the severity of these barriers to survival an ordinary least squares (OLS) regression is estimated for firm growth, which is defined as firm employment in 1986 divided by firm employment in 1976. It should be emphasized that while Hall (1987) purposely corrected the growth equations to correct for the omission of exiting firms, in this case we purposely want to exclude the impact of exiting firms on the growth rates in order to shed light on the question; *do differences in barriers to survival across industries systematically influence the growth rates exhibited by those firms which ultimately survive?* That is, we are not interested here in whether the growth rates of all new firms vary systematically across industries, but rather, whether the growth rates of *surviving* entrants vary systematically from industry to industry.

As explained in the previous section, the traditional measures of entry barriers, which here are extended to pose as barriers to survival, are the extent of scale economies and product differentiation (Bain, 1956). Measurement of the extent of scale economies in an industry has proven to be challenging at best (Scherer and Ross, 1990; Caves et al., 1975). Here we adapt the standard Comanor and Wilson (1967) proxy for measuring the minimum efficient scale (MES) level of output, which is defined as the mean size of the largest plants in each industry accounting for one-half of the industry value of shipments, 1977. This measure is derived from the Census of Manufactures of the United States Bureau of the Census. While the Comanor and Wilson measure is crude and only a proxy at best, it has proven in numerous studies at least to reflect the extent to which scale economies play an important role in an industry (Scherer and Ross, 1990). As the MES increases, the more a firm of any given size must grow in order to realize maximum efficiency, or at least to attain a size similar to those firms in the industry accounting for most of the shipments. Thus, a positive relationship is expected to emerge between the proxy measure of the MES level of output and the post-entry growth rate. At the same time, the economic consequences of not growing become greater for a firm of a given size as the MES increases. This suggests that the likelihood of survival should be negatively related to the extent of scale economies in the industry.

Of course, the influence of scale economies, or the mean size of the largest firms in the industry, on the ability of a new entrant to survive is relative to the startup size of the firm. In fact, two important characteristics of new-firm entrants are: (1) their small size, as evidenced by a mean startup size of 7.63 employees, and (2) the relatively low variance of the startup size around this mean. That is, most new manufacturing firms are small and employ in the neighborhood of seven employees. This startup size and its variance do not vary dramatically across industries. Still, as the startup size of a new entrant increases relative to the MES level of output, the degree to which a firm needs to grow in order to eliminate cost disadvantages accruing from scale disadvantages decreases. This would suggest that firm size, measured as the number of employees in the startup year, 1976, should be positively related to the likelihood of survival but negatively related to the observed growth rates exhibited by surviving firms.

To measure the relative importance of innovative activity in the industry,

188 Entrepreneurship, Innovation and Economic Growth

the total innovation rate is defined as the total number of innovations recorded in 1982 divided by industry employment. The small-firm innovation rate is defined as the number of innovations contributed by firms with fewer than 500 employees divided by small-firm employment.[4] As explained in the previous section, previous work by Geroski (1989a) has found that entry tends to be greater in more innovative industries. And evidence provided by Acs and Audretsch (1990) suggests that entry is even greater in innovative industries where small firms tend to be particularly innovative. But not all or even most of these new entrants produce a product that will ultimately be viable in the market. That means that most of the new entrants are confronted with being based on a mismatch between their product and market demand. As Geroski (1995, p. 21) predicts, "The slower is the process of learning and the more turbulent is the market environment, the more likely it is that firms will fail to cope." Thus, the likelihood of survival confronting new entrants in general should be lower in highly innovative industries and particularly in industries where the small-firm innovative rate is high.

In addition to the more standard measures of structural barriers, the industry growth rate is also included as an influence on the likelihood of survival and post-entry growth rates. If industry growth (either in the positive or negative sense) is unanticipated it will result in higher price-cost margins (in the case of positive growth Bradburd and Caves, 1982), thus facilitating a higher likelihood of survival than otherwise would be the case. The industry growth rate measured is the value of shipments in 1986 divided by the 1976 value of shipments.

Finally, by using the firm as the unit of observation a systematic measurement error may be introduced. The number of employees for the entire firm recorded by the *firm size* variable will actually tend to overstate systematically the actual size of the individual plants. That is, the gap between the MES level of output and what is recorded as the firm size will tend to be less than the actual gap between the MES level of output and the size of individual plants. The measure of firm size will tend to overstate systematically the size of the actual plants comprising the entire firm, so that the likelihood of survival will tend to be systematically lower than would be predicted by the *firm size* variable, while the growth rates will tend to be systematically greater. A dummy variable taking on the value of one for firm

---

[4] The innovation data are from the United States Small Business Administration's Innovation Data Base. The data base consists of 8074 innovations introduced into the United States in 1982. Of the manufacturing innovations for which firm size could be identified, 55.81% came from large firms (with at least 500 employees), while 44.19% came from small firms (with fewer than 500 employees). The 1982 innovations resulted from inventions made, on average, five years earlier. A detailed analysis of the distribution of innovations according to significance levels and firm size can be found in Acs and Audretsch (1990, chapter 2).

organizations consisting of multi-plants was created to control for such cases. The systematic overstatement of firm size for multi-plant enterprises works in the opposite direction of any effects accruing from multi-plant scale economies and should result in a negative coefficient in the survival (logit) regression and a positive coefficient in the OLS growth rate regression.

As Table 3 shows, the results for the two-year and ten-year post-entry performance generally confirm the hypotheses tested. However, an interesting result emerges when a conditional survival logit regression is estimated for those 3130 entrants having survived until 1984. That is, the 1984–1986 logit regression is conditional upon the firm still existing as of 1984 and then subsequently either continuing to survive until 1986 or else exiting. Most strikingly, the coefficients of the total innovation rate and small-firm innovation rate flip from being negative, as is the case when the overall cohort of 1976 new entrants is analyzed, to being positive (although only the coefficient of the small-firm innovation rate can be considered to be statistically significant). This would suggest that, conditional upon having survived eight years, those firms still remaining in an industry which is highly innovative have a greater and not a lower likelihood of surviving an additional two years. This does imply that being in an innovative environ-

Table 3
Regressions of survival and growth for 1976 entrants (t-statistics in parentheses)

| | Time Period | | | | | |
| | 1976–1986 | | 1976–1978 | | 1984–1986 | |
	Survival (logit)	Growth (OLS)	Survival (logit)	Growth (OLS)	Survival (logit)	Growth (OLS)
Total innovation	−1.233	0.301	−0.136	0.331	0.110	0.008
rate	(−1.90)	(1.54)	(−2.66)	(2.26)	(1.29)	(0.97)
Small-firm	−0.140	0.210	−0.142	0.294	1.388	0.142
innovation rate	(−2.50)	(2.07)	(−2.72)	(2.83)	(1.86)	(1.03)
Mean largest	−0.002	0.002	−0.002	0.001	0.0002	0.0003
plant size	(−3.71)	(1.79)	(−5.15)	(2.98)	(0.79)	(0.97)
Firm size	0.003	−0.003	0.003	−0.002	0.001	0.001
	(2.77)	(−2.86)	(2.59)	(−3.10)	(1.34)	(0.42)
Industry growth	0.214	0.257	0.203	0.194	0.246	0.259
	(2.92)	(1.71)	(2.22)	(1.69)	(4.39)	(1.72)
Organization	−0.394	0.416	−0.498	0.693	−0.310	0.399
structure	(−2.24)	(1.21)	(−3.71)	(3.58)	(−1.42)	(1.07)
Intercept	−1.512	1.897	−1.511	1.142	−1.203	2.34
	(−8.47)	(6.02)	(−7.62)	(4.32)	(−4.38)	(9.96)
R^2	–	0.162	–	0.092	–	0.055
F	–	12.31	–	10.21	–	5.12
Log-likelihood	−5979	–	−6107	–	−4371	–
N	11322	2534	11322	8300	3130	2534

ment provides entrants with a greater likelihood of finding a niche and therefore compensating for scale and other size-related disadvantages – but only if they have survived the first few years subsequent to entry. It is also interesting to note that the impact of scale economies on the likelihood of survival, on the condition that the firm is still in existence after eight years, is negligible (the sign of this coefficient has also flipped and is positive). Similarly, neither the innovative environment nor the extent of scale economies, as proxied by the mean size of the largest plants in the industry, apparently exerts any influence on either the likelihood of survival or the growth rates.

Comparing the impacts of the traditional measures of structural barriers between the post-entry performance of the entire cohort of new entrants in 1976 and the cohort of entrants surviving eight years until 1984 suggests that these structural characteristics – scale economies and product differentiation – may serve as a barrier to survival within the first few years subsequent to entry but that the impact of these barriers has dissipated within eight years subsequent to entry.

5. Conclusion

The findings of this paper generally confirm Geroski's (1995, p. 23) reconciliation of the paradox posed by the simultaneous occurrence of "high entry barriers with high entry rates." As Geroski (1995, p. 24) suggests, "If, however, barriers to entry are thought of as an obstacle which prevents new firms from surviving long in a market, then the data present less of a puzzle." In fact, the evidence from this paper implies that two of the traditional characteristics of structural barriers, scale economies and product differentiation, do constitute a *barrier to survival*. However, the impact of these barriers on the likelihood of survival is apparently not permanent, but rather weakens as the entrant gains experience in the industry, or at least as the post-entry time period increases.

The impact of a highly innovative environment in shaping the post-entry performance of firms is somewhat ambiguous. On the one hand, as Geroski (1991, 1995) notes, "entry is often used as a vehicle for introducing new innovations." The ability of new entrants to differentiate their products through innovative activity and otherwise is clearly a key strategic instrument deployed by entrants to offset scale disadvantages and to occupy small-scale product niches. On the other hand, the results of this study clearly indicate that a highly innovative environment serves as a barrier to survival within the first few years subsequent to entry.

The reconciliation of this puzzle is also provided by Geroski, (1995, p. 24) who argues that, "Barriers to entry appear similar in character to costs of adjustment, and they are particularly pressing for those entrants who only have a limited time in which to prove themselves. What results is a kind of a time-cost trade-off, in which entry is more expensive (for a given level of entry barriers) the more quickly an entrant attempts to penetrate the market. If this is indeed the case, then the nature of entry barriers means that entry contests may take on the character of a war of attrition." That is, just because entrants are induced into an industry by the prospect of innovative activity does not at all guarantee that they succeed. To those firms unable to adjust, the highly innovative environment ends up being a siren call – the lure of a differentiated and innovative product becomes the force driving the unsuccessful entrants out of the industry. In this scene, it is the inability of many, if not most of the new entrants to adjust sufficiently to produce a product that is viable, which is simply a characteristic of a highly innovative environment, that constitutes a barrier to survival. But within several years subsequent to entry a reversed relationship between the innovative environment and the likelihood of survival can be observed. Having survived a period of time subsequent to entry (eight years in this study) may indicate that those surviving entrants have, at least to some extent, successfully adjusted and are able to produce a viable product. What was then a hostile environment and ultimately a barrier to survival to the exiting firms can now be observed to constitute a mechanism for promoting the survival of the remaining firms. Thus, the inherent ambiguity of an innovative environment in shaping the post-entry performance is that, on average, it tends to serve as a barrier to survival, and it certainly will rank among one of the main reasons for those entrants not being able to adjust or otherwise offer a viable product ultimately exiting out of the industry. But, for those firms that successfully innovate and differentiate their product a highly innovative environment provides a haven of opportunities and a mechanism for compensating for scale and other size-related disadvantages.

Acknowledgements

An earlier version of this paper was presented at the May 1994 conference on the *Post-Entry Performance of Firms*, sponsored by the Bank of Portugal. I am grateful to the suggestions of José Mata and two referees.

References

Acs, Z.J. and D.B. Audretsch, 1988, Innovation in large and small firms: An empirical analysis, American Economic Review, 78, 678–690.
Acs, Z.J. and D.B. Audretsch, 1990, Innovation and small firms (MIT Press, Cambridge, MA).

Arrow, K.J., 1962, Economic welfare and the allocation of resources for invention, in: R.R. Nelson, ed., The rate and direction of inventive activity (Princeton University Press, Princeton, New Jersey), 609–626.

Audretsch, D.B., 1991, New-firm survival and the technological regime, Review of Economics and Statistics 73, 441–450.

Audretsch, D.B., 1995, Innovation and industry evolution (MIT Press, Cambridge, Mass.).

Audretsch, D.B. and T. Mahmood, 1995, New-firm survival: New results using a hazard function, Review of Economics and Statistics 77, 97–103.

Bain, J., 1956, Barriers to new competition (Harvard University Press, Cambridge, Mass.).

Baldwin, J.R. and M. Rafiquzzaman, 1995, Selection versus evolutionary adaptation: Learning and post-entry performance, International Journal of Industrial Organization, 13, 501–522

Baldwin, J.R., 1995, The dynamics of industrial competition: A North American perspective (Cambridge University Press, Cambridge).

Baldwin, W.L. and J.T. Scott, 1987, Market structure and technological change (Harwood Academic, London).

Boden, R. and B.D. Phillips, 1985, Uses and limitations of USEEM/USELM data (Office of Advocacy, United States Small Business Administration, Washington, DC).

Bradburd, R. and R.E. Caves, 1982, A closer look at the effect of market growth on industries' profits, Review of Economics and Statistics 64, 635–645.

Caves, R.E., J. Khalizadeh-Shirazi, and M.E. Porter, 1975, Scale economies in statistical analyses of market power, Review of Economics and Statistics 57, 133–140.

Caves, R.E. and M.E. Porter, 1977, From entry barriers to mobility barriers, Quarterly Journal of Economics 91, 241–261.

Cohen, W.M. and R.C. Levin, 1989, Empirical studies of innovation and market structure, in: R. Schmalensee and R. Willig, eds., Handbook of industrial organization, Vol. 2 (North-Holland, Amsterdam) 1059–1107.

Comanor, W.S. and T.A. Wilson, 1967, Advertising, market structure, and performance, Review of Economics and Statistics 49, 423–440.

Dunne, T., M.J. Roberts, and L. Samuelson, 1988, Patterns of firm entry and exit in U.S. manufacturing industries, Rand Journal of Economics 19, 495–515.

Dunne, T., M.J. Roberts, and L. Samuelson, 1989, The growth and failure of U.S. manufacturing plants, Quarterly Journal of Economics 104, 671–698.

Evans, D.S., 1987a, Tests of alternative theories of firm growth, Journal of Political Economy 95, 657–674.

Evans, D.S., 1987b, The relationship between firm growth, size and age: Estimates for 100 manufacturing industries, Journal of Industrial Economics 35, 567–581.

Geroski, P.A., 1989a, Entry and the rate of innovation, Economics of Innovation and New Technology 1, 203–214.

Geroski, P., 1989b, Entry, innovation and productivity growth, Review of Economics and Statistics 71, 572–578.

Geroski, P.A., 1991, Market dynamics and entry (Blackwell, Oxford).

Geroski, P.A., 1995, What do we know about entry? International Journal of Industrial Organization, 13, 421–440.

Gort, M. and S. Klepper, 1982, Time paths in the diffusion of product innovations, Economic Journal 92, 630–653.

Hall, B., 1987, The relationship between firm size and firm growth in the U.S. manufacturing sector, Journal of Industrial Economics 35, 583–606.

Mata, J. and P. Portugal, 1994, Life duration of new firms, Journal of Industrial Economics 27, 227–246.

Mata, J., P. Portugal and P. Guimaraes, 1995, The survival of new plants: Start-up conditions and post-entry evolution, International Journal of Industrial Organization, 13, 459–481.

Mueller, D.C., 1976, Information, mobility, and profit, Kyklos 29, 419-448.

Mueller, D.C., 1991, Entry, exit, and the competitive process, in: P. Geroski and J. Schwalbach, eds., Entry and market contestability: An international comparison (Blackwell, Oxford), 1-22.

Nelson, R.R. and S.G. Winter, 1982, An evolutionary theory of economic change (Harvard University Press, Cambridge, Mass.).

Pavitt, K., M. Robson and J. Townsend, 1987, The size distribution of innovating firms in the U.K.: 1945-1983, Journal of Industrial Economics 55, 291-316.

Porter, M.E., 1979, The structure within industries and companies' performance, Review of Economics and Statistics 61, 214-227.

Scherer, F.M. and D. Ross, 1990, Industrial market structure and economic performance, 3rd edition (Houghton Mifflin, Boston).

United States Small Business Administration, Office of Advocacy, 1987, Linked 1976-1984 USEEM user's guide (Washington, DC).

Wagner, J., 1994, The post-entry performance of new small firms in German manufacturing industries, Journal of Industrial Economics 62, 141-154.

Williamson, O.E., 1975, Markets and hierarchies: Antitrust analysis and implications (Free Press, New York).

Winter, S.G., 1984, Schumpeterian competition in alternative technological regimes, Journal of Economic Behavior and Organization 5, 287-320.

16

THE JOURNAL OF INDUSTRIAL ECONOMICS   0022-1821
Volume XLIX   March 2001   No. 1

DOES ENTRY SIZE MATTER? THE IMPACT OF THE LIFE CYCLE AND TECHNOLOGY ON FIRM SURVIVAL*

RAJSHREE AGARWAL† AND DAVID B. AUDRETSCH‡

A wave of empirical studies has recently emerged showing that smaller-scale entry is confronted with a lower likelihood of survival than their larger counterparts. The purpose of this paper is to examine whether the relationship between size of a firm when entering an industry and the likelihood of survival holds under different technological conditions and across the different stages of the industry life cycle. The empirical evidence suggests that the relationship between firm size and the likelihood of survival is shaped by technology and the stage of the industry life cycle. While the likelihood of survival confronting small entrants is generally less than that confronting their larger counterparts, the relationship does not hold for mature stages of the product life cycle, or in technologically intensive products. In mature industries that are still technologically intensive, entry may be less about radical innovation and possibly more about filling strategic niches, thus negating the impact of entry size on the likelihood of survival.

I. INTRODUCTION

A RICH BODY of empirical evidence, spanning numerous countries and time periods, has provided sufficient evidence for several leading scholars (Caves [1998], Sutton [1997], Geroski [1995]) to infer stylized facts and stylized relationships about the basic elements concerning firm dynamics and industry evolution, or the manner in which firms enter into an industry, grow or stagnate and ultimately survive or exit from the industry. The stylized facts emerging from the new literature have been sufficiently compelling as to contradict what was previously classified as a Law—Gibrat's Law, which assumes that firm growth is independent of size—and motivate an entire article in the *Journal of Economic Literature* by Sutton [1997], explaining how something as certain as a Law could be refuted when subjected to empirical scrutiny.

The reconciliation of the Law with the empirical evidence is based on

*We are grateful to the helpful suggestions and comments of the editor and two anonymous referees of this journal. All errors and omissions remain our responsibility.

†Authors' affiliation: Dept. of Economics, CBA, 325E, University of Central Florida, Orlando, FL 32816-1400, USA.
email: agarwal@bus.ucf.edu

‡Institute of Development Strategies, SPEA, Suite 201, Indiana University, Bloomington, IN 47405, USA.
email: daudrets@indiana.edu

© Blackwell Publishers Ltd. 2001, 108 Cowley Road, Oxford OX4 1JF, UK, and 350 Main Street, Malden, MA 02148, USA.

21

what Geroski [1995] (p. 434) finds so convincing that it constitutes what he terms as a stylized result: 'Both firm size and age are correlated with the survival of entrants.' Because small firms have a lower likelihood of survival than their larger counterparts, and the likelihood of small-firm survival is directly related to growth, firm size is found to be negatively related to growth, thereby refuting Gibrat's Law.

While these relationships have now taken on the status of Stylized Results, they also challenge a number of other widely held theories in addition to Gibrat's Law. For example, the theory of small-firm strategic niches, posited by Porter [1979] and Caves and Porter [1977] argues that by occupying strategic niches, small firms do not need to grow in order to survive. Rather, small firms can remain small and avoid being confronted by a lower likelihood of survival by occupying a strategic niche.

The purpose of this paper is to reconcile these two views about the role of small firms in industry dynamics. We suggest that both views are, in fact, correct, but that each view tends to be specific for a particular phase of the industry life cycle, and to the technological intensity of the industry. What has emerged as a Stylized Result in Geroski's impressive review of the literature—that the likelihood of survival is greater for larger firms than for small firms—should hold in the formative stages of the life cycle but not in the mature stages, and in products that are relatively low in technological intensity. By contrast, the theory of strategic niches—which holds that firms can remain small and face no disadvantage with respect to the likelihood of survival—should hold in the mature phase of the life cycle, and in products characterized as high-technology.

In the second section of this paper, we present the theories and evidence suggesting that the likelihood of survival is positively related to firm size. In the third section, we link together recent theories and empirical evidence about the dynamics of firms over the industry life cycle and argue that the role of entrants evolves over the life cycle in such a way as to influence the post-entry performance of entrants. The data base, measurement issues and estimation techniques are presented in the fourth section. In the fifth section we compare survival and hazard rates for high-technology and low-technology firms over different stages of the industry life cycle. In the final section a summary and conclusions are provided.

II. ENTRY SIZE AND FIRM SURVIVAL

As both Geroski [1995] and Sutton [1997] emphasize in their surveys on intra-industry firm dynamics, a large body of empirical evidence has consistently found that the likelihood of firm survival is not independent of firm size. Virtually every study undertaken has found that firm size is positively related to the likelihood of survival. The only study that has not confirmed a positive relationship is for the five new Bundesländer in the former East Germany, which is clearly a special case (Harhoff and Stahl [1994]).

As Sutton makes clear in his article, these studies are generally specified so that size in period t, typically the entry year, is linked to growth in the subsequent time period. This lagged specification follows from the basic assumption underlying Gibrat's Law, that the 'probability that the next opportunity is taken up by any particular active firm is proportional to the current size of the firm' (Sutton, 1997, p. 43). These studies span a wide range of time periods and countries, such as the United States (Dunne, Roberts and Samuelson [1988 and 1989], Audretsch [1991 and 1995], Audretsch and Mahmood [1995], Doms, Dunne and Roberts [1995], Agarwal [1997]); Canada (Baldwin [1995], Baldwin and Rafiquzzaman [1995]); Portugal (Mata, Portugal, and Guimaraes [1995], Mata and Portugal [1994]); and Germany (Wagner [1994]).

The major theoretical interpretation of the observed positive relationship between firm size and the likelihood of survival first builds on the model of noisy selection introduced by Jovanovic [1982] and extended by Ericson and Pakes [1998]. Jovanovic, and Ericson and Pakes present a theory in which the entrants face costs that are not only random but also differ across firms. A central feature of the models is that an entrant does not know its own cost structure. Rather, the relative efficiency of each entrant is discovered through the process of learning from actual market experience. The true ability of the managerial competence of the entrepreneurs is only discovered subsequent to entry into the industry. Those entrepreneurs who discover that their ability exceeds their expectations expand the scale of their business, whereas those discovering that their post-entry performance is less than commensurate with their expectations will contract the scale of output and possibly exit from the industry.

Thus, the major function of an entrant is to gain a toehold in the industry in order to provide a platform for learning about or discovering the viability of the ideas and competence upon which the firm was founded. Evidence from the United States (Audretsch [1995], Dunne, Roberts and Samuelson [1988 and 1989]); Portugal (Mata and Portugal [1994]) and Germany (Wagner [1994]) suggests that the mean size of entrants is remarkably small. While the minimum efficient scale (MES) varies substantially across industries, and even to some degree across various product classes within any given industry, the observed size of most new manufacturing firms is sufficiently small to ensure that the bulk of entrants are operating at a suboptimal scale of output.

An implication of the theory of firm selection is that firms may enter at a small, even suboptimal, scale of output and then, if merited by subsequent performance, expand. Those entrants that are successful will grow, whereas those that are not successful will remain small and may ultimately

24   RAJSHREE AGARWAL AND DAVID B. AUDRETSCH

be forced to exit from the industry if they are operating at a suboptimal scale of output.

The greater the entry size in a given industry, the less will be the cost disadvantage imposed by an inherent size disadvantage, and the greater will be the likelihood of survival confronting the new entrant. As Geroski (1995, p. 23) points out, 'Perhaps the most striking thing that we know about entry is that small-scale, de novo entry seems to be relatively common in most industries, but that small-scale, de novo entrants generally have a rather short life expectancy. That is, entry appears to be relatively easy, but survival is not.' This interpretation is certainly consistent with a second observation by both Sutton [1997] and Geroski [1995] drawn from the empirical literature testing the validity of Gibrat's law—firm growth is negatively related to size. The consequences of not growing, in terms of a cost disadvantage, are negatively related to entry size. The larger the size of the firm, the higher is the likelihood of survival for any given growth rate.

III.   THE ROLE OF THE INDUSTRY LIFE CYCLE

Recent theories and empirical evidence (Agarwal and Gort [1996], Agarwal [1998], Klepper [1996], and Klepper and Miller [1995]) on industry evolution suggest that the role of entrants may not be invariant to the stage of the industry life cycle. Rather, the underlying reason motivating entry evolves over the life cycle of the industry. As Utterback and Anthony [1975] point out, in the formative stage of the life cycle, no singular product design or concept dominates the industry. Firms must experiment with the product design in short production runs, making significant modifications after observing consumer response. According to Williamson (1975, p. 215), 'The first or early formative stage involves the supply of a new product of relatively primitive design, manufactured on comparatively unspecialized machinery, and marketed through a variety of exploratory techniques. Volume is typically low. A high degree of uncertainty characterizes business experience at this stage.' Thus, in the formative stages of the life cycle, firms enter principally to compete for the dominant product design for that industry.

By contrast, as the industry evolves towards the mature and declining stages, the product design becomes more standardized and uniform, and the premium attached to technological superiority recedes. According to Williamson (1975, p. 216), in the mature and declining stages, 'Management, manufacturing, and marketing techniques all reach a relatively advanced degree of refinement. Markets may continue to grow, but do so at a more regular and predictable rate. Established connections with customers and suppliers (including capital market access) all operate to buffer changes and thereby to limit large shifts in market shares. Significant innovations tend to be fewer and are mainly of an improvement variety.' As Audretsch [1995] shows, mature industries, such as auto-mobiles, tend to be characterized by a relatively low ratio of new product innovations per R&D dollar expended. By contrast, emerging industries are characterized by a high ratio of new product innovations relative to R&D expended. Agarwal [1998] finds that patenting activity increases in the initial stages of the life-cycle, and subsequently declines during the mature period.

Many of the recent conclusions about the role of entrants ignore the influence of the industry life cycle. But the industry life-cycle theory suggests that, in fact, the role of entry as a vehicle for new innovations evolves systematically over the life-cycle. This is because the underlying knowledge conditions vary systematically over the industry life cycle. In the mature and declining stages of the life cycle, new economic knowledge generating innovative activity is relatively routine and can be com-mercialized within the context of the incumbent hierarchical bureau-cracies. By contrast, in the formative life cycle stages, innovations comes from knowledge that is not of a routine nature and therefore tends to be rejected by the hierarchical bureaucracies of incumbent corporations. Nelson and Winter [1982] describe these different underlying knowledge conditions as reflecting two distinct technological regimes: 'An entre-preneurial regime is one that is favorable to innovative entry and un-favorable to innovative activity by established firms; a routinized regime is one in which the conditions are the other way around' (Winter [1984]).[1]

Gort and Klepper [1982] argue that the relative innovative advantage between entrants and incumbent enterprises depends upon the source of information generating innovative activity. If information based on non-transferable experience in the market is an important input in generating innovative activity, then incumbent firms will tend to have the innovative advantage over entrants. This is characteristic of mature industries, where the accumulated stock of non-transferable information is the product of experience within the market—which, by definition, firms outside of the main incumbent organizations cannot possess.

By contrast, when information outside of the routines practiced by the incumbent firms is a relatively important input in generating innovative activity, entrants will have the innovative advantage over incumbent firms. Arrow [1962], Mueller [1976], and Williamson [1975] have all emphasized that when information created outside of the incumbent firms cannot be easily transferred to those incumbent enterprises, presumably due to agency and bureaucracy problems, the holder of such knowledge must enter the industry by starting a new firm in order to appropriate the expected value of that knowledge.

[1] See also Malerba and Orsenigo [1996], and Dosi *et al.* [1995].

There is considerable evidence that the role of innovation in motivating entrants varies between the entrepreneurial and routinized technological regimes (Audretsch [1995]). Because these technological regimes correspond to the formative and mature stages of the industry life cycle, entry is more likely to be based on innovative activity in the formative stages than in the mature stages. Thus, Geroski's [1995] pronouncement that 'entry is often used as a vehicle for introducing new innovations' certainly should reflect the formative stages of the industry life cycle but not the mature or declining stages. In the formative stage, entrants are vying for the dominant product design. While the likelihood is low, success brings subsequent high rates of growth.

By contrast, in the mature stage, the window of opportunity for setting product standards through innovative activity has been closed. Entry in the mature stage of the life cycle is less about (radical) innovative activity and more about occupying a strategic niche. The theories of Porter [1979], Caves and Porter [1977] and Newman [1978], that small and large enterprises co-exist simultaneously in an industry because of the ability of small firms to occupy strategic niches are most applicable in the mature phase of the life cycle.[2] According to the theory of strategic niches, firms can remain small and maintain levels of profitability in excess of those enjoyed by large firms by occupying product niches that are inaccessible to their larger counterparts. By occupying a strategic niche in the mature stage of the life cycle, an entrant is able to avoid the inherent scale disadvantages confronting small firms in earlier stages of the life cycle. Thus, size should be an advantage in reducing the likelihood of failure in the formative stages of the industry life cycle, but not in the mature phase. If this is not the case, and product differentiation plays a more important role prior to the emergence of a dominant design in the earlier life cycle stages, this should be verified by the failure of a statistical relationship to emerge between firm size and the likelihood of survival in the formative stages.

IV. DATA, MEASUREMENT AND ESTIMATION TECHNIQUES

The greatest impediment to examining how the technological regime impacts the relationship between firm size and the likelihood of survival has been an inability to identify the industry life cycle stage and link such a measure to firm-specific longitudinal observations. The data base used in this paper to accomplish both of these elements is based on the identification of the entry and exit of firms listed in *Thomas Register of American Manufacturers*. The *Thomas Register*, which dates back to 1906, is used

---

[2] As Geroski [1995] points out, occupying a niche can be interpreted as an innovative activity, since the small firm is engaging in some type of economic activity not pursued by larger counterparts.

primarily by purchasing agents. Lavin [1992], in extensively describing various sources of business information, states that the *Thomas Register* is the best example of a directory which provides information on manufacturers by focusing on products.[3] According to Lavin, 'The *Thomas Register* is a comprehensive, detailed guide to the full range of products manufactured in the United States. Covering only manufacturing companies, it strives for a complete representation within that scope.'

This study includes, as listed in Appendix 1, a sub-set of 31 of the 46 the products selected from the *Thomas Register* by Gort and Klepper [1982]. In addition, two new products—contact lenses and video cassette recorders—are included as they have gained prominence over the last two decades.[4]

A total of 3,431 firms is pooled across products for the survival analysis. Firms are subjected to checks to ensure actual entry rather than a renaming/relocation of existing firms.[5] A change in the name of the firm is tracked by checking its address, and vice versa for a change in address.[6] A change in both name and address, however, is treated as a new entry, since no other checks are possible for verifying prior existence. The margin of error is assumed to be small for such cases. When identifiable, mergers between two firms are treated as an exit of the smaller and continuance of the larger firm.[7] Thus, an important qualification of this database is that

---

[3] The importance of imports in manufacturing has increased over the last few decades. The *Thomas Register* includes foreign manufacturers of the product if the firm maintains an office or distribution channel for its product in the United States.

[4] While the study draws from the same pool of products as the Gort-Klepper study, the data are developed independently. Fifteen of the 46 products in the Gort-Klepper study could not be used for new data development for various reasons. Some products, like Nylon, Telemeters, Computers and Solar Batteries had breaks in consistency either because the listing was missing in the *Thomas Register*, or due to substantial changes in definition of product over the years. Products like DDT and cryogenic tanks were omitted since they were discontinued over the years for which the analysis was extended (from 1973 to 1991). Other categories like streptomycin and penicillin were discarded in favor of a broader product group Antibiotics. Finally, a few products were not included in the analysis due to time limitations on the development of data.

[5] To minimize possible data-entry errors, the database of firms for each product was developed independently by two sets of research assistants. The databases were then compared to rectify mistakes and ensure that the records were accurate.

[6] For instance, a firm (AMETEK) dropped out of a market in the same year that another firm appeared in the same city and state with a slightly different street address. An inspection of the name KETEMA confirmed the idea that it was one and the same firm (Ketema is an anagram (spelled backwards) of Ametek).

[7] In some cases, we were able to identify mergers between two firms due to a change in listing that either (a) clearly identified one of the firms as a subsidiary of the other, or (b) consisted of a name change that combined the names of individual firms. Some of the mergers and acquisitions may represent failing firms, while others may be highly successful. Data limitations do not allow us to make a distinction between the two types of firms. To the extent that the newly created firm represents the capitalized value of both firms that merged, the survival rates would reflect the attributes of both firms.

exit includes mergers and acquisitions. This qualification applies to almost every study undertaken analyzing exit, both in the cross section (Dunne, Roberts and Samuelson [1988 and 1989], Hall [1988]) and time series (Klepper [1995], Klepper and Miller [1995]). Virtually all of the studies included in the comprehensive literature reviews by Caves [1998] in the *Journal of Economic Literature*, Geroski [1995] in the *International Journal of Industrial Organization*, and Sutton [1996] in the *Journal of Economic Literature*, include only studies that suffer from this important data qualification. Only preciously few studies, such as Harhoff, Stahl and Woyvode [1998], have developed a data base distinguishing among the different types of exit. While their important data base and analysis paves the road for future research, it is almost unique in terms of the studies comprising the literature up to now (see also Holmes and Schmitz [1995], and Schary [1995]). We should also emphasize that, as in the Klepper [1996] and Gort and Klepper [1982] studies, the unit of observation for entry includes de novo firms as well as new businesses by existing firms.

We measure the entry size of the firm by the current dollar asset size reported in the *Thomas Register* at its time of entry. Since the time period over which firm entry is sampled encompasses almost the entire twentieth century, we first adjust the asset categories for inflation and express them in 1982 dollars, and then classify them into five categories.[8] These asset categories, expressed in 1982 dollars are (1) less than $2 million, (2) $2 to 4 million, (3) $4 to 6 million, (4) $6 to $8 million, and (5) greater than $8 million.[9] In the empirical analysis that follows, we identify size in two ways. We use the above size categories as ordinal measures of entry size in the proportional hazards regression. For the survival rate analysis, we distinguish between 'small' and 'large' firms by classifying firms as small if they are in the real value adjusted smallest asset category (55 percent of the firms are in this entry size category).[10]

The stage of the product life cycle is identified by the net entry of firms into the product market. Following Gort and Klepper [1982], and Agarwal and Gort [1996], we define the formative stages of the product life cycle to be the period of positive net entry, while the mature stages reflect the period of shake-out of firms (negative net entry) and the ensuing stable

[8] The producer price index (all commodities) is used as a deflator, since it is the only PPI that dates back to the beginning of the century. Using the consumer price index as a deflator does not change the results in the paper.

[9] The choice of the threshold values on the open ended lowest and highest asset category is restricted by the available information on current asset size for the early years in the study.

[10] We also experimented with alternative operationalizations of size by identifying firms as small if their size is less than the 60th percentile of the size distribution for all firms entering in a given decade; using midpoints of the size intervals and their logarithmic transformations. The results are robust to the different specifications.

period (approximate zero entry). Appendix 2 describes the general discriminant analysis procedure that was used to identify the appropriate classification of the years in the product life cycle stage. Appendix 1 presents the year that each product entered the mature stage, and in addition reports the number of firms within the formative and mature stages for every product in the analysis.

The stage of the product life cycle, as explained earlier, captures differences in an entrepreneurial regime vs. a routinized regime. Thus, the stage proxies for differences over time in the level of technological intensity within a product category. However, product categories can also differ in technological intensity levels, i.e. while more major innovations occur during the formative stages of all product, products may also have higher or lower levels of overall technological intensity over the entire product life cycle. Accordingly, we classify the products cross-sectionally as high-technology or low-technology based on their technological intensity in the *mature stage* of the product life cycle. Choosing the mature rather than the formative stage for the cross-sectional distinction, we believe, is a better indication of cross-sectional differences in technological intensity, since it is more representative of the 'steady state' level of the product. We use the study by Hadlock, Hecker and Gannon [1991] which uses the proportion of R&D employment in the corresponding 3-digit SIC code as a basis for distinction.[11] Appendix 1 tabulates the technological index of each product. About two-thirds of the products are classified as being high-tech, while one-third is low-tech.

To examine whether the relationship between firm size and the likelihood of survival is invariant to the stage of the life cycle, we use life-table analysis and the Cox proportional hazards regression. The effect on survival of the variable of interest, entry size, may well be attenuated by the growth of the firm. Accordingly, we restrict our analysis to the first ten years of the firm's survival. Thus firms that survive eleven years or more are treated as right censored, as are firms less than ten years of age that still existed in 1991, the last year for which data were compiled.

Life-table analysis allows us to compute both survival rates and hazard rates for the firms. A τ- year survival rate is defined as the fraction of the total number of firms that survived at least τ years. The hazard rate gives the number of firms that die conditional on their age, i.e., it represents the probability of failure given that the firm has survived τ years. Three tests for homogeneity, the non-parametric Log-rank and Wilcoxon tests, and the parametric Likelihood ratio tests are conducted to check for significance of differences between large and small entry size

---

[11] The study classifies industries based on technological intensity using data in 1987, by which time all products in the sample had reached the mature stage.

survival rates within the different competitive environments based on stage and technological activity.

The Cox proportional hazards regression is used to estimate the effect of entry size, stage and level of technological activity and to compute risk ratios for each of the variables of interest. The hazard function of a firm $h_f(t)$ is expressed as:

(1) $$h_f(t) = h(t; x_f) = h_0(t) \exp(x_f' \beta)$$

where $h_0(t)$ is an arbitrary and unspecified baseline hazard function reflecting the probability of failure conditional on the firm's having survived until time t after entry into the market, x_f is a vector of measured explanatory variables for the fth firm, and β is the vector of unknown regression parameters to be estimated. Negative coefficients and risk ratios less than one imply that the hazard rate decreases and the probability of survival increases with increases in the value of the variable, while positive coefficients and risk ratios greater than one imply an increase in the hazard rate function and a decrease in the probability of survival.

Finally, we use kernel estimated hazard rates for a graphical depiction of the relationship of the size and age of firm to survival in the context of the different competitive environments. The hazard rates generated from the life-table analysis are smoothed using kernel estimation, a powerful non-parametric technique that identifies regularities in hazard rate patterns without imposing a particular structure as a result of parametric restrictions. We use a gaussian density function for the kernel, and the parameter that controls the width of the kernel is held constant at 0.25 across all kernel estimations to ensure comparability of hazard rate functions across the different competitive environments (see Silverman [1986] for details on kernel estimation techniques).

V. EMPIRICAL RESULTS

Table I presents descriptive statistics on the key variables used in the analysis. On an average, firms tracked for the first ten years survived seven years. Sixty-two percent of the firms entered in the formative stage, and seventy percent of entrants were in high-tech industries. The ordinal entry size shows a skewed distribution towards smaller firms (mean = 2.10), which is also reflected by the fact that 55 percent of the firms in the sample are classified in the smallest asset category.

Table II presents results from the life table analysis. Survival rates for small and large entrants are distinguished based on their stage of entry and the level of technological intensity. The first row shows that when neither the time of entry nor the technological intensity is distinguished, survival rates for large entrants are significantly higher than for the small entrants in the sample. This result is certainly consistent with Geroski's

TABLE I
DESCRIPTIVE STATISTICS

Variable	Number	Mean	Std. Deviation	Minimum	Maximum
Span of survival	3431	7.07	3.80	1	11
Life cycle Stage (Formative = 1)	3431	0.62	0.48	0	1
Technological Intensity (High Tech = 1)	3431	0.70	0.45	0	1
Ordinal Size	3431	2.10	1.46	1	5
Small firm Dummy (Small = 1)	3431	0.55	0.49	0	1

[1995] stylized fact about the positive relationship between firm size and the likelihood of survival. However, what the following rows show is that when the competitive environment within which the firms operate are classified by product life cycle and technological intensity, the survival rates for small and large entrants diverge significantly from this stylized fact.[12]

For products in the formative life-cycle stage, 93 percent of the small entrants survived one year; 67 percent survived five years, and about one-half survived a decade. By contrast, the survival rates of the larger entrants in the formative-stage products were all higher—96 percent for one year, 74 percent for five years, and 54 percent for ten years. One sees a strong and consistent support for the stylized result that the likelihood of survival is greater for larger entrants in the formative years of the product life cycle, and all three tests reject the hypothesis of homogeneity at the one-percent level.

The advantage that size bestows on the likelihood of survival disappears, however, in the mature life-cycle stage. All of the three tests of homogeneity fail to reject the hypothesis of homogeneity, with the ten year survival rate for small entrants actually being slightly higher than their larger-sized counterparts. Thus, the theory of strategic niches might be more applicable in mature industries.

Table II shows that the impact of firm size at entry on survival also varies between low- and high-technology products. Size clearly bestows an advantage to larger entrants in low-tech products. All three tests reject the hypothesis of homogeneity. Small entrants start with a survival rate

---

[12] The tests for homogeneity check for significant differences across entry size within the competitive environment the firm faces based on life cycle stage and technological intensity. The fact that survival rates differ significantly across life cycle stages and technological intensity has been documented in Agarwal [1996] and Agarwal [1997].

RAJSHREE AGARWAL AND DAVID B. AUDRETSCH

TABLE II
SURVIVAL RATES OF SMALL AND LARGE ENTRANTS

Survival Rates (standard errors) for	Small Entry Size				Large Entry Size				Tests of Homogeneity		
	Number	1 year	5 year	10 year	Number	1 year	5 year	10 year	Log-Rank (p-value)	Wilcoxon (p-value)	Likelihood-Ratio (p-value)
All Firms	1880	92.51 (0.61)	66.03 (1.12)	48.66 (1.22)	1551	94.95 (0.56)	71.41 (1.19)	50.85 (1.37)	5.21 (0.02)	10.12 (0.001)	4.63 (0.03)
Formative Stage	1175	92.91 (0.75)	67.43 (1.38)	50.82 (1.50)	972	95.55 (0.66)	74.07 (1.42)	54.43 (1.65)	5.99 (0.01)	10.01 (0.002)	5.68 (0.02)
Mature Stage	705	91.84 (1.05)	63.50 (1.93)	44.29 (2.13)	579	93.93 (1.01)	66.44 (2.13)	43.20 (2.49)	0.14 (0.71)	0.92 (0.34)	0.05 (0.82)
Low-Tech Product	592	90.24 (1.23)	60.94 (2.07)	45.63 (2.20)	420	93.00 (1.25)	69.72 (2.32)	49.77 (2.63)	4.61 (0.03)	8.25 (0.004)	4.70 (0.03)
High-Tech Product	1288	93.56 (0.68)	68.36 (1.33)	50.06 (1.47)	1131	95.68 (0.61)	72.04 (1.39)	51.25 (1.61)	1.44 (0.22)	3.03 (0.08)	1.17 (0.28)
Formative, Low-Tech	412	94.22 (1.40)	62.39 (2.40)	47.62 (2.54)	277	94.22 (1.40)	70.59 (2.75)	52.72 (3.09)	3.82 (0.05)	6.29 (0.01)	3.89 (0.05)
Formative, High-Tech	763	94.33 (0.83)	70.18 (1.67)	52.58 (1.85)	695	96.08 (0.73)	75.49 (1.66)	55.11 (1.95)	3.31 (0.07)	3.55 (0.06)	3.44 (0.06)
Mature, Low-Tech	180	90.12 (2.28)	56.97 (4.07)	39.46 (4.46)	143	90.55 (2.50)	68.06 (4.09)	42.27 (4.92)	1.13 (0.28)	2.14 (0.14)	1.25 (0.26)
Mature, High-Tech	525	92.41 (1.17)	65.57 (2.18)	45.83 (2.43)	436	95.03 (1.06)	65.95 (2.46)	43.59 (2.88)	0.03 (0.85)	0.04 (0.84)	0.11 (0.73)

that is approximately three percent lower than larger entrants in the first year of their existence, and the situation worsens to a nine percent difference in five year survival rates. After ten years, the disadvantage persists, with small firm survival rate at 46 percent, while 50 percent of large firms survive the interval. However, the differences between the small and large firm survival rates are considerably less in high-tech products than for low-tech products, and only one of the three tests reject the hypothesis at the ten-percent level. More importantly, the differences in survival rates are not as dramatic as observed in low-tech products. The differential between small and large entrants, at its highest, is less than four percent (for five-year survival rates). In addition, comparing firms that enter in low-tech vs. high-tech products, we see that survival rates are consistently higher for small firms that enter high-tech products, while there is little difference in survival rates of large sized entrants. Thus, the one, five and ten-year rates show that not only do small entrants enjoy survival rates almost equal to the large firms in high-tech products, they also have a comparative advantage in high-tech areas when compared to their counterparts in low-tech products.

When the products are classified according to both life-cycle stage and technological intensity, we see that large entrants have a comparative advantage in the formative years of both low and high-tech markets, as all three tests uniformly reject the hypothesis of homogeneity. It is also worth noting that while entering in the formative years of high-tech products gives a small entrant a lower probability of survival relative to larger firms, the absolute levels of survival are the highest among small firm survival rates across other environments. In the mature period of low-tech markets, while larger firms seem to have higher survival rates than smaller entrants, none of the tests show statistical significance. For mature high-tech products, survival rates of small and large entrant firms are roughly the same, and again, all three tests fail to reject the hypothesis of homogeneity.

Hazard rate analysis provides a more cogent picture of the above results. We present the kernel smoothed hazard rates in Figures 1 and 2, and provide the empirical analysis using proportional hazards regressions in Table III.[13] Figure 1 shows the hazard rates of small and large entrants for the life cycle stages and level of technology for products separately, while Figure 2 takes into account interaction effects of stage and technology. In Table III, we provide the results from the Cox proportional hazards regression, which allows us to assess the effect of the relevant

---

[13] We use a two class categorization for the graphs in Figures 1 and 2 similar to the analysis in Table 2, with small firms being those that are in the lowest real asset category. For the proportional hazards regressions, an ordinal measure of size based on all available categories is used.

34   RAJSHREE AGARWAL AND DAVID B. AUDRETSCH

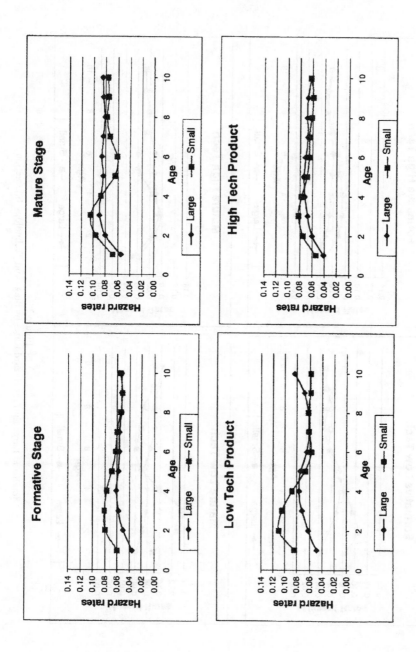

Figure 1
Small and Large Entrant Hazard Rates by Stage and Technology

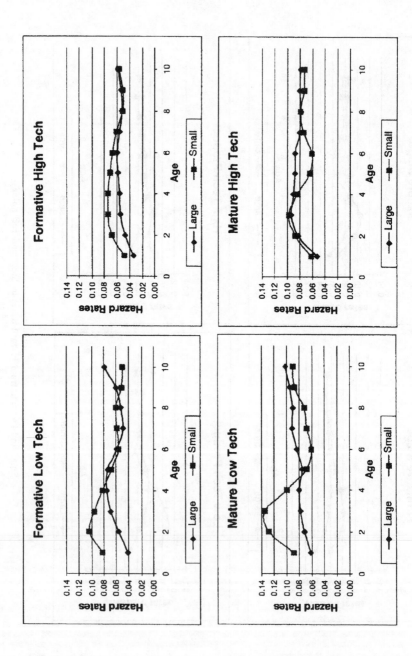

Figure 2

Small and Large Entrant Hazard Rates by Stage and Technology Interaction

RAJSHREE AGARWAL AND DAVID B. AUDRETSCH

TABLE III
COX PROPORTIONAL HAZARDS REGRESSIONS

Regression	Variable	Coefficient (Standard Error)	Risk Ratio	Industry Effects Chi-Square	Model Chi-square (p value)
1	Entry size	−0.05** (0.02)	0.95	–	29.75 (0.0001)
	Stage of entry	−0.21** (0.05)	0.81		
	Tech. intensity	−0.13* (0.06)	0.88		
2	Entry size	−0.04* (0.02)	0.96	97.98 (0.0001)	112.03 (0.0001)
	Stage of entry	−0.17** (0.06)	0.85		
3	Entry size in formative stage	−0.05* (0.02)	0.95	114.56 (0.0001)	118.91 (0.0001)
4	Entry size in mature stage	−0.03 (0.03)	0.97	46.08 (0.02)	46.96 (0.03)
5	Entry size in low-tech product	−0.08* (0.04)	0.92	23.74 (0.008)	29.69 (0.001)
6	Entry size in high-tech product	−0.03** (0.02)	0.97	69.63 (0.0001)	71.82 (0.0001)
7	Entry size in formative, low-tech	−0.04** (0.04)	0.96	29.20 (0.001)	28.13 (0.003)
8	Entry size in formative, high-tech	−0.07** (0.03)	0.94	80.18 (0.0001)	86.19 (0.0001)
9	Entry size in mature, low-tech	−0.08 (0.07)	0.92	9.16 (0.51)	10.15 (0.52)
10	Entry size in mature, high-tech	−0.02** (0.03)	0.98	35.85 (0.005)	36.31 (0.006)

Regressions 2 through 10 include industry dummies. The Chi-square values reported in the second last column represent regressions with only industry dummies, while the model chi-square values represent regressions that include the variables specified in the equation and industry dummies. * denotes statistical significance at the .05 level and **denotes statistical significance at the .01 level.

variables on the entire hazard rate function, and computes the risk ratio for the variable in question.

Before we begin with the analysis by stage and technological activity, it is worth emphasizing that what is now termed the *Jovanovic Effect*—the fact that firms need time to discover their own efficiency levels—is seen in the rise of mortality rates in the infant years for all of the firm hazard rates in Figures 1 and 2. In addition, the effect of entry size on hazard rates erodes over the age of the firm, and in all cases, the hazard rates tend to overlap after eight years at the latest, indicating most probably the effects of growth on continued survival. Thus, small entrants that survive past the first six or seven years seem to be at no greater risk than firms that enter with a larger size. This finding is also implicit in the tests of homogeneity in Table II, since the Wilcoxon test statistics are usually the most significant.[14] The infant mortality rate, however, is uniformly higher for small entrants relative to their larger counterparts in every case. After the initial rise though, both the levels and the patterns of the hazard rates differ substantially across the different environments defined by life cycle stage and technological intensity. Finally, the model chi-squares reported in Table III for regressions when only industry dummies are included show that hazard rates differ significantly across the products in almost all the environments.

Table III summarizes the results from several regressions. We present the coefficient estimates, their *p*-values, the risk ratio and the model chi-square for each regression. Note that a negative coefficient implies decreases in hazard rate, and the effect of the variable on the hazard rate is captured by the deviation of the risk ratio from 1. In order to ensure that the results are not an artifact of industry composition effects, all the regressions except for the first one include industry fixed effects. Regression 1 shows the multivariate results for entry size, technological intensity, and stage of product life cycle. Since the technological intensity for the product is measured at the industry level, Regression 1 excludes the industry dummies. The effect of entry size and stage in the presence of industry dummies are reported in Regression 2. All the coefficients are negative and strongly significant, indicating that hazard rates are lower in formative stages, in high-tech products, and for larger entry sizes. Entering a high-tech product reduces a firm's hazard rate by 12 percent. From Regressions 1 and 2, we see that increases in size bestow an advantage by reducing the hazard rate by four to five percent, and entering in the formative years decreases the hazard rate by 15 to 19 percent. The above results are all consistent with the established stylized facts on technological intensity, life-cycle and size effects.

More importantly though, the effect of entry size on survival changes dramatically when the life-cycle stage and technological intensity are included in the estimation. As seen already in Table I, size at time of entry matters in the formative years, and in low-tech products. Regressions 3 and 4 show the effect of entry size across stage of product life cycle. As was seen in Table II, while larger entrants benefit in the formative years

---

[14] Note that the Wilcoxon test statistic gives more weight to deviations between survival rates during the early years (age).

with a five percent decrease in hazard rate, there is no significant difference in hazard rates for the mature stages. Figure 1 shows that small entrants begin with a higher mortality rate relative to larger entrants in the formative stage, but as firms age, the gap declines slowly and the hazard rates overlap past age six. In contrast, small firm mortality rates in the mature period have a lower differential relative to larger entrants, the hazard rate rapidly declines and after crossing the large firm hazard rate at age four, is consistently lower at later ages.

Size matters in low-tech products; Regression 5 shows than increases in entry size results in a eight percent decrease in hazard rates. However, there is no significant difference attributable to entry size in high-tech products, as is evidenced in Regression 6. Thus, smaller firms are not disadvantaged relative to their larger counterparts in high-tech products. Figure 1 reveals the pattern of hazard rates in high and low technological products; large entrants seem to have a roughly similar hazard rate function at about six to seven percent in both types of products, while small entrant hazard rates experience different hazard rates. In low-tech products, small firm hazard rates experience the highest infant mortality rates, but then decline monotonically to cross the hazard rates of larger entrants around age five. In high-tech products, the divergence between large and small entrants is low, and the overlap between the two occurs earlier, around age four.

Finally, the results in Regressions 7 through 10 in Table III, and Figure 2 focus on the effect of entry size in environments that represent the interaction of technological intensity and stage. Consistent with the observations in Table II, there is no advantage bestowed by increases in entry size in the mature period of high-tech markets. Figure 2 shows that hazard rates of small firms are roughly the same as those of large entrants at infancy, but rapidly decline in this environment and are consistently lower after age four. The results in Regression 10 mirror the finding of no significant statistical difference, and in addition show a risk ratio of 0.98, the lowest observed effect of size on hazard rates. Surprisingly though, a larger size aids survival by decreasing hazard rates with statistical significance only in the formative years of high-tech products (Regression 8). This result becomes clearer when one sees the pattern that the hazard rates follow in Figure 2. For firms entering in the formative years of high-tech products, while the initial differential between large and small entrants is not as high as those observed in other environments, the disadvantage faced by small entrants persists for a longer time; the hazard rates do not overlap until age 7. In contrast, while the small entrant hazard rates in low-tech markets, both during the formative and mature stage, are much higher than large entrant hazard rates during infancy, they rapidly decline to intersect large firm hazard rates at age 5 and are slightly lower from then on. It is worth noting though, that while the relative differential between small and large entrants is significant in the formative years of high-tech products, small entrants seem to have the lowest *absolute* level of hazard rates when compared to small entrants in other environments.

Collectively, the regressions and the graphical analysis indicate that small entry size is a disadvantage in general, but small entrants that enter in high-tech markets, or in mature years of the product life cycle, show no significant differences in their hazard rates relative to larger entrants. Further, smaller entrants have the least size disadvantage in the mature stages of high-tech markets relative to large firms (with hazard rates actually lower after age four). And while smaller entrants have a relative disadvantage of size in the formative years of high-tech markets, they enjoy the highest absolute level of survival rate relative to other small counterparts in this environment. This seems to lend more credence to the hypothesis that while size and ability to undertake high R&D expenditures increase the probability of survival in product markets characterized by uncertainty, small firms have the greatest likelihood of survival where opportunities for niche marketing abound, as in the case of high-tech products in the mature period.

VI.   CONCLUSIONS

An empirical regularity—that small firms are confronted with a lower likelihood of survival than their larger counterparts—has recently emerged with such consistency that it has been given the status of a Stylized Result. (Geroski [1995], Caves [1998], and Sutton [1997]). In this paper, we find that this Stylized Result holds—but not for all industries and situations. Rather, technology and the industry life cycle are instrumental in shaping industry dynamics and, in particular, the role that entrants in an industry play.

Survival rates for large entry size firms are significantly higher for both the formative years, and the low-tech products. On the other hand, advantages bestowed by size seem to be less relevant in the mature stage, or in highly technical products.

In the formative stages of an industry, entrants do tend to play the role that is characterized by this Stylized Fact. The entrant is typically competing for a viable product—success brings about growth, which is a requisite for survival. By contrast, in the mature phase of the life cycle, and particularly in technically advanced industries, small firms are no longer under pressure to grow in order to increase the likelihood of survival. Rather, they enjoy the same likelihood of survival as their larger counterparts. Presumably, this reflects the ability of small firms to occupy strategic niches in mature high-tech industries in a manner that is less typical in the formative stages of the life cycle.

Thus, the evidence found in this paper suggests that general pronouncements about small and large firm survival are hazardous. This is because the role of new and incumbent firms varies considerably over the industry life cycle and with the technological demands of that industry. Because entrants are motivated by a different force and are responding to a different stimulus in the formative stages of the life cycle than in the mature stages, their role in industry dynamics is also different. Future research needs to pay more attention to the heterogeneity introduced by the evolution over time that exists not just within an industry but also across industries.

APPENDIX A

PRODUCTS IN STUDY, YEAR OF INTRODUCTION, CORRESPONDING SIC CODE AND TECHNOLOGICAL INDEX

Product Name	Year of Commercial Introduction[1]	Industry SIC Code[2]	Tech. Index[3]	Year of Onset of Mature Stage	Number of Entrants in Formative Stage	Number of Entrants in Mature Stage
Antibiotics	1948	283	1	1961	36	35
Artificial Xmas Trees	1938	399	0	1952	44	22
Ball-point Pens	1948	395	0	1983	162	59
Betaray Gauges	1956	382	1	1972	13	8
Cathode Ray Tubes	1935	367	1	1962	65	60
Combination Locks	1912	342	0	1977	68	35
Contact Lenses	1936	385	0	1981	52	21
Electric Blankets	1916	363	0	1964	42	15
Electric Shavers	1937	363	0	1943	52	26
Electrocardiographs	1942	384	1	1961	20	21
Freezers	1946	363	0	1957	83	44
Freon Compressors	1935	358	0	1975	66	8
Gas Turbines	1944	351	1	1959	138	36
Guided Missiles	1951	376	1	1964	231	99
Gyroscopes	1915	381	1	1969	77	44
Heat Pumps	1954	358	0	1969	48	59
Jet Engines	1948	372	1	1967	39	40
Microfilm Readers	1940	386	1	1975	94	36
Nuclear Reactors	1955	344	1	1966	49	33
Outboard Motors	1913	351	1	1923	23	65
Oxygen Tents	1932	384	0	1961	35	13
Paints	1934	285	1	1969	129	62
Phonograph Records	1908	365	1	1928	95	131
Photocopying Machines	1940	386	1	1970	42	57
Piezoelectric Crystals	1940	367	1	1962	59	34
Polariscopes	1928	381	1	1959	27	15
Radar Antenna Assemblies	1952	366	1	1965	62	51
Radiant Heating Baseboards	1947	363	0	1963	37	21
Radiation Meters	1949	382	1	1967	29	36
Recording Tapes	1952	365	1	1980	99	40
Rocket Engines	1958	372	1	1969	21	22
Styrene	1938	282	1	1984	66	20
Video Cassette Recorders	1974	365	1	1985	44	16

[1] Based on the *Thomas Register of American Manufacturers.*
[2] SIC Codes obtained from the *Alphabetical list of SIC codes, Census of Manufactures 1987 Manual* and from *Predicasts.*
[3] Technological Index based on Hadlock, Hecker and Gannon [1991] classification of 3-digit SIC industries as technological by the proportion of R&D employment using data for 1987.

APPENDIX B
PROCEDURE TO IDENTIFY FORMATIVE AND MATURE STAGES

The procedure that we used to identify the formative and mature stages is the same as the generalization of the standard discriminant analysis used in Gort and Klepper [1982] to separate the five stages in the product life cycle. To distinguish between the formative stage (positive net entry) and the mature period (negative net entry with ensuing period of approximately zero net entry), we first examined the data on annual net entry rates for each product. To determine the cut-off year for each product, we first partitioned the series into three categories—the first and third category contained the years where the net entry rate clearly reflected the formative and mature stages respectively. The net entry rates of the T consecutive 'in-between' years of the second category were then labeled $x_1, x_2, \ldots, x_T$. The problem was then to choose an optimal dividing year j such that observations $x_1, x_2, \ldots, x_j$ are classified in the formative stage, and $x_{j+1}, x_{j+2}, \ldots, x_T$ are classified in the mature stage. This was accomplished using a three step procedure:

1. For each $j = 1, 2, \ldots, T$, we computed

(1)
$$d_1(j) = \sum_{i=1}^{j} x_i/j$$

$$d_2(j) = \sum_{i=j+1}^{T} x_i/(T-j)$$

2. The choice of the dividing year was limited to those values of j for which

(2)
$$|d_1(j) - \mu_1| \leq |(\mu_1 - \mu_2)/2|$$
$$|d_2(j) - \mu_2| \leq |(\mu_1 - \mu_2)/2|$$

where μ_1 and μ_2 represent the mean rate of net entry in categories 1 and 2. If there were no values of j satisfying (2), then all observations were classified in the formative stage if $|d_1(T) - \mu_1| < |d_1(T) - \mu_2|$ and in the mature stage otherwise.

3. If there were multiple values of j satisfying (2), then we selected the value of j from this set that maximized $|d_1(j) - d_2(j)|$

Step 2 requires that the mean of the observations classified in each of the two stages is closer to the sample mean of the observations initially classified in those stages than in the alternative stage. Step 3 ensures that, among the classifications that would satisfy 2, the classification that is chosen maximizes the difference between the means of the points classified in the two alternative stages.

REFERENCES

Agarwal, R., 1998, 'Evolutionary Trends of Industry Variables', *International Journal of Industrial Organization,* 16, pp. 511–526.

Agarwal, R., 1997, 'Survival of Firms over the Product Life Cycle', *Southern Economic Journal*, 3, pp. 571–584.

Agarwal, R., 1996, 'Technological Activity and the Survival of Firms', *Economics Letters*, 52, pp. 101–108.

Agarwal, R., 1998, 'Small Firm Survival and Technological Activity', *Small Business Economics*, 11, pp. 215–224.

Agarwal, R. and Gort, M., 1996, 'The Evolution of Markets and Entry, Exit and Survival of Firms', *Review of Economics and Statistics*, 78, pp. 489–498.

Arrow, K. J., 1962, 'Economic Welfare and the Allocation of Resources for invention', in R. R. Nelson (ed.), *The Rate and Direction of Inventive Activity* (Princeton University Press, Princeton), pp. 609–625.

Audretsch, D. B., 1995, *Innovation and Industry Evolution* (MIT Press, Cambridge).

Audretsch, D. B., 1991, 'New Firm Survival and the Technological Regime', *Review of Economics and Statistics*, 73, pp. 441–450.

Audretsch, D. B. and Mahmood, T., 1995, 'New Firm Survival: New Results Using a Hazard Function', *Review of Economics and Statistics*, 76, pp. 97–103.

Baldwin, J. R., 1995, *The Dynamics of Industrial Competition* (Cambridge University Press, Cambridge).

Baldwin, J. R. and Rafiquzzaman, M., 1995, 'Selection versus Evolutionary Adaptation: Learning and Post-Entry Performance', *International Journal of Industrial Organization*, 13, pp. 501–522.

Caves, R. and Porter, M. E., 1977, 'From Entry Barriers to Mobility Barriers', *Quarterly Journal of Economics*, 91, pp. 241–261.

Doms, M., Dunne, T. and Roberts, M. J., 1995, 'The Role of Technology Use in the Survival and Growth of Manufacturing Plants', *International Journal of Industrial Organization*, 13, pp. 523–542.

Caves, R. E., 1998, 'Industrial Organization and New Findings on the Turnover and Mobility of Firms', *Journal of Economic Literature*, 36, pp. 1947–1982.

Dosi, G., Marsili, O., Orsenigo, L. and Salvatore, R., 1995, 'Learning, Market Selection and the Evolution of Industrial Structures', *Small Business Economics*, 7, pp. 411–436.

Dunne, T., Roberts, M. J. and Samuelson, L., 1988, 'Patterns of Firm Entry and Exit in U.S. Manufacturing Industries', *Rand Journal of Economics*, 19, pp. 495–515.

Dunne, T., Roberts, M. J. and Samuelson, L., 1989, 'The Growth and Failure of U.S. Manufacturing Plants', *Quarterly Journal of Economics*, 104, pp. 671–698.

Geroski, P. A., 1995, 'What Do We Know About Entry?' *International Journal of Industrial Organization*, 13, pp. 450–456.

Gort, M. and Klepper, S., 1982, 'Time Paths in the Diffusion of Product Innovations', *Economic Journal*, 92, pp. 630–653.

Hadlock, P., Hecker, D. and Gannon, J., 1991, 'High Technology Employment: Another View', *Monthly Labor Review*, 114, pp. 26–30.

Harhoff, D. and Stahl, K., 1994, 'Unternehmensentwicklung in den neuen Bundeslaendern—Erste empirische Ergebnisse', in Heinz Koenig and Viktor Steiner (eds.), *Arbeitsmarktdynamik und Unternehmensentwicklung in Ostodeutschland* (Nomos Verlagsgesellschaft, Baden-Baden), pp. 207–244.

Harhoff, D., Stahl, K. and Woyvode, 1998, 'Legal Form, Growth and Exit of West German Firms', *Journal of Industrial Economics*, 67, pp. 434–452.

Holmes, T. and Schmitz, J., 1995, 'On the Turnover of Business Firms and Business Managers', *Journal of Political Economy*, 103, pp. 1005–1038.

Jovanovic, B., 1982, 'Selection and Evolution of Industry', *Econometrica*, 50, pp. 649–670.

Klepper, S., 1995, 'Evolution, Market Concentration and Firm Survival', (revised as 'Firm Survival and the Evolution of Oligopoly', 1999), unpublished manuscript.

Klepper, S., 1996, 'Entry, Exit, Growth and Innovation over the Product Life Cycle', *American Economic Review*, 86, pp. 560–581.

Klepper, S. and Miller, J. H., 1995, 'Entry, Exit and Shakeouts in the United States in New Manufactured Products', *International Journal of Industrial Organization*, 13, pp. 567–591.

Lavin, M. R., 1992, *Business Information: How to Find It, How to Use It*, 2nd ed. (Oryx Press, Phoenix).

Malerba, F. and Orsenigo, L., 1996, 'The Dynamics and Evolution of Industries', *Industrial and Corporate Change*, 5, pp. 51–88.

Mata, J. and Portugal, P., 1994, 'Life Duration of New Firms', *Journal of Industrial Economics*, 27, pp. 227–246.

Mata, J., Portugal, P. and Guimaraes, P., 1995, 'The Survival of New Plants: Start-up Conditions and Post-Entry Evolution', *International Journal of Industrial Organization*, 13, pp. 459–481.

Mueller, D. C., 1976, 'Information, Mobility, and Profit', *Kyklos*, 29, pp. 419–448.

Nelson, R. R. and Winter, S. G., 1982, *An Evolutionary Theory of Economic Change* (Harvard University Press, Cambridge).

Newman, H., 1978, 'Strategic Groups and the Structure-Performance Relationship', *Review of Economics and Statistics*, 61, pp. 214–227.

Pakes, A. and Ericson, R., 1998, 'Empirical Applications of Alternative Models of Firm and Industry Dynamics', *Journal of Economic Theory*, 79, pp. 1–45.

Porter, M. E., 1979, 'The Structure within Industries and Companies' Performance', *Review of Economics and Statistics*, 61, pp. 214–227.

Schary, M., 1991, 'The Probability of Exit', *Rand Journal of Economics*, 22, pp. 339–353.

Silverman, B. W., 1986, *Density Estimation for Statistics and Data Analysis* (Chapman and Hall, New York).

Sutton, J., 1997, 'Gibrat's Legacy', *Journal of Economic Literature*, 35, pp. 40–59.

Thomas Register of American Manufacturers (Thomas Publishing Co., New York).

Wagner, J., 1994, 'The Post-Entry Performance of New Small Firms in German Manufacturing Industries', *Journal of Industrial Economics*, 62, pp. 141–154.

Utterback, J. and Abernathy, 1975, 'A Dynamic Model of Process and Product Innovation', *OMEGA*, 3, pp. 639–656.

Williamson, O. E., 1975, *Markets and Hierarchies: Antitrust Analysis and Implications* (The Free Press, New York).

Winter, S. G., 1984, 'Schumpeterian Competition in Alternative Technological Regimes', *Journal of Economic Behavior and Organization*, 5, pp. 287–320.

17

NEW FIRM SURVIVAL: NEW RESULTS USING
A HAZARD FUNCTION

David B. Audretsch and Talat Mahmood*

Abstract—A limitation of Audretsch's 1991 study of new-firm survival was the level of aggregation to industries. This precluded linking establishment-specific characteristics, such as organizational structure and size, to post-entry performance. The purpose of this paper is to relate the post-entry performance of individual establishments not only to their technological and market structure environments, but also to establishment-specific characteristics. We do this by estimating a hazard duration function for more than 12,000 individual establishments in U.S. manufacturing started in 1976 by tracking their subsequent performance over a ten-year period. We conclude that establishment-specific characteristics, which Audretsch was not able to capture in his earlier study, play an important role in shaping the exposure to risk confronting new establishments.

I. Introduction

ONE of the most striking stylized facts regarding the dynamics of industries that has emerged from empirical studies is that the survival rates of businesses are positively related both to establishment size and age.[1] Many, if not most, of these studies, however, did not specifically examine whether or not business survival varies across specific industries. Audretsch (1991) found that survival rates do, in fact, vary considerably across industries, and that they are shaped by the conditions of technology and demand underlying the industry. This result was important because it provided at least some reconciliation to the apparent paradox emerging from a wave of recent empirical studies finding that the entry of new firms is not substantially deterred in capital-intensive industries which exhibit scale economies.[2] That is, while new firms apparently still enter industries where scale economies play an important role, the likelihood of survival is correspondingly lower.

An important qualification and limitation of Audretsch's (1991) study is that the survival rates are at the level of industry and not business. This made it impossible to identify the actual post-entry performance of individual establishments and link it to establishment-specific characteristics, such as ownership status and size. The purpose of this paper is to identify explicitly the post-entry performance of new businesses by linking their likelihood of survival to the conditions of technology and demand underlying the industry within which they operate, as well as to establishment-specific characteristics. We do this in the framework of a hazard duration estimation model.

In the second section of this paper, the likelihood of firm survival is put into the context of the hazard model introduced by Cox (1972 and 1975). Measurement issues are considered in the third section. The main hypotheses linking establishment-specific as well as technological and market structure characteristics to the hazard rate are discussed in the fourth section. In the fifth section, the hazard model with time varying covariates is estimated for over 12,000 new U.S. manufacturing establishments started in 1976. Finally, in the last section a summary and conclusions are provided. We find that the likelihood of a new business surviving is shaped not only by the underlying technological conditions and extent of scale economies, but also by business-specific characteristics, such as ownership status and size. In addition, there is at least some evidence indicating that the hazard rates are influenced by macroeconomic conditions.

Received for publication August 4, 1992, Revision accepted for publication March 29, 1994.

* Wissenschaftszentrum Berlin für Sozialforschung.

We thank two anonymous referees for helpful suggestions. Any errors or omissions remain our responsibility.

[1] After these results appeared in Evans (1987a and 1987b), and Hall (1987), they were confirmed in a host of other studies, including Dunne, Roberts and Samuelson (1988 and 1989), Baldwin and Gorecki (1991), Audretsch (1991), and Phillips and Kirchhoff (1989).

[2] See, for example, Acs and Audretsch (1990, chapter five), Evans and Siegfried (1992), Austin and Rosenbaum (1991), and three of the country studies contained in Geroski and Schwalbach (1991) and summarized in Cable and Schwalbach (1991).

II. The Likelihood of Survival and the Hazard Function

The model proposed by Audretsch (1991, 1995) suggested that survival rates for new businesses should be shaped by three general factors.[3] The first is the degree to which a new business is burdened by an inherent size disadvantage, or the extent to which its own level of output is below that of the minimum efficient scale (MES) level of output. The greater this gap is, the greater will be the cost disadvantage confronting the establishment, leading to a greater likelihood of exit. That is, given a long-run average cost function and MES in an industry, the smaller the scale at which an enterprise operates, the greater will be its cost disadvantage. Conversely, for any business of a given size, higher levels of the MES will result in a greater cost disadvantage.

The second factor is related to what Winter (1984) termed as the "technological regime." Under the routinized regime the technological and information conditions underlying the industry are more conducive to innovative activity from established incumbent enterprises. However, under the entrepreneurial regime new entrants tend to have the innovative advantage.[4] Under the routinized regime, a high technological requirement increases the amount of financial requirements needed to operate in the industry. However, under the entrepreneurial regime, a greater degree of uncertainty regarding not only the technical nature of the product but also the demand for that product may lead to wider divergences in the assessment of (potential) innovations and ultimately to the entry of new firms in order to capitalize on asymmetries in such assessments. Thus, while the R & D requirements may generally reduce the likelihood of a new firm surviving, under the entrepreneurial regime new firms may have a greater likelihood of survival through innovative activity.

The third factor influencing industry survival rates is industry growth which, as Bradburd and Caves (1982) found, tends to elevate price–cost margins. To the extent that price–cost margins are elevated, establishments will be able to operate at a suboptimal level of scale without being driven out of the industry.

If these characteristics are included in the matrix X, then the rate of hazard for an individual

establishment[5] can be formulated as

$$r_{ij} = h_{ij} * \exp(X_t^{ij} * \beta^{ij}) \tag{1}$$

where r_{ij} is the transition rate from the birth state i to the death state j. The baseline rate of hazard remains unspecified as h_{ij}, and is by definition identical for all transitions. The vector of covariates X_t^{ij} is allowed to vary with respect to time, t, so that β^{ij} is the vector of associated coefficients.

Equation (1) can be estimated using a method of partial likelihood. Because the transitions into death vary over time and are specific to the individual unit of observation, i.e. the establishment, the partial likelihood estimation model is

$$PL = \prod_{i \in R} \frac{\exp(X_{it}'\beta)}{\sum_{l \in N(t_i)} \exp(X_{lt}'\beta)}, \tag{2}$$

where R denotes the set of all non-censored episodes of single transition. The risk of death at t_i for the ith episode contained in R is $N(t_i)$. Equation (2) incorporates the covariates at each successive point in time to calculate the risk of exit confronting the ith establishment at time t. The coefficients of the model are estimated by maximizing the partial likelihood function. The approximation proposed by Breslow (1974) is used to incorporate the cases of ties,

$$PL = \prod_{i=1}^{K} \left\{ \frac{\exp(\beta S_i(t_i))}{\left[\sum_{J \in N(t_i)} \exp(\beta X_{it_i}) \right]^{m_i}} \right\} \tag{3}$$

where $S_i(t_i)$ is defined as the vector sum of the covariates for the episodes with events at t_i, and m_i represents the number of exits at t_i.

III. Measurement Issues

There have been three major data constraints rendering estimation of a hazard duration model virtually impossible for anything approaching a large sample of establishments. The first has been the lack of longitudinal data bases which identify the actual startup and closure dates of establishments. And those longitudinal data bases that do

---

[3] An anonymous referee pointed out that this applies more to manufacturing than to services.

[4] Empirical evidence supporting the existence of these two distinct technological regimes has been found by Acs and Audretsch (1988 and 1990).

[5] It should be noted that the term establishment refers to a manufacturing plant throughout this paper. An enterprise refers to a firm.

exist tend not to provide observations at close enough time intervals for a meaningful implementation of a hazard duration model. For example, while Dunne, Roberts, and Samuelson (1988 and 1989), Evans (1987a and 1987b), Hall (1987), Phillips and Kirchhoff (1989), and Baldwin and Gorecki (1991) all had access to such a longitudinal data set, none of these studies explicitly estimated the hazard duration model. One reason why the U.S. Bureau of Census data employed by Dunne, Roberts, and Samuelson do not lend themselves to estimation of the hazard duration model is that while observations over time are available, they are only identified at five-year intervals. The third data constraint is that observations need to be at the level of the individual establishment or enterprise. Thus, the estimation of survival rates for aggregated four-digit standard industrial classification (SIC) industries by Audretsch (1991) precluded estimation of the hazard duration function.

To overcome these data constraints we employ a data set providing biennial observations on establishments compiled by the U.S. Small Business Administration. The data base is derived from the Dun and Bradstreet market identifier file, which provides a virtual census on about 4.5 million U.S. establishments every other year between 1976 and 1986.[6]

The most basic unit of observation in this data base is the establishment, which is defined as a particular economic entity operating at a specific and single geographic location. While most establishments, especially new ones, are legally independent and therefore represent enterprises or firms, the legal status of others is identified as being owned by a parent firm through either a branch or subsidiary relationship. An important feature of the data base is that the ownership of establishments is linked to any parent firm. This makes it possible to distinguish between (1) single-establishment firms, in which case the establishment is an independent legal entity, (2) a branch or subsidiary belonging to a multi-estab-

lishment firm, or (3) the headquarters of a multi-establishment firm. Of the 12,251 new establishments recorded in 1976, 590 represented a branch or subsidiary of an existing enterprise, and 11,154 represented an independent single-establishment firm.

IV. Specification

To test the hypothesis that the risk of exit confronting each establishment is attributable to the underlying conditions of technology, the extent of scale economies, market demand, and business-specific characteristics, such as ownership and size, the hazard duration model with time varying covariates was estimated for the 12,251 new establishments in 1976. The post-entry performance of each of these establishments was then tracked for the subsequent ten years within the context of the hazard duration model.

To capture the extent to which the underlying technological regime is conducive to large or small establishments, we adapt the same measures as Audretsch (1991). The total innovation rate is defined as the total number of innovations recorded in 1982 divided by industry employment. The small firm innovation rate is defined as the number of innovations contributed by firms with fewer than 500 employees divided by small-firm employment.[7] The rates are used to standardize the amount of innovative and small-firm innovative activity in an industry for the size of that industry (as Acs and Audretsch do in their 1987 and 1990 studies). The exposure to risk confronting new establishments is presumably greater in industries where incumbent firms tend to have the innovative advantage. By contrast, where the small-firm innovative advantage tends to be high, the likelihood of exit should be lower.

The extent to which new establishments are confronted by a size disadvantage is reflected by their start-up size in 1976, measured in terms of

---

[6] While the raw Dun and Bradstreet data have been subject to considerable criticism, the U.S. Small Business Administration in conjunction with the Brookings Institution undertook a massive project to clean up the data. Several important studies have compared these data with analogous measures from the establishment data of the U.S. Census of Manufactures (Acs and Audretsch, 1990, chapter two; and Boden and Phillips, 1985).

[7] The innovation data are from the U.S. Small Business Administration's Innovation Data Base. The data base consists of 8,074 innovations introduced into the United States in 1982. Of the manufacturing innovations for which firm size could be identified, 55.81% came from large firms (with at least 500 employees), while 44.19% came from small firms (with fewer than 500 employees). A detailed analysis of the distribution of innovations according to significance levels and firm size can be found in Acs and Audretsch (1990, chapter 2).

employees, and the overall capital intensity of the industry, measured as the 1977 capital–labor ratio (from the U.S. Census of Manufactures). The measure of establishment size is normalized by the MES. That is, given an industry level MES, as the establishment size decreases, the inherent cost disadvantage resulting from operating at a suboptimal scale of output increases. Thus, the exposure to risk confronting a new establishment rises as the size falls. Similarly, given any start-up size, an increased capital intensity, which is commonly associated with the extent of scale economies,[8] will also increase the cost disadvantage and therefore the exposure to risk confronting a new establishment.

In his 1991 study, Audretsch found no evidence that market growth, which presumably elevates price–cost margins, influences survival rates. Here we include not only the industry growth rate, defined as the percentage change in employment, over the time period corresponding to each observation, but also the industry price–cost margin. The price–cost margin is defined as value of shipments minus labor costs, minus costs of materials, all divided by value of shipments. Elevated price–cost margins will tend to compensate for size-related cost disadvantages, thereby reducing the risk confronting new establishments. We also include the average wages paid in the industry for each year, measured as wages divided by number of employees. Industries with higher wages tend to reflect a greater investment in certain labor-related sunk costs, such as training and firm-specific human capital. The propensity to exit such industries, ceteris paribus, should be somewhat reduced.[9] These measures are from the *Annual Survey of Manufactures*.

Because Audretsch's (1991) study was aggregated to the level of the industry, he was not able to link mean industry survival rates to establishment-specific characteristics, such as ownership structure and size. The ownership structure of the establishment is captured by including a

dummy variable taking on the value of one for branches and subsidiaries that belong to a multi-establishment enterprise and zero for establishments which represent independent firms. Because an established firm already has experience about the specific economic conditions and managerial competence, when a branch or subsidiary plant is opened it should face a systematically lower likelihood of failure. That is, the hazard rate would be expected to be systematically greater for new establishments which are independent enterprises and systematically lower for new branch or subsidiary plants opened by an incumbent enterprise.

Audretsch (1991) also implicitly assumed that macroeconomic conditions leave survival rates unaffected. Here we explicitly examine the link between the business cycle and the exposure to risk, by including the macroeconomic unemployment rate (from the 1990 *Economic Report of the President*) and the real interest rate (measured as the six-month Treasury bill and also from the 1990 *Economic Report of the President*), both of which may elevate the hazard rate.

V. Empirical Results

Table 1 shows the regression results estimating the Cox Model for the hazard function of 12,251 new U.S. manufacturing establishments started in 1976. The subscript i denotes a cross-sectional variable at the level of the establishment or corresponding industry, and t denotes a time-specific variable. Some of the variables, such as the innovation rates, are specific to the industry within which a particular establishment operates and do not vary over time. Other variables, such as the ownership dummy, also do not vary over time, but are specific to an actual establishment and not an industry. Still other measures, such as wages, and the price–cost margin, vary both with respect to the industry and over time, but do not vary across particular establishments within any given industry. And finally, the two macroeconomic variables, the unemployment and interest rates, are constant across both establishments and industry, and vary only with respect to time.

The results suggest that the exposure of new establishments to risk tends to be greater in highly innovative environments. While the coefficient of the small firm innovation rate is negative, it can-

TABLE 1.—REGRESSION RESULTS FOR COX MODEL WITH TIME VARYING COVARIATES[a]

Independent Variables	(1)	(2)	(3)	(4)
Total Innovation Rate (i)	0.168	0.107	0.166	0.105
	(4.119)	(2.597)	(4.062)	(2.533)
Small Firm Innovation	−0.001	−0.002	−0.001	−0.002
Rate (i)	(−0.662)	(−1.064)	(−0.683)	(−1.085)
Establishment Size (i)	−0.001	−0.001	−0.001	−0.001
	(−2.153)	(−2.300)	(−2.262)	(−2.421)
Capital Intensity	0.004	0.003	0.004	0.003
	(4.405)	(3.612)	(4.359)	(3.551)
Ownership Dummy (i)	0.115	0.104	0.116	0.105
	(1.924)	(1.746)	(1.941)	(1.762)
Unemployment Rate (t)	—	—	0.066	0.066
			(4.765)	(4.791)
Interest Rate (t)	—	—	−0.017	−0.017
			(−3.038)	(−3.224)
Growth Rate (it)	−0.049	−0.035	−0.047	−0.033
	(−1.393)	(−1.013)	(−1.339)	(−0.945)
Wages (it)	−0.040	−0.041	−0.040	−0.041
	(−8.174)	(−8.353)	(−8.213)	(−8.396)
Price–Cost Margin (it)	0.097	—	0.117	—
	(0.530)		(0.639)	
Price–Cost Margin*	—	0.013	—	0.012
Concentration (it)		(5.471)		(5.562)

Note: t = Statistics within parentheses. i = industry and t = time.

not be considered to be statistically significant. The positive coefficient of capital intensity confirms the findings by Audretsch (1991) that the likelihood of survival tends to be lower in industries where scale economies play an important role. What Audretsch could not capture, however, is that establishments can reduce their exposure to risk, at least to some extent, by increasing the start-up size, as indicated by the negative and statistically significant coefficient of the establishment size. That is, entrants are intentionally rational and presumably use what information they have about their chances for success. A large start-ups size presumably reflects an expectation of a greater likelihood of success and vice versa.[10]

Taken together, these two variables suggest that as the gap between the MES and start-up size increases, the hazard rate also rises. As the gap diminishes, the exposure to risk confronting new establishments tends to become less.[11]

Because he was limited to the aggregated industry level, Audretsch (1991) was unable to identify the apparent impact that ownership

[10] We are grateful to an anonymous referee for pointing this out to us.
[11] Including an interactive variable where capital intensity is divided by the standardized start-up size produces a statistically insignificant coefficient.

structure has on survival. The hazard rate is significantly higher for establishments which are a branch or subsidiary of an existing enterprise than for new independent enterprises.

The exposure to risk of an establishment appears to be more influenced by the price–cost margin than by the industry growth rate. The rather surprising positive impact of price–cost margins on the hazard rate may be attributable to the fact that price–cost margins tend to be elevated in more concentrated industries, where it may be easier to detect and punish new entrants. In any case, substituting a multiplicative variable including both of these effects still produced a positive relationship. This result is consistent with the model by Lippman and Rumelt (1982) where a stochastic likelihood of success confronting new entrants will still induce high entry as long as abnormal profits can be earned. As they show, the success probability must be low for a long-run equilibrium level of high concentration to exist.

The positive coefficient of the unemployment rate suggests that the hazard rate for new establishments tends to be greater during periods of higher unemployment, or what is commonly associated with macroeconomic downturns. However, the negative coefficient of the real interest rate indicates there is no evidence suggesting that higher interest rates increase the exposure to risk confronting new establishments. One explanation for this counter-intuitive result is that most new businesses are not that dependent on external capital.[12] Another is that five time periods are simply not sufficient to disentangle complicated links between the macroeconomic environment and microeconomic performance at the level of the individual establishment. Of course, a still simpler explanation may be multicollinearity between the macroeconomic growth rate and the real interest rate.[13]

The above results indicate that, after controlling for establishment-specific and industry-specific characteristics, the hazard rate tends to be greater for new firms than for new branch plants opened by existing enterprises. However, it is also possible that the relationship between each of the explanatory variables and the hazard rate is also influenced by establishment ownership status. An established firm's new plant is presumably founded by a managerial unit that is better informed about economic conditions and also has an established managerial competence. One would therefore expect its likelihood of survival to be less dependent on environmental conditions, at least those that are specific to the industry. When the four specifications for the hazard function from table 1 are estimated separately for subsamples alternatively comprised of (1) only new firms and (2) only new branch and subsidiary establishments opened by existing enterprises, this is confirmed because none of the regression coefficients for the second subsample, consisting of new branch and subsidiary establishments is statistically significant.[14] At the same time, the signs and levels of significance of the

coefficients of the explanatory variables for the first subsample, consisting of new firms, are virtually identical to those reported in table 1. Thus, there is considerable evidence that environmental conditions shape the post-entry performance of new firms but not necessarily of new plants opened by existing firms. These results support Jovanovic's (1982) assumption that entrepreneurs starting new firms know the distribution of abilities, and therefore the likelihood of success, but not their own abilities until they actually gain experience. Only after a new firm is started does the entrepreneur gain the necessary experience enabling her to identify the likelihood of success, as captured by the hazard function. Once a firm has been established, its knowledge embraces an ability to allow for the effect on hazard rates of the major systematic factors (leaving only project-, or plant-, specific random factors to cause failures).

VI. Conclusions

While Audretsch (1991) was able to identify the manner by which survival rates vary according to the conditions of underlying technology, scale economies, and demand, the aggregated nature of the data—at the industry level—made it impossible to link establishment-specific characteristics, such as the ownership structure and start-up size to the likelihood of survival. By examining the post-entry performance of more than 12,000 U.S. manufacturing establishments started in 1976 through the lens of the hazard duration model, we find that characteristics specific to the individual establishment influence the exposure to risk. In particular, the evidence suggests that both the structure of ownership and start-up size can substantially shape the likelihood of survival.

While the results of this paper do confirm the general findings of Audretsch (1991), they also point to the importance of establishment-specific characteristics in shaping the post-entry performance of businesses. An important qualification is that the results apply only to the manufacturing sector. More detailed longitudinal data sets need to be developed to link the technological and product strategies of individual businesses to their post-entry performance. Such data sets and analyses will surely yield worthwhile insights regarding the manner in which firms and industries evolve over time.

---

[12] For example, a March 1993 survey carried out by Louis Harris & Associates found that only 12% of managers and owners of companies with 6 to 500 employees considered "difficulty in obtaining" financing to be the "most serious problem" for their company. By contrast, about one-third of the respondents named "health cost' and "government regulations," and one-fifth named "finding and keeping qualified employees" as the most serious problem (cited in *Business Week*, April 19, 1993, p. 66).

[13] It should be pointed out that the impact of the real interest rate on the likelihood of survival may vary considerably between manufacturing and the service sector.

[14] The establishment dummy variable used in table 1 cannot be included in tables reporting the regression results for the Cox Model with the time varying covariates for the subsamples consisting of (1) only new firms and (2) only new branch and subsidiary plants opened by existing enterprises. These tables can be obtained upon request from the authors.

REFERENCES

Acs, Zoltan J., and David B. Audretsch, "Innovation Market Structure and Firm Size," this REVIEW 69 (4) (Nov. 1987), 567–575.

———, "Innovation in Large and Small Firms: An Empirical Analysis," *American Economic Review* 78 (4) (Sept. 1988), 678–690.

———, *Innovation and Small Firms* (Cambridge, MA: MIT Press, 1990).

Audretsch, David B., "New-Firm Survival and the Technological Regime," this REVIEW 60 (3) (Aug. 1991), 441–450.

———, *Innovation and Industry Evolution* (Cambridge MA: MIT Press, 1995).

Austin, John S., and David I. Rosenbaum, "The Determinants of Entry and Exit Rates into U.S. Manufacturing Industries," *Review of Industrial Organization* 5 (2) (Summer 1990), 211–223.

Baldwin, John, and Paul Gorecki, "Entry, Exit and Productivity Growth," in Paul Geroski and Joachim Schwalbach (eds.), *Entry and Market Contestability: An International Comparison* (Oxford: Basil Blackwell, 1991), 244–256.

Boden, Richard, and Bruce D. Phillips, "Uses and Limitations of USEEM / USELM Data" (Washington, D.C.: Office of Advocacy, U.S. Small Business Administration, Nov. 1985).

Bradburd, Ralph, and Richard E. Caves, "A Closer Look at the Effect of Market Growth on Industries Profits," this REVIEW 64 (Nov. 1982), 635–645.

Breslow, N., "Covariance Analysis of Censored Survival Data," *Biometrics* 30 (1) (Mar. 1974), 88–99.

Cable, John, and Joachim Schwalbach, "International Comparisons of Entry and Exit," in Paul Geroski and Joachim Schwalbach (eds.), *Entry and Market Contestability: An International Comparison* (Oxford: Basil Blackwell, 1990), 257–281.

Caves, Richard E., and Michael E. Porter, "Barriers to Exit," in Robert T. Masson and P. D. Qualls (eds.), *Essays on Industrial Organization in Honor of Joe S. Bain* (Cambridge, MA: Ballinger, 1976), 39–69.

Caves, Richard E., J. Khalilzadeh-Shirazi and M. E. Porter, "Scale Economies in Statistical Analyses of Market Power," this REVIEW 57 (2) (May 1975), 133–140.

Cox, David R., "Regression Models and Life Tables," *Journal of the Royal Statistical Society* 34 (May/Aug. 1972), 187–220.

———, "Partial Likelihood," *Biometrics* 62 (1975), 269–275.

Dunne, Timothy, Mark J. Roberts, and Larry Samuelson, "Patterns of Firm Entry and Exit in U.S. Manufacturing Industries," *Rand Journal of Economics* 104 (4) (Nov. 1988), 671–698.

Evans, David S., "The Relationship between Firm Growth, Size and Age: Estimates for 100 Manufacturing Industries," *Journal of Industrial Economics* 35 (2) (June 1987a), 567–581.

———, "Tests of Alternative Theories of Firm Growth," *Journal of Political Economy* 95 (4) (Aug. 1987b), 657–674.

Evans, Laurie Beth, and John J. Siegfried, "Entry and Exit in United States Manufacturing Industries from 1977 to 1982," in David B. Audretsch and John J. Siegfried (eds.), *Empirical Studies in Industrial Organization: Essays in Honor of Leonard W. Weiss* (Boston: Kluwer Academic Publishers, 1992), 253–274.

Geroski, Paul, and Joachim Schwalbach (eds.), *Entry and Market Contestability: An International Comparison* (Oxford: Basil Blackwell, 1991).

Hall, Bronwyn H., "The Relationship between Firm Size and Firm Growth in the U.S. Manufacturing Sector," *Journal of Industrial Economics* 35 (June 1987), 583–605.

Jovanovic, Boyan, "Selection and Evolution of Industry," *Econometrica* 50 (7) (May 1982), 649–670.

Lippman, S. A., and R. P. Rumelt, "Uncertain Imitability: An Analysis of Interfirm Differences in Efficiency Under Competition," *Bell Journal of Economics* 13 (2) (Autumn 1982), 418–438.

Scherer, F. M., and David Ross, *Industrial Market Structure and Economic Performance*, 3rd ed. (Boston: Houghton Mifflin, 1990).

Winter, Sidney G., "Schumpeterian Competition in Alternative Technological Regimes," *Journal of Economic Behavior and Organization* 5 (Sept.–Dec., 1984), 287–320.

[18]

The Dynamic Role of Small
Firms: Evidence from the U.S.

David B. Audretsch

ABSTRACT. This paper provides a conceptual and empirical account of the dynamic role of SMEs in the U.S. economy. Evidence is provided to show that SMEs are important sources of employment growth and innovation. For example, the net employment gain during 1990–95 is shown to be greater among smaller firms than among larger firms. Furthermore, while large firms often produce a larger number of patents per firm, the patenting rate for small firms is typically higher than that for large firms when measured on a per-employee basis. It is noted that public policy is shifting away from traditional measures which were based on a static conception of industrial organization and thus emphasized anti-trust, regulation and public ownership solutions, towards measures which are geared towards supporting the dynamic role of SMEs. These measures focus on providing an enabling environment for enterprise start-ups, job creation, knowledge spillovers and technological change.

1. Introduction

As recently as the 1980s, there were serious concerns about the ability of the United States to withstand competition in the global economy, to create jobs, and to continue to develop economically. Lester Thurow bemoaned that the United States was "losing the economic race,"[1] because, "Today it's very hard to find an industrial corporation in America that isn't in really serious trouble basically because of trade problems. . . . The systematic erosion of our competitiveness comes from having lower rates of growth of manufacturing productivity year after year, as compared with the rest of the world" (Thurow, 1985, p. 23). W. W. Restow predicted a revolution in economic policy, concluding that, "The United States is entering a new political era, one

Ameritech Chair of Economic Development
Institute of Development Strategies
Indiana University
SPEA, Suite 201
Bloomington
IN 47405-2100
U.S.A.

in which it will be preoccupied by increased economic competition from abroad and will need better cooperation at home to deal with this challenge."[2] The influential study, *Made in America*, directed by the leaders of the MIT Commission on Industrial Productivity (Dertouzos and others, 1989), even reached the conclusion that for the United States to restore its international competitiveness it had to adapt the types of economic policies targeting the leading corporations in Japan and Germany.

The 1990s proved those economists and scholars mistaken, or at least too zealous in their inclinations. The last decade has seen a remarkable reemergence of competitiveness, innovative activity, and job generation in the United States not seen in many years. Not only was this economic turnaround largely unanticipated by many scholars and members of the policy community, but what was even more surprising than the resurgence itself was the primary source of the resurgence; that is, small firms.

As scholars began the arduous task of documenting the crucial role played by small and medium enterprises (SMEs) in the United States as a driving engine of growth, job creation, and competitiveness in global markets (Audretsch, 1995), policy makers responded with a bipartisan emphasis on policies to promote SMEs.[3] For example, in his 1993 State of the Union Address to the country, President Bill Clinton proposed, "Because small business has created such a high percentage of all the new jobs in our nation over the last 10 or 15 years, our plan includes the boldest targeted incentives for small business in history. We propose a permanent investment tax credit or the small firms in this country."[4] The Republican response to Clinton was, "We agree with the president that we have to put more people to work, but remember this: 80 to 85 percent of

 Small Business Economics **18**: 13–40, 2002.
© 2002 *Kluwer Academic Publishers. Printed in the Netherlands.*

the new jobs in this country are created by small business. So the climate for starting and expanding businesses must be enhanced with tax incentives and deregulation, rather than imposing higher taxes and more governmental mandates."[5]

One of the puzzles posed by the important contribution of small firms to the resurgence of the U.S. economy is that the share of economic activity, measured in terms of share of total establishments, employment, or output, has not dramatically increased over the last 20 years (Acs and Audretsch, 1993). In fact, a meticulous comparison documenting the role of SMEs across a broad spectrum of countries revealed that the share of economic activity accounted for by SMEs is considerably less than in, for example, Japan, Germany, the United Kingdom, Italy, and The Netherlands.

If SMEs are so important to the U.S. economy, then how come SMEs account for such a small share of economic activity, at least relative to other economies? The answer to this question lies in a crucial distinction between the static role and the dynamic role of SMEs.

In the second section of this paper we contrast the static role and dynamic role of SMEs. In the third section we examine the policies that have contributed to promoting the dynamic contributions of SMEs. Finally, in the fourth section, a summary and conclusions are provided.

2. Evolution of SMEs

Static and dynamic context

Two disparate views about the impact of small firms on economic efficiency have emerged in the economics literature. On the one hand is the traditional, static, view in the field of industrial organization that views small firms as imposing excess costs on the economy as a result of a scale of production that is too small to be efficient. According to this traditional view, the inefficient scale of operations results in lower levels of productivity for small firms and lower wages for their workers. The shift in economic activity that has taken place over the previous two decades away from large corporations and toward new and small firms may be interpreted as causing a decrease in the standard of living of Americans. Shifting

employment out of high-productivity and high-wage firms and into lower productivity and lower-wage (small) firms, according to this traditional view, reduces the well-being of the American population, and any policies that shift economic activity out of small firms and back into large corporations should be encouraged, since they will increase the American standard of living.

On the other hand is the nontraditional, dynamic, view. With the hindsight of some 15 years, it is clear that the dynamic view of small-firm efficiency is more consistent with not just the recent wave of theories about the evolutionary role of small and new firms, but also with the compelling empirical evidence that analyzes firms and industries through a dynamic lens (Caves, 1998).

The purpose of this paper is to explain this dynamic role played by small firms in the U.S. economy. A particular emphasis is placed on the contribution of small firms to innovation, job generation, and international competitiveness.

Static role

The static role of SMEs in the United States is documented in Table I. The source of the data is the Longitudinal Establishment and Enterprise (LEEM) file, which is produced jointly by the U.S. Small Business Administration (SBA) and the U.S. Bureau of the Census. A more thorough and detailed explanation and documentation of the LEEM database can be found in Audretsch (1995).

According to the SBA, the definition of a small firm is one with fewer than 500 employees. In every major economic sector, most of the businesses are SMEs. For example, in manufacturing, only around 49,000 of the 388,000 businesses (establishments) are owned by large firms.

In Table II the distribution of employment by firm size is shown. Because a larger firm employs more people than a SME, the firm-size distribution measured by employment is not as skewed as in Table I, where it is measured by the number of establishments. Still, most Americans work in SMEs. However, the share of employment accounted for by SMEs varies considerably across major economic sectors. For example, in construction only a small share of employment is in large firms. By contrast, in manufacturing around two-thirds of employment is in large corporations.

In Tables I and II establishments are classified according to the size of the enterprise to which they belong. Table III shows that if the establishments are classified according to establishment size, then an even greater share of establishments are accounted for by SMEs. Similarly, Table IV shows that the employment share of SMEs is even greater if the employment were classified according to the size of the establishment and not the size of the enterprise.

One of the most striking findings emerging in this static view of industrial organization is that small firms generally operate at a level of output that is too small to sufficiently exhaust scale

TABLE I

LEEM establishment distribution by firm size and establishment industry: 1995

Firm size	Establishment industry									
	Agra-services	Mining	Construc-tion	Manufac-turing	TCPU	Wholesale	Retail	FIRE	Services	Uncoded
0	22,539	2,238	96,543	27,212	28,875	40,618	126,378	52,374	236,236	25,352
1–4	49,759	10,029	306,478	100,551	96,342	172,102	468,307	261,041	1,078,044	21,973
5–9	19,262	3,417	111,382	60,442	34,663	79,305	229,549	60,036	395,712	3,188
10–19	9,967	2,576	62,891	52,575	23,759	59,668	153,936	33,534	217,715	1,097
20–49	3,707	2,084	35,052	48,424	18,514	48,351	116,609	28,471	142,859	404
50–99	785	951	9,111	22,033	8,446	21,676	50,563	17,995	62,258	30
100–249	399	809	4,275	18,612	7,901	18,983	47,050	18,332	62,210	18
250–499	168	603	1,360	9,923	5,055	10,275	31,708	11,729		
500–999	214	625	931	8,376	4,683	9,302	29,065	12,139		
1000+	946	3,991	3,810	40,229	56,194	56,624	305,629	132,215		
Total	107,746	27,323	631,833	388,377	284,432	516,904	1,558,794	627,866	2,378,412	52,067

Source: Tabulations of the prototype Longitudinal Establishment and Enterprise (LEEM) file, a joint project of the Office of Economic Research, Office of Advocacy, Small Business Administration, and the Center for Economic Studies of the Bureau of the Census, U.S. Department of Commerce (Acs and Armington, 1998, Table 6.3c).

TABLE II

LEEM employment distribution by firm size and establishment industry: 1995

Firm size	Establishment industry									
	Agra-services	Mining	Construc-tion	Manufac-turing	TCPU	Wholesale	Retail	FIRE	Services	Uncoded
0	0	0	0	0	0	0	0	0	0	0
1–4	103,692	20,160	642,722	227,470	199,212	369,679	1,040,824	501,333	2,244,789	36,717
5–9	126,586	22,410	728,147	404,733	223,611	513,430	1,478,920	373,335	2,540,323	20,399
10–19	130,322	33,794	837,695	714,023	302,064	732,703	1,878,676	377,532	2,705,654	14,330
20–49	101,525	53,395	1,108,886	1,433,918	457,795	1,053,428	2,653,287	521,661	3,448,373	11,360
50–99	45,497	37,959	574,168	1,308,089	339,675	684,409	1,693,721	412,520	2,561,140	1,851
100–249	36,888	44,129	485,825	1,796,540	393,102	700,693	1,440,357	492,592	3,564,147	2,490
250–499	15,172	31,067	210,453	1,276,358	235,453	373,365	768,499	322,560	2,468,592	253
500–999	10,856	38,658	141,812	1,274,762	234,024	262,512	640,040	311,394	2,311,945	2,243
1000+	59,104	345,734	397,192	10,172,347	3,538,287	1,914,731	9,481,931	3,670,767	12,851,941	2,156
Total	629,642	627,306	5,036,900	18,608,240	5,923,233	6,604,950	21,076,255	6,983,694	34,696,904	91,799

Source: Tabulations of the prototype Longitudinal Establishment and Enterprise (LEEM) file, a joint project of the Office of Economic Research, Office of Advocacy, Small Business Administration, and the Center for Economic Studies of the Bureau of the Census, U.S. Department of Commerce (Acs and Armington, 1998, Table 6.4c).

16

TABLE III
LEEM establishments classified by firm size and by establishment size

Employment size class	1990		1994		1995	
	Number of establishments by firm size	Number of establishments by establishment size	Number of establishments by firm size	Number of establishments by establishment size	Number of establishments by firm size	Number of establishments by establishment size
0	592,101	619.153	655,566	694,967	658,365	695,344
1–4	2,393,133	2,679,308	2,520,339	2,838,407	2,564,626	2,882,658
5–9	969,135	1,237,084	981,598	1,285,158	996,956	1,298,392
10–19	598,851	769,619	608,316	799,077	617,718	817,335
20–49	415,667	508,292	438,295	526,365	444,475	543,906
50–99	174,448	175,357	192,803	177,913	193,848	185,259
100–249	160,002	97,709	178,683	101,940	178,589	107,308
250–499	94,725	24,323	105,074	25,657	105,392	27,194
500–999	82,052	9,590	87,258	9,765	91,039	10,333
1000+	645,902	5,581	697,125	5,808	722,746	6,025
Total	6,126,016	6,126,016	6,465,057	6,465,057	6,573,754	6,573,754

Source: Tabulations of the prototype Longitudinal Establishment and Enterprise (LEEM) file, a joint project of the Office of Economic Research, Office of Advocacy, Small Business Administration, and the Center for Economic Studies of the Bureau of the Census, U.S. Department of Commerce (Acs and Armington, 1998, Table 6.1).

TABLE IV
LEEM employment by firm size and by establishment size

Employment size class	1990		1994		1995	
	Number of establishments by firm size	Number of establishments by establishment size	Number of establishments by firm size	Number of establishments by establishment size	Number of establishments by firm size	Number of establishments by establishment size
1–4	5,108,303	5,843,895	5,311,360	6,127,769	5,386,598	6,192,612
5–9	6,242,213	8,158,925	6,325,466	8,485,239	6,431,894	8,574,605
10–19	7,534,444	10,343,097	7,537,382	10,738,355	7,726,793	10,992,228
20–49	10,401,095	15,375,515	10,364,280	15,905,109	10,753,628	16,435,592
50–99	7,295,147	12,027,638	7,321,621	12,224,648	7,659,029	12,755,332
100–249	8,268,752	14,610,283	8,590,755	15,276,124	8,956,763	16,070,791
250–499	5,272,697	8,306,581	5,523,148	8,757,727	5,701,772	9,280,853
500–999	4,807,014	6,550,174	5,128,503	6,661,977	5,228,246	7,019,910
1000+	38,495,464	12,209,021	40,584,831	12,510,398	42,434,190	12,956,990
Total	93,425,129	93,425,129	96,687,346	96,687,346	100,278,913	100,278,913

Source: Tabulations of the prototype Longitudinal Establishment and Enterprise (LEEM) file, a joint project of the Office of Economic Research, Office of Advocacy, Small Business Administration, and the Center for Economic Studies of the Bureau of the Census, U.S. Department of Commerce (Acs and Armington, 1998, Table 5.7).

economies, even when the standard definition of a small firm employing fewer than 500 employees is applied. A large number of studies found that because the minimum efficient scale (MES) of output, or the lowest level of output where the minimum average cost is attained, large-scale production is typically required to exhaust scale economies in manufacturing. Any enterprise or establishment that was smaller than required by the MES was branded as being *suboptimal* or inefficient, in that it produced at average costs in excess of more efficient larger firms. Weiss (Audretsch and Yamawaki, 1991, p. 403) assumed that "The term 'suboptimal' capacity describes a condition in which some plants are too small to be efficient."

The importance of scale economies in the typical manufacturing industry relegated most small firms to being classified as suboptimal.[6] For example, Weiss (1964) found that suboptimal plants accounted for about 52.8 percent of industry value-of-shipments, Scherer (1973) found that 58.2 percent of value-of-shipments emanated from the suboptimal plants in 12 industries, and Pratten (1971) identified the suboptimal scale establishments accounting for 47.9 percent of industry shipments. After reviewing the literature on the extent of suboptimal firms, Weiss concluded that, "In most industries the great majority of firms is suboptimal. In a typical industry there are, let's say, one hundred firms. Typically only about five to ten of them will be operating at the MES level of output, or anything like it."[7]

What are the economic welfare implications? Weiss (1979, p. 1137) argued that the existence of small firms that are suboptimal represented a loss in economic efficiency and therefore advocated any public policy that ". . . creates social gains in the form of less suboptimal capacity." This actually translated into an ingenious argument against market power, since empirical evidence suggested that the price umbrella provided by monopoly power encouraged the existence of suboptimal capacity firms. Weiss (1979) went so far as to argue that the largest inefficiency associated with market power was not the higher prices charged to consumers but rather that it facilitated the existence of suboptimal scale small firms.

Wages and productivity would be expected to reflect the degree to which small firms are less efficient than larger firms. There is a large body of empirical evidence spanning a broad range of samples, time periods, and even countries that has consistently found wages (and nonwage compensation as well) to be positively related to firm size. Probably the most cited study is that of Brown et al. (1990, pp. 88–89). They conclude that, "Workers in large firms earn higher wages, and this fact cannot be explained completely by differences in labor quality industry, working conditions, or union status. Workers in large firms enjoy better benefits and greater security than their counterparts in small firms. When these

factors are added together, it appears that workers in large firms do have a superior employment package." Indeed, Audretsch (1995) shows that the mean manufacturing wage in small firms that can be classified as being suboptimal is only 80.5 percent as high as their larger, optimal counterparts.

Seen through the static lens provided through traditional industrial organization and labor economics, the economic welfare implications of the recent shift in economic activity away from large firms and towards small enterprises is unequivocal. Overall economic welfare is decreased since productivity and wages will be lower in smaller than in larger firms. As Weiss (1979) argued in terms of efficiency and Brown et al. (1990) in terms of employee compensation, the implication for public policy is to implement policies to shift economic activity away from small firms and toward larger enterprises.

Dynamic view

Coase (1937) was awarded a Nobel Prize for explaining why a firm should exist. But why should more than one firm exist in an industry?[8] One answer is provided by the traditional economics literature focusing on industrial organization. An excess level of profitability induces entry into the industry. And this is why the entry of new firms is interesting and important, because the new firms provide an equilibrating function in the market in that the levels of price and profit are restored to the competitive levels. The new firms are about business as usual. They simply equilibrate the market by providing more of it.

An alternative explanation for the entry of new firms was provided for by Audretsch (1995). Audretsch shows how new firms entered the industry not simply to increase output by being a smaller replica of the large incumbent enterprises but by serving as *agents of change*. This suggested that small firms, at least in some situations, were not about being smaller clones of the larger incumbents but rather about serving as *agents of change* through innovative activity.

The starting point for most of these theories of innovation is the firm.[9] In such theories the firms are exogenous and their performance in generating technological change is endogenous.[10] For example, in the most prevalent model found in the literature of technological change, the model of the *knowledge production function*, formalized by Griliches (1979), firms exist exogenously and then engage in the pursuit of new economic knowledge as an input into the process of generating innovative activity.

The most decisive input in the knowledge production function is new economic knowledge. As Cohen and Klepper conclude, the greatest source generating new economic knowledge is generally considered to be R&D.[11] Certainly a large body of empirical work has found a strong and positive relationship between knowledge inputs, such as R&D, on the one hand and innovative outputs on the other.

The knowledge production function has been found to hold most strongly at broader levels of aggregation. The most innovative countries are those with the greatest investments to R&D. Little innovative output is associated with lesser developed countries, which are characterized by a paucity of production of new economic knowledge. Similarly, the most innovative industries also tend to be characterized by considerable investments in R&D and new economic knowledge. Industries such as computers, pharmaceuticals, and instruments are not only high in R&D inputs that generate new economic knowledge but also in innovative outputs (Audretsch, 1995). By contrast, industries with little R&D, such as wood products, textiles, and paper, also tend to produce only a negligible amount of innovative output. Thus, the knowledge production model linking knowledge generating inputs to outputs certainly holds at the more aggregated levels of economic activity.

Where the relationship becomes less compelling is at the disaggregated microeconomic level of the enterprise, establishment, or even line of business. For example, While Acs and Audretsch (1990) found that the simple correlation between R&D inputs and innovative output was 0.84 for four-digit standard industrial classification (SIC) manufacturing industries in the United States, it was only about half, 0.40, among the largest U.S. corporations.

The model of the knowledge production function becomes even less compelling in view of the recent wave of studies revealing that small enterprises serve as the engine of innovative activity in certain industries. These results are startling, because as Scherer (1991) observes, the bulk of industrial R&D is undertaken in the largest corporations. Small enterprises account only for a minor share of R&D inputs. Thus the knowledge production function seemingly implies that, as the *Schumpeterian Hypothesis* predicts, innovative activity favors those organizations with access to knowledge-producing inputs; that is, the large incumbent organization. The more recent evidence identifying the strong innovative activity raises the question, *Where do new and small firms get the innovation producing inputs; that is, the knowledge?*

One answer, proposed by Audretsch (1995), is that, although the model of the knowledge production function may still be valid, the implicitly assumed unit of observation – at the level of the firm – may be less valid. The reason why the knowledge production function holds more closely for more aggregated degrees of observation may be that investment in R&D and other sources of new knowledge spills over for economic exploitation by third-party firms.

A large literature has emerged focusing on what has become known as the *appropriability problem*.[12] The underlying issue revolves around how firms that invest in the creation of new economic knowledge can best appropriate the economic returns from that knowledge (Arrow, 1962). Audretsch (1995) proposes shifting the unit of observation away from exogenously assumed firms to individuals; that is, agents with endowments of new economic knowledge. But when the lens is shifted away from focusing on the firm as the relevant unit of observation to individuals, the relevant question becomes, *How can economic agents with a given endowment of new knowledge best appropriate the returns from that knowledge?*

The appropriability problem confronting the individual may converge with that confronting the firm. Economic agents can and do work for firms, and even if those economic agents do not, the economic agents can potentially be employed by an incumbent firm. In fact, in a model of perfect information with no agency costs, any positive economies of scale or scope will ensure that the appropriability problems of the firm and individual converge. If an agent has an idea for doing something differently than is currently being practiced by the incumbent enterprises – both in terms of a new product or process and in terms of organization – then the idea, which can be termed as an innovation, will be presented to the incumbent enterprise. Because of the assumption of perfect knowledge, both the firm and the agent would agree on the expected value of the innovation. But to the degree that any economies of scale or scope exist, the expected value of implementing the innovation within the incumbent enterprise will exceed that of taking the innovation outside of the incumbent firm to start a new enterprise. Thus, the incumbent firm and the inventor of the idea would be expected to reach a bargain by splitting the value added to the firm contributed by the innovation. The payment to the inventor – either in terms of a higher wage or some other means of remuneration – would be bounded between the expected value of the innovation if it is implemented by the incumbent enterprise on the upper end and by the return that the agent could expect to earn if the agent used it to launch a new enterprise on the lower end. Thus, each economic agent would choose how to best appropriate the value of this endowment of economic knowledge by comparing the wage the agent would earn if the agent remains employed by an incumbent enterprise, w, to the expected net present discounted value of the profits accruing from starting a new firm, π. If these two values are relatively close, then the probability that the agent would choose to appropriate the value of this knowledge through an external mechanism such as starting a new firm, $\Pr(e)$, would be relatively low. On the other hand, as the gap between w and π becomes larger, the likelihood of an agent choosing to appropriate the value of this knowledge externally through starting a new enterprise becomes greater, or

$$\Pr(e) = f(\pi - w).$$

The model proposed by Audretsch (1995) refocuses the unit of observation away from firms deciding whether to increase their output from a level of zero to some positive amount in a new industry to individual agents in possession of new knowledge that, owing to uncertainty, may or may not have some positive economic value. It is the uncertainty inherent in new economic knowledge, combined with asymmetries between the agent

possessing that knowledge and the decision making vertical hierarchy of the incumbent organization with respect to its expected value, that potentially leads to a gap between the valuation of that knowledge.

How the economic agent chooses to appropriate the value of this knowledge, that is either within an incumbent firm or by starting or joining a new enterprise, will be shaped by the knowledge conditions underlying the industry. Under the routinized technological regime the agent will tend to appropriate the value of new ideas within the boundaries of incumbent firms. Thus, the propensity for new firms to be started should be relatively low in industries characterized by the routinized technological regime.

By contrast, under the entrepreneurial regime the agent will tend to appropriate the value of new ideas outside of the boundaries of incumbent firms by starting a new enterprise. Thus, the propensity for new firms to enter should be relatively high in industries characterized by the entrepreneurial regime.

Audretsch (1995) suggests that divergences in the expected value regarding new knowledge will, under certain conditions, lead an agent to exercise what Hirschman (1970) has termed as *exit* rather than *voice*, and depart from an incumbent enterprise to launch a new firm. But who is right, the departing agents or those agents remaining in the organizational decision making hierarchy who, by assigning the new idea a relatively low value, have effectively driven the agent with the potential innovation away? *Ex post* the answer may not be too difficult. But given the uncertainty inherent in new knowledge, the answer is anything but trivial *a priori*.

Thus, when a new firm is launched, its prospects are shrouded in uncertainty. If the new firm were to be built around a new idea (i.e., potential innovation), then it is uncertain whether there is sufficient demand for the new idea or if some competitor will have the same or even a superior idea. Even if the new firm were to be formed to be an exact replica of a successful incumbent enterprise, it is uncertain whether sufficient demand for a new clone, or even for the existing incumbent, will prevail in the future. Tastes can change, and new ideas emerging from other firms will certainty influence those tastes.

Finally, an additional layer of uncertainty pervades a new enterprise. It is not known how competent the new firm really is, in terms of management, organization, and workforce. At least incumbent enterprises know something about their underlying competencies from experience. A new enterprise is burdened with uncertainty as to whether it can produce and market the intended product as well as sell it. In both cases the degree of uncertainty will typically exceed that confronting incumbent enterprises.

This initial condition of not just uncertainty, but greater degree of uncertainty vis-à-vis incumbent enterprises in the industry is captured in the theory of firm selection and industry evolution proposed by Jovanovic (1982). Jovanovic presents a model in which the new firms, which he terms *entrepreneurs*, face costs that are not only random but also differ across firms. A central feature of the model is that a new firm does not know what its cost function is (i.e., its relative efficiency) but rather discovers this cost function through the process of learning from its actual post-entry performance. In particular, Jovanovic (1982) assumes that entrepreneurs are unsure about their ability to manage a new-firm startup and therefore their prospects for success. Although entrepreneurs may launch a new firm based on a vague sense of expected post-entry performance, they only discover their true ability – in terms of managerial competence and of having based the firm on an idea that is viable on the market – once their business is established. Those entrepreneurs who discover that their ability exceeds their expectations expand the scale of their business, whereas those discovering that their post-entry performance is less than commensurate with their expectations will contact the scale of output and possibly exit from the industry. Thus, Jovanovic's model is a theory of *noisy selection*, where efficient firms grow and survive and inefficient firms decline and fail.

The role of learning in the selection process has been the subject of considerable debate. It has been referred to as the *Larackian* assumption that learning refers to adaptations made by the new enterprise. In this sense, those new firms most flexible and adaptable will be the most successful in adjusting to whatever the demands of the market are. As Nelson and Winter (1982, p. 11) point out, "Many kinds of organizations commit resources to learning; organizations seek to copy the forms of their most successful competitors."

Conversely, the interpretation that the role of learning is restricted to discovering if the firm has the *right stuff* in terms of the goods it is producing as well as the way the goods are being produced. Under this interpretation the new enterprise is not necessarily able to adapt or adjust to market conditions, but receives information based on its market performance with respect to its *fitness* in terms of meeting demand most efficiently vis-à-vis rivals. The theory of organizational ecology proposed by. Hannan and Freeman (1989) most pointedly adheres to the notion that, "We assume that individual organizations are characterized by relative inertia in structure." That is, firms learn not in the sense that they adjust their actions as reflected by their fundamental identity and purpose, but in the sense of their perception. What is then learned is whether or not the firm has the right stuff, but not how to change that stuff.

The theory of firm selection is particularly appealing in view of the rather startling size of most new firms. For example, the mean size of more than 11,000 new-firm startups in the manufacturing sector in the United States was found to be fewer than eight workers per firm (Audretsch, 1995).[13] While the MES varies substantially across industries, and even to some degree across various product classes within any given industry, the observed size of most new firms is sufficiently small to ensure that the bulk of new firms will be operating at a suboptimal scale of output. Why would an entrepreneur start a new firm that would immediately be confronted by scale disadvantages?

An implication of the theory of firm selection is that new firms may begin at a small, even suboptimal, scale of output, and then if merited by subsequent performance expand. Those new firms that are successful will grow, whereas those that are not successful will remain small and may ultimately be forced to exit from the industry if operating at a suboptimal scale of output.

Subsequent to entering an industry, an entrepreneur must decide whether to maintain its output by expanding, contracting, or simply exiting. Two different strands of literature have identified several major influences shaping the decision to exit an industry. The first and most obvious strand of literature suggests that the probability of a business exiting will tend to increase as the gap between its level of output and the MES level of output increases.[14] The second strand of literature points to the role that the technological environment plays in shaping the decision to exit. As Dosi (1982) and Arrow (1962) argue, an environment characterized by more frequent innovation may also be associated with a greater amount of uncertainty regarding not only the technical nature of the product but also the demand for that product. As technological uncertainty increases, particularly under the entrepreneurial regime, the likelihood that the business will be able to produce a viable product and ultimately be able to survive decreases.

An important implication of the dynamic process of firm selection and industry evolution is that new firms are more likely to be operating at a suboptimal scale of output if the underlying technological conditions are such that there is a greater chance of making an innovation (i.e., under the entrepreneurial regime). If new firms were to successfully learn and adapt, or are just plain lucky, then those firms will grow into viably sized enterprises. If not, then those firms will stagnate and may ultimately exit from the industry. This suggests that entry and the startup of new firms may not be greatly deterred in the presence of scale economies. As long as entrepreneurs perceive that there is some prospect for growth and ultimate survival, such entry will occur. Thus, in industries where the MES is high, it follows from the observed general small size of new-firm startups that the growth rate of the surviving firms would presumably be relatively high.

At the same time, those new firms not able to grow and attain the MES level of output would presumably be forced to exit from the industry, resulting in a relatively low likelihood of survival. In industries characterized by a low MES, neither the need for growth nor the consequences of its absence are as severe, so that relatively lower growth rates but higher survival rates would be expected. Similarly, in industries where the probability of innovating is greater, more entrepreneurs may actually take a chance that they will succeed by growing into a viably sized enterprise. In such industries one would expect that the growth of successful enterprises would be greater, but that

the likelihood of survival would be correspondingly lower.

That the role of SMEs seen through a dynamic lens is considerably different than through a static one is made clear in Table V, which shows the percentage change between 1990 and 1995 in employment owing to new firms (births), exits (deaths), additional employment in existing firms (expansions), and decreases in employment in existing firms (contractions). For example, there was a 12.76 percent increase in employment owing to the birth of new firms in manufacturing between 1990 and 1995. However, employment change owing to births was considerably greater by SMEs than by large corporations. There were nearly one-third new jobs created by new firms with fewer than 20 employees. Similarly, there was an increase in employment of SMEs of 144.69 percent resulting from the startup of new firms.

However, there was also a considerable number of jobs lost as a result of firms going out of business, classified as deaths in Table V. The overall employment birth rate of 12.76 percent in manufacturing was more than offset by a loss in employment owing to a death rate of 15.92 percent. Just as the birth rate is greater for smaller enterprises, so is the death rate. The share of 1990 employment lost owing to firms exiting was 12.79 percent for large corporations, 19.37 percent for enterprises having between 20 and 499 employees, and 28.69 percent for enterprises with fewer than 20 employees.

The expansion rate is also inversely related to firm size, with the smallest enterprises exhibiting an expansion rate of nearly one-third, while the large corporations exhibited an expansion rate of just over 10 percent. However, the contraction rate follows a different pattern than do the birth, death, and expansion rates. This is because the contraction rate is actually the greatest for large corporations and the lowest in enterprises with fewer than 20 employees. The high contraction rate for corporations, 16.62, percent reflects the high degree of corporate downsizing that has occurred in the 1990s.

The high degree of corporate downsizing combined with relatively low employment birth and expansion rates resulted in a net decrease in employment in large corporation of 8.47 percent

22

TABLE V
1990–1995 employment changes by establishment change type, industry, and firm size (base year method)

Industry	Firm employment	1990 establishment employment	Births	Deaths	Expansions	Contractions	Net
			(as a percentage of 1990 employment in same employment size category)				
Manufacturing	<20	1,354,055	30.38	−28.69	31.27	−11.72	21.25
	20–499	5,863,336	14.31	−19.37	18.67	−13.05	0.57
	500+	11,956,053	10.01	−12.79	10.93	−16.62	−8.47
	All	19,173,444	12.76	−15.92	14.73	−15.18	−3.61
Other productive	<20	2,559,336	38.51	−34.52	26.15	−14.39	15.75
	20–499	2,831,202	17.61	−25.47	14.54	−22.08	−15.41
	500+	1,127,345	20.49	−24.12	13.89	−24.22	−13.97
	All	6,517,883	26.32	−28.79	18.98	−19.43	−2.93
Distributive	<20	6,059,802	34.29	−33.39	20.65	−11.90	9.66
	20–499	9,075,659	27.57	−25.14	13.04	−14.82	0.65
	500+	11,054,412	31.74	−21.16	12.61	−14.41	8.79
	All	26,189,873	30.89	−25.37	14.62	−13.97	6.17
Services	<20	8,911,767	35.54	−27.36	27.20	−12.23	23.14
	20–499	13,467,494	30.79	−21.61	19.89	−15.82	13.24
	500+	19,164,668	28.88	−17.77	15.67	−14.91	11.87
	All	41,543,929	30.93	−21.07	19.51	−14.63	14.73
All	<20	18,884,960	35.17	−30.36	25.25	−12.38	17.68
	20–499	31,237,691	25.57	−22.56	17.18	−15.58	4.61
	500+	43,302,478	24.18	−17.42	13.53	−15.50	4.79
	All	93,425,129	26.87	−21.76	17.12	−14.89	7.34

Source: Tabulations of the prototype Longitudinal Establishment and Enterprise (LEEM) file, a joint project of the Office of Economic Research, Office of Advocacy, Small Business Administration, and the Center for Economic Studies of the Bureau of the Census, U.S. Department of Commerce (Acs and Armington, 1998, Table 8.1a).

between 1990 and 1995. At the same time, the high employment birth and expansion rates combined with lower death and contraction rates resulted in a net increase in employment, 21.25 percent for firms with fewer than 20 employees.

The dynamic pattern of employment creation in manufacturing is typical for the entire U.S. economy. In every major sector (1) the birth rate of SMEs exceeds that in large corporations, (2) the death rate of SMEs exceeds that of large corporations, (3) the expansion rate of SMEs exceeds that of large corporations, (4) the contraction rate of large corporations exceeds that of SMEs, and (5) the net employment gain is the greatest in SMEs.

Table VI shows that while the numbers of enterprises and new enterprises have been growing over time, the rate of growth has been fairly constant. The dynamic contribution of SMEs documented in Table IV does not seem to be restricted to just

several years but is now characteristic of the U.S. economy.

Table VII shows that SMEs contribute not only the greatest amount of net employment creation but also the greatest amount of turbulence. The sum of employment creation plus destruction is identified as reallocation in Table VII.

Analysis of SMEs through a dynamic framework reveals that their impact is considerably more significant than when analyzed through a static framework.

Innovation

Not only was the large corporation thought to have superior productive efficiency, but conventional wisdom also held the large corporation to serve as the engine of technological change and innovative activity. After all, Schumpeter (1942, p. 106), "What we have got to accept is that the large-scale

TABLE VI

Change in the number of U.S. businesses with employees, fiscal years 1982–1995 (thousands)

Year	Firms at end of each year	Successor firms	New firms	Sum: new and successor	Terminations	Net rate of growth (percent)
1995	6,057	164	819	983	871	1.09
1994	5,992	137	807	944	803	2.40
1993	5,851	136	776	911	801	1.93
1992	5,741	138	737	875	819	0.95
1991	5,687	140	724	864	818	0.84
1990	5,639	146	769	915	846	1.27
1989	5,568	153	743	896	826	1.10
1988	5,513	153	755	907	752	1.71
1987	5,420	163	775	939	717	3.64
1986	5,230	175	741	916	801	1.70
1985	5,142	166	722	888	746	2.67
1984	5,009	164	691	855	687	3.54
1983	4,837	171	633	804	720	1.26
1982	4,777	185	595	781	707	1.55

Source: Adapted by U.S. Small Business Administration, Office of Advocacy, from data provided by the U.S. Department of Labor, Employment and Training Administration, based upon state employment security agencies' quarterly reports, 1995.

TABLE VII

Establishment employment flows by initial year establishment size classification: 1994–1995
[percent change in establishment jobs (based on mean employment in size class)]

Initial establishment employment	1994 employment	Net	Creation	Destruction	Reallocation
1–4	6,127,769	18.2	36.2	−17.9	54.1
5–19	19,223,594	5.0	20.8	−15.8	36.6
20–49	15,905,109	3.5	17.5	−14.0	31.5
50–99	12,224,648	3.2	15.9	−12.7	28.6
100–499	24,033,851	2.1	13.5	−11.5	25.0
500–999	6,661,977	−0.6	10.2	−10.8	21.0
1,000–4,999	9,934,405	−0.9	8.0	−8.9	16.9
5,000+	2,575,993	1.5	10.1	−8.5	18.6
Total	96,687,346	3.6	16.6	−13.0	29.6

Mean establishment employment	1994 employment	Net	Creation	Destruction	Reallocation
1–4	7,125,242	4.4	33.4	−29.0	62.4
5–19	19,087,849	3.4	20.1	−16.7	36.7
20–49	15,683,617	4.1	17.6	−13.6	31.2
50–99	12,073,947	4.7	16.4	−11.7	28.1
100–499	23,798,729	4.0	13.8	−9.8	23.6
500–999	6,571,009	2.6	11.1	−8.6	19.7
1,000–4,999	9,818,110	2.2	9.0	−6.8	15.9
5,000+	2,528,843	1.1	7.3	−6.1	13.4
Total	96,687,346	3.6	16.6	−13.0	29.6

Source: Tabulations of the prototype Longitudinal Establishment and Enterprise (LEEM) file, a joint project of the Office of Economic Research, Office of Advocacy, Small Business Administration, and the Center for Economic Studies of the Bureau of the Census, U.S. Department of Commerce (Acs et al., 1999, Table 2).

establishment has come to be the most powerful engine of progress." A few years later, Galbraith (1956, p. 86) echoed Schumpeter's sentiment when he lamented, "There is no more pleasant fiction than that technological change is the product of the matchless ingenuity of the small man forced by competition to employ his wits to better his neighbor. Unhappily, it is a fiction."

Knowledge regarding both the determinants and the impact of technological change has been largely shaped by measurement. Measures of technological change have typically involved one of the three major aspects of the innovative process: (1) a measure of inputs into the process, such as R&D expenditures, or the share of the labor force accounted for by employees involved in R&D activities; (2) an intermediate output, such as the number of inventions that have been patented; or (3) a direct measure of innovative output.

The earliest sources of data, R&D measured, indicated that virtually all of the innovative activity was undertaken by large corporations. As patent measures became available, the general qualitative conclusions did not change, although it became clear that small firms were more involved with patent activity than with R&D. The development of direct measures of innovative activity, such as databases measuring new product and process introductions in the market, indicated something quite different. In a series of studies, Acs and Audretsch (1987, 1988, 1990) found that while large firms in manufacturing introduced a slightly greater number of significant new innovations than small firms, small-firm employment was only about half as great as large-firm employment, yielding an average small-firm innovation rate in manufacturing of 0.309, compared to a large-firm innovation rate of 0.202.

As Table VIII shows, the relative innovative advantage of small and large firms varies considerably across industries. In some industries, such as computers and process control instruments, small firms provide the engine of innovative activity. In other industries, such as pharmaceutical products and aircraft, large firms generate most of the innovative activity. Knowledge regarding both the determinants and the impact of technological change has been largely shaped by measurement.

Audretsch (1995) concluded that some indus-tries are more conducive to small-firm innovation while others foster the innovative activity of large corporations corresponds to the notion of distinct technological regimes; that is, the routinized and entrepreneurial technological regimes. According to Winter (1984, p. 297), "An entrepreneurial regime is one that is favorable to innovative entry and unfavorable to innovative activity by established firms; a routinized regime is one in which the conditions are the other way around."

New firm startups

Empirical evidence in support of the traditional model of entry, which focuses on the role of excess profits as the major incentive to enter, has been ambiguous at best, leading Geroski (1991, p. 282) to conclude, "Right from the start, scholars have had some trouble in reconciling the stories told about entry in standard textbooks with the substance of what they have found in their data. Very few have emerged from their work feeling that they have answered half as many questions as they have raised, much less that they have answered most of the interesting ones."

Perhaps one reason for this trouble is the inherently static model used to capture an inherently dynamic process. Neumann (1993, pp. 593–594) has criticized this traditional model of entry, as found in the individual country studies contained in Geroski and Schwalbach (1991), because they "are predicated on the adoption of a basically static framework. It is assumed that startups enter a given market where they are facing incumbents which naturally try to fend off entry. Since the impact of entry on the performance of incumbents seems to be only slight, the question arises whether the costs of entry are worthwhile, given the high rate of exit associated with entry. Geroski appears to be rather skeptical about that. I submit that adopting a static framework is misleading. . . . In fact, generally, an entrant can only hope to succeed if he employs either a new technology or offers a new product, or both. Just imitating incumbents is almost certainly doomed to failure. If the process of entry is looked upon from this perspective the high correlation between gross entry and exit reflects the inherent risks of innovating activities. . . . Obviously it is rather difficult to break loose from the inherited mode of

TABLE VIII

Number of innovations for large and small firms in the most innovative industries

Industry	Total innovations	Large-firm innovations	Small-firm innovations
Electronics computing equipment	395	158	227
Process control instruments	165	68	93
Radio and TV communication equipment	157	83	72
Pharmaceutical preparations	133	120	72
Electronic components	128	54	73
Engineering and scientific instruments	126	43	83
Semiconductors	122	91	29
Plastics products	107	22	82
Photographic equipment	88	79	9
Office machine	77	67	10
Instruments to measure electricity	77	28	47
Surgical appliances and supplies	67	54	13
Surgical and medical instrument	66	30	36
Special industry machinery	64	43	21
Industrial controls	61	15	46
Toilet preparations	59	41	18
Valves and pipe fittings	54	20	33
Electric housewares and fans	53	47	6
Measuring and controlling devices	52	3	45
Food products machinery	50	37	12
Motors and generators	49	39	10
Plastic materials and resins	45	30	15
Industrial inorganic chemicals	40	32	8
Radio and TV receiving sets	40	35	4
Hand and edge tools	39	27	11
Fabricated platework	38	29	9
Fabricated metal products	35	12	17
Pumps and pumping equipment	34	18	16
Optical instruments and lenses	34	12	21
Polishes and sanitation goods	33	13	19
Industrial trucks and tractors	33	13	20
Medicinal and botanicals	32	27	5
Aircraft	32	31	1
Environmental controls	32	22	10

Note: Large and small-firm innovations do not always sum to total innovations because several innovations could not be classified according to firm size.
Source: Audretsch (1995).

reasoning within the static framework. It is not without merit, to be sure, but it needs to be enlarged by putting it into a dynamic setting."

Still, one of the most startling results that have emerged in empirical studies is that entry by firms into an industry is apparently not substantially deterred or even deterred at all in capital-intensive industries in which scale economies play an important role (Audretsch, 1995).[15] While studies have generally produced considerable ambiguity concerning the impact of scale economies and other measures traditionally thought to represent

a *barrier to entry*, Audretsch (1995) found conclusive evidence linking the technological regime to startup activity. New-firm startup activity tends to be substantially more prevalent under the entrepreneurial regime, or where small enterprises account for the bulk of the innovative activity, than under the routinized regime, or where the large incumbent enterprises account for most of the innovative activity.[16] These findings are consistent with the view that differences in beliefs about the expected value of new ideas are not constant across industries but rather depend on the knowledge conditions inherent in the underlying technological regime.

Survival

Geroski (1995) and Audretsch (1995) point out that one of the major conclusions from studies about entry is that the process of entry does not end with entry itself. Rather, it is what happens to new firms subsequent to entering that sheds considerable light on industry dynamics. The early studies (Mansfield, 1962; Hall, 1987; Dunne et al. 1989; Audretsch, 1991) established not only that the likelihood of a new entrant surviving is quite low, but that the likelihood of survival is positively related to firm size and age. More recently, a wave of studies have confirmed these findings for diverse countries, including Portugal (Mata et al., 1995; Mata, 1994), Germany (Wagner, 1994), and Canada (Baldwin and Gorecki, 1991; Baldwin, 1995; Baldwin and Rafiquzzaman, 1995).

Audretsch (1991), Audretsch and Mahmood (1995) shifted the relevant question away from *Why does the likelihood of survival vary systematically across firms?* to *Why does the propensity for firms to survive vary systematically across industries?* The answer to this question suggests that what had previously been considered to pose a barrier to entry may, in fact, constitute not a barrier to entry barrier but rather a barrier to survival. The answer to these questions suggests that what had previously been considered to pose a barrier to entry may, in fact, constitute not an entry barrier but rather a barrier to survival.

Growth

What has become known as *Gibrat's Law*, or the assumption that growth rates are invariant to firm size, has been subject to numerous empirical tests (Sutton, 1997). Studies linking firm size and age to growth have also produced a number of stylized facts (Wagner, 1992). For small and new firms there is substantial evidence suggesting that growth is negatively related to firm size and age (Hall, 1987; Wagner, 1992, 1994; Mata, 1994; Audretsch, 1995). However, for larger firms, particularly those having attained the MES level of output, the evidence suggests that firm growth is unrelated to size and age.

An important finding of Audretsch (1991, 1995) and Audretsch and Mahmood (1995) is that although entry may still occur in industries characterized by a high degree of scale economies, the likelihood of survival is considerably less. People will start new firms in an attempt to appropriate the expected value of their new ideas, or potential innovations, particularly under the entrepreneurial regime. As entrepreneurs gain experience in the market they learn in at least two ways. First, they discover whether they possess the right stuff, in terms of producing goods and offering services for which sufficient demand exists, as well as whether they can produce the goods more efficiently than their rivals. Second, they learn whether they can adapt to market conditions as well as to strategies engaged in by rival firms. In terms of the first type of learning, entrepreneurs who discover that they have a viable firm will tend to expand and ultimately survive. But what about those entrepreneurs who discover that they are either not efficient or not offering a product for which there is a viable demand? The answer is that it depends on the extent of scale economies as well as on conditions of demand. The consequences of not being able to grow will depend, to a large degree, on the extent of scale economies. Thus, in markets with only negligible scale economies, firms have a considerably greater likelihood of survival. However, where scale economies play an important role, the consequences of not growing are substantially more severe, as evidenced by a lower likelihood of survival.

Dynamic contribution of SMEs

What emerges from the new evolutionary theories and empirical evidence on the economic role of new and small firms is that markets are in motion, with many new firms entering the industry and many firms exiting out of the industry. But is this motion horizontal, in that the bulk of firms exiting are composed of firms that had entered relatively recently, or vertical, in that a significant share of the exiting firms had been established incumbents that were displaced by younger firms? In trying to shed some light on this question, Audretsch (1995) proposes two different models of the evolutionary process of industries over time.

Some industries can be best characterized by

the model of the conical revolving door, where new businesses enter, but where there is a high propensity to subsequently exit from the market. Other industries may be better characterized by the metaphor of the forest, where incumbent establishments are displaced by new entrants. Which view is more applicable apparently depends on three major factors: the underlying technological conditions, scale economies, and demand. Where scale economies play an important role, the model of the revolving door seems to be more applicable. While the rather startling result just discussed that the startup and entry of new businesses is apparently not deterred by the presence of high scale economies, a process of firm selection analogous to a revolving door ensures that only those establishments successful enough to grow will be able to survive beyond more than a few years. Thus the bulk of new entrants that are not so successful ultimately exit within a few years subsequent to entry.

There is at least some evidence also suggesting that the underlying technological regime influences the process of firm selection and therefore the type of firm with a higher propensity to exit. Under the entrepreneurial regime new entrants have a greater likelihood of making an innovation. Thus, they are less likely to decide to exit from the industry, even in the face of negative profits. By contrast, under the routinized regime the incumbent businesses tend to have the innovative advantage, so that a higher portion of exiting businesses tend to be new entrants. Thus, the model of the revolving door is more applicable under technological conditions consistent with the routinized regime, and the metaphor of the forest, where the new entrants displace the incumbents, is more applicable to the entrepreneurial regime.

Why is the general shape of the firm-size distribution not only strikingly similar across virtually every industry – that is, skewed with only a few large enterprises and numerous small ones – but has persisted with tenacity not only across developed countries but even over a long period? The evolutionary view of the process of industry evolution is that new firms typically start at a very small scale of output and are motivated by the desire to appropriate the expected value of new economic knowledge. But, depending on the extent of scale economies in the industry, the firm may not be able to remain viable indefinitely at its startup size. Rather, if scale economies are anything other than negligible, then the new firm is likely to have to grow to survival. The temporary survival of new firms is presumably supported through the deployment of a strategy of compensating factor differentials that enables the firm to discover whether or not it has a viable product.

The empirical evidence supports such an evolutionary view of the role of new firms in manufacturing, because the post-entry growth of firms that survive tends to be spurred by the extent to which there is a gap between the MES level of output and the size of the firm. However, the likelihood of any particular new firm surviving tends to decrease as this gap increases. Such new suboptimal scale firms are apparently engaged in the selection process. Only those firms offering a viable product that can be produced efficiently will grow and ultimately approach or attain the MES level of output. The remainder will stagnate, and depending on the severity of the other selection mechanism – the extent of scale economies – may ultimately be forced to exit out of the industry. Thus, the persistence of an asymmetric firm-size distribution biased toward small-scale enterprise reflects the continuing process of the entry of new firms into industries and not necessarily the permanence of such small and suboptimal enterprises over the long run. Although the skewed size distribution of firms persists with remarkable stability over long periods, a constant set of small and suboptimal scale firms does not appear to be responsible for this skewed distribution. Rather, by serving as agents of change, new firms provide an essential source of new ideas and experimentation that otherwise would remain untapped in the economy.

3. Determinants of SME dynamism

Enabling environment

As Table VIII shows, the evidence revealing small enterprises to be the engine of innovative activity in certain industries, despite an obvious lack of formal R&D activities, raises the question, *Where do new and small firms get the innovation producing inputs; that is, the knowledge?* The answer proposed by Audretsch (1995) is from other, third-party, firms or research institutions, such as universities. Economic knowledge may *spill over* from the firm or research institution creating it for application by other firms (Acs et al., 1992).

That knowledge spillover is barely dispute. However, the geographic range of such knowledge spillovers is greatly contested. In disputing the importance of knowledge externalities in explaining the geographic concentration of economic activity, Krugman (1991) and others do not question the existence or importance of such knowledge spillovers.[17] In fact, they argue that such knowledge externalities are so important and forceful that there is no compelling reason for a geographic boundary to limit the spatial extent of the spillover. According to this line of thinking, the concern is not that knowledge does not spill over but that it should stop spilling over just because it hits a geographic border, such as a city limit, state line, or national boundary.

A recent body of empirical evidence clearly suggests that R&D and other sources of knowledge not only generate externalities, but studies by Audretsch and Feldman (1996), Almeida and Kogut (1997), Jaffe (1989), Audretsch and Stephan (1996), Feldman (1994a, b), and Jaffe et al. (1993) suggest that such knowledge spillovers tend to be geographically bounded within the region where the new economic knowledge was created. That is, new economic knowledge may spill over but the geographic extent of such knowledge spillovers is limited (Prevenzer, 1997).

Krugman (1991, p. 53) has argued that economists should abandon any attempts at measuring knowledge spillovers because ". . . knowledge flows are invisible, they leave no paper trail by which they may be measured and tracked." But as Jaffe et al. (1991, p. 578) point out, "knowledge flows do sometimes leave a paper trail," in particular in the form of patented inventions and new product introductions.

The innovations from Table VIII can be classified according to the four-digit SIC industry of the new product and the city where the innovating establishment was located. We adapt either the Consolidated Metropolitan Statistical Area (CMSA) or the Metropolitan Statistical Area (MSA) as the spatial unit of observation. The analysis here is based on 3969 new manufacturing product innovations for which the address of the innovating establishment could be identified.

The most innovative city in the United States was New York. Seven hundred and thirty-five, or 18.5 percent, of the total number of innovations in the country were attributed to firms in the greater New York City area. Four hundred and seventy-seven (12.0 percent) were attributed to San Francisco, California, and 345 (8.7 percent) to the Boston, Massachusetts, area and 333 (8.4 percent) to the Los Angeles, California, area. In total, 1,890, or 45 percent of the innovations, took place in those four consolidated metropolitan areas. In fact, all but 150 of the innovations included in the data base are attributed to metropolitan areas. That is, less than 4 percent of the innovations occurred outside of metropolitan areas. This contrasts with the 70 percent of the population that resided in those areas.

Of course, simply comparing the absolute amount of innovative activity across cities ignores the fact that some cities are simply larger than others. Cities vary considerably in size, and we expect that city scale will have an impact on innovative output. Table IX presents the number of innovations normalized by the size of the geographic unit. Population provides a crude but useful measure of the size of the geographic unit. Cities in Table IX are ranked in descending order by innovation rate or the number of innovations per 100,000 population. While New York has the highest count of innovation, it has the third highest innovation rate. The most innovative city in the United States, on a per capita measure of city size, was San Francisco, with an innovation rate of 8.90, followed by Boston, with an innovation rate of 8.69. By contrast, the mean innovation rate for the entire country is 1.75 innovations per 100,000 population. The distribution of innovation rates is considerably skewed. Only 14 cities are more innovative than the national average. Clearly, innovation appears to be a large city phenomenon.

Studies identifying the extent of knowledge spillovers are based on the knowledge production function. Jaffe (1989), and Audretsch and Feldman (1996), and Feldman and Audretsch (1999) modified the knowledge production function approach to a model specified for spatial and product dimensions:

$$I_{si} = IRD^{\beta_1} * UR_{si}^{\beta_2} * (UR_{si} * GC_{si}^{\beta_3}) * \varepsilon_{si} \qquad (1)$$

where I is innovative output, IRD is private cor-

TABLE IX
Counts of innovation normalized by population

Consolidated metropolitan statistical area	Innovations (1982)	1980 population (thousands)	Innovations per 100,000 population
San Francisco – Oakland	477	5368	8.886
Boston – Lawrence	345	3972	8.686
New York – Northern New Jersey	735	17539	4.191
Philadelphia – Wilmington	205	5681	3.609
Dallas – Fort Worth	88	2931	3.002
Hartford	30	1014	2.959
Los Angeles – Anaheim	333	11498	2.896
Buffalo – Niagara	35	1243	2.816
Cleveland – Akron	77	2834	2.717
Chicago – Gary	203	7937	2.558
Providence – Pawtucket	25	1083	2.308
Portland – Vancouver	25	1298	1.926
Cincinnati – Hamilton	30	1660	1.807
Seattle – Tacoma	37	2093	1.768
Pittsburgh	42	2423	1.733
Denver – Boulder	28	1618	1.731
Detroit – Ann Arbor	68	4753	1.431
Houston – Galveston	39	3101	1.258
Miami – Fort Lauderdale	13	2644	0.492

Source: 1980 Population is from the Statistical Abstract. Innovation data from Feldman and Audretsch (1999).

porate expenditures on R&D, *UR* is the research expenditures undertaken at universities, and *GC* measures the geographic coincidence of university and corporate research. The unit of observation for estimation was at the spatial level *s*, a state, and industry level *i*. Estimation of equation (1) essentially shifted the knowledge production function from the unit of observation of a firm to that of a geographic unit.

Implicitly contained within the knowledge production function model is the assumption that innovative activity should take place in those regions where the direct knowledge-generating inputs are the greatest, and where knowledge spillovers are the most prevalent. Audretsch and Feldman (1996) and Audretsch and Stephan (1996) link the propensity for innovative activity to cluster together to industry specific characteristics, most notably the relative importance of knowledge spillovers.

To actually measure the extent to which innovative activity in a specific four-digit SIC industry is concentrated within a geographic region, Audretsch and Feldman (1996) calculate gini coefficients for the geographic concentration of innovative activity. The gini coefficients are weighted by the relative share of economic activity located in each state. Computation of weighted gini coefficients enables us to control for size differences across states. The gini coefficients are based on the share of activity in a state and industry relative to the state share of the national activity for the industry. Of course, as Jaffe, Trajtenberg, and Henderson (1993) point out, one obvious explanation why innovative activity in some industries tends to cluster geographically more than in other industries is that the location of production is more concentrated spatially. Thus, in explaining why the propensity for innovative activity to cluster geographically varies across industries, we need first to explain, and then control for, the geographic concentration of the location of production.

There are three important tendencies emerging. First, there is no obvious simple relationship between the gini coefficients for production and innovation. Second, the gini coefficient of the number of innovations exceeds that of value added and employment in those industries exhibiting the greatest propensity for innovative activity to cluster spatially. By contrast, the gini coefficients of innovative activity for most industries is less than that for value added and employment.

Third, those industries exhibiting the greatest propensity for innovative activity to cluster are high-technology industries. There are, however, several notable exceptions. For example, in motor vehicle bodies, which is certainly not considered to be a high-technology industry, the geographic concentration of production of innovative activity is the seventh greatest. One reason may be the high degree of geographic concentration of production, as evidenced by gini coefficients for value added (0.9241) and employment (0.8089) that actually exceed that of innovative activity (0.6923). This points to the importance of controlling for the geographic concentration of production in explaining the propensity for innovative activity to spatially cluster. And finally, the gini coefficient for value added exceeds that for employment in virtually every industry.

Audretsch and Feldman (1996) measure three different types of new economic knowledge: industry R&D, university R&D, and skilled labor. A key assumption they make in examining the link between knowledge spillovers in an industry and the propensity for innovative activity to cluster is that knowledge externalities are more prevalent in industries where new economic knowledge plays a greater role.

One obvious complication in testing for this link is that innovative activity will be more geographically concentrated in industries where production is also geographically concentrated, simply because the bulk of firms are located within proximity. Even more problematic, though, is the hypothesis that new economic knowledge will tend to shape the spatial distribution of production as well as that of innovation. Indeed, we found that a key determinant of the extent to which the location of production is geographically concentrated is the relative importance of new economic knowledge in the industry. But even after controlling for the geographic concentration of production, the results suggest that industries in which knowledge spillovers are more pervasive – that is where industry R&D, university research and skilled labor are the most important – have a greater propensity for innovative activity to cluster than industries where knowledge externalities are less important.

A growing literature suggests that *who* innovates and *how much* innovative activity is under-taken is closely linked to the phase of the industry life cycle. Audretsch and Feldman (1996) suggest an additional key aspect to the evolution of innovative activity over the industry life cycle: *where* that innovative activity takes place. The theory of knowledge spillovers, derived from the knowledge production function, suggests that the propensity for innovative activity to cluster spatially will tend to be the greatest in industries where *tacit knowledge* plays an important role, and because it is tacit knowledge, as opposed to *information*, which can only be transmitted informally, and typically demands direct and repeated contact. The role of tacit knowledge in generating innovative activity is presumably the greatest during the early stages of the industry life cycle, before product standards have been established and before a dominant design has emerged.

The stage of the industry life cycle has been typically measured by tracking the evolution of an industry starting with its incipiency, based on a wave of product innovations. But the measures of geographic concentration and dispersion, for both innovation and the location of production, documented in the previous section, are available only for one point of time. That is, these measures provide a snapshot at a single point in time for each industry. Thus, the life cycle stage of each industry at this point in time needs to be measured. More specifically, industries that are highly innovative and where that innovative activity tends to come from small firms are better characterized as being in the introduction stage of the life cycle. Industries that are highly innovative and where the large firms tend to generate that innovative activity are better characterized by the growth stage of the life cycle. Industries that are low innovative and where large firms have a higher propensity to innovate are better characterized by the mature stage of the life cycle. And finally, industries that are low innovative and where small firms have a higher propensity to innovate are best characterized by the declining stage of the life cycle. The higher propensity to innovate of small enterprises vis-à-vis their larger counterparts may reflect the seeds of the introductory phase of the life cycle of new products emerging in what would otherwise be a declining industry.

This framework was used to classify 210 four-digit SIC industries into those four stages of the life cycle. High innovative industries were rather arbitrarily defined as those industries exhibiting innovative activity in excess of the mean. Low innovative industries were similarly defined as those industries with innovative rates less than the mean. The innovation rate is defined as the number of innovations divided by the number of employees in the industry (measured in thousands). The innovation rate is used rather than the absolute number of innovations to control for the size of the industry. That is, if two industries were to exhibit the same number of innovations but one industry were twice as large as the other, then it will have an innovation rate one-half as large as the other industry. To measure the relative innovative advantage of large and small firms, the small-firm innovation rate is compared to the large-firm innovation rate, where the small-firm innovation rate is defined as the number of innovations made by firms with fewer than 500 employees divided by small-firm employment and the large-firm innovation rate is defined as the number of innovations made by firms with at least 500 employees divided by large-firm employment.

By using this classification system, 62 of the industries were classified as being in the introductory stage of the life cycle (defined as highly innovative, and the small firms have the innovative advantage), 32 industries were classified as being in the growth stage of the life cycle (defined as highly innovative, and the large firms have the innovative advantage), 64 industries were defined in the mature stage of the life cycle (defined as low innovative, and the large firms have the innovative advantage), and 52 were defined in the declining stage of the life cycle (defined as low innovative, and the small firms have the innovative advantage).

The results provide considerable evidence suggesting that the propensity for innovative activity to spatially cluster is shaped by the stage of the industry life cycle. On the one hand, new economic knowledge embodied in skilled workers tends to raise the propensity for innovative activity to spatially cluster throughout all phases of the industry life cycle. On the other, certain other sources of new economic knowledge, such as university research, tend to elevate the propensity for innovative activity to cluster during the introduction stage of the life cycle but not during the

growth stage, but then again during the stage of decline.

Perhaps most striking is the finding that greater geographic concentration of production actually leads to more, and not less, dispersion of innovative activity. Apparently, innovative activity is promoted by knowledge spillovers that occur within a distinct geographic region, particularly in the early stages of the industry life cycle, but as the industry evolves toward maturity, decline may be dispersed by additional increases in concentration of production that have been built up within that same region. That is, the evidence suggests that what may serve as an *agglomerating influence* in triggering innovative activity to spatially cluster during the introduction and growth stages of the industry life cycle may later result in a *congestion effect*, leading to greater dispersion in innovative activity. In any case, the results of this paper suggest that the propensity for an innovative cluster to spatially cluster is certainly shaped by the stage of the industry life cycle.

Despite the general consensus that has now emerged in the literature that knowledge spillovers within a given location stimulate technological advance, there is little consensus as to exactly how this occurs. The contribution of the knowledge production function approach was simply to shift the unit of observation away from firms to a geographic region. But does it make a difference how economic activity is organized within the black box of geographic space? Political scientists and sociologists have long argued that the differences in the culture of a region may contribute to differences in innovative performance across regions, even holding knowledge inputs such as R&D and human capital constant. For example, Saxenian (1994) argues that a culture of greater interdependence and exchange among individuals in the Silicon Valley, California, region has contributed to a superior innovative performance than is found around Boston's Route 128, where firms and individuals tend to be more isolated less interdependent.

In studying the networks in California's Silicon Valley, Saxenian (1990, pp. 96–97) emphasizes that it is the communication between individuals that facilitates the transmission of knowledge across agents, firms, and even industries, and not just a high endowment of human capital and knowledge in the region: "It is not simply the concentration of skilled labor, suppliers and information that distinguish the region. A variety of regional institutions – including Stanford University, several trade associations and local business organizations, and a myriad of specialized consulting, market research, public relations, and venture capital firms – provide technical, financial, and networking services which the region's enterprises often cannot afford individually. These networks defy sectoral barriers: individuals move easily from semiconductor to disk drive firms or from computer to network makers. They move from established firms to startups (or vice versa) and even to market research or consulting firms, and from consulting firms back into startups. And they continue to meet at trade shows, industry conferences, and the scores of seminars, talks and social activities organized by local business organizations and trade associations. In these forums, relationships are easily formed and maintained, technical and market information is exchanged, business contacts are established, and new enterprises are conceived. . . . This decentralized and fluid environment also promotes the diffusion of intangible technological capabilities and understandings."[18]

While many social scientists tend to avoid attributing differences in economic performance to cultural differences, there has been a series of theoretical arguments suggesting that differences in the underlying structure between regions may account for differences in rates of growth and technological change. In fact, a heated debate has emerged in the literature about the manner in which the underlying economic structure within a geographic unit of observation might effect economic performance. One view, which Glaeser and others (1992) attribute to the Marshall-Arrow-Romer externality, suggests that an increased concentration of a particular industry within a specific geographic region facilitates knowledge spillovers across firms. This model formalizes the insight that the concentration of an industry within a city promotes knowledge spillovers between firms and therefore facilitates innovative activity. An important assumption of the model is that knowledge externalities with respect to firms exist, but only for firms within the same industry. Thus, the relevant unit of observation is extended from the

firm to the region in the tradition of the Marshall-Arrow model, and in subsequent empirical studies, but spillovers are limited to occur within the relevant industry.

By contrast, restricting knowledge externalities to occur only within the industry may ignore an important source of new economic knowledge: inter-industry knowledge spillovers. Jacobs (1969) argues that the most important source of knowledge spillovers are external to the industry in which the firm operates and that cities are the source of considerable innovation because the diversity of these knowledge sources is greatest in cities. According to Jacobs it is the exchange of complementary knowledge across diverse firms and economic agents that yields a greater return on new economic knowledge. She develops a theory that emphasizes that the variety of industries within a geographic region promotes knowledge externalities and ultimately innovative activity and economic growth.

The extent of regional specialization versus regional diversity in promoting knowledge spillovers is not the only dimension over which there has been a theoretical debate. A second controversy involves the degree of competition prevalent in the region, or the extent of local monopoly. The Marshall-Arrow-Romer model predicts that local monopoly is superior to local competition because it maximizes the ability of firms to appropriate the economic value accruing from their innovative activity. By contrast, Jacobs (1969) and Porter (1990) argue that competition is more conducive to knowledge externalities than is local monopoly.[19] It should be emphasized that by local competition Jacobs does not mean competition within product markets as has traditionally been envisioned within the industrial organization literature. Rather, Jacobs is referring to the competition for the new ideas embodied in economic agents. Not only does an increased number of firms provide greater competition for new ideas, but, in addition, greater competition across firms facilitates the entry of a new firm specializing in some particular and new product niche. This is because the necessary complementary inputs and services are likely to be available from small specialist niche firms but not necessarily from large vertically integrated producers.

The first important test of the specialization

versus diversity theories to date has focused not on the gains in terms of innovative activity, but rather in terms of employment growth. Glaeser and others (1992) employ a data set on the growth of large industries in 170 cities between 1956 and 1987 to identify the relative importance of the degree of regional specialization, diversity, and local competition ply in influencing industry growth rates. The authors find evidence that contradicts the Marshall-Arrow-Romer model but is consistent with the theories of Jacobs. However, their study provided no direct evidence as to whether diversity is more important than specialization in generating innovation.

Feldman and Audretsch (1999) identify the extent to which the organization of economic activity is either concentrated, or alternatively consists of diverse but complementary economic activities, and how this composition influences innovative output. We ask the question, *Does the specific type of economic activity undertaken within any particular geographic concentration matter?* To consider this question they link the innovative output of product categories within a specific city to the extent to which the economic activity of that city is concentrated in that industry or, conversely, diversified in terms of complementary industries sharing a common science base.

To systematically identify the degree to which specific industries share a common underlying science and technology base, we rely upon a deductive approach that links products estimated from their closeness in technological space. They use the responses of industrial R&D managers to a survey by Levin and others (1987). To measure the significance of a scientific discipline to an industry, the question was asked, *How relevant were the basic sciences to technical progress in this line of business over the past 10–15 years?* The survey uses a Likert scale of 1 to 7, from least important to most important, to assess the relevance of basic scientific research in biology, chemistry, computer science, physics, math, medicine, geology, mechanical engineering, and electrical engineering. Any academic discipline with a rating greater than 5 is assumed to be relevant for a product category. For example, basic scientific research in medicine, chemistry, and chemical engineering is found to be relevant for product innovation in drugs (SIC 2834).

They then used cluster analysis to identify six groups of industries that rely on similar rankings for the importance of different academic disciplines. Those six groups reflect distinct underlying common scientific bases.

Table X presents the prominent cities within each science-based industrial cluster. Again, the listing of prominent cities recalls the well known association between cities and industries. For example, Atlanta, Georgia, was a prominent center for innovation that used the common science base of agra-business. While the national innovation rate was 20.34 innovations per 100,000 manufacturing workers, agra-business in Atlanta was almost five times as innovative. A chi-squared test of the independence of location of city and science-based industrial activity reveals that neither the distribution of employment nor the distribution of innovation is random. Industries that rely on a common science base exhibit a tendency to cluster together geographically with regard to the location of employment and the location of innovation. We conclude that the distribution of innovation within science-based clusters and cities appears to reflect the existence of science-related expertise.

To test the hypothesis that the degree of specialization, or alternatively diversity, as well as the extent of local competition within a city shapes the innovative output of an industry, we estimate a model where the dependent variable is the number of innovations attributed to a specific four-digit SIC industry in a particular city. To reflect the extent to which economic activity within a city is specialized, we include as an explanatory variable a measure of industry specialization, which was used by Glaeser and others (1992) and is defined as the share of total employment in the city accounted for by industry employment in the city, divided by the share of U.S. employment accounted by that particular industry. This variable reflects the degree to which a city is specialized in a particular industry relative to the degree of economic activity in that industry that would occur if employment in the industry were randomly distributed across the United States. A higher value of this measure indicates a greater degree of specialization of the industry in that particular city. Thus, a positive coefficient would indicate that increased specialization within

34   *David B. Audretsch*

TABLE X
Innovation in science-based industry clusters

Cluster	Prominent cities	Mean industry innovations per 100,000 workers
Agra-business	Atlanta	92.40
	Dallas	41.15
	Chicago	33.03
	St. Louis	91.74
Chemical engineering	Dallas	38.09
	Minneapolis	66.67
	San Francisco	43.89
	Wilmington	85.47
Office machinery	Anaheim-Santa Ana	92.59
	Minneapolis	31.86
	Rochester	72.20
	Stanford	68.40
Industrial machinery	Anaheim-Santa Ana	54.95
	Cincinnati	66.01
	Cleveland	141.51
	Passaic, NJ	90.90
High-tech computing	Boston	73.89
	Houston	62.08
	San Jose	44.88
	Minneapolis	181.74
Biomedical	Boston	38.71
	Cleveland	68.76
	Dallas	35.22
	New York	188.07

a city is conducive to greater innovative output and would support the Marshall-Arrow-Romer thesis. A negative coefficient would indicate that greater specialization within a city impedes innovative output and would support Jacobs' theory that diversity of economic activity is more conducive to innovation than is specialization of economic activity.

To identify the impact of an increased presence of economic activity in complementary industries sharing a common science base on the innovative activity of a particular industry within a specific city, a measure of the presence of science-based related industries is included. This measure is constructed analogously to the index of industry specialization and is defined as the share of total city employment accounted for by employment in the city in industries sharing the science base divided by the share of total U.S. employment accounted for by employment in that same science base. This

variable measures the presence of complementary industries relative to what the presence would be if those related industries were distributed across the United States. A positive coefficient of the presence of science-based related industries would indicate that a greater presence of complementary industries is conducive to greater innovative output and would lend support for the diversity thesis. By contrast, a negative coefficient would suggest that a greater presence of related industries sharing the same science base impedes innovation and would argue against Jacobs' diversity thesis.

The usual concept of product market competition in the industrial organization literature is typically measured in terms of the size-distribution of firms. By contrast, Jacobs' concept of *localized competition* emphasizes instead the extent of competition for the ideas embodied in individuals. The greater the degree of competition among firms, the greater will be the extent of specialization among those firms and the easier it will be for individuals to pursue and implement new ideas. Thus the metric relevant to reflect the degree of localized competition is not the size of the firms in the region relative to their number (because, after all, many if not most manufacturing product markets are national or at least inter-regional in nature) but rather the number of firms relative to the number of workers. In measuring the extent of localized competition we again adopt a measure used by Glaeser and others (1992), which is defined as the number of firms per worker in the industry in the city relative to the number of firms per worker in the same industry in the United States. A higher value of this index of localized competition suggests that the industry has a greater number of firms per worker relative to its size in the particular city than it does elsewhere in the United States. Thus, if the index of localized competition exceeds one then the city is locally less competitive than in other U.S. cities.

In Feldman and Audretsch (1999) the regression model is estimated on the basis of the 5,946 city-industry observations for which data could be collected. The Poisson regression estimation method is used because the dependent variable is a limited dependent variable with a highly skewed distribution. By focusing on innovative activity for particular industries at specific locations, we find compelling evidence that specialization of economic activity does not promote innovative output. Rather, the results indicate that diversity across complementary economic activities sharing a common science base is more conducive to innovation than is specialization. In addition, the results indicate that the degree of local competition for new ideas within a city is more conducive to innovative activity than is local monopoly.

Public policy measures that affect SMEs

Globalization combined with the telecommunications revolution has drastically reduced the cost of transporting not just material goods but also information across geographic space. High wages are increasingly incompatible with information-based economic activity, which can be easily transferred to a lower cost location. By contrast, the creation of new ideas on the basis of tacit knowledge

cannot easily be transferred across distance. Thus, the comparative advantage of the high-cost countries of North America and Western Europe is increasingly based on knowledge-driven innovative activity. The spillover of knowledge from the firm or university creating that knowledge to a third-party firm is essential to innovative activity. Such knowledge spillovers tend to be spatially restricted. Thus, an irony of globalization is that even as the relevant geographic market for most goods and services becomes increasingly global, the increased importance of innovative activity in the leading developed countries has triggered a resurgence in the importance of local regions as a key source of comparative advantage.

As the comparative advantage in Western Europe and North America has become increasingly based on new knowledge, public policy toward business has responded in two fundamental ways. The first has been to shift the policy focus away from the traditional triad of policy instruments essentially constraining the freedom of firms to contract; that is, regulation, competition policy, or antitrust in the United States and public ownership of business. The policy approach of constraint was sensible as long as the major issue was how to restrain footloose multinational corporations in possession of considerable market power. This is reflected by the waves of deregulation and privatization along with the decreased emphasis of competition policy throughout the Organisation for Economic Co-operation and Development (OECD). Instead, a new policy approach is emerging that focuses on enabling the creation and commercialization of knowledge. Examples of such policies include encouraging R&D, venture capital, and new-firm startups.

The second fundamental shift involves the locus of such enabling policies, which are increasingly at the state, regional, or even local level. The downsizing of federal agencies charged with the regulation of business in the United Sates has been interpreted by many scholars as the eclipse of government intervention. But to interpret deregulation, privatization, and the increased irrelevance of competition policies as the end of government intervention in business ignores an important shift in the locus and target of public policy. The last decade has seen the emergence of a broad spectrum of enabling policy initiatives that fall outside of the jurisdiction of the traditional regulatory agencies. Sternberg (1996) documents how the success of a number of different high-technology clusters spanning a number of developed countries is the direct result of enabling policies, such as the provision of venture capital or research support. For example, the Advanced Research Program in Texas has provided support for basic research and the strengthening of the infrastructure of the University of Texas, which has played a central role in developing a high-technology cluster around Austin (Feller, 1997). The Thomas Edison Centers in Ohio, the Advanced Technology Centers in New Jersey, and the Centers for Advanced Technology at Case Western Reserve University, Rutgers University, and the University of Rochester have supported generic, precompetitive research. This support has generally provided diversified technology development involving a mix of activities encompassing a spectrum of industrial collaborators.

Such enabling policies that are typically implemented at the local or regional level are part of a silent policy revolution currently underway. The increased importance of innovative regional clusters as an engine of economic growth has led policy makers to abandon the policy cry frequently heard two decades ago, *Should we break up, regulate, or simply take over General Motors, IBM, and U.S. Steel,* for a very different contemporary version, *How can we grow the next Silicon Valley?*

One of the most important policies to promote SMEs at the federal level has been the Small Business Innovation Research (SBIR) program. The U.S. Congress enacted the SBIR in 1984. The Program provides a mandate that each participating government agency must spend a share of its research budget on contracts to small firms. This includes the major federal agencies, such as the Department of Defense, the National Institutes of Health, the National Science Foundation, Department of Energy, and the National Aeronautics and Space Administration. The Small Business Innovation Development Act of 1982[20] required that agencies with extramural R&D budget of $100 million or more set aside not less than 0.2 percent of that amount for the SBIR program. In addition, the Act provided for annual increases up to a ceiling of not less than 1.25

percent of the agencies' budgets. The amount of awards will total over $1.4 billion in 1999.

The SBIR consists of three phases. Phase I is oriented toward determining the scientific and technical merit along with the feasibility of a proposed research idea. Phase II extends the technological idea and emphasizes commercialization. Phase III involves additional private funding for the commercial application of a technology. Under the Small Business Research and Development Enhancement Act of 1992, funding in Phase I was increased to $100,000, and in Phase II to $750,000.

The SBIR was an offshoot of the Small Business Investment Company (SBIC) program, which provided more than $3 billion to young firms between 1958 and 1969. During this period this amounted to more than three times the total amount of private venture capital.

The SBIR represents about 60 percent of all public SME finance programs. Taken together, the public SME finance is about two-thirds as large as private venture capital. In 1995 the sum of equity financing provided through and guaranteed by public programs financing SMES was $2.4 billion, which amounted to more than 60 percent of the total funding disbursed by traditional venture funds in that year. Equally as important, the emphasis on SBIR and most public funds is on early stage finance, which is generally ignored by private venture capital. Some of the most innovative American companies received early stage finance from SBIR, including Apple Computer, Chron, Compaq, and Intel.

While systematic evidence has been compiled indicating that SMEs receiving SBIR support exhibit greater rates of growth than those that do not, there is also evidence suggesting that the SBIR alters the career choices of scientists and engineers. In particular, the evidence suggests that (1) a significant number of the firms would not have been started in the absence of SBIR, (2) a significant number of other firms are started because of the demonstration effect by the efforts of scientists to commercialize knowledge, (3) as a result of the demonstration effect by SBIR-funded commercialization, a number of other scientists alter their careers to include commercialization efforts, and (4) technology-based entrepreneurs start firms because they have ideas that they think are potentially valuable and not start firms and then search for useful ideas or products. This is reflected by the fact that not a single respondent on either the survey or from the case studies suggested that they would have tried to start the firm with a different idea in the absence of SBIR funding. However, once the firm exists, one-quarter of the respondents and one-sixth of the case studies indicated that they would have tried to continue the firm with a different idea in the absence of SBIR funding. These different results may suggest that the SBIR has a greater impact on commercializing ideas that otherwise would not find their way into the market on potential entrepreneurs than on existing small firms.

4. Conclusions

When viewed through the static lens provided by industrial organization, small firms place an efficiency burden on the economy. Their small scale of production inflicts a substantial loss in terms of higher production costs. However, when viewed through a more evolutionary lens, such static losses in production efficiency are more than offset in gains in dynamic efficiency. The greatest contribution to economic efficiency by small firms is dynamic and evolutionary in nature: Small firms serve as agents of change.

In the current debate on the relationship between employment and wages, it is typically argued that the existence of small firms that are suboptimal within the organization of an industry represents a loss in economic efficiency. However, this argument is based on a static analysis. When viewed through a dynamic lens a different conclusion emerges. One of the most striking results in the new literature is the finding of a positive impact of firm age on productivity and employee compensation, even after controlling for the size of the firm. Given the strongly confirmed stylized fact linking both firm size and age to a negative rate of growth (that is, the smaller and younger a firm the faster it will grow but the lower is its likelihood of survival), this new finding linking firm age to employee compensation and productivity suggests that not only will some of the small and suboptimal firms of today become the large and optimal firms of tomorrow, but there is at least a tendency for the low productivity and wage of

today to become the high productivity and wage of tomorrow.

The public policies emerging in the post-war period dealing with business have been shaped by the static view of industrial organization and therefore are essentially constraining in nature. There were three general types of public policies towards business: antitrust (competition policy), regulation, and public ownership. All three of those policy approaches toward the firm in the market restricted the firm's freedom to contract. While specific policy approaches tended to be more associated with one country than with others, such as antitrust in the United States or public ownership in France and Sweden, all developed countries shared a common policy approach of intervening to restrain what otherwise was perceived as too much market power held by firms. Public policies constraining the freedom of the firm to contract were certainly consistent with the *Weltanschauung* emerging from the theories and empirical evidence regarding the firm in the market during the post-war period. Left unchecked, the large corporation in possession of market power would allocate resources in such a way as to reduce economic welfare. Through state intervention the Williamsonian tradeoff between efficiency on the hand and fairness on the other would be solved in a manner that presumably would be more socially satisfying.

More recently the relevant policy question has shifted away from *How can the government constrain firms from abusing their market power?* to *How can governments create an environment fostering the success and viability of firms?* The major issues of the day have shifted away from concerns about excess profits and abuses of market dominance to the creation of jobs, growth, and international competitiveness. The concern about corporations is now more typically not that they are too successful and powerful but that they are not successful and powerful enough. Thus, the government policies of the 1990s have increasingly shifted away from *constraining* to *enabling*. Public policy in the United States is increasingly fostering efforts to create new firms to promote job creation and economic growth within their jurisdictions. While this policy emphasis on small and new firms as engines of dynamic efficiency may seem startling after decades at looking to the corporate giants to bestow efficiency is anything but new. Before the country was even half a century old, Alexis de Tocqueville, in 1835, reported, "What astonishes me in the United States is not so much the marvelous grandeur of some undertakings as the innumerable multitude of small ones."[21]

Acknowledgements

I am particularly grateful for the insightful suggestions made on draft versions of this paper by Farrukh Iqbal, Shujiro Urata, Migara De Silva, Al Berry, Christina Boari, Jeff Nugent, Bee Aw Roberts and Hideki Yamawaki.

Notes

[1] Lester Thurow, "Losing the Economic Race," *New York Review of Books*, September 1984, pp. 29–31.
[2] W.W. Restow, "Here Comes a New Political Chapter in America," *International Herald Tribune*, 2 January 1987.
[3] For example, U.S. News and World Report (16 August 1993) reported, "What do Bill Clinton, George Bush and Bob Dole have in common? All have uttered one of the most enduring homilies in American political discourse: That small businesses create most of the nation's jobs."
[4] Cited from Davis, Haltiwanger, and Schuh (1996b, p. 298).
[5] Representative Robert Michel, House Minority Leader, in the Republican Response to the 1993 State of the Union Address, cited from Davis et al. (1996, p. 298).
[6] While it was acknowledged that small firms were able to avoid direct competition by occupying strategic niches, Weiss (Audretsch and Yamawaki, 1991, p. 404) observed that, "The survival of smaller plants within any given industry may be due to their specialization in items with short production runs or to their service of small geographic markets within which their relatively small national market share is irrelevant. To the extent that such explanations hold, small plants are not necessarily suboptimal. However, such explanations seem unlikely to hold for a number of the industries where the percentage of suboptimal capacity is larger."
[7] Quotation from p. xiv of the Introduction in Audretsch and Yamawaki (1991).
[8] Coase (1937, p. 23) himself asked, "A pertinent question to ask would appear to be (quite apart from the monopoly considerations raised by Professor Knight), why, if by organizing one can eliminate certain costs and in fact reduce the cost of production, are there any market transactions at all? Why is not all production carried on by one big firm?"
[9] See for reviews of this literature Baldwin and Scott (1987), Scherer (1991), and Dosi (1988).
[10] See for example Scherer (1991), Cohen and Klepper (1991, 1992), and Arrow (1962).
[11] Cohen and Klepper (1991, 1992).
[12] See Baldwin and Scott (1987).

[13] A similar startup size for new manufacturing firms has been found by Dunne et al. (1989) for the United States, Mata (1994) and Mata and Portugal (1994) for Portugal and Wagner (1994) for Germany.
[14] For example, Weiss (1976, p. 126) argues that, "In purely competitive long-run equilibrium, no suboptimal capacity should exist at all."
[15] The country studies included in Geroski and Schwalbach (1991) also indicate considerable ambiguities between measures reflecting the extent of scale economies and capital intensity on the one hand, and entry rates on the other.
[16] While the concept of technological regimes does not lend itself to precise measurement, the major conclusion of Acs and Audretsch (1988, 1990) was that the existence of these distinct regimes can be inferred by the extent to which small firms are able to innovate relative to the total amount of innovative activity in an industry. That is, when the small-firm innovation rate is high relative to the total innovation rate, the technological and knowledge conditions are more likely to reflect the entrepreneurial regime. The routinized regime is more likely to exhibit a low small-firm innovation rate relative to the total innovation rate.
[17] Macki (1996) points out that these views are not original with Krugman (1991).
[18] Saxenian (1990, pp. 97–98) claims that even the language and vocabulary used by technical specialists is specific to a region, ". . . a distinct language has evolved in the region and certain technical terms used by semiconductor production engineers in Silicon Valley would not even be understood by their counterparts in Boston's Route 128."
[19] Porter (1990) provides examples of Italian ceramics and gold jewelry industries in which numerous firms are located within a bounded geographic region and compete intensively in terms of product innovation rather than focusing on simple price competition.
[20] Public Law 97–219, 22 July 1982.
[21] Quoted from *Business Week*, Bonus Issue, 1993, p. 12.

References

Acs, Zoltan J. and Catherine Armington, 1998, 'Longitudinal Establishment and Enterprise Microdata (LEEM) Documentation', Center for Economic Studies, U.S. Department of Commerce, Discussion Paper, 98-9 July 1998.

Acs, Zoltan J., Catherine Armington and Alicia Robb, 1999, 'Measures of Job Flow Dynamics in the U.S.', Center for Economic Studies, U.S. Department of Commerce, Washington DC, Discussion Paper 99-1 January 1999.

Acs, Z. J. and David B. Audretsch, 1987, 'Innovation, Market Structure and Firm Size', *Review of Economics and Statistics* **69**(4), 567–575.

Acs, Z. J. and David B. Audretsch, 1990, *Innovation and Small Firms*, Cambridge, Mass.: MIT Press.

Acs, Z. J. and David B. Audretsch, 1993, *Small Firms and Entrepreneurship: An East-West Perspective*, Cambridge, U.K.: Cambridge University Press.

Acs, Z. J. and David B. Audretsch, 1998, 'Innovation in Large and Small Firms: An Empirical Analysis', *American Economic Review* **78**(4), 678–690.

Acs, Z. J., David B. Audretsch and Maryann P. Feldman, 1992, 'Real Effects of Academic Research', *American Economic Review* 82(1), 363–367.

Almeida, P. and B. Kogut, 1997, 'The Exploration of Technological Diversity and the Geographic Localization of Innovation', *Small Business Economics* 9(1), 21–31.

Arrow, Kenneth J., 1962, 'Economic Welfare and the Allocation of Resources for Invention', in R. R. Nelson (ed.), *The Rate and Direction of Inventive Activity*, Princeton: Princeton University Press.

Audretsch, David B., 1991, 'New Firm Survival and the Technological Regime', *Review of Economics and Statistics* 73(3), 441–450.

Audretsch, David B., 1995, *Innovation and Industry Evolution*, Cambridge, Mass.: MIT Press.

Audretsch, David B. and Maryann P. Feldman, 1996, 'R&D Spillovers and the Geography of Innovation and Production', *American Economic Review* 86(3), 630–640.

Audretsch, David B. and Talat Mahmood, 1995, 'New-Firm Survival: New Results Using a Hazard Function', *Review of Economics and Statistics* 77(1), 97–103.

Audretsch, David B. and Paula E. Stephan, 1996, 'Company-Scientist Locational Links: The Case of Biotechnology', *American Economic Review* 86(3), 641–652.

Audretsch, David B. and Hideki Yamawaki (eds.), 1991, *Structure, Conduct and Performance: Leonard Weiss*, New York: New York University Press.

Baily, Martin Neil, Eric J. Bartelsman and John Haltiwanger, 1996, 'Downsizing and Productivity Growth: Myth or Reality?' *Small Business Economics* 8(4), 259–278.

Baldwin, John R., 1995, *The Dynamics of Industrial Competition*, Cambridge, U.K.: Cambridge University Press.

Baldwin, John R. and Paul K. Gorecki, 1991, 'Entry, Exit, and Production Growth', Iin P. Geroski and J. Schwalbach (eds.), *Entry and Market Contestability: An International Comparison*, Oxford: Basil Blackwell.

Baldwin, John R. and M. Rafiquzzaman, 1995, 'Selection Versus Evolutionary Adaptation: Learning and Post-Entry Performance', *International Journal of Industrial Organization* 13(4), 501–523.

Baldwin, W. L. and J. T. Scott, 1987, *Market Structure and Technological Change*, New York: Harwood.

Brown, Charles, James Hamilton and James Medoff, 1990, *Employers Large and Small*, Cambridge, Mass.: Harvard University Press.

Caves, Richard E., 1998, 'Industrial Organization and New Findings on the Turnover and Mobility of Firms', *Journal of Economic Literature* 36(4), 1947–1982.

Coase, R. H., 1937, 'The Nature of the Firm', *Economica* 4(4), 386–405.

Cohen, W. M. and S. Klepper, 1991, 'Firm Size Versus Diversity in the Achievement of Technological Advance', in Z. J. Acs and D. B. Audretsch (eds.), *Innovation and Technological Change: An International Comparison*, Ann Arbor: University of Michigan Press.

Cohen, W. M. and S. Klepper, 1992, 'The Tradeoff Between Firm Size and Diversity in the Pursuit of Technological Progress', *Small Business Economics* 4(1), 1–14.

Davis, Steven J., John Haltiwanger and Scott Schuh, 1996a,

Job Creation and Destruction, Cambridge, Mass.: MIT Press.

Davis, Steven J., John Haltiwanger and Scott Schuh, 1996b, 'Small Business and Job Creation: Dissecting the Myth and Reassessing the Facts', *Small Business Economics* 8(4), 297–315.

Dertouzos, Michael L., Richard K. Lester, Robert M. Solow and the MIT Commission on Industrial Productivity, 1989, *Made in America: Regaining the Productive Edge*, Cambridge, Mass.: MIT Press.

Dosi, G., 1982, 'Technological Paradigms and Technological Trajectories: A Suggested Interpretation of the Determinants and Directions of Technical Change', *Research Policy* 13(1), 3–20.

Dosi, G., 1988, 'Sources, Procedures, and Microeconomic Effects of Innovation', *Journal of Economic Literature* 26(3), 112–117.

Dunne, T., M. J. Roberts and L. Samuelson, 1989, 'The Growth and Failure of U.S. Manufacturing Plants', *Quarterly Journal of Economics* 104, 671–698.

Feldman, M., 1994a, 'Knowledge Complementarity and Innovation', *Small Business Economics* 6(3), 363–372.

Feldman, M., 1994b, *The Geography of Innovation*, Boston: Kluwer.

Feldman, Maryann P. and David B. Audretsch, 1999, 'Innovation in Cities: Science-Based Diversity, Specialization and Localized Competition', *European Economic Review* 43, 409–429.

Feller, Irwin, 1997, 'Federal and State Government Roles in Science and Technology', *Economic Development Quarterly* 11(4), 283–296.

Galbraith, John Kenneth, 1956, *American Capitalism*, Boston: Houghton Mifflin.

Geroski, Paul A., 1991, 'Some Data-Driven Reflections on the Entry Process', in Paul Georski and Joachin Schwalbach (eds.), *Entry and Market Contestability: An International Comparison*, Oxford: Basil Blackwell.

Geroski, Paul A., 1995, 'What Do We Know About Entry', *International Journal of Industrial Organization* 13(4), 421–440.

Geroski, Paul A. and Joachim Schwalbach (eds.), 1991, *Entry and Market Contestability: An International Comparison*, Oxford: Basil Blackwell.

Glaeser, E., H. Kallal, J. Scheinkman and A. Shleifer, 1992, 'Growth of Cities', *Journal of Political Economy* 100, 1126–1152.

Griliches, Zvi, 1979, 'Issues in Assessing the Contribution of R&D to Productivity Growth', *Bell Journal of Economics* 10 (Spring), 92–116.

Hall, Bronwyn H., 1987, 'The Relationship Between Firm Size and Firm Growth in the U.S. Manufacturing Sector', *Journal of Industrial Economics* 35 (June), 583–605.

Hannan, Michael T. and John Freeman, 1989, *Organizational Ecology*, Cambridge, Mass.: Harvard University Press.

Hirschman, Albert O., 1970, *Exit, Voice, and Loyalty*, Cambridge, Mass.: Harvard University Press.

Jacobs, J., 1969, *The Economy of Cities*, New York: Random House.

Jaffe, A., 1989, 'Real Effects of Academic Research', *American Economic Review* 79, 957–970.

Jaffe, A., Trajtenberg, M. and Henderson, R., 1993, 'Geographic Localization of Knowledge Spillovers as Evidenced by Patent Citations', *Quarterly Journal of Economics* **63**, 577–598.

Jovanovic, Boyan, 1982, 'Selection and Evolution of Industry', *Econometrica* **50**(2), 649–670.

Krugman, Paul, 1991, *Geography and Trade*, Cambridge, Mass.: MIT Press.

Levin, R. C., A. K. Klevorick, R. R. Nelson and S. G. Winter, 1987, *Appropriating the Returns From Industrial Research and Development. Brooking Papers on Economic Activity*, Washington, D.C., pp. 783–820.

Malecki, E. J., 1996, *Technology and Economic Development*, London: Longman.

Mansfield, Edwin, 1962, 'Entry, Gibrat's Law, Innovation, and the Growth of Firms', *American Economic Review* **52**(5), 1023–1051.

Mata, Jose, 1994, 'Firm Growth During Infancy', *Small Business Economics* **6**(1), 27–40.

Mata, J. and P. Portugal, 1994, 'Life Duration of New Firms', *Journal of Industrial Economics* **27**(3), 227–246.

Mata, Jose, Pedro Portugal and Paulo Guimaraes, 1995, 'The Survival of New Plants: Start-Up Conditions and Post-Entry Evolution', *International Journal of Industrial Organization* **13**(4), 459–482.

Nelson, Richard R. and Sidney G. Winter, 1982, *An Evolutionary Theory of Economic Change*, Cambridge, Mass.: Harvard University Press.

Neumann, Manfred, 1993, 'Review of Entry and Market Contestability: An International Comparison', *International Journal of Industrial Organization* **11**(4), 593–594.

Porter, M., 1990, *The Comparative Advantage of Nations*, New York: Free Press.

Pratten, C. F., 1971, *Economies of Scale in Manufacturing Industry*, Cambridge, U.K.: Cambridge University Press.

Prevenzer, M., 1997, 'The Dynamics of Industrial Clustering in Biotechnology', *Small Business Economics* **9**(3), 255–271.

Saxenian, A., 1990, 'Regional Networks and the Resurgence of Silicon Valley', *California Management Review* **33**, 89–111.

Saxenian, Anna Lee, 1994, *Regional Advantage*, Cambridge, Mass.: Harvard University Press.

Scherer, F. M., 1973, 'The Determinants of Industry Plant Sizes in Six Nations', *Review of Economics and Statistics* **55**(2), 135–175.

Scherer, F. M., 1991, 'Changing Perspectives on the Firm Size Problem', in Z. J. Acs and D. B. Audretsch (eds.), *Innovation and Technological Change. An International Comparison*, Ann Arbor: University of Michigan Press.

Schumpeter, Joseph A., 1942, *Capitalism, Socialism and Democracy*, New York: Harper and Row.

Sternberg, Rolf, 1996, 'Technology Policies and the Growth of Regions', *Small Business Economics* **8**(2), 75–86.

Sutton, John, 1997, 'Gibrat's Legacy', *Journal of Economic Literature* **35**(1), 40–59.

Thurow, Lester C., 1985, 'Healing with a Thousand Bandages', *Challenge* **28**, 19–28.

Tyson, Laura, Tea Petrin and Halsey Rogers, 1994, 'Promoting Entrepreneurship in Eastern Europe', *Small Business Economics* **6**(3), 165–184.

Wagner, Joachim, 1992, 'Firm Size, Firm Growth, and Persistence of Chance: Testing Gibrat's Law with Establishment Data from Lower Saxony, 1978–1989', *Small Business Economics* **4**(2), 125–131.

Wagner, Joachim, 1994, 'Small Firm Entry in Manufacturing Industries: Lower Saxony, 1979–1989', *Small Business Economics* **6**(3), 211–224.

Weiss, L. W., 1964, 'The Survival Technique and the Extent of Suboptimal Capacity', *Journal of Political Economy* **72**(3), 246–261.

Weiss, L. W., 1976, 'Optimal Plant Scale and the Extent of Suboptimal Capacity', in R. T. Masson and P. D. Qualls (eds.), *Essays on Industrial Organization in Honor of Joe S. Bain*, Cambridge, Mass.: Ballinger.

Weiss, Leonard W., 1979, 'The Structure-Conduct-Performance Paradigm and Antitrust', *University of Pennsylvania Law Review* **127**, 1104–1140.

Winter, Sidney G., 1984, 'Schumpeterian Competition in Alternative Technological Regimes', *Journal of Economic Behavior and Organization* **5**, 287–320.

[19]

Mansfield's Missing Link: The Impact
of Knowledge Spillovers
on Firm Growth

David B. Audretsch[1]
Erik E. Lehmann[2,3]

ABSTRACT. The purpose of this paper is to provide a link between two of the seminal contributions of Edwin Mansfield. The first focuses on the determinants of firm growth and the second is concerned with university-based knowledge spillovers. By linking both firm-specific characteristics as well as access to knowledge spillovers from universities, the empirical evidence found in this paper suggests that knowledge spillovers as well as firm-specific characteristics influence firm growth.

Key words: university spillovers, firm growth

JEL Classification: M13, L20, R30

1. Introduction

Among his many compelling contributions, Edwin Mansfield ranked among the pioneers in economics focusing the determinants of the evolutionary process by which firms are created and then grow through an evolutionary process. According to Mansfield (1962, p. 1023), "Because there have been so few econometric studies of the birth, growth and death of firms, we lack even crude answers to the following basic questions regarding

[1]Department Entrepreneurship, Growth, and Public Policy Max Planck Institute for Research into Economic Systems Jena Kahlaische Strasse 10, 07745 Jena, Germany.
Email: audretsch@mpiew-jena.mpg.de
[2]Department Entrepreneurship, Growth, and Public Policy Max dPlanck Institute for Research into Economic Systems Jena Kahlaische Strasse 10, 07745 Jena
Germany.
[3]Department of Economics
University of Konstanz
Box D-144, 78457 Konstanz
Germany.
E-mail: lehmann@mpiew-jena.mpg.de

the dynamic processes governing an industry's structure. What are the quantitative effects of various factors on the growth of firms represented by Gibrat's law of proportionate effect? What have been the effects of successful innovations on a firm's growth rate?" It required no fewer than two sweeping articles in the Journal of Economic Literature (Caves, 1998; Sutton, 1997) at the end of the last century to review the literature on empirical tests of firm growth and Gibrat's Law spawned by Mansfield's pioneering research.

Towards the end of his career, Mansfield (1995), also pioneered a very different research trajectory, which focused on external sources of R&D, and in particular universities, as inputs into firm innovation.[1] Mansfield's research was instrumental in triggering a more recent wave of studies identifying the role that knowledge spillovers play, and in particular, knowledge spillovers from universities in generating innovative activity (Audretsch and Stephan, 1996; Jaffe, 1989).

Despite the enormous literatures triggered by Mansfield's seminal contributions, these two research trajectories remain separate. As the Caves (1998) and Sutton (1997) review articles confirm, the plethora of econometric studies focusing on firm growth in general, and Gibrat's law in particular, never consider the impact of external research on the growth of firms. Instead, this entire literature consists almost exclusively of trying to link firm-specific characteristics, principally size and age, but also in some cases R&D and other types of innovative activity, to firm growth. Similarly, the literature on knowledge spillovers has concentrated mainly on performance measures such as innovation and R&D, but has yet to consider the impact on firm growth (Audretsch et al., 2005).

Journal of Technology Transfer, 30 1/2, 207–210, 2005.
© 2005 Springer Science+Business Media, Inc. Manufactured in The Netherlands.

The purpose of this paper is to provide the missing link between the literatures on firm growth and on university-based knowledge spillovers. In particular, we examine whether access to university-based knowledge spillovers has an impact on firm growth. In the second section we present the model relating not just firm characteristics, but also knowledge external to the firm, to firm growth. In the third section issues involving measurement are discussed. The results from estimating the growth rates of high-technology German firms are presented in Section 4. Finally, in the last section a summary and conclusion are provided. In particular, the results of this paper suggest that two of the seminal contributions made by Mansfield need to be linked together. Just as Mansfield discovered, not only is firm growth positively influenced by investments in knowledge, but accessing external knowledge generated by universities also contributes to firm growth.

2. Linking firm growth to university spillovers

Since the purpose of this paper is to link the two seminal contributions by Mansfield together, we introduce a model relating firm growth to characteristics specific to the enterprise as well as external knowledge from universities. The starting point is the most prevalent model for identifying the determinants of growth at the level of the firm, which has been based to test Gibrat's Law (Sutton, 1997).

Formalizing the relationship between size and growth, Gibrat's law assumes that the present size of firm i in period t may be decomposed into the product of a "proportional effect" and the initial firm size as:

$$\text{Size}_{i,t} = (1 + \varepsilon_t)\,\text{Size}_{i,t-1}, \qquad (1)$$

where $(1 + \varepsilon_t)$ denotes the proportional effect for firm i in period t. Here the random shock ε_t is assumed to be identically and independently distributed. Taking the natural log and assuming that for small ε, $\ln(1 + \varepsilon) \approx \varepsilon_t$,

$$\ln(\text{Size}_{i,t}) = \ln(\text{Size}_{i,0}) + \sum_{k=1}^{t} \varepsilon_{ik} \qquad (2)$$

It can be observed that as $t \to \infty$ a distribution emerges which is approximately log normal with properties that $\ln(\text{Size}_{i,t}) \sim N(t\mu\varepsilon,\, t\sigma^2{}_\varepsilon)$. Firm growth can then be measured as the difference between the natural log of the number of employees as:

$$\text{Growth}_{it} = \ln(S_{i,t}^\cdot) - \ln(S_{i,t-1}) \qquad (3)$$

where the difference in size for firm i between the current period t and the initial period $(t-1)$ equals Growth_{it}.

This equation can be empirically estimated by:

$$\text{Growth}_{i,t} = B_1 \ln(\text{Size}_{i,t-1}) + B_2 \ln(\text{Size}_{i,t-1})^2 + B_3 \text{Age}_{i,t-1} + \varepsilon_i \qquad (4)$$

where growth for firm i in period t is a function of initial firm size, size^2, age, and ε_i a stochastic error term.

Sutton (1997) and Caves (1998) survey and report on the large number of empirical studies estimating Equation (4). The evidence is systematic and compelling that both size and age are negatively related to firm growth.

Note that Equation (4) only considers characteristics specific to the enterprise. We extend this approach by including knowledge spillovers from universities,

$$\text{Growth}_{i,t} = B_1 \ln(\text{Size}_{i,t-1}) + B_2 \ln(\text{Size}_{i,t-1})^2 + B_3 \text{Age}_{i,t-1} B_4 \text{Knowledge}_{r,t-1} \qquad (5)$$
$$\times B_5 D_{ind} + \varepsilon_i$$

where D_{ind} is a vector of industry dummies controlling, for example, for the knowledge intensity of production in a specific sector. Knowledge$_r$, $t-1$ represents knowledge spillovers from universities.

3. Data set and descriptive statistics

To test the hypothesis that firm growth depends not only on firm size and age but also university spillovers, we use a unique dataset of 281 IPO firms in Germany. The dataset is collected combining individual data from IPO prospectuses, along with publicly available information from on-line data sources including the *Deutsche Boerse AG* (www.deutsche-boerse.com). We pooled this dataset by adding university-specific variables, which are individually collected from the 73 public universities in Germany. For each of those universities we collected the number of articles listed in the research database from the ISI (Information Sciences Institutes). Although this research database includes a small number of all the journals in one field, it ensures that it only contains the high-quality research journals. We further consider the amount of grants available to each respective university in 1997 (see Audretsch *et al.*, 2004).

We take the *log growth rates* of employees one year after the IPO as the dependent variable. The first two exogenous variables are firm age (AGE) and firm size (SIZE). Age is measured in years from foundation to IPO, and firm size by the number of employees before IPO. To capture effects from university spillovers we include the distance to the closest university as an exogenous variable. Since universities in Germany are more geographically concentrated compared to the US, we need a measure which is sensitive to small variations. The distance is measured in kilometers using the online database of the *German Automobile Club* (www.a-dac.de). All firms located within a radius of 1.5 km are classified as belonging to the distance category of 1 km.

In the first two models (models I, II), we estimate the following basic regressions to test Gibrat's Law, as proposed in the literature (see Sutton, 1997).

$$\text{(I)} \quad LnGrowth = const. + \beta_1 LnSize + \beta_2 LnSize^2$$
$$+ \beta_3 LnAge + \beta_4 LnAge^2 + \varepsilon$$

$$\text{(II)} \quad LnGrowth = const. + \beta_1 LnSize$$
$$+ \beta_2 LNAge + \varepsilon$$

Then we test for the impact of university spillovers as an additional explanatory variable for firm growth (models III, IV):

$$\text{(III)} \ LnGrowth = const. + \beta_1 LnSize + \beta_2 LNAge$$
$$+ (-1)\beta_3 University\ Spillovers$$
$$+ \varepsilon$$

$$\text{(IV)} \ LnGrowth = const. + \beta_1 LnSize + \beta_2 LnAge$$
$$+ (-1)\beta_3 University\ Spillovers$$
$$\times (LnUniversity\ Spending;$$
$$\times LnSSCI;\ LnSCI)$$

We multiplied with (-1) to capture the effect that the closer the distance towards the next university, the higher should be the growth rate of the respective firm. Model (V), which is not explicitly shown, captures all variables.

The descriptive statistics are depicted in Table I. The closest location between firms and universities is 1 km and the maximum distance is 177 km away from the nearest university. The data also demonstrate that most of the firms are strikingly young. Half of the firms in our sample are 8 years old or less. The firms also differ extremely in their size as measured by the number of employees before IPO. The mean firm before IPO employed about 180 workers. Finally, the table shows that on average the log growth rate is about 0.475. All the variables show high differences between the minimum and maximum values.

4. Empirical evidence

Table II presents the results from the four regressions. Models (I) and (II) replicate the standard tests of Gibrat's Law as known from the literature. The negative and statistically coefficient on firm size suggests that smaller firms grow faster than do their larger counterparts. The coefficient of firm age and firm age as well as the squared term shows no statistically significant impact on firm growth.

The estimation of model (III) shows no significant impact of university spillovers as measured by the distance towards the closest university of a firm. However, if we instrument this variable model (model IV) using the spending for the

TABLE I
Descriptive statistics

Variable	Mean	SD.	Min.	Max.
Distance (km)	16.69	23.45	1	177
Firm size (#employees)	180.20	256.52	2	1,700
Firm age (years)	10.27	11.11	0.1	107
Ln growth rates	0.4969	1.6121	−4.106	7.5183

TABLE II
Regressions on firm growth

	OLS (I)	OLS (II)	OLS (III)	OLS (V)	2SLS (IV)	2SLS (V)
LnSize	−0.7895 (2.75)[b]	−0.9290 (15.33)[c]	−0.9117 (14.10)[c]	−0.8537 (1.86)[b]	−0.8554 (10.22)[c]	−1.1272 (2.31)[c]
Ln Size2	−0.0152 (0.47)			−0.0059 (0.12)		0.03133 (0.58)
LnAge	0.0859 (1.29)	0.07390 (1.40)	0.0613 (1.19)	0.0731 (0.96)	0.1688 (2.00)[b]	0.1929 (1.83)[a]
LnAge2	−0.0114 (0.41)			0.0092 (0.34)		−0.0099 (0.31)
University spillover				−0.0430 (0.92)	0.7131 (1.78)[b]	0.7263 (1.79)[b]
Const.	4.3187 (7.03)[c]	4.5762 (17.27)[c]	4.4339 (13.75)[c]	4.3289 (4.11)[c]	5.430 (8.25)[c]	6.001 (4.43)[c]
R	0.4749	0.4779	0.4856	0.4860	0.0236	0.0094

This table presents the result from OLS on firm growth. The endogenous variable is growth rates of employees one year after the IPO. University Spillover is measured in log kilometers from the next university. This variable is instrumented in the 2SLS approach by the number of research spending, the number of papers published in the natural sciences and in the social sciences. All OLS-estimations are done using the White-heteroskedasticity robust estimator. Absolute *t*-values in parentheses, [a, b, c] Statistically significant at the 10, 5 1% level, respective. The coefficient of university spillovers are multiplied with (−1) to capture the positive effect of a close location towards the next university.

respective university as well as the academic papers published in the natural sciences and the social sciences, we find the missing link: Spillovers matter for firm growth. The closer the distance towards the next university and the higher the amount of academic papers published, the higher the growth rates of firms. This result is also robust in model 2SLS (V), which includes all the variables.

5. Conclusion

Perhaps had Edwin Mansfield's career been extended, he would have had the opportunity to bring together two of his seminal contributions—firm growth and university research spillovers. In this paper, we have followed in the footsteps of Mansfield by linking these two seminal contributions together. Not only does firm growth depend upon characteristics specific to the firm, but also on external characteristics as well, and in particular, the spillover of knowledge from universities. We would anticipate future research to further pursue the intellectual tradition pioneered by Ed Mansfield and further examine how firm growth is shaped by other types of knowledge spillovers external to the firm.

Note

1. An earlier study focusing on knowledge spillovers is Link and Rees (1991).

References

Audretsch, D.B. and P.E. Stephan, 1996, 'Company-Scientist Locational Links: The Case of Biotechnology,' *American Economic Review* **86** (3), 641–652.

Audretsch, D.B., M. Keilbach and E.E. Lehmann, 2005, *Entrepreneurship and Economic Growth*, London: Oxford University Press (forthcoming).

Audretsch, D.B., E.E. Lehmann, and S. Warning, 2004, 'University Spillovers: Does the Kind of Knowledge Matters?,' *Industry and Innovation* (forthcoming).

Caves, R., 1998, 'Industrial Organization and New Findings on the Turnover and Mobility of Firms,' *Journal of Economic Literature* **36** (4), 1947–1982.

Hall, B.H., A.N. Link, and J.T. Scott, 2003, 'Universities as Research Partners,' *Review of Economics and Statistics* (forthcoming).

Jaffe, A.B., 1989, 'Real Effects of Academic Research,' *American Economic Review* **79**, 957–970.

Link, A.N. and J. Rees, 1991, 'Firm Size, University-Based Research, and the Returns to R&D,' *Small Business Economics* **2**, 24–31.

Link, A.N., and B. Bozeman, 1991, 'Innovative Behavior in Small-Sized Firms,' *Small Business Economics* **3** (3), 179–184.

Mansfield, E., 1962, 'Entry, Gibrat's Law, Innovation, and the Growth of Firms,' *American Economic Review* **52**, 1023–1051.

Mansfield, E., 1995, 'Academic Research Underlying Industrial Innovations: Sources, Characteristics, and Financing,' *The Review of Economics and Statistics* **77**, 55–65.

Sutton, J., 1997, 'Gibrat's Legacy,' *Journal of Economic Literature* **35**, 40–59.

Technological Regimes, Industrial Demography and the Evolution of Industrial Structures

DAVID B. AUDRETSCH

(Georgia State University, Atlanta, GA 30303-3083, USA)

The purpose of this paper is to weave together the new theories and empirical evidence analyzing firms and industries in motion, or what has been termed 'industrial demographics'. In particular, the links between the technological regime underlying an industry and the observed patterns of industry demography are emphasized. Although a major conclusion of this new literature is that the structure of industries is perhaps better characterized by a high degree of fluidity and turbulence than stability, the patterns of industry demographics vary considerably from industry to industry. And what apparently shapes the evolution of firms particular to a specific industry is, as much as anything else, the knowledge conditions shaping the technological regime underlying that industry.

1. Introduction

Industrial and Corporate Change   Volume 6   Number 1   1997

Schumpeter (1942, p. 132) predicted that, due to scale economies in the production of new economic knowledge, large corporations would not only have the innovative advantage over small and new enterprises, but that ultimately the economic landscape would consist only of giant corporations: 'Innovation itself is being reduced to routine. Technological progress is increasingly becoming the business of teams of trained specialists who turn out what is required and make it work in predictable ways'. Certainly the perceived economic threat posed by the Soviet Union in the late 1950s and early 1960s was attributable to its ability to concentrate economic assets and exhaust scale economies to a degree that was unthinkable in the West, where a commitment to political democracy seemingly translated into a concomitant commitment to economic decentralization.

———————— *The Evolution of Industrial Structures* ————————

Perhaps the ascendancy of industrial organization as a field in economics during this period came from the recognition not only by scholars but also by policy makers that industrial organization matters. It became the task of the industrial organization scholars to sort out the issues involving this perceived trade-off between economic efficiency on the one hand and political and economic decentralization on the other. The scholars of industrial organization (see Scherer and Ross, 1990) responded by producing a mass of literature focusing on essentially three issues: (i) how much economic concentration is there? (ii) what are the economic welfare implications of an oligopolistic market structure? and (iii) given the evidence that economic concentration is associated with efficiency, what are the public policy implications? A characteristic of this literature was not only that it was obsessed with the concentration/oligopoly question but that it was essentially static in nature. There was considerable concern about what to do about the firms and industrial structures that existed, but little attention was paid to where they came from and where they were going. Williamson's classic 1968 article, 'Economies as an Antitrust Defense: The Welfare Tradeoffs,' became something of a final statement demonstrating this seemingly inevitable tradeoff between the gains in productive efficiency that could be obtained through increased concentration and gains in terms of competition that could be achieved through decentralizing policies, such as antitrust. But it did not seem possible to have both, certainly not in Williamson's completely static model.

Yet what has become striking about the industrial structure of the USA is not its stability, but rather the opposite—its dynamic, turbulent nature. The industrial landscape of the USA has been radically transformed in a relatively short period of time. A number of corporate giants such as IBM, US Steel, RCA and Wang have lost their aura of invincibility. Only slightly more than a decade ago Peters and Waterman, in their influential best-selling management book, *In Search of Excellence: Lessons from America's Best Run Companies,* identified IBM as the best-run corporation in America and possibly in the entire world. At the same time has come the breathtaking emergence of new firms that hardly existed two decades ago, such as Microsoft, Apple Computer, Intel, Dell and Compaq Computer. In the 1950s and 1960s it took two decades for one-third of the Fortune 500 to be replaced. In the 1970s it took one decade. By contrast, in the 1980s it took just five years for one-third of the Fortune 500 firms to be replaced.

Perhaps even more impressive than the handful of new enterprises that grow to penetrate the Fortune 500 are the armies of startups that come into existence each year—and typically disappear into oblivion within a few years.

In the 1990s there are around 1.3 million new companies started each year (Audretsch, 1995). That is, the modern economy is characterized by a tremendous degree of turbulence. It is an economy in motion, with a massive number of new firms entering each year but only a subset surviving for any length of time, and an even smaller subset that can ultimately challenge and displace the incumbent large enterprises.

Despite the high degree of fluidity and turbulence in modern economies, very little is actually known about the dynamic process through which industries and firms evolve over time. Perhaps this lack of knowledge motivated Mansfield (1962) some 30 years ago to make a plea for a greater emphasis on the dynamic process by which industries change over time:

> Because there have been so few econometric studies of the birth, growth, and death of firms, we lack even crude answers to the following basic questions regarding the dynamic processes governing an industry's structure. What are the quantitative effects of various factors on the rates of entry and exit? What have been the effects of successful innovations on a firm's growth rate? What determines the amount of mobility within an industry's size structure? (p. 1023)

In the intervening three decades a new literature has emerged focusing on industrial markets in motion. In particular, this literature examines the process by which new firms enter into industrial markets, either grow and survive or exit from the industry, and possibly displace incumbent corporations. At the heart of this evolutionary process is innovation, because the potential for innovative activity serves as the driving force behind much of the evolution of industries. It is innovative activity that explains why the patterns of industry evolution vary from industry to industry, depending upon the underlying knowledge conditions, or what Nelson and Winter (1982) term 'technological regimes'.

The purpose of this paper is to weave together the new theories and empirical evidence analyzing firms and industries in motion, or what has been termed 'industry demographics'. In particular, the links between the technological regime underlying an industry and the observed patterns of industry demography are emphasized. In the following section the traditional static view of industrial organization provided by the literature of industrial economics is portrayed. The concept of technological regimes and their influence on innovative activity is explained in the third section. The fourth section focuses on entry, and the fifth section on survival and growth. In the sixth section the role that wages and non-wage employee compensation plays is examined. The theories and evidence are synthesized in the seventh section to provide a coherent model of industrial organization within an evolutionary framework. Finally, in the eighth section a summary and conclusions are provided.

2. *The Static View of Industrial Organization*

Two stylized facts that have emerged from a plethora of studies pose something of a puzzle to scholars of industrial organization. The first, which has received considerable attention at least since the seminal study by Simon and Bonini (1958) more than three decades ago, is the persistence of an asymmetric firm-size distribution predominated by small enterprises. Ijiri and Simon (1977, p. 2) characterized this 'regularity in social phenomena that is both striking and observable in a number of quite diverse situations. It is a regularity in the size distribution of firms'.[1] In fact, virtually no other economic phenomenon has persisted as consistently as the skewed asymmetric firm-size distribution. Not only is it almost identical across every manufacturing industry, but it has remained strikingly constant over time, at least since the Second World War, and even across developed industrialized nations (Acs and Audretsch, 1993).

The persistence of this skewed asymmetric firm-size distribution is consistent with the common observation in industrial organization that the bulk of firms in most industries are operating at a suboptimal level of output. However, firm-size distribution is much less stable at the level of individual products (Klepper and Graddy, 1990; Klepper and Miller, 1995; Klepper, 1996). Building on his earlier studies on the extent of suboptimal scale plants and firms in industrial markets, Weiss (1991) concluded that, 'In most industries the great majority of firms is suboptimal. In a typical industry there are, let's say, one hundred firms. Typically only about five to ten of them will be operating at the MES (minimum effcient scale) level of output, or anything like it' (p. xiv). Not only did Weiss find that the MES level of output exceeds that of most firms (enterprises) and plants (establishments), but that, 'On the average, about half of total shipments in the industries covered are suboptimal in scale, and a very large percentage of output is from suboptimal plants in some unconcentrated industries'. The persistence of what has traditionally been classified as suboptimal plants to dominate the firm-size distribution in

---

[1] Ijiri and Simon (1977, pp. 1–2) observed that 'Nature, as it presents itself to the physical scientist, is full of clearly defined patterns...The patterns that have been discovered in social phenomena are much less neat. To be sure, economics has evolved a highly sophisticated body of mathematical laws, but for the most part, these laws bear a rather distinct relation to empirical phenomena...Hence, on those occasions when a social phenomenon appears to exhibit some of the same simplicity and regularity of pattern as is seen so commonly in physics, it is bound to excite interest and attention'.

industrial markets over time raises the question of not only why suboptimal scale plants exist but how they are able to exist.[2]

The second puzzling stylized fact has been established by a number of studies that have found that the entry of new firms into an industry is apparently not substantially deterred in industries where scale economies play an important role. Taken together, these two stylized facts raise two troubling questions: why is it that the preponderance of enterprises in virtually every US manufacturing industry is small? and why are entrepreneurs not more noticeably deterred from entering industries characterized by substantial scale economies? The traditional static view has been able to shed little light on resolving these two empirical paradoxes.

3. *Innovation and Technological Regimes*

The Knowledge Production Function

The starting point for most theories of innovation is the firm (for reviews see Scherer, 1984, 1992; Baldwin and Scott, 1987; Dosi, 1988; Cohen and Levin, 1989). In such theories the firms are exogenous and their performance in generating technological change is endogenous (e.g. Arrow, 1962, 1983; Scherer, 1984, 1991; Cohen and Klepper, 1991, 1992a,b). For example, in the most prevalent model found in the literature of technological change, the model of the knowledge production function, formalized by Griliches (1979), firms exist exogenously and then engage in the pursuit of new economic knowledge as an input into the process of generating innovative activity.

The most decisive input in the knowledge production function is new economic knowledge. As Cohen and Klepper conclude, the greatest source generating new economic knowledge is generally considered to be R&D (Cohen and Klepper, 1991, 1992a,b). Certainly a large body of empirical work has found a strong and positive relationship between knowledge inputs, such as R&D, on the one hand, and innovative outputs on the other hand.

Audretsch (1995) proposed shifting the unit of observation away from

───

[2] Weiss (1991, p. 404) observed that 'The survival of smaller plants within any given industry may be due to their specialization in items with short production runs or to their service of small geographic markets within which relatively small national market share is irrelevant. To the extent that such explanations hold, small plants are not necessarily suboptimal. However, such explanations seem unlikely to hold for a number of the industries where the percentage of suboptimal capacity is large'.

exogenously assumed firms to individuals—agents with endowments of new economic knowledge. As Graf (1957) observed four decades ago,

> When we try to construct a transformation function for society as a whole from those facing the individual firms comprising it, a fundamental difficulty confronts us. There is, from a welfare point of view nothing special about the firms actually existing in an economy at a given moment of time. The firm is in no sense a 'natural unit'. Only the individual members of the economy can lay claim to that distinction. All are potential entrepreneurs. It seems, therefore, that the natural thing to do is to build up from the transformation function of men, rather than the firms, constituting an economy. If we are interested in eventual empirical determination, this is extremely inconvenient. But it has conceptual advantages. The ultimate repositories of technological knowledge in any society are the men comprising it, and it is just this knowledge which is effectively summarized in the form of a transformation function. In itself a firm possesses no knowledge. That which is available to it belongs to the men associated with it. Its production function is really built up in exactly the same way, and from the same basic ingredients, as society's.

The Appropriability Problem Revisited

A large literature has emerged focusing on what has become known as the appropriability problem (see Baldwin and Scott, 1987; Cohen and Levin, 1989). The underlying issue revolves around how firms which invest in the creation of new economic knowledge can best appropriate the economic returns from that knowledge (Arrow, 1962). But when the lens is shifted away from focusing upon the firm as the relevant unit of observation to individuals, the relevant question becomes how can economic agents with a given endowment of new knowledge best appropriate the returns from that knowledge?

The appropriability problem confronting the individual may converge with that confronting the firm. Economic agents can and do work for firms, and even if they do not, they can potentially be employed by an incumbent firm. In fact, in a model of perfect information with no agency costs, any positive economies of scale or scope will ensure that the appropriability problems of the firm and individual converge. If an agent has an idea for doing something different than is currently being practiced by the incumbent enterprises— both in terms of a new product or process and in terms of organization—the idea, which can be termed an innovation, will be presented to the incumbent enterprise. Because of the assumption of perfect knowledge, both the firm and the agent would agree upon the expected value of the innovation. But to the degree that any economies of scale or scope exist, the expected value of implementing the innovation within the incumbent enterprise will exceed that of taking the innovation outside of the incumbent firm to start a new enterprise. Thus, the incumbent firm and the inventor of the idea would be expected to reach a bargain splitting the value added to the firm contributed by the innovation. The payment to the inventor—either in terms of a higher wage or some other means of remuneration—would be bounded between the expected value of the innovation if it is implemented by the incumbent enterprise on the upper end, and by the return that the agent could expect to earn if he used it to launch a new enterprise on the lower end. Or, as Knight (1921, p. 273) observed more than 70 years ago,

> The laborer asks what he thinks the entrepreneur will be able to pay, and in any case will not accept less than he can get from some other entrepreneur, or by turning entrepreneur himself. In the same way the entrepreneur offers to any laborer what he thinks he must in order to secure his services, and in any case not more than he thinks the laborer will actually be worth to him, keeping in mind what he can get by turning laborer himself.

Thus, each economic agent would choose how to best appropriate the value of his endowment of economic knowledge by comparing the wage he would earn if he remains employed by an incumbent enterprise, w, to the expected net present discounted value of the profits accruing from starting a new firm, p. If these two values are relatively close, the probability that he would choose to appropriate the value of his knowledge through an external mechanism such as starting a new firm, $\Pr(e)$, would be relatively low. On the other hand, as the gap between w and p becomes larger, the likelihood of an agent choosing to appropriate the value of his knowledge externally through starting a new enterprise becomes greater, or

$$\Pr(e) = f(p - w) \tag{1}$$

Asymmetric Knowledge, Transaction Costs and the Principal–Agent Relationship

As Knight (1921) and later Arrow (1962) emphasized, new economic knowledge is anything but certain. Not only is new economic knowledge inherently risky, but substantial asymmetries exist across agents both between and within firms (Milgrom and Roberts, 1987). This is to say that the expected value of a new idea, or what has been termed here as a potential innovation, is likely to be anything but unanimous between the inventor of that idea and the decision maker, or group of decision makers,[3] of the firm confronted with evaluating proposed changes or innovations. In fact, it is because information is not only imperfect but also asymmetric that Knight (1921, p. 268) argued that the primary task of the firm is to process information in order to reach a decision:

> With the introduction of uncertainty—the fact of ignorance and the necessity of acting upon opinion rather than knowledge—into this Eden-like situation (that is, a world of perfect information), its character is entirely changed...With uncertainty present doing things, the actual execution of activity becomes in a real sense a secondary part of life; the primary problem or function is deciding what to do and how to do it.

Alchian (1950) pointed out that the existence of knowledge asymmetries would result in the inevitability of mistaken decisions in an uncertain world. Later, Alchian and Demsetz (1972) attributed the existence of asymmetric information across firm employees as resulting in the problem of monitoring the contribution accruing from each employee and setting the rewards correspondingly. This led them to conclude that 'The problem of economic organization is the economical means of metering productivity and rewards' (Alchian and Demsetz, 1972, p. 783).

Combined with the bureaucratic organization of incumbent firms involved in making a decision, the asymmetry of knowledge leads to a host of agency problems, spanning incentive structures, monitoring and transaction costs. It is the existence of such agency costs, combined with asymmetric information, that not only provides an incentive for agents with new ideas to appropriate the expected value of their knowledge externally by starting new firms, but also with a propensity that varies systematically from industry to industry.

Coase (1937) and later Williamson (1975) argued that the size of an (incumbent) enterprise will be determined by answering what Coase (1937, p. 30) articulated as: 'The question always is, will it pay to bring an extra exchange transaction under the organizing authority?' In fact, Coase (1937, p. 24) pointed out that, 'Other things being equal, a firm will tend to be larger the less likely the (firm) is to make mistakes and the smaller the increase in mistakes with an increase in the transactions organized'.

Holmström (1989) and Milgrom (1988) have pointed out the existence of what they term a 'bureacratization dilemma', where 'To say that increased size

---

[3] For example, as of 1993 a proposal for simply modifying an existing product at IBM had to pass through 250 layers of decision making to gain approval ('Uberfördert und Unregierbar,' *Der Spiegel*, No. 14, 1993, p. 127).

brings increased bureaucracy is a safe generalization. To note that bureaucracy is viewed as an organizational disease is equally accurate' (Holmström, 1989, p. 320).

To minimize agency problems and the cost of monitoring, bureaucratic hierarchies develop objective rules. In addition, Kreps (1991) has argued that such bureaucratic rules promote internal uniformity and that a uniform corporate culture, in turn, promotes the reputation of the firm. These bureaucratic rules, however, make it more difficult to evaluate the efforts and activities of agents involved in activities that do not conform to such bureaucratic rules. As Holmström (1989, p. 323) points out,

> Monitoring limitations suggest that the firm seeks out activities which are more easily and objectively evaluated. Assignments will be chosen in a fashion that are conducive to more effective control. Authority and command systems work better in environments which are more predictable and can be directed with less investment information. Routine tasks are the comparative advantage of a bureaucracy and its activities can be expected to reflect that.

Williamson (1975, p. 201) has also emphasized the inherent tension between hierarchical bureaucratic organizations and the ability of incumbent organizations to appropriate the value of new knowledge for innovative activity outside of the technological trajectories associated with the core competence of that organization:

> Were it that large firms could compensate internal entrepreneurial activity in ways approximating that of the market, the large firm need experience no disadvantage in entrepreneurial respects. Violating the congruency between hierarchical position and compensation appears to generate bureaucratic strains, however, and is greatly complicated by the problem of accurately imputing causality.

This led Williamson (1975, pp. 205–206) to conclude that

> I am inclined to regard the early stage innovative disabilities of large size as serious and propose the following hypothesis: An efficient procedure by which to introduce new products is for the initial development and market testing to be performed by independent investors and small firms (perhaps new entrants) in an industry, the successful developments then to be acquired, possibly through licensing or merger, for subsequent marketing by a large multidivision enterprise...Put differently, a division of effort between the new product

innovation process on the one hand, and the management of proven resources on the other may well be efficient.

The Role of Technological Regimes

The degree to which agents and incumbent firms are confronted with knowledge asymmetries and agency problems with respect to seeking out new economic knowledge and (potential) innovative activity would not be expected to be constant across industries. This is because the underlying knowledge conditions vary from industry to industry. In some industries new economic knowledge generating innovative activity tends to be relatively routine and can be processed within the context of incumbent hierarchical bureaucracies. In other industries, however, innovations tend to come from knowledge that is not of a routine nature and therefore tends to be rejected by the hierarchical bureaucracies of incumbent corporations. Nelson and Winter (1974, 1978, 1982) described these different underlying knowledge conditions as reflecting two distinct technological regimes—the entrepreneurial and routinized technological regimes: 'An entrepreneurial regime is one that is favorable to innovative entry and unfavorable to innovative activity by established firms; a routinized regime is one in which the conditions are the other way around' (Winter, 1984, p. 297; see also Malerba, 1992; Malerba and Orsenigo, 1993).

Gort and Klepper (1982) argued that the relative innovative advantage between newly established enterprises and incumbent firms depends upon the source of information generating innovative activity. If information based on nontransferable experience in the market is an important input in generating innovative activity, then incumbent firms will tend to have the innovative advantage over new firms. This is consistent with Winter's (1984) notion of the routinized regime, where the accumulated stock of non-transferable information is the product of experience within the market—which, by definition, firms outside of the main incumbent organizations cannot possess.

By contrast, when information outside of the routines practiced by the incumbent firms is a relatively important input in generating innovative activity, newly established firms will tend to have the innovative advantage over incumbent firms. Arrow (1962), Mueller (1976) and Williamson (1975) have all emphasized that when such information created outside of the incumbent firms cannot be easily transferred to those incumbent enterprises—presumably due to the type of agency and bureaucracy problems described above—the holder of such knowledge must enter the industry by starting a new firm in order to exploit the expected value of his knowledge.

While the concept of technological regimes does not lend itself to precise measurement, the major conclusion of Acs and Audretsch (1988, 1990) and Audretsch (1991, 1995) was that the existence of these distinct regimes can be inferred by the extent to which small firms are able to innovate relative to the total amount of innovative activity in an industry. That is, when the small-firm innovation rate is high relative to the total innovation rate, the technological and knowledge conditions are more likely to reflect an entrepreneurial regime. A routinized regime is more likely to exhibit a low small-firm innovation rate relative to the total innovation rate. The existence of these two distinct technological regimes is documented in Audretsch (1995).

Table 1 indicates that the most innovative firms in the USA were among the largest corporations and that they generally had large investments in R&D. This is certainly consistent with the model of the knowledge production function. The R&D and firm size measures are from the *Business Week* sample of over 700 corporations for which R&D expenditures play an important role. A significant feature of this sample is that it includes more than 95% of the total company R&D expenditures undertaken in the USA.

As Table 2 shows, in the most innovative four-digit standard industrial classification (SIC) industries, large firms (defined as enterprises with at least 500 employees) contributed more innovations in some instances while in other industries small firms proved to be more innovative. For example, in both the electronic computing equipment and process control instruments industries, the small firms contributed most of the innovations. By contrast, in the pharmaceutical preparation industry and in aircraft the large firms were much more innovative.

Probably the best measure of innovative activity is the total innovation rate, which is defined as the total number of innovations per 1000 employees in each industry. The large-firm innovation rate is defined as the number of innovations made by firms with at least 500 employees divided by the number of employees (thousands) in large firms. The small-firm innovation rate is analogously defined as the number of innovations contributed by firms with fewer than 500 employees divided by the number of employees (thousands) in small firms.

The innovation rates, or the number of innovations per 1000 employees, have the advantage in that they measure large- and small-firm innovative activity relative to the presence of large and small firms in any given industry. That is, in making a direct comparison between large- and small-firm

TABLE 1. Most Innovative Firms

Firm	Number of Innovations	Sales (millions)	R&D expenditure (millions)	R&D/sales (%)
Hewlett Packard	55	981.0	89.5	9.1
Minnesota Mining & Mfg	40	3127.0	143.4	4.5
General Electric	36	13399.0	357.1	2.7
General Signal	29	548.0	21.2	3.9
National Semiconductor	27	235.0	20.7	8.8
Xerox	25	4054.0	192.5	4.9
Texas Instruments	24	1358.0	51.0	3.7
Pitney Bowes	22	461.0	10.5	2.3
RCA	21	4790.0	113.5	2.4
IBM	21	14437.0	945.0	5.5
Digital Equipment	21	534.0	48.5	9.1
Gould	20	773.0	23.1	3.0
Motorola	19	1312.0	98.5	7.5
Wheelabrator Frye	18	332.0	2.0	0.5
United Technologies	18	3878.0	323.7	8.3
Hoover	18	594.0	4.3	0.7
Honeywell	18	2750.0	154.2	5.9
Rockwell International	17	4943.0	31.0	0.5
Johnson & Johnson	17	2225.0	97.9	4.4
Eastman Kodak	17	4959.0	312.9	5.3
Data General	17	108.0	11.5	10.8
Exxon	16	44855.0	187.0	0.4
Du Pont	15	7222.0	335.7	4.5
Stanley Works	15	454.0	3.5	0.7
Sperry Rand	15	3041.0	153.5	5.4
Pennwalt	15	714.0	15.7	2.2
North American Philips	14	1410.0	22.5	1.5
Harris	14	479.0	21.1	4.4
General Motors	14	35725.0	1113.9	3.1
Becton Dickinson	14	455.0	17.8	3.9

———————————— *The Evolution of Industrial Structures* ————————————

TABLE 2. Number of Innovations for Large and Small Firms in the Most Innovative Industries, 1982

Industry	Total innovations	Large-firm innovations	Small-firm innovations
Electronics computing equipment	395	158	227
Process control instruments	165	68	93
Radio and TV communication equipment	157	83	72
Pharmaceutical preparations	133	120	72
Electronic components	128	54	73
Engineering and scientific instruments	126	43	83
Semiconductors	122	91	29
Plastics products	107	22	82
Photographic equipment	88	79	9
Office machinery	77	67	10
Instruments to measure electricity	77	28	47
Surgical appliances and supplies	67	54	13
Surgical and medical instruments	66	30	36
Special industry machinery	64	43	21
Industrial controls	61	15	46
Toilet preparations	59	41	18
Valves and pipe fittings	54	20	33
Electric housewares and fans	53	47	6
Measuring and controlling devices	52	3	45
Food products machinery	50	37	12

innovative activity, the absolute number of innovations contributed by large firms and small enterprises is somewhat misleading, since these measures are not standardized by the relative presence of large and small firms in each industry. Hence the innovation rates, which are compared across two-digit manufacturing sectors in Table 3, are presumably a more reliable measure of innovative intensity. While the large firms in US manufacturing introduced 2445 innovations and small firms contributed slightly fewer (1954), small-firm employment was only half as great as large-firm employment, yielding an average small-firm innovation rate of 0.309, compared with a large-firm innovation rate of 0.202.

TABLE 2. Continued

Industry	Total innovations	Large-firm innovations	Small-firm innovations
Motors and generators	49	39	10
Plastic materials and resins	45	30	15
Industrial inorganic chemicals	40	32	8
Radio and TV receiving sets	40	35	4
Hand and edge tools	39	27	11
Fabricated platework	38	29	9
Fabricated metal products	35	12	17
Pumps and pumping equipment	34	18	16
Optical instruments and lenses	34	12	21
Polishes and sanitation goods	33	13	19
Industrial trucks and tractors	33	13	20
Medicinals and botanicals	32	27	5
Aircraft	32	31	1
Environmental controls	32	22	10

Large and small-firm innovations do not always sum to total innovations because several innovations could not be classified according to firm size.

In a series of studies, Acs and Audretsch (1988, 1990) and Audretsch and Feldman (1996) found that market concentration negatively influences not only the total amount of innovative activity but also the relative innovative advantage of large and small enterprises, that is the technological regime underlying the particular industry. Whether an industry can be better characterized by the routinized technological regime or the entrepreneurial technological regime is shaped by: (i) the degree of capital intensity; (ii) the extent to which an industry is concentrated; (iii) the total amount of innovative activity in the industry; and (iv) the extent to which an industry is composed of small firms.

In particular, the routinized technological regime, where the large incumbent firms tend to have the relative innovative advantage, tends to be characteristic of industries that are capital-intensive, advertising-intensive, concentrated and highly unionized. By contrast, the entrepreneurial technological regime tends to be characteristic of industries that are highly innovative and composed predominantly of large firms.

The Evolution of Industrial Structures

TABLE 3. Innovation rates for Large and Small Firms, by Two-Digit SIC Sector, 1982[a]

Sector	Total innovations	Large-firm innovations	Small-firm innovations
Food	0.2119 (0.1741)	0.2555 (0.3120)	0.1361[b] (0.1905)
Textiles	0.0740 (0.0612)	0.0295 (0.0646)	0.1669[b] (0.1723)
Apparel	0.1253 (0.1553)	0.0639 (0.1222)	0.1439 (0.2076)
Lumber	0.1400 (0.2179)	0.0506 (0.0680)	0.1415 (0.2662)
Furniture	0.3053 (0.2917)	0.2412 (0.3759)	0.2592 (0.2243)
Paper	0.1616 (0.1651)	0.1931 (0.2821)	0.1214 (0.2691)
Printing	0.0426 (0.0350)	0.0468 (0.0452)	0.0313 (0.0552)
Chemicals	0.7592 (0.5945)	0.6272 (0.6297)	1.3547[b] (1.5641)
Petroleum	0.3386 (0.3797)	0.0476 (0.0824)	0.6173 (0.6591)
Rubber	0.1204 (0.0787)	2.1814 (4.1868)	0.1129 (0.1779)
Leather	0.1356 (0.1487)	0.0053 (0.0106)	0.1793[b] (0.1695)
Stone, clay and glass	0.2130 (0.1640)	0.1625 (0.2116)	0.2696 (0.1979)
Primary metals	0.1586 (0.2905)	0.1624 (0.3394)	0.3336 (0.8319)
Fabricated metal products	0.3224 (0.3109)	0.2878 (0.3357)	0.3619 (0.3862)
Machinery (non-electrical)	0.6039 (0.6728)	0.4860 (0.5673)	1.1491[b] (1.7965)
Electronics	0.3713 (0.3510)	0.2719 (0.3263)	0.7948[b] (0.7912)
Transportation equipment	0.1250 (0.1289)	0.1182 (0.1868)	0.1911 (0.3349)
Instruments	1.3586 (0.9939)	0.7442 (0.5367)	2.9987[b] (2.5253)

[a]Innovation rates are defined as the number of innovations divided by employment (thousands of employees). Standard deviations are listed in parentheses.

[b]The difference between the large and small firm innovation rates is statistically significant at the 90% level of confidence.

4. *Entry*

The Traditional View

Coase (1937) was awarded a Nobel Prize for explaining why a firm should exist. But why should more than one firm exist in an industry?[4] One answer is

[4] Coase (1937, p. 23) himself asked: 'A pertinent question to ask would appear to be (quite apart from the monopoly considerations raised by Professor Knight), why, if by organizing one can eliminate certain costs and in fact reduce the cost of production, are there any market transactions at all? Why is not all production carried on by one big firm?'

provided by the traditional economics literature focusing on industrial organization. An excess level of profitability induces entry into the industry. And this is why the entry of new firms is interesting and important—because the new firms provide an equilibrating function in the market, in that the levels of price and profit are restored to competitive levels.

In this traditional theory, outputs and inputs in an industry are assumed to be homogeneous. That is, the entry of new firms is about business as usual—it is just that with the new entrant there is more of it. For example, Geroski (1991a, p. 65) assumes that

> If we think of entry as an error-correction mechanism which is attracted by and serves to bid away excess profits, it is natural to suppose that entry will occur whenever profits differ from their long-run levels. Given this maintained hypothesis, observations of actual entry rates and current (or expected post-entry) profits can be used to make inferences about the unobservable of interest—long-run profits. In particular, entry in an industry is hypothesized to occur whenever expected post-entry profits exceed the level of profits protected in the long run.

This leads to the traditional model of entry:

$$E_{jt} = \lambda(P_{jt} - b_j) + m_{jt} \qquad (2)$$

where E_{jt} represents entry in industry j at time t, P_{jt} represents expected post-entry profits, b_j represents the level of profits protected in the long run by entry barriers b_j and m_{jt} represents stochastic disturbance. In this standard model of entry, which theoretically dates back to Bain (1956) and empirically to Orr (1974), λ measures the speed with which entrants respond to excess profits, and has the dimension of a flow per unit of time. The level of profits which can be sustained in perpetuity without attracting entry is b_j; it serves as a limit to what Geroski (1991a, pp. 65–66) terms 'limits profits' and is a natural measure of the height of barriers to entry.

The point to be emphasized here is that this traditional model assumes that the impact that the new entrant has on the market, and on equilibrium price and industry profits, is through the additional amount of output that is contributed. The fundamental motivation for entering an industry, either through a new firm or through diversified entry, as reflected in equation (2), is that profits exceed their long-run equilibrium level, even after accounting for structural barriers to entry.

In fact, little consensus has emerged in the growing plethora of studies trying to link industry profitability, growth and structural barriers to entry rates, as implied by equation (2). The level of industry profitability has been found to have only a weak and sometimes ambiguous impact on entry (reviewed in Geroski, 1995). A positive relationship has generally been found to exist between industry growth rates and entry rates. Presumably higher rates of growth enable incumbent enterprises to raise prices, thereby inducing more entry, or else raise expectations about future profits. For example, in five of the six countries (Germany, Norway, Portugal, Belgium and Korea) studied by Geroski and Schwalbach (1991), entry rates were found to be positively influenced by industry growth rates. Only for the UK did a negative relationship emerge between entry rates and industry growth.

One of the most startling results that has emerged in empirical studies is that entry by firms into an industry is apparently not substantially deterred or even deterred at all in capital-intensive industries in which scale economies play an important role (Acs and Audretsch, 1990, Ch. 5; Austin and Rosenbaum, 1990; Siegfried and Evans, 1992; Audretsch, 1995).

Empirical evidence in support of the traditional model represented by equation (2) is ambiguous at best, leading Geroski (1991b, p. 282) to conclude

> Right from the start, scholars have had some trouble in reconciling the stories told about entry in standard textbooks with the substance of what they have found in their data. Very few have emerged from their work feeling that they have answered half as many questions as they have raised, much less that they have answered most of the interesting ones.

Perhaps one reason for this trouble is the inherently static model used to capture an inherently dynamic process. Neumann (1993, pp. 593–594) criticized this traditional model of entry, as found in the individual country studies of Geroski and Schwalbach (1991), because they

> ...are predicated on the adoption of a basically static framework. It is assumed that startups enter a given market where they are facing incumbents which naturally try to fend off entry. Since the impact of entry on the performance of incumbents seems to be only slight, the question arises whether the costs of entry are worthwhile, given the high rate of exit associated with entry. Geroski appears to be rather skeptical about that. I submit that adopting a static framework is misleading...In fact, generally, an entrant can only hope to succeed if he employs either a new technology or offers a new product, or both. Just imitating incumbents is almost certainly doomed to failure. If the process of entry is looked upon from this perspective the high correlation between gross entry and exit reflects the inherent risks of innovating activities...Obviously it is rather difficult to break loose from the

inherited mode of reasoning within the static framework. It is not without merit, to be sure, but it needs to be enlarged by putting it into a dynamic setting.

The Evolutionary View

The model proposed by Audretsch (1995) refocuses the unit of observation away from firms deciding whether to increase their output from a level of zero to some positive amount in a new industry, to individual agents in possession of new knowledge that, due to uncertainty, may or may not have some positive economic value. It is the uncertainty inherent in new economic knowledge, combined with asymmetries between the agent possessing that knowledge and the decision making vertical hierarchy of the incumbent organization with respect to its expected value, that potentially leads to a gap between the valuation of that knowledge and its actual worth. How the economic agent chooses to appropriate the value of his knowledge—that is, either within an incumbent firm or by starting or joining a new enterprise—will be shaped by the knowledge conditions underlying the industry.

As Knight (1921, p. 199) pointed out, uncertainty is the result of possessing only partial or bounded knowledge: 'The essence of the situation is action according to opinion, of greater or less foundation and value, neither entire ignorance nor complete and perfect information, but partial knowledge'. In fact, it is the fundamental condition of incomplete knowledge that led Arrow (1974, 1985) to focus on the firm as an organization whose main distinction is processing information. As March and Simon (1993, p. 299) argued, 'Organizations process and channel information'. But as Arrow (1985, p. 303) emphasized,

> The elements of a firm are *agents* among whom both decision making and knowledge dispersed...Each agent observes a random variable, sometimes termed a *signal*...Each agent has a set of actions from which choice is to be made...We may call the assignment of signals to agents the *information structure* and the choice of decision rules the *decision information structure structure*.

Arrow goes on to note that the cost of acquiring that signal or information is nontrivial.

How will economic agents, and ultimately hierarchical organizations, respond when confronted by incomplete knowledge? Knight's (1921, p. 241) answer was 'differently', because agents differ 'in their capacity by perception and inference to form correct judgments as to the future course of events in the environment'. This is to say that different economic agents confronted by the same signal in Arrow's terms (1985), or simply incomplete information in Knight's terms, will respond differently because they have a different set of experiences from which to evaluate that incomplete information.

March and Simon (1993) argue that one of the main functions of an organization is to filter both the signal, or information, and the response in a way that is not only efficient but also unique to that organization. They do this by shaping the goals and loyalties of those agents participating in the organization; for example, 'They create shared stories—an organization ethos that includes common beliefs and standard practices' (March and Simon, 1993, p. 300). And they offer incentives for conduct that is consistent with the organizational goals.

Like Nelson and Winter (1982), March and Simon (1993, p. 309) emphasize the role of established routines in the functioning of organizations:

> Organizations turn their own experience as well as the experience and knowledge of others into rules that are maintained and implemented despite turnover in personnel and without necessary comprehension of their bases. As a result, the processes for generating, changing, evoking, and forgetting rules become essential in analyzing and understanding organizations.

As long as new information is consistent with the routines established in an organization, it will be processed by economic agents and a decision-making hierarchy in a manner that is familiar. New information under the routinized regime is familiar turf for organizations. A more fundamental problem arises, however, when the nature of that new information is such that it can no longer be processed by the familiar routines. Under these circumstances the organizational routines for searching out new relevant information and making (correct) decisions on the basis of that information break down. It is under such knowledge conditions that divergences tend to arise not only among economic agents in evaluating that information but also between agents and organizational hierarchies.

Thus, when the underlying knowledge conditions are better characterized by the routinized technological regime, there is likely to be relatively little divergence in the evaluation of the expected value of a (potential) innovation between the inventor and the decision-making bureaucracy of the firm. Under the routinized regime a great incentive for agents to start their own firms will not exist, at least not for the reason of doing something differently. When the underlying knowledge conditions more closely adhere to the entrepreneurial technological regime, however, a divergence in beliefs between the agent and the principal regarding the expected value of a (potential) innovation is more likely to emerge. Therefore, it is under the entrepreneurial regime that the startup of new firms is likely to play a more important role, presumably as a result of the motivation to appropriate the value of economic knowledge; due to agency problems, this knowledge cannot be easily and costlessly transferred to the incumbent enterprise.

Under the routinized technological regime the agent will tend to appropriate the value of his new ideas within the boundaries of incumbent firms. Thus, the propensity for new firms to be started should be relatively low in industries characterized by the routinized technological regime. By contrast, under the entrepreneurial regime the agent will tend to appropriate the value of his new ideas outside of the boundaries of incumbent firms by starting a new enterprise. Thus, the propensity for new firms to enter should be relatively high in industries characterized by the entrepreneurial regime.

This model analyzing the decision of how best to appropriate the value of new economic knowledge confronting an individual economic agent seems useful when considering the actual decision to start a new firm taken by entrepreneurs. For example, Chester Carlsson started Xerox after his proposal to produce a (new) copy machine was rejected by Kodak. Kodak based its decision on the premise that the new copy machine would not earn very much money, and in any case, Kodak was in a different line of business— photography. It is perhaps no small irony that this same entrepreneurial startup, Xerox, decades later turned down a proposal from Steven Jobs to produce and market a personal computer, because they did not think that it would sell, and, in any case, they were in a different line of business—copy machines (Carrol, 1993a). After 17 other companies turned down Jobs for virtually identical reasons, including IBM and Hewlett Packard, Jobs resorted to starting his own company, Apple Computers.

Similarly, IBM turned down an offer from Bill Gates, 'the chance to buy ten percent of Microsoft for a song in 1986, a missed opportunity that would cost $3 billion today' ('System Error,' *The Economist*, 18 September 1993, p. 99). IBM reached its decision on the grounds that 'neither Gates nor any of his band of thirty some employees had anything approaching the credentials or personal characteristics required to work at IBM' (Carrol, 1993b).

Divergences in beliefs with respect to the value of a new idea need not be restricted to what is formally known as a product or even a process innovation. Rather, the fact that economic agents choose to start a new firm due to divergences in the expected value of an idea applies to the sphere of managerial style and organization as well. One of the most vivid examples

―――――――――――― *The Evolution of Industrial Structures* ――――――――

involves Bob Noyce, who founded Intel. Noyce had been employed by Fairchild Semiconductor, which is credited with being the pioneering semiconductor firm. In 1957 Noyce and seven other engineers quit en masse from Schockley Semiconductor to form Fairchild Semiconductor, an enterprise that in turn is considered the start of what is today known as Silicon Valley. Although Fairchild Semiconductor had 'possibly the most potent management and technical team ever assembled' (Gilder, 1989, p. 89),

> Noyce couldn't get Fairchild's eastern owners to accept the idea that stock options should be part of compensation for all employees, not just for management. He wanted to tie everyone, from janitors to bosses, into the overall success of the company...This management style still sets the standard for every computer, software, and semiconductor company in the Valley today...Every CEO still wants to think tkat the place is run the way Bob Noyce would have run it. (Cringley, 1993, p. 39)

That is, Noyce's vision of a firm excluded the dress codes, reserved parking places, closed offices and executive dining rooms, along with the other trappings of status that were standard in virtually every hierarchical and bureaucratic US corporation. But when he tried to impress this vision upon the owners of Fairchild Semiconductor, he was flatly rejected. The formation of Intel in 1968 was the ultimate result of the divergence in beliefs about how to organize and manage the firm.

The key development at Intel was the microprocessor. When long-time IBM employee Ted Hoff approached IBM and later DEC with his new microprocessor in the late 1960s, 'IBM and DEC decided there was no market. They could not imagine why anyone would need or want a small computer; if people wanted touse a computer, they could hook into time-sharing systems' (Paifreman and Swade, 1991, p. 108).

While studies have generally produced considerable ambiguity concerning the impact of scale economies and other measures traditionally thought to represent a barrier to entry, Audretsch (1995) found conclusive evidence linking the technological regime to startup activity. New-firm startup activity tends to be substantially more prevalent under the entrepreneurial regime, or where small enterprises account for the bulk of the innovative activity, than under the routinized regime, or where the large incumbent enterprises account for most of the innovative activity. These findings are consistent with the view that differences in beliefs about the expected value of new ideas are not constant across industries but rather depend on the knowledge conditions inherent in the underlying technological regime.

5. *Survival and Growth*

Theory

The theory proposed by Audretsch (1995) suggests that divergances in the expected value regarding new knowledge will, under certain conditions, lead an agent to exercise what Hirschman (1970) termed *exit* rather than *voice*, and depart from an incumbent enterprise to launch a new firm. But who is right, the departing agents or those agents remaining in the organizational decision-making hierarchy who, by assigning the new idea a relatively low value, have effectively driven the agent with the potential innovation away?

Ex post the answer may not be too difficult. But given the uncertainty inherent in new knowledge, the answer is anything but trivial *a priori*.

Thus, when a new firm is launched, its prospects are shrouded in uncertainty. If the new firm is built around a new idea, i.e. potential innovation, it is uncertain whether there is sufficient demand for the new idea or if some competitor will have the same or even a superior idea. Even if the new firm is formed to be an exact replica of a successful incumbent enterprise, it is uncertain whether sufficient demand for a new clone, or even for the existing incumbent, will prevail in the future. Tastes can change, and new ideas emerging from other firms will certainly influence those tastes.

Finally, an additional layer of uncertainty pervades a new enterprise: it is not known how competent the new firm really is, in terms of management, organization and workforce. At least incumbent enterprises know something about their underlying competencies from past experience. Which is to say that a new enterprise is burdened with uncertainty as to whether it can produce and market the intended product as well as sell it. In both cases the degree of uneertainty will typically exceed that confronting incumbent enterprises.

This initial condition of not just uncertainty but greater degree of uncertainty *vis-à-vis* incumbent enterprises in the industry is captured in the theory of firm selection and industry evolution proposed by Jovanovic (1982). Jovanovic presented a model in which the new firms, which he termed *entrepreneurs*, face costs that are not only random but also differ across firms. A central feature of the model is that a new firm does not know what its cost function is—that is, its relative efficiency—but rather discovers this through the process of learning from its actual post-entry performance. In particular, Jovanovic (1982) assumed that entrepreneurs are unsure about their ability to manage a new-firm startup and therefore their prospects for success (Jovanovic, 1994). Although entrepreneurs may launch a new firm based on

──────────────── *The Evolution of Industrial Structures* ────────────────

a vague sense of expected post-entry performance, they only discover their true ability—in terms of managerial competence and of having based the firm on an idea that is viable on the market—once their business is established. Those entrepreneurs who discover that their ability exceeds their expectations expand the scale of their business, whereas those discovering that their post-entry performance is less than commensurate with their expectations will contract the scale of output and possibly exit from the industry. Thus, Jovanovic's model is a theory of noisy selection, where efficient firms grow and survive and inefficient firms decline and fail.

The role of learning in the selection process has been the subject of considerable debate. On the one hand there is what has been referred to as the *Larackian* assumption that learning refers to adaptations made by the new enterprise. In this sense, those new firms that are the most flexible and adaptable will be the most successful in adjusting to whatever the demands of the market are. As Nelson and Winter (1982, p. 11) pointed out, 'Many kinds of organizations commit resources to learning; organizations seek to copy the forms of their most successful competitors'. In fact, A. Pakes and R. Ericson (unpublished data) extended Jovanovic's original theory by incorporating strategies that entrepreneurs can pursue to accelerate the learning process, such as investing in knowledge-creation activities like R&D.

On the other hand there is the interpretation that the role of learning is restricted to discovering if the firm has the 'right stuff' in terms of the goods it is producing as well as the way they are being produced. Under this interpretation the new enterprise is not necessarily able to adapt or adjust to market conditions, but receives information based on its market performance with respect to its 'fitness' in terms of meeting demand most efficiently *vis-à-vis* rivals. The theory of organizational ecology proposed by Hannan and Freeman (1989) most pointedly adheres to the notion that 'We assume that individual organizations are characterized by relative inertia in structure'. That is, firms learn not in the sense that they adjust their actions as reflected by their fundamental identity and purpose but in the sense of their perception. What is then learned is whether or not the firm has the right stuff, but not how to change that stuff.

The theory of firm selection is particularly appealing in view of the rather startling size of most new firms. For example, the mean size of more than 11,000 new-firm startups in the manufacturing sector in the USA was found to be fewer than eight workers per firm (Audretsch, 1995).[5] While the minimum efficient scale (MES) varies substantially across industries, and even

─────────────────

[5] A similar startup size for new manufacturing firms was found by Dunne *et al.* (1988, 1989) for the USA; Mata (1993) and Mata and Portugal (1994) for Portugal; and Wagner (1994a,b) for Germany.

to some degree across various product classes within any given industry, the observed size of most new firms is sufficiently small to ensure that the bulk of new firms will be operating at a suboptimal scale of output. Why would an entrepreneur start a new firm that would immediately be confronted by scale disadvantages?

An implication of the theory of firm selection is that new firms may begin at a small, even suboptimal, scale of output and then, if merited by subsequent performance, expand. Those new firms that are successful will grow, whereas those that are not successful will remain small and may ultimately be forced to exit from the industry if they are operating at a suboptimal scale of output.

Subsequent to entering an industry, a firm must decide whether to maintain its output, expand, contract or exit. Two different strands of literature have identified several major influences shaping the decision to exit an industry. The first and most obvious suggests that the probability of a business exiting will tend to increase as the gap between its level of output and the MES level of output increases.[6] The second strand of literature points to the role that the technological environment plays in shaping the decision to exit. As Dosi (1982, 1988) and Arrow (1962) have argued, an environment characterized by more frequent innovation may also be associated with a greater amount of uncertainty regarding not only the technical nature of the product but also the demand for that product. As technological uncertainty increases, particularly under the entrepreneurial regime, the likelihood that the business will be able to produce a viable product and ultimately be able to survive decreases.

An important implication of the dynamic process of firm selection and industry evolution is that new firms are more likely to be operating at a suboptimal scale of output if the underlying technological conditions are such that there is a greater chance of making an innovation; that is, under the entrepreneurial regime. If new firms successfully learn and adapt, or are just plain lucky, they grow into viably sized enterprises. If not, they stagnate and may ultimately exit from the industry. This suggests that entry and the startup of new firms may not be greatly deterred in the presence of scale economies. As long as entrepreneurs perceive that there is some prospect for growth and ultimately survival, such entry will occur. Thus, in industries where the MES is high, it follows from the observed general small size of new-firm startups that the growth rate of the surviving firms would presumably be relatively high.

──────────

[6] For example, Weiss (1976, p. 126) argues that, 'In purely competitive long-run equilibrium, no suboptimal capacity should exist at all'.

──────────────── 72 ────────────────

At the same time, those new firms not able to grow and attain the MES level of output would presumably be forced to exit from the industry, resulting in a relatively low likelihood of survival. In industries characterized by a low MES, neither the need for growth nor the consequences of its absence are as severe, so that relatively lower growth rates but higher survival rates would be expected. Similarly, in industries where the probability of innovating is greater, more entrepreneurs may actually take a chance that they will succeed by growing into a viably sized enterprise. In such industries one would expect the growth of successful enterprises to be greater, but the likelihood of survival to be correspondingly lower.

Summarizing these arguments, the theory of firm selection and industry evolution leads to the following predictions, or hypotheses, concerning the likelihood of survival and growth rates of those surviving new firms:

1. The likelihood of new-firm survival should be lower in industries exhibiting greater scale economies. The growth rates observed in surviving firms in high MES industries should be greater.
2. The likelihood of firm survival should be higher for larger firms but growth rates should be lower.
3. The likelihood of firm survival should be lower under the entrepreneurial technological regime but the growth rates of surviving firms should be greater.
4. Both firm growth and the likelihood of survival should be greater in high-growth industries.

Empirical Evidence

Geroski (1995) points out that one of the major conclusions from studies about entry is that the process of entry does not end with entry itself. Rather, it is what happens to new firms subsequent to entering that sheds considerable light on industry dynamics. The early studies (Mansfield, 1962; Hall, 1987; Dunne et al., 1988, 1989; Audretsch, 1991) established not only that the likelihood of a new entrant surviving is quite low, but that the likelihood of survival is positively related to firm size and age. More recently, a wave of studies have confirmed these findings for diverse countries, including Portugal (Mata, 1994; Mata and Portugal, 1994), Germany (Wagner, 1994) and Canada (Baldwin and Gorecki, 1991; Baldwin, 1995; Baldwin and Rafiquzzaman, 1995).

Audretsch (1991), Mata (1994), Mata and Portugal (1994) and Audretsch and Mahmood (1995) shifted the relevant question away from 'Why does the likelihood of survival vary systematically across firms?' to 'Why does the propensity for firms to survive vary systematically across industries?' The answer to this question suggests that what had previously been considered to pose a barrier to entry may, in fact, constitute not an entry barrier but rather a barrier to survival.

What has become known as Gibrat's Law, or the assumption that growth rates are invariant to firm size, has been subject to numerous empirical tests. Studies linking firm size and age to growth have also produced a number of stylized facts (Wagner, 1992). For small and new firms there is substantial evidence suggesting that growth is negatively related to firm size and age (Hall, 1987; Wagner, 1992, 1994a,b; Mata, 1993; Audretsch, 1995). However, for larger firms, particularly those having attained the MES level of output, the evidence suggests that firm growth is unrelated to size and age.

An important finding of Audretsch (1991, 1995) and Audretsch and Mahmood (1995) is that although entry may still occur in industries characterized by a high degree of scale economies, the likelihood of survival is considerably less. People will start new firms in an attempt to appropriate the expected value of their new ideas, or potential innovations, particularly under the entrepreneurial regime. As entrepreneurs gain experience in the market they learn in at least two ways. First, they discover whether they possess the right stuff in terms of producing goods and offering services for which sufficient demand exists, as well as whether they can produce that good more efficiently than their rivals. Second, they learn whether they can adapt to market conditions as well as to strategies engaged in by rival firms. In terms of the first type of learning, entrepreneurs who discover that they have a viable firm will tend to expand and ultimately survive. But what about those who discover that they are either not efficient or not offering a product for which there is a viable demand? The answer is that it depends—on the extent of scale economies as well as on conditions of demand. The consequences of not being able to grow will depend, to a large degree, on the extent of scale economies. Thus, in markets with only negligible scale economies, firms have a considerably greater likelihood of survival. However, where scale economies play an important role the consequences of not growing are substantially more severe, as evidenced by a lower likelihood of survival.

6. *Compensating Factor Differentials*

How are the new firms, many of which operate at a suboptimal scale of output, able to exist? The answer, according to the studies on post-entry survival and growth, is that they cannot—at least not indefinitely. Rather, they must grow to at least approach the MES level of output. An alternative answer is provided by recent studies focusing on the relationship between firm size, age and employee compensation (Audretsch, 1995). By deploying a strategy of compensating factor differentials, where factor inputs are both deployed and remunerated differently than they are by the larger incumbent enterprises, suboptimal scale enterprises are to some extent able to offset their size-related cost disadvantages.

Just as it has been found that the gap between the MES and firm size lowers the likelihood of survival, there is evidence suggesting that factors of production, and in particular labor, tend to be used more intensively (that is, in terms of hours worked) and remunerated at lower levels (in terms of employee compensation). Taken together, the empirical evidence on survival and growth combined with that on wages and firm size suggests how it is that small, suboptimal scale enterprises are able to exist in the short run. In the initial period of learning, during which time the entrepreneur discovers whether he has the right stuff and whether he is able to adapt to market conditions, new firms are apparently able to reduce the cost of production in order to compensate for their small scale of production.

In the current debate on the relationship between employment and wages it is typically argued that the existence of small firms which are suboptimal within the organization of an industry represents a loss in economic efficiency. This argument is based on a static analysis; however, when viewed through a dynamic lens a different conclusion emerges. One of the most striking results is the finding of a positive impact of firm age on productivity and employee compensation, even after controlling for the size of the firm. Given the strongly confirmed stylized fact linking both firm size and age to a negative rate of growth (that is, the smaller and younger a firm, the faster it will grow but the lower is its likelihood of survival), this new finding linking firm age to employee compensation and productivity suggests that not only will some of the small and suboptimal firms of today become the large and optimal firms of tomorrow, but there is at least a tendency for the low productivity and wage of today to become the high productivity and wage of tomorrow.

7. *Industrial Organization through an Evolutionary Lens*

What emerges from the new theories and empirical evidence on innovation and industry evolution is that markets are in motion, with a lot of firms entering and a lot of firms exiting out of the industry (Dosi *et al.*, 1995; Malerba and Orsenigo, 1996). But is this motion horizontal, in that the bulk of firms exiting comprise firms that had entered relatively recently, or vertical, in that a significant share of the exiting firms had been established incumbents that were displaced by younger firms? In trying to shed some light on this question, Audretsch (1995) proposed two different models of the evolutionary process of industries over time. Some industries can be best characterized by the model of the conical revolving door, where new businesses enter but where there is a high propensity to subsequently exit from the market. Other industries may be better characterized by the metaphor of the forest, where incumbent establishments are displaced by new entrants. Which view is more applicable apparently depends on three major factors—the underlying technological conditions, scale economies and demand. Where scale economies play an important role, the model of the revolving door seems to be more applicable. Despite the rather startling result discussed above that the startup and entry of new businesses is apparently not deterred by the presence of high scale economies, a process of firm selection analogous to a revolving door ensures that only those establishments successful enough to grow will be able to survive beyond a few years. Thus the bulk of new entrants that are not so successful ultimately exit within a few years subsequent to entry.

There is at least some evidence also suggesting that the underlying technological regime influences the process of firm selection and therefore the type of firm with a higher propensity to exit. Under the entrepreneurial regime new entrants have a greater likelihood of making an innovation. Thus, they are less likely to decide to exit from the industry, even in the face of negative profits. By contrast, under the routinized regime the incumbent businesses tend to have the innovative advantage, so that a higher portion of exiting businesses tend to be new entrants. Thus, the model of the revolving door is more applicable under technological conditions consistent with the routinized regime, and the metaphor of the forest, where the new entrants displace the incumbents, is more applicable to the entrepreneurial regime. Why is the general shape of the firm-size distribution not only strikingly similar across virtually every industry—that is, skewed with only a few large enterprises and numerous small ones—but has persisted with tenacity not only across developed countries but even over a long period of time? The dynamic view of the process of industry evolution is that new firms typically start at a very small scale of output. They are motivated by the desire to appropriate the expected value of new economic knowledge. But, depending upon the extent of scale economies in the industry, the firm may not be able to remain viable indefinitely at its startup size. Rather, if scale economies are anything other than negligible, the new firm is likely to have to grow to survive. The temporary survival of new firms is presumably supported through the deployment of a strategy of compensating factor differentials that enables the firm to discover whether or not it has a viable product.

The empirical evidence supports such a dynamic view of the role of new firms in manufacturing, because the post-entry growth of firms that survive tends to be spurred by the extent to which there is a gap between the MES level of output and the size of the firm. However, the likelihood of any particular new firm surviving tends to decrease as this gap increases. Such new suboptimal scale firms are apparently engaged in the selection process. Only those firms offering a viable product that can be produced efficiently will grow and ultimately approach or attain the MES level of output. The remainder will stagnate and, depending upon the severity of the other selection mechanism—the extent of scale economies—may ultimately be forced to exit out of the industry. Thus, the persistence of an asymmetric firm-size distribution biased towards small-scale enterprise reflects the continuing process of the entry of new firms into industries and not necessarily the permanence of such small and suboptimal enterprises in the long run. Although the skewed size distribution of firms persists with remarkable stability over long periods of time, a constant set of small- and suboptimal-scale firms does not appear to be responsible for this skewed distribution.

8. *Conclusions*

Each of the topics addressed in this paper has provided a snapshot of an important aspect of the process of industry evolution, and particularly the role that innovation plays in shaping that process. These dynamic aspects involve the startup of new firms, survival, growth, the development of a strategy of compensating factor differentials and the extent to which new firms displace incumbent enterprises.

The fundamental theory common to all of these themes is that the dynamic process through which industries evolve is shaped, at least to some extent, by three major factors—technology, scale economies and demand. There is, in fact, substantial empirical evidence supporting the notion of distinct technological regimes. It can be inferred from this evidence that under the routinized regime there tends to be convergence regarding the expected value of new ideas, or potential innovations, across agents and decision-making hierarchies within the industry. By contrast, under the entrepreneurial regime there tends to be much more divergence regarding the expected value of new ideas, or potential innovations, across agents. It is differences in the extent to which new economic knowledge tends to converge or diverge across agents that, to a considerable degree, shapes the patterns of firm demography observed across industries.

If each economic agent were identical, such divergences in beliefs would not arise. The greater the degree of heterogeneity among agents, the greater the tendency for beliefs in evaluating uncertain information to converge. But individuals are not homogeneous. Rather, agents have varied personal characteristics and different experiences that shape the lens through which each agent evaluates where to get new information and how to assess it. That is, reasonable people confronted by the same information may evaluate it very differently, not just because they have different abilities but also because each has had a different set of life experiences which shape the decision-making process.

Thus, to some extent, the phenomenon of a new firm being established represents not just imperfect information but also a diverse population of economic agents. That is, diversity in the population of economic agents may ultimately lead to diversity in the types of firms populating the industrial structure. To some extent, these diverse firms represent experiments based on differing visions about what should be produced and how it should be produced.

Diversity, however, may also be the source of the high degree of turbulence that is apparently characteristic of at least the USA, if not of all leading developed nations.[7] That is, industrial markets are characterized by a high degree of churning. It should, however, be emphasized that there is to date no evidence that the industrial structure has actually become more turbulent over time. Without undertaking painstaking statistical research to compare the degree to which the structure of industries characterized by turbulence has changed over long periods of time, such conjectures remain just that—conjectures. After all, the observation that the structure of industries, at least in the USA, tends to be remarkably fluid and turbulent is not new. Before the country was even half a century old, Alexis de Tocqueville in 1835 reported, 'What astonishes me in the United States is not so much the marvelous grandeur of some undertakings as the innumerable multitude of small ones' (quoted from *Business Week*, Bonus Issue, 1993, p. 12).

The new learning on technological regimes and industry demography suggests that, with respect to the dynamic patterns of firms over time, there is, in fact, no tendency that can be generalized. Rather, the dynamic nature in which firms and industries tend to evolve over time varies substantially from industry to industry. And it is apparently differences in the knowledge conditions and

---

[7] For a direct analysis of the degree of turbulence in industrial markets, see Acs and Audretsch (1990, 1993) for the USA; Invernizzi and Revelli (1993) for Italy; and Beesley and Hamilton (1984) for Great Britain.

technology underlying the specific industry (that is, the nature of innovative activity) that account for variations in industry evolution across markets.

Acknowledgements

An earlier version of this paper was presented at the July 1994 IIASA workshop on Technological Regimes, Industrial, Demography and the Evolution of Industrial Structures, Laxenburg, Austria. I am grateful to the participants for their helpful comments and the suggestions of an anonymous referee, and in particular John Baldwin, Giovanni Dosi, Steven Klepper, Daniel Levinthal, Franco Malerba, Robert H. McGuckin, Dick Nelson, Luigi Orsenigo and Sid Winter. Any omissions or errors remain my responsibility.

References

Acs, Z. J. and D. B. Audretsch (1988), 'Innovation in Large and Small Firms: An Empirical Analysis,' *American Economic Review*, 78, 678–690.

Acs, Z. J. and D. B. Audretsch (1990), *Innovation and Small Firms.* MIT Press: Cambridge, MA.

Acs, Z. J. and D. B. Audretsch (1993), *Small Firms and Entrepreneurship: An International Comparison.* Cambridge University Press: Cambridge.

Alchian, A. (1950), 'Uncertainty, Evolution, and Economic Theory,' *Journal of Political Economy*, 58, 211–221.

Alchian, A. and H. Demsetz (1972), 'Production, Information Costs, and Economic Organization,' *American Economic Review*, 62, 777–795.

Arrow, K. J. (1962), 'Economic Welfare and the Allocation of Resources for Invention,' in R. R. Nelson (ed.), *The Rate and Direction of Inventive Activity.* Princeton University Press: Princeton, NJ, pp. 609–625.

Arrow, K. J. (1983), 'Innovation in Large and Small Firms,' in J. Ronen (ed.), *Entrepreneurship.* Lexington Books: Lexington, MA.

Audretsch, D. B. (1995), *Innovation and Industry Evolution.* MIT Press: Cambridge, MA.

Audretsch, D. B. (1991), 'New Firm Survival and the Technological Regime,' *Review of Economics and Statistics*, 73, 441–450.

Audretsch, D. B. and M. Feldman (1996), 'R&D Spillovers and the Geography of Innovation and Production,' *Americal Economic Review*, 86, 630–640.

Audretsch, D. B. and P. E. Stephan (1996), 'Company–Scientist Locational Links: The Case of Biotechnology,' *American Economic Review*, 86, 641–642.

Audretsch, D. B. and T. Mahmood (1995), 'New-Firm Survival: New Results Using a Hazard Function,' *Review of Economics and Statistics*, 77, 97–103.

Austin, J. S. and D. I. Rosenbaum (1990), 'The Determinants of Entry and Exit Rates into U.S. Manufacturing Industries,' *Review of Industrial Organization*, 5, 211–223.

Bain, J. (1956), *Barriers to New Competition.* Harvard University Press: Cambridge, MA.

Baldwin, J. R. (1995), *The Dynamics of Industrial Competition.* Cambridge University Press: Cambridge.

Baldwin, J. R. and M. Rafiquzzaman (1995), 'Selection versus Evolutionary Adaptation: Learning and Post-Entry Performance,' *International Journal of Industrial Organization*, 13, 501–522.

———————————— *The Evolution of Industrial Structures* ————————————

Baldwin, W. L. and J. T. Scott (1987), *Market Structure and Technological Change*. Harwood Academic Publishers: New York.

Beesley, M. E. and R. T. Hamilton (1984), 'Small Firms' Seedbed Role and the Concept of Turbulence,' *Journal of Industrial Economics*, 33, 217–232.

Carrol, P. (1993a), *Big Blues: The Unmaking of IBM*. Crown Publishers: New York.

Carrol, P. (1993b), 'Die Offene Sehlacht,' *Die Zeit*, No. 9, 24 September, p. 18.

Coase, R. H. (1937), 'The Nature of the Firm,' *Economica*, 4, 386–405.

Cohen, W. M. and R. C. Levin (1989), 'Empirical Studies of Innovation and Market Structure,' in R. Schmalensee and R. Willig (eds), *Handbook of Industrial Organization*, vol. II. North-Holland: Amsterdam.

Cohen, W. M. and S. Klepper (1991),'Firm Size versus Diversity in the Achievement of Technological Advance,' in Z. J. Acs and D. B. Audretsch (eds), *Innovation and Technological Change: An International Comparison*. University of Michigan Press: Ann Arbor, MI.

Cohen, W. M. and S. Klepper (1992a), 'The Tradeoff between Firm Size and Diversity in the Pursuit of Technological Progress,' *Small Business Economics*, 4, 1–14.

Cohen, W. M. and S. Klepper (1992b), 'The Anatomy of Industry R&D Intensity Distributions,' *American Economic Review*, 82, 773–799.

Dosi, G. (1982), 'Technological Paradigms and Technological Trajectories: a Suggested Interpretation of the Determinants and Directions of Technical Change,' *Research Policy*, 13, 3–20.

Dosi, G. (1988), 'Sources, Procedures, and Microeconomic Effects of Innovation,' *Journal of Economic Literature*, 26, 1120–1171.

Dosi, G., O. Marsili, L. Orsenigo and R. Salvatore (1995), 'Learning, Market Selection and the Evolution of Industrial Structures,' *Small Business Economics*, 7, 411–436.

Dunne, T., M. J. Roberts and L. Samuelson (1988), 'Patterns of Firm Entry and Exit in U.S. Manufacturing Industries,' *Rand Journal of Economics*, 19, 495–515.

Dunne, T., M. J. Roberts and L. Samuelson (1989), 'The Growth and Failure of U.S. Manufacturing Plants' *Quarterlyy Journal of Economics*, 104, 671–698.

Geroski, P. A. (1995), 'What Do We Know About Entry,' *International Journal of Industrial Organization*, 13, 450–456.

Geroski, P. A. (1991a), 'Domestic and Foreign Entry in the United Kingdom: 1983–1984,' in P. Geroski and J. Schwalbach (eds), *Entry and Market Contestability: An International Comparison*. Basil Blackwell: Oxford.

Geroski, Paul A. (1991b), 'Some Data-Driven Reflections on the Entry Process,' in P. Geroski and J. Schwalbach (eds), *Entry and Market Contestability: An International Comparison*. Basil Blackwell: Oxford, pp. 282–286.

Geroski, P. A. and J. Schwalbach (eds), *Entry and Market Contestability: An International Comparison*. Basil Blackwell: Oxford.

Gilder, G. (1989), *Microcosm*. Touchstone: New York.

Gort, M. and S. Klepper (1982), 'Time Paths in the Diffusion of Product Innovations,' *Economic Journal*, 92, 630–653.

Graf, J. de V. (1957), *Theoretical Welfare Economics*. Cambridge University Press: Cambridge.

Griliches, Z. (1979), Issues in Assessing the Contribution of R&D to Productivity Growth,' *Bell Journal of Economics*, 10, 92–116.

Hall, B. H. (1987), 'The Relationship between Firm Size and Firm Growth in the U.S. Manufacturing Sector,' *Journal of Industrial Economics*, 35, 583–605.

Hannan, M. T. and J. Freeman (1989), *Organizational Ecology*. Harvard University Press: Cambridge, MA.

Hirschman, A. O. (1970), *Exit, Voice, and Loyalty*. Harvard University Press: Cambridge, MA.

Holmström, B. (1989), 'Agency Costs of Innovation,' *Journal of Economic Behavior and Organization*, 12, 305–327.

Ijiri, Y. and H. A. Simon (1977), *Skew Distributions and Sizes of Business Firms*. North-Holland: Amsterdam.

Invernizzi, B. and R. Revelli (1993), 'Small Firms in the Italian Economy: Structural Change and Evidence of Turbulence,' in Z. Acs and D. B. Audretsch (eds), *Small Firms and Entrepreneurship: An East–West Perspective*. Cambridge University Press: Cambridge.

Jovanovic, B. (1982), 'Selection and Evolution of Industry,' *Econometrica*, 50, 649–670.

Jovanovic, B. (1994), 'Entrepreneurial Choice When People Differ in their Management and Labor Skills,' *Small Business Economics*, 6, 185–192.

Klepper, S. (1996), 'Entry, Exit, Growth and Innovation over the Product Life Cycle,' *American Economic Review*, 86, 560–581.

Klepper, S. and E. Graddy (1990), 'The Evolution of New Industries and the Determinants of Market Structure,' *Rand Journal of Economics*, 21, 27–44.

Klepper, S. and J. H. Miller (1995), 'Entry, Exit, and Shakeouts in the United States in New Manufactured Products,' *International Journal of Industrial Organization*, 13, 567–591.

Knight, F. H. (1921), *Risk, Uncertainty and Profit*. Houghton Mifflin: New York.

Kreps, D. (1991), 'Corporate Culture and Economic Theory,' in J. Alt and K. Sliepsle (eds), *Positive Perspectives on Political Economy*. Cambridge University Press: Cambridge.

Malerba, F. and L. Orsenigo (1993), 'Technological Regimes and Firm Behaviour,' *Industrial and Corporate Change*, 2, 74–89.

Malerba, F. (1992), 'Learning by Firms and Incremental Technical Change, *Economic Journal*, 94, 213–228.

Maleta, F. and L. Orsenigo (1996), 'The Dynamics and Evolution of Industries,' *Industrial and Corporate Change*, 5, 51–88.

Mansfield, E. (1962), 'Entry, Gibrat's Law, Innovation, and the Growth of Firms,' *American Economic Review*, 52, 1023–1051.

March, J. C. and H. A. Simon (1993), 'Organizations Revisited,' *Industrial and Corporate Change*, 2, 299–316.

Mata, J. and P. Portugal (1994), 'Life Duration of New Firms,' *Journal of Industrial Economics*, 27, 227–246.

Milgrom, P. (1988), 'Employment Contracts, Influence Activities and Organization Design,' *Journal of Political Economy*, 96, 42–60.

Milgrom, P. and J. Roberts (1987), 'Information Asymmetries, Strategic Behavior, and Industrial Organization,' *American Economic Review*, 77, 184–193.

Mueller, D. C. (1976), Information, Mobility, and Profit,' *Kyklos*, 29, 419–448.

Nelson, R. R. and S. G. Winter (1974), 'Neoclassical vs. Evolutionary Theories of Economic Growth: Critique and Prospectus,' *Economic Journal*, 84, 886–905.

Nelson, R. R. and S. G. Winter (1978), 'Forces Generating, and Limiting Concentration under Schumpeterian Competition,' *Bell Journal of Economics*, 9, 524–548.

Nelson, R. R. and S. G. Winter (1982), *An Evolutionary Theory of Economic Change*. Harvard University Press: Cambridge, MA.

Neumann, M. (1993), 'Review of Entry and Market Contestability: an International Comparison,' *International Journal of Industrial Organization*, 11, 593–594.

Orr, D. (1974), 'The Determinants of Entry: A Study of the Canadian Manufacturing Industries,' *Review of Economics and Statistics*, 56, 58–66.

Palfreman, J. and D. Swade (1991), *The Dream Machine: Exploring the Computer Age*. BBC Books: London.

Scherer, F. M. (1984), *Innovation and Growth: Schumpeterian Perspectives*. MIT Press: Cambridge, MA.

——————————— *The Evolution of Industrial Structures* ———————————

Scherer, F. M. (1992), 'Schumpeter and Plausible Capitalism,' *Journal of Economic Literature*, 30, 1416–1433.

Scherer, F. M. and D. Ross (1990), *Industrial Market Structure and Economic Performance*, 3rd edn. Houghton Mifflin: Boston, MA.

Schumpeter, J. A. (1942), *Capitalism, Socialism and Democracy*. Harper & Row: New York.

Siegfried, J. J. and L. B. Evans (1992), 'Entry and Exit in U.S. Manufacturing Industries from 1977 to 1982,' in D. B. Audretsch and J. J. Siegfried (eds), *Empirical Studies in Industrial Organization: Essays in Honor of Leonard W. Weiss*. Kluwer Academic: Boston, MA.

Simon,H. and C. Bonini (1958), 'The Size Distribution of Business Firms,' *American Economic Review*, 48, 607–617.

Wagner, J. (1992), 'Firm Size, Firm Growth, and Persistence of Chance: Testing Gibrat's Law with Establishment Data from Lower Saxony 1978–1989,' *Small Business Economics*, 4, 125–131.

Wagner, J. (1994a), 'Small-Firm Entry in Manufacturing Industries,' *Small Business Economics*, 5, 211–214.

Wagner, J. (1994b), 'The Post-Entry Performance of New Small Firms in German Manufacturing Industries, *Journal of Industrial Economics*, 62, 141–154.

Weiss, L. W. (1991), In D. B. Audretsch and H. Yamawaki (eds), *Structure, Conduct and Performance*. New York University Press: New York.

Williamson, O. E. (1968), 'Economies as an Antitrust Defense: The Welfare Tradeoffs,' *American Economic Review*, 58, 18–36.

Williamson, O. E. (1975), *Markets and Hierarchies: Antitrust Analysis and Implications*. The Free Press: New York.

Winter, S. G. (1984), 'Schumpeterian Competition in Alternative Technological Regimes,' *Journal of Economic Behavior and Organization*, 5, 287–320.

PART V

ECONOMIC GROWTH

[21]

Regional Studies, Vol. 38.8, pp. 949–959, November 2004

Carfax Publishing
Taylor & Francis Group

Entrepreneurship Capital and Economic Performance

DAVID B. AUDRETSCH* and MAX KEILBACH†

*Max-Planck Institut zur Erforschung von Wirtschaftssystemen, Kahlaische Str. 10, D-07745 Jena, Germany.
Email: audretsch@mpiew-jena.mpg.de

†Max-Planck Institut zur Erforschung von Wirtschaftssystemen, Kahlaische Str. 10, Research Group on Entrepreneurship,
Growth and Public Policy, D-07745 Jena, Germany.
Email: keilbach@mpiew-jena.mpg.de

(Received September 2003: in revised form June 2004)

AUDRETSCH D. B. and KEILBACH M. (2004) Entrepreneurship capital and economic performance, *Regional Studies* **38**, 949–959. The neoclassical model of the production function, as applied by Solow when building the neoclassical model of growth, linked labour and capital to output. More recently, Romer and others have expanded the model to include measures of knowledge capital. This paper introduces a new factor, entrepreneurship capital, and links it to output in the context of a production function model. It explains what is meant by entrepreneurship capital and why it should influence economic output. A production function model including several different measures of entrepreneurship capital is then estimated for German regions. The results indicate that entrepreneurship capital is a significant and important factor shaping output and productivity. The results suggest a new direction for policy that focuses on instruments to enhance entrepreneurship capital.

Production function   Entrepreneurship capital   Regional economic performance

AUDRETSCH D. B. et KEILBACH M. (2004) Le capital entrepreneurial et la performance économique, *Regional Studies* **38**, 949–959. Le modèle néo-classique de la fonction de production selon Solow, qui l'a employé dans le but de construire le modèle néo-classique de croissance, relie le travail et le capital au rendement. Plus récemment, Romer, parmi d'autres, a développé le modèle afin de comporter des mesures du capital de connaissance. Cet article cherche à présenter un nouveau facteur, le capital entrepreneurial, et à le relier au rendement économique sur la base d'un modèle de fonction de production. D'abord, cet article cherche à expliquer la notion du capital entrepreneurial et les raisons pour lesquelles il pourrait influencer le rendement économqiue. Il s'ensuit une estimation d'un modèle de fonction de production qui se rapporte aux régions allemandes et qui utlise différents mesures du capital entrepreneurial. Les résultats montrent que le capital entrepreneurial excerce un effet positif et signifiant sur le rendement économique des regions. Ces résultats laissent supposer une nouvelle orientation pour la politique qui porte sur des outils destinés à augmenter le capital entrepreneurial.

Fonction de production   Capital entrepreneurial   Performance économique régionale

AUDRETSCH D. B. und KEILBACH M. (2004) Entrepreneurship Kapital und wirtschaftliche Leistungsfähigkeit, *Regional Studies* **38**, 949–959. Das neoklassische Modell der Produktionsfunktion, wie es von Solow zur Konstruktion des neoklassischen Wachstumsmodell benutzt wurde, verband Arbeit und Kapital mit wirtschaftlichem Output. In jüngster Zeit haben Romer und andere das Modell dahingehend erweitert, dass Wissenskapital einbezogen wird. In diesem Aufsatz wird ein weiterer Faktor eingeführt, der des Entrepreneurship Kapitals und die Produktionsfunktion mit diesem Faktor erweitert. Der Aufsatz erklärt zunächst, was mit Entrepreneurship Kapital gemeint ist, und inwiefern es den wirtschaftlichen Output einer Region beeinflussen kann. Es wird sodann ein Produktionsfunktionsmodell einschließlich mehrerer verschiedener Maße für Entrepreneurship Kapital für deutsche Regionen geschätzt. Die Ergebnisse weisen darauf hin, dass Entrepreneurship Kapital einen signifikanten und wichtigen Beitrag zur Beeinflussung des wirtschaftlichen Outputs der Regionen darstellt. Die Ergebnisse legen nahe, neue Wege der Wirtschaftspolitik zu beschreiten, die sich auf Instrumente zur Erhöhung des Entrepreneurship Kapitals konzentrieren.

Produktionsfunktion   Entrepreneurship Kapital   Regionalwirtschaftliche Leistungsfähigkeit

AUDRETSCH D. B. y KEILBACH M. (2004) Capital entrepreneurial y comportamiento económico, *Regional Studies* **38**, 949–959. El modelo neoclásico de la función de producción, tal como ha sido aplicado por Solow para desarrollar el modelo neoclásico de crecimiento, vinculó trabajo y capital a producción. Más recientemente, Romer y otros han expandido el modelo para incluír medidas de capital intelectual. En este artículo nosotros introducimos un nuevo factor, el capital empresarial, y lo vinculamos a la producción en el contexto de un modelo de función de producción. Este artículo explica qué es a lo que nosotros nos referimos cuando hablamos de capital empresarial y por qué debería influir en la producción económica. A

0034-3404 print/1360-0591 online/04/080949-11 ©2004 Regional Studies Association
http://www.regional-studies-assoc.ac.uk

DOI: 10.1080/0034340042000280956

continuación se estima un modelo de función de producción que incluye varias medidas diferentes de capital empresarial para las regiones alemanas. Los resultados indican que el capital empresarial es un factor importante y significativo a la hora de determinar producción y productividad. Estos resultados sugieren una nueva dirección para las políticas que se centran en instrumentos dirigidos a aumentar el capital empresarial.

Función de producción   Capital empresarial   Comportamiento económico regional

JEL classifications: M13, O32, O47

> The Entrepreneur is the single most important player in a modern economy.
>
> (LAZEAR, 2002, p. 1)

INTRODUCTION

Ever since SOLOW (1956) based his model of economic growth on the neoclassical production function with its key factors of production, capital and labour, economists have relied upon the model of the production function as a basis for explaining the determinants of economic growth. ROMER's (1986) critique of the Solow approach was not with the basic model of the neoclassical production function, but rather with what Romer perceived to be omitted from that model – knowledge. Not only did Romer along with LUCAS (1988) and others argue that knowledge was an important factor of production, along with the traditional factors of labour and capital, but because it was endogenously determined as a result of externalities and spillovers, it was particularly important.

The purpose of the paper is to suggest that another key factor has been omitted from the neoclassical production function: entrepreneurship capital. Entrepreneurship has typically been referred to as an action, process or activity. It is proposed that it can also be considered to constitute a stock of capital, since it reflects a number of different factors and forces, legal, institutional and social, which create a capacity for this activity (HOFSTEDE *et al.*, 2002). ACS and AUDRETSCH (2003) suggest that entrepreneurship capital might be something of a missing link in explaining variations in economic performance. However, while a rich literature has emerged identifying the determinants of entrepreneurship, led by the pioneering study of EVANS and LEIGHTON (1989), the link between entrepreneurship capital and performance remains largely anecdotal or based on case studies. For example, SAXENIAN (1994) provides compelling case study evidence attributing the superior performance of Silicon Valley, CA, USA, to a high capacity for promoting entrepreneurship, which could be viewed as a rich endowment of entrepreneurship capital.

BAUMOL (2002, pp. 58–59) has argued that entrepreneurial activity might account for a significant amount of the growth left unexplained in traditional production function models. While the traditional factors of labour and capital, and even the addition of knowledge capital, are important in shaping output, the capacity to harness new ideas by creating new enterprises is also essential to economic output. A counter-example is instructive. In the former Soviet Union, while the exact measures of the stocks of capital and labour, and even knowledge, were questionable, their existence was not. By contrast, entrepreneurship capital, at least as it could be legally applied, was minimal.

The paper is organized as follows. The second section is devoted to defining entrepreneurship capital and to explaining why is should be linked to output in the context of a production function model. The third section specifies the production function to be estimated and it exposes the data. A production function model is estimated for German regions in the fourth section. The final section provides a summary and conclusion. In particular, the evidence suggests that various measures of entrepreneurship capital in fact contribute to output. Those regions with a higher level of entrepreneurship capital exhibit higher levels of output and productivity, while those with a paucity of entrepreneurship capital tend to generate lower levels of output and productivity.

ENTREPRENEURSHIP CAPITAL

What is entrepreneurship capital?

While it has become widely acknowledged that entrepreneurship is a vital force in the economies of developed countries, there is little consensus about what actually constitutes entrepreneurial activity. Scholars have proposed a broad array of definitions, which when operationalized have generated a number of different measures (HEBERT and LINK, 1989). Similarly, there is no generally accepted definition of entrepreneurship for the developed countries of the Organisation for Economic Co-operation and Development (OECD, 1998). The failure of a single definition of entrepreneurship to emerge undoubtedly reflects the fact that it is a multidimensional concept. The actual definition used to study or classify entrepreneurial activities reflects a particular perspective or emphasis. For example, definitions of entrepreneurship typically vary between the economic and management perspectives. From the economic perspective, Hebert and Link distinguish between the supply of financial capital, innovation, allocation of resources among alternative uses and decision-making. Thus, an entrepreneur is someone encompassing the entire spectrum of these functions: 'The entrepreneur is someone who specializes in taking responsibility for and making judgmental decisions that affect the location, form, and the use of goods, resources or institutions' (HEBERT and LINK, 1989, p. 213).

The most prevalent and compelling views of entrepreneurship focus on the perception of new economic opportunities and the subsequent introduction of new ideas in the market. Just as entrepreneurs are agents of change, entrepreneurship is thus about the process of change. This corresponds to the definition of entrepreneurship proposed by the OECD (1998, p. 11):

Entrepreneurs are agents of change and growth in a market economy and they can act to accelerate the generation, dissemination and application of innovative ideas. ... Entrepreneurs not only seek out and identify potentially profitable economic opportunities but are also willing to take risks to see if their hunches are right.

Or as GARTNER and CARTER (2003) state:

Entrepreneurial behavior involves the activities of individuals who are associated with creating new organizations rather than the activities of individuals who are involved with maintaining or changing the operations of on-going established organizations.

While the entrepreneur undertakes a definitive action, starting a new business, his/her action cannot be viewed in a vacuum devoid of context. Rather, as AUDRETSCH *et al.* (2002) show, the determinants of entrepreneurship are shaped by a number of forces and factors, including legal and institutional and also social factors. The study of social capital and its impact on economic decision-making and actions stems from classic literatures in economics and sociology in which social and relational structure influence market processes (GRANOVETTER, 1983). SAXENIAN (1994) and THORTON and FLYNNE (2003) attribute the high economic performance of Silicon Valley not only to single individuals, but also to their interaction within formalized networks (e.g. firms) and unformalized ones:

It is not simply the concentration of skilled labour, suppliers and information that distinguish the region. A variety of regional institutions – including Stanford University, several trade associations and local business organizations, and a myriad of specialized consulting, market research, public relations and venture capital firms – provide technical, financial, and networking services which the region's enterprises often cannot afford individually. These networks defy sectoral barriers: individuals move easily from semiconductor to disk drive firms or from computer to network makers. They move from established firms to start-ups (or vice versa) and even to market research or consulting firms, and from consulting firms back into start-ups. And they continue

to meet at trade shows, industry conferences, and the scores of seminars, talks, and social activities organized by local business organizations and trade associations. In these forums, relationships are easily formed and maintained, technical and market information is exchanged, business contacts are established, and new enterprises are conceived. ... This decentralized and fluid environment also promotes the diffusion of intangible technological capabilities and understandings.

(SAXENIAN, 1990, pp. 96–97)[1]

The present paper defines entrepreneurship capital as a region's endowment with factors conducive to the creation of new businesses. This involves aspects such as a high endowment with individuals willing to take the risk of starting up a new business. It also implies the existence of a regional milieu that encourages start-up activities such as an innovative milieu, the existence of formal and informal networks, but also a general social acceptance of entrepreneurial activity and the activity of bankers and venture capital agents willing to share risks and benefits involved. Such contexts generating a high propensity for economic agents to start new firms can be characterized as being rich in entrepreneurship capital. Other contexts, where the start-up of new firms is inhibited, can be characterized as being weak in entrepreneurship capital.

Impacts of entrepreneurship capital

Entrepreneurship capital can be expected to exert a positive impact on economic output for a number of reasons. The first is that it is a mechanism for knowledge spillovers. ROMER (1986), LUCAS (1988, 1993) and GROSSMAN and HELPMAN (1991) establish that knowledge spillovers are an important mechanism underlying endogenous growth. However, they shed little light on the actual mechanisms by which knowledge is transmitted across firms and individuals. The answer to this question is important, because a policy implication commonly drawn from the new economic growth theory is that as a result of convexities in knowledge and the resultant increasing returns, knowledge factors, such as research and development (R&D), should be publicly supported. While this may be valid, it is also important to recognize that the mechanisms for spillover transmission may also play a key role and might also serve as a focus for public policy enhancing economic growth and development.

The literature identifying mechanisms actually transmitting knowledge spillovers is sparse and remains underdeveloped. However, one important area where such transmission mechanisms have been identified involves entrepreneurship. Entrepreneurship involves the start-up and growth of new enterprises.

Why should entrepreneurship serve as a mechanism for the spill over of knowledge from the source of origin? At least two major channels or mechanisms for knowledge spillovers have been identified in the literature. Both spillover mechanisms revolve around the issue of appropriability of new knowledge. COHEN and LEVINTHAL (1989) suggest that firms develop the capacity to adapt new technology and ideas developed in other firms and, therefore, can appropriate some of the returns accruing to investments in new knowledge made externally. This view of spillovers is consistent with the traditional model of the knowledge production function, where the firm exists exogenously and then undertakes (knowledge) investments to generate innovative output.

By contrast, AUDRETSCH (1995) proposes shifting the unit of observation away from exogenously assumed firms to individuals, such as scientists, engineers or other knowledge workers, i.e. agents with endowments of new economic knowledge. When the lens is shifted away from the firm to the individual as the relevant unit of observation, the appropriability issue remains, but the question changes: How can economic agents with a given endowment of new knowledge best appropriate the returns from that knowledge? If the scientist or engineer can pursue the new idea within the organizational structure of the firm developing the knowledge and appropriate roughly the expected value of that knowledge, he/she has no reason to leave the firm. On the other hand, if he/she places a greater value on his/her ideas than does the decision-making bureaucracy of the incumbent firm, he/she might choose to start a new firm to appropriate the value of his/her knowledge. Small enterprises can compensate for their lack of R&D through spillovers and spin-offs. Typically, an employee from an established large corporation, often a scientist or engineer working in a research laboratory, will have an idea for an invention and ultimately for an innovation. Accompanying this potential innovation is an expected net return from the new product. The inventor would expect to be compensated for his/her potential innovation accordingly. If the company has a different, presumably lower, valuation of the potential innovation, it might decide either not to pursue its development, or that it merits a lower level of compensation than that expected by the employee.

In either case, the employee will weigh the alternative of starting his/her own firm. If the gap in the expected return accruing from the potential innovation between the inventor and the corporate decision-maker is sufficiently large, and if the cost of starting a new firm is sufficiently low, the employee might decide to leave the large corporation and establish a new enterprise. Since the knowledge was generated in the established corporation, the new start-up is considered to be a spin-off from the existing firm. Such start-ups typically do not have direct access to a large R&D laboratory. Rather, these small firms succeed in exploiting the knowledge and experience accrued from the R&D laboratories with their previous employers.

The research laboratories of universities provide a source of innovation-generating knowledge that is available to private enterprises for commercial exploitation. JAFFE (1989) and AUDRETSCH and FELDMAN (1996) find that the knowledge created in university laboratories 'spills over' to contribute to the generation of commercial innovations by private enterprises. ACS *et al.* (1994) find persuasive evidence that spillovers from university research contribute more to the innovative activity of small firms than to the innovative activity of large corporations.

In the metaphor provided by HIRSCHMAN (1970), if a voice proves ineffective within incumbent organizations and loyalty is sufficiently weak, a knowledge worker might resort to exit the firm or university where the knowledge was created to form a new company. In this spillover channel, the knowledge production function is actually reversed. The knowledge is exogenous and embodied in a worker. The firm is created endogenously in the worker's effort to appropriate the value of his/her knowledge through innovative activity. Thus, entrepreneurship serves as the mechanism by which knowledge spills over from the source by the creation of a new firm where it is commercialized.

A second way that entrepreneurship capital exerts a positive influence on economic output is through increased competition by an increased number of enterprises. JACOBS (1969) and PORTER (1990) argue that competition is more conducive to knowledge externalities than is local monopoly. It should be emphasized that by local competition, Jacobs does not mean competition within product markets as has traditionally been envisioned within the industrial organization literature. Rather, Jacobs is referring to the competition for the new ideas embodied in economic agents. Not only does an increased number of firms provide greater competition for new ideas, but also greater competition across firms facilitates the entry of a new firm specializing in some particular new product niche. This is because the necessary complementary inputs and services are likely to be available from small specialist niche firms, but not necessarily from large, vertically integrated producers.

Both FELDMAN and AUDRETSCH (1999) and GLAESER *et al.* (1992) find empirical evidence supporting the hypothesis that an increase in competition, as measured by the number of enterprises, in a city increases the growth performance of that city.

A third way that entrepreneurship capital generates economic output is by providing diversity among the firms. Not only does entrepreneurship capital generate a greater number of enterprises, but also it increases the variety of enterprises in the location. A key assumption made by HANNAN and FREEMAN (1989) in the population ecology literature is that each new organization represents a unique approach. A series of theoretical arguments suggests that the degree of diversity, as opposed to homogeneity, in a location will influence the growth potential.

The theoretical basis linking diversity to economic performance is provided by JACOBS (1969), who argues that the most important source of knowledge spillovers is external to the industry in which the firm operates and that cities are the source of considerable innovation because the diversity of these knowledge sources is greatest in cities. According to Jacobs, it is the exchange of complementary knowledge across diverse firms and economic agents that yields a greater return on new economic knowledge. Jacobs develops a theory that emphasizes that the variety of industries within a geographic region promotes knowledge externalities and ultimately innovative activity and economic growth.

The first important test linking diversity to economic performance, measured in terms of employment growth, was by GLAESER *et al.* (1992), who used a data set on the growth of large industries in 170 cities between 1956 and 1987 to identify the relative importance of the degree of regional specialization, diversity and local competition play in influencing industry growth rates. They find evidence that diversity promotes growth in cities. FELDMAN and AUDRETSCH (1999) identify the extent to which the extent of diversity influences innovative output. They link the innovative output of product categories within a specific city to the extent to which the economic activity of that city is concentrated in that industry or, conversely, diversified in terms of complementary industries sharing a common science base.

Entrepreneurship capital therefore can contribute to output and growth by serving as a conduit for knowledge spillovers, increasing competition and by injecting diversity. Inclusion of measures of entrepreneurship capital would be expected to be positively related to output.

PRODUCTION FUNCTION MODEL AND MEASUREMENT ISSUES

The goal of the paper is to state that a region's endowment with entrepreneurship capital exerts a positive impact on the region's economic output. It bases a test of this hypothesis on an often tested approach, i.e. it augments a production function with entrepreneurship capital. Using a specification of the Cobb–Douglas type, one obtains:

$$Y_i = \alpha K_i^{\beta_1} L_i^{\beta_2} R_i^{\beta_3} E_i^{\beta_4} e^{\epsilon_i} \qquad (1)$$

where K is the factor of physical capital, L is labour, R is knowledge capital, E is entrepreneurship capital and i refers to German regions. Data derive from a cross-section of 327 West German *Kreise* (regions) for 1992, if not indicated otherwise. Table 1 has some summary statistics for these variables. The sources and construction of the data are as follows (for further details, see KEILBACH, 2000):

- Output: measured as gross value added corrected for purchases of goods and services, Value Added Tax (VAT) and shipping costs. Statistics are published every 2 years for *Kreise* by the Working Group of the Statistical Offices of the German *Länder* (Federal States) under 'Volkswirtschaftliche Gesamtrechnungen der Länder'.

- Physical capital: stock of capital used in the manufacturing sector of the *Kreise* has been estimated using a perpetual inventory method, which computes the stock of capital as a weighted sum of past investments. In the estimates, a β-distribution was used with $p = 9$ and a mean age of $q = 14$. The type of survival function as well as these parameters was provided by the German Federal Statistical Office, Wiesbaden. This way, we attempted to obtain maximum coherence with the estimates of the capital stock of the German producing sector as a whole as published by the Federal Statistical Office. Data on investment at the level of *Kreise* are published annually by the Federal Statistical Office in the 'E I 6' series. These figures, however, are limited to firms of the producing sector, excluding the mining industry, with more than 20 employees. The vector of the producing sector as a whole was estimated by multiplying these values such that the capital stock of Western Germany – as published by STATISTISCHES BUNDESAMT (1993) – was attained. Note that this procedure implies that estimates for *Kreise* with a high proportion of mining might be biased. Note also that for protection purposes, some *Kreise* did not publish data on investment (like, for example, the city of Wolfsburg, whose producing sector is dominated by the car-maker Volkswagen). Therefore, five *Kreise* are treated as missing.

- Labour: data are published by the Federal Labor Office, Nuremberg, which reports number of employees liable to social insurance by *Kreise*.

- Knowledge capital: expressed as number of employees engaged in R&D in the public (1992) and the private (1991) sectors. With this approach, the examples of GRILICHES (1979), JAFFE (1989) and AUDRETSCH and FELDMAN (1996) are followed. Data have been communicated by the Stifterverband für die Wissenschaft, Essen, under obligation of data protection. With these data, it was impossible to make a distinction between research and development employees in both the producing and non-producing sectors. Regression results, therefore, will implicitly include spillovers from R&D of the non-producing sector to the producing sectors. It is presumed, however, that this effect is rather low.

- Entrepreneurship capital: measurement of entrepreneurship capital is no less complicated than is measuring the traditional factors of production. Just as measuring capital, labour and knowledge invokes numerous assumptions and simplifications, creating a metric for entrepreneurship capital presents a

Table 1. *Summary statistics of variables used in regression*

	Mean	Standard deviation	Minimum	Maximum
Gross Domestic Product (Y) (DM millions)	2351.89	2621.77	95.00	22 258.00
Capital (K) (DM millions)	4248.25	5038.72	211.20	37 295.64
Number of employees (L)	27 022.48	24 080.32	2562	171 938
Number of R&D employees (R)	840.76	2223.75	0	29 863
Entrepreneurship capital (E)[a]	9.406	2.805	4.793	24.635
High-technology (HT) E[a]	0.755	0.398	0.011	6.004
Information and Communication Technology (ICT) E[a]	0.565	0.310	0.157	2.520

Note: [a]Entrepreneurship capital is measured as the sum of the number of start-ups in the respective industry in 1989–92 divided by 1000 of the population. Hence, on average, there were 9.4 start-ups per 1000 population in all industries in these years.

challenge. Many of the elements that determine entrepreneurship capital in the present definition defy quantification. In any case, entrepreneurship capital, like all the other types of capital, is multifaceted and heterogeneous. However, it manifests itself singularly: the start-up of new enterprises. Thus, using new-firm start-up rates as an indicator of entrepreneurship capital, the latter being an unobservable (i.e. latent) variable, is proposed. *Ceteris paribus*, higher start-up rates reflect higher levels of entrepreneurship capital. Entrepreneurship capital is computed as the number of start-ups in the respective region relative to its population, which reflects the propensity of inhabitants of a region to start a new firm. From the background of the present definition of entrepreneurship capital, alternative measures would be possible. A number of aspects of this definition being difficult to quantify, a natural candidate would be a region's stock of young firms. However, this measure would implicitly reflect exit and shakeout dynamics. Hence, a measure along these lines would inevitably be influenced by factors external to entrepreneurship capital such as the quality of management or business ideas and, thus, be biased. The number of start-ups is therefore considered as being the most appropriate measure of entrepreneurship capital.

The data on start-ups are taken from the start-up panel that is developed by the Centre for European Economic Research (ZEW), Mannheim, Germany on the basis of data provided biannually from the largest German credit-rating agency, Creditreform (Neuss, Germany). These data contain virtually all entries – hence start-ups – in the German Trade Register, especially for firms with large credit requirements as, for example, high-technology firms.[2] By now, there are 1.6 million entries for Western Germany. Since the number of start-ups is subject to a greater level of stochastic disturbance over short periods, it is prudent to compute the measure of entrepreneurship capital based on start-up rates over a longer period. The number of start-ups between 1989 and 1992 is therefore used.

One might argue that in the set-up of equation (1),

the use of entrepreneurship capital invokes a simultaneity problem in the sense that it is not only entrepreneurship capital that drives output, but also high output drives start-ups. The argument would imply that entrepreneurs move to locations where economic performance is high. However, a similar argumentation would hold for all variables used in this approach. If this effect holds for entrepreneurs, it will certainly also apply to labour, but probably even more to capital, which is a sum of past monetary investments and money migrating more easily across borders, hence moving more quickly to productive regions. Thus, the present measure of entrepreneurship capital fits well with the tradition of production function regressions. The use of lagged start-up rates avoids some of the degree of simultaneity between output and entrepreneurship.

While the present paper argues that entrepreneurship capital should include start-up activity in any industry, some scholars have suggested that it should only apply to start-ups involving innovative activity. Therefore, two modified measures of entrepreneurship are computed. The first restricts entrepreneurship capital to include only start-up activity in high-technology manufacturing industries (whose research and development intensity is above 2.5%). The second restricts entrepreneurship capital to include only start-up activity in the information and communication industries, i.e. firms in the hard- and software business. Some of these industries are also classified under high-technology manufacturing. Hence, there exists an intersection between the two measures. The measures will place more emphasis on the aspect of risk involved in the present definition of entrepreneurship capital since R&D-intensive activities are more uncertain in outcome and a larger financial commitment is also necessary to engage in R&D-intensive industries. Therefore, the expected monetary loss is larger.

The spatial distribution of the measure of entrepreneurship capital based on all industries is shown in Fig. 1. It makes evident that entrepreneurship capital is a phenomenon of agglomerated regions, Frankfurt, Munich, Hamburg and Düsseldorf, with their surrounding regions showing the highest start-up intensity. This is reflected in the correlation matrix shown in

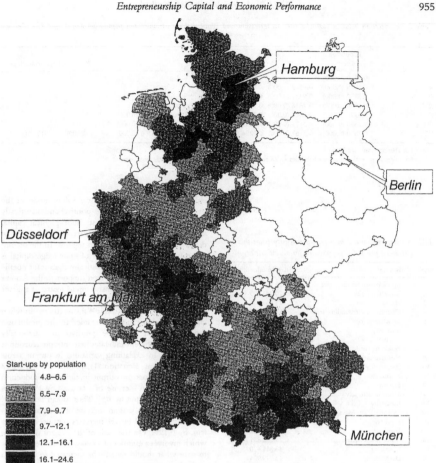

Fig. 1. *Spatial distribution of entrepreneurship capital measured as the number of start-ups in all industries in 1989–92 per 1000 population*

Table 2 where entrepreneurship capital shows a positive and significant correlation with population density, measured as inhabitants per square kilometre.

Table 3 ranks the regions according to their endowment with entrepreneurship capital. This makes again evident that Frankfurt, Munich, Hamburg and Düsseldorf, together with their surrounding regions, are those with the strongest endowment. This ranking will differ slightly, though not fundamentally if start-ups in high-technology manufacturing industries or in ICT industries are used instead of start-ups in all industries.

This is indicated by the positive and significant correlations between all three measures of entrepreneurship shown in Table 2. Tables A1 and A2 (in the Appendix) show the ranking of regions (showing again the 20 strongest and 20 weakest regions) when using the two alternative measures of entrepreneurship capital.

EMPIRICAL RESULTS

Estimation of the production function model of equation (1) produced the results shown in Table 4. The

Table 2. *Correlation between variables used in regression and between these variables and population density for 327 German Kreise*

	Population density	Y	K	L	R	E	High-technology E
Y	0.5539 (0.000)						
K	0.5978 (0.000)	0.9172 (0.000)					
L	0.5252 (0.000)	0.9437 (0.000)	0.9244 (0.000)				
R	0.5068 (0.000)	0.7838 (0.000)	0.7250 (0.000)	0.6922 (0.000)			
E	0.3376 (0.000)	0.2671 (0.000)	0.2133 (0.000)	0.2203 (0.000)	0.3036 (0.000)		
HT E	0.2668 (0.000)	0.3179 (0.000)	0.2292 (0.000)	0.2756 (0.000)	0.3404 (0.000)	0.8153 (0.000)	
ICT E	0.2870 (0.000)	0.3167 (0.000)	0.2224 (0.000)	0.2579 (0.000)	0.3396 (0.000)	0.8164 (0.000)	0.9138 (0.000)

Notes: For abbreviations, see Table 1.
Numbers in parentheses are probabilities (p) of correlations not differing significantly from zero.

Table 3. *Regions ranked by start-up intensity (start-ups in 1989–92 per 1000 population) for all industries*

Rank	Region	Start-up intensity
1	Munich, surrounding area	24.634561
2	Düsseldorf, city	20.241409
3	Hamburg, city	19.669706
4	Offenbach, surrounding area	18.606913
5	Wiesbaden, city	17.671311
6	Starnberg	17.101142
7	Munich, city	16.081293
8	Frankfurt am Main, city	15.956175
9	Hochtaunuskreis	15.866653
10	Speyer, city	15.395183
11	Passau, city	15.254072
12	Freising	14.850592
13	Memmingen, city	14.805079
14	Landsberg a. Lech	14.792960
15	Offenbach am Main, city	14.620285
16	Segeberg	14.572237
17	Diepholz	14.435722
18	Main-Taunus-Kreis	14.232831
19	Ebersberg	13.811470
20	Dachau	13.779904
...		
308	Wesermarsch	6.006103
309	Wolfsburg, city	6.001654
310	Cham	5.991514
311	Sankt Wendel	5.919445
312	Neckar-Odenwald-Kreis	5.912736
313	Donnersbergkreis	5.896884
314	Schweinfurt	5.896509
315	Emsland	5.774027
316	Uelzen	5.758620
317	Salzgitter, city	5.668607
318	Lichtenfels	5.551670
319	Trier-Saarburg	5.541770
320	Herne, city	5.526887
321	Grafschaft Bentheim	5.428270
322	Höxter	5.287556
323	Bremerhaven, city	5.258049
324	Tirschenreuth	5.198918
325	Coburg	5.193940
326	Cuxhaven	5.168823
327	Kusel	4.793161

equation estimates the traditional Solow model of the production function. As the positive and statistically significant coefficients suggest, both physical capital and labour are important factors of production in determining output in German regions. In the second column of Table 4, the factor of knowledge capital is added. The positive and statistically significant coefficients of all three variables lend support to the Romer view that knowledge-intensive inputs matter as a factor of production.

The third column of Table 4 shows the results when entrepreneurship capital is included in the production function model (1). The positive and statistically significant coefficient indicates that entrepreneurship is a key factor in explaining variations in output across German regions. Equation (1) specifies the impact of production factors on output in terms of production elasticities, i.e. an increase of a factor *j* by 1% implies an increase of output by $\beta_j\%$. Thus, it can be deduced from the estimates that an increase of a region's entrepreneurship capital by 1% increases output, *ceteris paribus*, by 0.12%. On the basis of the present definition, which involves a number of aspects, it is not yet possible to state what should actually be increased to increase a region's entrepreneurship capital; this is left for further research. However, the estimates evidence that the impact of entrepreneurship capital is stronger than that of knowledge capital, the production elasticity of entrepreneurship capital being roughly five times larger than that of knowledge capital. This would imply that investments in entrepreneurship capital are more productive compared with investments in knowledge capital, which in turn would suggest a shift in public policy to increasing entrepreneurship capital. Of course, this first evidence should be interpreted carefully. In addition, estimates do not allow the derivation of specific policy measures; however, they give important directions for further research.

Table 4, columns (4) and (5), shows the results for equation (1) if start-up rates in high-technology manufacturing or in ICT industries are used instead of the start-up rates of all industries. The results indicate

Table 4. *Results of the estimation of the production function model (1) for German counties: the dependent variable is Gross Domestic Product* (Y)

	(1)	(2)	(3)	(4)	(5)
Y	−2.755*** (0.000)	−2.380*** (0.000)	−1.863*** (0.000)	−1.620*** (0.000)	−1.549*** (0.000)
K	0.270*** (0.000)	0.261*** (0.000)	0.258*** (0.000)	0.265*** (0.000)	0.267*** (0.000)
L	0.805*** (0.000)	0.755*** (0.000)	0.767*** (0.000)	0.753*** (0.000)	0.756*** (0.000)
R		0.034** (0.011)	0.026* (0.063)	0.021 (0.133)	0.019 (0.179)
E			0.120** (0.026)		
HT E				0.043*** (0.003)	
ICT E					0.105*** (0.001)
Adjusted R^2	0.9108	0.9124	0.9134	0.9156	0.9150

Notes: For abbreviations, see Table 1.

Numbers in parentheses denote the probability (*p*) of estimates being stochastically equal to zero. Hence, statistically significant for the two-tailed test: *90%, **95% and ***99% levels of confidence

that using these two alternative measures of entrepreneurship capital still generates a positive and statistically significant coefficient, suggesting that entrepreneurship capital is an important addition to the model of the production function.

SUMMARY AND CONCLUSION

Subsequent to publication of SOLOW's (1956) seminal paper depicting the neoclassical model of the production function as a basis for analysing economic growth, a series of new policy directions were developed to enhance the two traditional factors of production, physical capital and labour. Similarly, endogenous growth theory has triggered a new policy direction focusing on enhancing knowledge capital through investments in R&D, education and human capital. The present paper suggests that these approaches neglect an important factor that also shapes the economic performance of a region: the entrepreneurship capital of that region. It gives a definition of entrepreneurship capital and measures the regions' endowment with this factor by the regions' start-ups of new businesses in different industries, taking this as an indicator of the underlying latent variable. Based on a Cobb–Douglas production function, empirical evidence is found that entrepreneurship capital indeed exerts a positive impact on regions' output as measured in terms of Gross Domestic Product. This finding holds for different measures of entrepreneurship capital, be they general or more risk oriented. Indeed, a larger production elasticity is measured for entrepreneurship capital than for the present measure of knowledge capital, suggesting that the impact of a 1% increase in entrepreneurship capital on Gross Domestic Product is larger than the increase of knowledge capital by the same amount.

The results suggest, at least in the case of Germany, a different and new policy direction: the enhancement of entrepreneurship capital. While these findings certainly do not contradict the conclusions of earlier studies linking growth to factors such as labour, capital and knowledge, the present evidence points to an additional factor, entrepreneurship capital, that also plays an important role in the model of the production function. Although on the basis of analysis the present authors cannot yet provide detailed policy recommendations such as, for example, what specific measures should be taken and what aspect of entrepreneurship capital they should address, it can be stated that under certain conditions, policies focusing on enhancing entrepreneurship capital can prove to be more effective than those targeting more traditional factors. A detailed analysis of the components of entrepreneurship capital and how public policy can address them will be dealt with in further research. This research needs to map out more precisely the exact links and channels that policy can influence and augment entrepreneurship in such a way as to raise productivity and growth, as suggested by the results of the present paper.

Acknowledgements – The paper was written during a research stay at the Centre for European Economic Research (ZEW) in Mannheim, Germany. The authors gratefully acknowledge the support from the ZEW and financial support of the Deutsche Forschungsgemeinschaft (DFG) within the research focus Interdisziplinäre Gründungsforschung under Contract Number STA 169/10-1.

NOTES

1. SAXENIAN (1990, pp. 97–98) claims that even the language and vocabulary used by technical specialists can be specific to a region: 'a distinct language has evolved in the region and certain technical terms used by semiconductor production engineers in Silicon Valley would not even be understood by their counterparts in Boston's Route 128'.

2. Firms with low credit requirements, with a low number of employees or with unlimited liability legal forms are registered only with a time lag. These are typically retail stores or catering firms. For more detail on the ZEW foundation panels, see HARHOFF and STEIL (1997).

APPENDIX

Table A1. Regions ranked by start-up intensity (start-ups in 1989–92 per 1000 population) of high-technology manufacturing industries

Rank	Region	High-technology manufacturing start-up intensity
1	Tuttlingen	6.00451
2	Munich	5.82258
3	Aachen, krfr. St.	5.17982
4	Ravensburg	4.42391
5	Landsberg a. Lech	4.38991
6	Starnberg	4.04163
7	Enzkreis	3.77389
8	Miesbach	3.61141
9	Ebersberg	3.58143
10	Solingen, krfr. St.	3.55480
11	Bad Tölz-Wolfratshausen	3.54417
12	Offenbach	3.51651
13	Darmstadt, krfr. St.	3.45167
14	Bodenseekreis	3.44225
15	Speyer, krfr. Stadt	3.43462
16	Fürstenfeldbruck	3.39916
17	Aachen	3.38475
18	Herford	3.38254
19	Segeberg	3.37696
20	Rottweil	3.33336
...		
308	Salzgitter, krfr. Stadt	0.50916
309	Werra-Meissner-Kreis	0.50894
310	Gifhorn	0.50387
311	Neuburg-Schrobenhausen	0.47102
312	Haßberge	0.46271
313	Cochem-Zell	0.46240
314	Trier-Saarburg	0.45116
315	Hersfeld-Rotenburg	0.45077
316	Schwalm-Eder-Kreis	0.41891
317	Uelzen	0.41881
318	Donnersbergkreis	0.39844
319	Wittmund	0.36625
320	Wolfsburg, krfr. Stadt	0.31505
321	Aschaffenburg, krfr. St.	0.30290
322	Kusel	0.25294
323	Regen	0.24462
324	Lüchow-Dannenberg	0.19536
325	Emden, krfr. St.	0.19303
326	Freyung-Grafenau	0.12302
327	Kitzingen	0.11511

Table A2. Regions ranked by start-up intensity (start-ups in 1989–92 per 1000 population) of ICT industries (hardware, software, consulting, database services)

Rank	Region	ICT industry start-up intensity
1	Munich	2.519525
2	Offenbach	2.030401
3	Starnberg	1.835573
4	Ebersberg	1.561137
5	Karlsruhe, krfr. St.	1.483696
6	Freising	1.472786
7	Darmstadt, krfr. St.	1.423815
8	Hamburg	1.383457
9	Hochtaunuskreis	1.366637
10	Fürstenfeldbruck	1.332686
11	Wiesbaden, krfr. St.	1.319147
12	Munich, krfr. St.	1.309578
13	Aachen, krfr. St.	1.218066
14	Landsberg a. Lech	1.214881
15	Darmstadt-Dieburg	1.160630
16	Main-Taunus-Kreis	1.139757
17	Frankfurt am Main, krfr. St.	1.105130
18	Koblenz, krfr. Stadt	1.095390
19	Rheingau-Taunus-Kreis	1.091414
20	Offenbach am Main, krfr. St.	1.081712
...	...	
308	Cloppenburg	0.241666
309	Wilhelmshaven, krfr. St.	0.241149
310	Emsland	0.234035
311	Lichtenfels	0.228346
312	Wesermarsch	0.225632
313	Trier-Saarburg	0.225581
314	Kelheim	0.224252
315	Bremerhaven, krfr. St.	0.221633
316	Salzgitter, krfr. Stadt	0.212148
317	Südwestpfalz	0.209798
318	Freyung-Grafenau	0.209128
319	Helmstedt	0.206010
320	Neustadt a.d. Waldnaab	0.202612
321	Kusel	0.202350
322	Wittmund	0.201439
323	Regen	0.195700
324	Cham	0.178735
325	Coburg	0.177571
326	Donnersbergkreis	0.159375
327	Cuxhaven	0.157092

REFERENCES

ACS Z. J. and AUDRETSCH D. B. (2003) *The International Handbook of Entrepreneurship*. Kluwer, Dordrecht.

ACS Z. J., AUDRETSCH D. B. and FELDMAN M. P. (1994) R&D spillovers and recipient firm size, *Review of Economic and Statistics* **76**, 336–340.

AUDRETSCH, D. B. (1995) *Innovation and Industry Evolution*. MIT Press, Cambridge, MA.

AUDRETSCH D. B. and FELDMAN M. P. (1996) R&D spillovers and the geography of innovation and production, *American Economic Review* **86**, 630–640.

AUDRETSCH D. B., THURIK R., VERHEUL I. and WENNEKERS S. (2002) *Entrepreneurship: Determinants and Policy in a European–U.S. Comparison*. Kluwer, Boston.

BAUMOL W. J. (2002) *Free Market Innovation Machine: Analysing the Growth Miracle of Capitalism*. Princeton University Press, Princeton.

COHEN W. and LEVINTHAL D. (1989) Innovation and learning: the two faces of R&D, *Economic Journal* **99**, 569–596.

EVANS, D. S. and LEIGHTON, L. S. (1989) Some empirical aspects of entrepreneurship, *American Economic Review* **79**, 519–535.

FEDERAL STATISTICAL OFFICE (annually) E I 6 series.

FELDMAN M. P. and AUDRETSCH D. B. (1999) Innovation in cities: science based diversity, specialization and localized competition, *European Economic Review* **43**, 409–429.

GARTNER W. B. and CARTER N. M. (2003) Entrepreneurship behavior: firm organizing processes, in ACS Z. J. and AUDRETSCH D. B. (Eds) *The International Handbook of Entrepreneurship*, pp. 195–221. Kluwer, Dordrecht.

GLAESER E., KALLAL H., SCHEINKMAN J. and SHLEIFER A. (1992) Growth of cities, *Journal of Political Economy* **100**, 1126–1152.

GRANOVETTER M. S. (1983) The strength of weak ties: a network theory revisited, in COLLINS R. (Ed.) *Sociological Theory*, pp. 201–233. Jossey-Bass, San Francisco.

GRILICHES Z. (1979) Issues in assessing the contribution of R&D to productivity growth, *Bell Journal of Economics* **10**, 92–116.

GROSSMAN G. M. and HELPMAN E. (1991) *Innovation and Growth in the Global Economy*, MIT Press, Cambridge MA.

HANNAN M. T. and FREEMAN J. (1989) *Organizational Ecology*. Harvard University Press, Cambridge, MA.

HARHOFF D. and STEIL F. (1997) Die ZEW-Gruendungspanels: Konzeptionelle Ueberlegungen und Analysepotential, in HARHOFF D. (Ed.) *Unternehmensgruendungen – Empirische Analysen fuer die alten und neuen Bundeslaender*, 7. Nomos, Baden-Baden.

HEBERT R. F. and LINK A. N. (1989) In search of the meaning of entrepreneurship, *Small Business Economics* **1**, 39–49.

HIRSCHMAN A. O. (1970) *Exit, Voice, and Loyalty*. Harvard University Press, Cambridge, MA.

HOFSTEDE G., NOORDERHAVEN N. G., THURIK A. R., WENNEKERS A. R. M., UHLANER L. and WILDEMAN R. E. (2004) Culture's role in entrepreneurship, in ULIJN J. and BROWN T. (Eds) *Innovation, Entrepreneurship and Culture: The Interaction between Technology, Progress and Economic Growth*, pp. 162–203. Edward Elgar, Brookfield.

JACOBS, J.(1969) *The Economy of Cities*. Vintage, New York.

JAFFE A. B. (1989) Real effects of academic research, *American Economic Review* **79**, 957–970.

KEILBACH M. (2000) *Spatial Knowledge Spillovers and the Dynamics of Agglomeration and Regional Growth*. Physica, Heidelberg.

LAZEAR E. (2002) *Entrepreneurship*. Working Paper No. 9109. National Bureau of Economic Research, Cambridge, MA.

LUCAS JR R. E. (1993) Making a miracle, *Econometrica* **61**, 251–272.

LUCAS R. E. (1988) On the mechanics of economic development, *Journal of Monetary Economics* **22**, 3–39.

ORGANISATION FOR ECONOMIC CO-OPERATION AND DEVELOPMENT (1998) *Fostering Entrepreneurship*. OECD, Paris.

PORTER M. (1990) *The Comparative Advantage of Nations*. Free Press, New York.

ROMER P. M. (1986) Increasing returns and long-run growth, *Journal of Political Economy* **94**, 1002–1037.

SAXENIAN A. (1990) Regional networks and the resurgence of Silicon Valley, *California Management Review* **33**, 89–111.

SAXENIAN A. (1994) *Regional Advantage*. Harvard University Press, Cambridge, MA.

SOLOW R. (1956) A contribution to the theory of economic growth, *Quarterly Journal of Economics* **70**, 65–94.

STATISTISCHES BUNDESAMT (1993) *Statistisches Jahrbuch 1993*. Metzler-Poeschel, Stuttgart.

THORTON P. H. and FLYNN K. H. (2003) Entrepreneurship, networks and geographies, in ACS Z. J. and AUDRETSCH D. B. (Eds) *The International Handbook of Entrepreneurship*, pp. 401–433. Kluwer, Dordrecht.

What's New about the New Economy? Sources of Growth in the Managed and Entrepreneurial Economies

DAVID B. AUDRETSCH[a] and A. ROY THURIK[b]

([a]Institute for Development Strategies, Indiana University, SPEA 201, Bloomington, IN 47401, USA. Email: daudrets@indiana.edu and [b]Tinbergen Institute at Erasmus University Rotterdam (EUR), Centre for Advanced Small Business Economics (CASBEC), EIM Business and Policy Research, Zoetermeer, 3000 DR Rotterdam, The Netherlands. Email: thurik@few.eur.nl)

The purpose of this paper is to document the fundamental shift that is taking place in OECD countries. This shift is from the managed economy to the entrepreneurial economy. While politicians and policymakers have made a plea for guidance in the era of entrepreneurship, scholars have been slow to respond. This paper attempts to make a first step identifying and articulating these differences. We do this by contrasting the most fundamental elements of the newly emerging entrepreneurial economy with those of the managed economy. We identify 14 trade-offs confronting these two polar worlds. The common thread throughout these trade-offs is the increased role of new and small enterprises in the entrepreneurial economy. A particular emphasis is placed on changes in economic policy demanded by the entrepreneurial economy vis-à-vis the managed economy.

1. Introduction

Economic growth and employment creation are twin horns of not just the European dilemma but of what looms as the major challenge confronting the West. Over 10% of the workforce in the European Union was unemployed in 1999. Individual countries have responded to the twin horns of the growth–employment dilemma with a broad spectrum of policy approaches. Led by France and Germany, continental European countries have generally pursued policies of maintaining the status quo economic models, while the United

Industrial and Corporate Change   Volume 10   Number 1   2001

Kingdom and the Netherlands have been bolder at modifying their economic models.

This divergence of policy approaches across countries is new. In the first three postwar decades, the countries of Western Europe and North America pursued economic policies which though not identical had a high degree of similarity. As Galbraith (1956) articulated, something of a convergence had taken place throughout the Western economies in the way that the model of 'managed capitalism' was developing. It seemed that all countries were converging toward economies dominated by a handful of powerful enterprises, constrained only by the countervailing powers of the state and workers.[1] The 1950s and 1960s were an era of high and increasing concentration of economic activity. Perhaps the ascendancy of industrial organization as a field in economics during this period came from the need to address what became known as the *concentration question*. Scholars of industrial organization responded by producing a mass of literature focusing on essentially three issues: (i) How much economic concentration actually exists? (ii) What are the economic welfare implications of an oligopolistic market structure? (iii) Given the evidence that economic concentration is associated with efficiency, what are the public policy implications? Oliver Williamson's classic 1968 article, 'Economies as an Antitrust Defense: The Welfare Trade-offs', became something of a final statement, demonstrating what appeared to be an inevitable trade-off between the gains in productive efficiency that could be obtained through increased concentration and gains in terms of competition, and implicitly democracy, that could be achieved through decentralizing policies.

The fundamental issue of public policy at that time was how to live with this apparent trade-off between concentration and efficiency on the one hand, and decentralization and democracy on the other. The public policy question of the day was: *how can society reap the benefits of the large corporation in an oligopolistic setting while avoiding, or at least minimizing, the costs imposed by a concentration of economic power?* The policy response was to constrain the freedom of firms to contract. Such policy restraints typically took the form of public ownership, regulation, and competition policy or antitrust. At the time, considerable attention was devoted to what seemed like glaring differences in policy approaches to this apparent trade-off by different countries. France and Sweden resorted to government ownership of private business. Other countries, such as the Netherlands and Germany, tended to emphasize regulation. Still other countries, such as the Untied States, had a greater emphasis on antitrust. In fact, most countries relied upon elements of

[1] This view was certainly represented in the influential book written by Jean-Jacques Servan-Schreiber in 1968, *The American Challenge*.

all three policy instruments. While the particular instrument may have varied across countries, they were, in fact, manifestations of a singular policy approach—how to restrict and restrain the power of the large corporation. What may have been perceived as a disparate set of policies at the time appears in retrospect to comprise a remarkably singular policy approach—a managed economy.

Quantitative and qualitative changes in the job market were the first hint of a shifting economic system (Blanchard and Katz, 1997; Siebert, 1997). One manifestation has been a divergence in job creation and reduction of unemployment across countries, between the forerunners that have shifted towards a newly emerging economy, like the Netherlands, Denmark and the United Kingdom, and the laggards still obsessed with perfecting the managed economy, like Germany, or rethinking the managed economy, like France (Nickell, 1997). This newly emerging economy we will term the *entrepreneurial economy*. Why have the policies central to the entrepreneurial economy, such as deregulation, privatization and labor market flexibility, not diffused rapidly to other countries still burdened with unemployment and stagnant growth? As the OECD points out in the 1997 *Employment Outlook*, 'the failure of continental European countries to adopt its recommendations reflects their fear of increased earnings inequality. The question is whether it is possible to deregulate without suffering these malign effects.' The problem is that the alleged benefits from structural change are accompanied only at a perceived cost in terms of important economic goals, such as income equality, the social safety net, a high level of public goods available to all, and a high level of mean wages. To reap the gains from structural change in terms of greater competitiveness, economic growth and ultimately increased employment demands a loss, or at least a perceived loss, of certain other economic policy goals.

In response to the rising unemployment coupled with the stagnant growth of the past decade, this singular policy approach has broken down. The consequences of economic restructuring are enormous and encompass virtually every dimension of economic life. To characterize fundamental differences between the old and emerging systems is a formidable task for both policy makers as well as scholars. While traces of this shift can be found in different lines of research across a broad spectrum of fields within and beyond economics, there are also insightful references in the popular press as well as the political debate addressing the most pressing policy issues of our day. Many of these references are under the rubric of the *New Economy*. In response to their direct accountability to the public, policymakers have been quicker to acknowledge the emergence of changing economic forces.

Although politicians and policymakers have made a plea for guidance in the era of entrepreneurship, scholars have been slower to respond. The purpose of this paper is to make a first step in identifying and articulating these differences and to suggest that a fundamental shift in Europe, along with the other OECD countries, is taking place. This shift is from the managed economy to the entrepreneurial economy. We do this by contrasting the most fundamental elements of the newly emerging entrepreneurial economy with those of the managed economy. Contrasting the managed economy with the entrepreneurial economy is not, however, symmetric. While scholars have accumulated decades of meticulous research documenting, analyzing and explaining the many manifestations of the managed economy, the entrepreneurial economy is sufficiently new as to preclude anything approaching comparable scholarship. Thus, while we are able to stand on the shoulders of giants when describing the managed economy, systematic knowledge about the emerging entrepreneurial economy remains more limited. The aim of this paper is to motivate subsequent research by outlining some of the main differences between the two. We do this by contrasting the most fundamental elements of the newly emerging entrepreneurial economy with those of the managed economy. Fourteen trade-offs confronting these two polar worlds are identified. The common thread throughout these trade-offs is the increased role of new and small enterprises in the entrepreneurial economy.

We speculate that these 14 trade-offs are all manifestations of a shifting source of comparative advantage away from capital and labor towards knowledge-based economic activity. Just as the comparative advantage in economic activity based on capital and labor rendered the managed economy as an appropriate response, the shift to knowledge-based economic activity is the driving force underlying the emergence of the entrepreneurial economy. While the requisite research to validate or refute this conjecture remains to be undertaken, the point of this article is to suggest not only that a systematic and pervasive set of distinct manifestations differentiate the managed economy from the emerging entrepreneurial economy, but also that these differences are profound and fundamental in nature. This article is therefore more descriptive in nature and calls upon analytical contributions from a broad range of other studies to weave together a consistent framework in differentiating the entrepreneurial from the managed economy.

2. The Trade-offs

The managed economy, as characterized by Chandler (1977, 1990), thrived for nearly three-quarters of a century. Why has an alternative system, which

———————————— *What's New about the New Economy?* ————————————

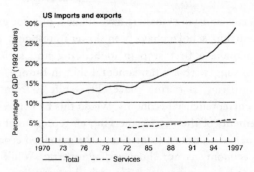

FIGURE 1. US imports and exports. Source: *Economic Report of the President* (February 1998), taken from http://www.neweconomyindex.org/index.html.

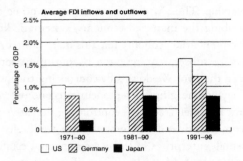

FIGURE 2. Average FDI inflows and outflows. Source: Organization for Economic Co-operation and Development, *Reviews of Foreign Direct Investment—United States* (Paris, 1995), taken from www.neweconomyindex.org/index.html.

we term the entrepreneurial economy, emerged? The answer has to do with globalization. While globalization is a multidimensional phenomenon encompassing a broad spectrum of economic and social dimensions, virtually all measures of trade, foreign direct investment and integration indicate a sharp increase in recent years. For example, Figure 1 shows that trade has become increasingly important over time for the United States. Similarly, Figure 2 shows that foreign direct investment is also gaining in importance.

The emergence of the entrepreneurial economy is a response to two fundamental aspects of globalization. The first is the advent of low-cost but highly skilled competition in Central and Eastern Europe as well as Asia. The second is the telecommunications and microprocessor revolution, which has greatly reduced the cost of shifting standardized economic activity out of high-cost locations, such as Europe, and into lower-cost locations elsewhere in the world.

A consequence of globalization is that the comparative advantage of high-wage countries is no longer compatible with routinized economic activity, which can be easily transferred to lower-cost regions outside Western Europe. Maintenance of high wages requires knowledge-based economic activity that cannot be costlessly diffused across geographic space. The first group of trade-offs we examine focuses on characterizing the forces underlying the managed and entrepreneurial economies. This group consists of three trade-offs. The first is between localization and globalization. The second trade-off is between change and continuity. Change goes together with knowledge-based activity, and knowledge-based activity results in innovations that are more radical and less incremental. An inherent characteristic of knowledge is high uncertainty, which individuals assess differently. Differences in the evaluation of knowledge result in an increased role of new and small firms. Small firms were viewed negatively in the managed economy because their suboptimal size imposed a less efficient use of resources. The third trade-off of this group compares the view that increased employment requires a reduction in wages with the view in the entrepreneurial economy that higher wages can accompany increased employment.

The second group also consists of three trade-offs, which characterize differences in the underlying environment. Turbulence, diversity and heterogeneity are central to the entrepreneurial economy. By contrast, stability, continuity and homogeneity were the cornerstones of the managed economy. These differences are examined in trade-offs 4–6.

There are four trade-offs in the fourth group, which focuses on how firms function in the entrepreneurial and managed economies. Trade-off 7 examines motivation versus control. The boundary between the firm and the industry is the subject of trade-off 8—market exchange versus firm transaction. The interface between firms is the focus of trade-off 9, where competition and co-operation are viewed as complements or substitutes. The tenth trade-offs focuses on the roles of flexibility and scale economies.

The final group consists of four trade-offs involving government policy. They cover the goal of policy (stimulation versus regulation), the target of policy (inputs versus outputs), the locus of policy (local versus national) and financing policy.

2.1 Localization versus Globalization

The meaning of geographic space differs between entrepreneurial and managed economies. In the managed economy, the standardization of products and production reduces the importance of regional-specific characteristics and idiosyncrasies. This is because of the difference in the most important factors of production between the managed and entrepreneurial economies. As represented by the neoclassical production function, production in the managed economy results from the inputs of land, labor and capital (Romer, 1992). While these traditional inputs still play a role in the entrepreneurial economy, knowledge has emerged as the most important factor of production. A recent literature from the new growth theory argues that knowledge differs inherently from the traditional factors of production in that it cannot be costlessly transferred across geographic space (Krugman, 1991a,b; Lucas, 1993). This is why under the entrepreneurial economy geography plays a more important role in that knowledge tends to be developed in the contexts of localized production networks embedded in innovative clusters.

In rediscovering the importance of economic geography, Krugman (1991a, p. 5) asks, 'What is the most striking feature of the geography of economic activity? The short answer is surely concentration . . . production is remarkably concentrated in space.' Perhaps in response to Krugman's concern, a literature in economics has recently emerged which focuses on the implications of the spatial concentration of economic activity for economic growth. Theoretical models posited by Romer (1990), Lucas (1993) and Krugman (1991a,b) link increasing returns to scale yielded by externalities within a geographically bounded region to higher rates of growth. The empirical evidence clearly suggests that R&D and other sources of knowledge not only generate externalities, but also that such knowledge spillovers tend to be geographically bounded within the region where the new economic knowledge was created (Jaffe, 1989; Jaffe *et al.*, 1993; Audretsch and Feldman, 1996; Audretsch and Stephan, 1996). That is, new economic knowledge may spill over, but the geographic extent of such knowledge spillovers is limited.[2]

As Figure 3 shows, internet use has exploded in the last decade. The importance of location and geographic proximity in a world increasingly dom-

---

[2] An important finding of Jaffe (1989) and Audretsch and Feldman (1996) is that investment in R&D by private corporations and universities spills over for economic exploitation by third-party firms. In these studies the knowledge production function was modified where the innovative activity within a geographical unit of observation—a state—was related to the private corporate expenditures on R&D within that state as well as the research expenditures undertaken at universities. Not only was innovative activity found to increase in the presence of high private corporate expenditures on R&D, but also as a result of research expenditures undertaken by universities within the geographic area. In order to explicitly identify the recipients of R&D spillovers, Acs, Audretsch and Feldman (1994) estimated separate knowledge production functions for large and small firms. Their results suggested that the innovative output of all firms rises along with an increase in the amount of R&D inputs, in both private corporations and university laboratories. However, R&D expenditures made by private companies play a particularly important role in providing inputs to the innovative activity of large firms; and expenditures on research made by universities serve as an especially key input for generating innovative activity in small enterprises.

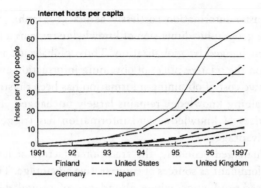

FIGURE 3. Internet hosts per capita.

inated by email, fax machines and electronic communications superhighways may seem surprising and even paradoxical at first glance. After all, the new telecommunications technologies have triggered a virtual spatial revolution in terms of the geography of production.

The resolution of this paradox lies in the distinction between knowledge and information. While the marginal cost of transmitting *information* may be invariant to distance, presumably the marginal cost of transmitting *knowledge*, and especially *tacit knowledge*, rises with distance. Von Hipple (1994) demonstrates that high context, uncertain knowledge, or what he terms as *sticky knowledge*, is best transmitted via face-to-face interaction and through frequent contact. Proximity matters in transmitting knowledge because as Arrow (1962) pointed out some three decades ago, tacit knowledge is inherently non-rival in nature, and knowledge developed for any particular application can easily spill over and be applied for different purposes. Similarly, Griliches (1992, p. 29) has defined knowledge spillovers as 'working on similar things and hence benefiting much from each other's research.' As Glaeser *et al.* (1992) have observed, 'intellectual breakthroughs must cross hallways and streets more easily than oceans and continents'. Stephan (1996) explains the role that working together in close proximity plays in generating new breakthroughs in science.[3]

The dichotomy between knowledge and information does not contradict globalization. However, globalization has not had symmetric impacts on knowledge and information. On the one hand, globalization has made it

———————

[3] The dichotomy between information and tacit knowledge does not mirror the more traditional dichotomy between high and low technology industries. Just as there are aspects of high technology industries that are well defined and standardized and can therefore be outsourced, there are also elements of low technology industries that are not well defined and cannot be outsourced. For example, certain types of software programming is outsourced to India and Eastern Europe, while the genesis for ideas in entertainment clusters in just several locations.

possible to transfer information costlessly across geographic space. On the other hand, the geographic dimension of knowledge remains a local phenomenon, largely unchanged by globalization. Thus, globalization has exerted a powerful shift on the relative prices of obtaining information and knowledge. While the relative cost of obtaining information has been drastically reduced, the cost of obtaining knowledge remains largely unchanged. This change in the relative prices of knowledge and information has triggered a shift in comparative advantage.

Under the managed economy, the traditional factors of land, labor and capital are predominant as sources of comparative advantage. This was clearly the case in mass production where abundance of capital determined the comparative advantage (Chandler, 1977). Local characteristics and regional idiosyncrasies are irrelevant as a knowledge source and therefore as a source of competitive advantage. In the managed economy, geography provides a platform to combine mobile capital with (immobile) lower-cost labor (Kindleberger and Audretsch, 1983). In the entrepreneurial economy the comparative advantage is based on innovative activity. An important source of this innovative activity is knowledge spillovers that cannot be easily diffused across geographic space. Local characteristics and regional idiosyncrasies provide a rich source of new knowledge in the entrepreneurial economy. The so-called *death of distance* resulting from globalization has shifted the comparative advantage of high-cost locations towards economic activity that cannot be costlessly diffused across geographic space. The creation and spillover of tacit knowledge is a localized phenomenon. Thus, in the entrepreneurial economy local proximity and regions have emerged as an important locus of economic activity.

2.2 Change versus Continuity

Cohen and Klepper (1992) identify an inherent trade-off between change on the one hand and continuity on the other. While the managed economy depended upon continuity (Chandler, 1977), the entrepreneurial economy provokes and thrives on change. Cohen and Klepper's (1992) theory extends the work of Richard Nelson (1981) about the importance of competition and diversity for technological change. Seen through the lens of evolutionary economics (Nelson and Winter, 1982) there are two key dimensions involved in the process of technological change: diversity and selection. The technological competence of each firm results in a particular technological trajectory. Innovative activity is generally within the boundaries established by the firm's core competence and its technological trajectory. Such innovative activity within the technological paradigm established by the firm's core competence provides the basis of continuity in the managed economy.

As Cohen and Klepper (1992) point out, large firms have a greater incentive to invest in R&D because they are better able to appropriate the returns through greater output and sales. At the same time they do not have a large incentive to try to extend innovative activity beyond the boundaries imposed by their technological trajectories. According to Cohen and Klepper (1992, p. 2),

> Dividing up industry output over a greater number of small firms increases the chances that any given approach to innovation will be pursued, thereby increasing the diversity of technological efforts in the industry. While increasing the number of firms does not necessarily benefit individual firms in the industry, it promotes technical advance and, hence, benefits society by increasing the number of productive approaches to innovation that are collectively pursued in the industry. From this perspective, the source of the social advantage associated with small firm size is not smallness per se but the greater number of firms that small size implies given some industry demand.

Thus, in the entrepreneurial economy, decentralized decision-making in an industrial structure comprised of smaller firms leads to a greater diversity of approaches. This diversity, in turn, generates greater opportunities for breaking out of the boundaries imposed by the lock-in along technological trajectories and ultimately to hit it big.

Concentrating knowledge resources in just several firms in the managed economy results in a concentration of innovative activity within just several technological trajectories. By contrast, unleashing knowledge by letting loose a horde of independent agents—deconcentration—in the entrepreneurial economy, results in a greater diversity of approaches across a broad range of technological trajectories. Which is more efficient? If the degree of uncertainty is relatively low, then concentrating knowledge results may result in greater technological change. But as the degree of uncertainty increases, a diversity of approaches, represented by a multiplicity of technological trajectories, becomes more important.

Innovation is present under both change and continuity. However, the locus of innovative activity differs considerably between the managed and entrepreneurial economies. This difference is shaped by a distinction between incremental and radical innovations. Innovations can be considered to be incremental when that they are compatible with the core competence and technological trajectory of the firm (Teece *et al.*, 1994).[4] The implementation of such incremental innovations does not require significant change in the firm or its personnel. By contrast, a radical innovation can be defined as extending beyond the boundaries of the core competence and technological trajectory of the firm. Both theoretical reasons and empirical evidence support the notion that firms are characterized by technological lock-in. Theoretically, implementation of a radical innovation would require significant changes in the firm and its personnel. As Hannan and Freeman (1989) conclude, 'We assume that individual organizations are characterized by relative inertia in structure.' Empirically, a rich set of case studies provides compelling evidence that incumbent firms tend to suffer from technological lock-in (Henderson and Clark, 1990; Christenson, 2000). The managed economy was designed to absorb change within a given technological paradigm, and hence the typical firm excelled at incremental innovation. By contrast, in the entrepreneurial economy, the capacity to break out of the technological lock-in imposed by existing paradigms is enhanced. Incumbent firms may still be subject to technological lock-in in the entrepreneurial economy, just as they were under the managed economy. However, the ability for individuals and groups of individuals to break out of the existing technological trajectories by starting a new firm is a fundamental characteristic differentiating the entrepreneurial from the managed economy. The main mechanism for breaking out of a locked-in technology is the ability of economic agents to start new firms. The firm's technological trajectory may be locked-in, but new technological trajectories are started as new firms are created.

The industry lifecycle theory introduced by Vernon (1966) is typically considered to link trade and foreign direct investment to the stage of the lifecycle. There do not appear to be direct implications for the relevance of radical versus incremental innovations. But a more thoughtful examination of the framework of the industry lifecycle suggests that the relative importance of radical versus incremental innovations is shaped by the industry lifecycle.

There have been various versions of what actually constitutes the industry lifecycle. For example, Williamson (1975, pp. 215–216) has depicted the industry lifecycle as,

Three stages in an industry's development are commonly recognized: an early exploratory stage, an intermediate development stage, and a mature stage. The first or early formative stage involves the supply of a new product of relatively primitive design, manufactured on comparatively

—————————————

[4] Archibugi and Pianta (1992) show that what holds for firms also holds for countries.

unspecialized machinery, and marketed through a variety of exploratory techniques. Volume is typically low. A high degree of uncertainty characterizes business experience at this stage. The second stage is the intermediate development state in which manufacturing techniques are more refined and market definition is sharpened, output grows rapidly in response to newly recognized applications and unsatisfied market demands. A high but somewhat lesser degree of uncertainty characterizes market outcomes at this stage. The third stage is that of a mature industry. Management, manufacturing, and marketing techniques all reach a relatively advanced degree of refinement. Markets may continue to grow, but do so at a more regular and predictable rate-established connections, with customers and suppliers (including capital market access) all operate to buffer changes and thereby to limit large shifts in market shares. Significant innovations tend to be fewer and are mainly of an improvement variety.

While not explicitly stated by Vernon (1966) or Williamson (1975), the role of R&D does not stay constant over the industry lifecycle. As Klepper (1996) shows, in the early stages of the lifecycle, R&D tends to be highly productive, so that there are increasing returns to R&D. In addition, the costs of radical innovation tend to be relatively low while the cost of incremental innovation and imitation tend to be relatively low. Because innovation in newly emerging industries tends to be more radical and less incremental, it is more costly to diffuse across geographic space for economic application in lower-cost locations.

By contrast, as an industry evolves over the lifecycle, the cost of radical innovation tends to increase relative to the cost of incremental innovation and imitation. Strong diminishing returns to radical innovative activity set in. This is not the case for incremental innovation and especially imitation. An implication is that it requires an increasing amount of R&D effort to generate a given amount of innovative activity as an industry matures over the lifecycle. At the same time, it requires a decreasing amount of R&D expenditure to transfer new technology to lower cost locations, because innovation activity tends to become less radical and more incremental (Dosi, 1982, 1988; Nelson, 1990, 1995).

This means that information generated by R&D in mature industries can be transferred to lower-cost locations for economic commercialization. By contrast, the knowledge resulting from R&D in newly emerging industries cannot be easily transferred to lower-cost locations for economic commercialization. The reason for the asymmetry between the ability to transfer the product of R&D lies in the inherent distinction between information and knowledge described above. Since R&D generates tacit knowledge in the earlier stages of the lifecycle, geographic proximity plays a more important role. Thus, under the managed economy incremental innovative activity along with diffusion played a more important role. This type of innovative activity, while often requiring large R&D investment, generated incremental changes in products along the existing technological trajectories. In the entrepreneurial economy, the comparative advantage of the high-cost location demands innovative activity earlier in the lifecycle. Early stage innovative activity consists of radical innovation, which is more involved in creating and developing new technological trajectories rather than following existing technological trajectories (Agarwal and Audretsch, 2001).

2.3 Jobs and High Wages versus Jobs or High Wages

One of the most striking policy dilemmas in the managed economy was that unemployment could be reduced only at the cost of lower wages. In the entrepreneurial economy the choice is less ambiguous. High employment can be combined with high wages, just as low wages do not necessarily imply high employment.

The policy dilemma between employment creation and wage levels was the response to the wave of corporate downsizing, which has left virtually no OECD country untouched. The US Labor Department recently reported that as a result of corporate downsizing more than 40 million jobs have disappeared in the United States since 1979. This includes over 20 million blue-collar jobs and somewhat fewer than 20 million white-collar jobs. Between 1980 and 1993, the 500 largest US manufacturing corporations cut nearly 5 million jobs, or one-quarter of their workforce (Audretsch, 1995). The rate of corporate downsizing has apparently increased over time. During most of the 1980s, about one in 25 workers lost a job. In the 1990s this has risen to one in 20 workers. Such downsizing has not been unique to the United States but has become increasingly rampant throughout Europe.

If corporate downsizing has been rampant throughout OECD countries, why is there such a large variance in unemployment rates? For example, unemployment in the United States, United Kingdom and the Netherlands has actually been falling. How can these seemingly incompatible phenomena be reconciled? Because the more entrepreneurial economies have been more successful at creating new jobs to compensate for jobs lost to corporate downsizing. It is small firms in general, and new firm start-ups in particular, that have been the locomotive of employment creation.[5] For example, Audretsch (1995) found that 1.3 million new jobs in manufacturing were in

TABLE 1. Entrepreneurship Rate in OECD Countries

	Level			Growth	
	1974	1986	1998	1986–74	1998–86
Austria	0.081	0.066	0.080	−0.015	0.013
Belgium	0.100	0.106	0.119	0.005	0.013
Denmark	0.081	0.063	0.064	−0.018	0.001
Finland	0.062	0.066	0.082	0.004	0.015
France	0.109	0.098	0.085	−0.011	−0.012
Germany (West)	0.073	0.069	0.085	−0.004	0.016
Greece	0.173	0.182	0.186*	0.009	0.003
Ireland	0.073	0.078	0.112	0.004	0.034
Italy	0.144	0.167	0.182	0.023	0.015
Luxembourg	0.100	0.078	0.059*	−0.022	−0.019
The Netherlands	0.097	0.082	0.104	−0.015	0.022
Portugal	0.110	0.108	0.152*	−0.002	0.044
Spain	0.116	0.115	0.130	−0.001	0.015
Sweden	0.071	0.066	0.082	−0.005	0.016
UK	0.077	0.089	0.109	0.012	0.020
Iceland	0.102	0.099	0.132	−0.004	0.033
Norway	0.092	0.084	0.071	−0.008	−0.014
Switzerland	0.065	0.070	0.091	0.005	0.021
USA	0.082	0.103	0.103	0.021	0.000
Japan	0.127	0.125	0.100	−0.002	−0.024
Canada	0.075	0.100	0.141	0.025	0.041
Australia	0.137	0.165	0.155	0.028	−0.011
New Zealand	0.098	0.110	0.142	0.012	0.032
Average	0.098	0.100	0.111		

The source of the data are OECD figures, adapted by EIM to improve upon international comparability. *Provisional. Agriculture is excluded. Germany is West Germany for 1974 and 1986. The total numbers of business owners for all countries in 1974, 1986 and 1998 are 30 337, 38 446 and 44 927 respectively (in thousands). The data set is referred to as COMPENDIA 2000.1. For further information contact André van Stel at EIM (ast@eim.nl).

fact created by small firms between 1976 and 1986, while the number of large manufacturing jobs actually decreased by 100 000. Subsequently, between 1987 and 1992, small companies (with fewer than 500) employees created all of the 5.8 million new jobs in the United States. Over that same period, large companies recorded a net loss of 2.3 million jobs

Konings (1995) found that for the United Kingdom there is a negative

[5] The literature on employment generation and firm size can be found in Davis *et al.* (1996a,b) and Carree and Klomp (1996).

relationship between gross job creation and plant size but a positive one between gross job destruction and plant size. Robson and Gallagher (1994) show that about one-third of all new employment in the United Kingdom between 1971 and 1981 was in firms with fewer than 20 employees. In the 1980s nearly one-half of all jobs were created in such firms (although they accounted for about one-fifth of total employment in 1985). And between 1987 and 1991 large firms in the United Kingdom, like their counterparts in the United States, were net job shedders. Small firms contributed all of the new employment. Hughes (1993) provides evidence suggesting that this was in part due to downsizing of the largest firms in the economy, and in part due to an actual expansion of economic activity contributed by small firms. Baldwin and Picot (1995) have found virtually identical results for Canada.

Table 1 shows that there has been considerable disparity among OECD countries in business ownership rates both across countries and over time. The magnitude of this shift and speed of adjustment varies considerably across countries. Econometric evidence undertaken by Audretsch *et al.* (2001) suggests that those countries that have shifted industry structure towards smaller firms in a more rapid fashion have been rewarded by higher growth rates (see also Thurik, 1996; Carree and Thurik, 1998, 1999; Audretsch and Thurik, 2000).

While systematic empirical evidence has been gathered across a broad range of countries documenting that small firms generate most of the new jobs, similar studies also provide compelling evidence that small firms are also a large source of job destruction. Taken together, these studies suggest that the industrial structure has become more turbulent (Caves, 1998).

In the managed economy, the job creation contributed by small firms was associated with lower wages. There is a large body of consistent empirical evidence linking the size of a firm to wages. Probably the most cited study is that of Brown *et al.* (1990, pp. 88–89), who conclude that,

> Workers in large firms earn higher wages, and this fact cannot be explained completely by differences in labor quality, industry, working conditions, or union status. Workers in large firms also enjoy better benefits and greater job security than their counterparts in small firms. When these factors are added together, it appears that workers in large firms do have a superior employment package.

This apparent trade-off between wages and employment is the result of static, cross-section studies taken at a single point in time. A different picture emerges when a dynamic analysis is introduced. This dynamic analysis suggests that, in knowledge-based industries, people start firms to pursue new but uncertain ideas. The only way they can discover if these new ideas are viable is through the trial-and-error experience provided by the market (Jovanovic, 1982; Ericson and Pakes, 1995; Pakes and Ericson, 1998). They subsequently learn, or discover, through experience, whether or not the idea is viable. If it is viable, the firm will survive and grow. If it is not viable, the firm stagnates and ultimately exits. An important line of research, spanning a broad spectrum of time periods and countries, supports this dynamic view of industries (Geroski, 1995; Caves, 1998). Start-up activity is high in almost every OECD country. Audretsch (1995) has shown that it is greater in industries where there is a higher degree of uncertainty than in industries where there is less uncertainty. In addition, there is systematic evidence that negative relationships exist between firm age and growth, and firm size and growth, as well as positive relationships between firm size and the likelihood of survival, and firm age and the likelihood of survival (Geroski, 1995). This evidence supports the dynamic view of industries that people start firms to experiment with new ideas. Most of these experiments fail, but some succeed, resulting in lower survival rates but high growth rates of the new entrants.

Recent research based on longitudinal data sets, shows that the wages and productivity of new firms in knowledge-based industries increase as the firm ages (Baldwin, 1995; Audretsch *et al.*, 2001). This implies that, as new firms mature, the small low wage firm of today becomes the high wage firm of tomorrow. Similarly, the small low productivity firm of today becomes the high productivity firm of tomorrow (Baily *et al.*, 1996). New and small firms are in motion. Through growth, new firms generate not just greater employment but also higher wages. The growth of new firms ensures that the greater employment does not come at a cost of lower wages, but rather the opposite—higher wages. Thus, while small firms generated employment at a cost of lower wages in the managed economy, in the entrepreneurial economy small firms create both more jobs and higher wages.

2.4 Turbulence versus Stability

The managed economy of the postwar period was characterized by remarkable stability. This stability was characterized by product homogeneity and durability of demand, resulting in a constant population of firms, and a low turnover rate of both jobs and workers. This stability was conducive to mass production. Just as Taylorism provided a managerial mechanism for ensuring the stability and reliability of workers in the production process, competition focused on the dimension of prices but not necessarily product differentiation (Chandler, 1977).

In the 1950s and 1960s it took two decades to replace one-third of the Fortune 500. In the 1970s it took one decade. And in the 1980s one-third of the Fortune 500 firms were replaced within just five years. Perhaps even more impressive than the handful of new enterprises that grow to penetrate the Fortune 500 are the armies of start-ups that come into existence each year—and typically disappear into oblivion within a few years. In the 1990s around 1.3 million new companies were started each year in the United States (Audretsch, 1995).

Why is the entrepreneurial economy characterized by less stability and more turbulence? The answer has to do with the sources and commercialization of new ideas. As Nelson and Winter (1982) emphasize, the role of diversity and selection has been at the heart of generating change. The process of creating diverse ideas and selecting across these diverse ideas is important in both the managed and entrepreneurial economies. However, what differs is the management and organization of the process by which diversity is created as well as the selection mechanism. In the managed economy, research activities are organized and scheduled in departments devoted towards novel products and services. The management of change fitted into what Nelson and Winter (1982) call the *routines* of a firm. According to Schumpeter (1942, p. 132), 'Innovation itself is being reduced to routine. Technological progress is increasingly becoming the business of teams of trained specialists who turn out what is required and make it work in predictable ways.' The ability of the existing corporations to manage the process of change pre-empted any opportunities for entrepreneurs to start new firms. This meant that relatively few firms were started and few firms failed, resulting in a remarkably stable industrial structure. Chandler (1990) examined the largest 200 firms in the United States, Britain and Germany over the first half of this century and found that they maintained a remarkably stable position. Teece (1993, p. 214) interprets these findings: 'Chandler's data on rankings of the largest industrial firms (for 1917, 1930, 1948 for Great Britain; 1913, 1928, 1953 for Germany) indicate considerable stability in rankings—at least as compared to what economic theory would predict. The firms that were leaders (as measured by asset size) in their industrial groupings often remained there over long periods.' Similarly, the share of total US manufacturing assets accounted for by the largest 100 corporations increased from about 36% in 1924, to 39% after the Second World War to over 50% by the end of the 1960s. This development caused Scherer (1970, p. 44) to state that, 'Despite the (statistical) uncertainties, one thing is clear. The increasing domestic dominance of the 100 largest manufacturing firms since 1947 is not a statistical illusion.' Similarly, Mueller (1989) has shown that the profits of the largest corporations tended to persist in the long run during the postwar period.

In the entrepreneurial economy, the process of generating new ideas, both within and outside of R&D laboratories, creates a diversity of opinions about the value of these new ideas. Differences in the evaluation of new ideas leads individual agents to pursue their commercialization external to the established firm in the form of a new independent venture. The diversity of new ideas and experiments with their commercialization manifests itself externally as well as internal to incumbent firms. The selection between viable and non-viable ideas is then the result of the market process and not restricted to internal decisions imposed by decision-making hierarchies. The drive to appropriate the expected value of knowledge embodied in individual economic agents results in commercialization of ideas in the form of new firms. But not all of these start-ups are successful. A large body of empirical studies shows (Geroski, 1994) that (i) start-up rates are greater in innovative industries than in non-innovative industries, and (ii) the likelihood of survival is lower in innovative industries (for a study of the services see Audretsch *et al.*, 1999). Audretsch (1995) finds that one-third of all US manufacturing firms are less than six years old. However, these new start-ups account for only 5% of total manufacturing employment.

Taken together, this evidence provides a view of the entrepreneurial economy as being characterized by a tremendous degree of turbulence. It is an economy in motion, with a massive number of new firms entering each year, but only a subset surviving for any length of time, and an even smaller subset that can ultimately challenge and displace the incumbent large enterprises.

It is not just enterprises that are more turbulent in the entrepreneurial economy, but also both jobs and the commitments between firms and workers. Davis *et al.* (1996a, b) document a marked increase in the degree of worker turnover in the United States over a long period of time. At the same time, labor contracts have become more targeted towards specific tasks, typically for a limited period time, whereas in the managed economy labor contracts tended to be general for an indefinite time period. The new legal forms of employment contracts and practices—part-time workers, flex-workers, temporary workers, freelance workers, contract workers, consultants, etc.—represent an injection of entrepreneurial forces into the labor market (Eberts and Stone, 1992; Addison and Welfens, 1998). For example, Paque (1998) shows that the share of total employment accounted for by part-time workers has increased between 1973 and 1994 from 3.8% to 12.8%

in Belgium, from 4.9% to 14.9% in France, from 10.1% to 15.1% in Germany, from 16.0% to 23.8% in the United Kingdom, and between 1983 and 1994 from 21.4% to 35.0% in the Netherlands. The greater degree of uncertainty and turnover experienced by workers in the entrepreneurial economy mirrors the greater turbulence experienced by firms. Replacing long-term fixed contracts with new flexible forms of work contracts provides the essential vehicle propelling the transition from the managed to the entrepreneurial economy.

2.5 Diversity versus Specialization

There has been a series of theoretical arguments suggesting that the degree of diversity versus specialization may account for differences in rates of growth and technological change. There are two dimensions to this debate: the firm and the industry. More recently, it has been extended to geographic units, such as nations and regions. On the one hand, specialization of industry activities is associated with lower transactions costs and therefore greater (static) efficiency (the decrease in transactions costs results in a decrease in production costs). On the other hand, a diversity of activities is argued to facilitate the exchange of new ideas and therefore greater innovative activity and (dynamic) efficiency.

One view, which Glaeser *et al.* (1992) attribute to the *Marshall–Arrow–Romer* externality, suggests that an increased specialization of a particular industry facilitates knowledge spillovers across firms because all workers are engaged in identical activity. This model formalizes the insight that the concentration of an industry within a certain set of narrow economic activities promotes knowledge spillovers between firms and therefore facilitates innovative activity. An important assumption of the model is that knowledge externalities with respect to firms exist, but only for firms within the same activities.

By contrast, restricting knowledge externalities to occur only within the specialized industry may ignore an important source of new economic knowledge: inter-industry knowledge spillovers. Jacobs (1969) argues that the most important source of knowledge spillovers are external to the industry in which the firm operates and that cities are the source of considerable innovation because the diversity of knowledge sources is greatest in cities. This same view about the role of knowledge spillovers in cities is the basis of Lucas (1993). According to Jacobs, it is the exchange of complementary knowledge across diverse firms and economic agents that yields a greater return on new economic knowledge. She develops a theory that emphasizes that the variety of industries within a geographic region promotes knowledge externalities and ultimately innovative activity and economic growth.[6]

Recent studies have provided evidence testing for the impact of diversity versus specialization on the performance of regions, measured in terms of growth (Glaeser *et al.*, 1992) and in terms of innovative activity (Feldman and Audretsch, 1999). These studies provide systematic empirical support for the thesis that diversity is more conducive to knowledge spillovers and ultimately innovative activity and subsequent growth than is specialization.[7]

Because spillovers are an important source of knowledge-generating innovative activity, diversity is a prerequisite of the entrepreneurial economy. Sacrificing lower transaction costs for greater opportunities for knowledge spillovers is preferable. In the managed economy, there is less to be gained from the spillover of knowledge. The higher transaction costs associated with diversity yield little in terms of increased innovative activity, making specialization preferable in the managed economy.

2.6 Heterogeneity versus Homogeneity

A trade-off exists between the degree of heterogeneity and homogeneity within the population. In contrast to the trade-off between diversity and specialization, which focuses on firms, the trade-off involving population refers to individuals, which are the basis for decision-making within firms and as consumers. There are two dimensions shaping the degree of homogeneity/ heterogeneity. The first refers to the genetic make-up of individuals and their personal experiences (Nooteboom, 1994). The second dimension refers to the information set to which they are exposed. The managed economy is based on homogeneity; the entrepreneurial economy on heterogeneity. According to Nooteboom (1994, p. 330), 'The sources that produce diversity within the scope allowed for it, lie in the variance of backgrounds, motives and goals of entrepreneurship.'

To the extent that individuals in the population are identical, the costs of communication and transactions are minimized (Olson, 1982). Lower costs of transaction in communication result in (static) efficiency gains and facilitate

---

[6] The first important test of the specialisation versus diversity theories to date has focused not on the gains in terms of innovative activity, but rather in terms of employment growth. Glaeser *et al.* (1992) employ a data set on the growth of large industries in 170 cities between 1956 and 1987 in order to identify the relative importance of the degree of regional specialisation, diversity and local competition play in influencing industry growth rates. The authors find evidence that contradicts the Marshall–Arrow–Romer model but is consistent with the theories of Jacobs. However, their study provided no direct evidence as to whether diversity is more important than specialisation in generating innovation.

[7] Feldman and Audretsch (1999) provide systematic evidence that the gains from diversity hold for both the spatial and firm units of observation.

a higher probability of knowledge spilling over across individuals within the population. However, new ideas are less likely to emerge from communication across individuals in a perfectly homogeneous population because these individuals tend to be identical. This means that individuals in homogeneous populations tend to have access to the same information sets and to evaluate any information set in a similar fashion. Thus, a homogeneous population results in a higher probability of communications but those communications have a lower impact because there are fewer new ideas to spill over. A world of homogeneous economic agents promotes diffusion but not innovation.

In a heterogeneous population each individual has a unique genetic and experience profile, and has access to a unique information set (Olson, 1982). The unique genetic and experience profiles would result in a different evaluation across individuals even for a given set of information. However, a heterogeneous population is also characterized by differential access to information. This means that the costs of communications across individuals in a heterogeneous population tend to be difficult and costly, resulting in higher transaction costs and lower levels of efficiency than in a homogeneous population. At that same time, new ideas are more likely to emerge from communication in a heterogeneous than in a homogeneous world. An implication is that the likelihood of communication in a heterogeneous population is lower but such communication is more prone to produce novelty and innovation. It is differences not similarities that generate knowledge spillover. As W. M. Cohen and F. Malerba (unpublished data) argue, the 'tendency to variation is a chief cause of progress'.

The trade-off between diversity versus specialization focuses on the population of firms and industries. The trade-off discussed in this section is analogous and involves the population of people. The lower transactions costs resulting from a homogeneous population in the managed economy are not associated with a high opportunity cost, because knowledge spillovers are relatively unimportant in generating innovative activity. However, knowledge spillovers are a driving force in the entrepreneurial economy, which more than offset the higher transactions costs associated with a heterogeneous population. The relative degree of homogeneity or heterogeneity can be influenced by policies, such as those promoting immigration, mobility and education.[8]

2.7 Motivation versus Control

If the application of British inventions in the 1800s had served as the catalyst

---

[8] It may be that the appropriate role of education was to foster homogeneity in the managed economy, but heterogeneity in the entrepreneurial economy (Audretsch *et al.*, forthcoming).

for US industrialization, the revolution in management techniques—the modern corporate structure—enabled its implementation. According to Reich (1983, p. 26),

> Managerialism offered America a set of organizing principles at precisely the time when many Americans sensed a need for greater organization and these principles soon shaped every dominant American institution precisely as they helped those institutions become dominant. The logic of routine, large-scale manufacturing, first shaped its original business environment and then permeated the larger social environment.

Through the structure of the modern corporation, the new managerialism excelled at amassing large quantities of raw materials, labor and capital inputs, and at applying particular manufacturing processes, thereby achieving a very specific use of these resources. The essence of the managerialism was *command and control of labor effort*. Labor was considered to be indistinguishable from all other inputs, as long as scientific management was able to extract a full day's worth of energy for a full day's pay (Wheelwright, 1985). As tasks became increasingly specialized, the skill level required of workers under the mass-production regime became less important. What mattered most under Taylorism was the consistency and reliability of each precise cog; what mattered least was the decision-making capability of each unit. Thus, the labor input in the production process was reduced to routine (Chandler, 1990).

However, as the comparative advantage of the advanced industrialized countries in Europe and North America become increasingly based on new knowledge, the command and control approach to labor becomes less effective. What matters less is requiring an established set of activities from knowledge workers and what matters more is motivating these workers to facilitate the discovery and implementation of new ideas. The type of work environment fostering creativity is radically different from one simply harnessing the brute labor input of workers. A central feature of work is dealing with uncertainty. As uncertainty replaces predictability as the main characteristic of the work environment, workers who can deal with uncertain situations are more valuable in the entrepreneurial economy. This contrast between the new entrepreneurial and managed economies is reflected by the explosion of titles such as *Managing Chaos*, *Re-engineering*, *Management without Hierarchy*, and *De-Layering* in the popular management literature. Thus, in the entrepreneurial economy motivating employees to participate in the creation and commercialization of new ideas matters more than in simply controlling and regulating their behavior.

2.8 Market Exchange versus Firm Transaction

Dating back at least to Coase (1937), and more recently advanced by Williamson (1975), an analytical distinction has been made between exchange via the market and intra-firm transactions. Coase (1937) and later Williamson (1975) argued that the size of an enterprise will be determined by answering what Coase (1937, p. 30) articulated as, 'The question always is, will it pay to bring an extra exchange transaction under the organizing authority?' Both Coase (1937) and Williamson (1975) emphasize that uncertainty and imperfect information increase the costs of intra-firm transactions. As Knight (1921) argued, low uncertainty combined with transparency and predictability of information make intra-firm transactions efficient relative to market exchange. However, in an era where uncertainty is high and information is imperfect, market exchange tends to be more efficient than intra-firm transactions. In the managed economy, which was dominated by a high degree of certainty and predictability of information, transactions within firms tended to be more efficient than market exchange. This is consistent with the well-documented increase in both vertical integration and conglomeration during the post-war period (Chandler, 1977). In the entrepreneurial economy, both of these trends have been reversed (Carlsson, 1989). As Carlsson and Taymaz (1994) show, there has been a decrease in both mean firm size as well as the extent of vertical integration and conglomeration since the mid-1970s.

Coase was awarded a Nobel Prize for explaining why a firm should exist. But why should more than one firm exist in an industry?[9] One answer is provided by the traditional economics literature focusing on industrial organization in the managed economy. An excess level of profitability induces entry into the industry. And this is why the entry of new firms is interesting and important in the managed economy—because the new firms provide an equilibrating function in the market, in that the levels of price and profit are restored to the competitive levels. In the traditional theory, outputs and inputs in an industry are assumed to be homogenous. That is, the entry of new firms in the managed economy is about business as usual—it is just that

[9] Coase (1937, p. 23) himself asked, 'A pertinent question to ask would appear to be (quite apart from the monopoly considerations raised by Professor Knight), why, if by organising one can eliminate certain costs and in fact reduce the cost of production, are there any market transactions at all? Why is not all production carried on by one big firm?'

with the new entrant there is more of it. Geroski (1991a, p. 65) reflects the role of entry in the managed economy by asserting,

> If we think of entry as an error-correction mechanism which is attracted by and serves to bid away excess profits, it is natural to suppose that entry will occur whenever profits differ from their long-run levels. Given this maintained hypothesis, observations of actual entry rates and current (or expected post-entry) profits can be used to make inferences about the unobservable of interest—long-run profits. In particular, entry in an industry is hypothesized to occur whenever expected post-entry profits exceed the level of profits protected in the long run.

Empirical evidence in support of the model of entry in the managed economy is ambiguous at best. This leads Geroski (1991b, p. 282) to conclude,

> Right from the start, scholars have had some trouble in reconciling the stories told about entry in standard textbooks with the substance of what they have found in their data. Very few have emerged from their work feeling that they have answered half as many questions as they have raises, much less that they have answered most of the interesting ones.

Perhaps one reason for this trouble is the inherently static model used to capture an inherently dynamic process.[10]

In the entrepreneurial economy, the balance between market exchange and firm transactions leads to a different role for the entry of new firms. This is because the entrepreneurial economy is based more on the factor of new knowledge and less on the traditional factors of land, labor and capital upon which the managed economy thrived. There is an inherent difference between new knowledge and the traditional factors. As Knight (1921), and later Arrow (1962), emphasized, new economic knowledge is anything but certain. Not only is new economic knowledge inherently risky, but also substantial

---

[10] Manfred Neumann (1993, pp. 593–594) has criticized this traditional model of entry, as found in the individual country studies contained in Geroski and Schwalbach (1991), because they 'are predicated on the adoption of a basically static framework. It is assumed that start-ups enter a given market where they are facing incumbents which naturally try to fend off entry. Since the impact of entry on the performance of incumbents seems to be only slight, the question arises whether the costs of entry are worthwhile, given the high rate of exit associated with entry. Geroski appears to be rather sceptical about that. I submit that adopting a static framework is misleading. . . . In fact, generally, an entrant can only hope to succeed if he employs either a new technology or offers a new product, or both. Just imitating incumbents is almost certainly doomed to failure. If the process of entry is looked upon from this perspective the high correlation between gross entry and exit reflects the inherent risks of innovating activities. . . . Obviously it is rather difficult to break loose from the inherited mode of reasoning within the static framework. It is not without merit, to be sure, but it needs to be enlarged by putting it into a dynamic setting.'

asymmetries exist across agents both between and within firms (Milgrom and Roberts, 1987). The expected value of a new idea, or potential innovation, is likely to be anything but unanimous between the inventor of that idea and the decisionmaker, or group of decisionmakers, of the firm confronted with evaluating proposed changes or innovations.[11]

Combined with the bureaucratic organization of incumbent firms to make a decision, the asymmetry of knowledge leads to a host of agency problems, spanning incentive structures, monitoring and transaction costs. It is the existence of such agency costs, combined with asymmetric information, that not only provides an incentive for agents with new ideas to appropriate the expected value of their knowledge externally by starting new firms, but also with a propensity that varies systematically from industry to industry.[12]

To minimize agency problems and the cost of monitoring, bureaucratic hierarchies develop objective rules.[13] As Holmstrom (1989, p. 323) points out,

> Monitoring limitations suggest that the firm seeks out activities which are more easily and objectively evaluated. Assignments will be chosen in a fashion that is conducive to more effective control. Authority and command systems work better in environments, which are more predictable and can be directed with less investment information. Routine tasks are the

[11] It is because information is not only imperfect but also asymmetric that Knight (1921, p. 268) argued that the primary task of the firm is to process information in order to reach a decision: 'With the introduction of uncertainty—the fact of ignorance and the necessity of acting upon opinion rather than knowledge—into this Eden-like situation (that is a world of perfect information), its character is entirely changed. . . . With uncertainty present doing things, the actual execution of activity, becomes in a real sense a secondary part of life; the primary problem or function is deciding what to do and how to do it.'

[12] Alchian (1950) pointed out that the existence of knowledge asymmetries would result in the inevitability of mistaken decisions in an uncertain world. Later, Alchian and Demsetz (1972) attributed the existence of asymmetric information across the employees in a firm as resulting in a problem of monitoring the contribution accruing from each employee and setting the rewards correspondingly. This led them to conclude that, 'The problem of economic organisation is the economical means of metering productivity and rewards' (Alchian and Demsetz, 1972, p. 783). Coase (1937) and later Williamson (1975) argued that the size of an (incumbent) enterprise will be determined by answering what Coase (1937, p. 30) articulated as, 'The question always is, will it pay to bring an extra exchange transaction under the organising authority?' In fact, Coase (1937, p. 24) pointed out that, 'Other things being equal, a firm will tend to be larger the less likely the (firm) is to make mistakes and the smaller the increase in mistakes with an increase in the transactions organised.'

[13] Holmstrom (1989) and Milgrom (1988) have pointed out the existence of what they term as a *bureaucratization dilemma*, where, 'To say that increased size brings increased profit is a safe generalisation. To note that bureaucracy is viewed as an organisational disease is equally accurate' (Holmstrom, 1989, p. 320). In addition, Kreps (1991) has argued that such bureaucratic rules promote internal uniformity and that a uniform corporate culture, in turn, promotes the reputation of the firm. These bureaucratic rules, however, make it more difficult to evaluate the efforts and activities of agents involved in activities that do not conform to such bureaucratic rules.

comparative advantage of a bureaucracy and its activities can be expected to reflect that.

Williamson (1975, p. 201) has also emphasized the inherent tension between hierarchical bureaucratic organizations and the ability of incumbent organizations to appropriate the value of new knowledge for innovative activity outside of the technological trajectories associated with the core competence of that organization:

> Were it that large firms could compensate internal entrepreneurial activity in ways approximating that of the market, the large firm need experience no disadvantage in entrepreneurial respects. Violating the congruency between hierarchical position and compensation appears to generate bureaucratic strains, however, and is greatly complicated by the problem of accurately imputing causality.

This leads him to conclude that:

> I am inclined to regard the early stage innovative disabilities of large size as serious and propose the following hypothesis: An efficient procedure by which to introduce new products is for the initial development and market testing to be performed by independent investors and small firms (perhaps new entrants) in an industry, the successful developments then to be acquired, possibly through licensing or merger, for subsequent marketing by a large multidivision enterprise. . . . Put differently, a division of effort between the new product innovation process on the one hand, and the management of proven resources on the other may well be efficient. (Williamson, 1975, pp. 205–206)

The degree to which agents and incumbent firms are confronted with knowledge asymmetries and agency problems with respect to seeking out new economic knowledge and (potential) innovative activity would not be expected to be constant across industries. This is because the underlying knowledge conditions vary from industry to industry. In some industries new economic knowledge generating innovative activity tends to be relatively routine and can be processed within the context of incumbent hierarchical bureaucracies. In other industries, however, innovations tend to come from knowledge that is not of a routine nature and therefore tends to be rejected by the hierarchical bureaucracies of incumbent corporations. Nelson and Winter (1982) describe these different underlying knowledge conditions as reflecting two distinct technological regimes—the entrepreneurial and routinized technological regimes: 'An entrepreneurial regime is one that is favorable to innovative entry and unfavorable to innovative activity by established firms; a routinized regime is one in which the conditions are the other way around' (Winter, 1984, p. 297). As the comparative advantage of the advanced industrial economies shifts towards innovative industries, what is true for those industries holds for entire countries.[14]

In the managed economy, there is likely to be relatively little divergence in the evaluation of the expected value of a (potential) innovation between the inventor and the decision-making bureaucracy of the firm. A great incentive for agents to start their own firms will not exist. In the entrepreneurial economy, however, a divergence in beliefs between the agent and the principal regarding the expected value of a (potential) innovation is more likely to emerge.[15] It is in the entrepreneurial economy where the start-up of new firms is likely to play a more important role, presumably as a result of the motivation to appropriate the value of economic knowledge.

2.9 Competition and Co-operation as Complements versus Competition and Co-operation as Substitutes

While models of competition generally assume that firms behave autonomously, models of co-operation involve linkages among firms. These linkages take various forms, including joint ventures, strategic alliances, and formal and informal networks (Gomes-Casseres, 1996, 1997). In the managed economy competition and co-operation are viewed as being substitutes. This is because firms are vertically integrated and compete primarily in product markets. Co-operation between firms in the product market reduces the

[14] Gort and Klepper (1982) argued that the relative innovative advantage between newly established enterprises and incumbent firms depends upon the source of information generating innovative activity. If information based on non-transferrable experience in the market is an important input in generating innovative activity, then incumbent firms will tend to have the innovative advantage over new firms. This is consistent with Winter's (1984) notion of the routinized regime, where the accumulated stock of non-transferrable information is the product of experience within the market, which firms outside of the main incumbent organisations, by definition, cannot possess. By contrast, when information outside of the routines practised by the incumbent firms is a relatively important input in generating innovative activity, newly established firms will tend to have the innovative advantage over incumbent firms. Arrow (1962), Mueller (1976) and Williamson (1975) have all emphasized that when such information created outside of the incumbent firms cannot be easily transferred to those incumbent enterprises—presumably due to the type of agency and bureaucracy problems described above—the holder of such knowledge must enter the industry by starting a new firm in order to exploit the expected value of his knowledge.

[15] In the framework of Hirschman (1970), if an agent in possession of potentially valuable economic knowledge is unable to exercise voice within an existing firm, only loyalty will prevent him from exercising exit by starting a new firm.

number of competitors and lessens the degree of competition. In the entrepreneurial economy firms are vertically independent and specialized in the product market. The greater degree of vertical disintegration in the entrepreneurial economy means that co-operation among independent firms replaces internal transactions within a large, vertically integrated corporation. At the same time, there are more firms, resulting in an increase in both the competitive as well as the co-operative interface. The likelihood that a firm may end up competing or co-operating with another firm is greater in the entrepreneurial economy. In addition, new and enhanced configurations bring independent firms together in new and unexpected ways.

As Griliches (1992) has pointed out, knowledge spillovers come from different people working on similar things. A rich set of empirical evidence supports Griliches' conjecture in identifying that knowledge spillovers are promoted in clusters of economic activity (Audretsch and Feldman, 1996; Audretsch and Stephan, 1996). Thus, co-operation between individuals as well as between different firms generates the spillover of knowledge and new ideas. There is a large incentive for individuals and firms to interact co-operatively to create and explore new ideas that would otherwise remain undiscovered.

At the same time, there is a high degree of competition among firms for new ideas. Knowledge embodied in individuals and teams of individuals that is not used by one firm will be pursued by another firm if it is perceived as valuable. Thus, there is a high degree of competition for new ideas by the very firms that are co-operating to create those ideas. In addition, the increased interaction of firms and individuals facilitates the rapid diffusion of new ideas and the outcome of efforts to generate new ideas across individuals in different firms as well as within firms. In the managed economy, the monopolization of information was typically associated with power: 'Information is power' and is to be shared sparingly seemed to be the practice within large organizations.

In studying the networks in California's Silicon Valley, Saxenian (1990, pp. 96–97) emphasizes that it is the co-operation between individuals which facilitates the transmission of knowledge across agents, firms and even industries, and not just a high endowment of human capital and knowledge in the region:

> It is not simply the concentration of skilled labor, suppliers and information that distinguish the region. A variety of regional institutions—including Stanford University, several trade associations and local business organizations, and a myriad of specialized consulting, market research, public relations and venture capital firms—provide technical, financial, and

——————————— *What's New about the New Economy?* ———————————

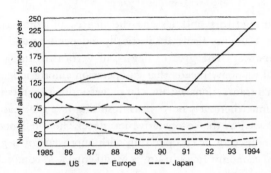

FIGURE 4. Industry technology alliances. Source: National Science Foundation, *Science and Engineering Indicators, 1996* (Washington, DC: US Government Printing Office, 1996), p. 158, taken from www.neweconomyindex.org/index.html.

networking services which the region's enterprises often cannot afford individually. These networks defy sectoral barriers: individuals move easily from semiconductor to disk drive firms or from computer to network makers. They move from established firms to start-ups (or vice versa) and even to market research or consulting firms, and from consulting firms back into start-ups. And they continue to meet at trade shows, industry conferences, and the scores of seminars, talks and social activities organized by local business organizations and trade associations. In these forums, relationships are easily formed and maintained, technical and market information is exchanged, business contacts are established, and new enterprises are conceived. . . . This decentralized and fluid environment also promotes the diffusion of intangible technological capabilities and understandings.[16]

There is at least some empirical evidence suggesting that co-operative activity has been increasing over time. As Figure 4 shows, the number of formal technology agreements has increased in the United States.

Thus, in the managed economy increasing the amount of co-operation reduces the degree of competition. There are simply fewer rivals competing in the product market. In the entrepreneurial economy, both competition and co-operation exist simultaneously. An increase in competition may actually generate an increase in co-operation in the search for knowledge spillovers.

[16] Saxenian (1990, pp. 97–98) claims that even the language and vocabulary used by technical specialists is specific to a region, 'a distinct language has evolved in the region and certain technical terms used by semiconductor production engineers in Silicon Valley would not even be understood by their counterparts in Boston's Route 128'.

2.10 Flexibility versus Scale

The classic manner for reducing cost-per-unit in economics under the managed economy was through expanding the scale of output, or through exploiting *economies of scale*. In product lines and industries where a large scale of production renders a substantial reduction in average cost, large firms will have an economic advantage, leading to a concentrated industrial structure. The importance of scale economies no doubt contributed to the emergence and dominance of large corporations in heavy manufacturing industries such as steel, automobiles and aluminum (Chandler, 1977).

The alternative source of reduced average costs under the entrepreneurial economy is through flexibility. As Teece (1993, p. 218) argues, 'Flexible specialization . . . and contracting may today yield greater advantages than economies of scale and scope generated internally.' Industries where demand for particular products is constantly shifting require a flexible system of production that can meet such a shifting demand. There are four major sources of flexibility: technological, organizational, demand side and qualitative. These four sources of flexibility result in a decrease in the importance of scale economies.

Technological flexibility refers to the emergence of certain new technologies, such as computer numerically controlled machine tools that facilitate flexible production. Systematic attempts to estimate the impact of these new technologies on the extent of scale economies (Carlsson, 1989; Carlsson and Taymaz, 1994) have resulted in the conclusion that the importance of scale economies has been drastically reduced in industries where such flexible technology has been implemented.

The second manifestation of flexibility is in terms of the organization of production. While the organization of production was centered upon mass production during the first three decades of the 20th century, an alternative system of industrial organization, flexible specialization, re-emerged during the last several decades of that century (Piore and Sabel, 1984). Flexible production consists of producing smaller numbers of specially designed goods of a specific quality for a niche market. Such goods typically command a higher price and cannot be so easily diffused to lower-cost production locations. The organization of industry centered around flexible specialization typically contains five key elements:

- *A reliance upon multi-purpose equipment.* General-purpose equipment enhances the flexibility to rapidly change the product specifications to meet specific demands of customers. This requires high levels of human capital and skilled labor.

- *Continual innovative activity*. Both the nature of the product(s) as well as production and organization methods are continually improved upon.
- *Clustering*. Groupings of enterprises, in both a product as well as a geographic dimension, provide a seedbed for the exchange of new ideas. Not only does physical proximity tend to facilitate the transmission of knowledge, but it also enhances the development of institutions and makes them more effective.
- *Networking*. Formal and informal links between enterprises, including subcontracting relationships, facilitate both increased economic specialization external to the firm as well as superior access to information.
- *Spillover effects*. Knowledge created within an enterprise spills over for use by other enterprises. Conversely, enterprises and individuals have access to external knowledge.

There is considerable evidence supporting the hypothesis that not only does flexible production provide a viable alternative to mass production as a system of industrial organization, but also that such systems centered around flexible production actually outperform those based on mass production. This evidence spans both developed and less developed countries (Piore and Sabel, 1984).[17]

The third type of flexibility refers to the ability of production to absorb demand fluctuations (Mills, 1984). There is a trade-off between efficiency, as measured by the costs of producing a given level of output, on the one hand, and flexibility, as measured by the costs of adjusting output, on the other hand. Large firms with high capital investment achieve a larger scale of output at a lower marginal cost than do small, labor-intensive enterprises. But the labor intensity of small firms enables them to adjust their current level of output at lower cost than their larger counterparts, which are capital and not labor intensive. As Brock and Evans (1989, p. 10) summarize, 'Smaller firms incur higher marginal production costs at a point in time than larger firms but include lower marginal adjust costs over time as demand fluctuates.'

The fourth type of flexibility refers to the ability for economic activity to

———

[17] One of the most striking examples of superior economic performance emerging from the industrial organization model of flexible production is provided by Emilia Romagna, a mixed agricultural–industrial region located in north central Italy with a population of around four million, and usually referred to as the 'Third Italy'. Through flexible production small firms have achieved a better economic performance than large enterprises by creating specialized industrialized districts where an agglomeration of producers in one industry work in close physical proximity. In what has become known as the 'Emilian Model of Production', the narrow division of labour common to large enterprises has been replaced by an organizational structure where employees perform a wide variety of different tasks (Piore and Sabel, 1984).

respond to qualitative changes in market demands. In a world of wealth and affluence, consumer demand is heterogeneous and fickle. Demand tends to proliferate across a broad spectrum of product class niches. The variances in consumer demand across product types and over time create a continuously changing set of product niches. Knowledge about these niches is uncertain for two reasons. First, the niches are difficult to observe and are changing. Second, the set of economic agents evaluating potential opportunities is heterogeneous. These two knowledge conditions are pivotal for understanding the entrepreneurial economy. This means that people are confronted with a variance in evaluations about the relevance of opportunities of the prospective ventures and, hence, the relevance of possible actions. Individuals who seek to appropriate the value of such knowledge by starting a new firm serve as *agents of change* by injecting flexibility into the economy. A common myth prevalent in the popular press is that small firms are more flexible than large firms. This belief suffers from a fallacy of composition. The mistake is committed at the unit of observation—the firm. Rather, the empirical evidence suggests that a population of firms, or an organization of industry consisting of diverse new and small firms, provides greater flexibility than does an organization of industry consisting of large corporations. Systematic empirical evidence is provided by Audretsch (1995) that the development and evolution of new industries is promoted by the presence of a large number of small firms, and by Audretsch and Thurik (2000) that national unemployment rates are lower in countries with a greater number of firms.

Scale economies were the engine that drove efficiency and growth in the managed economy. In the entrepreneurial economy the multiple dimensions of flexibility replace scale economies as the organizing principle for economic activity.

2.11 Stimulation versus Regulation

The public policies emerging in the postwar period of the managed economy dealing with the firm in the market were essentially constraining in nature. There were three general types of public policies towards business: antitrust (competition policy), regulation and public ownership. All three of these policy approaches restricted the firm's freedom to contract. While specific policy approaches tended to be more associated with one country than with others, such as antitrust in the United States, or public ownership in France and Sweden, all countries shared a common policy approach of intervening to restrain what otherwise was perceived as too much market power in the hands of firms.

Public policies constraining the freedom of the firm were certainly consistent with the *Weltanschauung* emerging from the theories and empirical evidence. Left unchecked, the large corporation in possession of market power would allocate resources in such a way as to reduce economic welfare. Through state intervention, the trade-off between efficiency on the hand and fairness on the other would be solved in a manner that presumably would be more socially satisfying. Galbraith (1956) is the seminal statement on the role of government in the managed economy, where state intervention typically involved the social partnership of big business, big government and big labor. This social partnership existed in nearly every Western economy.

In the entrepreneurial economy the relevant policy question has shifted away from 'How can the government constrain firms from abusing their market power?' to 'How can governments create an environment fostering the success and viability of firms?'[18] The major issues in the entrepreneurial economy have shifted away from concerns about excess profits and abuses of market dominance to international competitiveness, growth and employment. The concern about corporations is not that they are too successful and too powerful but that they are not successful enough. Jorde and Teece (1991) argued for the emasculation of the antitrust laws in order to enable American firms to co-operate and compete more effectively against their Japanese and European competitors.

As the waves of small start-ups in newly emerging high-technology industries demonstrate, the link between success and market power has been broken. The government policies of the entrepreneurial economy have increasingly shifted away from regulation to stimulation. Examples include the promotion of joint R&D programs, fostering efforts to innovate and the creation of new firms.

2.12 Targeting Inputs versus Targeting Outputs

Stimulation and regulation are not the only dimensions regarding the role of government policy in the managed and entrepreneurial economies. A second dimension involves targeting selected outputs or outcomes in the production process versus targeting selected inputs. Because of the relative certainty regarding markets and products in the managed economy, the appropriate policy response is to target outcomes and outputs. Specific industries along with particular firms could be promoted through government programs. The

---

[18] The Microsoft case suggests that the concern about market dominance is in terms of suppression of future innovative activity rather than profit levels.

targeting of specific firms in selected industries was clearly a successful policy for Japan in the postwar period and helped the Japanese achieve the competitive advantage in industries such as automobiles and electronics. As Joseph E. Stiglitz (1996) concludes from 'Some Lessons from the East Asian Miracle', 'government interventions acting together' (p. 151) account for at least part of the postwar Japanese growth miracle. The success of Japanese industrial policy in promoting a broad range of performance criteria, spanning trade performance to economic growth, has been painstakingly documented in a number of systematic empirical studies (Pugel, 1984; Audretsch and Yamawaki, 1988; Audretsch, 1989; Okuno-Fujiwara, 1991; Noland, 1993).

Targeting outputs has had a long tradition in Europe. As a response to 'the American Challenge', in the form of the dynamism, organization, innovation and boldness that characterize the giant American corporations, Servan-Schreiber (1968, p. 153) prescribed an R&D policy that would undertake 'the creation of large industrial units which are able both in size and management to compete with the American giants'. Because giant corporations were thought to be needed to amass the requisite R&D resources for innovation, Servan-Schreiber (1968, p. 159) argued that

> The first problem of an industrial policy for Europe consists in choosing 50 to 100 firms which, once they are large enough, would be the most likely to become world leaders of modern technology in their fields. At the moment we are simply letting industry be gradually destroyed by the superior power of American corporations.

This R&D policy prescription of targeting outputs is echoed in the 1988 Cecchini Report to the Commission of the European Union, where the anticipated gains from European integration are measured in terms of reduced costs achieved through increases in scale economies when firms are no longer limited to domestic markets and can instead operate on a larger European market.

How relevant are targeting outputs and outcomes today? One has to wonder what would have happened to the US computer semiconductor industry had IBM been selected as 'a national interest' around 1980 and promoted through favorable treatment as well as protected from threats like Apple Computer, Microsoft and Intel. Would the United States be as strong in the computer, semiconductor and software industries as it is today? While the proclamation, 'What is good for General Motors is good for America' may have been sensible in the managed economy, it no longer holds in the entrepreneurial economy.

The entrepreneurial economy is based less on the traditional inputs of land, labor and capital, and more on the input of knowledge. It is no longer certain what products should be produced, how they should be produced, and by whom. There are many indicators reflecting the shift towards greater uncertainty associated with knowledge-based economic activity. For example, Kortum and Lerner (1997, p. 1) point to 'the unprecedented recent jump in patenting in the United States', as evidenced by the rise in applications for the US patents by American inventors since 1985, which exceeds the increase in any other decade in this century. Throughout this century, patent applications fluctuated within a band between 40 000 and 80 000 per year. By contrast, in 1995 there were over 120 000 patent applications. Similarly, Berman *et al.* (1997) have shown that the demand for less skilled workers has decreased dramatically throughout the OECD, while at the same time the demand for skilled workers capable of dealing with uncertainty has exploded.

This increased degree of uncertainty increases the difficulty of selecting the correct outcomes and increases the likelihood that the wrong firm and industry will be targeted. Rather, the appropriate policy in what Krugman (1994) terms 'the Age of Uncertainty' is to target inputs, and in particular those inputs involved in the creation and commercialization of knowledge. Such policies involve basic and applied research at universities and research institutes, investment in the general level of education as well as advanced technical specialties, and the training and upgrading of the skill levels of workers.[19] While outcomes and outputs in the form of specific industries and even firms are targeted in the managed economy, the entrepreneurial economy calls for policy that creates an environment, or *Rahmenbedingungen*, facilitating the creation and commercialization of knowledge.

2.13 Local Policy versus National Policy

The rationale and target of policy—stimulation versus control and inputs versus outputs—are not the only aspects to differ between the managed and entrepreneurial economies. A third dimension involves the locus of policy. Under the managed economy, the appropriate locus of policy-making is at the national or federal level. While the targeted recipients of policy may be localized in one or a few regions, the most important policy-making institutions tend to be at the national level. By contrast, under the entrepreneurial

───────────────────

[19] For example, the Hope Scholarship in the state of Georgia enables all students to attend the state universities for free as long as they maintain a B average.

economy, the locus of government policy towards business tends to be decentralized and regional in nature.

In the managed economy, a federal or national locus of control of large, oligopolistic firms in command of considerable market power is appropriate. This is because the benefits and costs derived from that market power are asymmetric between the local region where the firm is located and the national market, where the firm sells its product. Not only is production concentrated in one or just several regions, but the workers along with ancillary suppliers also tend to be located in the same regions. These workers as well as the community at large, share the fruits accruing from monopoly power. Systematic empirical evidence (Weiss, 1966) shows that wages are positively related to the degree of market power held by a firm, even after controlling for unionization. Higher profits resulting from market power are shared by labor. Workers and firms in their region have the same interest.

As Olson (1982) shows, relatively small coalitions of economic agents benefiting from some collective action tend to prevail over a large group of dispersed economic agents each incurring a small cost from that action. The costs of organizing and influencing policy are relatively low for the small coalition enjoying the benefits but large for the group of dispersed economic agents. Government policies to control large oligopolistic firms with substantial market power are not as likely to be successful if they are implemented on the local level. Rather, as Olson (1982) predicts, a regional locus of policy towards business in the managed economy tends to result in the capture of policy by the coalition of local interests benefiting from that policy. Only by shifting the locus of policy away from the region to the national level can the capture of policy by special interest groups be minimized. This is because the negative effects of market power in the form of higher prices are spread throughout the national market while the benefits accruing from that power are locally concentrated.

The most important institutions administering antitrust policy and regulation, which were given a mandate by the US Congress to constrain the market power of big business during the era of the managed economy, were at the national level. Beginning with the Sherman Act of 1890 and the Interstate Commerce Act of 1890, which established the first federal regulatory agency, the mandate for the control of large oligopolistic enterprises with substantial market power was mainly at the level of the federal government (Audretsch, 1989). The Antitrust Division of the US Justice Department combined with the Federal Trade Commission to safeguard America against the abuse of market power, while a broad range of federal regulatory agencies, starting with the Interstate Commerce

—————————————— *What's New about the New Economy?* ——————————————

Commission and later the Federal Communications Commission and the Civil Aeronautics Boards, were created to regulate large, oligopolistic firms in concentrated markets. But starting during the Carter administration of the late 1970s and continuing in the administrations of presidents Reagan, Bush and Clinton, antitrust has been de-emphasized and a 20 year wave of deregulation has led to a downsizing and even closure of a number of the former regulatory agencies.

Many economists interpret the downsizing of the federal agencies charged with the regulation of business as the eclipse of government intervention. But to interpret the retreat of the federal government as the end of government intervention is to confuse the downsizing of government with a reshifting of the locus of government policy away from the federal level to the local level. The last two decades have seen the emergence of a set of policy initiatives at the local level. The new industrial policy of the entrepreneurial economy is decentralized and regional in nature. As Sternberg (1996) emphasizes in his review of successful technology policy in the four leading technological countries, the most important industrial policies in the last decades have been local not national. They have occurred in locations such as Research Triangle (Link, 1995), Austin, Texas, and Cambridge (UK). Sternberg (1996) shows how the success of a number of different high-technology clusters spanning the four most technologically advanced countries is the direct result of regional policy.

Eisinger (1990) asks the question, 'Do American states do industrial policy?' Lowery and Gray (1992) confirm Eisinger's affirmative answer by analyzing the impact of state industrial policy in the United States. They develop a new data set on gross state product and a new measure of state industrial policy activism. Their results suggest that the implementation of industrial policy at the state level tends to promote growth. For example, Feller (1997, p. 289) points out that 'In theory and implementation, state technology development programs —as in Texas, Ohio, New York, New Jersey, and Pennsylvania—may be viewed as bands on a wide spectrum from basic research to product development, with the ends reflecting quite different state strategies.'

The Advanced Research Program in Texas has provided support for basic research and the strengthening of the university infrastructure, which played a central role in developing the high-tech cluster around Austin. The Thomas Edison Centers in Ohio,[20] the Advanced Technology Centers in New Jersey, and the Centers for Advanced Technology at Case Western Reserve University,

———————————————————————————

[20] See Carlsson and Braunerhejelm (1999) for an analysis about the role of the Edison Biotechnology Center in creating biomedical clusters in Ohio.

Rutgers University and the University of Rochester have supported generic pre-competitive research.[21]

This shift in the locus of policy is the result of two factors. First, because the competitive source of economic activity in the entrepreneurial economy is knowledge, which tends to be localized in regional clusters, public policy requires an understanding of regional-specific characteristics and idiosyncrasies. As Sternberg (1996) concludes, regional strengths provide the major source of innovative clusters. The second factor is that the motivation underlying government policy in the entrepreneurial economy is growth and the creation of (high-paying) jobs, largely through the creation of new firms. These new firms are typically small and pose no oligopolistic threat in national or international markets. There are no external costs imposed on consumers in the national economy in the form of higher prices as is the case in the managed economy. There is no reason that the promotion of local economies imposes a cost on consumers in the national economy, so that local intervention is justified and does not result in any particular loss incurred by agents outside of the region.

2.14 Risk Capital versus Low-risk Capital

In the managed economy, the systems of finance in Europe have provided the existing companies with liquidity for investment.[22] This is particularly true in countries such as Germany, where the banks are allowed to hold equity positions in private companies (Cable, 1985). Many scholars have argued that allowing bank ownership of private companies has given Germany a superior mechanism linking finance to production (Mayer and Alexander, 1990; Edwards and Fischer, 1994). The evidence suggests this was true as long as Germany's comparative advantage was in traditional industries, such as automobile production, machine tools and metalworking (Audretsch and Elston, 1997). But as the comparative advantage in the European Union shifts away from managed industries towards entrepreneurial activities, the demand for finance also shifts away from financing investment in traditional industries towards high-risk ventures. This means that, under the entrepreneurial economy, the traditional means of finance are not longer appropriate. Of particular importance is venture capital, which has traditionally been a form of finance for high-risk, innovative new firms and the informal capital

―――――――――

[21] It should be emphasized that clearly, not all local interventions are effective.

[22] For a very thorough analysis on finance, see Hughes and Storey (1994), Storey (1994), and the special issues of *Small Business Economics* devoted to *European SME Financing* (Cressy and Olofsson, 1997), and to *Financing and Small Firm Dynamics* (Reid, 1996).

What's New about the New Economy?

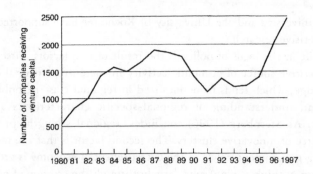

FIGURE 5. Number of companies receiving venture capital. Source: The National Venture Capital Association 1997 Annual Report (Arlington, VA: NVCA, 1998), prepared by Venture Economics (a division of Securities Data Company), taken from www.neweconomyindex.org/index.html.

market (Gaston, 1989; Gompers, 1999). As Figure 5 shows, venture capital has recently become more prevalent.

Informal risk capital is equity and near-equity invested by private individuals directly, i.e. informally, without formal intermediation (Mason and Harrison, 1997). Near-equity investments refer to loans or loan guarantees provided by individuals to firms where the individuals hold an equity. This has been referred to in the finance literature as informal debt or informal risk capital. Such informal risk capital is virtually the only source of risk or venture-type capital for most small and medium-sized enterprises, once their capital needs surpass family resources (Hughes, 1993). As Gaston points out, 'Informal capital markets are the leading sources of external source of external risk capital fuelling entrepreneurial start-ups and small business growth' (Gaston, 1989, p. 223).

Because the availability of venture capital and informal capital varies substantially across countries, new ventures flourish where they have the easiest access to finance. For example, the institution of venture capital is considerably more developed in the United States than in Europe. And the manner in which that venture capital is used also varies between Europe and the United States. The deficiency of venture capital and informal capital has impeded restructuring in the form of a liquidity constraint on people seeking finance to start a new company in a new industry.

The entrepreneurial economy requires a different system of finance to that in the managed economy. Since the managed economy was based on certainty in outputs as well as inputs, a strong connection between banks and firms fostered growth. Certainty has given way to uncertainty in the entrepreneurial economy, and therefore financial institutions must also change.

3. *Conclusions*

The continued rise in unemployment coupled with stagnant growth in Europe has triggered a plea by policy-makers for a rethink on the policy approach that ushered in European prosperity during the postwar era. Those countries that have succeeded in creating new jobs and reducing unemployment seem to have accomplished this at the cost of lower wages and a deterioration in civil society. The resulting policy debate has been miscast as the European model versus the American model. This debate is wrong because it confuses a fundamental shift in economic systems with what used to be a recognized and widely accepted policy trade-off. The policy debate should be instead cast as the entrepreneurial versus the managed economy.

The managed economy flourished for most of the 20th century. It was based on relative certainty in outputs, which consisted mainly of manufactured products, and in inputs, which consisted mainly of land, labor and capital. The twin forces of globalization have reduced the ability of the managed economies of Western Europe and North America to grow and create jobs. On the one hand has come the advent of new competition from low-cost but relatively highly educated and skill-intensive countries in Central and Eastern Europe as well as Asia. On the other hand, the telecommunications and computer revolutions have drastically reduced the cost of shifting not just capital but also information out of the high-cost locations of Europe and into lower-cost locations around the globe. Taken together, these twin forces of globalization mean that economic activity in a high-cost location is no longer compatible with routinized tasks. Rather, globalization has shifted the comparative advantage of high-cost locations to knowledge-based activities, and in particular search activities, which cannot be costlessly transferred around the globe.

Knowledge as an input into economic activity is inherently different from land, labor and capital. It is characterized by high uncertainty, high asymmetries across people and is costly to transact. The response to an economy where knowledge is the main source of comparative advantage is the entrepreneurial economy. This paper has identified 14 characteristics that differ between the entrepreneurial and managed economies, and provides a framework for understanding how the entrepreneurial economy fundamentally differs from the managed economy. Such a framework provides a lens through which to interpret economic events and formulate policy. Application of the wrong lens leads to the wrong policy choice. For example, under the managed economy firm failure is viewed negatively and as representing a drain on society's resources. According to this view, resources should not be invested in higher risk ventures. When viewed through the lens of the entrepreneurial economy, firm failure is interpreted differently. It is seen as an experiment, an attempt to go in a new direction in an inherently risky environment. An externality of failure is learning. In the entrepreneurial economy, failure accompanies the process of searching for new ideas. It similarly follows that the positive virtues of long-term relationships, stability, continuity under the managed economy give way to flexibility, change and turbulence in the entrepreneurial economy. What is a liability in the managed economy is, in some case, a virtue in the entrepreneurial economy.

The current policy debate has been erroneously miscast as more versus less government. The wave of government downsizing, combined with deregulation, privatization and the retreat of antitrust, has created an impression that there is no longer a role for government to play other than to get out of the way of private interests. What has been overlooked is the inherently different role of government policy in the entrepreneurial compared to the managed economy. The well-documented high-technology clusters of the world have not been created in a vacuum. The policies helping to shape such innovative clusters are not only different in that they are local, rather than national, but they also target inputs in the process of creating and commercializing knowledge, rather than outputs, such as particular firms.

Government policy in the managed economy was largely about control. High certainty dictated that it was known what to produce, how it should be produced and who would produce it. The role of government was to constrain the power of large corporations, which were needed for efficiency under mass production, but posed a threat to democracy through their concentration of power. Under the managed economy the policy debate centered on competition policies (antitrust), regulation and public ownership of business. In the entrepreneurial economy these constraining policies have become increasingly irrelevant. The central role of government policy in the entrepreneurial economy is enabling in nature. The focus is to foster the production and commercialization of knowledge. Rather than focus on limiting the freedom of firms to contract through antitrust, regulation and public ownership, government policy in the entrepreneurial economy targets education, increasing the skills and human capital of workers, and facilitating the mobility of workers and their ability to start new firms.

The economic failure of the Soviet Union and its Eastern European satellites was to a great extent a failure to participate in the micro-electronic revolution.[23] Computerized technology implied a shift away from a concentrated

[23] Sylos-Labini (1992, p. 63) observed that, 'In the last two or three decades, after a number of attempts that ailed at decentralising many activities and of giving more discretionary power to managers, the difficulties rose very rapidly and the Soviet economy entered a period of general crisis. Concentrating

and rigid structure and toward a fluid, decentralized system as the most efficient means of production, which constituted a direct threat to the political principle of centralizing all information and decision-making under Communism. While the demise of Communism has been widely celebrated as a victory for Western capitalism, what has been overlooked is that the system of capitalism dominating most of the 20th century—the managed economy—is now itself under attack by the same forces that undermined Communism.

The prevailing view about the gains to Europe through integration has been formulated in terms of lower costs resulting from a greater exploitation of scale economies. The 1988 Cecchini Report, building on the tradition of Servan-Schreiber (1968), measured these gains to Europe in terms of cost reduction. Through growth, mergers, combinations and rationalization, larger European firms will generate gains to European consumers in the form of lower costs. Convergence of institutions and nations in Europe is a goal, since this facilitates the single European markets and large-scale production and sales. Focusing on scale economies resulting from a large market size is a metric implicit in the managed economy. The analysis of this paper, focusing instead on the entrepreneurial economy, predicts that *the major economic benefits of European integration will come not through economies of scale, but rather through economies of diversity*. In an uncertain world, the diversity of European cultures and institutions is well positioned to generate a diversity of different approaches to economic problems. Diversity, not convergence, generates innovation and growth.

A series of empirical studies has identified that a pervasive shift in the industrial structure away from large corporations and towards small enterprises has taken place between the mid-1970s and early 1990s (see the country studies of Loveman and Sengenberger, 1991; Acs and Audretsch, 1993; Thurik, 1999). This shift occurred not just in one or a few of the developed countries but rather in virtually every single leading industrial country. Is such a shift desirable and should the resulting industrial structure be promoted or avoided? Prevailing economic theory provides a set of ambiguous answers, which essentially depend upon a number of trade-offs between what is gained and lost by shifting economic activity towards smaller enterprises. While this ambiguity cannot be easily resolved, in this paper we have attempted to identify at least the most important of these trade-offs. The empirical evidence from linking growth rates to changes in the industrial

economic, organisational, and scientific efforts on military production, the Soviet Union has succeeded, at least for a period, in not losing ground in this sector with respect to the United States and other Western countries. But even this sector—after the latest developments in electronics, which, especially in the

—————————— *What's New about the New Economy?* ——————————

structure suggests that the ongoing shift towards smaller enterprises tends to promote rather than retard economic growth.[24] Those countries that have introduced a greater element of entrepreneurship have been rewarded with additional growth.[25] It is now the task of policy makers also seeking to reward their economies with additional growth, to reformulate policy in harmony with the shift from the managed to the entrepreneurial economy.

Acknowledgements

This paper is the result of a series of visits by David Audretsch as a Visiting Research Fellow at the Tinbergen Institute in 1996, 1997 and 2000 and by Roy Thurik as the Ameritech Research Scholar at the Institute for Development Strategies, Indiana University in 1999 and 2000. We are grateful to the helpful suggestions by two anonymous referees and the editors of this journal. We would like to thank Martin Carree and André van Stel for their helpful comments, and the suggestions of Giovannie Dosi and Franco Malerba. Any errors or omissions remain the responsibility of the authors.

United States, owe much to the contribution of small firms—has shown increasing signs of weakness.' See also Nelson (1992).

[24] Carree and Thurik (1998, 1999) provide analyses showing the consequence of lagging behind in this restructuring process in manufacturing. Using a sample of 14 manufacturing industries in 13 European countries and 13 manufacturing industries in 12 European countries, respectively, they find that, on average, the employment share of large firms in 1990 has a negative effect on growth of output in the subsequent four-year period.

[25] Thurik (1996) shows that the percentage growth of GNP is explained using a structural shift. This shift is captured by the difference between the annual percentage growth of value-of-shipments of large firms (with employment of less than 500 employees) and the annual percentage growth of value-of-shipments of small firms (with employment of at least 500 employees), using data for three distinct time periods: 1988–90, 1989–92 and 1990–93 for all 12 old member countries of the European Union. See also Audretsch and Thurik (2000) where some calculations are presented showing that a rise in the number of entrepreneurs, i.e. self-employed per laborforce, leads to lower levels of unemployment. They use data material from 23 OECD countries including the 15 countries of the EU-15, Iceland, Norway, Switzerland, Canada, Australia, New Zealand, Japan and US for the period 1974–94. Further evidence is provided by Schmitz (1989) and Nickell (1996). Schmitz presents a theoretical endogenous growth model which relates entrepreneurial activity and economic growth. He shows that an increase of the proportion of entrepreneurs in the working force leads to an increase in long-run economic growth. Nickell studies the

References

Acs, Z. J. and D. B. Audretsch (eds) (1993), *Small Firms and Entrepreneurship: An East–West Perspective.* Cambridge University Press: Cambridge.

Acs, Z. J., D. B. Audretsch and M. P. Feldman (1994), 'R&D Spillovers and Recipient Firm Size,' *American Economic Review*, 82, 363–367.

Addison, J. T. and P. J. J. Welfens (eds) (1998), *Labor Markets and Social Security: Wage Costs, Social Security Financing and Labor Market Reforms in Europe.* Springer Verlag: Berlin.

Agarwal, R. and D. B. Audretsch (eds) (2001), 'Does Start-up Start Size Matter? The Impact of the Life Cycle and Technology on Firm Survival,' *Journal of Industrial Economics*, April.

Alchian, A. (1950), 'Uncertainty, Evolution, and Economic Theory,' *Journal of Political Economy*, 58, 211–221.

Alchian, A. and H. Demsetz (1972), 'Production, Information Costs, and Economic Organization,' *American Economic Review*, 62, 777–795.

Archibugi, D. and M. Pianta (1992), *The Technological Specialization of Advanced Countries.* Kluwer: Boston, MA.

Arrow, K. J. (1962), 'Economic Welfare and the Allocation of Resources for Invention,' in R. R. Nelson (ed.), *The Rate and Direction of Inventive Activity*, pp. 609–626. Princeton University Press: Princeton, NJ.

Audretsch, D. B. (1995), *Innovation and Industry Evolution.* MIT Press: Cambridge, MA.

Audretsch, D. B. (1989), *The Market and the State.* New York University Press: New York.

Audretsch, D. B. and J. A. Elston (1997), 'Financing the German Mittelstand,' *Small Business Economics*, 9, 97–110.

Audretsch, D. B. and M. P. Feldman (1996), 'R&D Spillovers and the Geography of Innovation and Production,' *American Economic Review*, 86, 630–640.

Audretsch, D. B. and P. E. Stephan (1996), 'Company-scientist Locational Links: the Case of Biotechnology,' *American Economic Review*, 86, 641–652.

Audretsch, D. B. and A. R. Thurik (2000), 'Capitalism and Democracy in the 21st Century: from the Managed to the Entrepreneurial Economy,' *Journal of Evolutionary Economics*, 10, 17–34.

Audretsch, D. B. and H. Yamawaki (1988), 'R&D Rivalry, Industrial Policy, and U.S.–Japanese Trade,' *Review of Economics and Statistics*, 70, 438–447.

Audretsch, D. B., L. Klomp and R. Thurik (1999), 'Do Services Differ from Manufacturing? The Post Entry Performance of Firms in Dutch Services,' in D. B. Audretsch and A. R. Thurik (eds), *Innovation, Industry Evolution and Employment.* Cambridge: Cambridge University Press.

Audretsch, D. B., G. van Leeuwen, B. J. Menkveld and R. Thurik (2001), 'Market Dynamics in the Netherlands: Competition Policy and the Role of Small Firms,' *International Journal of Industrial Organization*, 19, 795–822.

Audretsch, D. B., A. Lederer, Ingrid Verheul, R. Thurik and S. Wennekers (eds) (2001b), *Entrepreneurship: Determinants and Policies in the Global Economy.* Kluwer: Boston, MA (forthcoming).

Audretsch, D. B., M. A. Carree, A. van Stel and R. Thurik (2001c), 'Impeded Industrial Restructuring: the Growth Penalty,' discussion paper, Tinbergen Institute, Erasmus University Rotterdam (forthcoming).

Baily, M. N., E. J. Bartelsman and J. Haltiwanger (1996), 'Downsizing and Productivity Growth: Myth or Reality?' *Small Business Economics*, 8, 159–178.

Baldwin, J. and G. Picot (1995), 'Employment Generation by Small Producers in the Canadian Manufacturing Sector,' *Small Business Economics*, 7, 317–331.

Baldwin, J. R. (1995), *The Dynamics of Industrial Competition: A North American Perspective.* Cambridge University Press: Cambridge.

Berman, E., J. Bound and S. Machin (1997), 'Implications of Skill-biased Technological Change:

International Evidence,' working paper no. 6166, National Bureau of Economic Research (NBER): Cambridge.

Blanchard, O. and L. F. Katz (1997), 'What We Know and Do Not Know About the Natural Rate of Unemployment,' *Journal of Economic Perspectives*, 11, 51–72.

Birch, D. L. (1981), 'Who Creates Jobs?' *The Public Interest*, 65, 3–14.

Brock, W. A. and D. S. Evans (1989), 'Small Business Economics,' *Small Business Economics*, 1, 7–20.

Brown, C., J. Hamilton and J. Medoff (1990), *Employers: Large and Small*. Harvard University Press: Cambridge, MA.

Cable, J. (1985), 'Capital Market Information and Industrial Performance: the Role of West German Banks,' *Economic Journal*, 95, 118–132.

Carlsson, B. (1989), 'The Evolution of Manufacturing Technology and its Impact on Industrial Structure: an International Study,' *Small Business Economics*, 1, 21–38.

Carlsson, B. and P. Braunerhejelm (1999), 'Industry Clusters: Biotechnology/Biomedicine and Polymers in Ohio and Sweden,' in D. B. Audretsch and R. Thurik (eds), *Innovation, Industry Evolution, and Employment*, pp. 182–215. Cambridge University Press: Cambridge.

Carlsson, B. and E. Taymaz (1994), 'Flexible Technology and Industrial Structure in the US,' *Small Business Economics*, 6, 193–209.

Carree, M. and L. Klomp (1996), 'Small Business and Job Creation: a Comment,' *Small Business Economics*, 8, 317–322.

Carree. M. A. and A. R. Thurik (1998), 'Small Firms and Economic Growth in Europe,' *Atlantic Economic Journal*, 26, 137–146.

Carree. M. A. and A. R. Thurik (1999), 'Industrial Structure and Economic Growth,' in D. B. Audretsch and A. R. Thurik (eds), *Innovation, Industry Evolution and Employment*, pp. 86–110. Cambridge University Press: Cambridge.

Caves, Richard E. (1998), 'Industrial Organization and New Findings on the Turnover and Mobility of Firms,' *Journal of Economic Literature*, 36, 1947–1982.

Cecchini, P. (1988), *The European Challenge*. Gower Press: London.

Chandler A. D. Jr (1977), *The Visible Hand: The Managerial Revolution in American Business*. Harvard University Press: Cambridge, MA.

Chandler, A. (1990), *Scale and Scope: The Dynamics of Industrial Capitalism*. Harvard University Press: Cambridge, MA.

Christensen, C. M. (2000), *The Inventor's Dilemma: When New Technologies Cause Great Firms to Fail*. Harper Collins: New York.

Coase, R. H. (1937), 'The Nature of the Firm,' *Economica*, 4, 386–405.

Cohen, W. M. and S, Klepper (1992), 'The Tradeoff between Firm Size and Diversity in the Pursuit of Technological Progress,' *Small Business Economics*, 4, 1–14.

Cressy, R. and C. Olofsson (1997), 'European SME Financing: an Overview,' *Small Business Economics*, 9, 87–96.

Davis, S. J., J.Haltiwanger and S.Schuh (1996a), *Job Creation and Destruction in US Manufacturing*. MIT Press: Cambridge, MA.

Davis, S. J., J. Haltiwanger and S. Schuh (1996b), 'Small Business and Job Creation: Dissecting the Myth and Reassessing the Facts,' *Small Business Economics*, 8, 259–278.

Dosi, G. (1982), 'Technological Paradigms and Technological Trajectories: a Suggested Interpretation of the Determinants and Directions of Technical Change,' *Research Policy*, 13, 3–20.

—————————— *What's New about the New Economy?* ——————————

Dosi, G. (1988), 'Sources, Procedures, and Microeconomic Effects of Innovation,' *Journal of Economic Literature*, 26, 1120–1171.

Eberts, R. W. and J. A. Stone (1992), *Wage and Employment Adjustment in Local Labor Markets*. W. E. Upjohn Institute: Kalamazoo, MI.

Edwards, J. S. and K. Fischer (1994), *The German Financial System*. Cambridge University Press: Cambridge.

Eisinger, P. (1990), 'Do the American States do Industrial Policy?' *British Journal of Political Science*, 20, 509–535.

Ericson, R. and A. Pakes (1995), 'Markov-perfect Industry Dynamics: a Framework for Empirical Work,' *Review of Economic Studies*, 62, 53–82.

Feldman, M. P. and D. B. Audretsch (1999), 'Innovation in Cities: Science-based Diversity, Specialization and Localized Competition,' *European Economic Review*, 43, 409–429.

Feller, I. (1997), 'Federal and State Government Roles in Science and Technology,' *Economic Development Quarterly*, 11, 283–296.

Galbraith, J. K. (1956), *American Capitalism: The New Industrial State*. Houghton Mifflin: Boston, MA.

Gaston, R. J. (1989), 'The Scale of Informal Capital Markets,' *Small Business Economics*, 1, 223–230.

Geroski, P. A. (1991a), 'Domestic and Foreign Entry in the United Kingdom: 1983–1984,' in P. Geroski and J. Schwalbach (eds), *Entry and Market Contestability: An International Comparison*, pp. 63–88. Basil Blackwell: Oxford.

Geroski, P. A. (1991b), 'Some Data-driven Reflections on the Entry Process,' in P. Geroski and J. Schwalbach (eds), *Entry and Market Contestability: An International Comparison*, pp. 282–286. Basil Blackwell: Oxford.

Geroski, P. A. (1995), 'What Do We Know about Entry?,' *International Journal of Industrial Organization*, 13, 421–440.

Geroski, P. and J. Schwalbach (eds) (1991), *Entry and Market Contestability: An International Comparison*. Basil Blackwell: Oxford.

Glaeser, E. L., H. D. Kallal, J. A. Scheinkman and A. Shleifer (1992), 'Growth of Cities,' *Journal of Political Economy*, 100, 1126–1152.

Gomes-Casseres, B. (1996), *The Alliance Revolution: The New Shape of Business Rivalry*. Harvard University Press: Cambridge, MA.

Gomes-Casseres, B. (1997), 'Alliance Strategies of Small Firms,' *Small Business Economics*, 9, 33–44.

Gompers, P. (1999), *The Venture Capital Cycle*. MIT Press: Cambridge, MA.

Gort, M. and S. Klepper (1982), 'Time Paths in the Diffusion of Product Innovations,' *Economic Journal*, 92, 630–653.

Griliches, Z. (1992), 'The Search for R&D Spillovers,' *Scandanavian Journal of Economics*, 94(suppl.), 29–47.

Hannan, M. T. and J. Freeman (1989), *Organizational Ecology*. Harvard University Press: Cambridge, MA.

Henderson, R. and K. B. Clark (1990), 'Architectural Innovation: the Reconfiguration of Existing Product Technologies and the Failure of Established Firms,' *Administrative Science Quarterly*, 5(35), 9–30.

Hirschman, A. O. (1970), *Exit, Voice, and Loyalty*. Cambridge University Press: Cambridge.

Holmstrom, B. (1989), 'Agency Costs and Innovation,' *Journal of Economic Behavior and Organization*, 12, 305–327.

Hughes, A. (1993), 'Industrial Concentration and Small Firms in the United Kingdom: the 1980s in Historical Perspective,' in Z. J. Acs and D. B. Audretsch (eds), *Small Firms and Entrepreneurship: an East–West Perspective*, pp. 15–37. Cambridge University Press: Cambridge.

Hughes, A. and D. J. Storey (1994), *Finance and the Small Firm*. Routledge: London.

Jacobs, J. (1969), *The Economy of Cities*. Random House: New York.

Jaffe, A. B. (1989), 'Real Effects of Academic Research,' *American Economic Review*, 79, 957–970.

Jaffe, A. B., M. Trajtenberg and R. Henderson (1993), 'Geographic Localization of Knowledge Spillovers as Evidenced by Patent Citations,' *Quarterly Journal of Economics*, 63, 577–598.

Jorde, T. M. and D. J. Teece (1991), 'Antitrust Policy and Innovation: Taking Account of Performance Competition and Competitor Cooperation,' *Journal of Institutional and Theoretical Economics*, 147, 118–144.

Jovanovic, B. (1982), 'Selection and Evolution of Industry,' *Econometrica*, 50, 649–670.

Kindleberger, C. P. and D. B. Audretsch (eds) (1983), *The Multinational Corporation*. MIT Press: Cambridge, MA.

Klepper, S. (1996), 'Entry, Exit, Growth, and Innovation over the Product Life-cycle,' *American Economic Review*, 86, 562–583.

Knight, F. H. (1921), *Risk, Uncertainty and Profit*. Houghton Mifflin: New York.

Konings, J. (1995), 'Gross Job Flows and the Evolution of Size in UK Establishments,' *Small Business Economics*, 7, 213–220.

Kortum, S. and J. Lerner (1997), 'Stronger Protection or Technological Revolution: What is Behind the Recent Surge in Patenting?,' working paper no. 6204, National Bureau of Economic Research (NBER), Cambridge.

Kreps, D. (1991), 'Corporate Culture and Economic Theory,' in J. Alt and K. Shepsle (eds), *Positive Perspectives on Political Economy*. Cambridge University Press: Cambridge, pp. 191–223.

Krugman, P. (1991a), *Geography and Trade*. MIT Press: Cambridge, MA.

Krugman, P. (1991b), 'Increasing Returns and Economic Geography,' *Journal of Political Economy*, 99, 483–499.

Krugman P. (1994), *The Age of Uncertainty*. MIT Press: Cambridge, MA.

Link A. (1995), *A Generosity of Spirit*. Duke University Press: Durham, NC.

Loveman, G. and W. Sengenberger (1991), 'The Re-emergence of Small-scale Production: an International Perspective,' *Small Business Economics*, 3, 1–38.

Lowery, D. and V. Gray (1992), 'Holding Back the Tide of Bad Economic Times: the Compensatory Impact of State Industrial Policy,' *Social Science Quarterly*, 73, 483–495.

Lucas, R. E. Jr (1993), 'Making a Miracle,' *Econometrica*, 61, 251–272.

Mason, C. M. and R. T. Harrison (1997), 'Business Angel Networks and the Development of the Informal Venture Capital Market in the UK: Is There Still a Role for the Public Sector?,' *Small Business Economics*, 9, 111–123.

Mayer, C. and I. Alexander (1990), 'Banks and Security Market: Corporate Financing in Germany and the United Kingdom,' *Journal of Japanese and International Economics*, 4, 181–194.

Milgrom, P. (1988), 'Employment Contracts, Influence Activities and Organization Design,' *Journal of Political Economy*, 96, 42–60.

Milgrom, P. and J. Roberts (1987), 'Information Asymmetries, Strategic Behavior, and Industrial Organization,' *American Economic Review*, 77, 184–193.

Mills, D. (1984), 'Demand Fluctuations and Endogenous Firm Flexibility,' *Journal of Industrial Economics*, 14 (September), 55–71.

Mueller, D. C. (1976), 'Information, Mobility, and Profit,' *Kyklos*, 29, 419–448.

Mueller, D. C. (1989), *The Persistence of Profits*. Cambridge University Press: Cambridge.

Nelson, R. R. (1981), 'Assessing Private Enterprise: an Exegesis of Tangled Doctrine,' *Bell Journal of Economics*, 12, 93–111.

Nelson, R. R. (1990), 'Capitalism as an Engine of Progress,' *Research Policy*, 19, 190–214.

Nelson, R. R. (1992), 'U.S. Technological Leadership: Where Did It Come From and Where Did It Go?' in F. M. Scherer and M. Perlman (eds), *Entrepreneurship, Technological Innovation and Economic Growth: Studies in the Schumpeterian Tradition*, pp. 25–50. University of Michigan Press: Ann Arbor, MI.

Nelson, R. R. (1995), 'Co-evolution of Industry Structure, Technology and Supporting Institutions, and the Making of Comparative Advantage,' *International Journal of the Economics of Business*, 2, 171–184.

Nelson, R. R. and S. G. Winter (1982), *An Evolutionary Theory of Economic Change*. Harvard University Press: Cambridge, MA.

Neumann, M. (1993), 'Review of Entry and Market Contestability: an International Comparison,' *International Journal of Industrial Organization*, 11, 593–594.

Nickell, S. J. (1996), 'Competition and Corporate Performance,' *Journal of Political Economy*, 104, 724–746.

Nickell, S. J. (1997), 'Unemployment and Labor Market Rigidities: Europe versus North America,' *Journal of Economic Perspectives*, 11, 55–74.

Noland, M. (1993), 'The Impact of Industrial Policy on Japan's Trade Specialization,' *Review of Economics and Statistics*, 75, 241–248.

Nooteboom B. (1994), 'Innovation and Diffusion in Small Firms,' *Small Business Economics*, 6, 327–347.

OECD (1997), *Employment Outlook*. OECD: Paris.

Okuno-Fujiwara, M. (1991), 'Industrial Policy in Japan: a Political Economy View,' in P. Krugman (ed.), *Trade with Japan: Has the Door Opened Wider?* pp. 271–296. University of Chicago Press: Chicago, IL.

Olson, M. (1982), *The Rise and Decline of Nations: Economic Growth, Stagflation and Social Rigidities*. Yale University Press: New Haven, CT.

Pakes, A. and R. Ericson (1998), 'Empirical Applications of Alternative Models of Firm and Industry Dynamics,' *Journal of Economic Theory*, 79, 1–45.

Paque, K.-H. (1998), 'Structural Unemployment in Europe: A Bird's-eye View,' in J. T. Addison and P. J. J. Welfens (eds), *Labor Markets and Social Security: Wage Costs, Social Security, Financing and Labor Market Reforms in Europe*, pp. 17–44. Springer Verlag: Berlin.

Piore, M. J. and C. F. Sabel (1984), *The Second Industrial Divide: Possibilities for Prosperity*. Basic Books: New York.

Pugel, T. A. (1984), 'Japan's Industrial Policy: Instruments, Trends, and Effects,' *Journal of Comparative Economics*, 8, 420–435.

Reich, R. B. (1983), *The Next American Frontier*. Times Books: New York.

Reid, G. C. (1996), 'Financial Structure and the Growing Small Firm: Theoretical Underpinning and Current Evidence,' *Small Business Economics*, 8, 1–7.

Robson, G. B. and C. C. Gallagher (1994), 'Change in the Size Distribution of UK Firms,' *Small Business Economics*, 6, 299–312.

Romer, P. (1990), 'Endogenous Technological Change,' *Journal of Political Economy*, 94, 71–102.

Romer, P. M. (1994), 'The Origins of Endogenous Growth,' *Journal of Economic Perspectives*, 8, 3–22.

Saxenian, A. (1990), 'Regional Networks and the Resurgence of Silicon Valley,' *California Management Review*, 33, 89–111.

Scherer, F. M. (1970), *Industrial Market Structure and Economic Performance*. Rand McNally: Chicago, IL.

Schmitz, J. A. (1989), 'Imitation, Entrepreneurship, and Long-run Growth,' *Journal of Political Economy*, 97, 721–739.

Schumpeter, J. A. (1942), *Capitalism, Socialism and Democracy*. Harper & Row: New York.

Servan-Schreiber, J.-J.(1968), *The American Challenge*. Hamish Hamilton: London.

Siebert, H. (1997), 'Labor Market Rigidities: at the Root of Unemployment in Europe,' *Journal of Economic Perspectives*, 11, 37–54.

Stephan, P. E. (1996), 'The Economics of Science,' *Journal of Economic Literature*, 34, 1199–1262.

Sternberg, R. (1996), 'Technology Policies and the Growth of Regions,' *Small Business Economics*, 8, 75–86.

Stiglitz, J. E. (1996), 'Some Lessons from the East Asian Miracle,' *World Bank Research Observer*, 11, 151–177.

Storey, D. J. (1994), *Understanding the Small Business Sector*. Routledge: London.

Sylos-Labini, P. (1992), '*Capitalism, Socialism, and Democracy* and Large-scale Firms,' in F. M. Scherer and M. Perlman (eds), *Entrepreneurship, Technological Innovation, and Economic Growth*, pp. 55–64. University of Michigan: Ann Arbor, MI.

Teece, D. J. (1993), 'The Dynamics of Industrial Capitalism: Perspectives on Alfred Chandler's Scale and Scope,' *Journal of Economic Literature*, 31, 199–225.

Teece, D., R. Rumult, G. Dosi and S. Winter (1994), 'Understanding Corporate Coherence: Theory and Evidence,' *Journal of Economic Behavior and Organization*, 23, 1–30.

Thurik, A. R. (1996), 'Small Firms, Entrepreneurship and Economic Growth,' in P. H. Admiraal (ed.), *Small Business in the Modern Economy*, pp. 126–152. Blackwell: Oxford.

Vernon, R. (1966), 'International Investments and International Trade in the Product Lifecycle,' *Quarterly Journal of Economics*, 80, 190–207.

Von Hipple, E. (1994), 'Sticky Information and the Locus of Problem Solving: Implications for Innovation,' *Management Science*, 40, 429–439.

Weiss, L. W. (1966), 'Concentration and Labor Earnings,' *American Economic Review*, 56, 105–116.

Wheelwright, S. C. (1985), 'Restoring Competitiveness in US Manufacturing,' *California Management Review*, 27, 113–121.

Williamson, O. (1968), 'Economies as an Antitrust Defence: the Welfare Trade-offs,' *American Economic Review*, 58, 18–36.

Williamson, O. (1975), *Markets and Hierarchies: Antitrust Analysis and Implications*. The Free Press: New York.

Winter, S. (1984), 'Schumpeterian Competition in Alternative Technological Regimes,' *Journal of Economic Behavior and Organization*, 5, 287–320.

[23]

KYKLOS, Vol. 55 – 2002 – Fasc. 1, 81–98

Impeded Industrial Restructuring:
The Growth Penalty

David B. Audretsch, Martin A. Carree,
Adriaan J. van Stel and A. Roy Thurik*

I. INTRODUCTION

Explanations for economic growth have generally been restricted to the realm of macroeconomics (Romer 1990, Krugman 1991). However, a different scholarly tradition linking growth to industrial organization dates back at least to Schumpeter (1934). According to this tradition, performance, measured in terms of economic growth, is shaped by the degree to which the industry structure most efficiently utilizes scarce resources. But what determines this optimal structure? There is a long-standing tradition in the field of industrial organization devoted towards identifying the determinants of industry structure. As early as 1948, Blair stated that technology is the most important determinant of industry structure[1]. Scherer and Ross (1990) and Chandler (1990) expand the

* Institute for Development Strategies, Indiana University, Tinbergen Institute at Erasmus University Rotterdam (EUR), Centre for Economic Policy Research (CEPR), London and EIM Business and Policy Research, Zoetermeer, email: daudrets@indiana.edu; Centre for Advanced Small Business Economics (CASBEC) at Erasmus University Rotterdam, Maastricht University and EIM Business and Policy Research, Zoetermeer, email: M.Carree@MW.UNIMAAS.NL; Centre for Advanced Small Business Economics (CASBEC) and Tinbergen Institute, Erasmus University Rotterdam and EIM Business and Policy Research, Zoetermeer, email: AST@eim.nl; Centre for Advanced Small Business Economics (CASBEC) and Tinbergen Institute, Erasmus University Rotterdam and EIM Business and Policy Research, Zoetermeer, email: thurik@few.eur.nl. This paper is the result of a series of visits by David Audretsch as a Visiting Research Fellow at the Tinbergen Institute in 1997 and 1998 and by Roy Thurik and Martin Carree as Ameritech Research Scholars at the Institute for Development Strategies, Indiana University in 1999 and 2000. Martin Carree is grateful to the Royal Netherlands Academy of Arts and Sciences (KNAW) for financial support. The authors are grateful to Ton Kwaak for making available the data set and to two anonymous referees for helpful comments on an earlier draft.

1. See Blair (1948, p. 121): 'The whole subject of the comparative efficiency of different sizes of business has long raised one of the most perplexing dilemmas in the entire body of economic theory. . . . But a beginning must be made sometime in tackling this whole size-efficiency problem on an empirical basis. The first step in any such undertaking would logically be that of studying the underlying technological forces of the economy, since it is technology which largely determines the relationship between the size of plant and efficiency'.

81

D. B. AUDRETSCH, M. A. CARREE, A. J. VAN STEL AND A. R. THURIK

determinants of optimal industry structure to include other factors as well as the underlying technology. Dosi (1988, p. 1157), in his systematic review of the literature in the *Journal of Economic Literature,* concludes that

'Each production activity is characterized by a particular distribution of firms'.

When the determinants of the underlying industrial structure are stable, the industry structure itself would not be expected to change. However, a change in the underlying determinants would be expected to result in a change in the optimal industry structure. Certainly, Chandler (1990) and Scherer and Ross (1990) identified a shift in optimal industry structure towards increased centralization and concentration throughout the first two-thirds of the previous century as a result of changes in the underlying technology along with other factors.

More recently, a series of studies has identified a change in the determinants underlying the industry structure that has reversed this trend. The most salient point of this change is that technology, globalization, deregulation, labor supply, variety in demand, and the resulting higher levels of uncertainty have rendered a shift in the industry structure away from greater concentration and centralization towards less concentration and decentralization. So, the industry structure is generally shifting towards an increased role for small enterprises. However, the extent and timing of this shift is anything but identical across countries. Rather, the shift in industry structures has been heterogeneous and apparently shaped by country-specific factors (Carree et al. 2002, Thurik 1996). Apparently, institutions and policies in certain countries have facilitated a greater and more rapid response to globalization and technological change, along with the other underlying factors, by shifting to a less centralized industry structure than has been the case in other countries. An implication of this high variance in industry restructuring is that some countries are likely to have industry structures that are different from 'optimal'.

While the evidence suggests that the restructuring paths of industry vary considerably across countries, virtually nothing is known about the consequences of lagging behind in this process. Do countries with an industry structure that deviates considerably from the optimal industry structure forfeit growth more than countries deviating less from the optimal industry structure? This question is crucial to policy makers, because if the opportunity cost, measured in terms of forgone growth, of a slow adjustment towards the optimal industry structure is low, the consequences of not engaging in a rapid adjustment process are relatively trivial. However, if the opportunity cost is high the consequences are more alarming. The purpose of this paper is to identify the impact of deviations in the actual industry structure from the optimal industry structure on growth.

82

IMPEDED INDUSTRIAL RESTRUCTURING

In the second Section of this paper, the shift in industry structure away from more to less concentrated production is documented and underlying explanations provided. In the third Section, we use a data base linking industry structure to growth rates for a panel of 18 European countries spanning five years to test the hypothesis that deviations from the optimal industry structure result in reduced growth rates. Finally, in the last Section conclusions are provided. In particular, we find that deviations from the optimal industry structure, measured in terms of the relative importance of small firms, have had an adverse effect on economic growth rates.

II. THE SHIFT IN INDUSTRY STRUCTURE

A wide range of studies identified systematic evidence documenting two imposing characteristics of industry structure over the first two-thirds of the previous century (Scherer and Ross 1990, Chandler 1990). The *first* is that the degree of centralization of production was steadily increasing over time. The *second* is that production was at its highest point of centralization and concentration in the 1970s. This reflected underlying technological and demand characteristics rendering large-scale production and organization more efficient.

1. Until 1970s: Large Businesses as the Engine of Growth

Giant corporations were seen as the sole and most powerful engine of economic and technological progress in the early post war period. Schumpeter (1950) provided an image of large corporations gaining the competitive advantage over small and new ones and of giant corporations ultimately dominating the entire economic landscape. This advantage would be due to scale economies in the production of new economic and technological knowledge. These scale economies would result from the organization of teams of highly trained specialists working on technological progress in a routinized fashion. The large corporation was thought to have both superior production efficiency and superior innovative efficacy. Galbraith (1956) pointed out that in his world of countervailing power large corporations are superior to small ones in nearly every aspect of economic behavior like productivity, technological advance, compensation and job security. In his world all major societal institutions contributed to the maintenance of the stability and predictability needed for mass production. In these worlds of Schumpeter and Galbraith there is little room for small

83

D. B. AUDRETSCH, M. A. CARREE, A. J. VAN STEL AND A. R. THURIK

scale, experimenting firms thriving on the uncertainty of technological advance, whimsical markets and the individual energy of an obstinate entrepreneur. Only large industrial units were thought to be able to compete on global markets producing global products.

The exploitation of economies of scale and scope was thought to be at the heart of dictating an industry structure characterized by concentration and centralization (Teece 1993). Chandler (1990) stresses the importance of investment in production, distribution, and management needed to exploit economies of scale and scope. Audretsch (1995) stresses the influence the image of the East-European economies and the perceived Soviet threat had on Western policy makers. An important concern in the late 1950s and early 1960s was the assumed strong technological progress emerging from huge and concentrated research and development programs being assembled in the Soviet Union and Eastern Europe. It was a period of relatively well-defined technological trajectories, of a stable demand and of seemingly clear advantages of diversification. Audretsch and Thurik (2001) characterize this period as one where stability, continuity and homogeneity were the cornerstones and label it the managed economy. Small businesses were considered to be a vanishing breed.

2. From 1970s on: Shift in Economic Activity Toward Small Firms

Perhaps it was the demise of the economies of Central and Eastern Europe and the former Soviet Union that made it clear that concentration and centralization were no longer the cornerstones of the most efficient industry structure. At the same time, more and more evidence became available that economic activity moved away from large firms to small, predominantly young firms. Brock and Evans (1989) provided an extensive documentation of the changing role of small business in the U.S. economy. They were the first to understand these new developments filling the void of economic research concerning formation, dissolution and growth of businesses and concerning the differential impact of regulations across business size classes. The new role of small firms and their new interaction with large ones is described in Nooteboom (1994). Various authors have provided empirical evidence for this new role. Blau (1987) showed that the proportion of self-employed in the U.S. labor force began to rise in the late 1970s. Acs and Audretsch (1993) and Carlsson (1992) provided a survey of evidence concerning manufacturing industries in countries in varying stages of economic development. Acs (1996) shows that the self-employment rate in OECD countries declined until 1977 and increased between then and 1987.

IMPEDED INDUSTRIAL RESTRUCTURING

Carree et al. (2002) show that for a sample of 23 OECD countries the average business ownership rate increased from 9.6% in 1976 to 11% in 1996[2].

There has been considerable documentation of the shift in the structure of American industry. Carlsson (1989) showed that the share of the Fortune 500 in total manufacturing employment dropped from 79% in 1975 to 73% in 1985. In the same period the share of these firms in total manufacturing shipments dropped from 83% to 78%. More recently, he shows that the employment share of the Fortune 500 dropped to 58% in 1996 and the latter to 75% (Carlsson 1999). Unfortunately, similar documentation for Europe has not been possible due to the absence of systematic data that is comparable across countries. However, Eurostat has begun to publish yearly summaries of the firm size distribution of EU-members at the two-digit industry level for the entire private sector, see Eurostat (1994 and 1996). The efforts of Eurostat are currently being supplemented by the European Network of SME Research (ENSR), a co-operation of 18 European institutes. This organization publishes a yearly report of the structure and the developments of the enterprise and establishment populations in the countries of the European Union[3].

3. Explaining the Shift in Industry Structure

Carlsson (1992) offers two explanations for the shift in the industry structure away from large corporations and towards small enterprises. The first deals with fundamental changes occurring in the world economy from the 1970s onwards. These changes relate to the intensification of global competition, the increase in the degree of uncertainty and the growth in market fragmentation. The second deals with changes in the character of technological progress. He shows that flexible automation has had various effects resulting in a shift from large to smaller firms. The shift in the nature of technological progress particularly involving flexible automation facilitated product differentiation and led to a new division of labor involving more cooperation and less competition between large and small firms. Piore and Sabel (1984) argue that in the 1970s firms and policy makers were unable to maintain the conditions necessary to preserve mass production. Mass production was based upon the input of special-purpose machines and of semi-skilled workers and the output of standardized products.

---

2. In this study, the business ownership rate is defined as the number of business owners or self-employed outside the agricultural sector (including owner-managers of incorporated businesses and excluding unpaid family workers), as a fraction of the total labour force.

3. See the various editions of *European Observatory* which provide an account of the state of small business in Europe like, for instance, EIM/ENSR (1997).

D. B. AUDRETSCH, M. A. CARREE, A. J. VAN STEL AND A. R. THURIK

A fundamental change in the path of technological development led to the oc-currence of vast diseconomies of scale. This market instability resulted in the demise of mass production and promoted flexible specialization. Piore and Sabel use the term *Industrial Divide* for the 'reversal of the trend' from that to-ward more large firms to that toward more small ones. Jensen (1993) refers to the *Third Industrial Revolution* when describing the same phenomenon. Me-redith (1987) discusses the advantages of a range of recently developed flexible production techniques for small-scaled enterprises. Audretsch and Thurik (2000) point at the role knowledge plays when explaining the shift from the managed economy to the entrepreneurial economy.

This shift away from large firms is not confined to manufacturing industries. Brock and Evans (1989) show that this trend has been economy-wide, at least for the United States. They offer four additional reasons as to why this shift has occurred: (1) the increase of labor supply; (2) changes in consumer tastes; (3) relaxation of (entry) regulations and (4) the fact that we are in a period of cre-ative destruction. Loveman and Sengenberger (1991) stress the influence of two other trends of industrial restructuring: decentralization and vertical disin-tegration of large companies and the formation of new business communities. Furthermore, they emphasize the role of private and public policies promoting the small business sector[4].

4. The Effect of the Shift

The extent to which this shift in industry structure has influenced economic performance has received limited attention. This has to do with a persistent lack in knowledge of market structure dynamics (Audretsch 1995). In other words, there is a lack in knowledge concerning questions like who enters and exits, what determines this mobility and what are its effects, in particular on eco-nomic performance. Here we are concerned with a key question in economics: why do industries or economies grow? As discussed earlier, traditionally, the prevalent assumption was that large enterprises are at the heart of the process of innovation and creation of welfare. This assumption is generally referred to as the *Schumpeterian Hypothesis*. Recently, the focus of attention has shifted

---

4. See also Carree et al. (2002) for a survey of the determinants of the shift away from a managed and toward an entrepreneurial economy. An important consequence of the shift in consumer tastes and the decentralization and vertical disintegration of large companies has been the in-creased share of the service sector. Because enterprises in the service sector are, on average, much smaller than in the manufacturing industry, this implies an increased share of small firms at the economy-wide level.

IMPEDED INDUSTRIAL RESTRUCTURING

towards whether the process of decentralization and deconcentration, which virtually every industrialized country has experienced in the last two decades, has had positive welfare implications. Audretsch (1995) calls this shift in orientation of our social-economic thinking 'the new learning'.

The link between the shift in the industry structure and subsequent growth can be investigated in two distinct ways. *First*, by investigating the range of consequences of the shift in the locus of economic activity. For instance, one may study whether this shift has been favorable to the rejuvenation of industries and the process of (radical) innovation[5]. Alternatively, one may focus on the importance of the role of small firms in enhancing competition[6]. A yet different perspective on the link between the shifting industry structure and performance has been to examine the relationship between small firms and job creation[7]. Lastly, the role of small firms as a vehicle for entrepreneurship has been the focal point for a series of studies. For example, Baumol (1990) provides an extensive account of the role that entrepreneurial activities and their consequences for prosperity play throughout history. Acs (1992) brings it all together in a short descriptive manner in a survey of some consequences of the shift of economic activity from large to smaller businesses. He claims that small firms play an important role in the economy as they are agents of change by their entrepreneurial activity, as they are a source of considerable innovative activity, as they stimulate industry evolution and as they create an important share of the newly generated jobs.

A *second* way to answer the question of how changes in the industry structure impact performance is to circumvent the intermediary variables of technological change, entrepreneurship, competitiveness and job generation to investigate a direct link between the shift and performance measures at the industry or economy-wide level. Some preliminary empirical results of the relation between changes in the firm size distribution and economic growth are presented in Thurik (1996). His analysis lacks a theoretical component but provides some indication of an increase in the economy-wide share of small firms positively affecting subsequent growth. Schmitz (1989) presents an endogenous growth model relating entrepreneurial activity and economic growth. An important implication of his model is that the equilibrium fraction of entrepreneurs is lower than the social optimal level, providing a rationale for policies stimulating en-

5. See Acs and Audretsch (1990), Audretsch (1995) and Cohen and Klepper (1992, 1996).
6. See Audretsch (1995), Oughton and Whittam (1997) and You (1995). Nickell (1996), Nickell et al. (1997) and Lever and Nieuwenhuijsen (1999) present evidence that competition, as measured by an increased number of competitors, has a positive effect on the rate of total factor productivity growth.
7. Davis, Haltiwanger and Schuh (1996) and Carree and Klomp (1996) provide some insights in the relationship between small firms and job creation.

D. B. AUDRETSCH, M. A. CARREE, A. J. VAN STEL AND A. R. THURIK

trepreneurial activity. Some evidence of a well-established historical (long-term) relationship between fluctuations in entrepreneurship and the rise and fall of nations is assembled by Wennekers and Thurik (1999). In this respect we also mention the work of Eliasson (1995) on economic growth through competitive selection. He demonstrates that such a relation may be characterized by significant time lags up to a couple of decades.

The evaluation of the various consequences of the shift in the locus of economic activity is necessary to establish whether it is desirable and whether it should be promoted by economic policy. However, this evaluation is complicated because none of these consequences is, in fact, independent of the other three and because the evaluation offers something of a series of trade-offs. Audretsch and Thurik (2001) contrast the most fundamental elements of the newly emerging entrepreneurial economy with those of the managed economy by identifying fifteen trade-offs that are essential for these two polar worlds. For instance, while total employment may rise due to new start-ups and declining average firm sizes, the lower average wages that small firms pay, may at least partly offset the welfare effect induced by the employment growth. By following the *second* way we are able to investigate whether there has been an *overall* growth-enhancing effect of the shift in the locus of economic activity from 'large' to 'small'. This is the subject of Section III.

III. ESTIMATING THE GROWTH PENALTY

In this Section we test the hypothesis that the extent of the gap between the actual industry structure and the optimal industry structure influences subsequent growth. We start with the assumption that a country's growth can be decomposed into two components: (i) growth that would have occurred with an optimal industry structure, and (ii) the impact on growth occurring from any actual deviations from that optimal industry structure. This can be represented by

$$\Delta GNP_{cp} = \Delta GNP_{cp}^* - \gamma \left| SFP_{cp-1} - SFP_c^* \right| \tag{1}$$

where the dependent variable is the actual rate of economic growth. ΔGNP_{cp}^* is the rate of economic growth in country c in the case where the actual industry structure, summarized by small firm presence (SFP_{cp}), is at the optimal level at the start of the period p. For ease of exposition we assume that the optimal industry structure in a country remains constant for the total period under investigation. This is not vital to our analysis. Since we are considering only short-term periods (maximum five years) this may be a reasonable assumption.

IMPEDED INDUSTRIAL RESTRUCTURING

Industry structure is multidimensional and spans a broad array of character-istics that defy measurement by a single statistic. However, as explained else-where (Audretsch and Thurik 2000, 2001), the most salient characteristic driv-ing the shift in industry structure from the managed to the entrepreneurial economy is that the relative role of small and entrepreneurial firms has in-creased. Thus, we capture changes in industry structures by changes in the rel-ative importance of small firms.

In equation (1) the parameter γ is positive. Deviations of the actual industry structure from the optimal industry structure negatively affect economic growth, both when the industry structure consists of too few or too many small firms. In either case there is a deviation from the optimal industry structure and number of small firms. Taking the first difference of equation (1) we obtain

$$\Delta GNP_{cp} = \Delta GNP_{cp-1} + \Delta\Delta GNP_{cp}^* - \gamma\left(\left|SFP_{cp-1}-SFP_c^*\right|-\left|SFP_{cp-2}-SFP_c^*\right|\right) \quad (2)$$

In case both SFP_{cp-1} and SFP_{cp-2} are above the optimal small-firm share, the ex-pression between brackets reduces to ΔSFP_{cp-1}. Indeed, in case the small-firm share is too high, adding small firms to the industry structure reduces economic growth. In case both SFP_{cp-1} and SFP_{cp-2} are below the optimal small-firm share, the expression between brackets reduces to $- \Delta SFP_{cp-1}$. An increase in the small firm share when this presence is below optimal enhances economic performance. Therefore, the sign of the parameter of ΔSFP_{cp-1} reflects whether the small firm presence is below or above the optimal levels for the countries under consideration. In case the parameter is negative, the industry structure consists of too many small firms. In case the parameter is positive, the reverse holds and the industry structure consists of too few small firms.

We will denote the parameter of ΔSFP_{cp-1} as κ. Note that this is not the same parameter as γ, since the sign of κ is dependent on whether the actual small-firm share is above or below the optimal one. So, κ can be both positive and negative whereas γ is necessarily positive.

We make some further assumptions to transform equation (2) into an equation that can be estimated using the data at hand. First, we approximate ΔSFP_{cp-1} by $\Delta SF_{cp-1} - \Delta LF_{cp-1}$, the difference between the growth of small firms and large firms in terms of value-of-shipments. Second, we assume that ΔGNP_{cp}^* is idio-syncratic with respect to time and country. Therefore country dummies and time dummies (the last to correct for European wide business cycle effects) are in-cluded. Thus, $\Delta\Delta GNP_{cp}^*$ is approximated by time dummies only because the country dummies drop out when taking first differences. Third, we add an error term e_{cp}. Summarizing we have

D. B. AUDRETSCH, M. A. CARREE, A. J. VAN STEL AND A. R. THURIK

$$\Delta GNP_{cp} = \Delta GNP_{cp-1} + \sum_{p=1}^{P} \beta_p D_p + \kappa(\Delta SF_{cp-1} - \Delta LF_{cp-1}) + e_{cp} \qquad (3)$$

where D_p denote dummy variables for periods $p = 1, \ldots, P$. Factors specific to each time period are reflected by β_p. A high value of this parameter indicates an unexplained increase in the extent of economic growth. In case of a low β_p the reverse holds. The contribution of the shift in the size class distribution of firms to the percentage growth of GNP is represented by κ. The influence of this shift on GNP growth is lagged. This implies that $p = 1, \ldots, P$ runs from 1990 through 1994 when applying equation (3) to our European data set.

To estimate equation (3), we use data provided by the *European Observatory* (EIM/ENSR 1993, 1994, 1995, 1996 and 1997). The European Observatory provides data on the annual percentage growth of real gross value added of the (non-primary) private sector, the annual percentage growth of value-of-shipments of small- and medium-sized firms (with employment less than 250 employees), as well as the annual percentage growth of value-of-shipments of large firms (with employment of at least 250 employees). These data are available for five years (1989 through 1993) for all fifteen member countries of the European Union (Europe-15), Iceland, Norway and Switzerland (including Liechtenstein)[8].

Hence, our European data set consists of a total of 90 (18 countries times five years) observations. However, Germany had to be omitted for the entire period. Germany's then recent unification led to specific economic perturbations that render it inappropriate for inclusion in the estimation model. The remaining 85 observations are used for computing the regression coefficients. The lowest values of $\Delta SF_{cp} - \Delta LF_{cp}$ in the data set are -2.5%-point (Finland, 1993) and -1.8%-point (Norway, 1989), while the highest values are 2.1%-point (Finland, 1989) and 1.9%-point (United Kingdom, 1989). The mean value is -0.2%-point. The period 1990–1994 is characterized by relatively vehement cyclical movements with 1992 being a recession year and 1994 being a year with an exceptional strong recovery.

In *Table 1* the regression results for the period 1990–1994 are presented. Equation (3) does not contain country dummies. The 'mean' country effect is reflected by coefficient α while D_{1991} is left out of all computations to avoid full multicollinearity[9]. The two dummy variables with a significant contribution are

---

8. The European Observatory database is largely based on the Eurostat publication *Enterprises in Europe*, which contains harmonised information for each of the countries listed above on the number of enterprises, employment, turnover, value added and labour costs, by industry and size class. For some countries, estimates have been made in case of incomplete data.

9. Instead of estimating coefficients for all P time dummies as suggested by equation (3), we actually estimate $P-1$ dummy coefficients and a constant term α.

IMPEDED INDUSTRIAL RESTRUCTURING

D_{1993} and D_{1994}. This reflects the strong economic recovery after the recession of 1992. We present both results with all time dummies included and with the two insignificant dummies excluded. In the first part of *Table 1* weighted least squares results are presented, with total employment as the weighting variable. In the second part of the table ordinary least squares results are presented.

In each of the cases we find a significantly positive coefficient (at the 5% significance level) for κ. Its value ranges from 0.55 for the first column of *Table 1* to 0.92 for the last column[10].

The empirical evidence suggests that the consequences for economic growth of not shifting the industry structure away from large business towards smaller ones are rather large. However, this result is qualified by the large standard deviation of the coefficient for κ. Another important qualification to these results is that measurement of the variables includes a number of estimates. Follow-up studies are required for corroboration of these results[11]. Still, the estimated κ is found to be significantly positive in all computations. We conclude, based on the empirical findings, that there is evidence that on average those countries that have experienced a shift in their industry structures away from large firms and towards small firms have also experienced greater economic growth, at least for a sample of Western European countries over a recent time period. Since our interpretation is that this shift is an indicator of the stage of the transition of the economy from a managed one to an entrepreneurial one, we conclude that European countries that progress on this transition track seem to have been rewarded with additional growth[12].

10. To control for possible country selection effects, we have run the regression 17 times independently, each time with one country excluded from the sample and with a model specification with only dummies for the years 1993 and 1994 in equation (3). The estimates of κ range from 0.53 (t-value 1.71) to 0.68 (t-value 2.67) using weighted least squares and from 0.73 (t-value 1.63) to 1.01 (t-value 2.43) using ordinary least squares.

11. Carree and Thurik (1998, 1999) provide complementary analyses showing the consequence of lagging behind in this restructuring process in manufacturing. Using a sample of 14 manufacturing industries in 13 European countries and 13 manufacturing industries in 12 European countries, respectively, they find that, on average, the employment share of large firms in 1990 has had a negative effect on growth of output in the subsequent four-year period.

12. It is conceivable that there is reversed causality, i.e. that the degree of industry restructuring is dependent on the level of economic growth. To correct for business cycle effects, we estimate the following equation: $\Delta SF_{cp} - \Delta LF_{cp} = \mu + \nu \Delta GNP_{cp} + \varepsilon_{cp}$ for the period 1989–1993. The estimated residuals of this equation, $\hat{\varepsilon}_{cp}$, can be seen as the variable $\Delta SF_{cp} - \Delta LF_{cp}$, corrected for business cycle effects. Equation (3) is now estimated for the period 1990–1994 (note that there is lag in (3)), with $\Delta SF_{cp} - \Delta LF_{cp}$ replaced by $\hat{\varepsilon}_{cp}$. The estimate of ν is 0.00 (t-value 0.01) using WLS and –0.04 (t-value –1.43) using OLS. As a consequence, the estimated value of κ in equation (3) is the same as in *Table 1* using WLS and is 0.62 (t-value 1.45) using OLS (only dummies for 1993 and 1994). After correcting for reversed causality, the estimate of κ equals 0.6 in all four versions of *Table 1*. We conclude that omission of the option of reversed causality hardly influences the size and sign of the effects as represented in *Table 1*.

D. B. AUDRETSCH, M. A. CARREE, A. J. VAN STEL AND A. R. THURIK

One has to be careful interpreting the estimation results for different countries. The estimated positive value of κ must be viewed as an average value of the (unobserved) κ_c's of the different countries. So, the positive value found for κ does not mean that in *all* countries in the sample an increase in small-firm presence is rewarded with additional growth. There may be countries in the sample where small-firm presence is indeed above the optimal level and consequently, a further increase in the number of small firms leads to a growth penalty instead of a growth reward. The estimation results do indicate, however, that for the majority of countries in the sample, the number of small firms was too low in the period under consideration. In translating the positive value of κ in terms of implications for different countries, policy makers should compare small-firm presence in their own country with that in surrounding countries. If *SFP* is relatively low, small-firm presence may be expected to be below optimum, given the positive value of κ. On the other hand, if *SFP* is relatively high, small-firm presence might exceed optimum, despite the estimated κ being positive.

Table 1

Regression Results for Equation (3): Relating Growth to Structure[1,2]

	Weighted least squares[3]		Ordinary least squares	
α	−0.93	−0.79	−1.22	−0.97
	(−2.30)	(−3.38)	(−1.84)	(−2.56)
β_{1990}	0.52		0.39	
	(0.89)		(0.41)	
β_{1992}	−0.08		0.37	
	(−0.14)		(0.39)	
β_{1993}	1.32	1.20	2.19	1.94
	(2.26)	(2.50)	(2.32)	(2.53)
β_{1994}	4.35	4.25	4.72	4.48
	(7.40)	(8.74)	(4.91)	(5.65)
κ	0.55	0.63	0.91	0.92
	(2.14)	(2.58)	(2.20)	(2.27)
R^2	0.441	0.422	0.318	0.317
Adjusted R^2	0.406	0.401	0.275	0.291
DW	2.05	2.04	1.72	1.72
N	85	85	85	85

Notes: [1] Regression for 17 European countries over the period 1990–1994. [2] DW is the Durbin-Watson statistic. T-values between parentheses. [3] Weighting variable for WLS is total employment

IMPEDED INDUSTRIAL RESTRUCTURING

The regression results are illustrated using *Figure 1*. We have grouped the growth-acceleration observations, $\Delta\Delta GNP = \Delta GNP_{cp} - \Delta GNP_{cp-1}$, on the basis of the degree to which the value-of-shipments shifted from large to small firms. That is, the $\Delta\Delta GNP$ observations have been sorted in order of the values of the (lagged) structural change variable, $\Delta SF - \Delta LF$. Both variables have been computed in deviation of the mean per year in order to correct for specific year effects. The 85 sorted observations have been divided into five groups of 17 observations. The averages of both $\Delta SF - \Delta LF$ and $\Delta\Delta GNP$ are displayed in *Figure 1*. We see that, on average, a larger shift toward smallness is associated with a higher growth acceleration.

Figure 1

Growth Accelerations and the Relative Shift Toward Small Firms[1]

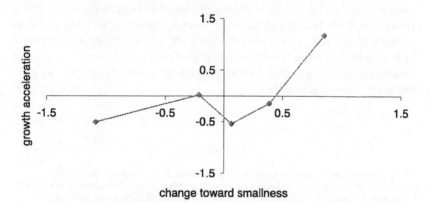

change toward smallness

Notes: [1] Averages of five groups of growth acceleration values ($\Delta\Delta GNP$), ordered on the basis of the degree of change toward small firms ($\Delta SF - \Delta LF$), both in deviation of yearly country-averages. Both axes are scaled in percentage points.

V. CONCLUSIONS

An extensive literature has linked the structure of industries to performance. However, little is known about the consequences of deviating from the optimal industry structure. The evidence provided in this paper suggests that, in fact, there is a cost of not adjusting industry structure towards the optimal. This cost is measured in terms of forgone economic growth.

D. B. AUDRETSCH, M. A. CARREE, A. J. VAN STEL AND A. R. THURIK

Most developed countries have experienced a shift towards a more decentralized industry structure in the last several decades. The magnitude of this shift and speed of adjustment varies considerably across countries. The evidence suggests that those countries that have shifted industry structure towards decentralization in a more rapid fashion have been rewarded by higher growth rates[13].

Our analysis is based upon whether excess growth of small firms over their larger counterparts has led to additional macro-economic growth for member countries of the European Union in the early 1990s. The results of this investigation are meant to supplement the intuition of many policymakers that the changes in industrial structure have had some real effects on economic performance.

European public policy has been preoccupied with generating economic growth and reducing unemployment. The resulting policy debate has typically focused on macroeconomic policies and instruments. The results of this paper suggest that an additional set of instruments may also be valuable in generating growth – policies focusing on allowing the industry structure to adjust. As the evidence shows, just as countries reluctant to shift their industry structures will be penalized by lower growth rates, those nations able to harness the forces of technology and globalization by transforming their industry structures are rewarded by growth dividends.

REFERENCES

Acs, Z. J. (1992). Small business economics: a global perspective, *Challenge*. 35: 38–44.
Acs, Z. J. (1996). Small firms and economic growth, in: P. H. Admiraal (ed.), *Small Business in the Modern Economy, De Vries Lectures in Economics*. Oxford, UK: Blackwell Publishers.
Acs, Z. J. and D. B. Audretsch (1990). *Innovation and Small Firms*. Cambridge, MA: MIT Press.
Acs, Z. J. and D. B. Audretsch (1993). Conclusion, in: Z. J. Acs and D. B. Audretsch (eds.), *Small Firms and Entrepreneurship: an East-West Perspective*. Cambridge, UK: Cambridge University Press: 227–231.
Audretsch, D. B. (1995). *Innovation and Industry Evolution*. Cambridge, MA: MIT Press.

13. Fagerberg (2000) investigates the impact of a different dimension of industry structure, that of the distribution of economic activity across (manufacturing) industries. Using data for a sample of 37 countries over the 1973–1990 period, he finds empirical evidence for increases in the shares of the electrical machinery industry (containing electronics) in the total manufacturing sector to positively affect productivity growth in manufacturing. Fagerberg argues it to be a consequence of this industry having the highest productivity growth (4.7% per annum), on average, of all manufacturing industries and of technological progress in electronics to spill over to other manufacturing industries.

IMPEDED INDUSTRIAL RESTRUCTURING

Audretsch, D. B. and A. R. Thurik (2000). Capitalism and democracy in the 21st century: from the managed to the entrepreneurial economy, *Journal of Evolutionary Economics*. 10: 17–34.

Audretsch, D. B. and A. R. Thurik (2001). What's new about the new economy? Sources of growth in the managed and entrepreneurial economies, *Industrial and Corporate Change*. 10: 267–315.

Baumol, W. J. (1990). Entrepreneurship: productive, unproductive and destructive, *Journal of Political Economy*. 98: 893–921.

Blair, J. M. (1948). Technology and size, *American Economic Review*. 38: 121–152.

Blau, D. (1987). A time series analysis of self-employment, *Journal of Political Economy*. 95: 445–467.

Brock, W. A. and D. S. Evans (1989). Small business economics, *Small Business Economics*. 1: 7–20.

Carlsson, B. (1989). The evolution of manufacturing technology and its impact on industrial structure: an international study, *Small Business Economics*. 1: 21–37.

Carlsson, B. (1992). The rise of small business: causes and consequences, in: W. J. Adams (ed.), *Singular Europe, Economy and Policy of the European Community after 1992*. Ann Arbor, MI: University of Michigan Press: 145–169.

Carlsson, B. (1999). Small business, entrepreneurship, and industrial dynamics, in: Z. Acs (ed.), *Are Small Firms Important?* Dordrecht, NL: Kluwer Academic Publishers: 99–110.

Carree, M. A. and L. Klomp (1996). Small business and job creation: a comment, *Small Business Economics*. 8: 317–322.

Carree, M. A. and A. R. Thurik (1998). Small firms and economic growth in Europe, *Atlantic Economic Journal*. 26: 137–146.

Carree, M. A. and A. R. Thurik (1999). Industrial structure and economic growth, in: D. B. Audretsch and A. R. Thurik (eds.), *Innovation, Industry Evolution and Employment*. Cambridge, UK: Cambridge University Press: 86–110.

Carree, M. A., A. J. van Stel, A. R. Thurik and A. R. M. Wennekers (2002). Economic development and business ownership: an analysis using data of 23 OECD countries in the period 1976–1996, *Small Business Economics*, forthcoming.

Chandler, A. D. Jr. (1990). *Scale and Scope: The Dynamics of Industrial Capitalism*. Cambridge, MA: Harvard University.

Cohen, W. M. and S. Klepper (1992). The trade-off between firm size and diversity in the pursuit of technological progress, *Small Business Economics*. 4: 1–14.

Cohen, W. M. and S. Klepper (1996). A reprise of size and R&D, *Economic Journal*. 106: 925–951.

Davis, S. J., J. Haltiwanger and S. Schuh (1996). Small business and job creation: dissecting the myth and reassessing the facts, *Small Business Economics*. 8: 297–315.

Dosi, G. (1988). Sources, procedures and microeconomic effects of innovations, *Journal of Economic Literature*. 26: 1120–1171.

EIM/ENSR (1993). *The European Observatory for SMEs: first annual report*. Zoetermeer, NL: EIM.

EIM/ENSR (1994). *The European Observatory for SMEs: second annual report*. Zoetermeer, NL: EIM.

EIM/ENSR (1995). *The European Observatory for SMEs: third annual report*. Zoetermeer, NL: EIM.

EIM/ENSR (1996). *The European Observatory for SMEs: fourth annual report*. Zoetermeer, NL: EIM.

EIM/ENSR (1997). *The European Observatory for SMEs: fifth annual report*. Zoetermeer, NL: EIM.

Eliasson, G. (1995). Economic growth through competitive selection, paper presented at the 22nd Annual EARIE Conference, Juan les Pins, 3–6 September 1995.

Eurostat (1994). *Enterprises in Europe, third edition*. Luxembourg.

Eurostat (1996). *Industrial Trends Monthly Statistics 1996/6*. Luxembourg.

Fagerberg, J. (2000). Technological progress, structural change and productivity growth: A comparative study, *Structural Change and Economic Dynamics*. 11: 393–411.

Galbraith, J. K. (1956). *American Capitalism: the Concept of Countervailing Power*. Boston, MA: Houghton Mifflin.

D. B. AUDRETSCH, M. A. CARREE, A. J. VAN STEL AND A. R. THURIK

Jensen, M. C. (1993). The modern industrial revolution, exit, and the failure of internal control systems, *Journal of Finance*. 48: 831–880.

Krugman, P. (1991). *Geography and Trade*. Cambridge, MA: MIT Press.

Lever, M. H. C. and H. R. Nieuwenhuijsen (1999). The impact of competition on productivity in Dutch manufacturing, in: D. B. Audretsch and A. R. Thurik (eds.), *Innovation, Industry Evolution and Employment*. Cambridge, UK: Cambridge University Press: 111–128.

Loveman, G. and W. Sengenberger (1991). The re-emergence of small-scale production: an international comparison, *Small Business Economics*. 3: 1–37.

Meredith, J. (1987). The strategic advantages of new manufacturing technologies for small firms, *Strategic Management Journal*. 8: 249–258.

Nickell, S. J. (1996). Competition and corporate performance, *Journal of Political Economy*. 104: 724–746.

Nickell, S., P. Nicolitsas and N. Dryden (1997). What makes firms perform well?, *European Economic Review*. 41: 783–796.

Nooteboom, B. (1994). Innovation and diffusion in small firms, *Small Business Economics*. 6: 327–347.

Oughton, C. and G. Whittam (1997). Competition and cooperation in the small firm sector, *Scottish Journal of Political Economy*. 44: 1–30.

Piore, M. and C. Sabel (1984). *The Second Industrial Divide: Possibilities for Prosperity*. New York: Basic Books.

Romer, P. M. (1990). Endogenous technological change, *Journal of Political Economy*. 98: 71–101.

Scherer, F. M. and D. Ross (1990). *Industrial Market Structure and Economic Performance*. Boston, MA: Houghton Mifflin Company.

Schmitz, Jr., J. A., (1989). Imitation, entrepreneurship, and long-run growth, *Journal of Political Economy*. 97: 721–739.

Schumpeter, J. A. (1934). *The Theory of Economic Development*. Cambridge, MA: Harvard University Press.

Schumpeter, J. A. (1950). *Capitalism, Socialism and Democracy*. New York: Harper and Row.

Teece, D. J. (1993). The dynamics of industrial capitalism: perspectives on Alfred Chandler's scale and scope, *Journal of Economic Literature*. 31: 199–225.

Thurik, A. R. (1996). Small firms, entrepreneurship and economic growth, in: P. H. Admiraal (ed.), *Small Business in the Modern Economy, De Vries Lectures in Economics*. Oxford, UK: Blackwell Publishers.

Wennekers, S. and A. R. Thurik (1999). Linking entrepreneurship and economic growth, *Small Business Economics*. 13: 27–55.

You, J. I. (1995). Small firms in economic theory, *Cambridge Journal of Economics*. 19: 441–462.

SUMMARY

This paper documents that a process of industrial restructuring has been transforming the developed economies, where large corporations are accounting for less economic activity and small firms are accounting for a greater share of economic activity. Not all countries, however, are experiencing the same shift in their industrial structures. Little is known about the cost of resisting this restructuring process. The goal of this paper is to identify whether there is a cost, measured in terms of forgone growth, of an impeded restructuring process. The cost is measured by linking growth rates of European countries to deviations from the 'optimal' industrial structure. The empirical evidence suggests that countries impeding the restructuring process pay a penalty in terms of forgone growth.

IMPEDED INDUSTRIAL RESTRUCTURING

ZUSAMMENFASSUNG

Die vorliegende Studie zeigt, daß der Prozeß industrieller Umstrukturierung diejenigen unter den entwickelten Volkswirtschaften verändert hat, in denen wirtschaftliche Aktivitäten weniger von großen als von kleinen Unternehmen ausgehen. Nicht alle Länder erleben jedoch identische Umgestaltungen ihrer Industriestrukturen. Über die Kosten des Widerstands gegen Umstrukturierungsprozesse ist bislang wenig bekannt. Die vorliegende Studie zielt deshalb darauf ab, diese Kosten zu identifizieren und in ihrer Höhe abzuschätzen. Die Kosten werden empirisch als 'Verlust an Wachstum' gemessen, indem die Wachstumsraten europäischer Länder auf die Abweichungen von einer 'optimalen' Industriestruktur bezogen werden. Die empirischen Ergebnisse implizieren, daß Länder, die Umstrukturierungsprozesse behindern, einen Preis in der Form eingebüßten Wachstums bezahlen.

RÉSUMÉ

Cet article montre que le processus de restructuration industrielle a transformé les pays développés où les grandes entreprises ont une moindre part à l'activité économique, tandis que les PME en couvrent une plus grande partie. Cependant, cette restructuration industrielle n'est pas la même dans tous les pays. Les coûts encourus par les pays s'opposant à cette transformation sont à peine connus. Le but de cet article est donc d'identifier les coûts d'un processus de restructuration entravé et d'en estimer le montant. Ces coûts sont mesurés en termes de 'croissance manquée', en liant les taux de croissance de pays européens aux déviations d'une structure industrielle jugée 'optimale'. Les résultats empiriques suggèrent que les pays qui entravent le processus de restructuration en payent le prix sous forme de croissance manquée.

24

Regional Studies, Vol. 36.2, pp. 113–124, 2002

Carfax Publishing
Taylor & Francis Group

Growth Regimes over Time and Space

DAVID B. AUDRETSCH★ and MICHAEL FRITSCH†

★*Indiana University, Institute for Development Strategies, SPEA Suite 201, Bloomington, IN 47405–2100, USA.*
Email: daudrets@indiana.edu

†*Technical University of Freiberg, Faculty of Economics and Business Administration, Lessingstraße 45, D-09596 Freiberg,*
Germany. Email: fritschm@vwl.tu-freiberg.de

(Received October 2000; in revised form June and September 2001)

AUDRETSCH D. B. and FRITSCH M. (2002) Growth regimes over time and space, *Reg. Studies* **36**, 113–124. This paper seeks to shed new light on the policy debate about whether regional economic development policy should be targeted towards fostering new firm start-ups or nurturing large, incumbent enterprises. We extend the concept of technological regimes for innovative activity in the industrial economics literature to develop a concept of growth regimes for the unit of observation of regions. Based on data for 74 regions in West Germany over a two-decade period, we identify the existence of four distinct growth regimes: the entrepreneurial regime; the routinized regime; the revolving door regime; and the declining regime. The empirical evidence suggests that no single type of regime accounts for growth. Rather, regional growth can result in regions focusing on large enterprises or new enterprises. Thus, we conclude that diverse growth regimes exist across both time and space.

Regional growth   Entrepreneurship   Small firms   Innovation

AUDRETSCH D. B. et FRITSCH M. (2002) Facteurs de croissance sur le temps et dans l'espace, *Reg. Studies* **36**, 113–124. Cet article cherche à éclaircir le débat à propos du rôle de la politique de développement économique régional: devrait-elle cibler la création d'entreprise ou le développement des grandes entreprises existantes? La notion de régimes technologiques relatifs à l'innovation, tirée de la documentation sur l'économie industrielle, se voit étendre afin de développer la notion de régimes pour l'unité régionale observée. A partir des données auprès de 74 régions situées dans l'Allemagne de l'Ouest sur deux décennies, on identifie quatre régimes différents – le régime entreprise, le régime systématique, le régime transitoire et le régime déclin. Les preuves empiriques laissent voir que la croissance ne s'explique pas par un seul régime. Plutôt, la croissance régionale puisse avoir pour résultat des régions qui focalisent sur ou de grandes ou de nouvelles entreprises. Ainsi, on conclut que divers régimes existent sur le temps et dans l'espace.

Croissance régionale   Entreprise
Petites entreprises   Innovation

AUDRETSCH D. B. und FRITSCH M. (2002) Wachstumsregime in Zeit und Raum *Reg. Studies* **36**, 113–124. Der Beitrag behandelt die Frage, ob die Regionalpolitik auf die Stimulierung von Unternehmensgründungen oder die Förderung von bereits existierenden Betrieben konzentrieren sollte. Dabei erweitern wir das industrieökonomische Konzept der Technologischen Regime um eine regionale Dimension. Anhand von Daten für die Entwicklung von 74 westdeutschen Regionen über fast zwei Dekaden identifizieren wir vier verschiedene Entwicklungsregime – das entrepreneurhafte Regime, das routinisierte Regime, das Drehtür-Regime und das Niedergangs-Regime. Der empirische Befund zeigt, das tatsächlich solche Unterschiede hinsichtlich des regionalen Entwicklungsregimes bestehen, wobei es im Zeitablauf durchaus auch zu einem Wechsel des Regime-Typs kommen kann. Darüber hinaus legen die Ergebnisse der Schlussfolgerung nahe, dass der positive Einfluss von Gründungen auf die wirtschaftliche Entwicklung vor allem langfristiger Natur ist.

Regionales Wachstum   Unternehmertum
Kleine und mittelgroße Unternehmen   Innovation

INTRODUCTION

Which is the engine of regional growth – large, established enterprises or new firm start-ups? This question has emerged as one of the great policy debates confronting regional economic development in recent years. The answer to this question is crucial, because it dictates the focus for the investment of regional economic development resources. Academic studies such as HARRISON, 1994, 1995, argue that the major goals

of regional economic development policy, job creation and growth, are best met by large enterprises. According to HARRISON, 1995, p. 358; 'Small firms do not create the most jobs'. This line of thinking is certainly consistent with the regional economic development policies implemented in places like Alabama, which invested its economic development resources in attracting large corporations (Daimler Benz). While a number of empirical analyses of the relationship between start-up activity in a region and subsequent

0034-3404 print/1360-0591 online/02/020113-12 ©2002 Regional Studies Association
http://www.regional-studies-assoc.ac.uk

DOI: 10.1080/00343400220121909

employment change did not find any such significant impact (AUDRETSCH and FRITSCH, 1996; FRITSCH, 1997), other studies (such as REYNOLDS *et al.*, 1995; COOKE, 1996; FELDMAN, 1996; COOKE and WILLS, 1999) argue that new and small enterprises serve as the locomotive of regional growth and employment creation. Again, a broad array of examples (STERN-BERG, 1996; ETTLINGER and TUFFORD, 1996), such as Austin, Texas, suggest that many regions have successfully targeted new firm start-ups to be the engine of job creation and growth.

This debate is strikingly reminiscent of an analogous controversy in the field of industrial economics, where scholars and policy makers have argued for years about whether large or small enterprises are best suited for innovative activity. On the one hand, SCHUMPETER, 1942, p. 3, had proclaimed the large corporation as having the innovative advantage: 'What we have got to accept is that the large-scale establishment has come to be the most powerful engine of progress'. On the other hand, ROTHWELL, 1989; SCHERER, 1992, and others have argued that small firms are more innovative than their larger counterparts.

While they were developing, the literatures in regional economics and industrial economics seemed disparate and unconnected. More recently, however, a convergence may be taking place between these two literatures. This convergence reflects, as the new growth theory emphasizes (ROMER, 1986; KRUGMAN, 1991), the increased importance of innovative activity as a determinant of economic growth. As the comparative advantage of high-wage countries shifts to knowledge-based economic activity, the ability to generate innovative activity becomes linked with regional growth and employment creation (STERNBERG, 1996).

The purpose of this paper is to provide a reconciliation to the debate over the sources of regional growth by suggesting that, in fact, both sides are correct. New firm start-ups as well as large incumbent firms may make a significant contribution to economic development – but not in all regions and at all times. We draw upon a reconciliation in the industrial economics literature introduced by NELSON and WINTER, 1982, who argued that both large and small firms have the innovative advantage – but under contrasting technological regimes, which are shaped by the underlying knowledge conditions. By analogy, we introduce the concept of growth regimes, which suggests that in some regions large enterprises are more conducive to growth, while in other regions small enterprises are the engine of economic development. By linking growth rates to the relative importance of new firm start-ups and incumbent enterprises, as well as other regional characteristics, for 74 West German regions, we find compelling evidence for the existence of four distinct growth regimes. This suggests that the search for a unique holy grail of regional economic development may be misguided. Rather, there are multiple policy

paths to generating growth – the types of policies and instruments triggering growth in one region may be very different from those conducive to growth in a different region. This would suggest that diversity may be more appropriate for regional economic development policy than a singular policy approach.

FROM TECHNOLOGICAL TO GROWTH REGIMES

The theory of *growth regimes* is derived from the theories and empirical validation of *technological regimes*. The theory of technological regimes dates back at least to NELSON and WINTER, 1982, who tried to reconcile the earlier work by SCHUMPETER, 1911, with the seeming contradiction posed by his later ideas (SCHUMPETER, 1942). In his earlier thinking, Schumpeter argued that the creative destruction triggered by the start-up of new firms and the displacement of the incumbents resulted in a superior economic performance, in terms of innovation and growth. However, Schumpeter reversed his view in his subsequent work (SCHUMPETER, 1942) by suggesting that large corporations in a stable environment are more conducive to innovation and growth.

While a great, and sometimes bitter debate ensued contesting which of these 'two Schumpeters' was correct, NELSON and WINTER, 1982, provided a reconciliation by suggesting that they both are – but under the guise of very different technological regimes. According to WINTER, 1984, p. 297: 'An entrepreneurial regime is one that is favourable to innovative entry and unfavourable to innovative activity by established firms; a routinized regime is one in which the conditions are the other way around'. These different technological regimes distinguish between distinct knowledge conditions underlying an industry. As AUDRETSCH, 1995, explains, these knowledge conditions reflect three essential characteristics of the technology: the degree of uncertainty about the outcome of R & D (technologically as well as commercially); the extent of knowledge asymmetries; and the cost of transacting knowledge that is not just uncertain but also asymmetric. Under the routinized technological regime, the knowledge conditions bestow large, incumbent enterprises with the innovative advantage. Under the entrepreneurial regime, the knowledge conditions are more conducive to new and small enterprises.

GORT and KLEPPER, 1982, posited, and provided empirical evidence, that the relative innovative advantage between newly established enterprises and incumbent firms depends on the source of information generating innovative activity. If information based on non-transferable experience in the market is an important input in generating innovative activity, then incumbent firms will tend to have the innovative advantage over new firms. This is consistent with

WINTER's, 1984, notion of the routinized regime, where the accumulated stock of non-transferable information is the product of experience within the market, which firms outside of the industry, by definition, cannot possess.

By contrast, when information outside of the routines practiced by the incumbent firms is a relatively important input in generating innovative activity, newly established firms will tend to have the innovative advantage over the incumbent firms. ARROW, 1962; WILLIAMSON, 1975; and MUELLER, 1976, have all emphasized that when such information created outside of the incumbent firms cannot be easily transferred to those incumbent firms – presumably due to agency and bureaucracy problems (see WILLIAMSON, 1975; TIROLE, 1986; HOLMSTROM, 1989; KREPS, 1991; NONAKA, 1994; KROGH, 1998) – the holder of such knowledge must start a new firm to appropriate the market value of her or his knowledge.

Thus, under the routinized technological regime, there is little divergence in the evaluation of the expected value of new ideas between the inventor and the decision-making bureaucracy of incumbent firms. Hence, there is no great incentive for agents to start new firms, at least not for the reason of doing something differently. However, under the entrepreneurial technological regime, a divergence in beliefs between the agent and the principal evaluating the expected value of a new idea is more likely to emerge. Therefore, it is under the entrepreneurial regime where the start-up of new firms is likely to play a more important role, presumably as a result of the motivation to appropriate the value of economic knowledge that cannot be easily transferred to the incumbent enterprises.

A number of studies have provided considerable empirical evidence for the existence of distinct technological regimes (DOSI, 1982, 1988; ACS and AUDRETSCH, 1990; MALERBA, 1992; MALERBA and ORSENIGO, 1993; AUDRETSCH, 1995; DOSI et al., 1995; AGARWAL, 1998). In some industries small firms clearly have the innovative advantage, which is consistent with the entrepreneurial regime. In other industries large enterprises exhibit the innovative advantage, which is consistent with the routinized regime.

In introducing a theory of growth regimes, we extend the concept of the technological regime from the unit of observation of the industry to a geographic unit of observation. By analogy, the entrepreneurial growth regime exists in a region where growth is the result of a high importance of new firm start-ups and a turbulent enterprise structure. In an entrepreneurial regime, the knowledge conditions underlying the region combine with local institutions and policies, so that new ideas and innovative activity are typically implemented by the start-up of new firms. SAXENIAN, 1990, p. 96 ff., describes a case study of such an entrepreneurial growth regime:

It is not simply the concentration of skilled labour, suppliers and information that distinguish the region. A variety of regional institutions – including Stanford University, several trade associations, and local business organizations, and a myriad of specialized consulting, market research, public relations and venture capital firms – provide technical, financial, and networking services which the region's enterprises often cannot afford individually. These networks defy sectoral barriers: individuals move easily from semiconductor to disk drive firms or from computer to network makers. They move from established firms to start-ups (or vice versa) and even to market research or consulting firms, and from consulting firms back into start-ups.... This decentralized and fluid environment also promotes the diffusion of intangible technological capabilities and understandings.

GERTLER, 1995, has shown that geographic proximity promotes a transfer of tacit knowledge (NONAKA, 1994; KROGH, 1998). There is a considerable degree of correspondence between such an entrepreneurial regime in a region and the characterization of entrepreneurial industries that is given in the literature (WINTER, 1984; AUDRETSCH, 1995). These are mainly new industries in which start-ups make a considerable contribution to innovation activity and have relatively good prospects for survival and growth. We, therefore, expect that the proportion of innovative entries in young industries is comparatively high under a regional entrepreneurial regime, where young firms make a significant contribution to employment change.

By contrast, a routinized growth regime exists in a region where growth is the result of a stable enterprise structure and the predominance of large, incumbent enterprises. In the routinized regime, new firm start-ups play a relatively unimportant role and if new firms enter the market, their chances for survival and growth are much lower than in an entrepreneurial regime. The knowledge conditions in the region combine with the local institutions and policies so that growth is typically a manifestation of incumbent enterprises. For example, GRABHER, 1993, has documented how the institutions of the Rhine-Ruhr region nurtured the existing incumbent enterprises and impeded the potential threat posed by new entrants.

The theory of technological regimes applies only to industries where innovative activity plays an important role. Because their focus was on innovation, it made little sense for NELSON and WINTER, 1982, to develop these concepts for industries with little or no innovative activity. AUDRETSCH, 1995, however, observed the existence of industries which are not particularly innovative, but are characterized by a high degree of simultaneous entry and exit. At any point in time, both a high start-up rate as well as a high exit rate can be observed. He characterized these industries as exhibiting a *revolving door regime*. By analogy, any region exhibiting a relatively low growth rate but a high start-up rate can be characterized as a *revolving door regime*. We may suspect that under such a regime, entries tend to be non-innovative supplying roughly the same products by using about the same technology as the incumbent firms. This would imply that they do not have any significant technological advantage over their competitors which makes it rather unlikely that they will grow fast and generate a large number of jobs. Moreover, high numbers of entries *and* exits in a region would be a likely outcome if a relatively high share of the new firms produce mainly for the regional market so that they tend, if successful, to crowd out local competitors instead of creating additional employment in the region. The proportion of such types of entries may be relatively large in regions with high unemployment in which the push factors for becoming an entrepreneur are relatively strong.

A fourth regime exists in low-growth regions exhibiting little start-up activity, but where employment losses are attributable to the downsizing and plant closures of incumbent enterprises. Such regions are classified as belonging to a *downsizing regime*. The relatively low level of start-up activity here is insufficient to provide enough new jobs or income to substitute the losses in the incumbent firms. Therefore, these regions are in danger of experiencing some kind of 'entropic death' of their economic system, because too little seeding is done. Regions under a downsizing regime have much in common with regions characterized by a routinized regime. For example, knowledge conditions and survival chances of entrants may be rather similar in both cases. The crucial difference between the two types is that, under a routinized regime, the incumbent firms perform relatively well, while in the downsizing case they are likely to be declining. In the first case, the dominant industry is growing. Therefore, we may expect that regions with a routinized regime show a tendency to transform into a downsizing regime as the industry ages and is replaced by a new industry. Due to unfavourable entry conditions and the correspondingly low level of start-ups under a routinized regime, this development may be much more likely than a transformation into an entrepreneurial or a revolving door regime.

MEASUREMENT AND CLASSIFICATION OF GROWTH REGIMES

To shed light on the question – do distinct growth regimes exist over time and space? – we employ a somewhat ad hoc classification of regions into the four different types. Our database is constructed from the German Social Insurance Statistics, as described and documented by BRIXY and FRITSCH, 2002. In particular, this database enables us to capture different measures of enterprise dynamics – start-up rates, closure rates, turbulence rates, net-entry rates, as well as employment change. All of these measures are available

for the 74 (West) German planning regions that are somewhat larger than labour market areas.[1] Another important characteristic of this database is that the information is available for a relatively long time period, from 1983–98. In Figs. 1 and 2, each of these regions is classified as an entrepreneurial regime, revolving door regime, routinized regime or downsizing regime.[2]

A regime is classified as an entrepreneurial regime if the start-up rate[3] and growth rate both exceed their median values. A region is classified as a revolving door regime if the start-up rate exceeds the median but the employment (private sector) growth rate is below the median employment growth rate. A region is classified as the routinized regime if the start-up rate is below the median, but the growth rate is in the upper 50%. Finally, the downsizing regime includes regions where both the start-up and growth rates are in the lower 50%. We refer to relative growth here because employment change was negative in all regions in the 1993–98 period. Because such a classification may be somewhat arbitrary, two alternative combinations of criteria were applied in order to identify more extreme cases, hoping that the relevant characteristics of the growth regimes would become more visible. According to the first alternative, only those regions were selected that were among the upper/lower 40% with regard to both criteria. A second alternative selected only the regions among the upper/lower 30% for classification.

For classifying the regions into the four regimes, an important adjustment was made to control for the fact that not only does the composition of industries vary considerably across regions, but the relative importance of start-ups and incumbent enterprises also varies systematically across industries. For example, start-up rates are higher in the service sector than in manufacturing industries. This means that the relative importance of start-ups and incumbents in a region is confounded by the composition of industries in that region. This would result in a bias of overestimating the existence of an entrepreneurial regime in regions with a high composition of industries where start-ups play an important role, and underestimating the presence of the entrepreneurial regime in regions with a high composition of industries where new-firm start-ups are relatively unimportant.

To correct for the confounding between the regional composition of industries with the relative importance of start-ups and incumbent enterprises, a shift-share procedure, as described by ASHCROFT *et al.*, 1991, was deployed to develop a measure of sector adjusted start-up activity. This sector adjusted number of start-ups is defined as the number of new firms in a region that can be expected to be observed if the composition of industries was identical across all regions. Thus, the measure adjusts the raw data by imposing the same composition of industries on each region (see the Appendix for details).

Figs. 1 and 2 show the classification of each region

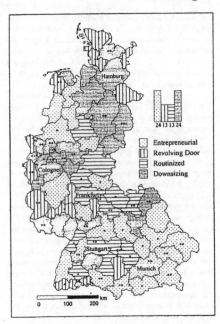

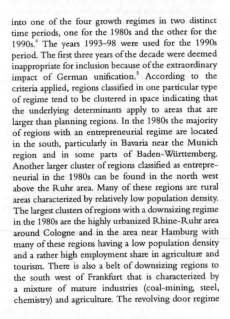

Fig. 1. Distribution of regional growth regimes in West Germany in the 1980s

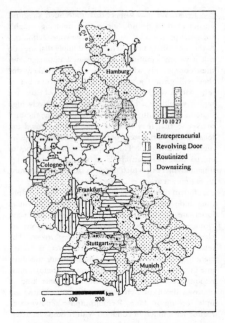

Fig. 2. Distribution of regional growth regimes in West Germany in the 1990s

into one of the four growth regimes in two distinct time periods, one for the 1980s and the other for the 1990s.[4] The years 1993–98 were used for the 1990s period. The first three years of the decade were deemed inappropriate for inclusion because of the extraordinary impact of German unification.[5] According to the criteria applied, regions classified in one particular type of regime tend to be clustered in space indicating that the underlying determinants apply to areas that are larger than planning regions. In the 1980s the majority of regions with an entrepreneurial regime are located in the south, particularly in Bavaria near the Munich region and in some parts of Baden-Württemberg. Another larger cluster of regions classified as entrepreneurial in the 1980s can be found in the north west above the Ruhr area. Many of these regions are rural areas characterized by relatively low population density. The largest clusters of regions with a downsizing regime in the 1980s are the highly urbanized Rhine-Ruhr area around Cologne and in the area near Hamburg with many of these regions having a low population density and a rather high employment share in agriculture and tourism. There is also a belt of downsizing regions to the south west of Frankfurt that is characterized by a mixture of mature industries (coal-mining, steel, chemistry) and agriculture. The revolving door regime

includes mainly regions with a low or medium population density while among the regions classified as routinized we find some dynamic centres of economic activity like Stuttgart and Frankfurt. Looking at the distribution of regional growth regimes in the 1990s (Fig. 2), there are quite a number of changes between categories but the picture is not completely different. Bavaria and particularly the regions in the south east of Munich still appear to be the heartland of the entrepreneurial regime, while Stuttgart and a number of adjacent regions are now classified as downsizing. Also a number of regions north and east of Frankfurt that had been routinized in the 1980s are now in the downsizing category. Hamburg and a neighbouring region (Bremen) have succeeded in recovering from downsizing to entrepreneurial and also a number of revolving door regions in the 1980s are classified as entrepreneurial in the 1990s.

Table 1 makes it clear that neither a high start-up rate nor a high turbulence rate is sufficient for relatively high growth. Turbulence is defined as the number of start-ups plus the number of closures in a certain period. The turbulence rate describes the fluctuation in the number of businesses in a certain period and may be interpreted as a measure for the intensity of

David B. Audretsch and Michael Fritsch

Table 1. Characteristics of regional growth regimes in the 1980s[1]

Regional characteristics	Growth regime			
	Entrepreneurial	Revolving door	Routinized	Downsizing
Start-up rate	6·14 (6·33; 6·60)[3]	6·30 (6·40; 6·84)	4·86 (4·82; 4·43)	4·79 (4·53; 4·52)
Closure rate	5·05 (5·34; 5·56)	5·32 (5·38; 5·51)	4·04 (4·03; 4·02)	4·35 (4·29; 4·26)
Turbulence rate	11·23 (11·69; 12·10)	11·65 (11·86; 12·35)	8·97 (8·85; 8·47)	9·06 (8·82; 8·79)
Net entry rate	1·09 (1·11; 1·06)	0·98 (1·04; 1·04)	0·83 (0·89; 0·85)	0·42 (0·30; 0·27)
Volatility rate	10·11 (10·68; 11·12)	10·64 (10·77; 11·02)	8·07 (8·06; 8·05)	8·71 (8·59; 8·51)
Employment change, 1983–89 (%)	9·85 (10·51; 11·01)	5·56 (5·13; 2·87)	9·06 (9·12; 10·45)	4·04 (3·74; 3·48)
Share of employment in establishments with < 50 employees, 1983 (%)	45·38 (45·54; 47·32)	44·07 (45·42; 49·26)	38·94 (39·92; 42·34)	35·60 (33·90; 34·98)
Unemployment rate 1983 (%)	7·79 (6·92; 5·99)	11·63 (11·86; 12·94)	6·84 (7·07; 7·31)	11·64 (12·06; 12·57)
Population density, 1983[2]	144·8 (124·4; 137·0)	205·0 (175·8; 125·9)	178·8 (175·1; 152·5)	353·3 (494·0; 415·4)
No. of regions	24 (16; 8)	13 (8; 4)	13 (8; 3)	24 (14; 12)

Notes: 1. Median values.
2. Inhabitants per km[2].
3. First value in parentheses: value for regions that are among the upper/lower 40% with regards to the criteria applied for classification; second value in parentheses: value for regions that are among the upper/lower 30%.

Sources: Information on unemployment rates and population density was taken from the regional database of the Bundesamt für Bauwesen und Raumordnung (Federal Office for Building and Regional Planning); all other data are own calculations based on Social Insurance Statistics.

market selection processes in a region. Volatility is defined as turbulence (start-ups plus closures) minus the absolute change in the number of establishments (net-entry). It is supposed to reflect the degree of turbulence that did not account for the observed changes in the number of establishments. It is also clear from Table 1 that low start-up activity does not necessarily condemn a region to low growth. While the downsizing regime exhibits both low start-up and growth rates, under the routinized regime, higher growth is achieved in the absence of significant start-up activity. One remarkable difference between regions belonging to the routinized category and the downsizing regions is the higher net-entry rate,[6] indicating better conditions for survival under a routinized regime. That closure rates as well as turbulence rates tend to be highest in regions characterized by an entrepreneurial or a revolving door regime is presumably a result of the high level of start-ups there; new businesses tend to have high failure rates and successful start-ups may force incumbent firms to exit the market. This may also explain the relatively high degree of the volatility rates in high start-up regions.

That we find the highest share of employment in small businesses with less than 50 employees in regions with a high level of start-ups corresponds to the empirical observation made in diverse studies of new firm formation that there is a pronounced correspondence of small firm employment in a region and entry (see REYNOLDS *et al.*, 1994, for an overview). The main explanation for this relationship is probably that many founders of new firms have worked in relatively small firms before starting their own business. Moreover, new businesses tend to start small and if a certain region experiences high start-up rates over a longer time period, this may lead to a high proportion of employ-

ment in small firms. As was to be expected, unemployment rates are higher in the regions with relatively slow growth or severe decline. That we find the highest population density in the downsizing regions results from the high proportion of old industrialized regions in this category. In contrast to that, many (but not all!) of the high-start-up regions are rather rural areas.

The same patterns across the four different growth regimes can be observed in Table 2 for the 1990s as well, although some of the regions were characterized by different growth regimes than in the 1980s (see Figs. 1 and 2). In both time periods, the differences between the four types with regard to small firm employment, unemployment rates and population density tend to be more pronounced when comparing the more extreme cases that are among the upper/lower 30% or 40% according to the criteria used for classification. Note that no significant differences among the four types of regions could be found with respect to industry structure, the qualifications of the workforce and innovation activity.

CHANGES OF GROWTH REGIME OVER TIME

Table 3 shows the distribution of regions across the four regimes in both decades. Over 60% of the regions characterized by the entrepreneurial growth regime in the 1990s were also characterized by the entrepreneurial growth regime in the 1980s. Over 30% of the regions characterized by the routinized growth regime in the 1990s were also characterized by the routinized growth regime in the 1980s. Thus, there was a considerable degree of regime change between the two decades. Looking for patterns of such regime change, we find that eight out of the 13 revolving door regions of the

Table 2. *Characteristics of regional growth regimes in the 1990s*[1]

Regional characteristics	Growth regime			
	Entrepreneurial	Revolving door	Routinized	Downsizing
Start-up rate	5·95 (6·44; 6·53)[3]	6·26 (6·16; 5·98)	5·08 (5·08; 4·24)	4·98 (4·62; 4·60)
Closure rate	5·54 (5·84; 6·07)	5·81 (5·81; 5·75)	4·55 (4·55; 3·59)	4·67 (4·43; 4·36)
Turbulence rate	11·55 (11·99; 12·74)	12·06 (11·96; 11·71)	9·63 (9·62; 7·83)	9·65 (9·12; 9·03)
Net entry rate	0·49 (0·43; 0·55)	0·39 (0·36; 0·38)	0·53 (0·53; 0·65)	0·28 (0·26; 0·24)
Volatility rate	11·08 (11·63; 12·14)	11·61 (11·61; 11·51)	9·09 (9·09; 7·18)	9·21 (8·86; 8·73)
Employment change, 1993–98 (%)	−2·43 (−1·85; −0·40)	−5·96 (−6·36; −7·75)	−3·01 (−2·55; −2·14)	−7·26 (−7·64; −7·94)
Share of employment in establishments with < 50 employees, 1993 (%)	49·45 (51·66; 52·41)	44·70 (45·34; 46·11)	41·95 (41·52; 42·03)	41·55 (40·10; 39·27)
Unemployment rate, 1993 (%)	7·50 (7·27; 9·10)	8·43 (7·50; 7·53)	7·64 (7·62; 9·61)	8·02 (9·70; 10·78)
Population density, 1993[2]	153·2 (126·9; 141·9)	355·9 (304·6; 227·0)	185·7 (166·9; 111·3)	237·9 (321·7; 527·5)
No. of regions	27 (18; 11)	10 (7; 3)	10 (6; 1)	27 (18; 12)

Notes: 1. Median values.

2. Inhabitants per km[2].

3. First value in parentheses: value for regions that are among the upper/lower 40% with regards to the criteria applied for classification; second value in parentheses: value for regions that are among the upper/lower 30%.

Sources: See Table 1.

Table 3. *Distribution of regions across regimes in the 1980s and the 1990s*[1]

Growth regime in the 1980s	Growth regime in the 1990s				Row total
	Entrepreneurial	Revolving door	Routinized	Downsizing	
Entrepreneurial	15 (11; 5)[2]	3 (2; 2)	4 (1; 0)	2 (2; 1)	24 (16; 8)
	62·5 (68·8; 62·5)	12·5 (12·5; 25·0)	16·7 (6·3; 0)	8·3 (12·5; 12·5)	100
	55·6 (64·7; 55·6)	30·0 (40·0; 66·7)	40·0 (20·0; 0)	7·4 (10·53; 7·69)	32·4 (34·8; 29·6)
Revolving door	8 (5; 3)	5 (3; 1)	0 (0; 0)	0 (0; 0)	13 (8; 4)
	61·5 (62·5; 75·0)	38·5 (37·5; 25·0)	0 (0; 0)	0 (0; 0)	100
	29·6 (29·4; 33·3)	50·0 (60·0; 33·3)	0 (0; 0)	0 (0; 0)	17·6 (17·4; 14·8)
Routinized	0 (0; 0)	0 (0; 0)	4 (2; 1)	9 (2; 1)	13 (8; 3)
	0 (0; 0)	0 (0; 0)	30·8 (25·0; 33·3)	69·2 (75·0; 66·7)	100
	0 (0; 0)	0 (0; 0)	40·0 (40·0; 50·0)	33·3 (31·6; 15·4)	17·6 (17·4; 11·1)
Downsizing	4 (1; 1)	2 (0; 0)	2 (1; 1)	16 (11; 10)	24 (14; 12)
	16·7 (7·1; 8·3)	8·3 (0; 0)	8·3 (14·3; 8·3)	66·7 (78·6; 83·3)	100
	14·8 (5·9; 11·1)	20·0 (0; 0)	20·0 (40·0; 50·0)	59·3 (57·9; 76·9)	32·4 (30·4; 44·4)
Column total	27 (17; 9)	10 (5; 3)	10 (5; 2)	27 (19; 13)	74 (46; 27)
	36·5 (37·0; 33·3)	13·5 (10·9; 11·1)	13·5 (10·9; 7·4)	36·5 (41·3; 48·2)	100
	100	100	100	100	100

Notes: 1. Rows are: number of cases; row percentage; column percentage.

2. First figure in parentheses: share of regions that were among the upper/lower 40% in the 1980s with regards to the criteria applied for classification; second value in parentheses: share of regions that were among the upper/lower 30% in the 1980s.

1980s became entrepreneurial in the 1990s. Of the more extreme cases with values among the upper/lower 30% in the 1980s, two out of the three (five out of the eight) extreme revolving door regions of the 1980s were classified as entrepreneurial in the 1990s. It is also quite remarkable that none of the revolving door regions of the 1980s was classified as routinized or downsizing in the subsequent decade. This may be seen as an indication for long run effects of a relatively high level of start-up activity: perhaps it took a considerable number of years for some of the revolving door regions of the 1980s to succeed in harvesting the fruit of the high level of start-up activity in the 1990s. It is also remarkable that none of the regions with a routinized regime in the 1980s became entrepreneurial or a revolving door-type region in the 1990s. Even more

striking is that nine out of the 13 regions that had been classified as routinized in the 1980s fell into the downsizing category in the 1990s. These results raise the question: is this decline a long-run effect of having a relatively low level of start-ups in a region?

Comparing the regions between the 1980s and 1990s also suggests that the majority (62·5% and 66·7%, respectively) of the regions that were in the entrepreneurial or the downsizing category in the 1980s were also the same type in the 1990s. The degree of path dependency is apparently much higher for these two kinds of growth regimes. This may indicate that the entrepreneurial and the downsizing regimes represent more a sort of equilibrium position than do the revolving door and the routinized regimes, which, by contrast, appear to be more transitional in character. It is also remarkable that both the entrepreneurial as well as the downsizing regime serve as a starting position for a transformation into all of the other types of regimes. In contrast, transitions from the revolving door and the routinized regime appear to represent moves down a one-way street leading to an entrepreneurial or a downsizing regime only. If this hypothesis is correct and only the entrepreneurial and the downsizing regimes represent somewhat stable combinations of start-up activity and employment change, this would imply a strong positive relationship between new firm formation and regional growth in the long run, even though no such short-run relationship can be ascertained. Due to the relatively small number of regions in our sample, however, such interpretations remain somewhat speculative.

Applying a simple Markow chain model based on the probabilities of transition from one type of growth regime to another, we calculated the final distribution of regions to growth regimes is 37·04% as entrepreneurial, 12·53% as revolving door, 13·39% as routinized and 37·04% as downsizing. This distribution suggests a concentration of regions in the two polar cases, the entrepreneurial and downsizing regimes.

Looking at the characteristics of the regions according to their allocation to the different growth regimes in the 1980s and the 1990s, we find a clear pattern with regard to population density, indicating relatively unfavourable conditions for employment growth in regions with high density (Table 4).[7] One clear indication for this is that those regions under a downsizing regime in the 1980s that became entrepreneurial or revolving door in the 1990s had a much lower level of population density than those downsizing regions of the 1980s that were classified as routinized or downsizing in the 1990s. Furthermore, those entrepreneurial regions of the 1980s that experienced relatively bad performance with regard to employment in the subsequent decade and had to be classified as revolving door in the 1990s were much more densely populated than those

regions that fell into the entrepreneurial category in both periods. Accordingly, revolving door regions that became entrepreneurial in the 1990s had a relatively low population density; in those cases that remained revolving door, population density was relatively high. Because population density in a region is highly correlated with a number of factors like the wage level, real estate prices, quality of communication infrastructure, diversity of the labour market, qualification of the workforce, share of small businesses as well as with certain characteristics of the industry structure in the respective region (e.g. proportion of service employment), the causes behind this statistical relationship with employment change remain somewhat unclear.

START-UP ACTIVITY AND REGIONAL EMPLOYMENT CHANGE

As noted earlier, many of the previous studies (see AUDRETSCH and FRITSCH, 1996; FRITSCH, 1997) had found no evidence linking start-up activity to subsequent growth for German regions. But the earlier analyses were for the 1980s. There are compelling reasons to suspect that Germany has changed between the two decades.[8] Thus, in Table 5 we estimate employment growth in each region and link it to the start-up rate. We control for population density in these models due to the statistical impact on employment change that we find for this variable in our data. Population density here represents all kinds of regional influences, such as availability of qualified labour, house prices, local demand and the level of knowledge spillovers. Including population density instead of indicators for these individual effects into the regression avoids the problem of multicollinearity caused by relatively high levels of correlation among these factors. Moreover, we find a higher level of statistical significance compared to estimates based on separate indicators for the different effects of location. Other indicators for regional charac-

Table 4. *Characteristics of regions according to growth regime in the 1980s and 1990s*

Growth regime in the 1980s	Growth regime in the 1990s	Population density, 1983[1]
Entrepreneurial	Entrepreneurial	121·1
	Revolving door	365·3
	Routinized	164·9
	Downsizing	160·2
Revolving door	Entrepreneurial	125·9
	Revolving door	335·2
Routinized	Routinized	147·3
	Downsizing	186·7
Downsizing	Entrepreneurial	281·1
	Revolving door	247·0
	Routinized	494·0
	Downsizing	309·6

Note: 1. Number of inhabitants per km[2].

Table 5. *Determinants of regional employment change in the 1980s and the 1990s[1]*

	Regional employment change, 1983–89 (%)		Regional employment change, 1993–98 (%)	
Constant	5·043*	4·252	−9·591**	−11·013**
	(2·02)	(1·38)	(4·00)	(4·21)
Average start-up rate	0·401	—	1·090**	—
	(0·98)		(2·70)	
Average sector adjusted start-up rate	—	0·605	—	1·308**
		(1·20)		(3·02)
Population density	−0·001	−0·003*	−0·002**	−0·002*
	(1·65)	(2·22)	(2·87)	(2·52)
R^2	0·034	0·100	0·213	0·230
F value	2·30	4·06**	10·85**	11·91**

Notes: 1. *T*-values in parentheses.
*Statistically significant at the 5%-level; **statistically significant at the 1%-level.

teristics not related to population density (e.g. qualification of regional workforce, level of innovation
activities, etc.) did not prove to be statistically significant
at any conventional level in explaining regional
employment change. As the results show, the start-up
rate has no statistically significant impact on growth for
the 1980s. In the model using 'original', non-sector
adjusted start-up rate, the rather low value of the R^{2adj}
indicates that not much is explained and the F value is
not statistically significant. In the alternative approach
using the sector adjusted start-up rate, population density is statistically significant at a 5% level with a
negative sign indicating unfavourable conditions for
employment in urbanized areas that we already mentioned above (see Table 4). The fit of this model is
somewhat better than of the model with the non-
adjusted start-up rate but the impact of new firm
formation activities on employment change is still
insignificant.

For the 1990s, a different result emerges. The
coefficient for the start-up rate has a significantly positive value indicating that those regions with a higher
start-up rate exhibit higher growth rates. As in the
estimations for the 1980s, we find a negative impact of
population density on employment change. For a cross-
section regression, the fit of the models is quite accept-
able. The difference between the coefficients for the
regional start-up rate in the 1980s and the 1990s
suggests that, in fact, Germany is changing over time,
where the engine of growth is shifting from a dual
regime – both the entrepreneurial and routinized
regimes – towards more of a focus on the entrepreneurial regime. The higher coefficients for the sector
adjusted start-up rate compared to the non-adjusted
rate indicate that the relationship between the start-
up rate and employment change is indeed somewhat
'disturbed' by differences with regard to the industry
structure between the regions. This clearly shows the
relevance of the sector adjustment procedure. Therefore, Table 6 shows only the results of regressions with
the adjusted start-up rates.

The regime trajectory of a region is linked to its
growth performance in the 1990s in Table 6. By
including a dummy variable reflecting regions with an
above average growth rate in the 1980s, equation (1)
shows that high growth regions in the 1980s also
tended to be high growth regions in the 1990s. But
even holding this path dependency constant, those
regions that experienced high start-up rates in the
1980s also exhibited high growth rates in the next
decade. This suggests that while both the routinized
and entrepreneurial regimes generated growth in the
1980s, regions with high start-up rates in the 1980s
had a greater likelihood of being high growth regions
in the 1990s. That is, one of the keys to a high growth
performance region in the 1990s was having a high
start-up rate in the 1980s. The non-significance of the
start-up rate in the 1990s in equation (1) may be caused

Table 6. *Entry and growth history as determinants of regional*
employment change in the 1990s[1]

| | Regional employment change 1993–98 | | |
	(1)	(2)	(3)
Constant	−12·099**	−12·341**	−13·407**
	(5·15)	(4·99)	(6·29)
Average sector adjusted	2·542**	—	1·510**
start-up rate, 1983–85	(2·95)		(4·27)
Average sector adjusted	−1·236	1·300**	—
start-up rate, 1993–95	(1·31)	(3·21)	
Population density, 1993	−0·001	−0·002	−0·001
	(1·53)	(1·81)	(1·49)
Above average			
employment change,			
1983–89 (yes = 1;	1·526*	2·280**	1·830**
no = 0)	(2·21)	(3·38)	(2·80)
R^{2adj}	0·395	0·329	0·389
F value	12·93**	12·91**	16·49**

Notes: 1. *T*-values in parentheses.
* Statistically significant at the 5%-level.
** statistically significant at the 1%-level.

by multicollinearity because start-up rates for different
time periods tend to be highly correlated. However,
omitting the start-up rate for the 1980s or the 1990s
from the model in order to account for such correlation
between these two variables, the coefficient for the
start-up rate in the 1980s (equation (3)) is higher
than that for the start-up in the 1990s (equation (2))
suggesting that the long run impact of a high start-up
rate is stronger than the short run effect. Moreover, we
find a higher share of explained variance for the model
with the start-up rate of the 1980s (equation (3) in
Table 6).

CONCLUSIONS

The results of this paper suggest that, in terms of
enterprise structure, there is no singular approach to
regional economic development policy. Rather, we
identify the existence of four distinct growth regimes.
Thus, there are multiple and diverse ways to attain the
same goal – employment creation and growth. Just as
some regions achieve relatively high growth rates by
concentrating on established, large enterprises, other
regions achieve the same goal by focusing on new firm
start-ups and a more turbulent enterprise structure.
This would suggest that the policy debate focusing on
whether large or small firms are better at creating
employment and growth is somewhat misguided. There
is, apparently, no singular policy approach to employment creation and growth. That is, growth regimes
apparently vary across time and space.

We also find evidence that long term influences play
an important role for regional development. Obviously,
regions that have once attained a relatively steep growth
path tend to follow this path for a longer time period.
At the same time, there is at least some evidence

suggesting that new firm start-ups and small firms are important for future growth. While both the entrepreneurial and routinized regimes provide growth, the results in this paper show that those regions with a high start-up rate in the 1980s exhibited higher growth rates in the subsequent decade. Moreover, we found that regions with a routinized regime face a high danger of subsequently becoming downsized and experiencing relatively low grow rates. Small firms and new firm start-ups may not be necessary for regional growth in the short run, but perhaps they are the seeds of future growth and are of central importance for long run economic development. This would suggest that, despite the differences in the characteristics of regional growth regimes, regional policy should focus on promoting new firm start-ups. This appears to be a necessary, if not sufficient, long term strategy for policy to foster regional growth.

Acknowledgements – We are indebted to Michael Niese for comments on an earlier version of this paper. He and Udo Brixy also provided energetic support in preparing the data. We also gratefully acknowledge comments and suggestions of three anonymous referees that have led to considerable improvements.

NOTES

1. The definition of the planning regions from the 1980s was used for the whole period to correspond with the early period in the database. This enabled a consistent empirical framework between the two time periods analysed in this paper. For this definition of the planning regions, see BUNDESFORSCHUNGSANSTALT FÜR LANDESKUNDE UND RAUMORDNUNG, 1987, pp. 7–10. The Berlin region was excluded due to changes in the definition of the region in the time period under inspection here. German unification in 1990 may have had a particular effect on start-up activity and employment change in regions along the border to the former East Germany. However, closer inspection shows that such effects, if existent, tend to be rather small and in any case not significant enough to justify exclusion of these regions.
2. It could be argued that the classification in growth regimes should only account for start-ups in the manufacturing sector because manufacturing constitutes the main part of a region's economic base. This argument, however, neglects the important role of the service sector in regional innovation systems. Moreover, including services in the analysis enables us to capture at least some degree of the structural change that took place in Germany between the 1980s and 1990s.
3. All rates measuring changes in the population of enterprises (start-up, closure, turbulence, net-entry, volatility) are calculated according to the labour market approach here, i.e. the number of start-ups etc. is divided by the number of persons in the regional workforce at the beginning of the respective period. See AUDRETSCH and FRITSCH, 1994, for different approaches of calculating such rates.

4. The start-up rate is the mean value of the sector-adjusted start-up rate for the private sector according to the labour market approach in the years 1983–85 and 1993–95. Employment change is the percentage change of private sector employment 1983–89 and 1993–98, respectively. The median value of the indicators was used for classification. A single asterisk indicates that the region is among the upper/lower 40% with regards to both criteria. A double asterisk signifies that the region is among the upper/lower 30% with regard to both criteria.
5. Moreover, reliable data for East Germany are only available beginning with the year 1993. Taking the 1993–98 period for the analysis of western German regions in the 1990s may facilitate comparisons with developments in East Germany in that decade. The results of such comparisons are reported elsewhere.
6. Net entry is the number of start-ups minus the number of closures.
7. Some of these average figures should, however, be interpreted with caution because there are only a few underlying cases (regions).
8. The FEDERAL MINISTRY OF ECONOMICS AND TECHNOLOGY, 1999, shows that, in West Germany, employment decreased between 1991–95 in manufacturing industries where employment had increased in the 1980s. As a result, the new policy goal of the Ministry is 'solutions to take advantage of the opportunities offered by globalization for sustained growth, innovation, and new, forward-looking jobs, for making Germany more attractive for creating broader scope for self-reliance and independent action, and thus successfully fighting unemployment' (*ibid.*, p. 15).

APPENDIX

The procedure applied for sector adjustment of regional start-up rates

For eliminating the effect of industry structure in a region on start-up activity, we apply a shift-share procedure (see ASHCROFT *et al.*, 1991). Industry structure is measured on the basis of the number of establishments per industry, not employment. In a first step, we calculate for each region i the hypothetical number of establishments hne_{ij} in industry j:

$$hne_{ij} = E_i * S_j \text{ with } E_i = \sum_j e_{ij} \text{ and } S_j = \frac{E_j}{E} = \frac{\sum_i e_{ij}}{\sum_{ij} e_{ij}}$$

(1)

In this equation, e_{ij} is the observed number of establishments of industry j in region i. E_i represents the overall number of establishments in region i and S_j is the share of establishments of industry j with regard to total number of private sector establishments in West Germany. The hypothetical number of start-ups in region i can be calculated by multiplying the hypothetical number of establishments of each industry in the region (hne_{ij}) with the start-up rate of the respective industry in West Germany as a whole StR_j. This leads to:

$$HNSt_i = \sum_j hne_{ij} * StR_j = \sum_j B_i * StR_j$$

$$\text{with } StR_j = \frac{St_i}{E_j} = \frac{\sum_i st_{ij}}{\sum_i e_{ij}} \tag{2}$$

This hypothetical number of start-ups ($HNSt_i$) is not influenced by deviations of the regional industry structure from the national average and other region-specific factors. To estimate the impact of a deviation of a region's industry structure on the number of start-ups, we multiply the difference between the hypothetical and the observed number of establishments in each

industry by the national start-up rate of the respective industry. Summing up the results over all industries, we obtain the number of start-ups induced by differences between the industry structure of the respective region and the national average ($HISt_i$).

$$HISt_i = \sum_j (e_{ij} - hne_{ij}) * StR_j \tag{3}$$

Subtracting this number from the observed number of start-ups yields the sector-adjusted number of start-ups in the region. We can assume this number is independent of diverging industry structures in the regions.

For the private economy as a whole, the difference between the sector adjusted number of start-ups and the original number of start-ups was between 0·3% and 9·8%; for details see FRITSCH and NIESE, 2000.

REFERENCES

ACS Z. J. and AUDRETSCH D.B. (1990*) Innovation and Small Firms*. MIT Press, Cambridge, MA.

AGARWAL R. (1998) Small firm survival and technological activity, *Small Business Econ.* **11**, 215–24.

ARROW K. J. (1962) Economic welfare and the allocation of resources for invention, in NELSON R. R. (Ed) *The Rate and Direction of Inventive Activity*, pp. 609–25. Princeton University Press, Princeton, NJ.

ASHCROFT B., LOVE J. H. and MALLOY E. (1991) New firm formation in the British counties with special reference to Scotland, *Reg. Studies* **25**, 395–409.

AUDRETSCH D. B. (1995) *Innovation and Industry Evolution*. MIT Press, Cambridge, MA.

AUDRETSCH D. B. and FRITSCH M. (1994) On the measurement of entry rates, *Empirica* **21**, 105–13.

AUDRETSCH D. B. and FRITSCH M. (1996) Creative destruction: turbulence and economic growth, in HELMSTÄDTER E. and PERLMAN M. (Eds) *Behavioral Norms, Technological Progress, and Economic Dynamics: Studies in Schumpeterian Economics*, pp. 137–50. University of Michigan Press, Ann Arbor, MI.

BRIXY U. and FRITSCH M. (2002) Betriebsdatei der Beschäftigtenstatistik der Bundesanstalt für Arbeit (The Establishment File of the Social Insurance Statistics of the Federal Agency for Employment), in FRITSCH M. and GROTZ R. (Eds) *Datenquellen zum Gründungsgeschehen in Deutschland – Darstellung und vergleichende Analysen (Data Sources on New Firm Formation in Germany – Description and Comparative Analysis)*, forthcoming (in German).

BUNDESFORSCHUNGSANSTALT FÜR LANDESKUNDE UND RAUMORDNUNG (1987) *Aktuelle Daten zur Entwicklung der Städte, Kreise und Gemeinden 1986*. Bonn.

COOKE P. (1996) The new wave of regional innovation networks: analysis, characteristics and strategy, *Small Business Econ.* **8**, 159–71.

COOKE P. and WILLS D. (1999) Small firms, social capital and the enhancement of business performance through innovation programmes, *Small Business Econ.* **13**, 219–34.

DOSI G. (1982) Technological paradigms and technological trajectories: a suggested interpretation of the determinants and directions of technical change, *Research Policy* **13**, 3–20.

DOSI G. (1988) Sources, procedures, and microeconomic effects of innovation, *J. Econ. Lit.* **26**, 1,120–71.

DOSI G., MARSILI O., ORSENIGO L. and SALVATORE R. (1995) Learning, market selection and the evolution of industrial structures, *Small Business Econ.* **7**, 411–36.

ETTLINGER N. and TUFFORD M. (1996) Evaluating small firm performance in local context, *Small Business Econ.* **8**, 139–57.

FEDERAL MINISTRY OF ECONOMICS AND TECHNOLOGY (1999) *Economic Report '99*. Bonn.

FELDMAN M. P. (1996) Introduction to special issue on geography and regional economic development: the role of technology-based small and medium sized firms, *Small Business Econ.* **8**, 71–74.

FRITSCH M. (1997) New firms and regional employment change, *Small Business Econ.* **9**, 437–48.

FRITSCH M. and NIESE M. (2000) Der Einfluss der Branchenstruktur auf das Gründungsgeschehen – Eine Analyse für die westdeutschen Raumordnungsregionen1983–1997 (The impact of industry structure on start-up activity – an analysis for West German planning regions 1983–1997), *Geographische Zeitschrift* **88**, 234–50.

GERTLER M. S. (1995) 'Being there': proximity, organization, and culture in the development and adoption of advanced manufacturing technologies, *Econ. Geogr.* **71**, 1–26.

GORT M. and KLEPPER S. (1982) Time paths in the diffusion of product innovations, *Econ. J.* **92**, 630–53.

GRABHER G. (1993) *The Embedded Firm: On the Socio-economics of Industrial Networks*. Routledge, London.

HARRISON B. (1994) *Lean and Mean*. Basic Books, New York.

HARRISON B. (1995) Symposium on Harrison's 'lean and mean': what are the questions?, *Small Business Econ.* **7**, 357–63.

HOLMSTROM B. (1989) Agency costs and innovation, *J. Econ. Behavior & Organization* **12**, 305–27.

KREPS D. (1991) Corporate culture and economic theory, in ALT J. and SLIEPSLE K. (Eds) *Positive Perspectives on Political Economy*, pp. 82–97. Cambridge University Press, Cambridge.

KROGH G. V. (1998) Care in knowledge creation, *Calif. Mgt. Rev.* **40**, 133–55.

KRUGMAN P. (1991) *Geography and Trade*. MIT Press, Cambridge, MA.

MALERBA F. (1992) Learning by firms and incremental technical change, *Econ. J.* **94**, 213–28.

MALERBA F. and ORSENIGO L. (1993) Technological regimes and firm behavior, *Ind. & Corporate Change* **2**, 45–72.

MUELLER D. C. (1976) Information, mobility, and profit, *Kyklos* **29**, 419–48.

NELSON R. R. and WINTER D. G. (1982) *An Evolutionary Theory of Economic Change*. Harvard University Press, Cambridge, MA.

NONAKA I. (1994) A dynamic theory of organizational knowledge creation, *Organization Science* **5**, 14–37.

REYNOLDS P. D., MILLER B. and MAKI W. R. (1995) Explaining regional variation in business births and deaths: U.S. 1976–1988, *Small Business Econ.* **7**, 389–407.

REYNOLDS P. D., STOREY D. J. and WESTHEAD P. (1994) Cross national comparison of the variation on the new firm formation rates, *Reg. Studies* **27**, 443–56.

ROMER P. M. (1986) Increasing return and long-run growth, *J. Pol. Econ.* **94**, 1,002–37.

ROTHWELL R. (1989) Small firms, innovation and industrial change, *Small Business Econ.* **1**, 39–50.

SAXENIAN A. (1990) Regional networks and the resurgence of Silicon Valley, *Calif. Mgt. Rev.* **33**, 89–112.

SCHERER F. M. (1992) Schumpeter and plausible capitalism, *J. Econ. Lit.* **30**, 1,416–33.

SCHUMPETER J. A. (1911) *Theorie der wirtschaftlichen Entwicklung, Eine Untersuchung über Unternehmergewinn, Kapital, Kredit, Zins und den Konjunkturzyklus (The Theory of Economic Development: An Inquiry into Profits, Capital, Credit, Interest, and the Business Cycle)*. Duncker & Humblot, Berlin.

SCHUMPETER J. A. (1942) *Capitalism, Socialism and Democracy*. Harper & Row, New York.

STERNBERG R. (1996) Technology policies and the growth of regions: evidence from four countries, *Small Business Econ.* **8**, 75–86.

TIROLE J. (1986) Hierarchies and bureaucracies, *J. Law, Econ. & Organization* **2**, 181–214.

WILLIAMSON O. E. (1975) *Markets and Hierarchies*. The Free Press, New York.

WINTER S. G. (1984) Schumpeterian competition in alternative technological regimes, *J. Econ. Behavior & Organization* **5**, 287–320.

25

1042-2587
Copyright 2004 by
Baylor University

Does Entrepreneurship Capital Matter?

David B. Audretsch
Max Keilbach

Economics has identified three types of capital as the drivers of economic growth—physical capital, human capital, and knowledge capital. This article introduces the concept of entrepreneurship capital and suggests that it is also an important factor shaping the economic performance of an economy. We define entrepreneurship capital as those factors influencing and shaping an economy's milieu of agents in such a way as to be conducive to the creation of new firms. The hypothesis that entrepreneurship capital is positively linked to economic growth is then tested by examining the relationship between several different measures of entrepreneurship capital and regional economic performance, measured as per-capita income for Germany. The empirical evidence suggests that there is indeed a positive link between entrepreneurship capital and regional economic performance. These results suggest a new direction for public policy that focuses on instruments to enhance entrepreneurship capital.

Introduction

One of the basic questions in economics has to do with what drives the economic performance of an economy. While the neoclassical tradition identified investment in physical capital as the driving factor (Solow, 1956), the endogenous growth theory (Romer, 1986, 1990) put the emphasis on the process of the accumulation of knowledge, and hence the creation of knowledge capital. The concept of *social capital* (Putnam, 1993; Coleman, 1988) can be considered as a further extension because it identifies a social component to those factors shaping economic growth and prosperity. According to Putnam (2000, p. 19), "Whereas physical capital refers to physical objects and human capital refers to the properties of individuals, social capital refers to connections among individuals—social networks and the norms of reciprocity and trustworthiness that arise from them. In that sense social capital is closely related to what some have called 'civic virtue.' The difference is that 'social capital' calls attention to the fact that civic virtue is most powerful when embedded in a sense network of reciprocal social relations. A society of many virtues but isolated individuals is not necessarily rich in social capital."

Putnam also challenged the standard neoclassical growth model by arguing that social capital was also important in generating economic growth: "By analogy with notions of physical capital and human capital—tools and training that enhance individual produc-

---

Please send all correspondence to: David B. Audretsch at daudrets@indiana.edu and to Max Keilbach at Keilbach@mpiew-jena.mpg.de.

tivity—social capital refers to features of social organization, such as networks, norms, and trust, that facilitate coordination and cooperation for mutual benefits."

A large and compelling literature has emerged linking social capital to entrepreneurship (Aldrich & Martinez, 2003; Thorton & Flynne, 2003). According to this literature, entrepreneurial activity should be enhanced where investments in social capital are greater (Amin, 2000; Simmie, 2003; Smith, 2003). However, while it was clear that Putnam was providing a link between social capital and economic welfare, this link did not directly involve entrepreneurship. The components of social capital that Putnam placed the greatest emphasis on were associational membership and public trust. While these may be essential for social and economic well being, it was not obvious that they involved entrepreneurship, per se.

The purpose of this article is to suggest that what has been called social capital in the entrepreneurship literature may actually be a more specific subcomponent, which we introduce as *entrepreneurship capital*. Entrepreneurship has typically been defined as an action, process, or activity. By entrepreneurship capital of an economy or a society we mean a regional milieu of agents that is conducive to the creation of new firms. This involves a number of aspects such as social acceptance of entrepreneurial behavior but of course also individuals who are willing to deal with the risk of creating new firms[1] and the activity of bankers and venture capital agents that are willing to share risks and benefits involved. Hence entrepreneurship capital reflects a number of different legal, institutional, and social factors and forces. Taken together, these factors and forces constitute the entrepreneurship capital of an economy, which creates a capacity for entrepreneurial activity (Hofstede et al., 2002). Thus, entrepreneurship capital manifests itself by the creation of new firms.

It should be emphasized at the outset that entrepreneurship capital should not be confused with social capital. The major distinction is that, in our view, not all social capital may be conducive to economic performance, let alone entrepreneurial activity. Some types of social capital may be more focused on preserving the status quo and not necessarily directed at creating challenges to the status quo. By contrast, entrepreneurship capital could be considered to constitute one particular subset of social capital. While social capital may have various impacts on entrepreneurship, depending on the specific orientation, entrepreneurship capital, by its very definition, will have a positive impact on entrepreneurial activity.

In the second section of this article the link between entrepreneurship capital and economic growth is explained. In the third section an empirical test based on a simple model is introduced, along with the data and methodology. Finally, in the last section a summary and conclusions are provided. In particular, the empirical results provide compelling evidence that economic performance is positively related to the presence of entrepreneurship capital. While these findings do not enable us to shed any light on what exactly constitutes entrepreneurship capital, or which type of public policies would best enhance entrepreneurship capital, they do shed light on the current race among public policy makers to "create the next Silicon Valley" in an effort to promote entrepreneurial activity.

---

1. As Gartner and Carter (2003) state, "Entrepreneurial behavior involves the activities of individuals who are associated with creating new organizations rather than the activities of individuals who are involved with maintaining or changing the operations of on-going established organizations."

Regional Economic Performance and Entrepreneurship Capital

The main contribution of the social capital literature is that endowments with "traditional factors" such as capital, labor, and (since not too long) knowledge are not adequate to sufficiently explain economic performance. Rather, as Putnam argues, social interaction facilitates the creation of communities, personal commitments, and social fabric. A sense of belonging and the concrete experience of social networks, which involves relationships of trust and tolerance, will ultimately be transmitted into economic performance.

As explained in the previous section, in this article we suggest that the notion of entrepreneurship capital may be more useful in the entrepreneurship literature. Entrepreneurship capital refers to a specific type of social capital that explicitly generates the startup of new enterprises.

Even if the concept of entrepreneurship capital might be acknowledged, the exact link between entrepreneurship capital and economic performance is less than certain. In an article in the *Harvard Business Review*, Ferguson (1988, p. 61), actually argued that entrepreneurship would actually reduce rather than increase economic performance. He considered entrepreneurship in Silicon Valley to be a drag on economic performance, because the "fragmentation, instability, and entrepreneurialism are not signs of well-being. In fact, they are symptoms of the larger structural problems that afflict U.S. industry. In semiconductors, a combination of personnel mobility, ineffective intellectual property protection, risk aversion in large companies, and tax subsidies for the formation of new companies contribute to a fragmented 'chronically entrepreneurial' industry. U.S. semiconductor companies are unable to sustain the large, long-term investments required for continued U.S. competitiveness. Companies avoid long-term R&D, personnel training, and long-term cooperative relationships because these are presumed, often correctly, to yield no benefit to the original investors. Economies of scale are not sufficiently developed. An elaborate infrastructure of small subcontractors has sprung up in Silicon Valley. Personnel turnover in the American merchant semiconductor industry has risen to 20 percent compared with less than 5 percent in IBM and Japanese corporations. . . . Fragmentation discouraged badly needed coordinated action—to develop process technology and also to demand better government support."

The opposite view, suggesting that entrepreneurship capital will have a positive impact on economic performance, is provided by Saxenian (1994), who examines the same region, Silicon Valley, "It is not simply the concentration of skilled labor, suppliers and information that distinguish the region. A variety of regional institutions— including Stanford University, several trade associations and local business organizations, and a myriad of specialized consulting, market research, public relations and venture capital firms—provide technical, financial, and networking services which the region's enterprises often cannot afford individually. These networks defy sectoral barriers: individuals move easily from semiconductor to disk drive firms or from computer to network makers. They move from established firms to startups (or vice versa) and even to market research or consulting firms, and from consulting firms back into startups. And they continue to meet at trade shows, industry conferences, and the scores of seminars, talks, and social activities organized by local business organizations and trade associations. In these forums, relationships are easily formed and maintained, technical and market information is exchanged, business contacts are established, and new enterprises are conceived. . . . This decentralized and fluid environment also promotes the diffusion of intangible technological capabilities and understandings" (Saxenian, 1990, pp. 96–97). Saxenian claims further (pp. 97–98) that even the language and vocabulary used by technical specialists can be specific to the entrepreneurship capital associated with that region, "... a distinct language has evolved in the region and certain technical terms used by semiconductor production engineers in Silicon Valley would not even be understood by their counterparts in Boston's Route 128." Amin and Thrift (2003) address this phenomenon as well, denoting it "institutional thickness." A similar observation for the Cambridge, United Kingdom, cluster has been provided by Keeble (1997), Keeble et al. (1999) and Keeble and Wilkinson (1999).

These arguments put in economic terms, suggest that entrepreneurship capital can be seen as a mechanism for knowledge spillovers because it facilitates the exchange and flow of ideas. Just as Romer (1986) addressed what he perceived to be a shortcoming in the Solow (1956) model—the lack of an explicit contribution by knowledge—we would argue that a shortcoming of the Romer model is that the spillover of knowledge is assumed to be automatic. But this assumption by Romer is inconsistent with Arrow's (1962) claim that knowledge is not automatically transmitted into commercial knowledge. The factor of knowledge differs from the traditional economic factors of labor and capital in that it is characterized by a significantly greater degree of uncertainty, more asymmetries, and higher costs of transactions across agents and organizations. These knowledge conditions create greater divergences in the perceived valuation of new ideas, resulting in a high variance of expected values associated with those new ideas. If a new idea is not highly valued by an incumbent firm, knowledge workers, such as scientists and engineers, may resort to starting a new enterprise in order to appropriate the potential value of their own knowledge. Thus, the decision to start a new firm also involves the (potential) spillover of knowledge from the incumbent enterprise to the startup.

The literature identifying mechanisms that actually transmit knowledge spillovers is sparse and remains underdeveloped. However, one important area where such transmission mechanisms have been identified involves entrepreneurship, i.e., the startup and growth of new enterprises. In the metaphor provided by Albert O. Hirschman (1970), if voice proves to be ineffective within incumbent organizations, and loyalty is sufficiently weak, a knowledge worker may resort to exiting the firm or university where the knowledge was created in order to form a new company.[2] In this spillover channel, the knowledge production function is actually reversed. The knowledge is exogenous and embodied in a worker. The firm is created endogenously in the worker's effort to appropriate the value of his knowledge through innovative activity. Thus, entrepreneurship serves as the mechanism by which knowledge spills over from the source creating a new firm where it is commercialized.

Regions with a high degree of entrepreneurship capital facilitate the startup of new firms based on uncertain and asymmetric ideas. On the other hand, regions with a low degree of entrepreneurship capital impede the ability of individuals to start new firms. Thus, entrepreneurship capital promotes the spillover of knowledge by facilitating the startup of new firms. Acs et al. (2003) refer to the gap between knowledge and commercialized knowledge as the knowledge filter. By commercializing ideas that otherwise would not be pursued and commercialized, entrepreneurship serves as one mechanism facilitating the spillover of knowledge. Thus, entrepreneurship capital promotes economic performance by serving as a conduit of knowledge spillovers. As Meister and Werker (2004), Bode (2004), and Pinch et al. (2003) have emphasized, the localized nature of knowledge spillovers would suggest that the impact of knowledge capital should also be localized.

---

2. See Audretsch (1995) for a more detailed analysis of this issue.

Production Function Model and Measurement Issues

As stated in the introduction, the goal of this article is to identify the impact of entrepreneurship capital on regional economic performance. We use a standard measure of economic performance, labor productivity, i.e., a region's economic output relative to its labor force. Dividing output by the input of labor corrects for the size of a region, hence increases the pertinence of this measure. We link this measure of regional economic performance to the traditional factors of capital, labor, and knowledge, along with our (new) factor of entrepreneurship capital by using a Cobb-Douglas production function of the form

$$Y_i = \alpha K_i^{\beta_1} L_i^{1-\beta_1} R_i^{\beta_2} E_i^{\beta_3}.$$

Based on this function, dividing output by labor we obtain

$$(Y_i/L_i) = \alpha(K_i/L_i)^{\beta_1} R_i^{\beta_2} E_i^{\beta_3}, \tag{1}$$

where Y represents economic output, L represents *labor* (hence Y/L is labor productivity), K represents the factor of *physical capital* (K/L being the capital intensity of the region), R represents *knowledge capital*, and E represents *entrepreneurship capital*. The subscript i refers to German regions. Equation 1 represents the classical Cobb-Douglas production function in its intensive form under the assumption that the production elasticities of capital and labor sum to unity. β_j represents output elasticities of the respective variables, i.e., an increase of the corresponding variable by 1% increases the left-hand side (labor productivity) by $\beta_j\%$.

Our data will consist of a cross section of 327 West German regions, or *Kreise*, for the year 1992 (if not indicated otherwise). Sources and construction of the data are as follows. We measure *Output* as Gross Value Added corrected for purchases of goods and services, VAT, and shipping costs. Statistics are published every two years for *Kreise* by the Working Group of the Statistical Offices of the German Länder, under "Volkswirtschaftliche Gesamtrechnungen der Länder." Data on *labor* are published by the Federal Labor Office, Nürnberg, which reports number of employees liable to social insurance by *Kreise*.

The stock of *physical capital* used in the manufacturing sector of the *Kreise* has been estimated using a perpetual inventory method, which computes the stock of capital as a weighted sum of past investments. Data on investments at the level of German *Kreise* are published annually by the Federal Statistical Office in the series "E I 6." These figures however are limited to firms of the producing sector, excluding the mining industry, with more than 20 employees. The vector of the producing sector as a whole has been estimated by multiplying these values such that the value of the capital stock of Western Germany—as published in the Statistical Yearbook—was attained. Note that this procedure implies that estimates for *Kreise* with a high proportion of mining might be biased.

Knowledge Capital is measured as the number of employees engaged in R&D in the public (1992) and in the private sector (1991). R&D inputs have been used in a number of previous studies as a proxy indicator of knowledge capital (Griliches, 1979; Jaffe, 1989; Audretsch & Feldman, 1996). The data were obtained by the *Stifterverband für die Wissenschaft* under obligation of secrecy. With these data, it was impossible to make a distinction between R&D employees in the producing and nonproducing sectors. Regression results therefore will implicitly include spillovers from R&D of the nonproducing sector to the producing sectors. We presume, however, that this effect is rather low.

Measurement of *entrepreneurship capital* is no less complicated than is measuring the traditional factors of production. Just as measuring capital, labor, and knowledge invokes numerous assumptions and simplifications, creating a metric for entrepreneurship capital presents a challenge. Many of the elements determining entrepreneurship capital defy quantification and as our definition has emphasized, entrepreneurship capital is a multifaceted and heterogeneous phenomenon.[3] Direct measurement of entrepreneurship capital would include a broad spectrum of institutions, policies, historical, social, and cultural traditions, as well as personal characteristics associated with the particular region. Such measurement, if accurately and correctly undertaken, would clearly be nontrivial, and of great significance. While we anticipate future research will rise to the challenge of directly measuring entrepreneurship capital, in this article we instead rely on an indicator that is a reflection or a manifestation of entrepreneurship capital—the number of new firms started in a region relative to the size of that region.

There are several important qualifications which must be emphasized using this indicator of entrepreneurship capital. First, it does not at all directly measure entrepreneurship capital, but indirectly reflects an underlying economic phenomenon that, as of now, cannot be measured. However, ceteris paribus, new-firm startups would be expected to be relatively low in those regions with a low stock of entrepreneurship capital, but higher in those regions endowed with a high stock of (the unmeasurable) entrepreneurship capital. Second, startup rates are a flow measure reflecting the stock variable entrepreneurship capital. This should not be interpreted as suggesting that entrepreneurship capital is being measured as a flow. Rather, it suggests that the underlying latent stock of entrepreneurship capital generates a flow of new-firm startups that can be observed and measured. That a flow measure is used to reflect an underlying latent stock factor is not without precedent. In fact, the use of R&D expenditures is often used to reflect the underlying stock of knowledge that is also latent and cannot be directly measured.

With these two important qualifications in mind, we compute an indicator of entrepreneurship capital as the *number of startups in the respective region relative to its population*, which reflects the propensity of inhabitants of a region to start a new firm. In addition, to avoid stochastic disturbance implicit in this approach, we compute this measure based on startup rates over a longer time period. In particular, we use the number of startups between 1989–1992, thus covering four periods. The choice of these periods and the length of the lag involved are driven by data restrictions, 1992 being the base year of our analysis and our data on startups starting in 1989.[4] The data on startups are taken from the ZEW foundation panels that are based on data provided biannually by *Creditreform*, the largest German credit-rating agency. This data contains virtually all entries—hence startups—in the German Trade Register, especially for firms with large credit requirements, such as high-technology firms.[5] As of 2003 there were 1.6 million entries for West Germany.

One might argue that our measure of entrepreneurship capital is endogenous in the sense that regions with higher labor productivity will generate a higher number of star-

---

3. Actually, this applies for physical capital too. The measure of capital condenses such diverse input factors as buildings, machinery, as well as raw materials and supplies into one singular measure.

4. A correlation analysis has shown that measures of entrepreneurship capital involving more periods are highly correlated with the one we used. This implies that adding more periods would not improve the quality of the measure of entrepreneurship capital.

5. Firms with low credit requirements, with a low number of employees, or with unlimited legal forms are registered only with a time lag. These are typically retail stores or catering firms. See Harhoff and Steil (1997) for more detail on the ZEW foundation panels.

Table 1

Correlation between Variables and Population Density for 327 German *Kreise*

	Population Density	Y/L	K/L	R	Startups All	Startups High Tech
Y/L	0.2040					
	(0.000)					
K/L	0.3842	0.2478				
	(0.000)	(0.000)				
R	0.5068	0.2072	0.2811			
	(0.000)	(0.000)	(0.000)			
Entrepr. Cap. (E)	0.3367	0.1117	0.0501	0.3036		
	(0.000)	(0.044)	(0.366)	(0.000)		
High-Tech E	0.2668	0.1716	0.0437	0.3404	0.8153	
	(0.000)	(0.002)	(0.431)	(0.000)	(0.000)	
ICT E	0.2870	0.1881	0.0304	0.3396	0.8164	0.9138
	(0.000)	(0.001)	(0.584)	(0.000)	(0.000)	(0.000)

Notes: p-values in brackets denote probability of correlation to be nondifferent to zero. As long as these are below 0.05 (0.1), the correlation is significant at the 5% (10%) level.

tups rather than the other way around. However, this argument would certainly apply to physical capital as well. The argument could even be stronger, since monetary invest-ments (which build up capital) will flow across regions more easily than persons (hence entrepreneurs). Thus, the application of the production function is consistent with previ-ous studies in the growth literature. Equally important, the use of lagged values of startup rates enables us to avoid problems of simultaneity and endogeneity between output and entrepreneurship capital. This lagged relationship reflects causality between entrepre-neurship capital in one period and economic output in subsequent periods.

In our definition of entrepreneurship capital given above, we stated that a region's entrepreneurship capital is also related to its capacity to deal with the risk involved with the creation of new businesses. To address this aspect, we compute two more measures of entrepreneurship capital that involve risk in a stronger way since they concern high-tech- or R&D-oriented activities. The first one restricts entrepreneurship capital to include only startup activity in high-technology manufacturing industries (whose R&D-intensity is above 2.5%). The second measure restricts entrepreneurship capital to include only startup activity in the ICT industries, i.e. firms in the hardware and software business. Some of these industries are also classified under high-technology manufacturing.

Table 1 shows a matrix of correlations between all variables involved in this study. A few interesting insights follow from this table. First (from column 1), as the high cor-relation indicates, entrepreneurship capital tends to be higher in densely populated areas, suggesting that it is an urban phenomenon. Second, the correlation rates between the mea-sures of entrepreneurship capital and labor productivity are rather low (though signifi-cant). Third, it is interesting to observe, that while all of the different indicators of entrepreneurship capital are highly and positively correlated, in fact the correlation coef-ficients among those variables and the measure of knowledge capital is positive but rather low (though significant). This provides at least an indication that startups are slightly stronger in regions with a greater proportion of R&D employees, and would suggest that

Table 2

Results of Estimation of Model (1) for German Regions

	(1)	(2)	(3)	(4)	(5)	(6)	(7)	(8)
Constant	-1.888	-2.2340	-1.1249	-0.9627	-0.8606	-1.6671	-1.4603	-1.3589
	(0.000)	(0.000)	(0.000)	(0.000)	(0.000)	(0.000)	(0.000)	(0.000)
K/L	0.332	0.2662	0.3188	0.3094	0.3126	0.2659	0.2709	0.2736
	(0.000)	(0.000)	(0.000)	(0.000)	(0.000)	(0.000)	(0.000)	(0.000)
R		0.039				0.0344	0.0270	0.0266
		(0.000)				(0.000)	(0.000)	(0.000)
Entrepreneurship (E)			0.1676			0.1145		
			(0.000)			(0.032)		
High-Tech E				0.1326			0.0951	
				(0.000)			(0.000)	
ICT E					0.1401			0.1038
					(0.000)			(0.000)
F-Test	46.44	34.50	29.01	35.35	36.34	24.80	26.63	27.26
	(0.000)	(0.000)	(0.000)	(0.000)	(0.000)	(0.000)	(0.000)	(0.000)
Adjusted R^2	0.122	0.170	0.146	0.174	0.178	0.178	0.190	0.195

Notes: p-values in parentheses denote probability of estimate to be nondifferent to zero. As long as these are below 0.05, the estimate differs significantly from zero at the 5% level.

an R&D employee might have a greater propensity to start a new business. The weak but positive correlation, on the other hand, might indicate that other factors will also have an influence on the regional startup activities.

Empirical Results

Estimation of Equation 1 produced the results displayed in Table 2. To test for robustness, different specifications were estimated. In the first column, results are shown for the estimation of regional productivity in Germany using the traditional Cobb-Douglas model, (relating output to capital and labor) in its intensive form. The implicitly estimated output elasticities for capital (β_1) and labor ($1 - \beta_1$) are in the usual range.[6] As has been consistently verified in previous studies, those regions with a higher capital intensity exhibit greater levels of productivity. In the second column knowledge capital is added. The positive and statistically significant coefficient of this variable lends support to the Romer view that knowledge matters as a factor of production and generates higher levels of productivity.

For columns 3 to 5, we added the three different indicators of entrepreneurship capital. All three estimations provided positive and significant results. This supports our hypothesis that entrepreneurship capital is positively linked to economic performance. It

---

6. Cobb and Douglas (1928) estimated a production elasticity of 0.75 for labor and 0.25 for capital, implying that an increase of labor (capital) input by 1% increases output by 0.75% (0.25%). Virtually all of subsequent estimates that have been done for different regions or industries have found results in ranges between 0.25 and 0.33 for capital and 0.66 to 0.75 for labor.

is interesting to observe that the estimated output elasticities of the different measures of entrepreneurship capital (β_3) are larger than the output elasticities of knowledge capital (β_2). More precisely, the effect of a 1% increase in the indicator of entrepreneurship capital on regional labor productivity is three to four times larger than a 1% increase of R&D.

Columns 6 to 8 combine the measure of knowledge along with the three different indicators reflecting entrepreneurship capital. All of the estimated coefficients are statistically significant at the 5% level. Hence both variables—the indicators of knowledge capital and of entrepreneurship capital—have a joint positive impact on a region's labor productivity. Still, the impact of entrepreneurship capital seems relatively larger in the sense that its estimated production elasticity is three to four times larger than that of knowledge capital. A policy implication of this finding is that it would be more efficient to increase a region's entrepreneurship capital rather than its R&D input. However, this is only preliminary evidence, to be interpreted carefully. Subsequent research needs to be undertaken to identify specifically (a) what actually constitutes entrepreneurship capital, and (b) which, if any, public policies could actually be undertaken to promote entrepreneurship capital.

Summary and Conclusions

In this article, we have attempted to link entrepreneurship to the economic performance of a society. To do so, we introduce the concept of entrepreneurship capital as a subcomponent, or specific aspect, of social capital. Entrepreneurship capital differs from social capital in that it focuses solely on those aspects of social capital that promote entrepreneurial activity. There are other aspects of social capital that actually may inhibit entrepreneurship. However, this article clearly follows the social capital tradition, fuelled by the writings of Putnam and Coleman, among others, by arguing that a high presence of entrepreneurship capital will enhance economic performance.

Since the degree of entrepreneurship capital in an economy ultimately manifests itself in the form of newly created businesses, we measure it indirectly, as being reflected by the amount of business startups in that economy relative to the respective population. Using data from German regions, we find convincing evidence consistent with the hypothesis that entrepreneurship is positively linked to economic performance.

There are two important qualifications in concluding this article. First, entrepreneurship capital is not directly measured, but rather is inferred by the observable degree of startup activity. While we are not able to directly measure entrepreneurship capital, we are able to infer something about relative magnitudes across regions based on a manifestation of that entrepreneurship capital—startup activity within that region. Second, the amount of entrepreneurship capital in a region is taken as being exogenous. The article never considers why entrepreneurship capital varies across regions and which factors actually shape entrepreneurship capital. We leave this for further research.

Taken together, these two qualifications suggest the sole public policy implication from the article. Public policies promoting entrepreneurship capital would be expected to have a positive impact on economic performance. However, which types of public policy instruments are best suited to promote entrepreneurship capital are beyond the scope of this article. On the basis of our definition, all policy measures that increase an economy's entrepreneurship capital will be useful. In a recent study, Storey (2003) identified a broad range of public policy measures spanning a broad spectrum of countries that have been used to promote entrepreneurship.

However, the results of this article do provide an important interpretation of those public policies that have been undertaken to promote entrepreneurship in most, if not virtually all cities and regions in the developed countries. They clearly represent an attempt to increase the amount of entrepreneurship capital and therefore improve economic performance. Such policy attempts might be considered to constitute the new entrepreneurship policies and will no doubt be the focus of a growing area of research in the future.

REFERENCES

Acs, Z., Audretsch, D., Braunerhhjem, P., & Carlsson, B. (2003). The Missing Link: The Knowledge Filter, Entrepreneurship and Endogenous Growth, Stockholm: Center for Economic Policy Research.

Aldrich, H.E. & Martinez, M. (2003). Entrepreneurship as Social Construction In Z.J. Acs & D.B. Audretsch (eds.), *Handbook of Entrepreneurship Research.* Dordrecht: Kluwer Academic Publishers.

Amin, A. (2000). Industrial Districts. In E. Sheppard & T. Barnes (eds.), *Companion to Economic Geography.* Oxford: Blackwell.

Amin, A. & Thrift, N. (2003). *Cultural Economy Reader,* Blackwell Oxford, UK.

Arrow, K. (1962). The Economic Implication of Learning by Doing. *Review of Economics & Statistics,* 80, 155–173.

Audretsch, D.B. (1995). *Innovation and Industry Evolution,* MIT Press Cambridge, MA.

Audretsch, D.B. & Feldman, M.P. (1996). R&D Spillovers and the Geography of Innovation and Production. *American Economic Review,* 86(3), 630–640.

Bode, E. (2004). The spatial pattern of localized R&D spillovers: An empirical investigation for Germany. *Journal of Economic Geography,* 4(1), 43.

Cobb, C.W. & Douglas, P.H. (1928). A Theory of Production. *American Economic Review* (Supplement), 18, 139–165.

Coleman, J.C. (1988). Social capital in the creation of human capital, *American Journal of Sociology,* 94, S95–S120.

Ferguson, C.H. (1988). From the People Who Brought You Voodoo Economics. *Harvard Business Review,* May/June 1998, 66(3).

Foelster, S. (2000). Do Entrepreneurs Create Jobs? *Small Business Economics,* 14(2), 137–148.

Gartner, W.B. & Carter, N.M. (2003). Entrepreneurship Behavior: Firm Organizing Processes. In Z.J. Acs & D.B. Audretsch (eds.), *The International Handbook of Entrepreneurship.* Dordrecht: Kluwer Academic Publishers.

Griliches, Z. (1979). Issues in Assessing the Contribution of R&D to Productivity Growth. *Bell Journal of Economics,* 10(Spring), 92–116.

Harhoff, D. & Steil, F. (1997). Die ZEW-Gründungspanels: Konzeptionelle Überlegungen und Analysepotential In D. Harhoff (ed.), *Unternehmensgründungen—Empirische Analysen für die alten und neuen Bundeslaender,* 7, Baden-Baden.

Hirschman, A.O. (1970). *Exit, Voice, and Loyalty,* Cambridge: Harvard University Press.

Hofstede, G., Noorderhaven, N.G., Thurik, A.R., Wennekers, A.R.M., Uhlaner, L., & Wildeman, R.E. (2002). Culture's Role in Entrepreneurship. In J. Ulijn & T. Brown (eds.), *Innovation, Entrepreneurship and Culture: The Interaction between Technology, Progress and Economic Growth,* Edward Elgar, Brookfield UK.

Jacobs, J. (1961). *The Death and Life of Great American Cities*, New York: Vintage Books.

Jaffe, A.B. (1989). Real Effects of Academic Research. *American Economic Review*, 79(5), 957–970.

Keeble, D. (1997). Small Firms, Innovation and Regional Development in Britain in the 1990s, *Regional Studies*, 31(3), 281–293.

Keeble, D., Lawson, C., Moore, B., & Wilkinson (1999). Collective Learning Process, Networking and "Institutional Thickness" in the Cambridge Region. *Regional Studies*, 33(4), 319–332.

Keeble, D. & Wilkinson, F. (1999). Collective Learning and Knowledge Development in the Evolution of Regional Clusters of High Technology SMEs in Europe. *Regional Studies*, 33(4), 295–303.

Meister, C. & Werker, C. (2004). Physical and organizational proximity in territorial innovation systems. *Journal of Economic Geography*, 4(1), 1–2.

Pinch, S., Henry, N., Jenkins, M., & Tallman, S. (2003). From Industrial Districts to Knowledge Dissemination and Competitive Advantage in Industrial Agglomerations. *Journal of Economic Geography*, 3(4), 373.

Putnam, R.D. (1993). *Making Democracy Work. Civic traditions in modern Italy*, Princeton, NJ: Princeton University Press.

Putnam, R.D. (2000). *Bowling Alone. The Collapse and Revival of American Community*. New York: Touchstone Books.

Romer, P. (1986). Increasing Returns and Economic Growth. *American Economic Review*, 94, 1002–1037.

Romer, P. (1990). Endogenous Technical change. *Journal of Political Economy*, 98, S71–S102.

Saxenian, A. (1990). Regional Networks and the Resurgence of Silicon Valley. *California Management Review*, 33, 89–111.

Saxenian, A. (1994). *Regional Advantage*, Cambridge: Harvard University Press.

Simmie, J. (2003). Innovation and Urban Regions as National and International Nodes for the Transfer and Sharing of Knowledge. Regional Studies, 37(6/7), 607.

Smith, H. (2003). Knowledge Organizations and Local Economic Development: The Case of Oxford and Grenoble. *Regional Studies*, 37(1), 33.

Solow, R. (1956). A Contribution to The Theory of Economic Growth. *Quarterly Journal of Economics*, 70, 65–94.

Storey, D. (2003). Small and Medium Sized Enterprises and Public Policies. In Z. Acs & D. Audretsch (eds.), *Handbook of Entrepreneurship Research*. Dordrecht: Kluwer Academic Publishers.

Thorton, P.H. & Flynne, K.H. (2003). Entrepreneurship, Networks and Geographies. In Z. Acs & D. Audretsch (eds.), *Handbook of Entrepreneurship Research*. Dordrecht: Kluwer Academic Publishers.

David B. Audretsch is at Indiana University, CEPR and the Max Planck Institute for Research into Economic Systems in Germany.

Max Keilbach is at the Max Planck Institute for Research into Economic Systems in Germany.

We are grateful to the editors of this special issue and two anonymous referees for helpful comments.

PART VI

POLICY

[26]

Entrepreneurship Policy and the Strategic Management of Places

David B. Audretsch

The role of entrepreneurship in society has changed drastically over the last half-century. During the immediate post-World War II period the importance of entrepreneurship seemed to be fading away. When Jean Jacques Servan-Schreiber (1968: 159) warned Europeans of the *American Challenge* in 1968, it was not from small entrepreneurial firms, but exactly the opposite – from the "dynamism, organisation, innovation, and boldness that characterize the giant American corporations." By that time, a generation of scholars had systematically documented and supported the conclusion of Joseph A. Schumpeter (1942: 106): "What we have got to accept is that the large-scale establishment or unit of control has come to be the most powerful engine of progress and in particular of the long-run expansion of output." John Kenneth Galbraith (1956: 86) put it this way: "There is no more pleasant fiction than that technological change is the product of the matchless ingenuity of the small man forced by competition to employ his wits to better his neighbor." Servan-Schreiber (1968: 159) thus prescribed that Europeans create "large industrial units which are able both in size and management to compete with the American giants."

An earlier version of this paper was presented at the April 2001 conference on entrepreneurship and public policy at the Kennedy School of Government, Harvard University. I am grateful for the suggestions of David Hart, Maryann P. Feldman, and Charles Wessner.

20

Public policy toward business in this period revolved around finding solutions to the perceived trade-off between scale and efficiency
on the one hand, and decentralization and inefficiency on the other
hand. The three main policy mechanisms deployed to achieve the required balance in the industrialized countries were antitrust (or competition policy, as it was called in Europe), regulation, and public ownership of business. A heated debate emerged about which approach
best promoted large-scale production while simultaneously constraining the ability of large corporations to exert market power, but there
was much less debate about public policy toward small business and
entrepreneurship. The only issue was whether public policymakers
should simply allow small firms to disappear as a result of their inefficiency or intervene to preserve them on social and political grounds.
Those who perceived small firms to be contributing significantly to
growth, employment generation, and competitiveness were few and far
between.

This situation has been reversed completely in recent years. Entrepreneurship has come to be perceived as an engine of economic
and social development throughout the world. For example, Romano
Prodi, president of the European Commission, proclaimed recently
that the promotion of entrepreneurship was a central thrust of
European economic strategy. The rationale: "Our lacunae in the
field of entrepreneurship need to be taken seriously because there is
mounting evidence that the key to economic growth and productivity
improvements lies in the entrepreneurial capacity of an economy"
(Prodi 2002: 1).

The purpose of this chapter is to explain how and why the role of
entrepreneurship policy has changed. The next section explains why
public policy toward business after World War II focused on constraining the freedom of large corporations to contract, while small firms
were treated as relics to be preserved. In section three I explain how
this traditional policy approach changed as a result of globalization,
producing what I call the "strategic management of places." I then explore the role that entrepreneurship plays in the strategic management
of places and analyze a range of approaches to entrepreneurship policy.
The chapter reaches the conclusion that a new mandate for governance
has emerged that is (1) enabling rather than constraining, (2) more

local and less centralized, and (3) focused on knowledge inputs rather than on targeting outputs or specific firms.

PUBLIC POLICY TOWARD BUSINESS AFTER WORLD WAR II

The pervasive fear of the Soviet Union that emerged as the Cold War succeeded World War II went beyond concerns about military competition and the space race. Many in the West worried that the launching of *Sputnik* demonstrated the superior organization of Soviet industry. Facilitated by centralized planning, the Soviet economy apparently generated rates of growth higher than those of Western economies, threatening, ultimately, to "bury" (as Soviet Premier Nikita Khruschev famously put it) the free market competition. After all, the nations of Eastern Europe, and the Soviet Union in particular, had a "luxury" inherent in their systems of centralized planning – a concentration of economic assets on a scale beyond anything imaginable in the West, where the commitment to democracy seemingly imposed a concomitant commitment to economic decentralization.

Western economists and policymakers of the day were nearly unanimous in their acclaim for large-scale enterprises. It is an irony of history that this consensus mirrored a remarkably similar giantism embedded in Soviet doctrine, fueled by the writings of Marx and ultimately implemented by the iron fist of Stalin. This was the era of mass production when economies of scale seemed to be the decisive factor in determining efficiency. This was the world so colorfully described by John Kenneth Galbraith (1956) in his theory of countervailing power, in which big business was held in check by big labor and by big government. This was the era of the man in the gray flannel suit (Riesman 1950) and the organization man (Whyte 1960), when virtually every major social and economic institution acted to reinforce the stability and predictability needed for mass production (Piore and Sabel 1984; Chandler 1977).

Scholars spanning a broad spectrum of academic fields and disciplines generated a massive literature that attempted to sort out the perceived trade-off between economic efficiency on the one hand and political and economic decentralization on the other. The large corporation was thought not only to have superior productive efficiency, but was also assumed to be the engine of technological innovation.

Ironically, the literature's obsession with oligopoly was combined with an analysis that was essentially static. There was considerable concern about what to do about the existing industrial structure, but little attention paid to where it came from and where it was going. Oliver Williamson's classic 1968 article, "Economies as an Antitrust Defense: The Welfare Tradeoffs," became something of a final statement demonstrating that gains in productive efficiency could be obtained through increased concentration and that gains in terms of competition, and implicitly democracy, could be achieved through decentralizing policies. But it did not seem possible to have both, certainly not in Williamson's completely static model.

The key public policy question of the day was "How can society reap the benefits of the large corporation in an oligopolistic setting while avoiding or at least minimizing the costs imposed by a concentration of economic power?" The answer centered on constraining the freedom of large firms to contract through public ownership, regulation, and antitrust. Different countries blended these three policy instruments in very different proportions. France and Sweden were in the vanguard of government ownership of business. The Netherlands and Germany, by contrast, emphasized regulation. The United States placed more weight on antitrust. Although these differences loomed large to scholars at the time, at this remove they are better seen as manifestations of a common policy approach that aimed to restrict the power of the large corporation.

Even advocates of small business agreed that small firms were less efficient than big companies. These advocates were willing to sacrifice a modicum of efficiency, however, because of other contributions – moral, political, and otherwise – made by small business to society. Small business policy was thus "preservationist" in character. The passage of the Robinson-Patman Act in 1936, for instance, was widely interpreted as one effort to protect small firms such as independent retailers that would otherwise have been too inefficient to survive in open competition with large corporations.[1] According.to

---

[1] According to the Robinson-Patman Act, "It shall be unlawful for any person engaged in commerce, in the course of such commerce, either directly or indirectly, to discriminate in price between different purchasers of commodities of like grade and quality." The A&P super market chain, for instance, was found in violation of the Robinson-Patman Act for direct purchases from suppliers and for performing its own wholesale

Richard Posner (1976: 57), "The Robinson-Patman Act ... is almost uniformly condemned by professional and academic opinion, legal and economic." Similarly, Robert Bork (1978: 382) observed, "One often hears of the baseball player who, although a weak hitter, was also a poor fielder. Robinson-Patman is a little like that. Although it does not prevent much price discrimination, at least it has stifled a great deal of competition."

Preservationist sentiments were also at work in the passage of the Small Business Act of 1953. Congress authorized the creation of the Small Business Administration with an explicit mandate to "aid, counsel, assist and protect ... the interests of small business concerns."[2] This legislation was clearly an attempt by the Congress to halt the continued disappearance of small businesses and to preserve their role in the U.S. economy. Thus, in the traditional, managed economies of the postwar era, small firms and entrepreneurship were viewed as a luxury, perhaps needed by the West to ensure that decision-making remained decentralized, but in any case obtained only at a cost to efficiency. Despite the preservationist policy, however, the role of small business continued to diminish subsequent to World War II. The employment share of small firms in all industries declined from 55.1 percent in 1958 to 52.5 percent in 1977. Declines in the small business employment share reached double digits for minerals, retail, and wholesale, and single digits for construction, manufacturing, and services.

GLOBALIZATION AND THE STRATEGIC MANAGEMENT OF PLACES

A half-century later, this consensus has been shattered by the complex of forces captured in the term "globalization." The shift in economic activity from a local or national sphere to an international or global orientation ranks among the most profound trends of the recent period. Paradoxically, though, larger markets have weakened large firms. Unraveling this paradox requires some explanation.

functions. Although these activities resulted in lower distribution costs, the gains in efficiency were seen as being irrelevant because small business was threatened.

[2] U.S. Small Business Administration, "47 Years Of Service To America's Small Business," *http://www.sba.gov/aboutsba/sbahistory.html.*

One driving force underlying globalization has been technology. Observing the speed at virtually no cost with which information can be transmitted across geographic space via the internet, fax machines, and electronic "superhighways," *The Economist* recently proclaimed on its cover "The Death of Distance." The advent of the microprocessor combined with its application in telecommunications has altered the economic meaning of national borders and transformed the geography of production.

Globalization would not have occurred to the degree that it has, however, if the fundamental changes were restricted to technology. It took political revolutions in many parts of the world to reap the benefits of technological change. Throughout the Cold War, military and ideological antagonism combined with internal political instability to render potential investments in Eastern Europe and much of the developing world risky and impractical. International trade and investment were therefore generally confined to Europe and North America, and later a few of the Asian countries, principally Japan and the "four tigers" of South Korea, Taiwan, Singapore, and Hong Kong. Trade with countries behind the Iron Curtain was restricted and in some cases prohibited. Even trade with Asia was highly regulated and restricted. Investments in Latin America and the Middle East were undermined by episodes of nationalization in which foreign investors were expropriated.

The fall of the Berlin Wall and subsequent downfall of communism in Eastern Europe and the former Soviet Union changed the outlook radically. Within just a few years it became possible not just to trade with but also to invest in countries such as Hungary, the Czech Republic, Poland, and Slovenia as well as China, Vietnam, and Indonesia. India, too, became accessible as a trading and investment partner after economic reforms in the early 1990s. The opening of these areas to the world economy brought the long post-World War II equilibrium to a sudden end. The gaping wage differentials that existed while the Berlin Wall stood were suddenly exposed. Massive populations craving to enjoy the high levels of consumption that had become the norm in Western Europe and North America were willing to work for much less than their Western counterparts. Of course, the productivity of labor is vastly greater in the developed world, which compensates to a significant degree for such large wage differentials. Still, the magnitude of the differences caused trade and investment flows to swell hugely. Traditional measures of trade (exports and imports), foreign direct investment (inward and outward), international capital flows, and intercountry labor mobility have all trended strongly positive.

Many companies have responded to the opportunities made possible by the events of 1989. Confronted with low-cost competition in foreign locations, producers in the high-cost countries had three options as they sought to retain their leading positions: (1) reduce wages and other production costs sufficiently to compete with the low-cost foreign producers, (2) substitute equipment and technology for labor to increase productivity, and (3) shift production out of high-cost locations and into low-cost locations.

Many of the European and American firms that have successfully restructured resorted to the last two alternatives. Substituting capital and technology for labor along with shifting production to low-cost locations has resulted in waves of corporate downsizing throughout Europe and North America. For example, between 1979 and 1995 more than 43 million jobs were lost in the United States as a result of corporate downsizing. This figure includes 24.8 million blue-collar jobs and 18.7 million white-collar jobs. The 500 largest U.S. manufacturing corporations cut 4.7 million jobs between 1980 and 1993, or one quarter of their work force (Audretsch 1995). Perhaps most disconcerting, the rate of corporate downsizing has apparently increased over time in the United States, even as the unemployment rate has fallen. During most of the 1980s, about one in twenty-five workers lost a job. In the 1990s the share rose to one in twenty workers. Companies have shed labor to preserve their viability; many have thrived as a result.

The experience has not been different in Europe. Pressed to maintain competitiveness in traditional industries, where economic activity can be easily transferred across geographic space to access lower production costs, the largest and most prominent German companies have been downsizing their domestic employment. For example, Siemens decreased employment in Germany by 12 percent between 1985 and 1995, even as it increased the amount of employment outside Germany by 50 percent. The numbers for Volkswagen, Hoechst, and BASF are variations on the same theme.

The result of this wave of downsizing in Germany in the 1990s has been levels of unemployment – four million – not seen since the 1940s.

The impact was not confined to individual firms, but spread across entire industries and geographical regions. Stuttgart, which is home to Daimler-Chrysler (formerly Daimler-Benz), experienced an increase in manufacturing employment throughout the 1970s, 1980s, and into the 1990s. After reaching a peak of around 480,000 in 1991, manufacturing employment fell by more than one-third, to around 350,000 by the mid-1990s. The resulting unemployment triggered cries of betrayal from the critics of large corporations.[3] But this is a mistake. Corporations were simply trying to survive in global competition made fierce by easy access to low-cost inputs.

Much of the policy debate responding to globalization revolved around a perceived trade-off between maintaining higher wages but suffering greater unemployment on the one hand, and attaining higher levels of employment at the cost of lower wage rates on the other. There is, however, another alternative. It does not require sacrificing wages to create new jobs, nor does it require fewer jobs to maintain wage levels and the social safety net. This alternative involves shifting economic activity out of the traditional industries where the high-cost countries of Europe and North America have lost their comparative advantage and into those industries where comparative advantage is compatible with both high wages and high levels of employment – knowledge-based and innovative economic activity.

The locus of action in this strategy is not firms, but places. As long as corporations were inextricably linked to their regional location by substantial sunk costs, such as capital investment, the competitiveness of a region was identical to the competitiveness of the corporations located in that region. "What is good for General Motors is good for America" may have been controversial even a half-century ago, but few would have disagreed that "What is good for General Motors is good for Detroit." And so it was with U.S. Steel in Pittsburgh and Volkswagen in Wolfsburg. As long as the corporation thrived, so would the region. That world is gone. At the heart of the strategic management of places is the development and enhancement of factors of

---

[3] As the German newspaper *Die Zeit* (2 February, 1996: p. 1) pointed out in a front page article, "When Profits Lead to Ruin – More Profits and More Unemployment: Where is the Social Responsibility of the Firms?", the German public has responded to the recent waves of corporate downsizing with accusations that corporate Germany is no longer fulfilling its share of the social contract.

production that cannot be transferred across geographic space at low cost – principally, although not exclusively, knowledge and ideas.

THE SPATIAL BASIS OF THE KNOWLEDGE ECONOMY

Knowledge spills over from its initial producers to many secondary users. This fact is barely disputed. The big question is whether these spillovers have geographic limits such that locally produced knowledge can be retained and exploited locally. In a world of e-mail, fax machines, and cyberspace, the claim that geographic location is important to the process linking knowledge spillovers to innovative activity may seem surprising and even paradoxical. The resolution to the paradox posed lies in a distinction between knowledge and information. *Information*, such as the price of gold in New York, or the value of the yen in London, can be easily codified and has a singular meaning and interpretation. By contrast, *knowledge* is vague, difficult to codify, and often only serendipitously recognized. Whereas the marginal cost of transmitting information across geographic space has been rendered irrelevant by the telecommunications revolution, the marginal cost of transmitting knowledge, and especially tacit knowledge, rises with distance.

Von Hippel (1994) demonstrates that high context, uncertain knowledge (which he terms "sticky" knowledge) is best transmitted via face-to-face interaction and through frequent and repeated contact. Geographic proximity matters in transmitting knowledge because, as Kenneth Arrow (1962) pointed out four decades ago, such tacit knowledge is inherently nonrival in nature. Knowledge developed for any particular application can easily spill over and have economic value in very different applications. As Glaeser and colleagues (1992, p. 1126) have observed, "intellectual breakthroughs must cross hallways and streets more easily than oceans and continents."

The importance of local proximity for the transmission of knowledge spillovers has been observed in many different contexts. Recent scholarship has overcome the data constraints highlighted by Krugman (1991a) to provide precise estimates of the extent of knowledge spillovers and to link them to the geography of innovative activity. The empirical evidence consistently supports the notion that knowledge spills over from university research laboratories and from industry R&D laboratories as well. Location and proximity clearly matter in exploiting these knowledge spillovers. Jaffe, Trajtenberg, and Henderson (1993), for instance, found that patent citations tend to occur more frequently within the state in which patented inventions were made than outside of that state. Audretsch and Feldman (1996) found that the propensity of innovative activity to cluster geographically tends to be greater in industries where new economic knowledge plays a more important role. Prevezer (1997) and Zucker, Darby, and Armstrong (1998) show that in biotechnology, an industry based almost exclusively on new knowledge, firms tend to cluster together in just a handful of locations, a finding extended by Andrew Toole in this volume. Audretsch and Stephan (1996) demonstrate that an outside scientist is more likely to be located in the same region as the firm that he advises when the relationship involves the transfer of new economic knowledge. However, when a scientist is providing a service to a company that does not involve knowledge transfer, local proximity is much less important.

In addition, there is reason to believe that knowledge spillovers are not homogeneous across firms. In estimating the impact of knowledge spillovers on the innovative activity of large and small enterprises separately, Acs, Audretsch, and Feldman (1994) provide some insight into the puzzle posed by the recent wave of studies identifying vigorous innovative activity emanating from small firms in certain industries. How are these small, and frequently new, firms able to generate innovative output while undertaking negligible amounts of investment in knowledge-generating inputs, such as R&D? The answer appears to be that they exploit knowledge created by expenditures on research in universities and on R&D in large corporations, a finding affirmed by Nathan Rosenberg in his contribution to this volume. These findings suggest that the innovative output of all firms rises along with an increase in the amount of R&D inputs, both in private corporations as well as in university laboratories. However, R&D expenditures made by private companies play a particularly important role in providing knowledge inputs to the innovative activity of large firms, whereas expenditures on research made by universities serve as an especially key input for generating innovative activity in small enterprises. Apparently large firms are more adept at exploiting knowledge created in their own laboratories, while their smaller counterparts have a comparative advantage at exploiting spillovers from university laboratories.

David B. Audretsch

THE ROLE OF ENTREPRENEURSHIP

That small entrepreneurial firms would emerge as more important in the knowledge economy seems to be contrary to many of the conventional theories of innovation. The starting point for most theories of innovation is the firm. In such theories the firms are exogenous and their performance in generating technological change is endogenous (Arrow 1962). For example, in the most prevalent model found in the literature of technological change, the model of the knowledge production function, formalized by Zvi Griliches (1979), firms exist exogenously and then engage in the pursuit of new economic knowledge as an input into the process of generating innovative activity. Knowledge as an input in a production function is inherently different from the more traditional inputs of labor, capital and land. Whereas the economic value of the traditional inputs is relatively certain, knowledge is intrinsically uncertain and its potential value is asymmetric across economic agents.[4] The most important source of new knowledge usually considered in this framework is R&D. Other sources of new economic knowledge include a high degree of human capital, in the form of a skilled labor force and a high presence of scientists and engineers.

There is considerable empirical evidence supporting the model of the knowledge production function. The empirical link between knowledge inputs and innovative output becomes stronger as the unit of observation gets larger. Among countries, for example, the relationship between R&D and patents is very strong. The most innovative countries, such as the United States, Japan, and Germany, also make large investments in R&D. By contrast, little patent activity is associated with developing countries, which have very low R&D expenditures. The link between R&D and innovative output is also very strong when the unit of observation is the industry. The most innovative industries, such as computers, scientific instruments, and pharmaceuticals also tend to be the most R&D-intensive. Audretsch (1995) finds a simple correlation coefficient of 0.74 between R&D inputs and innovative output at the level of four-digit standard industrial classification (SIC) industries.

---

[4] Arrow (1962) pointed out that this is one of the reasons for inherent market failure.

However, when the knowledge production function is tested at the firm level, the link between knowledge inputs and innovative output becomes tenuous and weakly positive in some studies and nonexistent or even negative in others. The model of the knowledge production function becomes particularly weak when small firms are included in the sample. This is not surprising, since formal R&D is concentrated among the largest corporations, whereas a series of studies (for example, Acs and Audretsch 1990) has clearly documented that small firms account for a disproportional share of new product innovations given their low R&D expenditures. The breakdown of the knowledge production function at the level of the firm raises the question, *Where do innovative firms with little or no R&D get the knowledge inputs?* This question becomes particularly relevant for small and new firms that undertake little R&D themselves, yet contribute considerable innovative activity in newly emerging industries such as biotechnology and computer software (Audretsch 1995). One answer that has recently emerged in the economics literature is that they draw on other firms and research institutions such as universities. Economic knowledge spills over to these firms from these outside organizations.

Why should knowledge spill over from the source of origin? At least two major channels or mechanisms for knowledge spillovers have been identified in the literature. Both of these spillover mechanisms revolve around the issue of appropriability of new knowledge. Cohen and Levinthal (1989) suggest that firms develop the capacity to adapt new technology and ideas developed in other firms and are therefore able to appropriate some of the returns accruing to investments in new knowledge made externally.

By contrast, Audretsch (1995) proposes shifting the unit of observation away from exogenously assumed firms to individuals, such as scientists, engineers, or other knowledge workers – agents with endowments of new economic knowledge. When the lens is shifted away from the firm to the individual as the relevant unit of observation, the appropriability issue remains, but the question becomes, *How can economic agents with a given endowment of new knowledge best appropriate the returns from that knowledge?* If the scientist or engineer can pursue the new idea within the organizational structure of the firm developing the knowledge and appropriate roughly the expected value of that knowledge, he has no reason to leave the firm. On the other hand, if he

places a greater value on his ideas than does the decision-making bureaucracy of the incumbent firm, he may choose to start a new firm to
appropriate the value of his knowledge. In the metaphor provided by
Albert O. Hirschman (1970), if voice proves to be ineffective within
incumbent organizations, and loyalty is sufficiently weak, a knowledge
worker may exit from the firm or university where the knowledge was
created. In this spillover channel the knowledge production function
is actually reversed. The knowledge is exogenous and embodied in
a worker. The firm is created endogenously in the worker's effort to
appropriate the value of his knowledge through innovative activity.

What emerges from this line of scholarship on entrepreneurship is
that markets are in motion, with a lot of firms entering and exiting
knowledge-intensive industries. But is this motion horizontal, so that
the bulk of firms exiting are firms that had entered relatively recently,
or vertical, such that a significant share of the exiting firms had been
established incumbents that were displaced by younger firms? In trying
to shed some light on this question, Audretsch (1995) proposes two
different models of the evolutionary process of industries over time.
Some industries can best be characterized by the model of the conical
revolving door, where new businesses are started, but there is also
a high propensity for them to subsequently exit the market. Other
industries may be better characterized by the metaphor of the forest,
where incumbent establishments are displaced by new entrants.

Which view is more applicable apparently depends on three major factors: underlying technological conditions, scale economies, and
demand. Where scale economies play an important role, the model of
the revolving door seems to be more applicable. Although start-up and
entry of new businesses are apparently not deterred by the presence
of high scale economies (in itself a rather startling result), a process of
firm selection analogous to a revolving door ensures that only those
establishments successful enough to grow will be able to survive beyond more than a few years. The bulk of new entrants that are not so
successful ultimately exit within a few years after entry.

When new entrepreneurial firms employ a strategy of innovation,
they typically start at a very small scale of output. They are motivated by
the desire to appropriate the expected value of new economic knowledge. But if scale economies in the industry are large, the firm may not
be able to remain viable indefinitely at its start-up size. In this case, the

new firm must grow to survive. The temporary survival of new firms is presumably supported by a strategy of compensating factor differentials that enables the firm to discover whether or not it has a viable product.

The empirical evidence has found that the postentry growth of firms that survive tends to be spurred by the extent to which there is a gap between the minimum efficient scale of output and the size of the firm. Innovation also figures in the selection process. New firms employing a strategy of innovation to attain competitiveness are apparently engaged in the selection process. Only those new firms offering a viable product that can be produced efficiently will grow and ultimately approach or attain the minimum efficient scale of output. The remainder will stagnate and exit the industry. Thus, in highly innovative industries, there is a continuing process of entry of new firms, but not necessarily the continuation of the same small firms over the long run. Although the skewed size distribution of firms persists with remarkable stability over long periods of time, a constant set of small entrepreneurial firms does not appear to be responsible. Rather, by serving as agents of change, small entrepreneurial firms provide an essential source of new ideas and experimentation that otherwise would remain untapped in the economy.

A series of studies have identified a positive link between entrepreneurial activity and growth for spatial units of observation[5] ranging from the city and region (Carree 2002; Fritsch 1997; National Commission on Entrepreneurship 2001b; Reynolds et al. 2000; Reynolds, Hay, Bygrave, Camp, and Autio 2000) to the country (Carree, van Stel, Thurik and Wennekers 2000; Carree and Thurik 1999). In particular, Fritsch (1997) and Reynolds (1999) provide compelling evidence that fast growing regions are experiencing higher levels of entrepreneurial activity, as measured by start-up rates and turbulence rates. Carree and Thurik (1999) provide empirical evidence from a 1984–1994 cross-sectional study of the twenty-three member countries of the Organization for Economic Co-operation and Development (OECD), which reveals that increased entrepreneurship, as measured by business ownership rates, is associated with higher rates of employment growth

---

[5] Spatial units of observation refer to a geographic dimension such as a city, county, region, or country.

at the country level. Similarly, the Global Entrepreneurship Monitor (GEM) Study (Reynolds, Hay, Bygrave, Camp, and Autio 2000) also establishes an empirical link between the degree of entrepreneurial activity and economic growth, as measured by employment, at the country level. Thus, there are not only theoretical arguments but also empirical evidence that suggest that the growth of places is positively associated with an entrepreneurial advantage. The strategic management of places emerged in order for places to capitalize on the growth associated with entrepreneurship. As a consequence, a new role for government emerged.

ENTREPRENEURSHIP POLICY

The link between entrepreneurial activity and growth for spatial units of observation, which has only systematically been established by scholars in recent years, captured the attention of policymakers much earlier. They witnessed the decline of large manufacturing corporations that had once been the mainstay of employment growth in industries such as steel, autos, and tires, in places like Pittsburgh, Detroit, and Akron. Their eyes told them that the regions enjoying the highest rates of growth and job creation also exhibited the highest rates of entrepreneurial activity. The emergence of knowledge as a source of competitiveness, combined with the propensity for knowledge to remain localized, resulted in a new policy opportunity for places – cities, regions, states, and countries. The policy goal of growth and employment creation could be attained, it was hoped, by strategically managing the climate of these places so as to generate entrepreneurial activities and thus economic growth.

The policy mandate for promoting entrepreneurship was based on the market failure associated with knowledge activities. Arrow (1962) recognized that knowledge was inherently a public good, so that its production generated externalities. As Audretsch and Feldman (1996) point out, however, local proximity is essential for accessing these knowledge spillovers. Thus, both knowledge-based firms and workers place a greater value on locations with clusters than those without clusters. Because of knowledge spillovers, the value of an entrepreneurial firm is greater in the (local) presence of other entrepreneurial firms (Audretsch and Stephan 1996). Yet individual firms and workers are reluctant to invest in the creation of such a cluster, which involves the creation of other entrepreneurial firms, because of their inability to appropriate the returns from such a cluster, due to the public nature of knowledge. Policymakers, whose interest lies in generating growth for a particular location, had to step in.

Market failure also stimulated policy through the positive economic value created in entrepreneurial firms that ultimately failed. The high failure rates of new firm start-ups has been widely documented (Bruderl et al. 1992; Carroll 1983; Hannan and Freeman 1989), and the failure rates in knowledge-based activities are especially great (Audretsch 1995). These rates are not surprising since knowledge activities are associated with a greater degree of uncertainty than traditional economic activities. The failure of a knowledge-based firm does not necessarily mean, however, that no value was created by that firm. Evidence suggests that ideas created by failed firms and projects often become integral parts of successful products and projects in successful firms (Holbrook 1995; Holbrook et al. 2000). For example, although Fairchild Semiconductor failed, the ideas generated by the firm were used by numerous other firms and helped to spawn Silicon Valley. The externalities associated with failed firms lead to market failure in the valuation of (potential) new enterprises between private investors and policymakers. The private investor can only appropriate her investment if the particular firm succeeds. If the firm fails but knowledge externalities contribute to the success of other firms, the private investor still does not appropriate anything from her investment. However, the public policy perspective is considerably different. From the public policy perspective it does not matter which firms succeed, as long as some do. Thus, policymakers should be willing to address the market failure associated with high rates of firm failure.

As comparative advantage has become increasingly based on new knowledge, public policy has responded in two fundamental ways. The first has been to shift the policy focus away from the traditional triad of instruments that constrained the freedom of firms to contract – regulation, antitrust, and public ownership of business. The policy approach of constraint was sensible as long as the major issue was how to restrain large corporations in possession of considerable market power. That this policy is less relevant in a global economy is reflected by the waves of deregulation and privatization throughout the OECD.

The new policy approach enables the creation and commercialization of knowledge through R&D, venture capital, and entrepreneurship.

Sternberg (1996) has shown that a number of government-sponsored technology programs have triggered entrepreneurial ventures, a finding further supported in the chapter by Auerswald and Branscomb in this volume. These programs aim to eliminate particular bottlenecks in the development and financing of new firms. Sternberg (1996) examines the impact that seventy innovation centers have had on the development of technology-based small firms. He notes that the majority of the entrepreneurs find advantages from locating at an innovation center.

The second fundamental change involves shifting the locus of such enabling policies to the state, regional, or even local level. The downsizing of national agencies charged with the regulation of business in many of the OECD countries has been interpreted by many scholars as the eclipse of government intervention. But to interpret deregulation, privatization, and the increased irrelevance of antitrust as the end of government intervention in business ignores an important shift in the locus and target of public policy. The last decade has seen the emergence of a broad spectrum of enabling policy initiatives that fall outside the jurisdiction of the traditional regulatory agencies. Sternberg (1996) shows that the success of several high-technology clusters spanning a number of developed countries is the direct result of enabling policies, such as the provision of venture capital or research support. For example, the Advanced Research Program in Texas has provided support for basic research and the strengthening of the infrastructure of the University of Texas, which has played a central role in developing a high-technology cluster around Austin (Feller 1997). The Thomas Edison Centers in Ohio, to cite another case, link leading universities and medical institutions, businesses, foundations, and civic and state organizations in Ohio in order to create new business opportunities (Carlsson and Braunerhjelm 1999).

The plethora of science, technology, and research parks provide further examples of entrepreneurship policy at work. Lugar and Goldstein (1991) conducted a review of research parks and concluded that such parks are created to promote the competitiveness of a particular region. Lugar (2001: 47) further noted that, "The most successful parks . . . have a profound impact on a region and its competitiveness."

A distinct exemplar of this effect is the Research Triangle Park in North Carolina. In the 1950s, the traditional industries of North Carolina, such as furniture, textiles, and tobacco, had lost international competitiveness, resulting in declines in employment and stagnation in real incomes. In 1952, only Arkansas and Mississippi had lower per capita income than North Carolina. A movement emerged in this period that advocated exploiting the rich knowledge base of the region, formed by the three major universities (Duke University, University of North Carolina-Chapel Hill, and North Carolina State University), for economic development (Link and Scott, 2003). This movement arose initially in the business community, but it eventually fell into the hands of the Governor's office, which carried it to fruition (Link 1995). Empirical evidence provides strong support that the initiative creating the Research Triangle Park has led to fundamental changes in the region. Link and Scott (2003) document the growth in the number of high-technology companies there from none in 1958 to fifty by the mid-1980s and over 100 by 1997. At the same time, employment in these companies increased from zero in the late 1950s to over forty thousand by 1997. Lugar (2001) credits the Research Triangle Park with directly and indirectly generating one-quarter of all jobs in the region between 1959 and 1990, and shifting the nature of those jobs toward high value-added knowledge-based activities.

One of the most interesting examples of entrepreneurship policy for the strategic management of places involves the establishment of five EXIST regions in Germany, where start-ups from universities and government research laboratories are encouraged (Bundesministerium fuer Bildung und Forschung 2000). The program has the explicit goals of (1) creating an entrepreneurial culture, (2) commercializing scientific knowledge, and (3) increasing the number of innovative start-ups and SMEs. Five regions were selected among many applicants for START funding: (1) Rhein-Ruhr region (bizeps program), (2) Dresden (Dresden exists), (3) Thueringen (GET UP), (4) Karlsruhe (KEIM), and (5) Stuttgart (PUSH!).

CONCLUSIONS

The role of entrepreneurship and small business policy has evolved considerably since World War II. What was once considered to be a necessary drain on Western economies has become a central strategic instrument for competitiveness in global markets. Globalization has shifted the comparative advantage in the OECD countries away from land, labor, and capital toward knowledge. This shift has triggered a divergence between the competitiveness of firms and the competitiveness of locations. As the strategic management of firms dictated a response to globalization of outward foreign direct investment combined with employment downsizing at high-cost locations, public policy has responded by developing the strategic management of places. Entrepreneurship policy plays a central role in the strategic management of places, because entrepreneurial activity is the conduit between investments in knowledge and economic growth at the particular location.

Just as it has been important to understand how to manage entrepreneurial firms, it has now become at least as important to understand how to achieve an entrepreneurial society. Although this emphasis on small entrepreneurial firms as engines of dynamic efficiency may seem startling after decades of looking to the corporate giants as engines of growth and development, it in fact may not be so new. That great observer of early American life, Alexis de Tocqueville, reported in 1835, "What astonishes me in the United States is not so much the marvellous grandeur of some undertakings as the innumerable multitude of small ones."

References

Acs, Zoltan J., and David B. Audretsch. 1990a. *Innovation and Small Firms.* Cambridge, MA: MIT Press.

Acs, Zoltan, David Audretsch and Maryann P. Feldman. 1994. R&D Spillovers and Recipient Firm Size. *Review of Economics and Statistics* 76:336–340.

Arrow, K. 1962. Economic Welfare and the Allocation of Resources for Invention. In R. Nelson, ed., *The Rate and Direction of Inventive Activity.* Princeton: Princeton University Press.

Audretsch, D. 1995. *Innovation and Industry Evolution.* Cambridge, MA: MIT Press.

Audretsch, D., and M. P. Feldman. 1996. R&D Spillovers and the Geography of Innovation and Production. *American Economic Review* 86:630–640.

Audretsch, D., and P. Stephan. 1996. Company-Scientist Locational Links: The Case of Biotechnology. *American Economic Review* 86:641–652.

Bork, Robert H. 1978. *The Antitrust Paradox: A Policy at War with Itself.* New York: Basic Books.

Bruderl, J., P. Preisendorfoer, and R. Ziegler. 1992. Survival Chances of Newly Founded Business Organizations. *American Sociological Review* 57:227–242.

Bundesministerium fuer Bildung und Forschung. 2000. *Zur Technologischen Leistungsfaehigkeit Deutschlands* [On the Technological Capabilities of Germany]. Bonn: Bundesministerium fuer Bildung und Forschung.

Carlsson, B., and P. Braunerhjelm. 1999. Industry Clusters: Biotechnology/Biomedecine and Polymers in Ohio and Sweden. In D. B. Audretsch and A. R. Thurik, eds. *Innovation, Industry Evolution, and Employment.* New York: Cambridge University Press.

Carree, M. A. 2002. Does Unemployment Affect the Number of Establishments? *Regional Studies* 36:389–398.

Carree, M. A., and A. R. Thurik. 1999. Industrial Structure and Economic Growth. In D. B. Audretsch and A. R. Thurik, eds., *Innovation, Industry Evolution, and Employment.* New York: Cambridge University Press.

Carree, M. A., A. van Stel, A. R. Thurik, and S. Wennekers. 2000. Economic Development and Business Ownership: An Analysis Using Data of 23 OECD Countries in the Period 1976–1996. Institute for Development Strategies Discussion Paper 00-6. Bloomington: University of Indiana.

Carroll, G. 1983. A Stochastic Model of Organizational Mortality. *Social Science Research* 12:309–329.

Chandler, Alfred D., Jr. 1977. *The Visible Hand: The Managerial Revolution in American Business.* Cambridge, MA: Harvard University Press.

Cohen, W., and D. Levinthal. 1989. Innovation and Learning. *Economic Journal* 99:569–596.

Feller, I. 1997. Federal and State Government Roles in Science and Technology. *Economic Development Quarterly* 11:283–296.

Fritsch, M. 1997. New Firms and Regional Employment Change. *Small Business Economics* 9:437–448.

Galbraith, John K. 1956. *American Capitalism*. Rev. ed. Boston; Houghton Mifflin.

Glaeser, E., H. Kallal, J. Scheinkman, and A. Shleifer. 1992. Growth of Cities. *Journal of Political Economy* 100:1126–1152.

Griliches, Z. 1979. Issues in Assessing the Contribution of R&D to Productivity Growth. *Bell Journal of Economics* 10:92–116.

Hannan, M. T., and J. H. Freeman. 1989. *Organizational Ecology*. Cambridge, MA: Harvard University Press.

Hirschman, Albert O. 1970. *Exit, Voice, and Loyalty*. Cambridge, MA: Harvard University Press.

Holbrook, D. 1995. Government Support of the Semiconductor Industry. *Business and Economic History* 24:133–168.

Holbrook, D., W. M. Cohen, D. A. Hounshell, and S. Klepper. 2000. The Nature, Sources, and Consequences of Firm Differences in the Early History of the Semiconductor Industry. *Strategic Management Journal* 21:1017–1041.

Jaffe, A., M. Trajtenberg, and R. Henderson. 1993. Geographic Localization of Knowledge Spillovers as Evidenced by Patent Citations. *Quarterly Journal of Economics* 63:577–598.

Krugman, P. 1991a. Increasing Returns and Economic Geography. *Journal of Political Economy* 99:483–499.

Link, A. N. 1995. *A Generosity of Spirit*. Durham, NC: Duke University Press.

Link, A. N., and J. T. Scott. 2003. The Growth of Research Triangle Park. *Small Business Economics*.

Lugar, M. 2001. The Research Triangle Experience. In C. Wessner, ed., *Industry-Laboratory Partnerships*. Washington, D.C.: National Academy Press.

Lugar, M., and H. Goldstein. 1991. *Technology in the Garden*. Chapel Hill: The University of North Carolina Press.

National Commission on Entrepreneurship. 2001b. *High-Growth Companies*. Washington, D.C.: NCOE.

Piore, Michael J., and Charles F. Sabel. 1984. *The Second Industrial Divide*. New York: Basic Books.

Posner, Richard A. 1976. *The Robinson-Patman Act: Federal Regulation of Price Differences*. Washington, D.C.: American Enterprise Institute.

Prevezer, M. 1997. The Dynamics of Industrial Clustering in Biotechnology. *Small Business Economics* 93:255–271.

Prodi, Romano. 2002. For a New European Entrepreneurship. Paper delivered to the Instituto de Empressa Madrid, February.

Reynolds, Paul D. 2000. National Panel Study of Business Startups: Background and Methodology. *Advances in Entrepreneurship, Firm Emergence and Growth* 4:153–227.

Reynolds, Paul D., Michael Hay, and S. Michael Camp. 1999. *Global Entrepreneurship Monitor 1999*. Kansas City, MO: Kauffman Foundation.

Reynolds, P. D., M. Hay, W. D. Bygrave, S. M. Camp, and E. Autio. 2000. *Global Entrepreneurship Monitor*. Kansas City, MO: Kauffman Center for Entrepreneurial Leadership.

Riesman, David. 1950. *The Lonely Crowd*. New Haven: Yale University Press.

Schumpeter, Joseph A. 1942. *Capitalism, Socialism and Democracy*. New York: Harper Brothers.

Servan-Schreiber, J.-J. 1968. *The American Challenge*. London: Hamish Hamilton.

Sternberg, R. 1996. Technology Policies and the Growth of Regions. *Small Business Economics* 82:75–86.

Von Hippel, E. 1994. Sticky Information and the Locus of Problem Solving. *Management Science* 40:429–439.

Whyte, William H. 1960. *The Organization Man*. Hammondsworth, Middlesex, U.K.: Penguin.

Williamson, Oliver E. 1968. Economies as an Antitrust Defense. *American Economic Review* 58:18–36.

Zucker, L. G., M. R. Darby, and J. Armstrong. 1998. Geographically Localized Knowledge: Spillovers or Markets? *Economic Inquiry* 36: 65–86.

The Emergence of
Entrepreneurship Policy

Brett Anitra Gilbert
David B. Audretsch
Patricia P. McDougall

ABSTRACT. Since the 1980s, many regulatory agencies were either downsized or closed and waves of publicly owned enterprises were privatized. Some scholars interpret this as signaling the retreat of government intervention. We suggest, however, that rather than retreating, public policy towards business is undergoing a profound shift. Specifically, a new set of policies designed to promote entrepreneurial activity has come to the forefront, that focuses on enabling the startup and viability of entrepreneurial firms rather than constraining existing enterprises.

1. Introduction

Government intervention has been a constant reality shaping the business environment throughout U.S. history (Chandler, 1977). Since as far back as the late 1800s, public policy towards business has been preoccupied with harnessing the market power of large corporations through a triad of policy instruments including regulation, antitrust and government ownership. The 1980s, however, ushered in the downsizing or closing of many regulatory agencies including the Civil Aeronautics Board, the Interstate Commerce Commission and the Federal Trade Commission.

Final version accepted on Octobert 28, 2003

Brett Anitra Gilbert and Patricia P. McDougall
Kelley School of Business
Indiana University
1309 E. Tenth Street
Bloomington, IN 47405
U.S.A.
E-mail: bgilbert@indiana.edu;
mcdougal@indiana.edu

David B. Audretsch
School of Public and Environmental Affairs
Indiana University
1315 E. Tenth Street
Bloomington, IN 47405
U.S.A.
E-mail: daudrets@indiana.edu

The privatization of scores of previously publicly owned enterprises also occurred. To some this may have appeared to be a signal of the retreat of government intervention, but in this paper we suggest a very different view.

The argument we will make is that a profound shift in government policies toward business is occurring, and a new policy agenda designed to promote entrepreneurial activity is coming to the forefront. By contrast to traditional policy instruments that worked primarily to constrain big business, contemporary policy instruments or what we will refer to as entrepreneurial policies, are enabling in nature and center on new and small businesses. Additionally, traditional policy instruments were generally implemented at the federal level. Entrepreneurship policies are implemented at all levels of government and are growing in utilization warranting greater attention and understanding than is currently available. This paper hopes to fill this gap in understanding.

The order of this paper will consist of a brief historical description of the role of public policy towards business, followed by a theoretical framework explaining the factors causing government intervention and the shift to the new paradigm. Several descriptions of entrepreneurship policies will be provided.

2. Theoretical framework

2.1. *The historical context*

Prior to the middle of the nineteenth century, production was undertaken primarily in small-scale craft establishments that often were family owned. The minimum efficient scale (MES), or smallest level of output where the minimum average cost was attained, was low generally and involved only a handful of few employees. Towards the turn of

Small Business Economics 22: 313–323, 2004.
© 2004 *Kluwer Academic Publishers. Printed in the Netherlands.*

the century, however, large-scale production rendered small firms more or less inherently inefficient (Chandler, 1977). The viability of small-scale family enterprises was sufficiently jeopardized through the advent of large corporations and accompanying managerial revolution.

From the American Industrial Revolution, the corporation emerged as the most efficient instrument of resource management. The organizational structure of the modern corporation post the U.S. Civil War birthed a new managerialism that excelled at applying manufacturing processes and amassing large quantities of raw materials, labor and capital inputs. This resulted in lower-cost production particularly for large scale operations than previously had been available. The increased efficiency of the larger corporations decreased prices in the product market, and the new competition from the emerging large corporations thrust many family-owned small businesses into an inefficient operating size.

2.2. *Structure-performance framework for emergence of entrepreneurship policy*

Chandler (1962) provided a framework to explain variations in firm performance. According to Chandler's framework, firm performance is shaped by the organization and structural characteristics of the enterprise. An analogous framework has been developed in the field of industrial organization (Scherer and Ross, 1990) to explain variations in performance for the unit of observation of industries or markets. According to the industrial organization framework (Scherer and Ross, 1990) industry or market performance is shaped by the underlying industry structure. That market structure is in turn influenced by the importance of key factors which are used in that industry. Thus, the elements of the structure-performance framework are:

2.2.1. *Market requirements*
The relative importance of the different types of factor inputs such as raw materials, unskilled labor, and capital determine the key factors for competing in a market.

2.2.2. *Market structure*
Market structure is shaped by the underlying factors of production. In an industry where capital and scale economies are important in the production process, a concentrated market structure characterized by oligopoly or monopoly often results. Whereas monopolistic markets are limited in structural factors, an oligopolistic market structure is accentuated by numerous structural factors, such as the degree of product differentiation, extent of entry barriers, degree of vertical integration, cost structures and breadth of diversification. By contrast, in industries where capital and scale economies do not play a significant role, the market tends to be less concentrated and more atomistic in nature.

2.2.3. *Market performance*
The industrial organization literature has sought to identify the impact of market structure on industry performance (Scherer and Ross, 1990). This literature has generated considerable numbers of studies seeking to answer one of two primary issues, namely (1) what is the degree of market power, concentration and oligopoly (market structure) and how has it been evolving over time; and (2) what is the impact of market power, concentration and oligopoly on performance measures such as prices and profits in particular.

Results of this literature is far too complex and idiosyncratic to summarize here, however, one general finding provided by Scherer and Ross (1990) was that there is a tradeoff between market power and performance, such that lower levels of market power, resulted in higher industry performance.

2.2.4. *Government response*
Increased market power through concentration results in production efficiency gains. However, such gains come through reduced competition. The implication for public policy was to find mechanisms for harnessing the productive efficiencies associated with large-scale production in concentrated markets while minimizing the negative aspects emanating from oligopolistic enterprises in concentrated industries. In particular, U.S. government policy evolved into a triad of public policy instruments to control big business – regulation, antitrust and public ownership.

The unsatisfactory performance emanating from large-scale production in concentrated markets induced policy intervention. While a lively debate raged among scholars about which specific instrument was more effective (Scherer and Ross, 1990), each instrument shared a common element in that it restricted the freedom of firms to contract.

As the superior efficiency of large-scale production over small business became obvious, a political debate emerged about what to do about the small business problem. One view held that the disappearance of small business should not be impeded, since it reflected the outcome of the efficiency enhancing market process (Chandler, 1977). The other view argued the importance of small businesses for political and social reasons. Policy efforts during the late nineteenth century therefore, were targeted towards preserving inefficient small businesses.

The passage of the Robinson-Patman Act is widely interpreted as one effort to protect small firms that would otherwise have been too inefficient to survive.[1] It also was passed with the goal of protecting small, independent retailers from the more efficient large chains.[2] According to Judge Richard Posner (1976), "The Robinson-Patman Act . . . is almost uniformly condemned by professional and academic opinion, legal and economic." Similarly, (former) Judge Robert Bork (1978, p. 382) observed that, "One often hears of the baseball player who, although a weak hitter, was also a poor fielder. Robinson-Patman is a little like that. Although it does not prevent much price discrimination, at least it has stifled a great deal of competition."

Similarly, preservationist efforts also appeared to be at work in the creation of the U.S. Small Business Administration. In the Small Business Act of July 10, 1953, Congress authorized the creation of the Small Business Administration, with an explicit mandate to "aid, counsel, assist and protect . . . the interests of small business concerns."[3] The Small Business Act was clearly an attempt by the Congress to halt the continued disappearance of small businesses and to preserve their role in the U.S. economy. Like the Robinson-Patman Act, the Small Business Act was clearly targeted to preserve the viability of existing status quo small businesses.

Political motivations as the driving force behind the creation of policy instruments towards small business seem like a plausible explanation behind the urgency of small business preservation, however, in the next few sections we will offer an alternative rationale. Figure 1 represents a pictorial depiction of our rationale.

2.3. *Enter catalysts – technology and globalization*

2.3.1. *Globalization*

As virtually all measures of trade, foreign direct investment and integration indicate (Porter, 1986), the degree of globalization has increased sharply over the last century. Conventional wisdom would have predicted that increased globalization would present a more hostile environment for small business (Vernon, 1970). In fact, Caves (1982) argued that the additional costs of globalization, that would be incurred by small business would "constitute an important reason for expecting that

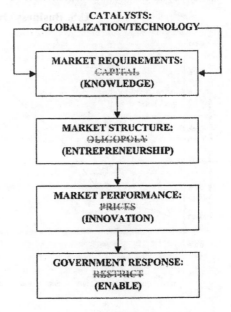

Figure 1.

foreign investment will be mainly an activity of large firms".

Empirical evidence by Horst (1972) in particular seemed to confirm that after controlling for industry effects, the only factor significantly influencing the propensity to engage in foreign direct investment was firm size, leading Chandler (1990) to conclude that, "to compete globally you have to be big."

Furthermore, Gomes-Casseres (1997, p. 33) acknowledged that, "[s]tudents of international business have traditionally believed that success in foreign markets required large size. Small firms were thought to be at a disadvantage compared to larger firms, because of the fixed costs of learning about foreign environments, communicating at long distances, and negotiating with national governments." It is interesting to note, therefore, that the rise of the global economy apparently created tremendous opportunities for large and small firms alike. As Figure 2 shows, despite the increasing wave of globalization, entrepreneurial activity (as measured by the business ownership rate) reversed

its long-term decline and began to increase by the mid-1970s, a period consistent with the acknowledged beginnings of the globalization era (Bartlett and Ghoshal, 1999).

Whereas large firms benefited from rapid globalization by being able to exploit opportunities for economies of scale and scope (Bartlett and Ghoshal, 1999), small firms apparently benefited by taking advantage of opportunities left unexplored in the domestic market, as well as opportunities then available internationally.

2.3.2. *Technology*

Technology is often attributed as one of the driving forces behind globalization (Bartlett and Ghoshal, 1999). With each wave of technological change, the bar of knowledge required to obtain that level of sophistication changes. The result is generally a greater need for human capital, which has given rise to the increase in knowledge workers. Berman et al. (1997) showed that demand for less skilled workers has decreased dramatically, while demand for skilled workers has

U.S. Business Ownership Rate, 1972-1996

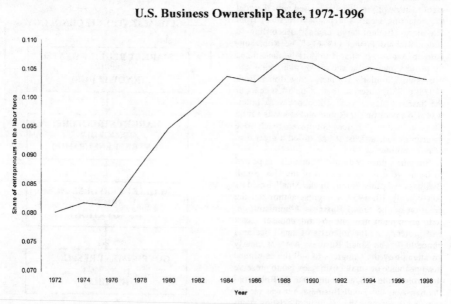

Figure 2.

exploded. Additionally, throughout the twentieth century patent applications fluctuated between 40,000 and 80,000 per year. In 1995, however, over 120,000 patent applications were filed. Conclusively, there has been an unprecedented jump in patent activities in the United States since 1985 (Kotrum and Lerner, 1997).

This shift, however, has not been without its costs. Audretsch and Feldman (1996) demonstrated that knowledge-based economic activity is costly to transfer across geographic space. The advent of information technologies, such as the internet, has reduced the cost of transferring codified information, such as the price of stocks in New York, or the temperature in Tokyo, to virtually zero. However, knowledge, and in particular those ideas that cannot be codified and require a large tacit element, cannot be transferred easily across geographic space using these new information technologies. Instead, face-to-face communication requiring geographic proximity is conducive to the transmission of ideas and tacit knowledge. As a result, knowledge generation appears to have localized.

A series of studies have identified a positive link between entrepreneurial activity and growth for spatial units of observation[4] ranging from the city and region (Carree, 2001; Fritsch, 1997; National Commission on Entrepreneurship, 2001; Reynolds, 1999; Reynolds et al., 1995) to the country (Carree et al., 2000; Carree and Thurik, 1999; Thurik, 1999). While Fritsch (1997) and Reynolds (1999) provided compelling evidence that the regions are experiencing higher levels of entrepreneurial activity measured by startup rates and turbulence rates, Thurik (1999) provided empirical evidence from a 1984–1994 cross-sectional study of the 23 countries that are part of the Organization for Economic Co-operation and Development (OECD), that increased entrepreneurship, as measured by business ownership rates, was associated with higher rates of employment growth at the country level.

Similarly, the Global Entrepreneurship Monitor (GEM) Study Reynolds et al. (2000) established an empirical link between the degree of entrepreneurial activity and economic growth, as measured by employment, at the country level. Thus, not only have theoretical arguments made the implication that the growth of places is positively associated with establishing an entrepreneurial advantage, but empirical evidence has as well. Subsequently, "places" developed a greater need for strategic management in order to capitalize on the growth associated with entrepreneurship. Because geographic proximity plays a greater role for the transmission of knowledge, which is costly and difficult to transmit, than for traditional factors (i.e. labor or capital), which are transmitted (relatively) more easily across geographic space (Porter and Wayland, 1995), a different set of policies implemental by the governments of places was required to foster entrepreneurial environments.

2.4. *Emergence of enabling policies*

When knowledge is the predominant factor of production, a different market structure emerges. Knowledge is inherently different from traditional factors of production, such as land, labor and capital (Arrow, 1962) in that it is uncertain, asymmetric, associated with greater transactions costs and therefore more difficult to evaluate across agents. Case studies (Holbrook et al., 2000) have documented how differences in evaluation of ideas result in the startup of numerous new companies providing evidence that new and small firms are the vehicles for at least some of the new ideas. High context, uncertain ideas, or what Von Hipple (1994) terms "sticky knowledge", is best transmitted via face-to-face interaction and through frequent and repeated contact. Geographic proximity is valuable in this sense because as Arrow (1962) acknowledged, tacit knowledge is inherently non-rival in nature; knowledge developed for any particular application can easily spill over for use by a third-party firm. Glaeser et al. (1992, p. 1126) also observed that, "intellectual breakthroughs must cross hallway and streets more easily than oceans and continents."

There is considerable evidence that knowledge spillovers result in both a geographic clustering of innovative activity (Audretsch and Feldman, 1996; Jaffe et al., 1993) as well as an increase in startups across innovative industries, such as semiconductors (Almeida and Kogut, 1997), and biotechnology (Audretsch and Stephan, 1996; Zucker et al., 1998). The link between entrepreneurial activity (business ownership rates) and growth of various geographic regions, ranging from cities to counties and countries could not escape the notice of regional and local policy makers. Thus efforts began to develop new policy initiatives that focused on the startup and growth of new firms. Waves of deregulation and privatization replaced regulation and public ownership in the U.S. as well as across other OECD countries (OECD, 1997). Initiatives also emerged to promote the production and commercialization of knowledge, rather than to simply allow the market to produce knowledge on its own. The impetus for these initiatives could be linked to the market failure associated with knowledge-based activities.

There are tremendous costs and uncertainty associated with the generation of knowledge that oftentimes results in firm failure (Audretsch, 1995). Because a firm's knowledge capabilities may be conditional upon the geographic proximity of complementary knowledge firms, and value from such firms would be created even if an entrepreneurial startup fails, it benefits locales to create such an environment. The failure of a knowledge-based firm does not imply that the firm created no value. In fact, evidence suggests that ideas created by failed firms and projects often become integral parts of successful products and projects in successful firms (Holbrook, 1995; Holbrook et al., 2000). Fairchild Semiconductor, though it failed, generated ideas that were used by numerous other firms and has been attributed as the catalyst spawning Silicon Valley.[5]

The externalities sometimes associated with failed firms, also creates a market failure in the valuation of (potential) new enterprises by private investors and policy makers. Whereas the private investor can only appropriate her investment if the particular firm succeeds, a failed firm that generates knowledge externalities contributes to the success of other firms. A private investor, however, appropriates nothing from the original investment. Similarly, individual firms or workers would have little incentive to invest in the development of a geographic cluster, or the geographic concentration of entrepreneurial firms. As knowledge inherently is a public good whose production generates externalities (Arrow, 1962), the inability of a third party to appropriate returns from such is a given (Jaffe et al., 1993).

From the perspective of public policy, by contrast, whether individual firms succeed is of little importance as long as some firms do and growth for the locale occurs. Thus, the shift to knowledge, combined with the propensity for knowledge to remain localized, resulted in a new policy opportunity for places – cities, regions, states and countries. It also resulted in a fundamental change in the role of government from that of an overseer of business, constraining the freedom of firms to contract, to that of a partner to business, enabling and fostering the development of new and small firms. This shift in policy emphasis as a response to a changing source of competitiveness from the traditional factors of capital and labor to the emerging factor of knowledge is depicted in Figure 1. This shows that when competitiveness was generated from capital and labor, the policy response towards large enterprises was restricted in nature, while small business was the target of preservationist policy. By contrast, when knowledge is the source of competitiveness in emerging markets, policy shifts towards enabling the startup and growth of new enterprises, or what can be termed as entrepreneurship policy.[6]

2.5. *Entrepreneurship policies – U.S.*

Examples of entrepreneurship policies abound at the local, regional, state & federal levels within the U.S. as well as other countries. While certainly not an exhaustive list, we present examples at each level in Table I. This section begins with a discussion of entrepreneurial policies pursued at the local level.

2.5.1. *Local level*

Sternberg (1996) documents how the success of a number of different high-technology clusters spanning a number of different local contexts is the direct result of policies such as the provision of venture capital or research support. The Advanced Technology Centers in New Jersey, and the Centers for Advanced Technology at Case Western Reserve University, Rutgers University and the University of Rochester have supported generic, pre-competitive research stimulating entrepreneurial startups (Sternberg, 1996). A striking example is evident in the history of Austin, Texas.

TABLE I
Examples of enabling policies

Level enacted	Example
National:	Small Business Innovation & Research (SBIR)
State:	Ohio Edison Program
Regional:	Research Triangle, NC
Local:	Austin, TX.
Specific examples, other countries:	START Program: Germany
	Special Purpose Credit Funds: Korea

In the early-1980s, Microelectronics and Computer Technology Corporation (MCC), persuaded by the efforts of University of Texas at Austin officials, local business leaders, and local and state government officials, decided to locate its headquarters to Austin. This not only brought Austin to the spotlight as a potential location for high-technology activities, but also initiated the university-industry partnership that is still evident today (Schmandt, 2001). Furthermore, a concentrated government policy effort to target the transfer of technology from the University of Texas and other research institutions to new-firm startups also exists. One of those policy initiatives, the Advanced Research Program in Texas, has provided support for basic research and infrastructure improvement at the University of Texas, and played a central role in developing a high-technology cluster around Austin (Feller, 1997). The success of these efforts has been attributed to the support of leadership at the local level as well as at the state level (Schmandt, 2001).

2.5.2. *Regional level*

The plethora of science, technology and research parks to emerge are perhaps the best representation of policies implemented to impact a regional level (Lugar and Goldstein, 1991). Lugar (2001, p. 47) noted that, "The most successful parks . . . have a profound impact on a region and its competitiveness." A distinct exemplar of this effect is found in the Research Triangle Park in North Carolina. The traditional industries in North Carolina – furniture, textiles, and tobacco – had all lost international competitiveness, resulting in declines in employment and stagnated real incomes. In 1952, only Arkansas and Mississippi had lower per capita incomes. A movement emerged to use the rich knowledge base of the

region, formed by the three major universities – Duke University, University of North Carolina-Chapel Hill and North Carolina State (Link and Scott, 2001, p. 2).

This movement, though initiated by North Carolina businessmen looking to improve industrial growth, was taken over by the Governor's office, which supported the efforts through fruition (Link, 1995). Empirical evidence provides strong support that the initiative creating Research Triangle has led to fundamental changes in the region. For example, Link and Scott (2001) documented that the growth in the number of research companies in the Research Triangle Park has increased from zero in 1958, to 50 by the mid-1980s, and to over 100 by 1997. Concurrently, employment from the Research Triangle companies increased from zero in the late 1950s to over 40,000 by 1997. Research Triangle Park has been attributed with directly and indirectly generating one-quarter of all jobs in the region between 1959 and 1990, as well as shifting the nature of those jobs towards high value-add knowledge activities (Lugar, 2001).

2.5.3. *State level*

Efforts at the state level have been just as prolific, but one state provides a particularly interesting case study. The Edison Technology Program of Ohio was established by the State of Ohio, as a means of transferring technology from universities and government research institutes to new firm startups. Carlsson and Brunerhjelm (1999) explain how the Edison BioTechnology Center serves an important dual role as a "bridging institution" between academic research and industry and between new startups and potential sources of finance. The Edison Centers in particular, try to link the leading universities and medical institutions, businesses, foundations, to civic and state organizations in Ohio in order to create new business opportunities. Numerous centers exist across the state. Similarly, the Edison Program has established a bridging institution to support polymer research and technology in Ohio. Carlsson and Brunerhjelm (1999) credit the program for the startup of new high technology firms in Ohio.

2.5.4. *Federal level*
The Small Business Innovation Research (SBIR) program was enacted by the U.S. Congress in the early 1980s as a response to the loss of American competitiveness in global markets. Congress ordered each federal agency to allocate approximately four percent of its annual budget to funding innovative small firms as a mechanism for restoring American international competitiveness. Thus, the SBIR was essentially a mandate to the major R&D agencies in the United States to allocate a share of the research budget to innovative small firms (Cooper, 2001). The results evaluating the SBIR program (Lerner and Kegler, 2000; Lerner, 1999; Wessner, 2000) indicate the following:

> The benefits of the SBIR extend beyond the impact on the individual recipient firm. The social rate of return, which incorporates this external positive impact, exceeds the positive rate of return. There was no evidence of a negative rate of return associated with the SBIR, but compelling evidence that the SBIR program has had a positive impact on developing the U.S. biotechnology industry. The benefits have been documented as:
>
> *   The survival and growth rates of SBIR recipients have exceeded those of firms not receiving SBIR funding.
> *   The SBIR induces scientists involved in biomedical research to change their career path. By applying the scientific knowledge to commercialization, these scientists shift their career trajectories away from basic research towards entrepreneurship.
> *   The SBIR awards provide a source of funding for scientists to launch start-up firms that otherwise would not have had access to alternative sources of funding.
> *   SBIR awards have a powerful demonstration effect. Scientists commercializing research results by starting companies induce colleagues to consider applications and the commercial potential of their own research.

2.6. *Entrepreneurship policies – global*

Although our discussion has primarily emphasized policies implemented at U.S. levels of govern-

ment, policies to promote entrepreneurial activity are not unique to the United States. Even so, the development and implementation of policies to promote entrepreneurship in other countries were perhaps at least to some degree, triggered by the growing awareness of the positive impact of entrepreneurship on regional competitiveness in certain U.S. areas, such as Silicon Valley and Route 128 (Saxenien, 1994). While cataloging all policies in each country would exceed the scope of this paper, several examples from various countries deserve mention.

2.6.1. *Europe*
The German Ministry of Economics and Technology (1999) attributed the high unemployment and stagnant growth rates plaguing Germany during the 1990s to a lack of entrepreneurial activity. The policy response, therefore, involved a plethora of instruments to stimulate the startup of new enterprises, particularly in high-technology industries. One of the most interesting examples involves the establishment of five EXIST regions in Germany, where startups from universities and government research laboratories are encouraged (BMBF, 2000). The program has the explicit goals of (1) creating an entrepreneurial culture, (2) the commercialization of scientific knowledge, and (3) increasing the number of innovative start-ups and SMEs. Five regions were selected among many applicants for START funding. They include the (1) Rhein-uhr region (bizeps program), (2) Dresden (Dresden exists), (3) Thueringen (GET UP), (4) Karlsruhe (KEIM), and (5) Stuttgart (PUSH!).

2.6.2. *Asia*
"Virtually nowhere has the relative role of small and medium enterprises . . . changed as much over time as in South Korea" (Nugent and Yhee, forthcoming). By the mid-1970s, Korea was characterized by "the extreme dominance in economic and public policy of its large *chaebol* (conglomerate firms)" (Nugent and Yhee, forthcoming). Kim and Nugent (1999) document how public policy shifted from supporting and promoting the *chaebol* prior to the 1970s, to promoting small business and new startups by the 1980s and 1990s. One goal of these policies was to compensate for the "earlier neglect of SMEs" (Nugent and Yhee,

forthcoming). In particular, the new constitution in the 1980s mandated that the government promote small firms.

In the 1990s, policy shifted towards promoting high-technology entrepreneurship in Korea. The new entrepreneurial policies resulted in the introduction of specific-purpose credit funds to foster venture capital for high-tech startups. In addition, numerous programs were introduced to assist mature small firms in updating their technology. An ambitious system for identifying and providing various kinds of support for "promising SMEs" was established. Various tax breaks to small firms, such as accelerated depreciation allowances, deductions from taxable income, tax moratoria, and tax rate reductions, were also implemented.

According to Nugent and Yhee (forthcoming), there has been a proliferation of technical research centers and institutes organized as either government or nonprofit agencies. There is at least some empirical evidence suggesting that these types of government programs have contributed to a greater role of small firms in Korea (Nugent and Yhee, forthcoming). The share of manufacturing employment accounted by small business (with fewer than 300 employees), increased from 45.7 percent in 1975, to 61.7 percent in 1990, and finally to 69.3 percent by 1997 (Nugent and Yhee, forthcoming).

3. Conclusion

The Employment Act of 1946 made public policy responsible for growth and employment in the United States. In particular, The Act stated that it is "The continuing policy and responsibility of the . . . government to use all practical means . . . to foster the general conditions under which there will be afforded useful employment opportunities." To meet this mandate, the government turned to monetary and fiscal policy as the main instruments to achieve the Act's goals of attaining full employment and high economic growth. This meant that growth and employment policies were essentially under the jurisdiction of the federal government and less relevant for regional and local governments.

Globalization and the shift towards knowledge as the source of competitiveness rendered the traditional policy instruments less effective. These instruments, alone, could no longer guarantee high growth and employment, certainly not for all regions and locations. Thus, policy makers started looking for new sources of growth and jobs. The links between entrepreneurship, employment and growth did not escape the attention of policy makers. As globalization resulted in the loss of jobs and stagnation to local and regional economies, policy makers specifically at the state and local levels responded by developing new policy instruments to help them implement the strategic management of regions. These new policy instruments have generally focused on entrepreneurship as an engine of economic development. And as a result, a new public policy agenda to promote entrepreneurship has been implemented at virtually all levels of government.

Although it has been argued that entrepreneurship policies were developed as a stopgap measure to absorb workers displaced by corporate downsizing (Storey, 1991), this paper argues that entrepreneurship policies instead are emerging as one of the most essential instruments for economic growth. Thus, just as monetary and fiscal policy were the mainstays for creating employment and growth in the post-war economy, entrepreneurship policy is likely to emerge as the most important policy instrument for a global and knowledge-based economy.

Notes

[1] According to the Robinson-Patman Act, "It shall be unlawful for any person engaged in commerce, in the course of such commerce, either directly or indirectly, to discriminate in price between different purchasers of commodities of like grade and quality. . . ."

[2] For example, A&P was found in violation of the Robinson-Patman Act for direct purchases from suppliers and from performing its own wholesale functions. While these activities resulted in lower distribution costs, the gains in efficiency were seen as being irrelevant because small business was threatened.

[3] http://www.sba.gov/aboutsba/sbahistory.html.

[4] Spatial units of observation refer to a geographic dimension such as a city, county, region, or country.

[5] Holbrook et al. (2000) provide extensive documentation of this phenomenon.

[6] For further discussion of entrepreneurship policy see Lundstroem and Stevenson (2002).

References

Almeida, P. and B. Kogut, 1997, 'The Exploration of Technological Diversity and the Geographic Localization of Innovation', *Small Business Economics* 9, 21–31.

Arrow, K. J., 1962, 'Economic Welfare and the Allocation of Resources for Invention', in R. R. Nelson (ed.), *The rate and Direction of Inventive Activity*, Princeton: Princeton University Press, pp. 609–626.

Audretsch, D. B., 1995, *Innovation and Industry Evolution*, Cambridge, MA: MIT Press.

Audretsch, D. B. and M. D. Feldman, 1996, 'R&D Spillovers and the Geography of Innovation and Production', *American Economic Review* 86, 630–639.

Audretsch, D. B. and P. E. Stephan, 1996, 'Company-Scientist Locational Links: The Case of Biotechnology', *American Economic Review* 86, 641–652.

Berman, E., J. Bound and S. Machin, 1997, Implications of Skill-Based Technological Change: International Evidence. Working Paper 6166, National Bureau of Economic Research (NBER), Cambridge.

Bork, R. H., 1978, *The Antitrust Paradox*, New York: Basic Books.

Carlsson, B. and P. Braunerhjelm, 1999, 'Industry Clusters: Biotechnology/Biomedicine and Polymers in Ohio and Sweden', in D. B. Audretsch and R. Thurik (eds.), *Innovation, Industry Evolution, and Employment*. Cambridge: Cambridge University Press, pp. 182–215.

Carree, M., 2001, 'Does Unemployment Affect the Number of Establishments? A Regional Analysis for U.S. States', *Regional Studies*, forthcoming.

Carree, M. A. and A. R. Thurik, 1999, 'Industrial Structure and Economic Growth', in D. B. Audretsch and A. R. Thurik (eds.), *Innovation, Industry Evolution and Employment*, Cambridge: Cambridge University Press, pp. 86–110.

Carree, M. A., A. van Stel, A. R. Thurik and S. Wennekers, 2000, Economic Development and Business Ownership: An Analysis Using Data of 23 OECD Countries in the Period 1976–1996. Institute for Development Strategies Discussion Paper 00-6.

Caves, R. E., 1982, *Multinational Enterprise and Economic Analysis*, Cambridge: Cambridge University Press.

Chandler, A., 1990, *Scale and Scope: The Dynamics of Industrial Capitalism*, Cambridge: Harvard University Press.

Chandler, Jr., A. D., 1977, *The Visible Hand: The Managerial Revolution in American Business*, Cambridge: Harvard University Press.

Cooper, R. S., Forthcoming, 'Purpose and Performance of the Small Business Innovation Research (SBIR) Program', *Small Business Economics*.

Feller, I., 1997, 'Federal & State Government Roles in Science & Technology', *Economic Development Quarterly* 11, 283–296.

Fritsch, M., 1997, 'New Firms and Regional Employment Change', *Small Business Economics* 9, 437–448.

German Federal Ministry of Economics and Technology, 1999, *Economic Report '99*. Bonn: Federal Ministry of Economics and Technology.

Glaeser, E. L., H. D. Kallal, J. A. Scheinkman and A. Shleifer, 1992, 'Growth of Cities', *Journal of Political Economy* 100, 1126–1152.

Gomez-Casseres, B., 1997, 'Alliance Strategies of Small Firms', *Small Business Economics* 9, 33–44.

Holbrook, D., 1995. 'Government Support of the Semiconductor Industry: Diverse Approaches and Information Flows', *Business and Economic History* 24, 133–168.

Holbrook, D., W. M. Cohen, D. A. Hounshell and S. Klepper, 2000, 'The Nature, Sources, and Consequences of Firm Differences in the Early History of the Semiconductor Industry', *Strategic Management Journal* 21, 1017–1041.

Horst, T., 1972. 'Firm and Industry Determinants of the Decision to Invest Abroad: An Empirical Study', *Review of Economic Statistics*, 258–266.

Jaffe, A. B., M. Trajtenberg and R. Henderson, 1993, 'Geographic Localization of Knowledge Spillovers as Evidenced by Patent Citations', *Quarterly Journal of Economics* 63, 577–598.

Kim, J. B. Nugent, 1999. 'Korean SMEs and Their Support Systems', in B. Levy, A. Berry and J. B. Nugent (eds.), *Fulfilling the Export Potential of Small and Medium Firms*, Boston: Kluwer.

Kortum, S. and J. Lerner, 1997, Stronger Protection or Technological Revolution: What is Behind the Recent Surge in Patenting? Cambridge, MA: Working Paper 6204, National Bureau of Economic Research (NBER).

Lerner, J., 1999, 'The Government as Venture Capitalist: The Long-Run Effects of the SBIR Program', *Journal of Business* 72, 285–297.

Lerner, J. and C. Kegler, 2000, 'Evaluating the Small Business Innovation Research Program: A Literature Review', in C. Wessner (ed.), *The Small Business Innovation Research Program (SBIR)*, Washington, DC: National Academy Press, pp. 307–327.

Link, A. N., 1995, *A Generosity of Spirit: The Early History of Research Triangle Park*, Durham: Duke University Press.

Link, A. N. and J. T. Scott, Forthcoming, 'The Growth of Research Triangle Park', *Small Business Economics*.

Lugar, M. and H. Goldstein, 1991, *Technology in the Garden: Research Parks and Regional Economic Development*, Chapel Hill, NC: The University of North Carolina Press.

Lugar, M., 2001, 'The Research Triangle Experience', in C. Wessner (ed.), *Industry-Laboratory Partnerships: A Review of the Sandia Science and Technology Park Initiative*, Washington, DC: National Academy Press, pp. 35–38.

National Commission on Entrepreneurship, 2001.

Nugent, J. B. and S. Yhee, Forthcoming, 'Small and Medium Enterprises in Korea: Achievements, Constraints and Policy Issues', *Small Business Economics*.

Organization for Economic Co-operation and Development (OECD), 1997, *The OECD Report on Regulatory Reform*, Paris: OECD.

Porter, M. E., 1986, 'Changing Patterns of International Competition', *California Management Review* 28(2), 9–40.

Porter, M. E. and R. E. Wayland, 1995, 'Global Competition and the Localization of Competitive Advantage', in

Advances in Strategic Management, vol. 11A, Greenwich, CT: JAI Press, pp. 63–105.

Posner, R. A., 1976. *The Robinson-Patman Act: Federal Regulation of Price Differences*, Washington, D.C.: American Enterprise Institute.

Reynolds, P. D., 1999, 'Creative Destruction: Source or Symptom of Economic Growth?', in Z. J. Acs, B. Carlsson and C. Karlsson (eds.), *Entrepreneurship, Small and Medium-Sized Enterprises and the Macroeconomy*, Cambridge: Cambridge University Press, pp. 97–136.

Reynolds, P. D., M. Hay, W. D. Bygrave, S. M. Camp and E. Autio, 2000, *Global Entrepreneurship Monitor*, Kansas City: Kauffman Center for Entrepreneurial Leadership.

Reynolds, P. D., B. Miller and W. R. Maki, 1995, 'Explaining Regional Variation in Business Births and Deaths: U.S. 1976–1988', *Small Business Economics* 7, 389–407.

Saxenian, A., 1994, *Regional Advantage: Culture and Competition in Silicon Valley and Route 128*, Cambridge, MA: Harvard University Press.

Schmandt, J., 2001, 'The Austin Experience', in C. W. Wessner (ed.), *A Review of the Sandia Science and Technology Park Initiative*, Washington, DC: National Academy Press, pp. 39–41.

Scherer, F. M. and D. Ross, 1990, *Industrial Market Structure and Economic Performance*, 3rd edition, Boston: Houghton-Mifflin.

Sternberg, R., 1996, 'Technology Policies and the Growth of Regions', *Small Business Economics* 8, 75–86.

Storey, D. J., 1991, 'The Birth of New Enterprises – Does Unemployment Matter? A Review of the Evidence', *Small Business Economics* 3, 167–178.

Thurik, A. R., 1999, 'Entrepreneurship, Industrial Transformation and Growth', in G. D. Libecap (ed.), *The Sources of Entrepreneurial Activity, in Advances in the Study of Entrepreneurship, Innovation and Economic Growth*, Vol. 11, Greenwich, CT: JAI Press, pp. 29–66.

United States Department of Commerce, Bureau of the Census, 1958, *Enterprise Statistics*, Washington, DC: U.S. Government Printing Office.

United States Department of Commerce, Bureau of the Census, 1977, *Enterprise Statistics*, Washington, DC: U.S. Government Printing Office.

Vernon, R., 1970, 'Organization as a Scale Factor in the Growth of Firms', in J. W. Markham and G. F. Papanek (eds.), *Industrial Organization and Economic Development*, Boston: Houghton Mifflin, pp. 47–66.

Von Hipple, E. 1994, 'Sticky Information and the Locus of Problem Solving: Implications for Innovation', *Management Science* 40, 429–439.

Wessner, C. (ed.), 2000, *The Small Business Innovation Research Program (SBIR)*, Washington, DC: National Academy Press.

Zucker, L. G., M. R. Darby and M. B. Brewer, 1998, 'Intellectual Human Capital and the Birth of U.S. Biotechnology Enterprises', *American Economic Review* 88, 290–306.

International Journal of Industrial Organization
19 (2001) 795–821

ELSEVIER

International Journal of
**Industrial
Organization**

www.elsevier.com/locate/econbase

Market dynamics in the Netherlands: Competition policy and the role of small firms [*]

David B. Audretsch[a,*], George van Leeuwen[b], Bert Menkveld[c],
Roy Thurik[d]

[a]*Ameritech Chair of Economic Development, Institute for Development Strategies,
Indiana University, and Centre for Economic Policy Research (CEPR) Bloomington, IN, USA*
[b]*Statistics Netherlands, Sector Statistical Methods, PO Box 959, 2270 AZ Voorburg, Netherlands*
[c]*Centre for Advanced Small Business Economics (CASBEC), Erasmus University Rotterdam,
Rotherdam, Netherlands*
[d]*EIM Small Business Research and Consultancy, PO Box 7001, 2701 AA Zoetermeer, Netherlands*

Abstract

A recent literature analyzing the dynamics of firms and industries suggests that the contribution of new and small firms to the dynamics of competition is significantly greater than found in a static analysis. Policy makers have responded by implementing a wide range of programs to reduce barriers to new-firm startup. At the same time, a number of European countries have maintained systems of collective agreements imposing industry-wide standards on the deployment and remuneration of inputs, particularly labor. The purpose of this paper is to examine whether the ability to deviate from the industry standards practiced by the incumbent firms promotes the viability of small and new firms. We examine this using a longitudinal data base from the Netherlands, where a system of rigid industry-wide collective agreements was abandoned in favor of greater flexibility. Whether or not the ability of small firms to deviate from the standards and practices of the incumbent firms in the industry promotes their viability in the Dutch context is instructive to other European countries, such as Germany and France. The latter countries have identified the startup of new firms as a central policy goal, but have maintained systems of industry-wide collective agreements. The important finding emerging from this paper is that wage flexibility promotes the viability of small firms and thus can be considered to be an instrument of competition policy in a dynamic context © 2001 Elsevier Science B.V. All rights reserved.

[*] The views expressed in this paper are those of the authors and do not necessarily reflect the policies of Statistics Netherlands.

*Corresponding author. Tel.: +1-812-855-6766.

E-mail address: daudrets@indiana.edu (D.B. Audretsch).

796   *D.B. Audretsch et al. / Int. J. Ind. Organ. 19 (2001) 795–821*

Keywords: Competition policy; Market structure dynamics; Small firms

JEL classification: L1; L4; L5; L60; O12

1. Introduction

From the perspective of the static model of industrial organization, the entry of new firms is important because they provide an equilibrating function in the market. In the presence of market power, the additional output provided by the new entrants restores the levels of profits and prices to their long-run competitive equilibrium. However, as Geroski (1995) points out in his comprehensive survey on 'What Do We Know About Entry?' the actual amount of output in markets contributed by new entrants is trivial. He reports from an exhaustive empirical literature that the share of total industry sales accounted for by new entrants typically ranges from 1.45 to 6.36%. This would seemingly suggest that new entrants contribute insufficient additional output to provide a competitive threat to incumbent firms. The implications for competition policy under this static perspective are that policies encouraging new-firm entry will contribute little in terms of fostering market competition. Thus, competition policies in both Europe and the United States have traditionally focused on reducing barriers to entry for existing incumbent enterprises rather than on reducing barriers to the startup of new enterprises.

However, a recent literature analyzing the dynamics of firms and industries suggests that the contribution of new and small firms to the dynamics of competition is significantly greater than found in a static analysis. There are two reasons why new-firm entry generates more competition in the dynamic than in the static context. The first is that the market shares of entrants, while being inconsequential in the startup and early years, often increase to significant levels within several years subsequent to entry. For example, Audretsch (1995) finds that, while the market penetration of new-firm startups is low, in some industries the penetration ratio has risen to nearly 20% within 5 years subsequent to entry. Analysis of longitudinal databases suggests that the market penetration of new firms has been understated by only considering their competitive impact in the entry year.

The second, and presumably more important reason why the contribution of new and small firms is of greater significance is as Geroski (1995) also points out, that 'entry is often used as a vehicle for introducing new innovations.' Ideas for new products, processes or organizations that cannot flourish or be pursued within the context of incumbent firms are sometimes pursued by the startup of a new firm. The startup of a new firm can represent the attempt to commercialize an untried idea. As Jovanovic (1982) argues in his model of noisy selection, new firms do not

D.B. Audretsch et al. / Int. J. Ind. Organ. 19 (2001) 795–821   797

know the viability of their enterprises but only discover this subsequent to start up struggling in the market and striving for performance. Startups learning from market experience that their product is viable, grow and ultimately survive; those learning that their products are not viable stagnate and exit. Thus, an important source of market competition in this dynamic context comes from the new products and processes being introduced in the market by new firms.

The dynamic contribution to competition emanating from new and small firms suggests that policies mitigating barriers to startup of new firms as well as barriers to entry by incumbent firms should be an equally important component of competition policies. By encouraging the entry of new firms, policy can generate new competition in the form of a greater number of firms experimenting with a greater variety of approaches. Increased variety generates greater competition, which through a process of selection, results in many firms exiting and fewer surviving by providing the best novel approaches (Cohen and Klepper, 1992; Audretsch and Thurik, 1999).

Policy makers have recently recognized the potential contribution to dynamic contribution that new firms can play. This has led to a shift in emphasis towards reducing barriers to startup. A wide range of programs has been introduced by governments on both sides of the Atlantic to reduce such barriers. For example, the Small Business Innovation Research (SBIR) in the United States program provides over $1.4 billion annually to high-technology small firms. European countries have similarly implemented a broad range of programs, spanning financial assistance, training, information, and alleviation of taxes and administrative burdens (EIM, 1998).

However, one of the greatest barriers to startup in the European context may be legal restrictions prohibiting new firms from deviating from the standard industry-wide practices followed by the large incumbent enterprises. These industry wide standards, referred to as collective agreements, impose rigidities spanning wage levels, hours worked, and technological and legal specifications. These industry-wide agreements may create significant barriers to new-firm startup because they preempt one of the most important competitive instruments of new firms – the ability to deviate from existing practices in a wide range of ways. New-firm entrants need to pursue a strategy of compensating factor differentials where they deploy and remunerate productive factors in a different manner from the incumbent firms. This is because most new entrants operate at such a small scale of output that they are confronted with an inherent cost disadvantage. One important aspect involves wage flexibility. The ability of a new entrant to pay a lower wage may provide a mechanism to compensate for higher costs due to an inefficient size. Wage flexibility may, in fact, be an essential instrument of dynamic competition policy by facilitating the startup of new firms that otherwise would be deterred.

The purpose of this paper is to examine whether the ability to deviate from the industry standards practiced by the incumbent firms promotes the viability of small and new firms. We examine this in the context of the Netherlands, because a system of rigid industry-wide collective agreements was abandoned in favor of greater flexibility.[1] Whether or not the ability of small firms to deviate from the standards and practices of the incumbent firms in the industry promotes their viability in the Dutch context is instructive to other European countries, such as Germany and France. The latter countries have identified the startup of new firms as a central policy goal, but have maintained systems of industry-wide collective agreements.

While industry-wide agreements span a broad range of dimensions, in this paper we focus on wages and the type of labor deployed. Under the system of industry-wide collective agreements in the Netherlands, wages and types of labor were standardized throughout the industry. However, since the 1980s, these industry-wide agreements were abandoned making it possible for new and small firms to deviate from the practices of incumbents. This enables us to analyze whether the ability of new and small firms to engage in a strategy of compensating factor differentials promotes their ability to exist.

A second but central policy question is that, even if wage flexibility promotes the viability of new and small firms, it may represent a net welfare loss due to lower wages. In his seminal article, 'Economies as an Antitrust Defense: The Welfare Tradeoffs,' Williamson (1968) clearly portrayed the antitrust dilemma as consisting of a tradeoff between efficiencies associated with size but a loss of competition on the one hand vs. greater enhanced competition, but less efficiency in the form of smaller enterprises, on the other hand. More recently, Brown et al. (1990) argue that the lower wages associated with small firms represent a net welfare loss. However, their analysis is based on static cross-section relationships between firm size and wages. Two important findings based on the dynamic framework of this paper are that (1) wage flexibility promotes the viability of small firms, and (2) both the compensation differential and the productivity differential between large and small firms tends to disappear as small firms age over time, even after controlling for the size of the firm. This new finding of the

---

[1] In the 1970s Dutch wage rates were high, combined with a low labor market participation rate, a low profit share in value added, rigid labor markets and a huge government budget deficit. Consensus and multilateral consultation between 'big labor, big business and big government' were deeply engrained in the industrial relations in the Netherlands during this period. This consensus contributed to what has been termed the 'Dutch Disease' in the early 1980s. It also led to its cure. A trilateral agreement was made in the early 1980s. 'Big business' abstained from massive layoffs, 'big labor' abstained from striving for ever higher wages and further refinement of the social safety system and 'big government' created order in its financial budget while maintaining sufficient social safety nets and encouraging companies to act in the public interest. This was done by providing tax cuts to companies while stimulating them to hire long-term unemployed, low-paid workers and providing other facilities like apprenticeship schemes and child care facilities. Workers agreed to accept more flexibility in their labor conditions. The trilateral agreement and the resulting improvement of economic performance are generally referred to as the 'Polder Model'.

influence of firm age on wages and productivity suggests not only that the less productive firm of today becomes the productive firm of tomorrow, but, equally important in terms of welfare economics, that the low wage of today becomes the high wage of tomorrow.

2. The productivity deficit of small firms

As Caves et al. (1975) and Scherer and Ross (1990, chapter eleven) both emphasize, estimating the extent of scale economies in an industry is a hazardous and imprecise undertaking. While a number of methodological approaches for estimating the industry MES have been introduced in the literature (Scherer and Ross, 1990, chapters eleven and four), here we follow the tradition in the industrial organization literature and adapt the method first introduced by Comanor and

Table 1
MES[a] measured in terms of sales, in Dutch, US and Japanese manufacturing sectors, 1991

Industry	Netherlands[b]		US[c]		Japan[c]	
	MES (1991 \$)	Sub-optimal share	MES (1991 \$)	Sub-optimal share	MES (1991 \$)	Sub-optimal share
Food	165.960	94.9	77.247	83.3	35.347	91.5
Textiles	58.077	95.3	53.793	86.4	11.024	90.1
Apparel	8.007	92.1	15.301	83.2	4.135	87.5
Lumber	11.486	96.3	5.832	79.6	6.940	86.9
Furniture	7.499	95.4	24.380	90.9	10.513	92.7
Paper	102.704	95.0	226.277	94.3	89.468	96.7
Printing	40.829	96.8	42.623	96.6	67.381	98.1
Chemicals	968.179	96.6	220.556	92.2	340.519	95.0
Rubber	50.987	97.1	32.837	86.6	163.664	98.6
Leather	6.748	97.0	30.779	84.2	5.519	86.0
Stone clay and glass	37.028	95.0	35.326	89.7	25.582	92.6
Primary metals	856.523	94.9	291.527	95.1	1038.575	98.3
Fabricated metal products	24.807	95.7	35.196	74.3	24.249	95.6
Machinery (non-electric)	38.103	94.8	109.454	96.3	154.450	98.4
Electrical equipment	106.285	97.6	170.889	93.2	347.558	98.6
Transportation equipment	261.648	97.2	1321.239	98.1	1284.744	99.1
Instruments	9.874	97.2	147.589	97.4	132.178	98.3
Miscellaneous	6.658	95.5	26.628	90.5	13.720	90.6
Entire manufacturing[d]	153.410	95.8	159.304	89.6	208.642	94.1

[a] The MES is determined at the two digit level. This mean is computed as a weighted mean of the MES values from the three digit industries.

[b] Source-Production Statistics, collected by the Department of Manufacturing and Construction of Statistics Netherlands.

[c] Source – Audretsch and Yamawaki (1992).

[d] Not weighted.

Wilson (1967), who approximated the MES by measuring the mean size of the plants accounting for the largest 50% of the industry value-of-shipments.[2] That is, the Comanor and Wilson measure yields the average size of the largest firms in the industry and is at least able to reflect whether the bulk of sales in an industry are made by larger or smaller firms.

It should be emphasized that this is not an exact measure of the actual MES. Rather, at best it is useful as an *index* in that it reveals relative differences in the extent of scale economies in a cross-industry context. That is, the MES index is useful in identifying that a certain industry, such as steel, has a greater extent of scale economies than, say, shoes. This proxy measure should *never* be interpreted as an exact measure of the actual MES in an industry. In any case, Scherer and Ross (1990, pp. 424–425) report that the various estimates of MES derived from industry census statistics correlated reasonably well with the presumably more precise engineering estimates for a limited sample of industries.

Using the 1991 Production Statistics, collected by the Department of Statistics of Manufacturing and Construction of Statistics Netherlands, the MES proxy was estimated.[3] The MES for Dutch manufacturing industries has been aggregated to two-digit manufacturing sectors for presentation purposes in Table 1. The computed MES is relatively large in chemicals, primary metals and transportation equipment. By contrast, the MES is relatively small in apparel, furniture and leather. This is also true in the United States and Japan.[4] In fact, the industry variations in the mean MES across sectors are quite the same among the three countries. In particular, the simple correlation of 0.86 between the computed MES in Japan and the United States suggests that, despite the conversion problem, the

---

[2] The Comanor and Wilson (1967) method for approximating the MES, while used by numerous researchers, is a slight variation on the original method introduced by Weiss (1963), who proxied the MES as the plant size accounting for one-half of the industry value-of-shipments. It follows that the Comanor and Wilson measure is systematically larger than the Weiss measure.

[3] An additional complication in computing the MES for the Netherlands is that total industrial sales for each manufacturing industry is not easily computed, because of a lack of universal data on all small firms. To estimate total sales of small firms, a procedure based on the so-called *ratio-estimator* was implemented. The procedure is based on a stratum, or a sub-group within a three-digit industry containing companies within a specific firm size class. The mean sales was computed for each stratum. The mean sales (of each stratum) was then multiplied by the number of firms in the auxiliary data set, which contains the universe of firms (in terms of numbers). This then provided by the estimate for the total sales in each stratum. In addition, any potential sample bias was corrected for by using a correction factor, based on combining the auxiliary data set with the data files identifying the mean number of employees. For companies that can be located in both data files, the mean number of employees per stratum was also computed. Using the auxiliary data files the mean number of employees per stratum was also computed. Dividing the mean sales by the mean employees provided a correction factor which was then used. Total sales in each industry was then calculated by summing all sales over the strata for the smallest firms and adding in the sales of the largest firms.

[4] The data for the United States are based on the 1982 *United States Census of Manufactures*. The data from Japan are based on the 1982 *Japanese Census of Manufactures*. They are both taken Audretsch (1995). To compare the computed MES for the Netherlands with that for the United States and Japan, the dollar estimates had to be obtained using a currency conversion exchange rate based on the 1993 *Yearbook of International Labor Statistics* from the International Labor Office, Geneva.

D.B. Audretsch et al. / Int. J. Ind. Organ. 19 (2001) 795–821   801

relative differences in the importance of scale economies are similar between the two countries. This similarity between the Netherlands and Japan is not so strong, as the simple correlation of 0.06 might suggest, and is even weaker between the United States and the Netherlands, as evidenced by the simple correlation coefficient of 0.30.

Next to the obviously crude method used to approximate the MES, there are also several other weaknesses which should be emphasized. The MES, when measured as total value of shipments, tends to be overstated in industries producing goods close to the final consumer and understated in industries producing goods that are predominantly used as intermediate inputs. That is, the level of the production process in the vertical chain is not controlled for in the value-of-shipments measure. In addition, comparing values of the MES across countries requires conversion into a common currency using the exchange rates for any given year. But the exchange rates, particularly with respect to Japan, are volatile from year to year. To avoid these problems, Table 2 lists the number of

Table 2

MES[a], measured in terms of employees, in Dutch, US and Japanese manufacturing sectors, 1991

Industry	Netherlands[b]		US[c]		Japan[c]	
	MES	Sub-optimal share	MES	Sub-optimal share	MES	Sub-optimal share
Food	557	94.9	295	83.3	130	91.5
Textiles	364	95.3	579	86.4	85	90.1
Apparel	196	92.1	251	83.2	70	87.5
Lumber	108	96.3	51	79.6	43	86.9
Furniture	61	95.4	309	90.9	74	92.7
Paper	457	95.0	1025	94.3	253	96.7
Printing	218	96.8	392	96.6	280	98.1
Chemicals	2567	96.6	798	92.2	741	95.0
Rubber	268	97.1	271	86.6	786	98.6
Leather	76	97.0	449	84.2	45	86.0
Stone clay and glass	315	95.0	284	89.7	136	92.6
Primary metals	5704	94.9	1555	95.2	2320	98.3
Fabricated metal products	164	95.7	280	74.3	126	95.6
Machinery (non-electric)	228	94.8	764	96.3	634	98.4
Electrical equipment	936	97.6	1432	93.2	1317	98.6
Transportation equipment	1459	97.2	6547	98.1	3057	99.1
Instruments	114	97.2	1454	97.4	728	98.3
Miscellaneous	55	95.5	249	90.5	756	90.6
Entire manufacturing[d]	770	95.8	943	89.6	643	94.1

[a] The MES is determined at the two digit level. This mean is computed as a weighted mean of the MES values from the three digit industries.

[b] Source-*Production Statistics*, collected by the Department of Manufacturing and Construction of Statistics Netherlands.

[c] Source – Audretsch and Yamawaki (1992).

[d] Not weighted.

employees associated with the MES firm. However, the employee measure is biased because it neglects the amount of capital input required to attain the MES. Thus, the MES tends to be understated in a highly capital-intensive industry and overstated in industries where the capital-labor ratio is relatively low. The limitations inherent in each of these measures explain why the rank order of industries according to the MES measured in terms of value-of-shipments does not exactly correspond to the rank order when the MES is measured in terms of employment.

There are at least four major reasons why the MES for any given industry should vary between nations. *First*, not all countries may be at the technological, management, and production frontier. *Second*, even if all three nations are at the technological frontier, variations in relative factor input prices will result in differences in the observed MES. *Third*, the aggregation of various productive activities under the umbrella of an encompassing industry classification will result in differences in the measured MES between the two countries, if the composition of various productive activities in the industry varies between nations. This is probably the explanation for the considerably greater MES measured in the American and Japanese transportation equipment sectors than in the Dutch transportation equipment sector. While considerable assembly production is included in the United States and Japan, the bulk of economic activity within this sector in the Netherlands involves the production of parts. *Fourth*, differences in domestic vertical and horizontal relationships as well as managerial techniques may result in variations in the computed MES across nations. For example, as Loveman and Sengenberger (1991) and Aoki (1988) point out, formal and informal subcontracting relationships are much more prevalent in Japanese manufacturing than in the United States or Western Europe. To the extent that Japanese plants tend to be less vertically integrated, the computed MES for a given Japanese industry will tend to be less than that for its American or Dutch counterpart. These four factors probably account for a considerable amount of the differentials in the aggregated mean MES for broad industrial sectors among the United States and Japan, which are shown in Table 1.

One common tendency exhibited in the Netherlands, as well as in the United States and Japan, is that the share of firms accounted for by sub-optimal scale firms is remarkably high. In all three countries the bulk of firms can be classified not only as being small, but as being so small that they can be classified as sub-optimal, at least according to the traditional definition found in the industrial organization literature.

3. Compensating factor differentials

The lower productivity associated with small firms displayed Tables 1 and 2 raises a question which has never been answered in the industrial organization literature: 'How are plants able to survive if they are operating at a scale that is

D.B. Audretsch et al. / Int. J. Ind. Organ. 19 (2001) 795–821   803

sub-optimal, in that their level of production is less than the MES level of output?' While it is true that small and new firms often resort to a strategy of filling a small product niche[5], or else serve as a supplier of parts to a larger downstream producer within the same industry, the systematically lower propensity of such new and small firms to survive confirms that they are confronted with at least some type of size disadvantage. And this size disadvantage should increase as the extent of scale economies in the industry increases.

That is, one reaction to the question of how sub-optimal firms manage to survive is that they do not, at least not with the same likelihood as larger firms (Baldwin and Rafiquzzaman, 1995; Mata, 1995). As previously mentioned, a growing and impressive literature has confirmed across a wide spectrum of countries, time periods and industries the existence of a positive relationship between the likelihood of survival and firm size. Similarly, those smaller firms surviving in the long run have been found to experience higher growth rates than their larger counterparts, so that presumably more than a few of them attain or at least approach the MES level of output. That is, small firms tend also to be young firms. The results of this literature clearly show that, while the probability of a young and small firm surviving is lower than that of a larger and more experienced firm, the growth rate of those young small firms that do survive tends to be greater than that of older and larger firms (Dunne et al., 1988, 1989).

Still, until smaller scale firms grow sufficiently to attain or at least approach the MES level of output, the question of how they manage to stay viable remains. The observation made by Brown and Medoff (1989) and Brown et al. (1990) that employee compensation tends to be systematically lower in small firms than in large ones provides at least on explanation.[6] Through providing a lower level of employee compensation than that provided by their larger counterparts, smaller scale plants can effectively offset their inherent cost disadvantages.[7] To the degree that sub-optimal scale firms are able to reduce the level of employee compensation

---

[5] Bradburd and Ross (1989).

[6] Similar results have been found by Oosterbeek and van Praag (1995) for the Netherlands. Teulings and Hartog (1998) conclude that the firm size effect is smaller in the Netherlands than in the US. For the Netherlands they obtain firm size elasticities of wages between 0.006 and 0.02, whereas Brown and Medoff (1989) obtain an elasticity of 0.03 for the US.

[7] An example of the strategy of compensating factor differentials is provided by the *Wall Street Journal* (1991, p. 1), which reports that 'Wall Street has been in love with Nucor Corp.', which has become the seventh largest steel company in the United States through its fifteen *mini-mill* plants. Nucor has pursued a strategy not only of '. . . declaring war on corporate hierarchy', but also by being '. . .terribly efficient, aggressively non-union and quite profitable. Most of its 15 mini-mills and steel fabrication operations are situated in small towns, where they have trained all sorts of people who never thought they'd make so much money. And Nucor has developed a revolutionary new plant that spins gleaming sheet steel out of scrapped cars and refrigerators.' In the case of Nucor, compensating factor differentials also apparently include the health and safety of the employees: 'Its worker death rate since 1980 is the highest in the steel industry . . . Nucor is a highly decentralized company with little corporate structure. It doesn't have a corporate safety director or uniform training programs, leaving safety up to plant managers.' One employee reports, ' If something's not right, and you can fix it in a half hour the wrong way and two hours the right way, you take the shorter way.'

below that paid by optimal-sized plants, the average cost will be correspondingly lower. Should the sub-optimal firm succeed in reducing employee compensation to a sufficient degree, it can actually lower its average cost to that faced by the larger firms, at which point it will be viable and able to survive in the long run.

Table 3 shows that sub-optimal firms do experience a considerable productivity disadvantage. Productivity is measured here as value added divided by employment. The productivity differential tends to be the greatest in those industrial sectors exhibiting the largest MES in Tables 1 and 2. Not only is the productivity the greatest in the Dutch industry exhibiting the largest computed MES-chemicals – but the gap between the optimal and sub-optimal firms is also the largest, where the large firms are nearly twice as productive as their smaller counterparts. By contrast, in industries with a very low computed MES, such as apparel, lumber, and furniture, the productivity gap between the optimal and sub-optimal plants is virtually non-existent. As might be expected, given the relatively high wage rate and other institutional rigidities in the Netherlands, the productivity gap between the optimal and sub-optimal firms is lower in the Netherlands than in either the United States or in Japan.

Table 3
Productivity ($) in optimal and sub-optimal plants for Dutch, US and Japanese manufacturing sectors, 1991

Industry	Netherlands[a] ($)		US[b] ($)		Japan[b] ($)	
	Optimal	Sub-optimal	Optimal	Sub-optimal	Optimal	Sub-optimal
Food	58.520	43.401	88.062	72.246	77.434	40.794
Textiles	63.470	45.232	36.237	36.847	43.599	36.392
Apparel	63.470	44.122	30.539	32.301	25.708	25.137
Lumber	43.835	47.175	39.207	33.005	47.150	35.374
Furniture	47.410	44.566	42.443	39.815	54.827	36.347
Paper	73.975	56.943	95.593	60.120	88.248	51.276
Printing	58.190	51.781	69.493	47.546	130.052	51.827
Chemicals	115.170	63.159	132.931	111.146	164.983	126.730
Rubber	61.820	50.283	61.068	48.055	79.470	44.093
Leather	51.205	47.341	34.315	31.438	41.682	36.897
Stone clay and glass	62.150	57.331	66.876	52.925	82.809	53.948
Primary metals	50.105	57.553	57.791	51.649	115.003	72.168
Fabricated metal products	57.750	49.228	62.651	48.873	72.674	46.977
Machinery (non-electric)	55.385	48.618	76.028	53.948	96.561	57.101
Electrical equipment	60.115	48.510	69.446	52.655	102.205	41.338
Transportation equipment	46.695	46.509	82.884	64.810	103.497	53.160
Instruments	40.755	58.330	91.200	61.194	64.289	42.408
Miscelleneous	49.885	51.060	57.092	40.840	61.549	41.749
Entire manufacturing[c]	58.882	50.618	66.325	52.189	80.652	49.650

[a] Source-*Production Statistics*, collected by the Department of Manufacturing and Construction of Statistics Netherlands.
[b] Source – Audretsch and Yamawaki (1992).
[c] Not weighted.

D.B. Audretsch et al. / Int. J. Ind. Organ. 19 (2001) 795–821   805

Table 4 confirms that employee compensation is lower in sub-optimal plants than in optimal plants in the Netherlands, as well as in the United States and in Japan. The differential in employee compensation generally reflects the differentials in productivity shown in Table 3. Thus, the Dutch sector exhibiting the greatest differential in productivity, chemicals, also exhibits the largest differential in labor compensation between optimal and sub-optimal scale firms. By contrast, in the sectors where there are virtually no differences in productivity between sub-optimal and optimal, such as apparel and furniture, there is also no difference in employee compensation.

Table 5 shows that the productivity gap between optimal and sub-optimal scale firms is the largest in Japan, second largest in the United States and the smallest in the Netherlands. At the same time, the gap in employment compensation between the optimal and sub-optimal scale firms is the greatest in Japan and virtually identical in the United States and the Netherlands.

Table 4

Employee compensation ($) in optimal and sub-optimal plants for Dutch, US and Japanese manufacturing sectors, 1991

Industry	Netherlands[a] ($)		US[b] ($)		Japan[b] ($)	
	Optimal	Sub-optimal	Optimal	Sub-optimal	Optimal	Sub-optimal
Food	36.241	22.755	25.852	21.666	23.406	17.754
Textiles	38.905	29.304	17.791	20.234	21.067	15.475
Apparel	23.143	28.305	14.290	14.741	14.192	12.522
Lumber	34.798	29.970	22.410	16.050	22.379	17.399
Furniture	32.301	26.917	20.109	18.913	23.271	18.821
Paper	41.458	33.133	34.306	26.046	33.940	22.253
Printing	40.404	32.689	27.253	21.884	46.262	25.631
Chemicals	48.285	36.852	36.437	28.896	39.221	32.176
Rubber	36.019	30.525	25.849	20.766	33.976	21.397
Leather	35.409	29.914	15.720	15.407	20.174	16.621
Stone clay and glass	37.795	31.690	29.129	23.359	30.029	21.253
Primary metals	39.904	34.077	39.448	27.659	40.176	30.308
Fabricated metal products	35.464	30.802	29.512	24.239	29.643	22.914
Machinery (non-electric)	37.018	32.745	32.931	27.032	37.363	27.227
Electrical equipment	38.940	30.635	31.823	23.511	32.654	19.968
Transportation equipment	35.131	29.692	40.385	30.416	38.046	27.018
Instruments	30.691	32.190	32.798	25.453	30.834	21.754
Miscellaneous	30.414	29.026	21.612	19.140	24.775	18.709
Entire manufacturing[c]	36.239	30.622	27.647	22.522	30.078	21.622

[a] Source-*Production Statistics*, collected by the Department of Manufacturing and Construction of Statistics Netherlands.

[b] Source – Audretsch and Yamawaki (1992).

[c] Not weighted.

Table 5
Productivity disadvantage and employee compensation advantage confronting optimal and sub-optimal jplants for Dutch, US and Japanese manufacturing sectors, 1991

Industry	Netherlands[a]		US[b]		Japan[b]	
	Productivity: sub-optimal/ optimal	Compensation: sub-optimal/ optimal	Productivity: sub-optimal/ optimal	Compensation: sub-optimal/ optimal	Productivity: sub-optimal/ optimal	Compensation: sub-optimal/ optimal
Food	0.73	0.63	0.82	0.84	0.53	0.69
Textiles	0.71	0.75	1.02	1.00	0.84	0.74
Apparel	0.69	1.22	1.06	1.03	0.98	0.88
Lumber	1.07	0.86	0.84	0.72	0.75	0.78
Furniture	0.93	0.83	0.94	0.94	0.66	0.81
Paper	0.76	0.80	0.63	0.76	0.58	0.66
Printing	0.88	0.81	0.68	0.80	0.40	0.55
Chemicals	0.54	0.76	0.84	0.79	0.77	0.82
Rubber	0.81	0.85	0.79	0.80	0.56	0.63
Leather	0.92	0.84	0.92	0.98	0.89	0.82
Stone clay and glass	0.91	0.84	0.79	0.80	0.65	0.71
Primary metals	1.14	0.85	0.89	0.70	0.64	0.75
Fabricated metal products	0.84	0.87	0.78	0.82	0.65	0.77
Machinery (non-electric)	0.87	0.88	0.71	0.82	0.59	0.73
Electrical equipment	0.87	0.78	0.76	0.74	0.41	0.61
Transportation equipment	0.99	0.85	0.78	0.75	0.51	0.71
Instruments	1.09	0.79	0.67	0.78	0.66	0.71
Miscellaneous	1.01	0.95	0.72	0.89	0.68	0.76
Entire manufacturing[c]	0.88	0.84	0.81	0.83	0.65	0.73

[a] Source – Production Statistics, collected by the Department of Manufacturing and Construction of Statistics Netherlands.
[b] Source – Audretsch and Yamawaki (1991).
[c] Not weighted.

D.B. Audretsch et al. / Int. J. Ind. Organ. 19 (2001) 795–821   807

As Tables 4 and 5 indicate, there is considerable evidence suggesting that a sub-optimal scale firm can exist by compensating for its inherent size disadvantages through deviating from the manner in which factor inputs are paid. As Brown et al. (1990) point out, smaller firms may be able to avoid labor rigidities imposed by unions and therefore subject employees to longer working hours. Similarly, a strategy of compensating factor differentials may be reflected in differing managerial organizations and methods of production. For example, as a result of their small size, sub-optimal plants may require less of a vertical hierarchy than their larger optimal counterparts, thereby reducing the amount of white-collar overhead cost. Carlsson arid Taymaz (1994) and Dosi (1988) have argued that small establishments are more adept at implementing flexible methods of production than larger plants, which are more likely to be burdened with rigid work rules. Caves and Pugel (1980) and Audretsch (1995) found evidence that small firms can offset their inherent size disadvantage through pursuing a strategy of product innovation and deploying factor inputs differently than their larger counterparts.

An important insight of Caves et al. (1975) was that the extent to which sub-optimal sized establishments are encumbered with an inherent cost disadvantage is determined not only by the extent to which the MES level of output is in excess of a sub-optimal plant output level, but also by the slope of the long-run average cost curve over the sub-optimal scale range. In fact, they introduced the *cost disadvantage ratio*, which they defined as average value-added per employee in establishments providing the lowest 50% of industry value-added, divided by the mean value-added per employee in establishments supplying the top half. The greater the computed cost disadvantage ratio, the greater will be the slope of the long-run average cost function in an industry. This suggests that in order for a sub-optimal firm to be viable, for any given size, the compensating differentials in terms of employee compensation, must be sufficiently greater to offset the greater cost disadvantage associated with a steeper long-run average cost curve.

Thus, the extent to which a sub-optimal scale firm shipping an output with a value of $VSHIP_{SO}$ falls short of the equivalent value-of-shipments corresponding to the MES level of output, or, $VSHIP_O$, will determine the degree to which the firm must compensate for its productivity disadvantage, by reducing its labor costs and deploying its resources differently from that practiced in optimal-sized firms, so that

$$VSHIP_{so} - VSHIP_o = \alpha_o + \alpha_l(W_{so} - W_o) + \sum_{i=1,I} \alpha_{2\,i}\,(F_{so} - F_o) + \alpha_3(VA_{so} - VA_o)$$

$$+ \sum_{i=1,J} \alpha_{4j}\,K_j + \mu_l \tag{1}$$

where W_{SO} and W_O represent the employee compensation in sub-optimal and optimal firms, F_{SO} and F_O represent the use of factor and managerial practices i in sub-optimal and optimal firms[8], and VA_{SO} and VA_O refer to the value-added per employee in sub-optimal and optimal firms. Finally, K refers to the j industry-specific characteristics influencing the extent to which sub-optimal firms must compensate for their cost disadvantages in order to be viable.

Eq. (1) can be most easily interpreted as identifying the extent to which wages must be lowered and factors deployed differently, such as investment strategy, in order for a sub-optimal firm of a given size to compensate for its size-induced productivity disadvantage. Three different phenomena determine the extent to which the payment of factors and their deployment must compensate for the inherent size disadvantage. The *first* is the degree to which the MES level of output exceeds that of the sub-optimal firm. The greater this difference becomes, the more wages must be reduced, and the greater is the extent to which other non-wage compensatory strategies must be deployed. That is, as the degree to which a firm is sub-optimal increases, the more a firm must compensate for its size-induced cost disadvantages. *Second,* for a given extent to which the MES level of output exceeds that of a sub-optimal firm, a greater slope of the long-run average cost function (negatively) causes an increases in the extent to which a strategy of compensating differentials must be deployed. *Finally,* certain industry-specific characteristics will presumably reduce or increase the extent to which a sub-optimal scale firm must compensate for a disadvantage of any given magnitude. For example, to the extent that the market price is elevated above long-run average costs, the need for a sub-optimal scale firm to compensate will be that much less.[9] More specifically, Bradburd and Caves (1982) have shown that high industry growth is associated with higher industry profitability and therefore presumably higher prices.

Audretsch (1995) and Caves and Pugel (1980) provide evidence that pursuing a strategy of product innovation is one mechanism that small and presumably sub-optimal businesses can deploy to compensate for size-induced disadvantages. However, an important conclusion of Audretsch (1995) is that the relative innovative advantage of small firms vis-à-vis their larger and more established counterparts is anything but constant across industries. Thus, the extent to which small firms need to compensate for their size disadvantages may be reduced somewhat in industries where small-firm innovative activity is particularly high.

A particular econometric challenge posed in estimating Eq. 1 is that, as Brown and Medoff's (1989) work makes clear, the gap in employee compensation between sub-optimal scale and optimal scale firms is largely determined by the size difference between the sub-optimal scale firm size and the MES level of output (Doms et al., 1997; Dunne and Schmitz, 1995; Troske, 1999). Similarly,

---

[8] These practices include the investment rate, advertising intensity, human resource management, etc.

[9] As Weiss (1976, p. 127) argues, to the degree that a certain market structure, '. . . results in prices above minimum long-run average cost, sub-optimal plants would be protected in the long run, especially if their cost disadvantages were mild.'

D.B. Audretsch et al. / Int. J. Ind. Organ. 19 (2001) 795–821   809

differentials in value-added-per employee between firms within an industry are determined, to a considerable extent, by differences in firm size. This suggests that, Eq. (1) must be estimated within the context of a simultaneous-three-equations-model, where the differences in value-added-per employee and employee compensation between sub-optimal and optimal scale firms, as well as the size differential, are endogenous variables.

Assuming linearity we obtain the following equation:

$$W_{so} - W_o = \beta_0 + \beta_1(VSHIP_{so} - VSHIP_o) + \beta_2(VA_{so} - VA_o) + \beta_3 AGE + \beta_4 ULAB + \mu_2 \tag{2}$$

where the additional variable AGE is the age of the firm and ULAB is an industry level measure for the amount of unskilled labor. The gap between optimal firm and sub-optimal firm employee compensation is estimated as being determined by the differentials in firm size and value-added per employee, along with the age of the firm and the share of the labor force accounted for by unskilled labor in the industry in which the firm is operating. Since it is more difficult to implement a strategy of compensating wage differentials for skilled than for unskilled labor it would be expected that the share of the labor force accounted for by unskilled labor should have a negative impact on the gap in employment compensation between sub-optimal and optimal scale firms.

Assuming linearity we obtain the third equation:

$$VA_{so} - VA_o = \delta_0 + \delta_1(VSHIP_{so} - VSHIP_o) + \delta_2(INV_{so} - INV_o) + \delta_3 AGE + \mu_3 \tag{3}$$

where the additional variable INV is a firm-level variable measuring the level of investment. The differential in value-added per employee, or productivity, between optimal and sub-optimal scale firms is estimated as being determined not only by the differential in firm size, but also by the differential investment activity, as well as the age of the firm. That is, a difference in plant size of a given amount will presumably result in a greater difference in value-added per employee when the differential in investment activity is also large.

4. Empirical results

4.1. Size differential

To estimate Eq. (1) and test the hypothesis that sub-optimal scale firms offset, at least to some extent, their size inherent disadvantages by deviating from the manner that larger firms deploy and compensate labor, the dependent variable, $VSHIP_{so} - VSHIP_o$, is formed by subtracting the value-of-shipment for 7716 firms from the computed value of VS_{MES} for the relevant three-digit industry. Employee compensation is measured as total employee wages plus non-wage compensation, including social security taxes paid by the firm, divided by the number of employees in that firm, for 1991. The difference in employee compensation between sub-optimal and optimal scale firms is then formed by subtracting the *employee compensation* of the MES sized firms from that of each sub-optimal firm. Thus, the gap in employee compensation is measured in terms of a negative number, so that a positive coefficient is expected indicating that a sub-optimal scale firm can compensate, at least partially, for its size-induced disadvantages by reducing workers wages and salaries below that paid by optimal sized firms.

The *productivity differential* between sub-optimal scale firms and firms having attained the MES level of output is analogously measured as the difference in the value-added-per employee, defined as manufacturing value added (in thousands of Dutch guilders) divided by the number of employees. A negative coefficient is expected and would reflect the need for differential strategies to be deployed by sub-optimal scale firms to compensate for a productivity disadvantage. That is, as the productivity disadvantage increases for a given sub-optimal firm size, a negative coefficient of this variable will contribute to determining the extent to which employee compensation must be reduced.

In addition, differences in *investment activity* are also included. Investment activity is proxied in terms of the depreciation costs associated with the cumulative stock of capital (in terms of thousands of Dutch guilders), divided by the number of employees in 1991. A negative coefficient of the differential between depreciated cumulative capital expenditures would suggest that sub-optimal firms resort to a strategy of higher capital investment to offset their size disadvantages.

As explained in the previous section, in addition to the above variables, which are specific to a particular firm, several industry-specific characteristics are also hypothesized to influence the extent to which sub-optimal scale firms engage in compensatory strategies to offset their size-induced disadvantages. *Market growth* is measured as the mean percentage growth of sales in each three-digit industry between 1985–1990. It is expected that a strategy of compensatory differentials is less important in industries experiencing high growth than in those industries growing more slowly. Finally, the degree to which small firms tend to have the *innovative advantage* over their larger counterparts is represented by a measure of the small-firm innovative advantage. The small-firm innovative advantage is measured as the mean R&D intensity of firms with fewer than 100 employees divided by the mean R&D intensity of all firms. The R&D intensity is measured as the total number of employees in the relevant three-digit industry occupied with R&D for the company, including formal, informal and external R&D, divided by total employment. A negative coefficient of the small-firm innovative advantage would indicate that in industries where the small firms tend to have the relative innovative advantage, less of a compensatory strategy is needed by sub-optimal firms to offset any given size disadvantages. A brief description and summary of all variables estimated in the three-equation model can be found in Table 6.

Table 6
Description of all variables

Firm levels	
Age	Number of months that a company is registered with the Central Statistics Office Netherlands. Registration began in 1967. A company changing core business will be registered as a new company in the new industry, 1991.
Investment	Depreciation costs (in Fl. 1000) of cumulative lagged investments (capital stock), divided by the number of employees, 1991.
Compensation	Total amount the employer has to compensate employees divided by total number of employees. This includes social security taxes and benefits paid to the government, 1991.paid to the government, 1991.
Employees	Number of employees, 1991.
Productivity	Value added (in Fl. 1000) divided by the number of employees, 1991.
Sales	Value of the total amounts of goods sold (in Fl. 1000), 1991.
Size difference	Sales of the sub-optimal firm minus the MES (sales), 1991.
Size difference scaled by MES	Sales of the sub-optimal firm minus the MES (sales) divided by the MES (%), 1991.
Industry levels	
MES	Mean sales (in Fl. 1000) of the largest companies in the industry, which have aggregate sales accounting for half of the total sales in the 3-digit industry. Three-digit industry variable, 1991.
Market growth	Mean market growth, measured as mean percentage growth of sales, 1985–1990. Three-digit industry variable.
Small firm innovative advantage	Mean R&D intensity of small firms ($< = 100$ employees) divided by mean R&D intensity of all firms. R&D intensity is measured as total number of employees involved in R&D for the company (formal, informal and external R&D) divided by total employment. Three-digit industry variable, 1988.
Unskilled labor	Total amount of blue-collar workers in a two-digit industry divided by then number of white-collar employees, 1987. Two-digit industry variable, 1987.

Based on the 7718 firms for which full records and compatible industry-specific variables are available, Eq. 1 is estimated first using the method of ordinary least squares (OLS), and the results are shown in the first column of Table 7. In fact, the coefficients of the compensation differential, productivity differential, market growth, and small-firm innovative advantage are all counter-intuitive. Of course, the OLS estimation treats the compensation and productivity differentials as if they were exogenous from the firm size differential (that is the differential between each firm and the computed MES in the relevant industry), which, as stressed in the previous section, is not a realistic assumption. Thus, in the two-stage least squares estimation (2SLS), both the compensation differential and the productivity differential are included as endogenous variables in a system of simultaneous equations. The actual estimates for the compensation differential and productivity differential will be examined in Sections 4.2 and 4.3. Under the 2SLS estimation the coefficient of the compensation differential becomes positive and statistically

Table 7
Regression results for differences between sub-optimal and optimal firm size, Eq. (1) (*t*-statistics in parentheses)[a]

	Unscaled[b]		Scaled by MES		Hypotheses Expected signs
	OLS	2SLS	Not corrected for hetero-skedasticity 2SLS	Corrected for hetero-skedasticity 2SLS	
Compensation	−0.458*	4.89*	0.539**	2.84**	+
Difference	(−1.96)	(2.13)	(3.96)	(13.3)	
Productivity	1.38**	−8.70**	0.165*	−0.560**	−
Difference	(13.3)	(−7.12)	(2.28)	(−9.49)	
Investment	−1.42**	16.5**	−0.307**	0.727**	−
Difference	(−3.89)	(7.26)	(−2.70)	(8.40)	
Market	27.6**	12.9**	0.631**	−2.419**	−
Growth	(16.4)	(4.15)	(4.00)	(−12.0)	
Small firm	23.6**	0.67	0.055	−4.39**	−
Innovation advantage	(6.99)	(0.11)	(0.20)	(−9.70)	
Sample size	7716	7716	7716	7716	
R^2	0.27	0.14	0.04	0.24	
F-value	125.94	54.14	15.12	102.83	

[a] Dummies for each 2-digit sector were used to compensate for differences between industries. These replace the intercept and are not reported for presentation purposes. The first two columns are divided by 1000 for presentation purposes.

[b] The regressions are weighted by the sample proportion.

*, Statistically significant for 95% level of confidence, two-tailed test.

**, Statistically significant for 99% level of confidence, two-tailed test.

significant, suggesting that the ability to reduce employee compensation facilitates the viability of smaller scale firms. Computing the elasticity at the mean shows that as the compensation gap shrinks by 1%, the firm will have to increase its size by 0.56% in order to maintain viability.

Similarly, under the 2SLS estimation the coefficient of the productivity differential becomes negative, implying that an increase in the productivity gap will force sub-optimal firms of any size to resort to a more intensive strategy of compensating factor differentials in order to compensate for the greater cost disadvantage. Or alternatively, it suggests that given a certain degree of compensating factor differentials, the size of any sub-optimal firm will have to increase as the productivity gap increases to maintain viability. Computing the elasticity at the mean suggests that as the productivity gap decreases by 1%, the size gap can correspondingly increase by a maximum of 1.09% for the firm to maintain its viability.

The positive and statistically significant coefficient of the investment differential suggests that smaller firms cannot compensate for size-inherent disadvantages by raising their investment intensities, relative to that of their larger counterparts. Perhaps production requires some minimum investment in capital goods. This suggests that capital goods requirements are a disadvantage to small firms. On the other hand, the positive and statistically significant coefficient of market growth suggests that the extent of a compensatory differential strategy for any firm needs to actually be greater in high growing markets than in more slowly or declining markets. Stated alternatively, given any degree of compensating factor differentials, as market growth increases, the size of a (sub-optimal) firm also needs to increase in order to maintain viability. Finally, the coefficient of the small-firm innovative advantage can not be considered to be statistically significant.

An alternative specification of Eq. (1) is to scale the difference between the size of a firm and the size associated with the MES level of output by MES. The advantage of scaling is that the dependent variables become measured free of dimensions in the same manner as all exogenous variables. In this case, the dependent variable to be estimated becomes $(VSHIP_{so} - VSHIP_o)/VSHIP_o$. However, this measure of the *relative* size gap is likely to suffer from heteroskedasticity, since the error term tends to be systematically larger as the relative size gap increases and thus the estimates need to be corrected for heteroskedasticity.[10] Estimation results of the scaled version of Eq. 1 can be found in the last two columns of Table 7.

In fact, as the final column of Table 7 indicates, the 2SLS estimation of the relative size gap, corrected for heteroskedasticity, produces coefficients for the *firm level* variables that are consistent with the unscaled 2SLS estimation. Both *industry level* variables show a change of sign and now show signs in accordance with the hypotheses. The coefficient of market growth is negative and statistically significant. This suggests that less of a strategy of compensating factor differentials is required in industries growing rapidly. The coefficient of the small-firm innovative advantage also becomes negative and statistically significant implying that less of a strategy of compensating factor differentials is required to maintain firm viability in industries where small firms have the innovative advantage. The observation that only the effect of industry level variables changes indicates that some industries have dominated the estimation results in the first three columns, because of a systematically greater residual variance.

4.2. Employee compensation differential

The estimated model for the differences in the employment compensation between optimal and sub-optimal firms is shown in Table 8. The differential in employment compensation between optimal and sub-optimal firms is estimated by

---

[10] Presence of heteroskedasticity was tested using the Breusch Pagan test statistic. The statistic took on a value of 175, far above 15.09, which is the 99th Percentile of the Chi-Square distribution with five degrees of freedom. Hence, the null hypothesis of constant variance is rejected at a 1% significance level.

Table 8
Regression results for differences in employment compensation between sub-optimal and optimal firms, Eq. (2) (*t*-statistics in parentheses)[a]

	Size difference unscaled[b] OLS	2SLS	Size difference scaled by MES 2SLS
Size difference	−0.00070	0.0073*	0.36**
	(−1.28)	(2.23)	(4.08)
Productivity difference	156**	97.2**	0.10**
	(38.8)	(12.35)	(12.4)
Age	23.1**	21.6**	0.011**
	(12.9)	(11.5)	(4.91)
Unskilled	−7660**	−8520**	−6.49**
Labor	(−6.02)	(−6.09)	(−5.70)
Sample size	7716	7716	7716
R^2	0.28	0.17	0.13
F-value	133.84	69.23	51.65

[a] Dummies for each 2-digit sector were used to compensate for differences between industries. These replace the intercept and are not reported for presentation purposes. The first two columns are multiplied by 1000 for presentation purposes.

[b] The regressions are weighted by the sample proportion.

*, Statistically significant for 95% level of confidence, two-tailed test.

**, Statistically significant for 99% level of confidence, two-tailed test.

the size differential [the dependent variable of Eq. (1)], the productivity differential, the age of the firm and the share of the labor force accounted for by unskilled labor, measured in 1987.[11] Based on the 2SLS estimation the results are qualitatively identical for both the unscaled compensation differential as well as the scaled differential. The positive and statistically significant coefficient of the size differential suggests that as the gap in firm size increases so does the gap in employee compensation.

Similarly, the positive and statistically significant coefficient for the productivity differential suggests that as the differential in productivity increases, holding the difference in firm size constant, the gap in the employment compensation between the optimal and sub-optimal firms also increases correspondingly. The negative and statistically significant coefficient of unskilled labor suggests that as the share of unskilled labor in the industry labor force increases, the compensation gap tends to increase. This suggests that a strategy of compensatory factor differentials is easier to implement in an industry where unskilled labor plays a more important role than in an industry where skilled labor plays a more important role.

The positive and statistically significant coefficient of the age of the firm

---

[11] The share of the labor force accounted for by unskilled labor is measured at the level of two-digit industries and repeated across common three-digit industries.

suggests that the compensation gap between the sub-optimal and optimal sized firms tends to fall as a firm matures, holding constant the size of that firm. This may reflect the propensity for firms to substitute a higher level of human capital and skilled labor as it matures over time and its prospects for longer-term survival improve. Alternatively, it may indicate that the ability for firms to suppress employee compensation below that of their larger and more established counterparts tends to deteriorate over time. A third potential explanation is that the impact of firm age on the compensation gap may be due to the fact that on average younger firms have younger employees. As the firm matures, also the age (and experience) of the average worker increases. In any case an increase in firm age by one year will increase employee compensation by $143. Alternatively, computing the elasticity at the mean suggests that an increase in firm age of 1% will lead to a decrease in compensation gap by 0.38%.

4.3. Productivity differential

The productivity differential between sub-optimal and optimal firms is estimated by the size differential, the degree of capital investment, and firm age. The results are presented in Table 9. The positive and statistically significant coefficient of the size difference in the OLS estimation suggests that as the gap between the size of a particular firm and that associated with a firm operating at the MES level of output increases, the productivity gap also increases. Surprisingly, this coefficient becomes reversed under the 2SLS estimation, both scaled and unscaled. The

Table 9
Regression results for differences in productivity between sub-optimal and optimal firms, Eq. (3) (*t*-statistics in parentheses)[a]*

| | Size difference unscaled[b] | | Size difference scaled by MES 2SLS |
	OLS	2SLS	
Size difference	0.023**	−0.014	−3.17**
	(16.8)	(−1.70)	(−5.90)
Investment	2120**	3100**	4.13**
Difference	(43.6)	(44.4)	(22.6)
Age	14.4**	31**	0.092**
	(3.15)	(6.11)	(6.89)
Sample size	7716	7716	7716
R^2	0.30	0.28	0.11
F-value	156	144.21	46.53

[a] Dummies for each 2-digit sector were used to compensate for differences between industries. These replace the intercept and are not reported for presentation purposes. The first two columns are multiplied by 1000 for presentation purposes.

[b] The regressions are weighted by the sample proportion.

*, Statistically significant for 95% level of confidence, two-tailed test.

**, Statistically significant for 99% level of confidence, two-tailed test.

positive and statistically significant coefficient of the investment differential suggests that by reducing the gap in investment per worker, a small firm can also reduce the productivity gap.

The positive and statistically significant coefficient of firm age suggests that, holding the firm size and investment intensity constant, as firms mature the productivity gap tends to decrease. This result is consistent with the finding from Table 8 suggesting that the compensation differential also tends to decrease as firms mature over time. An increase of one year in the life of a firm leads to an increase of productivity of $205 per worker. Alternatively, computing the elasticity at the mean yields a decrease in the productivity gap of 0.50% associated with a 1% increase in the age of the firm.

As previously mentioned, the positive influence of firm age on productivity may reflect the propensity for new firms to substitute skilled for unskilled labor as they mature, or alternatively, for firms to take advantage of *learning by doing* and *experience* to achieve greater productivity. In either case, the result is a clear association between the age of a firm and its levels of productivity and employee compensation, even after controlling firm size and investment.

4.4. Decomposing surviving and exiting firms

One of the concerns about comparing the wage and productivity performance to firm size is that at any one point in time, each size cohort consists of unsuccessful firms, in that they will ultimately fail, as well as successful ones, in that they will survive over an extended period. A result found repeatedly across a wide spectrum of nations (Evans, 1987; Hall, 1987; Audretsch, 1991; Audretsch and Mahmood, 1995; Wagner, 1996 and Mata, 1996) is that the likelihood of survival tends to increase systematically with firm size and firm age. These results suggest that cohorts of smaller firms, which also tend to be younger firms, will systematically include a greater share of firms that will ultimately fail than do the larger firm size classes. Presumably it is those firms which are the least productive and forced to compensate employees at lower levels that ultimately exit out of the industry.

Therefore, the inclusion of such firms which ultimately exit results in the estimation of a smaller mean productivity and employee compensation associated with the smaller firm size classes than would have been calculated had only surviving firms been included. It is conceivable that the observed relationships between firm size, employee compensation and productivity are simply attributable to the greater presence of inefficient firms within the smaller firm-size classes. This would suggest that the observed relationships are less the result of a strategy of compensating factor differentials being deployed by sub-optimal firms and more the result of including a higher proportion of unsuccessful firms in the cohorts containing the smaller firms.

To shed at least some light on distinguishing between the compositional effect from the strategy of factor compensation differentials, firms in existence in 1980

Table 10
Productivity and employee compensation for 1991 survivors and exiting firms (standard deviation in parentheses)

Size class (employees)	Number of observations		Productivity ($), 1980			Employee Compensation ($), 1980		
	Firms surviving until 1991	Firms exiting the industry	Firms surviving until 1991	Firms exiting the industry	t-value of difference	Firms surviving until 1991	Firms exiting the industry	t-value of difference
10–20	1276	1848	28.809 (12.251)	25.000 (11.442)	8.8	20.773 (5.040)	19.969 (5.759)	4.1
20–50	1608	1419	28.763 (36.286)	24.763 (12.140)	4.2	20.814 (4.332)	20.331 (4.975)	2.8
50–100	780	591	28.753 (11.683)	25.492 (12.357)	5.0	21.080 (3.859)	20.713 (5.256)	1.4
100–200	423	290	29.874 (14.407)	27.934 (24.241)	1.2	21.869 (3.789)	21.698 (4.181)	0.6
200–500	247	202	29.281 (9.929)	27.381 (15.171)	1.5	22.341 (3.628)	23.778 (13.367)	-1.5
500+	134	88	33.834 (16.603)	27.562 (11.920)	3.3	24.557 (3.895)	23.788 (3.457)	1.5
10+[a]	4468	4438	29.060 (23.959)	25.341 (13.201)	7.1	21.145 (4.442)	20.547 (5.980)	5.4

[a] Averaged over all firms in the dataset.

are divided into two major cohorts – those firms surviving through 1991 and those no longer in existence as of 1991. In forming and interpreting these two cohorts, two important qualifications must be emphasized. *First*, due to constraints within the Statistics Netherlands, it is not possible to include firms with fewer then ten employees, which is a crucial size class in a study focusing on the link between firm size and a strategy of compensating factor differentials. *Second*, a firm disappears from the files for a number of reasons on addition to simply going out of business. For example, firms acquired or involved in consolidations are recorded as exiting.

Table 10 shows that the likelihood of survival tends to increase along with firm size over the eleven-year period. The 1980 productivity of surviving firms is systematically greater than that for their competitors which exited prior to 1991 for all size classes. At the same time, the gap in mean productivity between smaller and larger firms still remains, even for the exiting firms, although it is considerably greater for the surviving ones. That is, on average the surviving firms are 14.7% more productive than their counterparts that exited. At the same time, the largest surviving firms are 17.4% more productive than the smallest firms. Thus, some of the propensity for smaller firm size classes to exhibit lower productivity levels can be attributed to the inclusion of a higher proportion of firms that will ultimately exit. But at the same time, even after including only surviving firms, the positive relationship between firm size and productivity still remains. And, the productivity gap is greater between the smallest and largest firms than between the surviving and exiting ones within any size class. In fact, it is within the largest firm size class that the productivity gap between surviving and exiting firms is the greatest, both in relative as well as in absolute terms.

The gap in employee compensation is also considerably greater across firm-size classes than within any particular size class. That is, employee compensation by surviving firms is 18.2% greater in the largest firm-size class than in the smallest. However, on average, there is only a 2.91% higher level of employee compensation in surviving firms than in exiting firms. Thus, differentials in employee compensation are far more attributable to firm size than to whether the firm ultimately survives or fails. The tendency for smaller firms to engage in a strategy of compensating factor differentials remains and does not vary greatly within a firm size class. Rather, it is the relatively large variations in employee compensation across firm size classes, for both surviving and exiting firms, that is consistent with the theory of compensating factor differentials.

5. Conclusions

An emerging literature has identified that new and small firms contribute to dynamic competition in at least two ways that are not captured by static competition (Audretsch and Thurik, 1999). The first is that their relatively modest small market shares upon entry tend to increase in subsequent years. The second, and probably more important impact is that new and small firms are a significant source of innovative activity. Policy makers have responded by introducing a broad spectrum of instruments designed to promote dynamic competition in the form of new and small firms (Audretsch and Thurik, 1999). The results of this paper suggest that an important policy instrument of dynamic competition is flexibility in terms of the manner in which factor inputs are deployed and compensated. Public policies and institutions forcing all firms to conform to identical standards in the way that factors are deployed and compensated, in particular labor, eliminate an important strategic instrument of new firms. Flexibility enables small and new firms to deploy a strategy of compensating factor differentials to at least partially offset their inherent size disadvantages. While wage flexibility has generally been debated in the realm of macroeconomic and labor market policies, the results of this paper suggest that it can make an important contribution to dynamic competition policy.

Both Williamson (1968) and Weiss (1991) represented the tradition in industrial organization concluding that the existence of small firms that are sub-optimal within the organization of an industry represented a loss in economic efficiency. More recently Caves and Barton (1990) use productivity frontier analysis to show that small firms are less efficient than their larger counterparts. Weiss (1979, p. 1137) advocated any public policy '. . .creates social gains in the form of less sub-optimal capacity.' Translating this lower efficiency into the impact on the labor market, Brown et al. (1990, pp. 88 and 89) conclude that, 'Workers in large firms earn higher wages, and this fact cannot be explained completely by differences in labor quality, industry, working conditions, or union status. Workers in large firms also enjoy better benefits and greater job security than their counterparts in small firms. When these factors are added together, it appears that workers in large firms do have a superior employment package.'

The policy conclusions by Weiss (1991) and Brown et al. (1990) that new-firm startups should be discouraged are based on a static analysis. However, when viewed through a dynamic lens, a different conclusion emerges. One of the most striking results of this study is the positive impact of firm age on productivity and employee compensation, even after controlling for the size of the firm. Given the strongly confirmed stylized fact linking both firm size and age to a negative rate of growth (that is the smaller and younger a firm is the faster it will grow), this new finding linking firm age to employee compensation and productivity suggests that not only will some of the small and sub-optimal firms of today become the large and optimal firms of tomorrow, but that there is at least a tendency for the low productivity and wage of today to become the high productivity and wage of tomorrow.

Thus, the evidence in this paper suggest that, at least for the case of the Netherlands, not only can policies promoting the startup and viability of new firms be viewed as instruments of competition policy, but that the impact on wages and productivity from such policies is considerably greater in a dynamic context than in a static context.

References

Aoki, M., 1988. Information, Incentives and Bargaining in the Japanese Economy. Cambridge University Press, Cambridge.

Audretsch, D.B., 1991. New-firm survival and the technological regime. Review of Economics and Statistics 60 (3), 441–450.

Audretsch, D.B., 1995. Innovation and industry evolution. MIT Press, Cambridge, MA.

Audretsch, D.B., Mahmood, T., 1995. New firm survival: new results using a hazard function. Review of Economics and Statistics 77, 97–103.

Audretsch, D.B., Thurik, A.R., 1999. Innovation, Industry Evolution and Employment. Cambridge University Press, Cambridge.

Audretsch, D.B., Yamawaki, H., 1992. Sub-optimal scale plants and compensating factor differentials in US and Japanese manufacturing. In: Audretsch, D.B., Seigfried, J.J. (Eds.), Emperical Studies in Industrial Organization: Essays in Honor of Leonard W. Weiss, Kluwer, Boston.

Baldwin, J.R., Rafiquzzaman, M., 1995. Selection versus evolutionary adaption: learning and post-entry performance. International Journal of Industrial Organization 13 (4), 501–522.

Bradburd, R., Caves, R.E., 1982. A closer look at the effect of market growth on industries profits. Review of Economics and Statistics 64 (4), 635–645.

Bradburd, R.M., Ross, D.R., 1989. Can small firms find and defend strategic niches? Review of Economics and Statistics 71, 258–262.

Brown, C., Medoff, J., 1989. The employer size wage effect. Journal of Political Economy 97 (4), 1027–1059.

Brown, C., Hamilton, J., Medoff, J., 1990. Employers Large and Small. Harvard University Press, Cambridge, MA.

Carlsson, B., Taymaz, E., 1994. Flexible technology and industrial structure in the US. Small Business Economics 6 (3), 193–210.

Caves, R.E., Barton, D., 1990. Efficiency in US Manufacturing Industries. MIT Press, Cambridge.

Caves, R.E., Khalilzadeh-Shirazi, J., Porter, M.E., 1975. From entry to mobility barriers. Quarterly Journal of Economics 91, 241–261.

Caves, R.E., Pugel, T.A., 1980. Intra-Industry Differences in Conduct and Performance: Viable Strategies in US Manufacturing Industries. New York University Press, New York.

Cohen, W.M., Klepper, S., 1992. The tradeoff between firm size and diversity in the pursuit of technological progress. Small Business Economics 4 (1), 1–14.

Comanor, W.S., Wilson, T.A., 1967. Advertising, market structure, and performance. Review of Economics and Statistics 9 (4), 423–440.

Dosi, G., 1988. Sources, procedures and microeconomic effects of innovation. Journal of Economic Literature 26 (3), 1120–1171.

Doms, M., Dunne, T., Troski, K.R., 1997. Workers, wages and technology. The Quarterly Journal of Economics 112, 253–290.

Dunne, T., Roberts, M.J., Samuelson, L., 1988. Patterns of firm entry and exit in US manufacturing industries. Rand Journal of Economics 19 (4), 495–515.

Dunne, T., Roberts, M.J., Samuelson, L., 1989. The growth and failure of US manufacturing plants. Quarterly Journal of Economics 104 (4), 671–698.

Dunne, T., Schmitz, Jr. J.A., 1995. Wages, employment structure and employer size-wage premia: their relationship to advanced-technology usage at US manufacturing establishments. Economica 62 (1), 89–108.

EIM, 1998. The European Observatory for SMEs. EIM, Zoetermeer.

Evans, D.S., 1987. Test of alternative theories of firm growth. Journal of Political Economy 95 (4), 657–674.

Geroski, P.A., 1995. What do we know about entry? International Journal of Industrial Organization 13 (4), 421–440.

Hall, B.H., 1987. The relationship between firm size and firm growth in the US manufacturing. Journal of Industrial Economics 35 (2), 583–605.

Jovanovic, B., 1982. Selection and evolution of industry. Econometrica 50 (2), 649–670.

Loveman, G., Sengenberger, W., 1991. The re-emergence of small-scale production: an international perspective. Small Business Economics 3 (1), 1–38.

Mata, J., 1995. Pedro Portugal and Paulo Guimaraes. The survival of new plants: start-up conditions and post-entry evolution. International Journal of Industrial Organization 13 (4), 459–481.

Mata, J., 1996. Small firm births and macroeconomic fluctuations. Review of Industrial Organization 11 (2), 173–182.

Oosterbeek, H., van Praag, M., 1995. Firm size wage differentials in the Netherlands. Small Business Economics 7, 65–74.

Scherer, F.M., Ross, D., 1990. Industrial Market Structure and Economic Performance, 3rd Edition. Houghton Mifflin, Boston.

Teulings, C., Hartog, J., 1998. Corporatism Or Competition. Cambridge University Press, Cambridge.

Troske, K.R., 1999. Evidence on the employer size-wage premium from worker-establishment matched data. Review of Economics and Statistics, 17–25.

Wagner, J., 1996. Firm size, firm age and job duration. Review of Industrial Organization 11 (2), 201–210.

Weiss, L.W., 1991. Structure, Conduct, and Performance. New York University Press, New York.

Weiss, L.W., 1963. Factors in changing Concentration. Review of Economics and Statistics 45 (1), 70–77.

Weiss, L.W., 1976. Optimal plant scale and the extent of suboptimal capacity. In: Masson Robert, T., Qualls, P.D. (Eds.), Essays On Industrial Organization in Honor of Joe S. Bain. Ballinger, Cambridge, MA.

Weiss, L.W., 1979. The structure-conduct-performance paradigm and antitrust. University of Pennsylvania Law Review 127, 1104–1140.

Williamson, O., 1968. Economies as an antitrust defense: The welfare tradeoffs. American Economic Review 58, 18–36.

International Journal of Industrial Organization
20 (2002) 1–17

International Journal of
Industrial
Organization

ELSEVIER

www.elsevier.com/locate/econbase

Does firm size matter? Evidence on the impact of liquidity constraints on firm investment behavior in Germany

David B. Audretsch[a], Julie Ann Elston[b,*]

[a]*Indiana University, SPEA, Suite 201, Bloomington, IN 47405, USA*
[b]*Department of Economics, University of Central Florida, Orlando, FL 32816-1400, USA*

Received 12 August 1998; received in revised form 24 September 1999; accepted 13 January 2000

Abstract

This paper examines the link between liquidity constraints and investment behavior for German firms of different sizes from 1970 to 1986. Results indicate that medium sized firms appear to be more liquidity constrained in their investment behavior than either the smallest or largest firms in the study, suggesting that the unique German infrastructure designed to assist the small firm has indeed succeeded in alleviating, to some degree, such liquidity constraints. Findings also support the hypothesis that the emerging competition and internationalism which characterized the German financial markets in the 1980s, have been improving access to capital for some groups of firms. © 2002 Elsevier Science B.V. All rights reserved.

JEL classification: G00; G3; L00

Keywords: Germany; Liquidity constraints; Size effects

1. Introduction

The notion that capital markets are inherently distinct from other markets has long been noted in the economics literature. What makes capital markets distinct is

*Corresponding author. Tel.: +1-407-823-2078; fax: +1-407-823-3269.
E-mail address: Julie.Elston@bus.ucf.edu (J.A. Elston).

the added feature of risk associated with the demand side of the market. Yet, it is only recently that attention has been devoted to one of the main implications of this risk inherent in loaning credit-capital markets do not, in fact, always clear. This has moved Alan S. Blinder (1988, p. 196) to observe that, 'A few years ago, in revising my graduate course reading list, I looked for some modern literature on liquidity constraints and investment. There was none.'

Since Blinder's (1988) dismal observation, a wave of studies have been published linking liquidity constraints to capital market conditions. A key theoretical contribution by Stiglitz and Weiss (1981) is that the propensity for an enterprise to be subject to credit rationing is not neutral with respect to firm size. Rather, as a result of adverse selection in a market with asymmetric information the likelihood of credit rationing tends to systematically increase as firm size decreases. For example, Fazzari et al. (1988), hereafter FHP, found systematic evidence that liquidity constraints tend to be more binding as firm size decreases. Further, after reviewing the empirical evidence, Chirinko (1993, p. 1904) concludes that, 'While the recently generated evidence points to the importance of financial structure and liquidity constraints, their sources and severity remain open questions.'

In fact virtually all of the empirical evidence linking liquidity constraints (inversely) to firm size has been restricted to the United States, the United Kingdom and a few other countries (Chirinko, 1993). Not only is little known about Germany, but there are reasons to believe that liquidity constraints are less binding, or even non-existent for some firms in Germany (Deeg, 1999). This is because the unique institutional structure of the German financial system may alleviate or avoid financing constraints. The German institutional structure has, among other traits, financial intermediaries that have close long-term relations to German firms in a way that do not exist in other countries such as the United States. Based on these institutional differences, the German system has been characterized as being bank-based, while the U.S. and United Kingdom represent prototypical market-based financial systems. Whether liquidity constraints can be avoided or at least mitigated under Germany's unique system of finance remains an empirical question which is the focus of this paper.

In particular, the purpose of this study is to explicitly examine the link between firm size and the extent to which liquidity constraints are imposed in Germany. We do this by examining investment behavior across firm size using the Q theory of investment model. In the second section of the paper we introduce theories relating firm size to investment and liquidity constraints and explain why the German institutional model of finance may produce results different from the Anglo-Saxon model. In the third section we explain the Q theory of investment and how it can be applied to shed light on the extent of liquidity constraints for specific firms. Measurement issues are discussed in the fourth section. In the fifth section a regression model is used to estimate investment behavior for 100 West German firms between 1970 and 1986. In the last section a summary and conclusions are presented. We find considerable evidence suggesting that medium-sized firms tend to experience a greater degree of liquidity constraints than do their smaller or larger counterparts in Germany. This refutes the hypothesis that under the German model of finance, only the smallest firms tend to be disadvantaged in terms of their access to funds.

2. Firm size, investment, and financial constraints

In reviewing the role of financial constraints on investment behavior, Chirinko (1993, p. 1902) observed that, 'The investment literature has been schizophrenic concerning the role of financial structure and liquidity constraints.' As FHP (1988, p. 141) point out, 'Empirical models of business investment rely generally on the assumption of a 'representative firm' that responds to prices set in centralized security markets. Indeed, if all firms have equal access to capital markets, firms' responses to changes in the cost of capital or tax-based investment incentives differ only because of differences in investment demand.' That is, the financial structure of a firm does not play an important role in investment decisions, since the firm can costlessly substitute external funds for internal capital. Under the assumption of perfect capital markets, then, firm-specific investment decisions are generally independent of the financial condition of that firm.

The assumption of perfect capital markets has, of course, been rigorously challenged. Once it is no longer assumed that capital markets are perfect, it also can no longer be assumed that external capital is a costless substitute for internal capital. An implication of this view is that the availability of internal finance, access to new debt or equity finance, and other financial factors may shape firm investment decisions.

Which view is correct? According to FHP (1988, p. 142), 'Conventional representative firm models in which financial structure is irrelevant to the investment decision may well apply to mature companies with well-known prospects. For other firms, however, financial factors appear to matter in the sense that external capital is not a perfect substitute for internal funds, particularly in the short run.'

There are compelling reasons why liquidity constraints become more severe as firm size decreases. Stiglitz and Weiss (1981) pointed out that, unlike most markets, the market for credit is exceptional in that the price of the good – the rate of interest – is not necessarily at a level that equilibrates the market. They attribute this to the fact that interest rates influence not only demand for capital but also the risk inherent in different classes of borrowers. As the rate of interest rises, so does the riskiness of borrowers, leading suppliers of capital to rationally decide to limit the quantity of loans they make at any particular interest rate. The amount of information about an enterprise is generally not neutral with respect to size. Rather, as Petersen and Rajan (1992, p. 3) observe, 'Small and young firms are most likely to face this kind of credit rationing. Most potential lenders have little information on the managerial capabilities or investment opportunities of such firms and are unlikely to be able to screen out poor credit risks or to have control over a borrower's investments.' If lenders are unable to identify the quality or risk associated with particular borrowers, Jaffe and Russell (1976) show that credit rationing will occur. This phenomenon is analogous to the lemons argument advanced by George Akerloff (1970). The existence of asymmetric information prevents the suppliers of capital from engaging in price discrimination between riskier and less risky borrowers. But, as Diamond (1991) argues, the risk associated with any particular loan is also not neutral with respect to the duration of the relationship. This is because information about the underlying risk inherent in any particular customer is transmitted over time. With experience a lender will condition the risk associated with any class of customers by characteristics associated with the individual customer.

Larger firms can finance capital expenditures from internal resources, issuance of equity, or debt. By contrast, smaller firms are limited in the extent of their internal earnings and the potential for issuing equity.[1] In Germany in particular since 1974, firms have been obligated by law to retain pension funds for employees. These funds, which can run into millions of deutsche marks, have become an important alternative source of firm financing, particularly for the larger firms.[2] It is expected that these funds would loosen the impact of liquidity constraints across firms, but particularly for the largest firms. Therefore in this study, any results indicating binding liquidity constraints after 1974 would suggest that the financial market imperfections limiting external finance are quite severe: sufficient to bind despite the new source of financing from employee pension funds.

A series of recent papers have found that liquidity constraints tend to have a greater impact on smaller enterprises than on their larger counterparts. In particular, small firms are more likely to be unable to obtain capital at market interest rates and therefore subject to credit rationing. FHP (1988) found that smaller publicly traded firms in the US face liquidity constraints and that such smaller enterprises in particular experience difficulties obtaining capital during periods of macroeconomic downturns. That is, *ceteris paribus*, the likelihood of a firm experiencing a liquidity constraint decreases along with increasing firm size. According to FHP, smaller firms tend to be more dependent upon internal finance

---

[1] See Franks and Mayer (1990) and Corbett and Jenkinson (1994) for details on differences and similarities between Anglo-Saxon and bank-based financial systems.

[2] We have chosen to include pension holdings as a source of funds, although we recognize that they could, alternatively, be treated as an obligation of the firm. Since there does not seem to be a consistent position in the literature, we have chosen to be consistent with the argument that availability of these funds may loosen liquidity constraints of the firm.

or bank loans than are their larger counterparts.[3] While the large firms in their study issued 99% of all new equity shares and 92% of all new corporate bonds, they accounted for only 74% of total manufacturing assets. Because smaller firms are more dependent upon loans from commercial banks, they are more prone to experiencing a credit crunch, especially during recessions. FHP find evidence suggesting that the credit sources for smaller firms tend to dry up more rapidly during economic downturns than do the credit sources for larger enterprises.

But Germany's financial infrastructure is not like other countries. In fact recent studies have suggested that the institutional structure of Germany precludes liquidity constraints from occurring.[4] There are two institutional features of the German financial system that sharply contrast with practices in the United States and the United Kingdom, both of which may impact the extent to which liquidity constraints occur. First, companies in Germany typically rely almost exclusively upon banks for external sources of finance. The external capital market remains relatively underdeveloped. And second, not only do the banks represent the major financial intermediary supplying capital to firms, but they are also extensively represented on the firm's supervisory boards[5]. Cable (1985, p. 119) refers to this peculiarity of the German financial system which links finance to supervision as a 'quasi-internal capital market'.

Several studies have noted that the spread in lending rates between the largest and the smallest firms is lower in Germany than in the UK or the US. This is due in part to the effect of strong local and regional bank networks that target as customers the small and medium firms. It is still unclear however, how much this spread in rates affects German firm investment behavior between different sizes of firms.

While considerable attention has been placed on the role that the *Big Three* private banks play[6] in terms of financing the largest manufacturing corporations of Germany,[7] considerably less emphasis has been placed on the other institutions comprising the German financial system. Vitols (1994) points out that, in fact, the

---

[3] Not surprisingly, small enterprises more frequently turn to commercial banks for funding of capital projects. But, as Stoll (1984) notes, smaller firms typically face higher credit costs than do their larger counterparts. For example, a Federal Reserve Board study of loan rates charged by commercial banks on loans made between November 3 and November 7, 1986 found that short-term loans at a fixed rate had an average rate of 11.2% for loans of less than $24,000. However, the rate fell steadily to a mean of 6.8% for loans exceeding $1 million. For loans with a floating rate, the differential was not quite as great. The smallest loans had an average rate of 9.7%, while the largest loans were for 7.5%. Very similar patterns were identified for long-term loans at both fixed and floating rates (United States Small Business Administration, 1987, Table A2.7, p. 91). Thus, the evidence clearly indicates that the cost of capital tends to fall as the size of the loan increases.

[4] See for example Cable (1985) and Soskice (1992).

[5] See Elston (1998) for a more detailed discussion of the scope of German bank influence on firms.

[6] The *Big Three* German banks are the Deutsche Bank, Dresdner Bank and the Commerzbank.

[7] See for example Cable (1985).

Big Three German banks only account for slightly less than one-tenth of all banking assets.[8] The bulk of credit from the *Big Three* private banks is channeled into the largest German firms. According to Vitols (1994, p. 7), 'These banks have traditionally confined their industrial lending activities to larger corporate accounts.' The largest financial institutions are the *Sparkassen*, which are essentially public savings banks, and the *Genossenschaftsbanken*, which essentially are co-operative banks. While the *Sparkassen* account for around 40% of all banking assets, the *Genossenschaftsbanken* account for about 15% of total banking assets (Deeg, 1992). These financial institutions are generally oriented towards financing the *German Mittelstand*, or small- and medium-sized firms in Germany. While the economic and political power of the *Big Three* German banks, particularly in terms of providing finance and direction to the largest firms of Germany, has tended to pre-empt the attention from overseas, what must be one of the better kept secrets of Germany is the magnitude and role that these other institutions play in shaping the overall financial landscape of Germany – particularly in providing finance to smaller enterprises.

The existence of these financial intermediaries channeling funds into the German *Mittelstand* has resulted in the emergence of mechanisms providing smaller banks access to long-term, fixed rate funds. As Vitols (1994, p. 12) points out, 'These mechanisms, which are less developed or absent in the United States and United Kingdom, include (1) special credit institutions which among other things issue bonds on national bond markets to refinance long-term fixed-rate loans to small firms, (2) refinancing and risk pooling mechanisms within both the savings bank and co-operative bank sectors, and (3) mechanisms allowing for the channeling of a high proportion of long-term savings held at insurance companies to the banks through bank bonds. Roughly two-thirds of long-term bank lending to small companies is refinanced through these three mechanisms.' According to Deeg (1999), the increasing bank competition has strengthened the long-term relationship between banks and small firms by inducing banks to provide more long-term funds and information to small firms.

It is the existence of this infrastructure of financial institutions, mandated with providing the German *Mittelstand* with finance, that supposedly defuses the problem of liquidity constraints confronting smaller enterprises as found by Evans and Jovanovic (1989) and FHP (1988), among others, to exist for the United States. As Petersen and Rajan (1992, p. 1) point out, 'One way to overcome frictions is for firms to build close relationships with the suppliers of capital. These relationships allow the lender to collect information about the borrower and their investments and to monitor the actions of the borrower.' Of course, whether the financial institutions under the German model are, in fact, able to avoid financial

---

[8] The Monthly Report of the Deutsche Bundesbank (April 1989, p. 15, Table 4.1) points out that the market share of the *Big Three* fell from 10.2% in 1970 and 10.6% in 1978, to 8.9% in 1988.

constraints imposed upon firms, and particularly smaller sized firms, is an empirical question, which will be answered in the following sections.

3. The Q Theory of Investment Model and Methodology

3.1. Q-theory of investment

We link the extent of financial constraints to firm investment behavior through the lens of the Q theory of investment.[9] The Q framework is based on the assumption that, in the absence of capital market imperfections (and taxes), the value-maximizing firm will continue to invest as long as the shadow price of a marginal unit of capital, Q, exceeds unity. The equilibrium level condition for a profit maximizing enterprise is met when the value of a marginal unit of capital is equated to the cost of replacement of that capital, ensuring that the marginal value of Q is unity. This measure of Q effectively controls for the assessment by the market of the investment opportunities available to the firm. As Chirinko (1993, p. 1903) points out, 'Even though financial market frictions impinge on the firm, Q is a forward-looking variable capturing the ramifications of these constraints on all the firm's decisions. Not only does Q reflect profitable opportunities in physical investment, but, depending on circumstances, Q capitalizes the impact of some or all finance constraints as well.'

3.2. Methodology

From Bond et al. (1997) we estimate an investment equation derived from an accelerator specification in the absence of adjustment costs and a constant returns to scale production function. In this model with the investment equation nested within the general dynamic regression model, we include lagged investment, sales, Q, and cash flow. We use the average Q to proxy for the unobservable Tobin's or marginal Q in order to control for the investment opportunities of the firm. As is standard in the investment literature, we use sales as a real proxy for output or productivity, and cash flow as a proxy for the liquidity constraints of the firm.

Under the standard application of the Q model of investment, the dependent variable is investment for firm j in time t. The investment behavior of each firm in each period is shaped primarily by the following variables. Q is defined as the market value of the firm over the replacement cost. This is calculated as the total market value of the firm's equity, divided by the value of the adjusted capital stock

---

[9] The Q theory of investment was introduced by Brainard and Tobin (1968) and Tobin (1969). Their studies focused on linking the financial sector of the economy to the real sector of the economy, where it was assumed that assets in the economy consist solely of money and capital.

of the firm plus inventories. From Hall (1991) and others, we recognize the difficulties in empirically implementing the Q model, but feel that it is important to estimate this well known specification within the German context for comparison.[10]

Cash flow is a proxy measure of the degree to which a firm is subjected to liquidity constraints, and is calculated as the net income of the firm in the previous period. Chirinko (1987), among others, have established the importance of including lagged investment in the model specification in order to control for the past level of investment by the firm. This is calculated as the annual change in the plant, property, and equipment for the firm. Finally the firm's net of tax sales is used as a measure of firm output.

Many have argued that Germany's unique system of corporate governance may impact the firm's ability to access capital markets. In order to control for the possible influence that concentrated ownership may have on firm investment and liquidity, we include a measure of the concentration of firm ownership in our investment model.

Thus, the model, stated in terms of first differences is specified as:

$$\frac{I_{jt}}{K_{jt}} = \beta_0 + \beta_1 \frac{I_{jt-1}}{K_{jt-1}} + \beta_2 Q_{jt-1} + \beta_3 \frac{CF_{jt-1}}{K_{jt-1}} + \beta_4 \frac{Y_{jt-1}}{K_{jt-1}} + \beta_5 \text{Conc}_{jt}$$
$$+ \beta_6 \log(\text{Size}_{jt}) + \varepsilon_t \tag{1}$$

where $I_{j,t-1}$ is investment for firm j in period $t-1$, $K_{j,t-1}$ is the capital stock of firm j in period $t-1$, $Q_{j,t-1}$ is the ratio of market to book value of firm j in period $t-1$, $CF_{j,t-1}$ is the net income of the firm or cash flow proxy for firm j in period $t-1$. $Y_{j,t-1}$ is the net sales of firm j in period $t-1$, Conc_{jt} is the ownership concentration of firm j in period t, and log (Size_{jt}) is the log of net sales of firm j in period t.

The regressions for each of the various size classes of firms are estimated with annual dummy variables in order to control for exogenous shocks in the data, such as the oil shocks of 1973, 1974, and 1979, and the move from a fixed to a floating exchange rate regime in 1973. We also used industry dummies to control for industry effects, and sorted the data by year which enabled us to examine the behavior of the firm over time. Nine broad industry dummies are constructed based on the primary specialization of the firm in: chemical, metal and metal goods, mineral and mineral products, mechanical engineering, electrical and instrument engineering, motor vehicles and transportation, food and tobacco, textiles, and 'other' manufacturing sectors.

From Arellano and Bond (1998) we estimated the model using a Generalized

---

[10] There are several difficulties in estimating the Q model, including the fact that the unobservable marginal Q is difficult to measure by proxy, even with the best of data, and that the Q model does not always perform well empirically as a predictor of investment.

Method of Moments (GMM) procedure from the DPD98 program in order to provide heteroscedastic-consistent parameter estimates. Estimations were run on first differenced data to remove firm-specific effects, and with instrumental variables of $t - 2$ lagged values of variables I_{jt}/K_{jt}, Q_{jt}, CF_t/K_{jt} and Y_{jt}/K_{jt} to account for endogeniety in the model.[11]

The impact of liquidity constraints on firm investment behavior can be inferred by estimating Eq. (1) for different years and different size classes of firms to shed light on the question, 'Are there any differences in terms of the investment sensitivity to liquidity constraints based on firm size in Germany?'

4. The data

One of the greatest impediments to measuring the impact of liquidity constraints on firm investment behavior in Germany has been the lack of a reliable and comprehensive panel data set. The Bonn Database is a new source of data tracking the financial performance of a comprehensive set of 719 German firms over from 1961 to 1989. Much of the firm level data are from annual financial reports of German industrial corporations quoted on the German stock exchange.[12] The initial year in the data base is 1961, because this was the first year that firms were required to publish sales data according to the 1959 Accounting Reform Act.[13] Data prior to 1970 is not used because much of the data for key variables are missing in this early time period. Because of mergers, bankruptcies, acquisitions, changes in legal status, double listing of consolidated and non-consolidated information for the same firm groups, only 295 unconsolidated firms remained in 28 industrial branches as of 1986.[14] From this population, a sample of 100 listed firms is used for which complete information was available on the concentration of firm ownership.

Note that we need to use listed firms only, in order to maintain consistency between our Q theory model and our empirical model which demands calculation of the value of the firm from stock price data. The sample we used is fairly

---

[11] From Bond et al. (1997) if the error term in levels is serially uncorrelated, then the error term in first differences is a Moving Average series of order 1, MA(1), and therefore instruments dated $t-2$ and earlier should be valid in the differenced equations. Under these assumptions, consistent parameter estimates can be obtained.

[12] The Bonn Database includes annual reports of firms, and information from the Handbuch der Aktiengesellschaften, Wer gehört zu wem, and the Statistisches Jahrbuch. The database was constructed at the Business and Economics Institute at the University of Bonn.

[13] The second legislation that effected accounting rules was the Corporation Act of 1965, under which the rules for the valuation of plant, equipment, and inventories, as well as profits, were tightened. According to Albach (1984), if BASF's 1981 equity was valued under U.S. SEC rules rather than under German law, the valuation would be 40% higher than reported according to the new German rules.

[14] Data after 1986 is not used because of the substantial changes in German accounting laws, which render the data incomparable without considerable revisions.

representative because in 1980 there were only about 459 listed AG and KgaA (incorporation identities indicating that they are publicly held) firms in Germany.[15]

The data for variables are measured in terms of millions of German deutsche marks. The market value of firm equity at time t, or V_t, is calculated by adding the end of year closing prices on stocks (P_t) times the number of outstanding shares of common stock (E_t) to the market value of preferred stock (S_t). The replacement cost of the firm was calculated as the adjusted total tangible fixed assets of the firm plus inventories. This includes the total tangible assets of the firm minus accumulated depreciation to property and current assets, undeclared valuation reserves, net losses, and capital stock subscriptions receivable. Adjusted definitions of capital and sales are based on the balance sheet format as prescribed by German law, which corresponds roughly to the historical cost. Capital stock was adjusted with a depreciation factor constructed from the index of actual to replacement cost of capital in each manufacturing sector from the German Statistical Yearbook. Unfortunately, calculation of assets does not include data from the firm's research and development activities because firms are not required by law to publish this information.

The cash flow of each firm is calculated as the net income (or loss) to the firm, plus depreciation and valuation reserves on fixed assets, intangible properties, and financial assets, plus changes in the year end reserve holdings for pensions. Gross sales, dividend payment information and retained earnings figures for the firms are taken from the balance sheet of each firm.

The concentration of firm ownership is measured from one to five, where the Concentration variable is set at 1 if the firms have the highest degree of ownership concentration with a single stockholder holding more than 75% of the firm's shares. If two or three stockholders hold more than 75% or the shares then Concentration is set at 2. Concentration is set at three if a single stockholder hold more than 50% of the shares, and four, if two or three stockholders own more than 50% of the shares. Concentration is set at 5 for all cases in which the concentration level is more dispersed than for category 4.[16]

Firms were placed into four size groups, roughly quartiles, based on the total number of employees in order to determine firm size effects. It was advantageous that by obtaining four groups of roughly equal size we were also able to define Size1 as those firms employing 500 persons or less – this criterion is consistent with the standard definition in the literature for small firms. The second quartile or Size2 firms contains those with more than 500 but 1300 or fewer employees, Size3

---

[15] See Edwards and Fischer (1994, p. 77).

[16] Note that 25% is a key percentage because it represents a minority blocking vote at shareholders meetings and German law requires disclosure of ownership for any party owning 25% or more of outstanding stock.

contains firms with more than 1300 but 5500 or fewer employees, and Size4 contains firms with more than 5500 employees.[17]

5. Empirical results

Tables 1 and 2 contain descriptive statistics on the data including the means and variable correlations. The mean of the concentration variable reveals that dispersion in ownership increases monotonically with firm size. Table 2 suggests that Sales (over capital stock) may be the best indicator of investment. In order to explicitly examine the link between liquidity constraints and investment behavior across firm size, we ran regressions on the data sorted by firm size and year.

The results of the estimations of the investment function over the period 1970–1986 are shown in Table 3. Of particular interest is the comparatively larger

Table 1
Means of investment variables[a]

Variables	Size1 (smallest)	Size2	Size3	Size4 (largest)
Y_{t-1}/K_{t-1}	−1.4485	1.1930	21.5150	373.3200
	(11.254)	(14.867)	(79.005)	(1681.3)
Q_{t-1}	−0.0289	0.0886	−0.0591	−0.0463
	(0.5197)	(0.5709)	(0.4696)	(0.3727)
CF_{t-1}/K_{t-1}	−4.3791	−2.7944	−1.0375	0.5518
	(8.9264)	(9.5978)	(9.6091)	(8.9360)
Log (Size$_t$)	310.18	867.0400	2179.0000	34014.0000
	(124.81)	(226.22)	(1256.6)	(42899)
Concentration$_t$	2.8534	2.8649	2.9815	3.5542
	(1.4452)	(1.5757)	(1.6129)	(1.5880)
Employees$_t$	310.1800	867.04	2719.0000	34014.0000
	(124.81)	(226.21)	(1256.6)	(42899)
Observations	392	444	423	424

[a] Means of key variables from 1970 to 1986 are listed, with standard deviations in parenthesis. Means were calculated for each firm size group as follows: the first quartile1 or Size1 is composed of firms with 500< =employees, Size 2 or quartile2 is defined (500<quartile2< = 1300) Size3 or quartile3 is defined (1300<quartile3< =5500), and Size4 or quartile4>5500.

---

[17] It should be emphasized that we are not examining very small firms, rather smaller vs. medium and larger firms in the context of the largest firms in Germany. While the smallest firm grouping is consistent with Small and Medium Sized Enterprise (SME) definitions in the literature, the general results should be interpreted in the light of examining firm size effects in the data.

Table 2
Correlation analysis[a]

Variable	I_{t-1}/K_{t-1}	Y_{t-1}/K_{t-1}	Q_{t-1}	CF_{t-1}/K_{t-1}	Log (Size$_t$)	Concentration$_t$
I_{t-1}/K_{t-1}	1.000					
	(0.000)					
Y_{t-1}/K_{t-1}	0.596	1.000				
	(0.000)	(0.000)				
Q_{t-1}	0.000	−0.005	1.000			
	(0.991)	(0.834)	(0.000)			
CF_{t-1}/K_{t-1}	0.040	0.013	−0.076	1.000		
	(0.116)	(0.613)	(0.004)	(0.000)		
Log (Size$_t$)	0.051	0.101	0.005	−0.004	1.000	
	(0.034)	(0.000)	(0.832)	(0.851)	(0.000)	
Concentration$_t$	0.004	0.079	−0.011	0.001	0.293	1.000
	(0.842)	(0.001)	(0.644)	(0.946)	(0.000)	(0.000)

[a] Correlations of key variables are listed. The correlation measures the strength of the relationship between variables, and the probability that the coefficient is zero is reported in parenthesis below.

and statistically significant coefficient of the Cash flow measure for the earlier years of the study. In 8 of the first 11 years of the study Cash flow is significant. From 1981 onward, there is just one Cash Flow coefficient significant at the 10% level, whereas all the cases before 1980 are significant at the 5% level. This evidence is broadly consistent with the hypothesis that German firms were subject to a lower degree of liquidity constraints during the 1980s in which the increasing competition in the German banking sector helped raise the supply of capital, possibly indicative of a fundamental shift in the financial regime in Germany. Coefficients on Q are positive as expected, and significant in 6 of the 17 years. These findings are consistent with the hypothesis that firms had incentives to invest in many of these years, but there does not appear to be any particular pattern to the incentives to invest over time.

In Table 4 we have regression results on quartiles of firms divided by size based on number of employees. We observe that Size2 and Size3 groups have relatively larger and more statistically significant cash flow coefficients compared to the smallest and largest firms, suggesting the impact of the liquidity constraints tends to be the greatest for the medium sized firms. The positive and significant coefficients on Q for Size1 suggests strong incentives to invest for the smallest firms, while negative and significant results for Size3 firms may suggest an incentive to disinvest.[18]

The difference in the impact of liquidity constraints on the investment behavior of the smallest and largest firms, compared with the two medium sized firm

---

[18] The negative and non-significant coefficients on Q may be indicative, among other things, of the weakness of empirical performance of Q as discussed in the Q literature.

Table 3
Investment equation by year[a]

Variables					Log (Size$_t$)	Concentration$_t$	M1[b]	Sargan[c] P-values
Year	I_{t-1}/K_{t-1}	Y_{t-1}/K_{t-1}	Q_{t-1}	CF_{t-1}/K_{t-1}				
1970	0.0008	0.0540*	0.6919*	0.0214	−0.0211	−0.1131	−6.02	0.214
	(0.260)	(4.172)	(2.341)	(1.168)	(−0.149)	(−1.450)		
1971	0.0003	0.1539*	0.0481	0.0075*	−0.0015	0.0090	−5.68	0.427
	(0.289)	(43.971)	(1.040)	(−3.437)	(−0.169)	(1.077)		
1972	0.0010	0.0166	0.8041	0.2330*	0.2936	−0.0026	−5.89	0.362
	(0.081)	(0.304)	(0.842)	(3.385)	(−0.696)	(−0.008)		
1973	−0.0008	0.0457**	0.1222	0.0767*	−0.0016	−0.1053	−5.99	0.805
	·(−0.133)	(1.849)	(−0.276)	(3.052)	(−0.009)	(−0.721)		
1974	−0.0016	0.1007*	0.0317	0.0445	0.2697	−0.178	−6.00	0.477
	(−0.190)	(3.037)	(0.046)	(1.329)	(1.170)	(−1.043)		
1975	−0.0071	0.0910*	0.2893*	0.0412	0.2745	−0.1323	−5.87	0.452
	(−1.204)	(2.874)	(2.424)	(1.162)	(1.309)	(−0.833)		
1976	−0.0084	0.0131	0.0849**	0.1132*	0.1908	0.0202	−5.67	0.635
	(−1.026)	(0.459)	(1.846)	(4.490)	(0.778)	(0.110)		
1977	−0.0106	0.0329	−0.6387	0.1060*	0.3297	−0.2800	−5.73	0.123
	(−1.219)	(0.882)	(−0.609)	(3.732)	(1.119)	(−1.407)		
1978	−0.0018	0.0122	0.2935	0.1208*	−0.1128	−0.0547	−5.76	0.321
	(−0.159)	(0.628)	(1.338)	(3.060)	(−0.378)	(−0.264)		
1979	−0.0051	0.0689*	0.2323**	0.0774*	−0.0427	−0.1561	−5.81	0.527
	(−0.521)	(2.132)	(1.676)	(3.190)	(−0.245)	(−1.093)		
1980	0.0015	0.0558*	0.1418	0.0787*	−0.4164	0.0865	−5.66	0.459
	(0.108)	(2.755)	(1.157)	(2.779)	(−1.493)	(0.438)		
1981	0.0071	0.0660*	0.1752	0.0294	−0.0120	−0.1528	−6.01	0.243
	(−0.745)	(4.789)	(1.385)	(1.199)	(−0.077)	(−1.251)		
1982	−0.0067	0.8983*	0.0741	0.0056	0.0753	−0.1189	−6.21	0.382
	(−0.714)	(5.413)	(1.171)	(−0.233)	(0.464)	(−1.049)		
1983	−0.0028	0.0680*	0.0434	0.0367	−0.1889	0.0413	−6.03	0.651
	(−0.252)	(5.698)	(0.078)	(1.471)	(−1.052)	(0.288)		
1984	−0.0043	0.0457*	0.3538**	0.0338	−0.1217	−0.1219	−6.21	0.756
	(−0.418)	(3.977)	(1.738)	(1.560)	(−0.619)	(−1.014)		
1985	−0.0236	0.0496*	0.0445	0.0471	−0.0043	−0.0225	−6.10	0.434
	(−0.846)	(2.467)	(1.033)	(0.739)	(−0.013)	(−0.096)		
1986	0.0032	0.1805*	1.245*	0.0521**	−0.2105	−0.0022	−6.03	0.672
	(0.483)	(8.274)	(2.453)	(1.732)	(−0.845)	(−0.013)		

*, t-statistic is significant at the 0.05; **, significant at the 0.10 levels.

[a] Investment equation was estimated using $t-2$ lagged values of I/K, CF/K and Y/K as instruments. The sample is comprised of 100 unconsolidated German firms from 1970 to 1986. T-values are reported in parenthesis below coefficients. Concentration is a measure of the ownership concentration of the firm, and Log (Size$_t$) is the log of total firm assets. Table reports P-values for the Sargan test – the probability of generating the calculated Sargan statistic under the null hypothesis of valid instruments. Reported M1 values can be used to test the null hypothesis of no autocorrelation. Regressions were estimated using nine industry dummies covering the German manufacturing sector.

[b] DPD98 reports tests for the absence of first-order and second-order serial correlation in the differenced residuals. Under this models particular assumptions about the form of the error term, we expect evidence of significant negative first order serial correction in the differenced residuals, which is confirmed by the M1 values.

[c] Reported P-values and non-reported Sargan statistic generally indicate valid instruments.

Table 4
Investment model by firm size groups[a]

Variables	Size1 (smallest)	Size2	Size3	Size4 (largest)
I_{t-1}/K_{t-1}	−0.0128*	−0.0050	−0.0048**	−0.0007
	(−4.891)	(−1.289)	(−1.703)	(−0.329)
Y_{t-1}/K_{t-1}	0.0086	0.0343*	0.0691*	0.1628*
	(1.061)	(3.710)	(7.378)	(19.574)
Q_{t-1}	0.1860*	0.2095	−0.8808*	−0.3780
	(2.248)	(0.931)	(−1.989)	(−1.375)
CF_{t-1}/K_{t-1}	0.0047	0.0798*	0.1187*	−0.0216**
	(1.111)	(7.173)	(6.481)	(−1.892)
Log (Size$_t$)	0.5474*	−0.3457	−1.0537*	0.9345*
	(7.356)	(−0.755)	(−2.366)	(5.552)
Concentration$_t$	0.0323	0.0244	−0.1522	−0.0152
	(1.000)	(0.351)	(−1.504)	(−0.241)
Sargan P-values[c]	0.364	0.072	0.647	0.526
M1[b]	−6.32	−5.81	−6.71	−7.40

*, t-statistic is significant at the 0.05 level; **, significant at the 0.10 level.

[a] Investment equation was estimated using $t-2$ lagged values of I/K, CF/K and Y/K as instruments. The sample is comprised of 100 unconsolidated German firms from 1970 to 1986. T-values are reported in parenthesis below coefficients. Concentration is a measure of the ownership concentration of the firm, and Log (Size$_t$) is the log of total firm assets. Reported P-values of the Sargan statistics tests the probability of generating the calculated Sargan statistics under the null hypothesis of valid instruments. M1 values are tests for first order (M1) serial correlation in the differenced residuals. Regressions were estimated using annual time dummies and nine industry dummies covering the German manufacturing sector.

[b] DPD98 reports tests for the absence of first-order and second-order serial correlation in the differenced residuals. Under this models particular assumptions about the form of the error term, we expect evidence of significant negative first order serial correction in the differenced residuals, which is confirmed by the M1 values.

[c] Reported P-values and non-reported Sargan statistic generally indicate valid instrument set.

groups, suggest that financial institutions of Germany do provide a system of finance that is different from the Anglo-Saxon model, specifically in that liquidity constraints could be attenuated for the smallest firms.

The findings are consistent with predictions by Deeg (1999) that the German financial system is becoming increasingly characterized as one consisting of several intertwined models of industrial finance. That is, as Germany's financial sector has became more acutely international and competitive, closer to the Anglo-Saxon model, larger firms have had an easier time gaining access to capital. While smaller firms have found that the market share for small business lending has shifted substantially from the commercial banking sector to the savings and credit cooperative sectors where they ' . . . continue to enjoy access to long-term and competitively priced capital'.[19] At the same time, this has largely left medium-sized firms as odd man out in the German financial system.

6. Conclusions

A wave of studies has recently emerged suggesting that the German model of finance is distinct from its Anglo-Saxon counterpart, in that the institutional structure is able to provide adequate liquidity to meet the long-term investment needs of enterprises (Corbett and Jenkinson, 1994; and Cable, 1985). The results presented in this paper suggest that may be true only for some firms, indicating a more complex relationship between firm size and liquidity constraints.

Smaller firms have relatively fewer liquidity constraints, apparently benefiting from the specialized institutional structure in Germany, which provides long-term and competitively priced capital to the SME. However, evidence does not support the hypothesis that the institutional structure of finance in Germany is able to avoid the impact of liquidity constraints for medium-sized firms, which had the most severe liquidity constraints in the study. Finally, the largest firms, not surprisingly, did not appear to be particularly liquidity constrained, consistent with their ability to easily access internal and external sources of funds.

Acknowledgements

We are grateful to participants of the 1999 "Funding Gaps" conference at the University of Warwick, and in particular our discussant Michael Devereux, for helpful comments on an earlier version of this paper. We are also grateful to John Scott and two anonymous referees, who provided helpful suggestions on earlier versions of this work, and to Steve Bond for providing a copy of the 1998 DPD program.

References

Akerloff, G.A., 1970. The market for lemons: quality uncertainty and the market mechanism. Quarterly Journal of Economics 84, 488–500.

---

[19] Deeg (1999) notes that over the last two and a half decades, all of the conditions in the market for business loans have changed in favor of greater firm independence from banks. This trend is particularly true for the largest firms, which presumably have better access to both internal and external capital.

Albach, H., 1984. Rates of return in German manufacturing industry: Measurement and policy implications. In: Mueller, D. (Ed.), Measuring Profitability and Capital Costs: An International Study. Lexington Press, Lexington KY, pp. 273–311.

Arellano, M., Bond, S., 1998. Dynamic Panel Data Estimation using DPD98 for Gauss: A Guide for Users, Institute for Fiscal Studies (IFS) Working paper no. 88/15.

Blinder, A.S., 1988. Financing constraints and corporate investment: Discussion and comments. Brookings Papers on Economic Activity, 196-200.

Bond, S., Elston, J.A., Mairesse, J., Mulkay, B., 1997. A comparison of empirical investment equations using company panel data for France, Germany, Belgium, and the UK. Working paper National Bureau of Economic Research (NBER), No. 5900.

Brainard, W., Tobin, J., 1968. Pitfalls in financial model building. The American Economic Review 58, 99–122.

Cable, J., 1985. Capital market information and industrial performance: The role of West German banks. Economic Journal 95, 118–132.

Chirinko, R., 1993. Business fixed investment spending: modelling strategies, empirical results, and policy implications. Journal of Economic Literature 31, 1875–1911.

Chirinko, R., 1987. Tobin's Q and financial policy. Journal of Monetary Economics XIX, 33–60.

Corbett, J., Jenkinson, T., 1994. The financing of industry, 1970–89: An international comparison. Center for Economic Policy Research discussion paper #948.

Deeg, R., 1992. Banks and the state in Germany: The critical role of subnational institutions in economic governance. Unpublished Ph.D. Dissertation, MIT.

Deeg, R., 1999. Finance Capitalism Unveiled: Banks and the German Political Economy. University of Michigan Press, Ann Arbor MI.

Diamond, D., 1991. Monitoring and reputation: The choice between bank loans and directly placed debt. Journal of Political Economy 99, 688–721.

Edwards, J.S., Fischer, K., 1994. The German Financial System. Cambridge University Press, Cambridge.

Elston, J.A., 1998. Investment, liquidity constraints and bank relationships: evidence from German manufacturing firms. In: Black, S.W., Moersch, M. (Eds.), Competition and Convergence in Financial Markets: The German and Anglo-Saxon Models. Elsevier Science, Amsterdam, pp. 135–150.

Evans, D., Jovanovic, B., 1989. An estimated model of entrepreneurial choice under liquidity constraints. Journal of Political Economy 97, 808–827.

Fazzari, S., Hubbard, R.G., Petersen, B.C., 1988. Financing constraints and corporate investment. Brookings Papers on Economic Activity, 141-195.

Franks, J., Mayer, C., 1990. Capital markets and corporate control: A study of France, Germany and the UK. Economic Policy 10, 191–231.

Hall, B., 1991. Firm level investment with liquidity constraints: What can the Euler equations tell us? Working paper, University of California-Berkeley.

Jaffe, D.M., Russell, T., 1976. Imperfect information, uncertainty and credit rationing. Quarterly Journal of Economics 90, 651–666.

Monthly Report of the Deutsche Bundesbank, 1989, Bonn.

Petersen, M.A., Rajan, R.G., 1992. The benefits of firm-creditor relationships: evidence from small business data. University of Chicago Working Paper #362.

Soskice, D., 1992. The institutional infrastructure for international competitiveness: a comparative analysis of the UK and Germany. In: Atkinson, A.B., Brunetta, R. (Eds.), The Economics of the New Europe. Macmillan, London.

Statistisches Jahrbuch. Federal Republic of Germany. Federal Statistics Office, Wiesbaden.

Stiglitz, J., Weiss, A., 1981. Credit rationing in markets with imperfect information. American Economic Review 71, 393–410.

Stoll, H.R., 1984. Small firms' access to public equity financing. In: Horvitz, P.M., Pettit, R.R. (Eds.),

Small Business Finance: Problems in the Financing of Small Business. JAI Press, Greenwich, CT, pp. 187–238.

Tobin, J., 1969. A general equilibrium approach to monetary theory. Journal of Money, Credit, and Banking 1, 15–29.

United States Small Business Administration, 1987. Washington, D.C.: U.S. Government Printing Office.

Vitols, S.I., 1994. German banks and the modernisation of the small firm sector: Long-term finance in comparative perspective. Unpublished manuscript, Wissenschaftszentrum Berlin für Sozialforschung.

Wer gehört zu wem, Commerzbank series, Frankfurt.

ELSEVIER

International Journal of Industrial Organization
19 (2001) 613–634

International Journal of
**Industrial
Organization**

www.elsevier.com/locate/econbase

Competition policy in dynamic markets

David B. Audretsch[a,*], William J. Baumol[b], Andrew E. Burke[c]

[a]*Institute for Development Strategies, Indiana University, SPEA 1315E, 10th Street, Room 201, Bloomington, IN 47405-1701, USA*
[b]*CV Starr Center, New York University and Princeton University, New York NY, USA*
[c]*University of Edinburgh, Edinburgh, UK*

Abstract

Competition and antitrust policies have been based on a scholarly tradition focusing on static models and static analyses of industrial organization. However, recent developments in the industrial organization literature have provided significant advances moving beyond the traditional static models and the pre-occupation with price competition. In particular, the field has now developed to consider the organization of industries in a dynamic context. These new approaches are dynamic in the sense that performance is related to variations in the products available to consumers, as well as variations in firm competencies, ranking, growth, entry and exit. The development of the industrial organization literature also incorporates models of industry and market evolution. The purpose of this paper is to provide a framework linking what is known in the industrial organization literature on the dynamics and evolution of markets to one of the major policy instruments — competition policy. This framework provides a basis for understanding the contributions of the contents of the Special Issue devoted to Competition Policy in Dynamic Markets. © 2001 Elsevier Science B.V. All rights reserved.

Keywords: Competition policy; Dynamic markets

JEL classification: L4; L5; O3; L1

*Corresponding author. Tel.: + 812-855-6766; fax: + 812-855-0184.
E-mail address: daudrets@indiana.edu (D.B. Audretsch).

0167-7187/01/$ – see front matter © 2001 Elsevier Science B.V. All rights reserved.
PII: S0167-7187(00)00086-2

1. Introduction

Competition (or antitrust[1]) law lays down rules for competitive rivalry. It comprises a set of directives that constrain the strategies available to firms. Most of these directives seek to prevent behaviour whose aim is either to reduce the rivalry of firms, or to exert monopolistic power. An ethos which holds that 'competition is good' underlies the purpose of the law. Even its various names — antitrust law (US) and competition law (EU) — indicate that the law relates primarily to interfirm rivalry. The US law is most explicit in its prohibition of particular types of interfirm co-operation. Similarly, lawyers who practice under these laws use the term 'anti-competitive' to describe business behaviour that violates antitrust law.

If there is any body of law that owes its existence to economics, it is surely antitrust law. It is therefore surprising that 'enhancement of welfare' is not explicitly adopted as the primary objective of this law. For traditional static economic analysis, this may not seem to be a major problem since perfect competition is often (if rather inaccurately) taken to be virtually synonymous with welfare maximisation. Thus, measures that increase the intensity of competition are automatically assumed to enhance welfare. Furthermore, legal practitioners and business managers can more easily evaluate the intensity of competition than the concomitant welfare effects. Thus, consideration of practicality may lead to emphasis on competition rather than welfare.

However, industrial economics has advanced substantially from its exclusively static foundations and its pre-occupation with *price* competition alone. In a dynamic economy competition in product and process innovations may have a more significant effect on welfare, at least in the long run, than does any likely variation in price. Developments in the productive efficiency of firms and the quality of their products, as well as their growth, and the ease, with which they can enter or exit, can be critical. The industrial organisation literature has also begun to incorporate much of the Austrian and evolutionary viewpoints into mainstream thought. Industrial organisation analysis differentiates among productive, un-productive and destructive firm rivalry and implies that the distinction does not lend itself to simple rules of thumb. 'Laws may suggest, but welfare must govern' may be an apt conclusion. In sum, the evolution of industrial economic thought has raised questions about the appropriateness of at least some of the current antitrust/competition laws and practices and their adherence to a static blueprint. The issue has become increasingly urgent as innovation and growth have increasingly characterised the markets of the industrialised economies (Audretsch, 1995).

The purpose of this special issue of this journal is to investigate this claim. Our

---

[1] We use the terms interchangeably throughout.

call for papers elicited a substantial number of submissions and we regret that we can only provide a select few of them here. We were forced to turn down many valuable papers but will no doubt encounter many of them in other reputable publications. It is noteworthy that, despite other differences, virtually all the papers submitted concurred with the view that current competition laws do not adequately promote welfare in dynamic markets.

Section 2 of this introductory article provides an overview of the recent evolution of industrial economic thought. Section 3 offers a characterization of the contents of this special issue. Section 4 illustrates the legal emphasis on static competition with reference to EU competition law. We conclude with a review of some of the questions the discussion raises about the current state of the US and EU antitrust laws.

2. Recent developments in the economics of industrial organisation

We turn next to an overview of the evolution of the economics of industrial organisation and its relation to competition policy. We will stress the difference between the static mainstream models and the modifications proposed for incorporation of the process of change, both in mainstream analysis and in more heterodox work. These intertemporal approaches include those employing game theory, as well as the work of the Austrian school and the recent dynamic analyses based on gross adjustment and evolutionary approaches to firm and market performance.

The origins of industrial economics are usually traced back to the work of Bain (1956) who introduced the Structure–Conduct–Performance (SCP) paradigm. In this framework, industries with high levels of concentration are taken to exhibit market power when firms charge monopolistic prices. These prices, in turn, affect economic performance (economic welfare). Thus, in Bain's schema the roots of economic inefficiencies are found in industry structure, since in the SCP paradigm causation runs from structure to conduct and then to economic performance.

The SCP literature was criticised by two groups. Economic theorists were unhappy that though SCP analyses were empirically based, they lacked rigorous foundation in economic theory (for a survey see Davies et al., 1989). Consequently, the Bain School of industrial organisation was sometimes dismissed as being based on 'lofty' intuition. However, the apparent success of the SCP approach in explaining phenomena of reality stimulated interest in the creation of a more robust theory of industrial organisation. This literature since the 1970s has recognized that conduct can influence structure and has abandoned the uni-directional flow of causation fundamental to the SCP framework (see Tirole, 1988, for a compendium of much of this research). The application of game theory to industrial organisation and an understanding of endogenous forces affecting market concentration indicated that structure is as much dependent on conduct, as conduct on structure. In many instances these attributes were shown to be simultaneously determined by the strategic action of firms. For example, endogenous barriers to entry, limit pricing and alteration of industry technology through R&D were found to affect industry structure. As a result, the strong correlation between conduct and structure reported in the empirical literature was no longer accepted as evidence that structure determines conduct, since it is equally consistent with the feedback loop hypothesis that conduct and structure mutually affect one another.

Game theory also illustrated that small adjustments in economic models can generate large changes in the competitiveness of firms' behaviour. For competition policy this implies that small variations in the basic circumstances of an industry can often be sufficient to make the difference between warranted and unnecessary regulation. Sutton (1991) described the ironic consequence of more rigorous theoretical analysis of markets when he observed:

> ... *within any particular model there are often many outcomes that can be supported as equilibria. This richness in modelling has made it much easier to provide a theoretical rationale for a wide range of observed phenomena: from predatory pricing to vertical restraints, our tool kit has been greatly enriched. The sting in the tail, however, lies in the old taunt, "With oligopoly, anything can happen."* [2]

Thus ideally, the theory even raised the possibility that a unique applied economic analysis may be necessary for the formulation of competition policy for each particular industry. However, despite the complexities of the new theory the main thrust of its prescription for competition policy remains intact in its conclusion that economic welfare is usually increased by movement from more monopolistic to more competitive circumstances. The main change lay in the revised criteria of competition and monopoly that now emphasized conduct rather than structure. This suggested that EU and US competition laws did not require redrafting but merely some re-interpretation. For example, the term 'dominant position' could no longer be equated with industry concentration, given the importance of potential entry.

The core of the game and non-game theoretical contributions to industrial organisation entailed a new emphasis on dynamics. Firms with dominant positions did not necessarily adopt prices that maximize immediate monopoly profits, since they had to consider the dynamic implications of such a strategy and the possibility that it would encourage entry (and hence competition) in the future. Similarly, firms were recognized to pursue long-term goals in conducting non-price strategies in activities such as R&D and advertising. This new emphasis was

---

[2] Sutton (1991), p xiii.

D.B. Audretsch et al. / Int. J. Ind. Organ. 19 (2001) 613–634   617

to prove important in terms of reliance of the design of competition policy upon the concept of perfect competition as the model for maximisation of welfare — making it almost the *raision d'etre* of antitrust law.

In general, economists have refrained from reliance on perfect competition as a guide to minimisation of welfare losses. Yet they have continued to think of it as the most illuminating model for guidance in policy formulation, partly because of their usual concerns about allocative inefficiency. Another plausible explanation of their continued affection for the perfect competition model is the encouragement to rent seeking provided by the presence of monopoly profits (which are sometimes labelled 'rents' since they originate from ownership of a monopoly resource) (see, for example, Tullock, 1967; Krueger, 1974; Posner, 1976). In this scenario monopoly rents induce agents to attempt to siphon-off some of these earnings (for example, through litigation or slack efficiency) which in turn forces monopolists to defend themselves, in the process using up resources that might otherwise be devoted to production. It is conceivable that such misallocated resources cumulatively can add up to a value in excess of the monopoly rent. But whatever their magnitude their mere existence makes monopoly losses exceed the standard dead-weight loss triangle. If so, even the theoretical monopoly that practices perfect price discrimination, and incurs no dead-weight losses, may yield economic welfare less than that provided by perfect competition.

In less theoretical terms, competition is favoured by economists and by the law because it forces firms to pursue efficiency, product improvement and vigorous innovation. In the words of Judge Learned Hand in the noted Alcoa decision (1945) "Possession of unchallenged economic power deadens initiative, discourages thrift and depresses energy . . . Immunity from competition is a narcotic, and rivalry a stimulant to industrial progress". In addition, non-economic objectives also underlie the widespread conviction that competition law should use perfect competition as a guide. Thus, in their text, Scherer and Ross (1990) tell us

> *We begin with political arguments, . . . because when all is said and done, they, and not economists' abstruse models, have tipped the balance of social consensus toward competition. One of the most important arguments is that the atomistic structure of buyers and sellers required for competition decentralises and disperses power.*[3]

Egalitarian objectives may also play a role. However, and whatever the reasons cited for the preferability of perfect competition, it must be recognized that even in theory this state of affairs is not a guarantee of welfare maximisation, even in the static model. Perhaps the most important reason is the widespread presence of

---

[3] Scherer and Ross (1990), pp 18–19.

substantial externalities and spillovers that, as is well known, can lead to inadequate investment in innovation and to serious resource depletion and degradation of the environment. But it has other deficiencies. For example, in the absence of subsidies, uniform pricing may prevent suppliers from covering their costs, notably their fixed and common outlays, even though their products, that offer a surplus to consumers, could be supplied viably under price discrimination. There are other more traditional arguments about the shortcomings of price competition in certain circumstances, as in the case of a natural monopoly operating in an unstable market (for an overview of this literature, see Sharkey, 1982).

In the new dynamic models of industrial organisation the usefulness of the perfect competition model becomes even more questionable. An early group of critics of this standard on dynamic grounds were the members of the Austrian school of economics, led by authors such as von Mises and Schumpeter and more recently by Demsetz, Shackle and Kirzner. The Austrians argue that economists in the classical tradition misuse the term 'competition' by applying it to a state of affairs rather than to a process. They argue that the static models of industrial organisation did more to explain where the market would end up (given some initial conditions) after enterprising activities were to cease, rather than explaining how it got there. However, they note that such static end-states are rarely relevant because ongoing entrepreneurship ensures that innovation hardly ever pauses sufficiently long for anything like static equilibrium to emerge. As Herbert and Link (1982), among many others, have pointed out there is no role for the entrepreneur in static economic theory:

> . . . *Neoclassical value theory . . . took ends as given, explained allocation of scarce resources to meet these given ends, and focused attention on equilibrium results rather than adjustment processes. It therefore left no room for entrepreneurial action; the entrepreneur became a mere automaton, a passive onlooker . . .* [4]

In the static model where technology and consumer demand is given, price (output) becomes the firm's main, if not its only, choice variable. The Austrians argue (for example, see Kirzner, 1973; Shackle, 1971) that in reality firms are engaged in a continuing dynamic competitive process, constantly creating and adopting new products and processes in order to gain a competitive advantage over their rivals. Firms that do obtain such an edge temporarily derive static monopoly power during the interval before imitating competitors replicate their innovation, or supersede it with one that is superior. Thus successful firms earn temporary monopoly profits as their reward for innovative activity. While in this scenario

---

[4] Herbert and Link (1982), p 52.

successful firms do obtain *ex-post* monopoly profits (with their associated static welfare losses), if there is ease of entry and exit (little sunk cost) firms in the industry must expect only normal profits *ex-ante*, as firms will enter the industry up to the point where an additional firm expects to make zero economic profits. *Ex-post* the 'losers' do incur losses and the 'winners' do earn positive economic profits, but that only spurs innovation and growth. As a result, the Austrian prescription for competition policy is that industries with negligible barriers to entry should be left to operate without constraint. The importance of market contestability is emphasized by Kirzner (1973):

> . . . *in the sense in which we have used the term 'competition' (a sense which, although sharply divergent from the terminology of the dominant theory of price, is entirely consistent with everyday business usage), the market process is indeed always competitive, so long as there is freedom to buy and sell in the market . . . we distinguish very sharply between a producer who is the sole source of supply for a particular commodity because he has a unique access to a necessary resource and one who is the sole source of supply as a result of his entrepreneurial activities (which can be duplicated by his competitors, if they so choose).*[5]

The Austrian school takes the view that if governments intervene to reduce the profits of winners this will reduce the incentive for existing firms and prospective entrants to engage in competitive innovation. The Austrians conclude that only where incumbent firms have substantial monopoly power and undertake little innovation should competition policy interfere and undertake regulation.[6] But even in such cases they are sceptical about the need for regulation because the presence of large profits is likely to attract enterprising competitors who will use innovation to facilitate their entry.

The Austrians have often been taken to be related to the Chicago school whose adherents also take the position that regulation is unnecessary when markets are contestable. Economists in the Chicago tradition tend to the view that many if not most markets tend to approximate perfect competition in the long-run (see Posner, 1979). Thus positive profits are considered a transitory phenomenon since their presence stimulates entry and hence leads to their demise. Therefore the Chicago school argues that regulation is generally unnecessary because market forces ensure that monopoly power will usually be short lived. The emphasis of the Austrians is somewhat different, arguing that market performance can be constrained by scarcity of entrepreneurial resources and that the lure of possible monopoly profits is necessary to give firms the incentive to utilise these resources

---

[5] Kirzner (1973), pp 20–21.
[6] Most usually state-owned monopolies.

in a manner beneficial to society. Thus, both advocate a *laissez faire* approach to regulation, but for very different reasons; the former on the presumption that the supply of entrepreneurs is infinite in the long-run while the latter concerns itself with the incentives needed to expand the limited supply of entrepreneurial resources.

As far as direct regulation of firms is concerned, the *laissez faire* argument received some possible support from Baumol et al. (1982) theory of contestable markets, which demonstrated that in industries with no barriers to entry, the threat of entry would not only restrain incumbents' market power, but also generally satisfy the requirements for static welfare maximisation. The theory has some roots in the work of Bain (1949) and rests on the premise that the toughness of price competition is influenced by potential as well as existing rivalry. If barriers to entry and exit are low, incumbent firms cannot afford the luxury of pricing above the competitive level since this will encourage entry. The authors of the theory, however, never claimed that most industries approximate the requirements of perfect contestability.[7] In any event, the authors of contestability theory did not take a position that fundamentally opposed regulation, and argued instead that the theoretical concept of perfect contestability, because it is compatible with the presence of large firms and scale economies, is a better model for regulatory measures than is the at least equally theoretical model of perfect competition.

The debate on the theory of market contestability has focused attention on the incentives for firms to enter an industry and to impose competitive pricing. However, little attention has been paid to the ability of entrants to compete effectively. If incumbents are to take the threat of entry seriously there must be a supply of capable entrants who are willing and able to respond to the profit opportunities created by monopolistic pricing. For example, in a contestable industry with a relatively high minimum efficient scale the supply of potential entrants may be restricted if they face liquidity constraints. In this case the incumbent may be able to charge monopolistic prices, regardless of market contestability, merely because there is an insufficient supply of able potential entrants.

In the Austrian framework competition always benefits welfare. They believe that since competitive advantages are gained primarily by improving product characteristics and/or reducing production cost, a new state resulting from such competitive acts must generally be Pareto superior to its predecessor. The Austrians conclude that economic welfare is thereby improved, even allowing for

---

[7] Baumol et al. (1982) example of a contestable airline market was soon challenged by authors such as Graham et al. (1983), Bailey et al. (1981) and Moore (1982). Morrison and Winston (1987) arrived at a compromise position, holding that although potential competition may not cause prices to descend to the competitive level, it may nonetheless provide some restraint on monopolistic pricing.

the role of market power in the process. It has subsequently been argued that their conclusion is incorrect on this issue, but a significant portion of the Austrian ideas has nevertheless been incorporated into mainstream industrial economics. To do this economists had to take dynamics into account, proceeding beyond the confines of static method.

Thus, the evolution of industrial economics from static to dynamic analysis entailed a rediscovery of much of the central Austrian argument. It is important to stress here that we are not referring to dynamic analysis of static competition, as in repeated games of price (output) competition (where technology and demand are given), with collusive (tacit or overt) and non-collusive strategies. Such dynamic analyses illuminate the complex character of inter-temporal static competition but do not capture the central attribute of Austrian dynamic competition — in which the prime instrument is technology itself. Instead, our primary concern is the literature on technological change, innovation, research, development and diffusion. The conceptual origins of this literature are usually attributed to Nordhaus (1969) although there is an earlier, mainly empirical, tradition with contributions such as those of Griliches (1957), Carter and Williams (1959), O'Brien (1964), and Mueller (1966). This literature focuses on particular issues such as patents, copyright, and other intellectual property rights and the manner of their utilisation. It also includes analysis of trademarks, although these have considerably different conceptual ramifications (see Landes and Posner, 1987). The economics of advertising also can be taken to constitute part of these forms of non-price competition.

In these analyses firms engage in enterprising behaviour in order to secure a competitive advantage over their (actual or anticipated) rivals. The research illustrates that there is something to be learned in this arena from the arguments of both the classical and the Austrian schools. The Austrians have made clear that product and process innovators who incur costs and take risks must be rewarded for their actions via positive economic profits in each static sub-period. At the same time, the classical tradition is correct in drawing attention to the static welfare losses generated by these positive profits as firms produce less than the perfectly competitive level of output. As is well documented in the literature on patents, there are few compelling reasons to suppose that dynamic competition will lead to the optimal monopoly profit in each period. Clearly, it can be either greater or less than that needed to yield the optimal degree of dynamic competition. Since the resources expended by losers may in some senses be wasted, there is no strong *a priori* reason to accept the Austrian presumption that such competition must always improve economic welfare. However, Lyons (1989) notes the consensus among economists that when the stimulation of innovation is necessary, some positive static profits are better than none:

Without the prospect of monopoly profits the incentive to invent would be very much reduced ... but it is almost certainly better than no protection at all for new ideas.[8]

Papers such as Gilbert and Newbery (1982) and Beil et al. (1995) have shown that the threat of entry can stimulate incumbents to increase innovative activity. However, a potential entrant who has the option of entering a market with the aid of some form of product or process innovation may have little incentive to do so if barriers to entry for subsequent imitators are sufficiently low to cause low *ex-post* profits. In this case the risk of entry is not worth taking. The intuitive explanation is identical to that in the literature on patents and copyright, where property rights ensure the possibility of some positive profits if the innovation is successful. Thus, efficient market regulation entails a sophisticated approach to property rights. On the one hand it must preserve these so that the incentive to engage in dynamic competition is maintained and on the other it must ensure that these rights are not employed to block entry to further rounds of dynamic competition. For example, this can occur through promotion of technological lock-in through the creation of network externalities emanating from protected innovation (Katz and Shapiro, 1981 and Arthur, 1989). Of course intervention such as this reduces the incentive for innovations involving network externalities. The dilemma for competition policy is that without prior knowledge of the economic benefits of such innovations and the minimum reward necessary to stimulate them one cannot ascertain with certainty whether such action will enhance or decrease economic welfare.

There are other ways in which entrepreneurial activity can hamper competition. Thus, through means such as unwarranted litigation seeking government intervention to prevent 'unfair' competition, innovation that raises competitors' costs or patents acquired to impede innovation by rivals, the generation of network externalities, etc., entrepreneurship can handicap innovation and reduce economic welfare.[9] Such activity can entail innovative exploitation of rent opportunities.

This line of analysis draws together a disparate body of literature which, although varied in focus, is consistent in refuting the common assumption that an increase in entrepreneurial activity is always welfare enhancing. Dynamic competition that gives rise to phenomena such as excessive product differentiation (Salop, 1979), excessive advertising (Sutton, 1991) and patent hoarding (Gilbert and Newbery, 1982) all serve as counterexamples. The analysis thus does indeed conflict with the presumption that dynamic competition is necessarily welfare enhancing. It immediately follows that even in dynamic markets where temporary monopoly profits serve to stimulate innovation regulation may be warranted if the

---

[8] Lyons (1989) p. 36.

[9] For example, Murphy et al. (1990) find a negative correlation between the size of the legal profession and economic growth in a sample of 91 countries.

profits are derived from undertakings such as those just described or by their existence encourage wasteful rent-seeking.

The economics of industrial organisation has also adopted a more disaggregated analysis of firm and market dynamics.[10] This new approach brought the writings on entrepreneurship and industrial economics closer together. It sought to explain the evolution of markets rather than dealing with snapshots of the concentration and performance of a market at given points in time. The analytic method entails a flow approach to performance of the firm, disaggregating the gross movements that underlie changes in market performance. At the core of this approach is the belief that to explain the dynamics of economic performance one must be able to take into account the mechanism of change within the firm and of its response to modifications in its external environment. The new dynamic approach to industrial organisation has its origins in the work of Penrose (1959) and is also based on the contributions of evolutionary economics (see, e.g., Teece, 1980; Nelson and Winter, 1982), economic history (e.g., Chandler, 1962; Lazonick, 1982) business strategy (e.g., Porter, 1980; Peteraf, 1993) and regional analyses (e.g., Krugman, 1991). The new literature seeks to explain the process of competition within a framework that is dynamic but is nevertheless consistent with mainstream analysis. Thus, like the Austrian approach, it recognises that there are critical resources necessary to exploit opportunities for profit via change and that these can vary among firms, time periods and geographic locations.[11] It was thereby recognised that market performance is as much influenced by variations in the ability of firms to exploit profit opportunities as it is by variations in the availability of profit opportunities.

The evolution of industrial economics from its static base to its current dynamic form, that recognises that competition can sometimes be destructive and that firm capability plays a major role in determining market performance, raises doubts about the efficacy of current competition laws. These concerns are exacerbated by the foundation of these laws in the policy implications of static analysis. The volume of papers submitted to this symposium and the concurrence of virtually all of them with the conclusion that their are serious grounds for concern, is certainly suggestive.

---

[10] The new dynamic approach to industrial organisation extends the focus from the one dimension considered in the traditional literature to three dimensions (see Thurik and Audretsch, 1996) viewing industry performance in terms of an industrial, geographical and temporal dimension. The analysis also decomposes net changes in market performance into contributing component parts such as firm entry, exit, survival and growth. The rise in the importance of small firms has also led to significant industrial economics research (see Acs and Audretsch, 1989; Brock and Evans, 1989; Reid, 1993; and Storey, 1994, for discussions of this literature). Much of the intuitive analysis of the economics of entrepreneurship plays a significant role in this literature.

[11] For example, new business ventures may be constrained by a lack of access to finance (Evans and Jovanovic, 1989).

3. On the papers in this issue

We turn next to a brief overview of the contents of this special issue and follow this with an overview of the questions raised for competition policy. The papers in this special issue concern themselves primarily with competition policy issues raised by three phenomena: variations in the capabilities of different firms, mergers and interfirm coordination, and the beneficial externalities generated by investment in R&D.

The issue begins with two related papers, one by Malerba, Nelson, Orsenigo and Winter, and the other by Pleatsikas and Teece. They examine the role of increasing returns and the evolution of firms' capabilities in high-tech sectors. Malerba, Nelson, Orsenigo, and Winter emphasise the role of evolving competences in firms' performance in a model of the US computer industry. Their analysis highlights that antitrust policy (as manifested in interventions to break up monopolistic firms) has limited impact in industries where increasing returns are prevalent. The paper also emphasises that the effectiveness of such an initiative will be affected by its timing. They derive an interesting result — that attempts to enhance the capability of resource constrained firms in a market with inherent increasing returns may not affect the long-term performance of the market but can improve performance in adjacent markets. This can occur if the firms with enhanced capability use it to enter an adjacent market and thereby avoid the consequences of an impending shakeout in their current market.

Pleatsikas and Teece critically assess traditional methods of analysing market definition and market power. They argue that these methods are inappropriate for high-tech industries which are typically characterised by high levels of product differentiation and dramatic shifts in firms' market positions. Pleatsikas and Teece claim that traditional methods tends to define markets too narrowly so that market power is exagerrated. They conclude by suggesting several alternative methods which attempt to account for the dynamics of high-tech industries.

The focus on firm capability continues in the next two papers, one by Burke and To, and the other by Boone. Burke and To illustrate how reductions in barriers to entry can lead to deterioration in market performance when the main threat of entry is posed by employees of the incumbents. In this model an incumbent's employees are considered to be the most likely entrants since they are most apt to have the requisite knowledge and skills, the business contacts, demonstrated ability and motivation. Where this is so reductions in barriers to entry can affect market performance by forcing firms to raise the wages of employees with entrepreneurial inclinations, in a bid to prevent entry. In the long run the resulting wage increases can reduce hirings and raise prices. The result refutes the general presumption that a reduction in barriers to entry must reduce prices.

Boone focuses on the role of variations in firms' cost levels on the relation between competition and R&D. His model entails a non-monotone relationship between competition and R&D, which holds quite generally across a number of

D.B. Audretsch et al. / Int. J. Ind. Organ. 19 (2001) 613–634   625

models. He further looks at the relation between competition and market structure. With asymmetric firms he demonstrates that when competition for consumers increases, industry concentration can rise as weaker firms are shaken out of the market. Thus, a decrease in concentration may indicate reduced competition among firms. This not only reverses the direction of causation in standard models but also the sign of the relationship between competition and concentration.

The view that coordinated decision making by competing firms either by agreement or through merger is not always a bad thing emerges from the next two contributions, one by Baumol, and the other by McGuckin and Hguyen. Baumol recalls that where R&D entails significant externalities, private returns may be insufficient to generate the amount of R&D called for by welfare maximisation. In this case, Baumol argues, co-operation between firms may help to internalise these externalities and proves that they can increase R&D activity. If the process involves technology trading by the firms, this can contribute to welfare in a second way — by increasing the speed with which new and improved technology is disseminated and more widely adopted.

The paper by McGuckin and Nguyen indicates that mergers are not typically undertaken to create static monopoly gains. Using US manufacturing data they find that ownership changes are not a primary vehicle for cuts in employment or plant closings, both of which would be likely if monopoly power was exploited through output reductions. Instead, the typical ownership change increases jobs and their quality as measured by wages.

The paper by Link and Scott also addresses the tendency to insufficiency of R&D when externalities are generated by innovation. However, these authors argue that in cases where private returns are insufficient to encourage adequate investment in welfare enhancing R&D industrial policy becomes appropriate. They suggest that financial aid for R&D be auctioned to firms, thereby ensuring that government support for R&D is reduced to the minimum marginal financial incentive necessary for welfare enhancing R&D to occur.

The following paper by Audretsch, van Leeuwen, Merkveld and Thurik illustrates that evolution of the capability of firms implies that the beneficial welfare effects of entry are underestimated. If one takes a static view, new firms may characteristically seem weak and hence they may appear capable of exerting only a limited influence on competition. However, Audretsch et al., take an intertemporal view and recognize that successful entrants are apt to become more capable with the passage of time. Thus their effect on competition becomes more significant in the longer run. They also argue that collective wage agreements can weaken dynamic competition because in their less capable and vulnerable stage, survival of new firms frequently requires them to have the opportunity to pay their employees less than established competitors do.

The paper by Neumann, Weigand, Gross, and Munter considers the dynamics of concentration when market size changes. They examine two forms of market growth relating to increased globalisation and income growth. In a model they demonstrate the key role of entry barriers, namely that an increase in market size will tend to cause deconcentration as long as entry is facilitated. This is complemented by an empirical analysis of the dynamics of German industry where they find that the deconcentration process appears to be impeded by significant entry barriers.

Finally, Konings, Van Cayseele and Warzynski assess the impact of temporal and regional variation in the form of competition policy on price-cost mark-ups in Belgium and The Netherlands. They find that competition policy seems to be less of a constraint on price-cost margins in The Netherlands than it is in Belgium. In general, they argue that the Dutch regulatory regime is less tough on monopolistic behaviour than its Belgian counterpart. They also find that the introduction of the EU style (conforming to Articles 81 and 82 of the EC Treaty) competition law to Belgium in 1993 appears to have had no measurable impact on Belgian price-cost margins.

Overall, three general themes have emerged from our overview of the literature. First, the dynamics of the competitive process are far more complex than its static structure. For competition policy it follows that dynamic welfare optimisation does not lend itself readily to simple rules of thumb, which are more readily possible for the case of monopoly viewed statically. This implies that effective competition law must take account of this heterogeneity and must adopt clear welfare objectives that make allowance for the flexibility required in applying the law to dynamic markets. In particular, it is important that the law require employment of a time horizon that is sufficiently long and does not consider only short-term consequences of the behaviour of firms or of government acts of intervention. This requires consideration of the principles that should underlie the choice of this time horizon and the appropriate discount rate. Second, the capability of firms plays a critical role in dynamic market performance. Indeed, this is one of the main reasons why dynamic competition is far more complex than static competition. Thus, broad competition policy may appropriately go beyond prohibition of various types of behaviour and discouragement of particular types of structure, seeking means to increase the number of firms and prospective entrants capable of competing effectively (perhaps using means such as enterprise policy and education). Third, the consequences of mergers, alliances and co-operation among firms require re-evaluation in a dynamic context. In the next section we examine some implications of this and other observations that emerge from the material we have surveyed for current EU competition law.

4. Dynamic competition policy: the EU approach as illustration

Next we discuss competition law and policy in the EU as an example of the implications of the discussions in this special issue. The main body of EU

D.B. Audretsch et al. / Int. J. Ind. Organ. 19 (2001) 613–634   627

competition law is comprised of Articles 81 and 82 of the EC Treaty[12] and the national competition laws of the EU Member States. Articles 81 and 82 govern trade between EU Member States, while national competition laws set the rules for intra-member state commerce. EU competition law is fairly uniform across the EU, as national legislatures have gradually amended domestic competition law, deliberately adapting it to the contents of Articles 81 and 82.

Given the dominant role of the model of static competition in the early years of industrial organisation analyses, it is not surprising to find that the European Union's competition law (which was framed in this era) pays homage to this viewpoint. Article 81 outlaws agreements that create market power, while Article 82 restrains the use of market power. To a significant extent, Article 81 attempts to affect industry structure by restricting agreements that facilitate concentration and the creation of market power, while Article 82 emphasises anti-competitive conduct by outlawing abuses of market power. We will deal with each in turn.

Article 81(1) — see below — prohibits (while Article 81(2) declares void) a particular set of agreements that seek to create or enhance market power. The list emphasises agreements associated with static monopoly. Thus, a traditional price fixing cartel would fall foul of Articles 81(1) a–c, which deal with price fixing, output restriction and market sharing, respectively. Similarly, Article 81(1) d prevents an upstream monopolist from undertaking discriminating agreements with downstream firms when they lead to monopolistic pricing in downstream markets. In the same fashion extension of monopoly power by tying the purchase of a product in a competitive market to a complementary product in a monopolistic market is outlawed by Article 81(1) e. In fact, Article 81(1) can serve as a useful device for students seeking to memorise the list of possible anti-competitive acts of a static monopolist, as recounted in an intermediate microeconomics text.

In contrast, dynamic monopoly behaviour, such as excessive innovation activity by an incumbent firm in order to prevent a resource-constrained entrant from evolving into a more capable competitor, is not explicitly prohibited by Article 81(1). Perhaps it can be argued that Article 81(1) b can be invoked here, but the difficulty is that — in line with the concern over the limiting of production by static monopolies — Article 81(1) b emphasises *insufficient* rather than *excessive* innovation. Moreover, Article 81(1) does not deal with welfare reducing strategies associated with dynamic competition, such as pre-emptive patenting, excessive advertising, innovative rent seeking, excessive product differentiation, and weakening of the capability of resource constrained competitors.

---

[12] The EU merger guidelines are set out in Regulation (EEC) No. 4064/89 while state aid and public enterprise are covered by Articles 86–89 of the EC Treaty.

4.1. Article 81

1. *The following shall be prohibited as incompatible with the common market: all agreements ... which have as their object or effect the prevention, restriction or distortion of competition within the common market, and in particular those which:*

> *(a) directly or indirectly fix purchase or selling prices or any other trading conditions;*
> *(b) limit or control production, markets, technical development, or investment;*
> *(c) share markets or sources of supply;*
> *(d) apply dissimilar conditions to equivalent transactions with other trading parties, thereby placing them at a competitive disadvantage;*
> *(e) make the conclusion of contracts subject to acceptance by other parties of supplementary obligations which, by their nature or according to commercial usage, have no connection with the subject of such contracts.*

Dynamic considerations are brought into play through Article 81(3), which declares that Article 81(1) *may* be inapplicable if an agreement

> *... contributes to improving the production or distribution of goods or to promoting technical or economic progress, while allowing consumers a fair share of the resulting benefit, and which does not:*

> *(a) impose on the undertakings concerned restrictions which are not indispensable to the attainment of these objectives;*
> *(b) afford such undertakings the possibility of eliminating competition in respect of a substantial part of the products in question.*

This article refers to the trade-off between dynamic and static efficiency familiar in the economics literature. It consequently acknowledges the need for a positive price-cost mark-up (and hence acceptance of second best allocative efficiency) to cover continuing sunk costs associated with R&D. However, Article 81(3) provides no unambiguous guidance on the right balance between these competing objectives. Of course, any economist will recognise that 81(3) must implicitly refer to economic welfare but the law does not mention it. Therefore, there is no legal declaration that clauses such as " ... allowing consumers a fair share ... " (Article 81(3)) should be interpreted in terms of economic welfare. In legal practice, economic welfare is mentioned, but the absence of explicit instructions gives substantial leeway to the Commission and the courts to choose what they consider to be the correct formulation. Furthermore, the law treats static inefficiency and the abuses that produce it as its main concern. Not surprisingly, therefore, the practice of EU competition law is frequently criticised for rulings that are inconsistent (possibly because of the absence of a clear social welfare objective) and biased in its emphasis of realised short-run profits over profits to be expected in the future (for examples see Korah, 1994).

Article 82 is virtually a mirror image of Article 81(1) except for the removal of article 81(1) c dealing with agreements to share markets. It provides no exemptions (such as those offered in Article 81(3) for Article 81). Even more than Article 81 — which gave some guidance on the requisites for exemption under 81(3) — Article 82 relies on the Commission and the courts to interpret this pivotal term. Article 82 also specifies no social welfare objective and the sub-articles of the law emphasise abuses associated with static inefficiency. For dynamic welfare, it is perhaps somewhat comforting that Article 82 is rarely used in legal practice because lawyers have found it too difficult to prove that a firm's actions constitute an abuse of market power. Instead, they usually opt for the easier task of demonstrating that the agreement behind the action is anti-competitive, as defined by Article 81.

4.2. Article 82

Any abuse by one or more undertakings of a dominant position . . . shall be prohibited . . . Such an abuse may, in particular, consist in:

(a) directly or indirectly imposing unfair purchase or selling prices or other unfair trading conditions;

(b) limiting production, markets or technical development to the prejudice of consumers;

(c) applying dissimilar conditions to equivalent transactions with other trading parties, thereby placing them at a competitive disadvantage;

(d) making the conclusion of contracts subject to acceptance by the other parties of supplementary obligations which, by their nature or according to commercial usage, have no connection with the subject of such contracts.

We have noted two shortcomings from the viewpoint of dynamic efficiency in EU law: lack of clarity on the social welfare objective of the laws and an emphasis on static efficiency. We have argued that the economic prescription for competition policy is relatively simple only if one ignores such phenomena as variation in the abilities of different firms to exploit particular profit opportunities and the evolution of such capability with the passage of time, or the manipulation of barriers to entry or the incentives for innovation and its possible abuse as a means to undermine competition.

630   *D.B. Audretsch et al. / Int. J. Ind. Organ. 19 (2001) 613–634*

5. Issues for competition policy in a dynamic world

It would clearly be premature and even presumptuous to attempt to provide a menu of policies for regulation and anti trust activity in a world economy in which evolution and change are the hallmarks. However, the materials in this volume certainly suggest a list of questions to be raised about traditional procedures and objectives as well as issues that must be resolved in the design of rational policy. The basic attribute that differentiates the dynamic approach to competition policy is a focus on innovation rather than prices and profits and on flexibility in resource utilisation rather than static efficiency in their assignment at a given moment. A reorientation toward flexibility means that policy makers must be less concerned about ensuring such things as the existence of 'the right number' of firms and more upon the ease with which that number can be changed. Increased attention to innovation may make interfirm coordination and bigness less undesirable than it would be in an economy in which change is rare and insignificant.

These considerations give rise to some obvious issues.

1. *Appropriate ease of entry:* a prime requisite for desirable flexibility in resource utilization is elimination of inappropriate impediments to entry. One approach is to use — perhaps co-ordinate — enterprise policy in order to increase the capability of new entrants. Another involves restricting incumbents' response to entry but here considerable care must be exercised. Denial of such flexibility to the incumbents patently does make entry more attractive and can serve to give the newcomers breathing space to develop their capability to a point where they can stand on their own. But at the same time this can encourage the use of resources by incapable and inefficient new enterprises that would not survive if the incumbents were permitted fuller freedom to compete. The danger, ultimately, is that one may end up with an arrangement governed by the infant industry argument, and that, as has many times been said, there is little incentive for the infants ever to grow up. The problem for a dynamic economy, then, is what limitations upon the behaviour of the incumbents, if any, and what incentives or capability support for the entrant, are truly welfare promoting.

2. *Appropriate interfirm coordination:* in a static model, the welfare reducing consequences of collusion among horizontal competitors are clear. However, where innovation rather than price is the prime means by which welfare can be increased the desirability of preventing coordination is not so clear. Theory suggests that a primary disincentive for investment in innovation is its substantial spillovers, the fact that a considerable proportion of the benefits of an innovation often go to others than those who have produced it. This is particularly likely to inhibit the innovation process when competitors are among the prime beneficiaries. Technology trading by rivals can help to internalise these externalities and can consequently be welfare increasing, particularly in the long run. Moreover, coordinating firms may be able to afford the outlays the innovation process

requires. The implication, then, is that the rules distinguishing permissible from impermissible coordination among competing firms must be rethought for a highly dynamic economy.

3. *Innovation, trade and monopoly power:* innovation has led to an explosion of the share of an economy's output and consumption that is exported and imported. Maddison (1995) estimates that since 1820 the *share* of world GDP that is involved in international trade has risen 13-fold, a truly incredible number. This rise is, of course, largely attributable to innovation in transportation and communication technology, and there is no reason to expect it to come to an end in the foreseeable future. This is and will continue to be a crucial influence increasing ease of entry. Industries that are highly concentrated when that attribute is examined in domestic terms alone are apt to be far from concentrated or at least substantially contestable in a global economy. The obvious issue is the way in which rivalry from abroad should be taken into account in competition policy.

4. *Anti-competitive innovation:* in a world in which innovation is the firm's prime competitive weapon, that weapon can sometimes be misused. Firms can, for example, engage in pre-emptive innovation and patenting in order to make it more difficult for entrants or even current rivals to provide viable innovations of their own. Or firms may engage in what may be deemed predatory innovation, for example, spending so much on R&D that rivals cannot afford to match the outlays and are driven from the market. What rules and procedures are appropriate to deal with such possible courses of action?

5. *Monopolisation in an innovative market:* it is sometimes claimed that in innovative industries monopoly power is generally highly transitory. This can reduce the incentive for the outlay of effort and resources on an attempt to acquire monopoly power by means other than innovation. Should competition policy explicitly be required to include the innovativeness of the industry, along with ease of entry and absence of concentration as evidence that monopoly power is unlikely and that where it occurs it is of limited importance because its duration is likely to be brief?

6. *Price discrimination where R&D costs are substantial and continuing:* in industries where innovation is a main instrument of competition, expenditure on the development of an invention can not be considered an irrelevant sunk cost that has been incurred once and for all. Survival of the firm requires continual large outlays on the innovation process. But these expenditures do not enter marginal costs. Uniform pricing based on marginal cost may evidently prevent recovery of the innovation outlays and destroy the firm. Only price discrimination may enable it to survive. How should competition policy adapt itself to this problem? When should price discrimination not be discouraged, and what circumstances will provide the firm with the power to adopt the required non-uniform prices?

Evidently, this list can easily be expanded. Its purpose is not to lay out the problems of design of competition policy for a dynamic economy in any detail, but to indicate the sorts of issues that it raises.

6. Conclusion

The special issue set out to investigate the claim that antitrust law addresses static inefficiencies but often neglects dynamic considerations. In this paper we reviewed the contents of the special issue and provided an overview of the evolution of the economics of industrial organisation from the viewpoint of competition policy. We found that EU competition laws do appear to emphasise static welfare optimisation. It is also apparent that an economic analysis of dynamic markets is more complex and yields a much richer depiction of competition, than that of static markets. But much work still needs to be done before economics is in a position to provide a defensible and comprehensive set of prescriptions for an economy whose most enduring attribute is rapid change. Yet it is easy to conclude that if one were to start all over again and design antitrust policy from scratch, the result would be rather different from current law and current practice.

Acknowledgements

The authors would like to thank Steve Martin for his support, encouragement and advice throughout the duration of this project.

References

Acs, Z.J., Audretsch, D.B., 1989. Editors' Introduction. Small Business Economics 1 (1), 1–5.
Arthur, W.B., 1989. Competing technologies, increasing returns and lock-in by historical events. Economic Journal 99 (2), 116–131.
Audretsch, D.B., 1995. In: Innovation and Industry Evolution. The MIT Press, Cambridge, MA.
Bailey, E., Graham, D., Kaplan, D., 1981. In: Deregulating the Airlines. The MIT Press, Cambridge, MA.
Bain, J.S., 1949. A note on pricing in monopoly and oligopoly. American Economic Review 39 (1), 448–469.
Bain, J.S., 1956. In: Barriers to New Competition. Harvard University Press, Cambridge, MA, USA.
Baumol, W.J., Panzar, J.C., Willig, R.D., 1982. In: Contestable Markets and the Theory of Industry Structure. Harcourt Brace Jovanovich, New York.
Beil, R.O., Kaserman, D.L., Ford, J.M., 1995. Entry and product quality under price regulation. Review of Industrial Organization 10 (3), 361–372.
Brock, W.A., Evans, D.S., 1989. Small business economics, small business economics 1 (1), 7–20.
Carter, C.F., Williams, B.R., 1959. The characteristics of technically progressive firms. Journal of Industrial Economics 7 (2), 87–104.

Chandler, A., 1962. In: Strategy and Structure, Chapters in the History of the American Industrial Enterprise. MIT Press, Cambridge, MA.

Davies, S., Lyons, B., Dixon, H., Geroski, P., 1989. In: Surveys in Economics: Economics of Industrial Organisation. Longman, London.

Evans, D.S., Jovanovic, B., 1989. An estimated model of entrepreneurial choice under liquidity constraints. Journal of Political Economy 97 (August), 808–827.

Gilbert, R.J., Newbery, D.M.G., 1982. Preemptive patenting and the persistence of monopoly. American Economic Review 72 (3), 514–526.

Graham, D., Kaplan, D., Sibley, D., 1983. Efficiency and competition in the airline industry. Bell Journal of Economics 14 (Spring), 118–138.

Griliches, Z., 1957. Hybrid corn: an exploration in the economics of technological change. Econometrica 25 (4), 501–522.

Herbert, R., Link, A., 1982. In: The Entrepreneur. Praeger, New York.

Katz, M.L., Shapiro, C., 1981. Network externalities, competition, and compatibility, American Economic Review 75(3).

Kirzner, I.M., 1973. In: Competition and Entrepreneurship. University of Chicago Press, Chicago.

Korah, V., 1994. In: EC Competition Law and Practice, 5th Edition. Sweet and Maxwell, London.

Krueger, A., 1974. The political economy of rent-seeking society. American Economic Review 64 (30), 291–303.

Krugman, P., 1991. Increasing returns and economic geography. Journal of Political Economy 99, 483–499.

Landes, W.M., Posner, R.A., 1987. Trademark law: an economic perspective. Journal of Law and Economics 30 (October), 265–309.

Lazonick, W., 1982. The cotton industry. In: Elbaum, B., Lazonick, W. (Eds.), The Decline of the British Economy. The Clarendon Press, Oxford.

Lyons, B., 1989. Barriers to entry. In: Davies, S., Lyons, B., Dixon, H., Geroski, P. (Eds.), Surveys in Economics: Economics of Industrial Organisation. Longman, London.

Maddison, A., 1995. In: Monitoring the World Economy 1820–1992. Organization for Economic Cooperation and Development, Paris.

Moore, T., 1982. US airline deregulation: its effect on passengers, capital and labor. Journal of Law and Economics 29 (April), 1–28.

Morrison, S., Winston, C., 1987. Empirical implications and tests of the contestability hypothesis. Journal of Law and Economics 30 (April), 53–66.

Mueller, D., 1966. Patents, research and development, and the measurement of inventive activity. Journal of Industrial Economics 15 (1), 26–37.

Murphy, K.J., Shleifer, A., Vishny, R., 1990. The allocation of talent: implications for growth. Manuscript, University of Chicago.

Nelson, R.R., Winter, S.G., 1982. In: An Evolutionary Theory of Economic Change. Harvard University Press, Cambridge, MA.

Nordhaus, W.D., 1969. Invention, growth, and welfare: a theoretical treatment of technological change. Cambridge, MA, USA.

O'Brien, D.P., 1964. Patent protection and competition in polyamide and polyester fibre manufacture. Journal of Industrial Economics 12 (3), 224–235.

Penrose, E., 1959. The Theory of the Growth of the Firm. Oxford.

Peteraf, M.A., 1993. The cornerstones of competitive advantage: a resource-base view. Strategic Management Journal 14, 179–191.

Porter, M.E., 1980. In: Competitive Strategy: Techniques for Analyzing Industries and Competitors. Free Press, New York.

Posner, R.A., 1976. The Robinson-Patman Act: Federal Regulation of Price Differences, City, American, Enterprise Institute.

Posner, R.A., 1979. The Chicago School of Economic Analysis. University of Pennsylvania Law Review 127 (4), 925–948.

Reid, G.C., 1993. In: Small Business Enterprise: An Economic Analysis. Routledge, London, New York.

Salop, S.C., 1979. Monopolistic competition with outside goods. Bell Journal of Economics 10 (1), 141–156.

Scherer, F.M., Ross, D., 1990. In: Industrial Market Structure and Economic Performance, 3rd Edition. Houghton Mifflin Company, Boston, MA.

Shackle, G.L.S., 1971. In: Economics For Pleasure. Cambridge University Press, Cambridge.

Sharkey, W.W., 1982. In: The Theory of Natural Monopoly. Cambridge University Press, Cambridge.

Storey, D., 1994. In: Understanding the Small Business Sector. Routledge, London.

Sutton, J., 1991. In: Sunk Costs and Market Structure. The MIT Press, London, UK.

Teece, D.J., 1980. Economics of scope and the scope of the enterprise. Journal of Economic Behaviour and Organisation 1 (3), 223–247.

Thurik, A.R., Audretsch, D.B., 1996. The dynamics of industrial organization. Review of Industrial Organization 11 (2), 149–153.

Tirole, J., 1988. In: The Theory of Industrial Organization. The MIT Press, Cambridge MA.

Tullock, G., 1967. The welfare costs of tariffs, monopolies and theft. Western Economic Journal 5, 221–232.

AGGLOMERATION AND THE LOCATION OF INNOVATIVE ACTIVITY

DAVID B. AUDRETSCH

Institute of Development Statistics, Indiana University, and the Centre for Economic Policy Research, London[1]

A paradox has been the emergence of the importance of local proximity and geographic clusters precisely at a time when globalization seems to dominate economic activity. The purpose of this paper is to resolve this paradox by explaining why and how geography matters for innovative activity and ultimately for the international comparative advantage. Globalization and the telecommunications revolution have triggered a shift in the comparative advantage of the leading developed countries towards an increased importance of innovative activity. This shift in comparative advantage has increased the value of knowledge-based economic activity. Since knowledge is generated and transmitted more efficiently via local proximity, economic activity based on new knowledge has a high propensity to cluster within a geographic region. This has triggered a fundamental shift in public policy towards business, away from policies constraining the freedom of firms to contract and towards a new set of enabling policies, implemented at the regional and local levels.

I. INTRODUCTION

That innovative activity has become more important is not surprising. What was perhaps less anticipated is that much of the innovative activity is less associated with footloose multinational corporations and more associated with high-tech innovative regional clusters, such as Silicon Valley, Research Triangle, and Route 122 around Boston. Only a few years ago the conventional wisdom predicted that globalization would lead to the demise of the region as a meaningful unit of economic analysis. Yet the ob-

session of policy-makers around the globe to 'create the next Silicon Valley' reveals the increased importance of geographic proximity and regional agglomerations. The purpose of this article is to explain why and how geography matters for innovative activity and ultimately for international comparative advantage.

The second section of this paper explains how globalization and the telecommunications revolution have triggered a shift in the comparative advantage of the leading developed countries towards an

[1] I would like to thank the editors of this journal and two anonymous referees.

18

D. B. Audretsch

increased importance of innovative activity. The importance of new knowledge as an input in generating innovative activity is explained in the third section, along with why knowledge is fundamentally different from the more traditional factors of production. These differences account for the propensity for knowledge to spill over from the source creating it to the firm commercializing it, which is explained in the fourth section. However, as is pointed out in the fifth section, there are important reasons why knowledge stops spilling over as it moves across geographic space, bestowing important economic benefits to geographic proximity and localization. In the sixth section the gains from agglomerations are explained by linking knowledge spillovers to innovative activity. In the seventh section, the black box of geographic space is penetrated to link the structure of economic activity within an agglomeration to the innovative performance of that region. Finally, policy implications are discussed in the concluding section. In particular, the increased importance of innovation has triggered a fundamental shift in public policy towards business, away from policies constraining the freedom of firms to contract and towards a new set of enabling policies, implemented at the regional and local levels.

II. INNOVATION AND COMPARATIVE ADVANTAGE

The traditional comparative advantage in mature, technologically moderate industries, such as metalworking, machine tools, and car production had provided an engine for growth, high employment, and economic stability throughout Western Europe for most of the post-war economic period. When the Berlin Wall fell in 1989, many people expected even greater levels of economic well-being resulting from the dramatic reduction of the economic burden in the West that had been imposed by four decades of Cold War. Thus, the substantial unemployment and general economic stagnation during the subsequent 8 years has come as a shock. Unemployment and relatively low growth are the twin economic problems confronting Europe. Over 11 per cent of the work-force in the European Union (EU) was unemployed in 1997, ranging from 6.1 per cent in the United Kingdom and 6.2 per cent in The Netherlands, to 11.1 per cent in Germany, 12.6 per cent in France, and over 20 per cent in Spain.[2]

The traditional comparative advantage has been lost in the high-cost countries of Europe and North America in the last decade for two reasons. The first has to do with globalization, or the advent of competition not just from the emerging economies in South-east Asia but also from the transforming economies of Central and Eastern Europe. The second factor has been the computer and telecommunications revolution. The new communications technologies have triggered a virtual spatial revolution in terms of the geography of production. According to *The Economist*, 'The death of distance as a determinant of the cost of communications will probably be the single most important economic force shaping society in the first half of the next century.'[3]

Much of the policy debate responding to the twin forces of the telecommunications revolution and increased globalization has revolved around a trade-off between maintaining higher wages but suffering greater unemployment, versus higher levels of employment but at the cost of lower wage rates. Globalization and the telecommunications revolution have rendered the comparative advantage in traditional moderate technology industries incompatible with high wage levels. At the same time, the emerging comparative advantage that is compatible with high wage levels is based on innovative activity. For example, employment has increased by 15 per cent in Silicon Valley between 1992 and 1996, even though the mean income is 50 per cent greater than in the rest of the country.[4]

The global demand for innovative products in knowledge-based industries is high and growing rapidly; yet the number of workers who can contribute to producing and commercializing new knowledge is limited to just a few areas in the world. Economic activity based on new knowledge generates higher wages and greater employment opportunities reflecting the exploding demand for new and improved products and services. There are many indicators reflecting the shift in the comparative

---

[2] OECD, *Employment Outlook* (1997).
[3] 'The Death of Distance', *The Economist* (30 September 1995).
[4] 'The Valley of Money's Delights', *The Economist* (29 March 1997, special section, p. 1).

advantage of the high-wage countries towards an increased importance of innovative activity. For example, Kortum and Lerner (1997, p. 1) document an unprecedented jump in patenting in the United States, as evidenced by the explosion in applications for United States patents by American inventors since 1985. Throughout this century, patent applications fluctuated within a band between 40,000 and 80,000 per year. By contrast, in 1995 there were over 120,000 patent applications. Similarly, Berman *et al.* (1997) have shown that the demand for less skilled workers has decreased dramatically throughout the OECD, while at the same time the demand for skilled workers has exploded.

III. THE KNOWLEDGE PRODUCTION FUNCTION

The starting point for most theories of innovation is the firm. In such theories the firms are exogenous and their performance in generating technological change is endogenous (Arrow, 1962). For example, in the most prevalent model found in the literature of technological change, the model of the knowledge production function, formalized by Zvi Griliches (1979), firms exist exogenously and then engage in the pursuit of new economic knowledge as an input into the process of generating innovative activity. The most decisive input in the knowledge production function is new economic knowledge. Knowledge as an input in a production function is inherently different from the more traditional inputs of labour, capital, and land. While the economic value of the traditional inputs is relatively certain, knowledge is intrinsically uncertain and its potential value is asymmetric across economic agents. The most important, although not the only, source of new knowledge is considered to be research and development (R&D). Other key factors generating new economic knowledge include a high degree of human capital, a skilled labour-force, and a high presence of scientists and engineers.

There is considerable empirical evidence supporting the model of the knowledge production function. However, the empirical link between knowledge inputs and innovative output apparently becomes stronger as the unit of observation becomes increasingly aggregated. For example, at the unit of observation of countries, the relationship between R&D

and patents is very strong. The most innovative countries, such as the United States, Japan, and Germany, also tend to undertake high investments in R&D. By contrast, little patent activity is associated with developing countries, which have very low R&D expenditures. Similarly, the link between R&D and innovative output, measured in terms of either patents or new product innovations, is also very strong when the unit of observation is the industry. The most innovative industries, such as computers, instruments, and pharmaceuticals, also tend to be the most R&D-intensive. Audretsch (1995) finds a simple correlation coefficient of 0.74 between R&D inputs and innovative output at the level of four-digit standard industrial classification (SIC) industries. However, when the knowledge production function is tested for the unit of observation of the firm, the link between knowledge inputs and innovative output becomes tenuous and only weakly positive in some studies, and even non-existent or negative in others. The model of the knowledge production function becomes particularly weak when small firms are included in the sample. This is not surprising, since formal R&D is concentrated among the largest corporations, but a series of studies (Acs and Audretsch, 1990) has clearly documented that small firms account for a disproportionate share of new product innovations, given their low R&D expenditures.

IV. KNOWLEDGE SPILLOVERS

The breakdown of the knowledge production function at the level of the firm raises the question: *Where do innovative firms with little or no R&D get the knowledge inputs?* This question becomes particularly relevant for small and new firms that undertake little R&D themselves, yet contribute considerable innovative activity in newly emerging industries such as biotechnology and computer software (Audretsch, 1995). One answer that has recently emerged in the economics literature is from other, third-party firms or research institutions, such as universities. Economic knowledge may spill over from the firm conducting the R&D or the research laboratory of a university (Baptista, 1997).

Why should knowledge spill over from the source of origin? At least two major channels or mechanisms for knowledge spillovers have been identified in the literature. Both of these spillover mechanisms revolve around the issue of appropriability of new knowledge. Cohen and Levinthal (1989) suggest that firms develop the capacity to adapt new technology and ideas developed in other firms and are therefore able to appropriate some of the returns accruing to investments in new knowledge made externally.

By contrast, Audretsch (1995) proposes shifting the unit of observation away from exogenously assumed firms to individuals, such as scientists, engineers, or other knowledge workers—agents with endowments of new economic knowledge. When the lens is shifted away from the firm to the individual as the relevant unit of observation, the appropriability issue remains, but the question becomes: *How can economic agents with a given endowment of new knowledge best appropriate the returns from that knowledge?* If the scientist or engineer can pursue the new idea within the organizational structure of the firm developing the knowledge and appropriate roughly the expected value of that knowledge, he or she has no reason to leave the firm. On the other hand, if he places a greater value on his ideas than does the decision-making bureaucracy of the incumbent firm, he may choose to start a new firm to appropriate the value of his knowledge. In the metaphor provided by Albert O. Hirschman (1970), if voice proves to be ineffective within incumbent organizations, and loyalty is sufficiently weak, a knowledge worker may resort to exiting the firm or university where the knowledge was created in order to form a new company. In this spillover channel the knowledge production function is actually reversed. The knowledge is exogenous and embodied in a worker. The firm is created endogenously in the worker's effort to appropriate the value of his or her knowledge through innovative activity.

V. THE IMPORTANCE OF LOCATION AND AGGLOMERATION

That knowledge spills over is barely disputed. In disputing the importance of knowledge externalities in explaining the geographic concentration of economic activity, Krugman (1991) and others do not question the existence or importance of such knowledge spillovers. In fact, they argue that such knowledge externalities are so important and forceful that there is no compelling reason for a geographic boundary to limit the spatial extent of the spillover. According to this line of thinking, the concern is not that knowledge does not spill over, but that it should stop spilling over just because it hits a geographic border, such as a city limit, state line, or national boundary. As illustrated by the title page of *The Economist* proclaiming 'The Death of Distance' (30 September 1995), the claim that geographic location is important to the process linking knowledge spillovers to innovative activity in a world of e-mail, fax machines, and cyberspace may seem surprising and even paradoxical. The resolution to the paradox posed by the localization of knowledge spillovers in an era where the telecommunications revolution has drastically reduced the cost of communication lies in a distinction between knowledge and information. *Information*, such as the price of gold on the New York Stock Exchange, or the value of the yen in London, can be easily codified and has a singular meaning and interpretation. By contrast, *knowledge* is vague, difficult to codify, and often only serendipitously recognized. While the marginal cost of transmitting information across geographic space has been rendered invariant by the telecommunications revolution, the marginal cost of transmitting knowledge, and especially tacit knowledge, rises with distance.

Von Hipple (1994) demonstrates that high context, uncertain knowledge, or what he terms 'sticky knowledge', is best transmitted via face-to-face interaction and through frequent and repeated contact. Geographic proximity matters in transmitting knowledge, because as Kenneth Arrow (1962) pointed out over three decades ago, such tacit knowledge is inherently non-rival in nature, and knowledge developed for any particular application can easily spill over and have economic value in very different applications. As Glaeser *et al.* (1992, p. 1126) have observed, 'intellectual breakthroughs must cross hallways and streets more easily than oceans and continents'.

The importance of local proximity for the transmission of knowledge spillovers has been observed in many different contexts. It has been pointed out that, 'business is a social activity, and you have to be where important work is taking place.'[5] A survey of nearly one thousand executives located in America's 60 largest metropolitan areas ranked Raleigh/ Durham as the best city for knowledge workers and for innovative activity.[6] The reason is that

A lot of brainy types who made their way to Raleigh/ Durham were drawn by three top research universities. . . . US businesses, especially those whose success depends on staying at the top of new technologies and processes, increasingly want to be where hot new ideas are percolating. A presence in brain-power centres like Raleigh/Durham pays off in new products and new ways of doing business. Dozens of small biotechnology and software operations are starting up each year and growing like *kudzu* in the fertile climate.[7]

VI. THE SPATIAL LINK BETWEEN KNOWLEDGE AND INNOVATION

Not only did Krugman (1991, p. 53) doubt that knowledge spillovers are not geographically constrained, but he also argued that they were impossible to measure because 'knowledge flows are invisible, they leave no paper trail by which they may be measured and tracked'. However, an emerging literature has overcome data constraints to measure the extent of knowledge spillovers and link them to the geography of innovative activity. Jaffe (1989), Feldman (1994), and Audretsch and Feldman (1996) modified the model of the knowledge production function to include an explicit specification for both the spatial and product dimensions:

$$I_{si} = IRD^{\beta_1} * (UR_{si})^{\beta_2} * \left[UR_{si} * (GC_{si})^{\beta_3} \right] * \varepsilon_{si} \quad (1)$$

where I is innovative output, IRD is private corporate expenditures on R&D, UR is the research expenditures undertaken at universities, and GC measures the geographic coincidence between university and corporate research. The unit of observation for estimation is at the spatial level, s, a state, and industry level, i. Jaffe (1989) used the number of inventions registered with the United States patent office as a measure of innovative activity. By contrast, Audretsch and Feldman (1996) and Acs *et*

al. (1992) developed a direct measure of innovative output consisting of new product introductions.

Estimation of equation (1) essentially shifts the model of the knowledge production function from the unit of observation of a firm to that of a geographic unit. The consistent empirical evidence that supports the notion knowledge spills over for third-party use from university research laboratories as well as industry R&D laboratories. This empirical evidence suggests that location and proximity clearly matter in exploiting knowledge spillovers. Not only have Jaffe *et al.* (1993) found that patent citations tend to occur more frequently within the state in which they were patented than outside of that state, but Audretsch and Feldman (1996) found that the propensity of innovative activity to cluster geographically tends to be greater in industries where new economic knowledge plays a more important role. Prevenzer (1997) and Zucker *et al.* (1994) show that in biotechnology, which is an industry based almost exclusively on new knowledge, the firms tend to cluster together in just a handful of locations. This finding is supported by Audretsch and Stephan (1996) who examine the geographic relationships of scientists working with biotechnology firms. The importance of geographic proximity is clearly shaped by the role played by the scientist. The scientist is more likely to be located in the same region as the firm when the relationship involves the transfer of new economic knowledge. However, when the scientist is providing a service to the company that does not involve knowledge transfer, local proximity becomes much less important.

The spatial link between knowledge inputs and innovative output can be seen in the Data Appendix which links knowledge inputs to innovative output. Since Krugman (1991, p. 57) has emphasized, 'States aren't really the right geographical units', the relevant geographic unit of observation is at the city level. The measure of innovative output is the number of patents registered by firms located within the city between 1988 and 1992. The Appendix also shows the education level, measured as the share of the labour-force in 1992 accounted for by workers

---

[5] 'The Best Cities for Knowledge Workers', *Fortune* (15 November 1993, p. 44).
[6] The survey was carried out in 1993 by the management consulting firm, Moran, Stahl & Boyer, of New York City.
[7] 'The Best Cities for Knowledge Workers', *Fortune* (15 November 1993, p. 44).

D. B. Audretsch

who have graduated from a 4-year college course (BA or higher). In addition, the number of research centres located in that city as of 1992 is listed. While the high number of patents issued to firms located at the heart of Silicon Valley in San José (10,138) and Los Angeles (9,598) is not particularly surprising, what is perhaps more striking is that the greatest number of patents (11,793) was issued to firms located in Chicago. One explanation may be that Chicago accounts for a greater number of research centres than any other city, with the exceptions of New York and Boston. Of course, Chicago is also a much larger city than San José. When patent rates, or the number of patents per 100,000 residents, are compared in the second column, San José emerges as the most innovative city in the United States. San José, in fact, has the second highest educational attainment level, where almost one-third of its workforce has a university degree or the equivalent. In general, a close relationship can be seen between the availability of knowledge resources in a city and its innovative performance.[8]

There is reason to believe that knowledge spillovers are not homogeneous across firms. In estimating equation (1) for large and small enterprises separately, Acs *et al.* (1994) provide some insight into the puzzle posed by the recent wave of studies identifying vigorous innovative activity emanating from small firms in certain industries. How are these small, and frequently new, firms able to generate innovative output while undertaking generally negligible amounts of investment into knowledge-generating inputs, such as R&D? The answer appears to be through exploiting knowledge created by expenditures on research in universities and on R&D in large corporations. Their findings suggest that the innovative output of all firms rises along with an increase in the amount of R&D inputs, both in private corporations as well as in university laboratories. However, R&D expenditures made by private companies play a particularly important role in providing knowledge inputs to the innovative activity of large firms, while expenditures on research made by universities serve as an especially key input for generating innovative activity in small enterprises. Apparently, large firms are more adept at exploiting knowledge created in their own laboratories, while their smaller counterparts have a comparative ad-

vantage at exploiting spillovers from university laboratories.

A conceptual problem arises with economies accruing to the knowledge transmission associated with agglomeration. Once a city, region, or state develops a viable cluster of production and innovative activity why should it ever lose the first-mover advantage? One answer, provided by Audretsch and Feldman (1996) is that the relative importance of local proximity and, therefore, agglomeration effects is shaped by the stage of the industry life cycle. A growing literature suggests that who innovates and how much innovative activity is undertaken is closely linked to the phase of the industry life cycle (Klepper, 1996). Audretsch and Feldman (1996) argue that an additional key aspect to the evolution of innovative activity over this life cycle is *where* that innovative activity takes place. The theory of knowledge spillovers, derived from the knowledge production function, suggests that the propensity for innovative activity to cluster spatially will be the greatest in industries where tacit knowledge plays an important role. As argued above, it is *tacit knowledge*, as opposed to *information*, which can only be transmitted informally, and typically demands direct and repeated contact. The role of tacit knowledge in generating innovative activity is presumably the greatest during the early stages of the industry life cycle, before product standards have been established and a dominant design has emerged. Audretsch and Feldman (1996) classify 210 industries into four different stages of the life cycle. The results provide considerable evidence suggesting that the propensity for innovative activity to cluster spatially is shaped by the stage of the cycle. On the one hand, new economic knowledge embodied in skilled workers tends to raise the propensity for innovative activity to cluster spatially throughout all phases of the industry life cycle. On the other hand, certain other sources of new economic knowledge, such as university research, tend to elevate the propensity for innovative activity to cluster during the introduction stage of the life cycle, but not during the growth stage, and then again during the stage of decline.

Perhaps most striking is the finding that greater geographic concentration of production actually

---

[8] The link between innovative output and knowledge inputs at the city level has been substantiated in an econometric model.

leads to more, and not less, dispersion of innovative activity. Apparently innovative activity is promoted by knowledge spillovers that occur within a distinct geographic region, particularly in the early stages of the industry life cycle, but, as the industry evolves towards maturity and decline, may be dispersed by additional increases in concentration of production that have been built up within that same region. The evidence suggests that what may serve as an agglomerating influence in triggering innovative activity to cluster spatially during the introduction and growth stages of the industry life cycle, may later result in a congestion effect, leading to greater dispersion in innovative activity. While the literature on economic geography has traditionally focused on factors such as rents, commuting time, and pollution as constituting congestion and dissipating agglomeration economies (Henderson, 1986), this type of congestion refers to lock-in with respect to new ideas. While there may have been agglomeration economies in automobiles in Detroit in the 1970 and computers in the Northeast Corridor in the 1980s, a type of intellectual lock-in made it difficult for Detroit to shift out of large-car production and for IBM and DEC to shift out of mainframe computers and into mini-computers. Perhaps it was this type of intellectual congestion that led to the emergence of the personal computer in California, about as far away from the geographic agglomeration of the mainframe computer as is feasible on the mainland of the United States. Even when IBM developed its own personal computer, the company located its fledgling PC facility in Boca Ratton, Florida, way outside of the mainframe agglomeration in the Northeast Corridor. Thus, there is at least some evidence suggesting that spatial agglomerations, just like other organizational units of economic activity, are vulnerable to technological lock-in, with the result being, in certain circumstances, that new ideas need new space.

VII. PENETRATING THE BLACK BOX OF GEOGRAPHIC SPACE

While a new literature has emerged identifying the important role that knowledge spillovers within a given geographic location play in stimulating innova-

tive activity, there is little consensus as to how and why this occurs. The contribution of the new wave of studies described in the previous section was simply to shift the unit of observation away from firms to a geographic region. But does it make a difference how economic activity is organized within the black box of geographic space? Political scientists and sociologists have long argued that the differences in the culture of a region may contribute to differences in innovative performance across regions, even holding knowledge inputs such as R&D and human capital constant. For example, Saxenian (1990) argues that a culture of greater interdependence and exchange among individuals in the Silicon Valley region has contributed to a superior innovative performance than is found around Boston's Route 128, where firms and individuals tend to be more isolated and less interdependent.

In studying the networks located in California's Silicon Valley, Saxenian (1990, pp. 96–7) emphasizes that it is the communication between individuals that facilitates the transmission of knowledge across agents, firms, and even industries, and not just a high endowment of human capital and knowledge in the region:

It is not simply the concentration of skilled labour, suppliers and information that distinguish the region. A variety of regional institutions—including Stanford University, several trade associations and local business organizations, and a myriad of specialized consulting, market research, public relations and venture capital firms—provide technical, financial, and networking services which the region's enterprises often cannot afford individually. These networks defy sectoral barriers: individuals move easily from semiconductor to disk drive firms or from computer to network makers. They move from established firms to start-ups (or vice versa) and even to market research or consulting firms, and from consulting firms back into start-ups. And they continue to meet at trade shows, industry conferences, and the scores of seminars, talks, and social activities organized by local business organizations and trade associations. In these forums, relationships are easily formed and maintained, technical and market information is exchanged, business contacts are established, and new enterprises are conceived. . . . This decentralized and fluid environment also promotes the diffusion of intangible technological capabilities and understandings.'[9]

---

[9] Saxenian (1990, pp. 97–8) claims that even the language and vocabulary used by technical specialists can be specific to a region: 'a distinct language has evolved in the region and certain technical terms used by semiconductor production engineers in Silicon Valley would not even be understood by their counterparts in Boston's Route 128'.

Such observations suggest a limitation inherent to the general knowledge production function approach described in the previous section. While economists tend to avoid attributing differences in economic performance to cultural differences, there has been a series of theoretical arguments suggesting that differences in the underlying structure between regions may account for differences in rates of growth and technological change. In fact, a heated debate has emerged in the literature about the manner in which the underlying economic structure within a geographic unit of observation might shape economic performance. This debate revolves around two key structural elements—the degree of diversity versus specialization and the degree of monopoly versus local competition.

One view, which Glaeser *et al.* (1992) attribute to the *Marshall–Arrow–Romer externality*, suggests that an increased concentration of a particular industry within a specific geographic region facilitates knowledge spillovers across firms. This model formalizes the insight that the concentration of an industry within a city promotes knowledge spillovers among firms and therefore facilitates innovative activity. To the degree that individuals in the population are identical and engaged in identical types of activities, the costs of communication and transactions are minimized. Lower costs of transaction in communication result in a higher probability of knowledge spilling over across individuals within the population. An important assumption of the model is that knowledge externalities with respect to firms exist, but only for firms within the same industry. Thus, the relevant unit of observation is extended from the firm to the region in the tradition of the Marshall–Arrow–Romer model, but the spillovers are limited to occur solely within the relevant industry.

By contrast, restricting knowledge externalities to occur only within the same industry may ignore an important source of new economic knowledge—inter-industry knowledge spillovers. After all, Griliches (1992, p. 29) has defined knowledge spillovers as, 'working on similar things and hence benefiting much from each other's research'. Jacobs (1969) argues that the most important sources of knowledge spillovers are external to the industry in

which the firm operates and that cities are the source of considerable innovation because the diversity of these knowledge sources is greatest in cities. According to Jacobs, it is the exchange of complementary knowledge across diverse firms and economic agents which yields a greater return on new economic knowledge. She develops a theory that emphasizes that the variety of industries within a geographic region promotes knowledge externalities and ultimately innovative activity and economic growth.

The extent of regional specialization versus regional diversity in promoting knowledge spillovers is not the only dimension over which there has been a theoretical debate. A second controversy involves the degree of competition prevalent in the region, or the extent of local monopoly. The Marshall–Arrow–Romer model predicts that local monopoly is superior to local competition because it maximizes the ability of firms to appropriate the economic value accruing from their investments in new knowledge. By contrast, Jacobs (1969) and Porter (1990) argue the opposite—that competition is more conducive to knowledge externalities than is local monopoly.[10] It should be emphasized that by local competition Jacobs does not mean competition within product markets, as has traditionally been envisioned within the industrial organization literature. Rather, Jacobs is referring to the competition for the new ideas embodied in economic agents. Not only does an increased number of firms provide greater competition for new ideas, but, in addition, greater competition across firms facilitates the entry of a new firm specializing in some particular new product niche. This is because the necessary complementary inputs and services are likely to be available from small specialist niche firms but not necessarily from large, vertically integrated producers.

The first important test of the specialization versus diversity debate measured economic performance in terms of employment growth. Glaeser *et al.* (1992) employ a data set on the growth of large industries in 170 cities between 1956 and 1987 in order to identify the relative importance of the degree of regional specialization, diversity, and local competition in influencing industry growth rates. The authors find evidence that contradicts the

---

[10] Porter (1990) provides examples of Italian ceramics and gold jewellery as industries in which numerous firms are located within a bounded geographic region and compete intensively for new ideas.

Marshall–Arrow–Romer model, but is consistent with the theories of Jacobs. However, their study provided no direct evidence as to whether diversity is more important than specialization in generating innovative activity.

Feldman and Audretsch (forthcoming) identify the extent to which the organization of economic activity is either concentrated, or alternatively consists of diverse but complementary economic activities, and how the underlying structure of economic activity influences innovative output. They link the innovative output of product categories within a specific city to the extent to which the economic activity of that city is concentrated in that industry, or conversely, diversified in terms of complementary industries sharing a common science base. Their results indicate that diversity across complementary economic activities sharing a common science base is more conducive to innovation than is specialization. In addition, their results indicate that the degree of local competition for new ideas within a city is more conducive to innovative activity than is local monopoly. Perhaps the most important conclusion from these two studies, however, is that more than simply an endowment of knowledge inputs is required to generate innovative activity. The underlying economic and institutional structure matters, as do the microeconomic linkages across agents and firms.

VIII. CONCLUSIONS

Globalization combined with the telecommunications revolution has drastically reduced the cost of transporting not just material goods but also information across geographic space. High wages are increasingly incompatible with information-based economic activity, which can be easily transferred to a lower cost location. By contrast, the creation of new ideas based on tacit knowledge cannot easily be transferred across distance. Thus, the comparative advantage of the high-cost countries of North American and Western Europe is increasingly based on knowledge-driven innovative activity. The spillover of knowledge from the firm or university creating that knowledge to a third-party firm is essential to innovative activity. Such knowledge spillovers tend to be spatially restricted. Thus, an irony of globalization is that even as the relevant geographic market for most goods and services becomes increasingly global, the increased importance of innovative activity in the leading developed countries has triggered a resurgence in the importance of local regions as a key source of comparative advantage.

As the comparative advantage in Western Europe and North America has become increasingly based on new knowledge, public policy towards business has responded in two fundamental ways. The first has been to shift the policy focus away from the traditional triad of policy instruments essentially constraining the freedom of firms to contract—regulation, competition policy or antitrust in the USA, and public ownership of business. The policy approach of constraint was sensible as long as the major issue was how to restrain footloose multinational corporations in possession of considerable market power. This is reflected by the waves of deregulation and privatization along with the decreased emphasis of competition policy throughout the OECD. Instead, a new policy approach emerges which focuses on enabling the creation and commercialization of knowledge. Examples of such policies include encouraging R&D, venture capital and new-firm start-ups.

The second fundamental shift involves the locus of such enabling policies, which are increasingly at the state, regional, or even local level. The down-sizing of federal agencies charged with the regulation of business in the United States and Great Britain has been interpreted by many scholars as the eclipse of government intervention. But to interpret deregulation, privatization, and the increased irrelevance of competition policies as the end of government intervention in business ignores an important shift in the locus and target of public policy. The last decade has seen the emergence of a broad spectrum of enabling policy initiatives that fall outside the jurisdiction of the traditional regulatory agencies. Sternberg (1996) documents how the success of a number of different high-technology clusters spanning a number of developed countries is the direct result of enabling policies, such as the provision of venture capital or research support. For example, the Advanced Research Program in Texas has provided support for basic research and the strengthening of the infrastructure of the University of Texas, which has played a central role in developing a high-technology cluster around Austin (Feller, 1997). The Thomas Edison Centers in Ohio, the Advanced Technology Centers in New Jersey, and the Centers for Advanced Technology at Case Western Reserve University, Rutgers University, and the University of Rochester have supported generic, pre-competitive research. This support has generally provided diversified technology development involving a mix of activities encompassing a broad spectrum of industrial collaborators.

Such enabling policies, that are typically implemented at the local or regional level, are part of a silent policy revolution currently under way. The increased importance of innovative regional clusters as an engine of economic growth has led policy-makers to abandon the policy cry frequently heard two decades ago, 'Should we break up, regulate, or simply take over General Motors, IBM and US Steel?' for a very different contemporary version, 'How can we grow the next Silicon Valley?'

DATA APPENDIX:
PATENT ACTIVITY OF MAJOR US CITIES

City	No. of patents	Patents/population	No. of research centres	Education level
Albany	3,086	350.33	115	23.60
Atlanta	2,776	86.80	205	26.10
Austin	2,121	231.01	174	30.70
Baltimore	2,400	98.14	225	23.10
Birmingham	223	25.81	72	19.70
Boston	9,013	179.05	650	28.80
Buffalo	1,498	124.98	23	18.80
Charlotte	953	77.13	25	19.60
Chicago	11,793	154.92	516	24.50
Cincinnati	2,353	149.73	141	19.90
Cleveland	3,871	174.21	118	18.50
Columbus	1,524	108.12	170	23.30
Dallas	4,557	159.65	126	26.90
Dayton	1,958	202.55	98	19.10
Denver	2,097	121.34	302	29.10
Detroit	8,652	200.46	361	17.70
Fort Lauderdale	1,395	105.58	108	18.80
Fort Worth	1,174	80.45	49	22.40
Grand Rapids	1,301	132.78	26	17.80
Greensboro	1,147	105.10	44	17.50
Hartford	1,925	165.45	62	26.00
Honolulu	250	28.63	115	24.60
Houston	5,765	163.00	199	25.00
Indianapolis	1,818	126.30	69	20.00
Jacksonville	323	33.59	20	18.60
Kansas City	883	53.92	140	23.20
Las Vegas	273	27.26	27	13.30
Los Angeles	9,598	104.99	515	22.30
Louisville	639	65.74	53	17.20
Memphis	473	45.19	85	18.70
Miami	1,011	50.07	108	18.80

City	No. of patents	Patents/population	No. of research centres	Education level
Milwaukee	2,685	182.80	106	21.30
Minneapolis	7,513	282.42	235	26.90
Nashville	417	40.18	117	21.40
New Orleans	647	49.69	73	19.30
New York	7,482	43.92	788	25.40
Norfolk	689	45.74	67	19.80
Oakland	4,445	205.66	283	29.90
Oklahoma	526	52.90	83	21.60
Orlando	957	71.56	33	20.40
Philadelphia	8,565	171.95	469	22.60
Phoenix	3,334	140.11	121	21.40
Pittsburgh	4,367	182.22	220	18.70
Portland	1,842	112.49	72	23.30
Raleigh-Durham	1,745	188.55	248	31.70
Richmond	940	103.80	41	23.80
Rochester	7,034	647.89	77	22.90
Sacramento	886	60.76	97	22.70
St Louis	2,473	97.57	136	17.70
Salt Lake City	1,398	122.29	109	22.90 .
San Antonio	517	37.20	56	19.30
San Diego	4,590	173.00	195	25.30
San Francisco	4,233	259.04	345	34.90
San José	10,138	665.14	91	32.60
Scranton	256	39.83	22	13.60
Seattle	3,424	157.67	153	29.50
Tampa	1,285	59.84	42	17.30
Tulsa	858	116.19	81	20.30
West Palm Beach	1,460	157.73	25	22.10

REFERENCES

Acs, Z., and Audretsch, D. (1990), *Innovation and Small Firms*, Cambridge, MA, MIT Press.
—   —Feldman, M. (1992), 'Real Effects of Academic Research', *American Economic Review*, **82**(1), 363–70.
—   — —(1994), 'R&D Spillovers and Recipient Firm Size', *Review of Economics and Statistics*, **100**(2), 336–40.
Arrow, K. (1962), 'Economic Welfare and the Allocation of Resources for Invention', in R. Nelson (ed.), *The Rate and Direction of Inventive Activity*, Princeton, NJ, Princeton University Press.
Audretsch, D. (1995), *Innovation and Industry Evolution*, Cambridge, MA, MIT Press.
—   Feldman, M. (1996), 'R&D Spillovers and the Geography of Innovation and Production', *American Economic Review*, **86**(4), 253–73.
—   Stephan, P. (1996), 'Company-Scientist Locational Links: The Case of Biotechnology', *American Economic Review*, **86**(4), 641–52.
Baptista, R. (1997), *An Empirical Study of Innovation, Entry and Diffusion in Industrial Clusters*, PhD dissertation, University of London (London Business School).
Berman, E., Bound, J., and Machin, S. (1997), 'Implications of Skill-Biased Technological Change: International Evidence', Working Paper No. 6166, National Bureau of Economic Research, Cambridge, MA.
Cohen, W., and Levinthal, D. (1989), 'Innovation and Learning: The Two Faces of R&D', *The Economic Journal*, **99**(3), 569–96.

Ellison, G., and Glaeser, E. (1997), 'Geographic Concentration in US Manufacturing Industries: A Dartboard Approach', *Journal of Political Economy*, (4), 889–927.

Feldman, M. (1994), 'Knowledge Complementarity and Innovation', *Small Business Economics*, **6**(3), 363–72.

— Audretsch, D. (forthcoming), 'Innovation in Cities: Science-Based Diversity, Specialization, and Localized Competition', special issue of the *European Economic Review,* edited by E. Helpman.

Feller, I. (1997), 'Federal and State Government Roles in Science and Technology', *Economic Development Quarterly*, **11**(4), 283–96.

Glaeser, E., Kallal, H., Scheinkman, J., and Shleifer, A. (1992), 'Growth of Cities', *Journal of Political Economy*, **100**, 1126–52.

Griliches, Z. (1979), 'Issues in Assessing the Contribution of R&D to Productivity Growth', *Bell Journal of Economics*, **10**, 92–116.

— (1992), 'The Search for R&D Spill-Overs', *Scandinavian Journal of Economics*, **94**, 29–47.

Henderson, V. (1986), 'Efficiency of Resource Usage and City Size', *Journal of Urban Economics*, **19**(1), 47–70.

Hirschman, A. O. (1970), *Exit, Voice, and Loyalty*, Cambridge, MA, Harvard University Press.

Jacobs, J. (1969), *The Economy of Cities*, New York, Random House.

Jaffe, A. (1989), 'Real Effects of Academic Research', *American Economic Review*, **79**, 957–70.

— Trajtenberg, M. L., and Henderson, R. (1993), 'Geographic Localization of Knowledge Spillovers as Evidenced by Patent Citations', *Quarterly Journal of Economics*, **63**, 577–98.

Klepper, S. (1996), 'Entry, Exit, Growth, and Innovation over the Product Life Cycle', *American Economic Review*, **86**(4), 562–83.

Kortum, S., and Lerner, J. (1997), 'Stronger Protection or Technological Revolution: What is Behind the Recent Surge in Patenting?', Working Paper No. 6204, National Bureau of Economic Research, Cambridge, MA.

Krugman, P. (1991), *Geography and Trade*, Cambridge, MA, MIT Press.

Porter, M. (1990), *The Comparative Advantage of Nations*, New York, Free Press.

Prevenzer, M. (1997), 'The Dynamics of Industrial Clustering in Biotechnology', *Small Business Economics*, **9**(3), 255–71.

Saxenian, A. (1990), 'Regional Networks and the Resurgence of Silicon Valley', *California Management Review*, **33**, 89–111.

Sternberg, R. (1996), 'Technology Policies and the Growth of Regions', *Small Business Economics*, **8**(2), 75–86.

Venables, A. J. (1996), 'Localization of Industry and Trade Performance', *Oxford Review of Economic Policy*, **12**(3), 52–60.

Von Hipple, E. (1994), 'Sticky Information and the Locus of Problem Solving: Implications for Innovation', *Management Science*, **40**, 429–39.

Zucker, L., Darby, M., and Armstrong, J. (1994), 'Intellectual Capital and the Firm: The Technology of Geographically Localized Knowledge Spillovers', Working Paper No. 9496, National Bureau of Economic Research, Cambridge MA.

29

Name index